Daniel P. Seaton

The Land of Promise

Or, The Bible Land and its Revelation

Daniel P. Seaton

The Land of Promise
Or, The Bible Land and its Revelation

ISBN/EAN: 9783337240417

Printed in Europe, USA, Canada, Australia, Japan

Cover: Foto ©Lupo / pixelio.de

More available books at **www.hansebooks.com**

D. P. SEATON, D. D., M. D.

THE LAND OF PROMISE;

OR,

THE BIBLE LAND AND ITS REVELATION.

ILLUSTRATED

WITH SEVERAL ENGRAVINGS OF SOME OF THE MOST
IMPORTANT PLACES IN PALESTINE AND SYRIA.

BY

D. P. SEATON, D. D., M. D.

PUBLISHING HOUSE OF THE A. M. E. CHURCH,
631 Pine Street, Philadelphia, Pa.
1895.

PREFACE.

THERE is no name given to a place more familiarly known than the title of this book. The Land of Promise is thought of, spoken of, and sought by millions of beings, who are seeking rest for their souls. The land which discloses the greatest religious thought, and furnishes the clearest information of the mercy and benevolence of Jesus Christ is the "Land of Promise." Many volumes have been written by learned authors on the great truths it reveals, but they have failed to exhaust its boundless historical developments. Every one who visits that country may find something of profound interest to write, which will give the world more information on the facts contained in the Holy Scriptures. The Land of Promise is the country in which the principal events revealed to man in the Bible were developed, and where the Lord Jesus spent the most of His time teaching the Way of Salvation. There have been critical examinations made of many of the sacred places in all parts of the country, and the majority of the localities of Bible reference, satisfactorily settled upon. There are new investigations being made constantly which furnish new historical matter for those who write books on the Bible developments of the country. On this account, every honest author can find something important for the enlightenment of his fellows, and thus lend a helping hand in lifting up mankind generally.

This book is intended to interest the masses; therefore the writer has taken great caution to prepare it in a form so plain, no one will fail to comprehend it. If we have succeeded in accomplishing the end in view, a work of untold good has been done, which will be gathering souls for the Kingdom of Heaven for many years to come. The Land of Promise is so replete with Bible history, no one who will take the time to visit it, can fail to see and learn more of its connection with God's Word in one day than he could in a whole year's study away from it. For years before the author made his first visit to Palestine, he made a close study of the history and geography of the country, and was under the impression he had become so familiar with it, that he could point out some of the sacred localities without the help of a guide; but on entering Joppa, he soon found himself incompetent to designate any of them. The history of the Bible was presented in an entirely different light, and so distinctly clear, his previous knowledge of the country seemed as but a simple speculation. The author has endeavored to present in this volume, an unbiased statement of men and things, as they appear now and were in ancient times. His object is to more fully impress men with the importance of accepting the Word of God upon the plain basis on which it is founded, and permit the truth to have full force in our world. He aims to produce several wonderful Bible characters as they were known to men in the times they lived in Palestine, and call to mind how the Lord dealt with them. We have presented the renowned Patriarch with his tents and herds, the King with sceptre ruling the nation, the bold Prophet proclaiming messages of terror to kings and subjects because of their gross sins, and many of the wonderful works of the Lord Jesus in the land.

The author had been repeatedly requested, for years before making his last visit through Palestine, to give a book to the world; but feeling it necessary to make another trip there and spend more time in taking observations, he deferred it until the last visit was finished. Now that we have completed the long-desired task, we shall feel more than repaid for the time and sacrifices made, if this work will accomplish half the good intended. We have taken pains to select texts for some of the most important subjects, so that the Bible student may easily turn to them and become more familiar with the Word of God. It has been our aim to accord to each race its proper place in history as nearly as possible; especially the Hamite, whom we have reasons to believe has been greatly slighted by many authors who have attempted to write his history as relates to Palestine. We dedicate this work, in the name of the Lord of Hosts, to the enlightenment of men.

WASHINGTON, D. C., 1895.

CONTENTS.

PART   **PAGES**

I.—HISTORICAL INTRODUCTION 1–12

The Historical and Physical Outline and Geography of Palestine and Syria—The Origin of Various Names—Boundary of Palestine Proper—As Compared with Other Lands—How Impressed when Approaching Joppa—Physical Formation of the Country—Mountains and Valleys—Carmel, Sharon and Esdraelon—Hills of Bashan—Coast Plains—Their Interception—Plain of Jericho—Its immense Fall—Rivers in Palestine and Syria—The Political Status of Syria and Palestine—Information Furnished by Books of Old Testament—The Law Given in Time of Moses—Friendship Between David and Hiram—Solomon and Hiram—The People Inclined to Idolatry—Work of the Jews after Captivity—Climate of Palestine and Syria—Skillfulness of Phœnicians.

II.—LIFE IN PALESTINE—PECULIAR CUSTOMS OF THE PEOPLE 13–19

Style of Dress—Costly Garments Owned by the Poor—Style of Dress of the Women of Bethlehem and Nazareth—Dress of Mohammedan Women—Farming Implements—How Plows are Made and Used—Armed Merchants and Shepherds—Long Standing Feuds—Land-Marks Respected—Historical Associations—First Settlers—How Homes are Built—Variety of Climate—People of Lebanon—Their Appearance—Their Manners—Their Relations as to Religion.

III.—OUTLINE HISTORY OF THE ISRAELITES 20–40

FROM THEIR ENTRANCE INTO THE LAND OF PROMISE TO THEIR DISPERSION.

General Character of Israelites—Their Criminal Waywardness—Allotments of Twelve Tribes—Their Religious and Political Revolutions—Situation of Tribes of Reuben, Gad, and Manasseh—Deborah's Criticism—Situation of Tribes of Judah, Ephraim, Simeon, Benjamin, and Dan—Situation of Tribes of Issachar, Asher, Zebulun, and Naphtali—Tribe of Levi—Its Official Relations to the Others—Their Cherished Treasure—The Tabernacle Removed from Gilgal to Shiloh—Great Feast Reunions—Shiloh, a Religious Court of Priests and Levites—Office of Levites—Office of Priests—Israel's Wayward Tendency the Signal of Their Decline—Israel given to Idolatry—Israel's Oppression a Divine Rebuke—Their Inter-Marriage with the Canaanites—Official Judges who Delivered Israel—Ehud of Benjamin, His Cunning Scheme—Ehud's Stratagem, His Escape—Philistines' Hostilities—Shamgar, a Deliverer of Israel—Shamgar, Judge of Israel—Trouble out North—Jabin, King of Hazor—Deborah the Prophetess—Engagement between Barak and Sisera—Triumph of Israel—Jael, Sisera's Destroyer—Israelites Afflicted by Moabites—Gideon and His Little Army—Position of the Midianites' Camp—Gideon's Attack—Death of Gideon—Invasion of Gilead by the Ammonites—Jephthah, the Victor—His Rash Vow—Trouble with the Philistines—Samson, the Mighty Hero—Samuel, the Last Judge—His Counsel to Israel—Israel's Anxiety for a King—Conduct of Joel and Abijah—Samuel Anoints Saul—The Turning Point in the Affairs of the Government—Samuel's Last Advice to Israel—Saul as King—David Chosen to Succeed Saul—Opposition to David—Its Final Result—Transfer of the Kingdom—David King of Israel—Solomon on the Throne—Revolt of Ten Tribes—Worshiping the Calves—Southern Kingdom—Prophets in Israel—Israelites Carried into Captivity—Assyrians Inhabiting Their

vi   CONTENTS.

PARTS   PAGES

Land—Samaritans Rejected—The Jews Return from Captivity—Discord between Jews and Samaritans—Services on Mount Gerizim—Nehemiah Rebuilding the Walls of Jerusalem—Ancient Samaritans—Visit to Samaritan Temple—Their Religious Devotions—The People, Their General Bearing—Tribes under Rehoboam and Jeroboam—Northern and Southern Districts—Silent Period—Condition of Jews when our Lord came on Earth—Jews Subject to Persia—Headquarters of Persian Monarch—A Strange Conquest—Rule of Ptolemies—Sanctuary Robbed—The Maccabees' Rule.

IV.—FROM JOPPA TO JERUSALEM 41–61

Situation of Joppa—Landing at Joppa—House of Simon the Tanner—Streets of Joppa—Orange Groves—American Colony at Joppa—Joppa Pilgrims—Preparation for their Festival—Traders in the City—Plain of Sharon—Old Highway—Lydda—Greek Church in Lydda—Ramleh—Tower of the Forty—View from the Tower—Valley of Ajalon—Ai—Israel's First Defeat—Ai Captured by Joshua—Joshua and Israelites go to Shechem—Gibeonites Visit Joshua—Kings' Confederacy—Joshua Responds to Gibeonites—Fate of Confederacy—Joshua's Prayer for Sun and Moon to Stand Still—Joshua's Victory—El-Jib or Gibeon—Bible Associations—History of Gibeon—Naby-Samwill or Ancient Mizpeh—Situation—View from the Mosque—Ancient Mizpeh—Present Village—Approaching Jerusalem from Joppa—Northern Confederacy—Jabin Forming a Confederacy—Jabin and His Allies—March to Lake Merom—Situation of Battle-field—The Great Battle—Joshua's Victory.

V.—ANCIENT AND MODERN JERUSALEM 62–100

Approaching Jerusalem—The Ancient and Modern Cities—Situation of Jerusalem—General Elevation of the City—Mountains Around the City—City Walls—Walls of To-day—Towers Along the Walls—Gates of the City—Present Jerusalem, the Modern City—Division of the City—Greek and Latin Churches—Population of Jerusalem—Its Sanitary Condition—How the Nights are Spent—Shining Light—The Jews' Wailing-place—Worship under the Church of England—Witnessing the Mournful Service—What Jerome Says of This Place—The Harem Area—Mosque of Omar—The Castle of Antonia—Mt. Moriah—Inscriptions on the Walls—Entering the Mosque of Omar—The Sacred Rock—Mohammed and Gabriel—Cave below the Mosque—Caleph Omar—Mosque of El-Aksa—Temple Courts and Foundations—Description of Temple—When Built—Its Furnishings—Old Foundations—Ancient Quarries—Ancient Jerusalem—Jebus Captured—Jerusalem the Resting-place of the Ark of God—Jerusalem During the Reign of Solomon—Decline of Jerusalem—Inhabitants Carried into Captivity—Prophecy of Isaiah Fulfilled—How Alexander the Great Met the People—Alexander and Antiochus—The Great Slaughter—Armenians to the Rescue—The Great War for Liberty—King Herod's Reign—Zion, the Centre Light—Zion, on Approaching Jerusalem—How Situated—Mt. Moriah, Ornan's Threshing-floor—David's Sin—Sacrifice Offered—Inhabitants of Mt. Moriah—Mt. Akra, Mt. Bezetha—Mt. Calvary—Extension of Walls of Jerusalem—Existence of Tombs within the Present City Walls—Great Questions Discussed—The Tomb of Christ—Church of Holy Sepulchre.

VI.—EVENTS IN AND ABOUT JERUSALEM—ITS MEMORABLE PLACES. 101–143

Description of Mount of Olives—Appearance from a Distance—Fuel Used in Palestine—A View of the Country from the Mountain—Disciples Taught how to Pray—Lazarus Raised—Bethany—Tomb of Lazarus—Our Lord en route to Jerusalem—Ride to Jerusalem—Christ's Entry into Jerusalem—Our Lord Deeply Moved with Compassion—The Garden of Gethsemane—Tomb of the Virgin Mary—Description of Tomb—Valley of Jehoshaphat—How Situated—Strong Faith of the People as to the Historical Places of Palestine—Absalom Proclaiming Himself King—David and His Friends—The Love Ittai had for David—The Returning of the Ark of God—David's Flight—David in Exile—Suicide of Ahithophel—David Numbers Those with Him and Forms Three Divisions—Absalom Hanged in the Forest—Breaking the News of His Death to David—David's Return—Absalom's Pillar—Valley of Hinnom—Valley of Giants—Hill

CONTENTS.

PART- PAGES

of Evil Counsel—Potter's Field—Idolatry of Israel—The Kingdom Embarrassed—Solomon's Early Blunder—His Decline in Piety—Pools and Fountains—The Great Cisterns—Pool of Siloam—Healing of the Blind Man—Pool of Bethesda—Healing of the Lame Man—Siege of Titus—Troops Stationed at the Foot of the Mount of Olives—Titus Marches to the City—Famine Raging—War Among the Inhabitants—Titus's Anxiety to Save the City—Prophecy Fulfilled Concerning the Destruction—Burial of the Dead—Towers of Antonia Captured—The Second Edifice in Flames—Titus Offers Terms of Peace—Final Demolition—The Triumphal Arch—David's Tomb—Attempts to Locate it Elsewhere—How Impressed on Entering—The Cœnaculum—Mosque of Neby Da'rid—Description of Upper Chamber—Tombs of St. James and Zacharias—Other Tombs—Absalom's Shaft—Tomb of Jehoshaphat—Tombs of Prophets and Judges—Tomb of Helena—Future of the Jews.

VII.—ANCIENT HEBRON 144-162

The Highway of Hebron and its Loneliness—General Description of the Country—Condition of the Land of Hebron—Tombs at Beth-Zur—The Highway to Hebron—Sad Reflections—Beth-Zur—Pleasant Reflections—Antiquity of Hebron—Inhabitants of Hebron—Different Names given to Hebron—Roads Leading to Hebron—Vineyards of Hebron—Watchtowers and Watchmen—Historic Pools—The Event Concerning Rechab and Baanah—Places of Interest to Tourists—Inhabitants of Hebron—Description of Streets—The Situation of Hebron—Feeling of the Inhabitants to Visitors—Meaning of the Word Hebron—The Author's Experience Concerning His Visit—Description of Ramah—Oak of Mamre—Ancient Hebron—Accommodations for Christians—Facts Connected with Hebron—Patriarchial Associations—Hebron as a Burial Place—Historical Associations of Hebron—Joseph's Mournful Return—Historical Associations—Jacob's Burial—The Mosque Machpelah—The Love of the Mohammedans for the Tomb—Treatment of Visitors who Visit Them—Description of the Mosque by the Prince of Wales—The Entrance to the Mosque—Description of the Shrine of Abraham and Sarah—Shrines of Jacob and Leah—Shrine of Joseph—Description of the Shrine of Joseph—Historical Association of Hebron—Value of the Investigation Made by the Prince of Wales—Desirable Situation and General Condition of the Land of Canaan—Ancient Inhabitants of Hebron—A Great Refuge City—The Custom of Blood Revenge—Cities of Refuge in which there were Judges—Names of Cities—Hebron the First Capital During David's Reign—Installation of David as King—Hebron as Headquarters of a Latin Bishopric—Possessed by the Moslems—Jews' Connection with Hebron—Treatment of the Author by Inhabitants—The Dominant Inhabitants of Hebron.

VIII.—FROM JERUSALEM TO BETHLEHEM 163-224

Places of Interest Along the Road—Valley of Giants—Well of the Wise Men—Tomb of Rachel—Well of David—Church of the "Holy Nativity"—Ancient Inns—Description of the Holy Nativity—Altar of the Magi—Joseph and Mary Journeying from Nazareth—The Advent of Jesus—Solomon's Porch—Solomon's Gardens and Orchards—Mar Saba—Site of the Convent—Places of Interest from Bethlehem to Jericho—The Well Bir Essuk—Character of the Bedouins—Wilderness of Judea—Wilderness of Engedi—Dead Sea—Mountains of Sodom—Cities of Sodom and Gomorrah—The Vale of Siddim—Location of Zoar—Earthquakes as a Work of Destruction—The Amorites—The Hot Springs—Judah and Israel Combined Against Moab—The Valley of the Jordan—Plain of Jericho—City of the Palm Trees—The Jordan River—The Faithfulness of the People of Palestine for their Church Services—Nebo and Pisgah—The View of Moses—Joshua Camped at Gilgal—The Three Jerichoes—Spring of Elisha—The Second Jericho—The Brook Cherith—The Highway to Jericho—Mount of Temptation.

IX.—FROM JERUSALEM TO SHECHEM 225-272

Preparation for the Journey—The Customs and Situation of the People in the Interior—Places of Interest on the Damascus Highway—Mount Scopus—The Last Sight of the Holy City—Scenes Along the Road—The Village of Sha'fat—Ancient Nob, Its Memorable Events—Gibeah, the Birth-place of Saul—Riz-

CONTENTS

PARTS   PAGE

Job's Devotion—The Levite and Benjamite—Ramah of Benjamin—Situation of Beeroth—Ramah and Its Population—The Character of the Mohammedans—Bethel and Its Condition—The Altar of Abraham and Jacob—Bethel a Judicial Station—Jeroboam's Idolatrous Worship—Dan and Bethel as Two Places for Worship—Reign of Josiah—The Reign of Ahab—The Reign of Solomon—Rehoboam's Reign Over Israel—The Reign of Pious Asa—Victory of the Cushite King—Number of Kings After Asa—Bethel, the Home of the Prophet—Present Situation of Bethel—Ancient Shiloh—History of Shiloh—Important Events at Shiloh—The Present Appearance of Shiloh—The Road from Shiloh to Lebonah—Ancient Tombs—The Plain of Mukhna—Mt. Hermon Seen From Mukhna—Well of Jacob—History of the Samaritans—Conversation Between Our Saviour and the Woman of Sychar—Temple on Mt. Gerizim—Jacob's Well and Its Surroundings—The Tomb of Joseph—Shechem and Sychar—Moses' Relation to Mt. Gerizim and Ebal—Historical Association of Mt. Gerizim and Ebal—View from Mt. Gerizim and Ebal—Backsheesh.

X.—SAMARIA—ANCIENT AND MODERN 273–339

The Road from Shechem to Samaria, or Sebastiyeh—The Pool of Samaria—Kings of Israel—Change of Dynasties—Jehu's Reign—Temple of Baal—The Syrian Invasion—Jehu Anointed—Death of Joram—Death of Jezebel—Reign of Jeroboam—Reign of Shallum—Pul, King of Assyria—Attack Upon Israel—Shalmaneser Invades Samaria—Description of Ancient Sites—The Situation and Environment of Dothan—Plain of Esdraelon—Mount Gilboa—Cities of Philistia—The Site of Ancient Jezreel—Naboth's Vineyard—Ancient Nain—Historical Associations—Visit to Shunem.

XI.—NAZARETH 340–356

Nazareth the Home of Our Lord—The Visit of Jesus to Galilee—Phœnician Possessions in Galilee—Hamitic Possessions in Galilee—Christ's Removal from Bethlehem—Childhood of Our Lord in Nazareth—Baptism of Jesus—First Miracle—Establishment of the Christian Church—Church of Annunciation—Feeding the Five Thousand—Christ's Social Life—Why Jesus was Rejected—Mount of Precipitation—The Ministry of Our Lord—Village of Gath-hepher.

XII.—MOUNT CARMEL 357–387

Description of Mount Carmel—The Athlit—Simon Bar-Cochebas, or "Son of the Star"—Situation of the Carmelite Convent—Location of Acre—Pasha of Acre—The Ladder of Tyre—Sidon the Mother of Tyre—Situation of Tyre—Shalmaneser's Invasion of Tyre—Nebuchadnezzar's Invasion of Tyre.

XIII.—DAMASCUS AND ENVIRONMENTS 388–399

Situation of Damascus—River Barada—Saul Arrested while on His Mission of Persecution—Its Buildings—Some of Her Rulers—First View of the City—Present Inhabitants—Annual Pilgrimage to Mecca—Principal Places of Amusement—The Great Café—Its Walls and Houses—Mohammedans' Hatred Towards Christians—The City Seized by Timour—The Street Called "Straight" and Others—The Great Mosque—House of Rimmon—Greek Inscription on Wall.

XIV.—THE SEA OF TIBERIAS AND NOTED PLACES ROUND ABOUT 400–440

Route from Nazareth to Tiberias—View of Mt. Tabor—Ascent of Mt. Tabor—Journey from Tabor to Tiberias—Caravan Road from Jerusalem to Damascus—Character of the Natives—The "Mount of Beatitudes" or "Horns of Hattin"—Time Spent in Galilee—The Environments of the Sea of Tiberias—Visit to Decapolis—Visit to Magdala—Visit to Cesarea Philippi—Mt. Hermon—Sea of Tiberias and Its Situation—Fish of the Sea of Galilee—Custom of the Fishermen—Town of Tiberias—Plain of Gennesaret—Springs of Lake Gennesaret—Old Testament Associations—Ancient Magdala—The Latin Convent—Ruins of Chorazin—The Two Bethsaidas.

ILLUSTRATIONS.

REV. D. P. SEATON, D.D., M.D.	. . Frontispiece.	
MAP OF PALESTINE	. . . . Facing page	1
VIEW OF JERUSALEM	"	62
JEWS' WAILING-PLACE	"	72
MOUNT ZION	"	91
CHURCH OF THE HOLY SEPULCHRE	"	99
MOUNT OF OLIVES.	"	102
GARDEN OF GETHSEMANE . .		108
THE TOWER OF DAVID		143
VIEW OF BETHLEHEM	"	163
CHURCH OF THE NATIVITY (INTERIOR), BETHLEHEM		169
CONVENT OF S. SABA		179
THE DEAD SEA	"	186
VIEW OF THE JORDAN . .	"	208
NABLOUS (SYCHAR OR SHECHEM)		265
NAZARETH		341
MOUNT TABOR	"	400
THE SEA OF GALILEE.	"	432

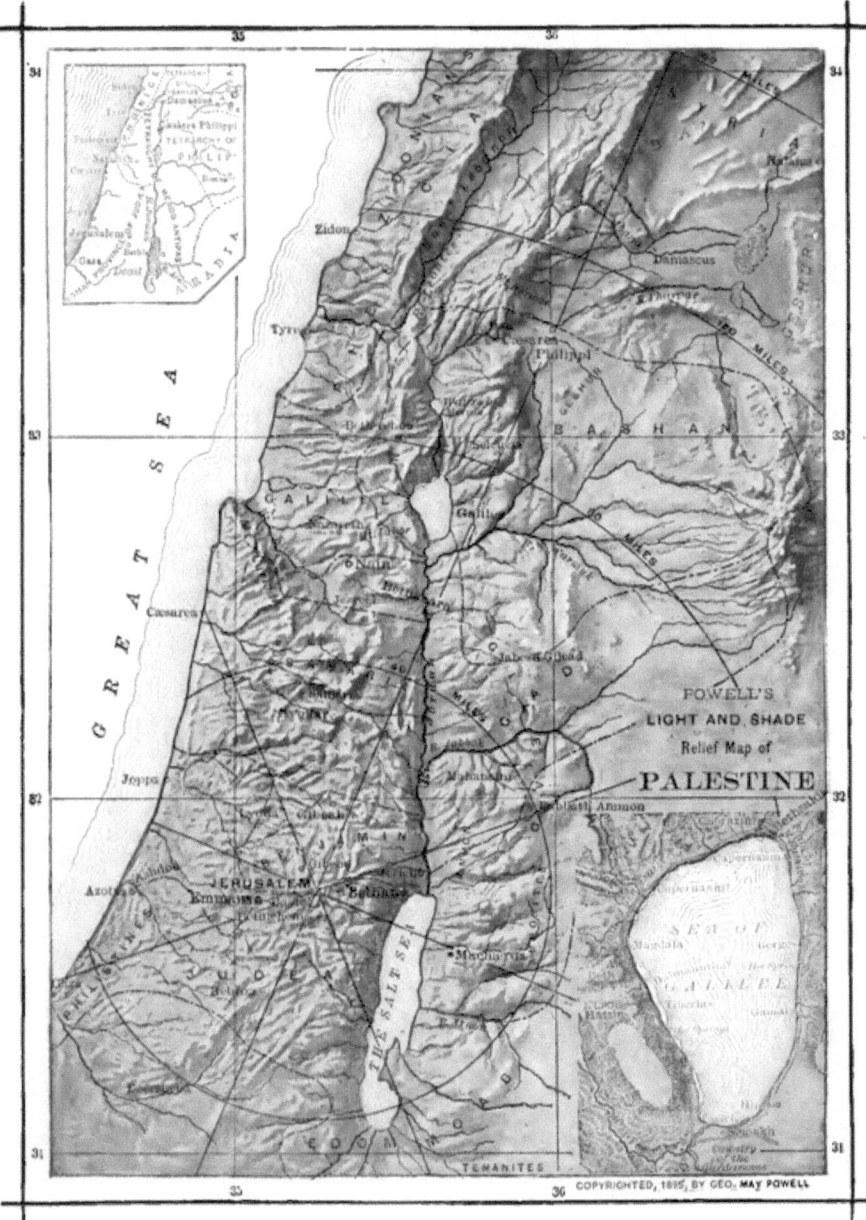

THE LAND OF PROMISE.

PART I.

HISTORICAL INTRODUCTION.

The Historical and Physical Outline and Geography of Palestine and Syria—The Origin of Various Names—Boundary of Palestine Proper—As Compared with Other Lands—How Impressed when Approaching Joppa—Physical Formation of the Country—Mountains and Valleys—Carmel, Sharon and Esdraelon—Hills of Bashan—Coast Plains—Their Interception—Plain of Jericho—Its Immense Fall—Rivers in Palestine and Syria—The Political Status of Syria and Palestine—Information Furnished by Books of Old Testament—The Law Given in Time of Moses—Friendship Between David and Hiram—Solomon and Hiram—The People Inclined to Idolatry—Work of the Jews after Captivity—Climate of Palestine and Syria—Skillfulness of Phœnicians.

THE ORIGIN OF VARIOUS NAMES.

THE cause of the various names, by which this country is known, originates from the people who composed its chief inhabitants; or some particular event which brought it into prominent notice.

It is called "The Land of Canaan;" this name was given it after the general name of the Sons of Canaan, the youngest son of Ham, and grand-son of Noah, who settled in the country in great numbers, divided the most inviting portions among themselves, greatly multiplied, and became a strong, warlike and thrifty people.

It is also called "The Promise Land;" from the promise God made Abraham, concerning the place his posterity should inhabit. St. Paul says of Abraham, that "By faith he became a sojourner in the land of promise, as in a land not his own, dwelling in tents, with Isaac and Jacob, heirs with him to the same promise."

It was, after the Hebrews entered and settled in the country, generally known as the land of Israel, from the general name given to the posterity of Jacob. After the revolt, the whole tract of country occupied by the chosen people was known by two general names: that portion inhabited by the loyal tribes was called "The Land of Judah," and that belonging to the revolters was called "The Land of Israel." It seems the whole land was finally called Judea. (See Heb. xi: 9; Psa. lxxvi: 1)

The whole tract of country inhabited by the Jews was, after their return from captivity, called the Holy Land; which seems to have been given and designated as the land selected of God to be the chief seat of His worship and the inheritance of those whom He had chosen; it was called "Holy Land," by Christians because Christ, the "Holy One," was born there; and the principles He came to teach and establish were first sent to the world from this country, by the Apostles, after the tragic scene of the agony of our Lord on the memorable day of His crucifixion.

This name is highly significant, and at once strikes the mind of one that some particular history belongs to this country which makes it peculiar and more noteworthy than any other land in the world.

Palestine is now generally adopted as the name of the "Promise Land," which is derived from the Philistines, who settled and greatly multiplied in the southern portion of the country along the coast; this name was at first (according to custom) confined to the territory occupied by them, but of late the whole land which the Israelites inhabited, both on the east and west of the Jordan, was known as Palestine. When this name is mentioned in the Bible, it refers to Philistia, or the territory occupied by the Philistines.

The boundary of "Palestine proper," is the Lebanon mountains on the north, by the great desert of Arabia on the east, on the south by Idumea and the Wilderness of Tih, and on the west by the Mediterranean Sea; it is about two hundred miles in length, an average of sixty miles in width, with an area of twelve thousand square miles (see Zach. ii: 12; Joel iii: 4; Exod. xv: 14; and Isa xiv: 29-31).

But Syria-Palestine is the name by which the "Promise Land was familiarly known in the time of Herodotus, whose writings precede all others known relative to the history of the Land of Promise." He is the first to bring this name into prominent mention. Although Syria and Palestine, connected under one sovereign, embrace less territory than some of our largest States, such as New York or Pennsylvania, there is no country in the world embracing so much history; because of which the whole civilized world have, from the earliest historic times to the present, directed their attention toward it, and have written thousands of valuable volumes from the contents of its exhaustless treasury of superior historical greatness.

Should we compare this small territory, which contains the most important issues of our world, to other lands, we must conclude that it was of all others the most secluded, as if hemmed in by God himself expressly for the protection of His people.

The whole of Syria, connected with the "Land of Promise," adds largely to the boundaries, as described above. It measures, according to careful estimation, three hundred and sixty miles from Asia-Minor on the north, to the Wilderness of Tih and ancient Edom on the south, with an area of twenty-eight thousand square miles. The first thing that forcibly struck my attention when approaching Joppa was the high border land along the coast, with a few intervening depressions at wide distances, through which great rocks were spread into the shoal water. I said, God has thrown up a mighty bulwark on the border land for the protection of His chosen people.

THE MOUNTAINS.

The physical formation of the country is very mountainous. A range of mountains runs through it from north to south. This mountain chain is intersected at several points by valleys and plains, so as to give us a physical and historical series of distinct ranges; the most lofty of them are on the north, and can be seen a long distance, especially by those going northward.

Ebal, Gerizim, Tabor, Carmel, Nazareth, Hermon, Lebanon, and Ante-Lebanon, are all approached, as the traveler proceeds northward, from east and south. The two last named were known in Jewish times as Lebanon, and the low land intercepting the double range as the Valley of Lebanon; and sometimes it is called by historians Cœle-Syria, which means the "Hollow Syria." Subsequently the name of this double range was changed by the early writers, so that the range on the west fronting the sea was called Lebanon, and the one sloping on the east toward Damascus was called Ante-Lebanon.

But it should be remembered the Bible makes no such denominational distinction; both ranges are known in it as Lebanon. The highest point of Mount Lebanon, which runs southwest from a broad opening between the sea and the eastern plain, caused by an abrupt termination of the Nusaiviyeh range at the Castle of Husn, runs as far south as the latitude of Tyre, at which point it is intersected by the "ravine of the Latiny." South of the river the Lebanon range is much wider and lower, and continues more and more so until it terminates in the plain of Esdraelon. Carmel, the lofty, runs between this plain and Sharon. On the coast and on the south of Esdraelon (see Josh. xi. 17) are the mountain ranges of Samaria and Judea, running through the centre of the country, and finally sink away in the desert a little to the north of Beersheba.

The neighboring range, or we may say the sister chain, is Ante-Lebanon, running parallel with Lebanon, and takes its rise in the plain of Hamah, about twenty miles east of the northern extremity of Lebanon, and gradually rises in elevation until it culminates at Mount Hermon, nine thousand feet above the sea level. Thence the ridge continues southward along the east land of the Jordan, through Gilead and Moab, to the mountains of Edom, and is succeeded by a ridge very much lower, it being only from two to three thousand feet at its greatest elevation.

"The hills of Bashan," to which considerable Bible distinction is given, are about thirty miles east of the Sea of Galilee, and have an elevation of about five thousand feet above the level of the Mediterranean; its modern name is Jehel ed-Druse.

PLAINS AND VALLEYS.

There are several plains and valleys in Palestine and Syria, which are of great historical importance; especially the plains of Esdraelon and Sharon; also, those of the Jordan and Jericho.

The coast plain is situated along the sea-border embracing Palestine and Syria, between the mountains and the sea, and is intercepted at three different points by the mountain slopes which border on the Mediterranean; these mountain extensions form elevations of considerable height, so that the plain is entirely barred off.

These breaks in the plain are caused by the projections of Carmel, the Casius, and the Ladder of Tyre. These elevations divide the coast plain, so that each division has a different name; the northern division is called the plain of Essus. The border land of Phœnicia extends from Casius to the Ladder of Tyre; from thence to Mount Carmel lies the beautiful expanse of the plain of Acre; then the Sharon plain extends south of Philistia; but some writers call this great plain Philistia, southward from Joppa.

In those portions of the plains where extensive table-land is prominent, the soil is rich and productive, especially in the eastern division; but near the sea the sand is very deep and difficult to travel, especially so between Kaibo and Beyrout, and to make three miles on a horse would be doing well. The most important and fertile plains away from the coast are the Hamah, the Damascus, the Hauran, and Moab. The plain of Esdraelon, through which the river Kishon flows, abounds in pastures and cultivated fields. The soil is rich and highly productive. This is the most historic plain in Palestine; it intersects the central range of mountains, running from Mount Lebanon southward.

The plain or valley of Lebanon, of which mention has been made, is situated between Lebanon and Ante-Lebanon, known as Cœle-Syria, and is one of the richest tracts of land in Syria. It yields from year to year very rich crops, and is estimated to be about ninety miles long and eleven broad. The inhabitants do not till the land extensively on account of the extortionate tax rule prevalent in that region. The valley of the Jordan is that depression running from north to south in Palestine, and increasing in depth southward. The river Jordan flows through it, and stimulates fertility on either side in all tillable land.

This valley, and that known as the plain of Jericho, is the same. It is situated between the lake Gennesaret on the north, and the Dead Sea on the south. It is not as wide as the plain along the coast, except on the southern extremity. Here it is about twelve miles wide; this is its most expansive portion.

It has an immense fall between the sea of Galilee and the Dead Sea. At this latter point, where it terminates, its depression is thirteen hundred feet below the level of the Mediterranean, which is the lowest known spot of ground on the face of the globe. Much of the land about Jericho, Gilgal, and along the Jordan, is desert; which is partly the result of lethargy, and partly from poverty. The whole plain, if properly cultivated, would produce bountifully; but the facilities for conducting agriculture are poor and far behind the age.

THE RIVERS OF PALESTINE AND SYRIA.

The greater number of the rivers are very small; no larger than many of the ordinary branches in America. They are mostly winter streams, that are produced by the rain coming down from the surrounding mountains; they become dry during the summer and early fall.

The most important of these rivers is the Jordan, which if it continued its course to the Dead Sea in a direct line would only run about ninety miles from its source; but having such an extraordinary crooked course, it is estimated to run at least two hundred miles. The Jordan, although but a small stream at its source, is fed by several tributaries along its course until it becomes wide and deep.

The Orontes ranks next in size to the Jordan; its source is in the plain of Baka'a at the foot of Ante-Lebanon, near the ruins of Lylon, and runs northward to the sea. On this account it is called "El-Asy, the Rebellious." It is also called El-Makluh, "the inverted." The course of the river is one hundred and forty-nine miles.

The next in size is the Litany; it takes its rise near Baalbek, and flows down the Baka'a, then flows into a deep bed intersecting the ridge of Mount Lebanon, and enters into the sea a little north of Tyre. The whole length of the Litany is only about fifty-five miles.

The Barada, the "Golden Flowing," is the next in point of importance; this is the Abana, or Amana of the Bible; one of the rivers of which Naaman proudly boasted when ordered to wash in the Jordan to be healed of his leprosy. It is the most celebrated river in Syria, and one of the most useful; its source is Ain Barada in the plain of Zehedani, but has several tributaries along the Ante-Lebanon, which more than double its volume. After running several miles through a very wild and lonely district it flows into the plain of Damascus, where many channels are made to receive their water for irrigation; and at length it enters into a lake about twenty miles east of the city.

Without Abana there would be but little cultivation about Damascus. It may be truthfully called the life of the great Syrian metropolis.

The other river near Damascus is Pharper, now called "Away," which pours its waters into the most southern of the three lakes east of the city; it enters and crosses the plain on the south of Damascus.

The Kishon is a river well worthy of mention, not so much for its size, but because of the Biblical and historic interest which clusters about it; when compared to rivers in general it has but little if any merit; it may be classed with the winter currents of Palestine, as it is almost dry during the summer in its upper course, but it is replenished in winter by the repeated heavy rains and swells to the top of its banks and often overflows.

Its sources are several periodical springs near Jezreel and Lejjun and flows through the plain of Esdraelon to the northwest, between Mount Carmel and the hills of lower Galilee, then enters into the Bay of Acre, north of Haifa. The Belus river, called by the natives Nahr Na'aman, also flows into the Bay of Acre; it has no Bible mention, but is historically mentioned as the site where the Phœnicians first discovered glass; it is one of the smallest streams in the land; its entire length is only about six miles.

There are several other smaller streams of which mention might be made, but they are of no particular importance, except two or three; these are the brooks Elah, Cherith and the Kedron; the history of these renowned streams are generally known to most lovers of sacred history. The pools and lakes will be noticed in other chapters.

THE POLITICAL STATUS OF SYRIA AND PALESTINE.

To attempt to write an outline history of the political government of Palestine would be certain failure, for it would involve an investigation of the administration of each ruler of the several dynasties who in succession occupied the throne from the first sovereigns known in history to the present. It is well known to historians that those countries were almost constantly changing rulers and often dynasties, each of whom had his own selfish ideas of administering the affairs of the government, and many of them ruled with an iron sceptre.

The Israelites under the leadership of Joshua crossed the Jordan and entered upon their promised possession, having Jehovah as their King and supreme dictator, about the year fourteen hundred and fifty. B. C., with an official in the person of the High Priest as minister and expounder of his will.

The historical books of the Old Testament furnish all the information necessary in relation to this subject. To establish its certainty, so that an outline statement would be instructive to the careful Bible reader, it is sufficient to state that from the time of Joshua to the installment of Saul, the Benjamite King of Israel, the government was in theory at least a Theocracy.

To what extent the Lord was recognized by the new nation as their King cannot be fully understood, but if we may be allowed to draw our conclusions from their conduct toward Him, it would seem they regarded Him as holding a kind of local relation to them especially, having nothing to do with the destiny of other nations and tribes round about them.

They did not appear to regard Him as the High, Holy and Infinite God, who made the heavens and the earth; such conceptions of their King were too lofty for them; therefore, they looked upon the gods of the idolators in many respects to be worthy of their most sacred and earnest devotion.

The combined efforts of the prophets in connection with repeated chastisement from God were not regarded as timely admonitions to restrain the people from confident trust in false gods. From the time of Joshua to that of the kings judges were appointed as the chief magistrates with limited authority; and in connection with these judicial superintendents each tribe was allowed to have an internal government for the regulation of domestic affairs, according to their several necessities.

It is said each of the tribes were divided into " families," and these again were divided into " households of fathers," and each section had its head or chief, called an " Elder " (Kitto). All legislation needful for the betterment of the domestic government could be enacted by any tribe according to its needs if it did not conflict with the general legislation for the observance of the whole people; but when a measure was introduced which was general in its bearing, it could not become a law without the sanction of all the tribes, which was usually done through their representatives.

This was an old law given in the time of Moses; it was in this way the people proceeded when they elected Saul, the Benjamite, King over them about the beginning of the eleventh century, B. C. The whole people, through their representatives, went from under the government of Jehovah to that of Saul, notwithstanding the protest of Samuel, whose keen foresight comprehended the dreadful dilemma in which they were placing themselves. See Josh. xxiii. 2 and xxiv. 1; Num. i. 16; Deut. xxix. 10.

King Saul was in power forty years, but proved himself unworthy of his position of high trust, and the kingdom was changed to the house of David, son of Jesse. Here the dynasty of Saul ended, for not one of his descendants was permitted to occupy the throne. David, who while a shepherd boy having been anointed to be successor to Saul, was made king over all Israel. at Hebron, about the middle of the eleventh century, B. C.

He may fittingly be called the war king, for just as soon as his kingdom was firmly established, he turned his attention to those powerful tribes and nations around him, and was bent on conquest. The Philistines, who had given the Hebrews much trouble, were brought under his control, and those powerful warlike people of the different tribes, dwelling amongst the mountains of Sinai, Edom, Gilead, Bashan, and the whole stretch of country from that bordering on Egypt to the Euphrates, was made subordinate to this mighty Hebrew king, except that known as Phœnicia on the north, who lived on amicable terms with David, and rendered valuable service to him.

Indeed it can be plainly seen that much of the success of the Hebrew kingdom was because of the efficient aid given them by the Phœnicians; these two nations composed of distinct social descendants lived side by side and amongst each other on terms of friendship.

David, King of Israel, and Hiram, King of Tyre, were strong

friends; as was Solomon, his successor, and there seems never to have been any serious trouble between them.

The distinguished King of Tyre was deeply interested in the construction and completion of the great temple at Jerusalem, and sent skilled workmen who were celebrated because of their superior genius in fine arts to assist the Hebrew workmen in fully completing the plan designed of the Lord as to the model of His house of worship.

Solomon was the last king who swayed the sceptre over all Israel; his successor was Rehoboam, in the beginning of whose reign ten of the tribes revolted and called a convention at Shechem, and selected Jeroboam, of the tribe of Ephraim, to be their king. With his reign the growing inclination of the people to worship idols was greatly encouraged; being anxious to draw the people from the temple worship at Jerusalem, he established two places for religious assemblies to conduct their festivals; one was Bethel, the other Dan. At each place King Jeroboam set up a molten calf, which was devoutly worshiped by the people as symbols of *Jehovah*, while he assumed the powers of the royal priesthood as well as king.

The kingdom of Israel continued about two hundred and fifty years, or until the year seven hundred and twenty-one, B.C., and was captured by Shalmaneser, king of Assyria. The kingdom of Judah continued about five hundred years, and was overthrown by Nebuchadnezzar, King of Babylon. Thus came to an end one of the most prosperous and historic nations of the world, which, from that day to the present, has not been able to regain the country chosen for them as an independent government.

They were permitted to return from captivity after the Kingdom of Babylon fell into the hands of Cyrus about the year five hundred and thirty-six, B.C. (See 1 Kings xii. 28, 29; 2 Kings xxv.). These emancipated Jews began to rebuild their demolished city, a second temple was built, and in process of time the whole city was surrounded by walls, and the chosen people finally became settled for a time in their own land; but it was not permanent, for they were again woefully subdued by the Romans in the year seventy, A. D., and finally became dispersed over the face of the whole earth, and their country, which was cunningly and restlessly sought by many powerful nations, successfully passed from one dominion to another, until at length it went under the control of the Turks, in whose custody it is at present.

Palestine and Syria are now divided into three Pashale'ks or Wilayets; each having a governor appointed by the Sultan to oversee the domestic affairs and guard the interest of Turkey. The Jews, who about eighteen hundred years ago were compelled to leave the cherished land of their fathers, have ever held it in sacred memory; thousands of these scattered people are returning from their dispersions and are settling in and about the Holy City.

Many of them have built comfortable homes in which to spend their lives; such was the rush for building sites by this people, an order was issued by the Turkish authorities, that no more land should be sold to them until further orders. The Jews of Palestine live mostly in Jerusalem, Hebron, Tiberias and Safed; these are known as their *Holy Cities*. Then thousands of pilgrims visit these places of sacred memory every year, at each of which they shed a tear, impress a kiss, and devoutly kneel in earnest supplications for the return of their former joys.

CLIMATE.

The variations of climate in Palestine and Syria are more numerous than in any other country in the world, covering the same number of square miles. Down in the extreme east and southeast it is unbearably warm in summer, and during the greater part of the winter, it is as warm as in many portions of America in summer.

There can scarcely be a place in any of the plains of the East Indies warmer than the valley of the Jordan, or the plain down about the Dead Sea. But as the heights of Judah are ascended going towards Jerusalem a perceptible and gratifying change is experienced in the climate; the changes in the atmosphere depend largely upon the elevations and nature of the soil. Jerusalem is about three thousand feet above the Dead Sea, and has the benefit of daily refreshing breezes, yet the city in the summer is oppressively warm; this is caused by the intense heat reflected from the white rocks which are in great numbers round about the city.

Persons going from our country to Jerusalem in the hot season are compelled to remain in-doors from early morn until near night-fall; therefore little or no satisfaction is given sight-seers.

The changes of the weather common to us throughout the year are not known in Palestine and Syria; the sky is almost cloudless from the last of April to the first of October, during which time the most of the springs and streams dry up and the whole face of the ground becomes parched and vegetation looks as if it had been burned by fire, except in a few spots where perennial streams flow.

During these seasons traveling is not only tedious, but dangerous; in February the rains are the most frequent; many times intermittent showers of fine hail fall thick and fast, so that it is necessary to protect the face from the injury one would sustain if left exposed. Snows are also common in the latter part of the winter; it sometimes falls a foot deep, but is of short duration, seldom lasting more than a day; the coldest weather is not severe, and people go all the year without shoes; we have seen them about Bethany and Jerusalem, walking about in the snow barefooted without hesitation.

There is but little ice seen in the coldest parts, except on the highest mountain peaks, where snows continue almost the year round, as on the highest peaks of Hermon and Lebanon. I call to mind my journey from Beyroute to Damascus; we had to cross the summit of Mt. Lebanon and in many places the snow was so deep I could stretch out my arm and gather it while sitting on my horse, sometimes reaching up to get it.

But on the southern slope, where the altitude is lower than two thousand feet, snows are seldom seen. The barley harvest begins as early as the middle of April, in the Jordan valley, and the wheat harvest about the first of May. In southern Palestine among the hills reaping begins about the first of June; and in Lebanon, where the altitude and climate is cooler, the harvest generally begins about the middle of June.

When the Hebrews entered the land they found the whole sea coast inhabited by a strong and vigorous people, who were conducting a most lucrative business in all parts of the inhabited world; they were the early settlers of the country and had made wonderful progress.

The Phœnicians, sometimes known as Sidonians and Tyrians, who inhabited the coast of Syria from Jeliel on the north to Acre on the south, were descendants of Canaan, and were of Hamitic stock or race; this powerful and energetic people were never expelled from their territory by the Hebrews, as were several of the tribes belonging to their race, but continued living on the most friendly terms with Israel during the whole time they possessed the "Promise Land," and were of great service to them in aiding them on the sea with their vessels, and in sending them skilled laborers to perform intricate work at Jerusalem.

There was such friendship existing between them that several intermarriages took place amongst them, especially the higher classes, and there are no reasonable grounds to doubt that such relation existed amongst the poorer people.

Color was not a barrier as in America; it was not this characteristic which regulated social relations, but rank and fitness were the ties which bound them. If the people of our country would copy their example society would greatly profit by it.

The Phœnicians were regarded as one of the most skillful and industrious people on the face of the earth; the Philistines were also a powerful race, who, of late years, have been traced by some historians to Japhetic origin. They were a people of warlike courage and greatly troubled Israel; it is thought they are identical with the Cherethites or Cretans in the Bible, but were mixed with other tribes, as has always been common in Palestine. (See 1 Sam. xxx. 14; Ezek. xxv. 16; Zeph. ii. 5.)

PART II.

LIFE IN PALESTINE—PECULIAR CUSTOMS OF THE PEOPLE.

Style of Dress—Costly Garment Owned by the Poor—Style of Dress of the Women of Bethlehem and Nazareth—Dress of Mohammedan Women—Farming Implements—How Plows are Made and Used—Armed Merchants and Shepherds—Long Standing Feuds—Land-Marks Respected—Historical Associations—First Settlers—How Homes are Built—Variety of Climate—People of Lebanon—Their Appearance—Their Manners—Their Relations as to Religion.

STYLE OF DRESS.

THE same style of dress obtains (with but few exceptions), among both sexes, as were known in the time of our Lord and the early Church fathers. The most of them wear loose garments something like those represented on ancient pictures as far back as patriarchal times. In some instances the costumes of the men and women vary such a little, it is hard to tell one from the other in the distance; but on approaching them they are easily distinguished. There seems to be but little changing to suit the weather, except the head-dress. More care is taken of it than of any other portion of the body; which, in cold weather, the natives carefully cover with a shawl, while their lower limbs are left unprotected. This is done by the merchant, the farmer, and the peasant. Men and women can be seen out when it is very cold having their heads wrapped so carefully that nothing but their eyes can be seen, and wearing short dresses, reaching just a little below their knees, without shoes or stockings on. The style being permanent, those who buy costly dresses are not put to the necessity of having them altered to suit the fashion. Sometimes women who live in very humble homes appear in very rich dress; so that persons who are not conversant with the custom of inheritance would think strange of the great outward display by some who are very poor. It is the case, for the most part those rich and costly dresses worn by poor women have been made for forty or fifty years, and passed to the possession of several different families; or some individual, who first owned it, bequeathed it to some poor relative with the understanding it was to be kept in the family as long as it was wearable. By this means one garment may continue in a family for fifty years, for they take the most cautious care of them, only wearing them on special occasions. The women of Bethlehem and Nazareth are exceptions to the rule as to the general style of dress; each has a fashion of her own; and no matter where they are seen, persons know them by the style of their dress. One very noticeable feature of the female attire is the way they dress their head. If we may be allowed to judge them by what their dwellings contain and what their heads are dressed with, we should conclude that many of them have about all they possess on their heads. They take silver coins and string them, as we do beads, and form a head-dress so arranged as to come down to their temples; many contain a hundred or more pieces. The coins generally are keep-sakes, given them by friends as birthday presents, and are regarded as sacred. Therefore, they are not liable to be stolen from them. Those who have the fortune to own a number of such gifts, pride them as a very valuable treasure, and would almost part with their life sooner than with one of them. The native women are seldom seen with a hat on; hence, when they appear in public, their head-dress can be seen at a very good advantage. These ornaments are not seen so conspicuously on Mohammedan women, because they are compelled to wear a veil so as to cover their faces from the sight of men. These veils are very ugly, and render the ladies very unpresentable to those whose civilization has been progressive. The men, we learn from ancient history, wore long garments of different colors, just as the females did; the white and purple being the favorite colors. Any one who has been to Palestine will conclude very readily that but slight changes have been made, if any, in the mode of dressing. The men wear now, as in olden times, a turban on the head instead of a hat. Many wear a red cap made of thick cloth, known as Turkish caps. It is not an uncommon thing to see people going through the country carrying their beds. This was an ordinary custom in the time of our Lord, and has been continued through the ages. Therefore, it was not a strange thing to see the man on his bed at the pool; but to see him restored without having been in the healing stream was wonderful.

FARMING IMPLEMENTS.

It will also be observed there is but little improvement in the instruments used for cultivating the ground. The same style of plow, hoe and other implements used in ancient times prevail now; and many of the fields under cultivation seem to be anything else but tillable land. It would appear to those who are not acquainted with produce-growing in Palestine that nothing could grow in many of the farming districts because they are so very mountainous and stony. But the husbandmen are thoroughly acquainted with the land and know just where and when to sow seed, and when it begins to grow it looks in many places as though it was coming up out of the very stones, such is the abundant growth. These farmers have lived so greatly isolated from the modern people and so far behind the march of civilization they would not know how to use the farming implements used in modern times. Their plows are the style of those used in the earliest times, and so small and light a small lad could carry one without being burdened. It simply consists of two poles which cross each other at the ends, near the ground; one of them is fastened to the yoke for drawing, the other is used by the driver as a plow-share at one end and the handle at the other; no plow has two handles, as is the case in modern countries. The plowman holds the handle in one hand and the ox-goad in the other, which consists of a pole seven or eight feet long, sharpened to a point at one end for the purpose of touching up the oxen; the other end is broadened to clean the soil from the plow. One seeing these implements would naturally remember the teachings of our Lord, "No man having put his hand to the plow and looking back is fit for the kingdom of Heaven;" and of His words to Saul of Tarsus, "It is hard for thee to kick against the pricks." It was with such an instrument Shamgar, the son of Anath, slew six hundred Philistines and won a triumphant victory for Israel. When the oxen are disposed to be unruly the driver sticks the sharp point of the goad into his flank, or should he kick he holds it so as to stick him. It is usual for several workmen to be in the same field, or if going to either of the large cities with produce they go in small companies.

ARMED MERCHANTS AND SHEPHERDS.

Sometimes a dozen or more shepherds are seen high up in the mountain slope watching their flocks, a number of husbandmen in one field plowing, or twenty or thirty merchants with camels and donkeys traveling up to Jerusalem or down to Damascus, or to some of the other cities with merchandise. Each man has either a sword or gun, a large Damascus knife, or some other deadly instrument of defence. It is a strange sight to those unaccustomed to such sights to meet those half wild men out in the lonely country with these deadly weapons exposed to view. Naturally the question is asked, Why do these men carry arms everywhere they go? The long guns are so arranged over their shoulders with a strap which can be adjusted in a moment. If they have pistols or daggers they are placed in a sash around them.

LONG-STANDING FEUDS.

There are many reasons given as a cause for their having them. It is said they take them for self-protection both against wild beasts and enemies, who may be seeking to rob them; then it is often the case that many have had quarrels with some one that have not been settled, or a family dispute that has been standing for two or three hundred years, that has been handed down from one generation to another, which is held against those who live now, just as strongly as if they had been the authors of the offence; and will be continued until some one of the descendants is revenged. So it can be seen the avenger of blood is still after them, and, therefore, they carry weapons to defend themselves in case of an attack. Sometimes a very small offence costs many lives. For if one is avenged the family and relatives of the one punished will seek revenge from the avenger, or some of his people, and will never be satisfied until some of his family share the fate of death by the survivors, though it may be a hundred years to come. Sometimes whole villages are thrown into strife and lasting enmity about something that occurred in a family; vengeance is sought, and year after year the inhabitants of each of the villages go from day to day armed in case of an attack. I was informed that it has been known that several members of a long line of relatives have been slain because of an outbreak that occurred three or four centuries past. If one man was killed, his relatives felt bound to kill some of the relatives of the man who killed him in return; and so the matter of outrage goes down from one generation to another. Just as small a thing as the capture of a stray goat has caused tumults and led whole neighborhoods into trouble and bloodshed.

LANDMARKS RESPECTED.

It is only those fields and orchards near the larger towns and cities that are fenced in either with stones or cactus fences; but the fields in which grain is sown are generally fenceless. At times only a heap of stones mark the boundary of the farmer's jurisdiction. This custom has existed from the early times, when the people, if they had a disposition, could extend their line by moving the stones. Yet they dare not do so lest they bring upon themselves the curse pronounced upon the man who moves his neighbor's landmark.

HISTORICAL ASSOCIATIONS.

There seems to be no difficulty about one farmer trespassing upon another; but the main evil is the liberty people take in riding over the fields after the seed has been sown; this is not done through ill-will, but because of a long-standing custom coming down through hundreds of ages. When that pattern woman, Ruth, went out to glean after the reapers she was not put to the embarrassment of climbing over fences and crossing boundary ditches, but simply passed from one stone limit to another, and her happiness was to light on a part of the field belonging to Boaz. These instances are but an introduction to the many customs daily met with, which were current in olden times. If the stranger should pass some of the vineyards at the season for trimming the vines he will see the dresser cutting off the dead branches and casting them in the fire to be burned. One is reminded of the teachings of Jesus: "I am the vine, ye are the branches, and my father is the husbandman; every branch in me that beareth not fruit he taketh away." Many of the old customs of the early Patriarchs are still followed by some classes of the people.

FIRST SETTLERS.

We know those of the earlier times had no fixed home, but dwelt in tents, as it was suitable to their occupation as keepers of flocks or shepherds. This is a common custom with hundreds and perhaps thousands of people in various parts of the country to-day. It is an ordinary thing to see a tent village settled near a good pasture, convenient to a spring or well. It is highly probable some of these nomads have never lived in a house in their lives. The most of their tents are so small one would be compelled to crawl into them.

HOW HOMES ARE BUILT.

When permanent homes began to be builded the people settled in small communities. This seems to have been the custom of the various Canaanitish tribes long before the Hebrews came in possession of the land. After they began to come in great numbers they founded towns and cities along the sea border and other favorable localities, even from Jericho to Sidon. The husbandmen usually live miles away from the land they cultivate. They believe it much safer and agreeable to live in small communities than to be dispersed here and there on their lonely farms, as they are not suited for permanent homes. They are prepared also to protect themselves against the violence of the lawless, whom they feared would rob them even of their existence, were they to live on separate farms miles apart, as is common in other countries. The houses in the interior are generally made of hard clay or mud, except in such places as Bethel or Samaria, where the people have gathered material for the erection of their little homes from the ruins of the original cities. This does not refer to the large inland towns, such as Hebron, Bethlehem, Shechem, and others that have always been business thoroughfares. These small huts are usually very low, having but one apartment, and without windows or chimney, and only a very low doorway.

VARIETY OF CLIMATE.

It is written that no country in the world of the same extent of territory has a greater variety of climate than Palestine and Syria, especially the latter. The lofty summit and high places along the Lebanon range are very cool and balmy in the hottest days of summer, while the valley of the Jordan and the shores of the Dead Sea are so very warm, one accustomed to a milder climate would be at once overpowered. Then during the winter, when the snow is impassable on the higher portions of Lebanon, the valley about it is fresh and green. January and February are the coldest months during the season, the snows being most frequent and deepest.

THE PEOPLE OF LEBANON—THEIR APPEARANCE AND MANNERS.

The inhabitants of Lebanon are robust and generally healthy, presenting a much nobler appearance than the dwarfs of the low-lands. The people throughout the country are polite to strangers, but caution is given by those who know them best not to receive their salutations as the true intent of their heart; for they will many times give a bow of friendship when their purpose is far from it. There is said to be a meaning in every gesture. When they lay their right hand upon their forehead, lips and breast in succession they indicate the following: "In thought, word and deed I am your servant;" and when they kiss one hand it is a representation of a greater humility. But these outward demonstrations of civility and friendship are only formal and empty. The whole inhabitants are divided into religious sects. It is that which has made the greatest distinction; every other preference is of a minor character.

THEIR RELIGIOUS RELATIONS.

The religious sects are by no means friendly towards each other, and it occurs that they sometimes become hostile. The Mohammedans are the most powerful, and take advantage of the minor sects whenever an opportunity is presented. They are taught to look with the most cruel contempt upon all others whose religion differs from theirs, and they know well how to practically observe their instructions. While the Mohammedans are divided into several sects, they are united on the question of opposing every other that is not inclined to their faith. There are so many excellent books written on the various sects, we deem it unnecessary to add anything in this volume.

PART III.

OUTLINE HISTORY OF THE ISRAELITES,
FROM THEIR ENTRANCE INTO THE LAND OF PROMISE TO THEIR DISPERSION.

General Character of Israelites—Their Criminal Waywardness—Allotments of Twelve Tribes—Their Religious and Political Revolutions—Situation of Tribes of Reuben, Gad, and Manasseh—Deborah's Criticism—Situation of Tribes of Judah, Ephraim, Simeon, Benjamin, and Dan—Situation of Tribes of Issachar, Asher, Zebulun, and Naphtali—Tribe of Levi—Its Official Relations to the Others—Their Cherished Treasure—The Tabernacle Removed from Gilgal to Shiloh—Great Feast Reunions—Shiloh, a Religious Court of Priests and Levites—Office of Levites—Office of Priests—Israel's Wayward Tendency the Signal of Their Decline—Israel given to Idolatry—Israel's Oppression a Divine Rebuke—Their Inter-Marriage with the Canaanites—Official Judges who Delivered Israel—Ehud of Benjamin, His Cunning Scheme—Ehud's Stratagem, His Escape—Philistines' Hostilities—Shamgar a Deliverer of Israel—Shamgar Judge of Israel—Trouble out North—Jabin, King of Hazor—Deborah the Prophetess—Engagement between Barak and Sisera—Triumph of Israel—Jael, Sisera's Destroyer—Israelites afflicted by Moabites—Gideon and His Little Army—Position of the Midianites' Camp—Gideon's Attack—Death of Gideon—Invasion of Gilead by the Ammonites—Jephthah, the Victor—His Rash Vow—Trouble with the Philistines—Samson, the Mighty Hero—Samuel, the last Judge—His Counsel to Israel—Israel's Anxiety for a King—Conduct of Joel and Abijah—Samuel Anoints Saul—The Turning Point in the Affairs of the Government—Samuel's last Advice to Israel—Saul as King—David Chosen to Succeed Saul—Opposition to David—Its Final Result—Transfer of the Kingdom—David King of Israel—Solomon on the Throne—Revolt of Ten Tribes—Worshiping the Calves—Southern Kingdom—Prophets in Israel—Israelites Carried into Captivity—Assyrians Inhabiting Their Land—Samaritans Rejected—The Jews Return from Captivity—Discord between Jews and Samaritans—Services on Mount Gerizim—Nehemiah Rebuilding the Walls of Jerusalem—Ancient Samaritans—Visit to Samaritan Temple—Their Religious Devotions—The People, Their General Bearing—Tribes under Rehoboam and Jeroboam—Northern and Southern Districts—Silent Period—Condition of Jews when our Lord came on Earth—Jews Subject to Persia—Headquarters of Persian Monarch—A Strange Conquest—Rule of Ptolemies—Sanctuary Robbed—The Maccabees' Rule.

THE GENERAL CHARACTER OF ISRAELITES.

BEFORE entering into a detailed account of the most prominent places that largely embrace the history of Palestine, it is of importance to give an outline survey of the general character of the Israelites, after entering upon their promised possessions, as a national organization. When Moses, the celebrated commander and law-giver of the Hebrews, died, Joshua, the brave and heroic leader, succeeded him, and triumphantly led the people into the "Land of Promise;" where they would have been, even to-day, one of the most progressive, prosperous, and wealthy nations on the face of the globe, if they had allowed the Lord to continue with them. But their superstitions, pride, idolatry, infidelity, and international strifes led them from the God of their fathers into grave offences of shame and dissolution, which broke down their government. They seemed not to know how to appreciate their independence, until they had been put under the sceptre of a foreign power. The Hebrews were the most unsettled and contentious people in the world, as a nation. If we carefully consider their history as detailed in the Holy Scriptures, and many other books written by brilliant and worthy authors, who have exhausted much time and energy in collecting facts touching the inner life of this people, it will be seen they were constantly contending against themselves; so that from the time of Joshua to that of our Lord, the religious and political revolutions were so tremendous that the whole nation had passed through an unenviable transition. They had lost all the bearing of the happy and prosperous people who went forth conquering throughout the land under the banner of the God of Hosts. When Jesus came among them, He found the whole nation full of corruption, superstition, and intensely gross darkness. This people, whose mighty arm of conquest had subdued nations and brought proud kings under the power of its sceptre, and struck all with great alarm who knew of their continued success, were themselves subject to the galling yoke of Roman domination. Their fame for conquest had vanished, and their country had been the hunting-ground for the nations round about them.

When the tribes had settled in the several districts allotted them they could have gone from one state of pleasing progress to another, for the condition and adaptations of each tribe were considered long before the allotment was made. It is reasonable to suppose that God, Himself, revealed to Jacob the territory each of the tribes should occupy. The aged patriarch, when dying, indicated what should be the possessions of each of his sons, although they had not been in Egypt more than about seventeen years. A passing notice of the districts, as allotted to the tribes, will show how well they were adapted to the capacity of each. Reuben and Gad were divided from the others by the river Jordan. This district was given them by their own choice. It may seem strange that these two tribes and half of that of Manasseh would have contented themselves to settle down on the east side of the Jordan, and beyond the bounds of Canaan proper, and become almost a distinct people, if it had not been so ordained by the Lord. The people living on the borderland were vicious, and entertained no friendly feelings for them; yet they were just as content to remain there as though the whole army had reached their destination. These tribes were keepers of flocks, and the country assigned them was splendidly adapted to their calling. It contained good pastures and a good supply of water and other conveniences necessary to properly care for their flocks. There was doubtless a stronger attachment between these two tribes than with the others, because they were usually camped together during their forty years' wanderings in the wilderness. They, under these circumstances, must have known each other better, and could dwell in peace.

One half of the tribe of Manasseh, having remained with them, made in all two tribes and a half of the twelve who did not live in Palestine. They located themselves, having Reuben on the south, Gad in the center, and the half tribe of Manasseh on the north. These people having been separated from their brethren, and living in almost absolute isolation, constantly burdened with the cares of pastoral life, lost much of their primitive devotion for their brethren on the west of the Jordan, and took no particular interest in the affairs of the nation. They were not conspicuous in the many wars fought by their brethren, nor did they seem to interest themselves as to the general prosperity of the other tribes. They were more stimulated with an ambition for personal gains than by patriotism. This is clear from their conduct towards the other tribes when they were wanted up north to assist in a conflict with the Canaanites. They stubbornly refused to go up to their help. Their attitude toward their fellows on the west caused Deborah, the Prophetess, to criticise them keenly in song after the victory had been won. "By the water-courses of Reuben there were great searchings of heart; why sittest thou among the sheep-folds to hear pipings of the flock?" Gilead abode beyond the Jordan. It is evident they were content with their own situation, and had no disposition to help those beyond the Jordan. Judah and Ephraim occupied the best portion of the southern and middle districts; around them clustered the most important history of the nation. Hebron, the headquarters of their historic development, was embraced in the allotment of Judah, who afterwards shared a part of their possessions to Simeon around Beersheba on the southwest. Ephraim had for his possession the territory that embraces Shechem on the north. The portions of

Benjamin and Dan were situated between Judah and Ephraim; the former occupied that portion of the country extending from the Jordan valley on the east, and southeast, northward to Ephraim, embracing Jericho, Gibeon and Bethel. Dan's portion extended northward from the two Beth-harans to the Mediterranean Sea, taking in a portion of the valley of Ajalon; also embracing Ramleh and Lydda, the Sharon plain and Joppa, and several other places important in Bible history. The half tribe of Manasseh, living west of the Jordan, was allotted a small district on the north of Ephraim, in connection with a number of towns in the districts of the adjoining tribes. The whole of the district of Galilee was apportioned to the remaining four tribes, Issachar, Asher, Zebulun and Naphtali. All the tribes received a special allotment, except the tribe of Levi, which was priestly, and was therefore dispersed amongst all the others in the forty-eight cities given them. This latter tribe was scattered throughout the nation to advise and check them from the commission of the various evils to which they were so greatly inclined. It is well known the Israelites had a most preciously cherished treasure, which they cautiously and sacredly guarded, and were careful as to its location, as it was highly necessary a proper and safe place should be selected for its safe keeping. We refer to the Tabernacle. Up to this time and onward for a long period the new inhabitants of the country had not been formed into a national brotherhood strictly; for as yet they were divided into tribes, each having a separate jurisdiction in the management of their political affairs, but sustaining a relation to each other peculiar to a nation. It may be said they were a confederation of distinctly organized settlements or communities. They had no federal capital and no human king. Under such circumstances it would seem that the Tabernacle would be a bone of contention among the tribes, each endeavoring to hold it within the confines of their own dominion. But such was not the case, for all the people were specially devoted to their moveable sanctuary and sacredly guarded its safety. There was a conference held by the most prominent of the people, and it was found important to remove it to some place convenient as possible to the people at large. Shiloh was, in their opinion, the most suitable place, and to it the sacred tent was taken. This they did before the tribes dispersed to their several allotments. The Tabernacle had remained at Gilgal from the time it was placed there, after the people crossed the Jordan. Any one having the map of Palestine can see the selection of Shiloh was wise, it being more central and convenient than any other, and close to the great highway leading through the main cities and towns in the land. This seems to have been the chief reason for making a selection of it for the permanent resting-place of their sacred treasure. There were three festivals celebrated yearly, which the able-bodied men were requested to attend. It can be seen, therefore, it was highly important the location of the sanctuary should be conveniently situated. Shiloh is in the territory of Ephraim, not far from the main thoroughfare leading to Damascus and Egypt, Jericho and Joppa, and about half way between Shechem and Bethel. The Tabernacle remained there the religious headquarters of the Israelites more than three hundred years. . But during the time of Eli it began to lose much of its former prestige, especially after the Philistines captured the Ark of the Covenant. The Tabernacle was a binding instrument; it kept the people together in religious sentiment, in sympathy, and in their fraternal relations, so that on meeting at their triennial religious services at Shiloh they most friendly and happily greeted each other, and devotedly renewed their ties of brotherhood.

When a people can meet upon a common level to pay their devotions to the Most High God, a union of friendship is stimulated that grows more and more from day to-day, until it becomes so strong it will be hard to break its influence. Such was the case with the Israelites. They were without national laws at that time to bind them as such, nor had they a human sovereign to rule over them, nor a centre from which the word of command was issued. But Shiloh served as a kind of religious court of Levites and priests; a capital to which the multitudes were drawn three times a year, and renewed their vows to the God of their fathers; recognizing Him as their supreme ruler and law-giver. Shiloh also served as a gathering place, where many things would be settled that caused unpleasantness among the people, growing out of local disputes, renewed former friendly relations, and prohibited the encroachments and ill-feelings, which the dividing of themselves into special territories would without doubt introduce and cherish. The Levites were instrumental in doing much towards keeping the people together fraternally. These officials were scattered through all the tribes, constantly teaching the people their whole duty towards each other, so that the tribes might be bound together in the strongest ties of fraternal brotherhood, promoting virtue and true piety. They were familiar with the laws and exercised the office of under-judges in the ordinary courts; they took charge of the Tabernacle and sacred vessels. The priests, who were the higher officials, were indispensable factors in aiding the people in the affairs of state as well as in their religious duties. They did much toward keeping the tribes together and in putting down many tendencies of bitter schisms that were brewing on account of jealousy. They were the chief spiritual directors of the tribes, and at times were called upon to be the judges of civil matters. They were God's messengers. He would make known His will to them, and they would teach the same to the people.

The unsatisfied appetite of the Israelites, stimulated by a passionate desire for a king of their own selection, began to disclose itself more decidedly at length, and continued to arouse the people until their ambition was gratified. It is noteworthy that during the whole period following Joshua, one trouble after another haunted the Israelites for many years: enmity, contention, murder and many other severe afflictions followed, because of repeated efforts of hostile nations around to destroy them. That the distressed Hebrews might have proper leaders during their great struggles, God appointed judges to protect and defend them at times of great distress and excitement. Their authority was bordering on kingly prerogatives; it extended to peace and war, or they had power to declare war and make peace as the case seemed to them expedient. They also had authority as chief magistrates to decide all cases of law coming under their notice, from which there was no appeal. The judges were not law-makers, but its executives. Soon after the death of Joshua Israel began to depart from God, and turn their minds towards idolatry, for which they were often rebuked; this would serve as a check for a time, but the same spirit would again incline them to seek the favor of other gods. This disposition took firm hold upon the hearts of the people and so controlled them that they yielded to its allurements by degrees, until at length the whole nation had to some extent devoted itself to idolatrous worship, and embraced it just as freely and fondly as did the heathen nations about them. For these glaring transgressions the Lord administered to them a stern rebuke, and allowed them to be sorely grieved by the people of Mesopotamia, the Moabites, the Canaanites, the Midianites, the Ammonites and Philistines. These several states at different periods greatly oppressed Israel and caused them to mourn on account of their transgressions. The book of Judges furnishes many narratives of the oppressions the people suffered as a stern rebuke from the Almighty for their persistence in rebelling against Him. Inter-marriage with the Canaanites was one of the influences that caused Israel to become entangled with heathen worship; and God permitted them to experience the bitter results of their folly, by withdrawing His guarding hand from them for a time, that they might see their extreme dependence upon Him and return to the true worship. The king of Mesopotamia overpowered them and held them under his iron sceptre for eight years, during which time Israel suffered greatly.

"The children of Israel did that which was evil in the sight of the Lord and forgot the Lord their God, and served the gods Baalim and Ashtaroth. Therefore, the anger of the Lord was kindled against Israel, and he sold them into the hand of Cushan-rishathaim." The lamentable experience of the Israelites under this deep oppression caused them to turn their attention to God, whom they had forsaken, and in tears of agony they appealed to Him for deliverance. The Lord heard them and gave them helpers. Othniel, son of Kenaz, rose up in the strength of God and delivered them from the iron arm of the king of Mesopotamia. Othniel was the first of the judges of Israel, and during the forty years he was in the official position the land enjoyed great peace. The next king who rose up against Israel was Eglon of Moab, who came into the country by the plain of Jericho in the border of Benjamin; he smote Israel and caused them to serve him eighteen years, and so bitter were their afflictions, they were again moved to seek refuge under the all-powerful hand of the Lord. He heard their cries and raised up Ehud of Benjamin to deliver them. This mighty man gathered the hosts of valiant men and came down with them from the heights of Ephraim and attacked the Moabites in their rear, and greatly discomfited them. There was great stratagem devised in preparing for this battle. Ehud was sent by the children of Israel to take a present, perhaps in connection with their taxes, to the king of Moab. Before starting he made a double-edged dagger, about as long as his arm, and hid it under his garment on his right side. It may be that he placed it there because he was left-handed. This seems the more plausible to me because he was a Benjamite, and to be left-handed was not unusual with them. But it is the opinion of some authors the dagger was placed on his right side to escape observation. I think, however, the opinion we have ventured is the correct one; for it is well known the men of Benjamin used to carry their sling-bag on their right side so as to get the stone in the hand from which they would throw it. When Ehud came to the palace with the present he sent those away who went with him, then he went back and said to the king, "I have a secret errand for thee, O king;" he was of the opinion an important message was to be delivered. He therefore commanded all to be silent, and sent his state servants away. Eglon was in his beautiful room that had been arranged for his special comfort, known as his summer cooling-room. When all was quiet and Eglon and Ehud were left to themselves, the Benjamite advanced to the king and said to him, "I have a message from God to thee." The king, in accordance with the custom of his day, rose to his feet to receive it. Just then Ehud pierced him deeply with his double-edged dagger, and the king fell heavily to the floor and died, without the knowledge of his chief officials or any one else. Ehud then closed and locked the doors and took the keys, quietly passed the guards, and finally made his escape. After a while the servants of the king returned to attend to him. Finding the doors locked, they supposed he was sleeping and said, " He covereth his feet." They returned to their quarters and remained an unusually long time without any signs of the king's presence. Becoming alarmed and suspicioning something was wrong with him, they began to look for a key to unlock the door and enter unbiddingly into his chamber; on entering they saw, to their great amazement and grief, their king lying dead on the earth. But Ehud was gone; and having escaped safely to his people, he blew the trumpet on Mount Ephraim. In response to the trumpet call they came to him. He said to them, " Follow after me, for the Lord hath delivered your enemies, the Moabites, into your hands." There were about ten thousand of the picked men of Moab, and not one of the men who oppressed Israel escaped the fury of the men of Ehud

PHILISTINES ROUTED.

After this successful engagement and triumphant victory, Israel enjoyed peace for about eighty years. The Philistines were very perplexing to the children of Israel and did them much harm. These enemies would watch favorable opportunities to intimidate the husbandmen just about the time their crops were ready to harvest. The Philistines would suddenly come down upon them and drive them from their fields in which they had labored so long and made great sacrifices to cultivate. It often occurred; they would be compelled to leave everything behind and flee for refuge among the rocks and caves. It is stated in Judges, " that in the days of Shamgar the highways were unoccupied." Such was the fear the people entertained of the Philistine robbers, they had abandoned the highways and made their journeys through the by-ways for safety. It occurred one day while Shamgar, the son of Anath, was working in the field with his companions, a company of Philistines came down with great fury upon them. The heroic Shamgar took up his ox-goad, an instrument used to urge the oxen and also to clean the plow, and single-handed slew six hundred of the intruders. They became wild with amazement and fled with great haste from the strong arms of the hero. Shamgar and those with him pursued the refugees and drove them to the confines of their own territory. This wonderfully strange defense delivered Israel from the terror of the Philistines, and they went once more to their work without fear and traveled the highways in peace. Shamgar, according to the most reliable sources, was the third judge of Israel after Ehud. His services to Israel were of great benefit both as judge and warrior

TROUBLE OUT NORTH.

The tribes living out north were greatly oppressed by Jabin, king of Hazor, who was a man of great power, wealth and influence. He was a formidable opponent of the Israelites, and greatly oppressed them twenty years. His army was large and well equipped with the most deadly instruments of warfare known in history. He had nine hundred chariots of iron. This great northern monarch treated the poor Hebrews without mercy, and held them in a state of sore depression. The people cried unto the Lord to help them, and he summoned Barak, son of Ahinoam of Kedesh, of the tribe of Naphtali, to deliver them. There was a remarkable woman in Israel who was both prophetess and judge, whose name was Deborah. She was a just and holy woman, and the Spirit of the Lord moved her to arouse Barak to strike an effectual blow for the deliverence of his people. Having received the message and the assurance of a triumphant victory, Barak gathered together ten thousand men from Zebulun and Naphtali, and stationed them on Mt. Tabor, from whence they descended upon Jabin's army (which was commanded by Sisera, his chief general, and stationed at the foot of the mountain), and threw them into great confusion. Sisera's army fled, followed by Barak; being greatly confused, they ran unguardedly into the brook Kishon, and were carried headlong into the Mediterranean Sea. It is said by Jewish writers that Barak was much alarmed when he saw the hosts of Jabin's men of war at the foot of Mt. Tabor, and would no doubt have become fainthearted, had not Deborah been by to encourage him and assure the people the Lord would give them victory. The timely encouragement of Deborah stimulated Barak to immediate action, and he descended the mount followed by his ten thousand men of war. "The Lord discomfited Sisera, and all his chariots and his host with the edge of the sword." Sisera, who was chief in command of Jabin's forces, got down from his chariot and ran to elude the pressing host of Barak, who were hard after him. But he was attracted by a female whose name was Jael; she invited Sisera, while fleeing, into her tent; he, supposing it to be a safe hiding-place, went in and hid himself.

The woman covered him with a cloak, and he, feeling himself secure from the apprehension of his pursuers, fell asleep; Jael took a long nail, that she used to fasten her tent, and, with powerful and effective blows, drove it through his temples, and fastened his head to the ground. Soon afterwards Barak was seen coming towards her tent, seeking the refugee; Jael ran to meet him, and said she would show him his enemy; he went with her into the tent and there he saw the man who had proudly stood at the head of Jabin's army pinned to the ground dead. Then the Israelites resolved to subdue this terrible foe by whom they had been troubled so long. "And the hand of the children of Israel prospered and prevailed against Jabin, king of Canaan." But the Israelites were soon found turning themselves from the God of their fathers and indulging in gross sins. Then the Midianites and Amalekites, children of the east, were induced to come over on account of the very fine crops and rich pastures of the plains of Sharon, Esdraelon and Philistia, spread themselves through the country as far as Gaza, and became masters of the beautiful and fertile country for seven years. These intruders dealt severely with Israel, many of them losing their homes and all their possessions. They were hunted down like wild beasts, so that Israel had to flee for refuge; some hid in caves, in dens and among rocks. The Midianites also would rob them of their produce, leaving nothing behind for man or beast. These are a few of the afflictions which disturbed the people before a deliverer was sent to them. At length God appointed or inspired Gideon, of the tribe of Manasseh, living in the country south of Esdraelon, to drive out the Midianites, who were increasing their outrageous impositions upon the Israelites. Then Gideon went forth in obedience to the will of God to fight the hosts of enemies, having but three hundred men upon whom he could depend when he had reached the place where the foe was camped. These men had lapped water at the brook as an evidence of their bravery and sincerity of purpose. But above all, God was with the valiant-hearted commander, and assured him a glorious victory. Gideon suddenly sprang upon the foe by night, whilst they were quietly sleeping, and greatly alarmed them. The Midianites had camped in the valley of Jezreel, just under the southern shoulder of little Hermon, which was a splendid situation for defence under ordinary circumstances. But the advantage of position, so necessary in war, was not a consideration with the leader and commander of the little army of three hundred men who went to battle without any physical weapons whatever. Having made full arrangements for the engagement, Gideon made a bold, determined and successful attack upon the enemies of Israel, and caused them to flee before him with frantic dismay. A messenger was sent to the men of Ephraim to pursue them with all possible haste, which they did, and slew Oreb and Zeeb, two of the princes of Midian. During this engagement the enemies of Israel suffered great loss, for "the sword of the Lord and of Gideon" was mighty in the destruction of the intruders. The people were so animated over the victory, and so charmed with the bravery of Gideon, they were ready to elect him their king; but such an office was far from his wish, and he promptly refused it. It was the Lord's victory, and he wanted Him to have the glory. This man of God died at a good old age, full of honor and great peace, and was laid to rest in the sepulchre with his fathers. This signal victory given the Israelites by the Lord did not make a lasting beneficial impression upon them; for they were so greatly inclined to idolatry, that, but a short while after the death of Gideon, they were again following the examples of the heathens and leaving the established worship of their fathers. They had forgotten Gideon, and cared nothing for his seventy sons left with them; nor did they seem to fondly remember the forty years of peace they had enjoyed, because of the services rendered them by the man of God, whom they would have honored with the office of king. Then there came another crisis; this was the invasion of Gilead, the country of Gad, Reuben and Manasseh by the Ammonites, who inhabited the country a little to the east of these tribes. Then Jephthah became their successful leader. He sent a messenger to the king of the Ammonites, demanding to know why he had invaded their country. In reply the king made an excuse for doing so on account of some quarrels that had occurred several hundred years prior, a matter the people then living had nothing to do with, and knew but little, if anything, about. Jephthah saw from the answer of the king there was no foundation to justify his procedure, and that there was evil intent in his heart; he therefore resolved to meet the Ammonites in the name of the Lord. He also made a vow to sacrifice to the Lord whatsoever he should first meet on approaching his house after the victory was won by him. He soon defeated the Ammonites and returned to his home crowned with glory. When he drew near his dwelling, filled with gratitude on account of the double victory he had won, his spirit was suddenly subdued, his only daughter came out to meet and embrace him, for he remembered his vow, which he felt himself bound to perform. The triumph of her father over the invading foes was so gladdening to the child that she made no demur. The question as to the manner Jephthah performed this vow has been obstinately and exhaustively discussed by several of the most brilliant and sagacious minds of our world; but it has not been definitely settled. It is thought by some that he really did sacrifice his daughter as a burnt-offering to the Lord. But when it is called to mind that no such sacrifice as human flesh was acceptable to God, and that it was the intention of the conqueror to present a sacrifice with which the Lord would be well pleased we are inclined to the opinion of those who discuss the question negatively, which seems to be the more plausible. There was another trouble broke out which was very serious to at least two of the tribes. The Philistines on the southwest rose up in great numbers and committed many depredations in Judah and Dan, and brought all the country round about under their sway, causing the people to endure great afflictions. But the Lord had at all times some one at hand to stand in the defence of Israel when they fervently prayed to Him. In this case Samson, the son of Manoah, of the tribe of Dan, was their deliverer. The conflict between the Hebrews and Philistines was strong and severe. At times the latter seemed to be increasing in power, and Israel many times smarted under their afflictions; and the condition of things indicated that the Philistines would soon become masters of the situation, who, with a relentless hand, were continually binding heavy burdens upon the disconsolate Israelites. But Samson was found to be a strong deliverer and saved his people from much distress. The people were still clamoring for a king, and nothing else would satisfy them. Their ambition for a monarch had thoroughly matured during the judgeship of Samuel, who was the last of those officials in Israel. It is generally conceded that he was the most efficient and energetic of all the Hebrew judges.

The political and moral condition of the people was at a very discouraging point when he began his administration; but Samuel lifted them from this deplorable state, freed them from the oppressions of tyrant foes, and established the true religious worship among them. His period was the closing of the judges and the dawning of the kingly age. When the duties of the office became too heavy for Samuel in his declining years, so that he felt himself physically incompetent to make his annual circuit through the country to administer justice as he had done, and feeling anxious as to the prosperity of the people, he appointed his two sons, Joel and Abijah, judges over Israel. But, instead of walking in the footsteps of their father, they were entirely to the contrary, being avaricious, reckless and untrue, having no disposition to care for the prosperity of any one but themselves. Being greedy for gain, they allowed themselves to take bribes, and would often punish the innocent and protect the guilty. Many times their decisions were given in favor of the men who furnished the most money. "And his sons (Samuel's) walked not in his ways, but turned aside after lucre, and took bribes and perverted judgment." The feeling among the people to have a king to rule over them had been growing stronger for a long time, and they became restlessly anxious for one during the administration of the sons of Samuel, and based the necessity of such a change upon the conduct of these unjust men. Samuel was much displeased with the growing and unyielding disposition of Israel, and endeavored to change their purpose, but could do nothing with them; a king they longed for, and a king they must have. Finding he could not change them, the aged judge took the case to God in prayer, that he might be properly directed what to do. Now the crisis is at hand; the Lord is about to grant the people their anxious wish, but informs Samuel that they must bear the responsibility of their own folly. God then directed him to anoint one, whom he would be directed by the Spirit, to be their king. One day Kish, the father of Saul, missed some of his donkeys and sent him to look for them. The young man and his servant traveled a three days' journey without success. Saul then concluded it would be better to return home, fearing his father would be troubled about him. But the servant remembering they were in the neighborhood of Ramah, the home of Samuel, he proposed to pay a visit to the "man of God;" and inasmuch as he was a prophet he might be able to inform them where the donkeys could be found. Saul agreed to the proposition; and as they were going up the hill towards Ramah, they met Samuel on his way to offer a sacrifice to the Lord. He had been impressed by the Spirit that he should meet a man that day whom he should anoint with oil, according to the honored customs of nations, setting apart a man to be king. As soon as the old sire saw Saul he knew he was the man; and just at that moment the Spirit impressed him to anoint the young man. After he was anointed he was to go to Gilgal with Samuel to offer sacrifice to the Lord; and when the people saw Saul among the prophets they marveled. When the time came for a king to be selected, Samuel called the people together at Mizpeh, and recounted to them the wonderful things the Lord had done for them from the time He led them forth from the land of Egypt, and how ungrateful they had shown themselves. They had at that time reached the most critical period of their history, for they were changing from a theocratical to a monarchical government. It was an auspicious moment, a turning point in the political affairs freighted with momentous results. The people were about to withdraw themselves from the superintendency of the Lord, and put their affairs under the jurisdiction of a man. The final duty of Samuel was to advise the people as to their duty to the king and the king's duty toward the people. Then Saul was chosen and installed king of Israel. Such were his many opportunities, he would have been the idol of the nation, and a great blessing to his subjects, had he allowed himself to be under the guidance of God. He began his administration with manliness and bravery; the victory he obtained over the Ammonites was a signal of the presence of the Lord with him and his people, and caused the new nation to rejoice in their king. But the flattering prospect with which Saul began his reign was soon clouded by confusion and trouble. King Saul had his headquarters in Gibeah, about four miles from Jerusalem; and although he was lifted to the highest and most honorable position in the gift of the people, he would often be engaged in domestic affairs. After the death of Saul, David of Bethlehem, succeeded him. He was anointed while a lad, long before the death of Saul, to be the second king of Israel, by good old Samuel, who was then in the evening of life. After the inauguration of David, he began his reign in Hebron, the great historical city of the tribe of Judah, to which he belonged.

The new king met with stubborn opposition from the tribes of the north and east, who for seven years and a half refused to submit to his authority, and clung with great zeal to the house of Saul. The persistent opposition these tribes made to the rule of David was the signal of a future trouble, and the corner-stone of the revolt under the rule of Rehoboam. For, notwithstanding David had been chosen by the Lord and was anointed by His direction to be the king of Israel, Ishbosheth, Saul's son, was so eager to succeed his father, he encouraged the rebellious spirit exhibited against the son of Jesse, and allowed himself to be illegally installed king over the dissatisfied tribes. This naturally introduced war, to force the rebels to loyalty. Ishbosheth established his headquarters in Mahanaim, among the hills of Gilead east of the Jordan, and the place in which David afterwards found refuge when he fled from his son Absalom. The son of Saul, and his party, did not hold out long; there were so many adversities in their way the hearts of the people failed, and by mutual consent they accepted David as king of the whole nation. The king, feeling the weight of his responsibility and himself too remote from the masses, sought a place more convenient for his seat of power. Jerusalem (Jebus) was fixed upon as a proper locality, it being twenty-six miles further north. The strongly fortified Mount Jebus was much desired, because of its adaptation for an impregnable fortress. The desire of the king was soon gratified, for Mount Jebus was ceded to him. David soon became known as a great warrior, and was feared by the nations round about him. Some of these nations formed alliances, and others were tributaries and brought him a great revenue. David also established the national worship at Jerusalem, making it the centre of the great religious festivals, to which the people went to pay their devotions to the Most High. When David drew near to the end of his life, he gave his son Solomon a most solemn charge, "then gathered up his feet and died." The Lord had given him the plan for building the Temple, which was transferred to Solomon, who carefully carried out all the requirements necessary to its completion. When finished, he solemnly dedicated it to the worship of God, with most impressive services. The youthful king displayed great wisdom and devout piety in the beginning of his reign; but as he grew older and more popular his conduct changed and he fell into many disgraceful snares, which brought the displeasure of God upon him, and introduced the final decline of the nation. When Solomon died, his son Rehoboam ascended the throne. The dissatisfaction which began in the beginning of his grandfather's reign, reached its height, and ten of the tribes revolted, utterly refusing to allow the new king to rule over them. The revolting ten tribes sent representatives up to Shechem to arrange for the election of another king, and the establishment of another kingdom. When these representatives met, they did not disclose their intention, but pretended they were going up there to harmonize the difficulty and acknowledge Rehoboam their rightful king. But it was found, when too late to remedy the matter, that it was the full and unyielding purpose of the ten tribes to revolt. It was the last stroke upon the wedge of discord, which rent the kingdom in twain, never again to be united. They proclaimed Jeroboam king of the ten tribes at Shechem; and fearing the people might be induced to abandon his kingdom if allowed free to associate with those who remained loyal to Rehoboam, especially if they continued their visits to Jerusalem as in former times to worship at the Temple, he persuaded them that it was too far to go from their distant homes up to the Holy City. He therefore made two molten calves for the people to worship, and said to them, "Behold the gods who brought you from the land of Egypt." To these idols he ordered that the people should bow and pay their religious devotions, which they did most fervently. The new kingdom, composed of the ten tribes, was called Israel; and the old kingdom, composed of the remaining two tribes, Judah and Benjamin, was called Judah. The latter partially maintained its original religious worship; but the former wholly departed from it. Jeroboam, for the accomplishment of his purpose, established two places of worship within the bounds of his kingdom; one was at Bethel on the southern extremity, the other at Dan out on the northern boundary. These twelve tribes were not only divided in government and religion, but were also divided socially. Their feelings of unfriendliness grew so strong, they were led to hate each other. The northern kingdom continued two hundred and fifty years, but its experiences were checkered and many times most bitter. The seat of government was changed several times; Shechem, Tirzah and Samaria, each for a while had the distinction of being the chief seat of power. The kingdom of Judah continued its capital at Jerusalem, and was not without its scourgings from time to time, because of the growing inclination of the people to depart from the God of their fathers and follow the example of the heathen. The kings of Judah were succeeded in an unbroken line in the house of David; but Israel did not adhere to any particular line of succession, therefore many radical changes were made, and many dynasties were in power during the two and a half centuries of its existence, as we shall see in another chapter.

We cannot fail to recognize the hand of God affectionately administering to Israel's protection and prosperity for a long while, notwithstanding the nation had left him and sought other gods. The priesthood continued in Judah, where they were needed to officiate in the religious ceremonies at the Temple, and do such other duties as was usual to those officials. Israel had no real need of the legitimate priests, therefore God sent the prophets to that people to arouse them from their slumber in which idolatry had placed them. The prophets often appeared and warned both king and people of the danger that would follow their sinfulness, and the calamities they would encounter. But their admonishments were mostly unheeded, and finally the cup of Israel's transgressions was filled to overflowing. Among the prophets sent to this people were Elijah, Elisha, and many others. These men of God labored hard to cause Israel to turn to the God of their fathers, but they could not so impress them. Finally the Lord left them to themselves, and soon they were carried away into captivity by the strong arm of the king of Assyria, and in that state drank the bitter cup of indignation, administered by their own hands. Then a strong people inhabited the land so suddenly relieved of its proud and rebellious occupants. Multitudes of Assyrians were transported to the land of Israel, who finally embraced (in part) the religion of their predecessors. These people were afterwards known as Samaritans. A small remnant of their descendants are now living in Shechem. When the inhabitants of Samaria and the adjacent country were carried away captive by Shalmaneser, king of Assyria, he sent colonies in their place from Babylonia, Cuthah, Hamath, Sepharvaim, and other towns in his dominion. When they came over and settled down in the land of Israel they found a remnant of them scattered here and there through the country. It is generally believed that they soon became socially drawn to the new colonists, and inter-marriages soon took place among them, so that in the process of time the whole people were amalgamated into one people. When the Jews returned from their captivity and found this strange race-type in the land, they were disposed to treat them with unfriendliness, not because they were a mixture of Jews and heathens, but on account of their religion. They were found to have embraced a portion of the Jewish worship, having sent to Assyria for an Israelitish priest to come and teach them the law of the Lord, but the greater number were but partially drawn from the heathen worship. When the walls of the Temple and the City of Jerusalem were about to be rebuilt, these people wished to assist, it is thought, on the ground of their being Jewish citizens. Their request was not complied with, and from that time onward there was a strong feeling of discord between the Jews and Samaritans. The latter then finding that Moses commanded in the law a special service should be held on Mt. Gerizim by Joshua and the people entering the "Land of Promise," and believing that Gerizim was the place designed for perpetual services, they set themselves at once about building a Temple there, and when it was finished they sacrificed according to the directions of the Mosaic law. They also rejected all sacred books of the Jews, except the Pentateuch. Sanballat, who was governor of Samaria, was very hostile to the Jews, and resorted to every stratagem to impede their progress. When Nehemiah came from Shushan and began to rebuild the walls of Jerusalem, Sanballat sent to inquire by what authority he did so, and offered many impediments to hinder his success. He was so odious in Jewish estimation that his name was held among them in great contempt, and all intercourse between the Jews and Samaritans was carefully avoided. The great Temple, so sacredly adored by this mixed race, was destroyed by Hyrcanus about one hundred and twenty-nine years before Christ, and was never fully restored, but the Samaritans continued to reverence the place as no other on earth; it was so esteemed in the time of our Lord they would ascend its rugged heights then, as they do now, on the return of their great festival season, and celebrate the passover with jubilating shouts. The remnant of the Samaritans, who still linger about Shechem, continue these most peculiar services on the brow of Gerizim every year, and draw crowds of people from the town to witness their celebration. They are a people strongly attached to each other, and will not intermarry. It is said they are dying out, and from the rate of reduction they have experienced during the last century, it is only a question of a comparatively short time before all of them will have died, and the race will be numbered with the past. They were a distinct race socially, and remain so to this day. They still cling to their old religious rites, and annually celebrate their feast of the passover on Mt. Gerizim. The site of their Ancient Temple is still located, but they hold their meetings in a small building on the slope of the Mount, known as the Samaritan Temple. They are very friendly to strangers, and seemingly take pleasure in showing their relics, which have been preserved from age to age, especially their old manuscripts. I had the pleasure of visiting this little Temple on the morning we left Shechem, and was shown the articles they keep on exhibition. The community is poor and fond of begging, which is not an uncommon thing in Palestine. They claim to have come down from their ancestors unmixed with any other of the race representatives, and pride themselves in being from the stock of genuine Samaritans. They have a very light complexion, and may be compared with the octoroons or very fair mulattoes. Their hair is long and straight, and features very pleasant. They are thoroughly devoted to their religion, and separate themselves from all other sects. These people became very numerous after their transportation here, so that on the return of the Jews from captivity they found this strange people occupying all the districts that had been alloted to Ephraim, Manasseh and Issachar, and was known as the middle districts of Palestine. Judah was on the south and Galilee on the north, so that persons going either way had to pass through Samaria. It embraced the modern districts of Aretas, Carmel, Shechem, and the City of Samaria. With this description before us it can be easily understood why Christ must needs go through Samaria, when He was going over to Galilee with His disciples. The Jews who returned from the captivity did not show themselves so deeply interested in the political affairs of the country as those who lived at the time of the capture of Jerusalem by the king of Babylon, nor were they very particular about hunting up, and dividing in separate communities, the members of the respective tribes, as had been done on the entrance of their fathers into the land.

The people were looked upon as Jews, or a vast brotherhood of the descendants of Abraham, constituting one of the two great divisions of the human race. This term, Jew, seems to have been specially applied to the two tribes who remained loyal to Rehoboam and his successors; it distinguished them from the ten tribes who revolted and crowned Jereboam king over the northern kingdom. The chief stimulant of the Jews on their re-occupancy of Palestine was to rebuild the demolished city and walls, and build again the sacred edifice to the worship of the Most High. There were members of each of the twelve tribes among those who returned, but they had at least a traditional knowledge of the ills their fathers endured by holding so tenaciously to the tribe to which they belonged rather than looking after the good of the whole people. They therefore settled in Jerusalem in great numbers, and from there planted themselves upon the environments, spreading out more as their numbers increased, until finally they passed beyond the territory of the central districts inhabited by the Samaritans and settled in the most remote northern province, known in the New Testament times as Galilee. This is the portion of the country in which Our Lord did the most of His "mighty works" and spent the greater part of His life. The people living in the south and southeast, some time after they had settled down and began to enjoy a good degree of prosperity, were inclined to ridicule and oppose their fellow-Jews who lived in the far north, and foster the old prejudice against them almost like that that divided the two kingdoms prior to the captivity. The Galileans were considered the most morally depraved people in the country, who belonged to the Jewish family, especially those living in Nazareth; even people in other portions of Galilee looked down upon them derisively, as will be seen in another chapter. The whole history of the Jews suddenly closed in the Old Testament Scriptures with the writings of Malachi, he being the last of the prophetic writers under the old dispensation. It is generally believed he was known as a prophet about one hundred and twenty years after the return of the Jews from their Babylonian captivity and four hundred years, B. C. But some writers estimate the time at four years earlier, and others thirty years later. The exact time is unsettled, but the general opinion favors the former estimation. Thus it is seen there was a long silence of nearly four and a quarter centuries from the time of Malachi to that of John the Baptist. During this long period of Bible silence the history of the Jews was written by uninspired men, known as ancient historians. During the transition from the old to the new dispensation the Jews lapsed into bold and gross wickedness, so that when our Lord came He found them full of selfishness, pride, lust and blindness. Josephus and other historians show in their writings that the history of the Jews was much less important during this long period of prophetic silence than in former times. They, having been subordinated by foreign powers, lost their national independence and became tributary to Persia and other kingdoms, and less prominent in the history of nations. The Persian monarch appointed a governor over them, whose headquarters were at Damascus, and the High Priest at Jerusalem was his deputy. The Jews highly favored this custom, because they were allowed to do just as though they were independent, except the payment of taxes, which was a very great annoyance to them. But the High Priest being a Jew, and one of those who was under this burden, did much toward allaying any attempt at rebellion among the people and encouraged them to be loyal. When Alexander the Great had conquered Persia and was making a siege upon Tyre, he sent up to Jerusalem, which was then a tributary to Persia, for troops, but the High Priest refused to aid him. This is an evidence of the strong attachment there was between Cyrus and his officials at Jerusalem. It is stated that he expressed his firm determination of adhering to the Persians, notwithstanding Alexander was conquering the world, and would, from his position at that time, soon be in Jerusalem. But it will be seen in another chapter that this same High Priest, against whom the great warrior had sworn vengeance, conquered him without striking a blow, and humbled him to the extent that he did not even attempt to lift up his arm against him or injure any of those under him. It is thought the victory won by the High Priest over Alexander on the day he was about to enter and destroy Jerusalem, was one of the greatest conquests ever won by a man through humiliation. The monarch's wrath was changed to tenderness, and the sceptre of iron with which he intended to govern the Jews was changed into a gentle and liberal one. The people were not burdened with taxes, nor did they lose any of the privileges they enjoyed under the Persian rule. After the death of Alexander the Ptolemies ruled Jerusalem. The poor Jews were so depressed it seems they made but little attempt towards their own defense for a long time. The Syrians, who lived on the north of Palestine, rapidly grew into power and brought the Jews under their sway. They were merciless and ruled their subjects with an iron sceptre.

The situation of the people grew more severe, so that their blood was so freely shed by their oppressors that it ran down the streets; their sanctuary was plundered and robbed of its rich and sacred treasures. At length the Maccabees rose up to defend the people, removed their heavy burdens, destroyed all traces of heathen worship that had been established, restored the true worship, and re-established the independence of the nation. The Jews experienced great peace under their rule, especially under Simon, the second brother; but this did not continue long; the nation was doomed to distress as a reward of its hands. When the Romans came into power in Palestine they held dominant sway over it, and caused the people to smart under their rigid rule, and they were found to be very much chagrined on account of Roman exactions when the Lord Jesus came amongst them. Jerusalem received its most deadly stroke during the great siege of Titus, from which she never finally recovered. Afterwards Jerusalem became a Christian city under Constantine the great, but has experienced many religious and political changes since.

PART IV.

FROM JOPPA TO JERUSALEM.

Situation of Joppa—Landing at Joppa—House of Simon the Tanner—Streets of Joppa—Orange Groves—American Colony at Joppa—Joppa Pilgrims—Preparation for their Festival—Traders in the City—Plain of Sharon—Old Highway—Lydda—Greek Church in Lydda—Ramleh—Tower of the Forty—View from the Tower—Valley of Ajalon—Ai—Israel's First Defeat—Ai Captured by Joshua—Joshua and Israelites go to Shechem—Gibeonites Visit Joshua—Kings' Confederacy—Joshua Responds to Gibeonites—Fate of Confederacy—Joshua's Prayer for Sun and Moon to Stand Still—Joshua's Victory—El-Jib or Gibeon—Bible Associations—History of Gibeon—Naby-Samwill or Ancient Mizpeh—Situation—View from the Mosque—Ancient Mizpeh—Present Village—Approaching Jerusalem from Joppa—Northern Confederacy—Jabin Forming a Confederacy—Jabin and His Allies—March to Lake Merom—Situation of Battle-field—The Great Battle—Joshua's Victory.

ANCIENT JOPPA.

JOPPA, some times called Yaffa, or Yafa, is one of the most important and interesting cities along the Mediterranean coast; it is situated on a low eminence immediately on sea-border. One viewing it from the deck of an approaching steamer, is favorably impressed with its picturesque appearance, and at once begins to consider its ancient history, which has made it memorable for thousands of years.

From the time of King David to the present, Joppa has been the sea-port for Jerusalem, it being the nearest and most convenient landing town on the sea from which merchandise could be transported to the "Great City."

Hiram, King of Tyre, shipped the cedar timber to this port, which was transported to Jerusalem to be used in the temple. From Joppa the Prophet Jonah started in his fruitless attempt to shirk the responsibility involved in the commission God gave him when ordered to Nineveh; who, instead of shipping to that port, started for Tarsus, and while in the midst of the sea, during the most eventful storm that ever swept over it, he was compelled to take passage in the abdomen of "a great fish" to Nineveh, and proclaim in its streets the message the Lord commanded him to give the people of that city.

Joppa was the home of the prophetess Dorcas, whom the Apostle Peter restored to life, and also of Simon "the Tanner," with whom he (Peter) lodged. It is not unlikely that the house on the margin of the sea, known as that of "Simon the Tanner," which is near the tanners' row, may be identical with the site on which the house stood that St. Peter lodged in, and on the top of which he sat while in that mysterious trance, when he saw the vision which convinced him that "God is no respecter of persons," but extended His blessings to all alike of whatever nation, race, tribe, condition, or complexion.

Ancient Joppa has been regarded as one of the oldest cities in the world. Pliny says: "It existed before the flood;" but Josephus traces it to Phœnician origin. As in the antique times, so now, Joppa is the landing-port for all travelers and merchandise going up to Jerusalem.

It has no harbor, therefore the landing of passengers at all times is unpleasant and often very dangerous, and for this reason the greatest caution is taken by sea-captains; they will not venture to stop at the usual anchoring places, or anywhere at this port, if the weather is foul. The steamships are generally anchored about one or two miles from the shore in the shoal water, where numerous rocks are prominent which have been ruinous to many vessels that were suddenly overtaken by storms, which broke them from their moorings, and, before they could be controlled, were broken to pieces among the rocks.

It has also happened several times that scores of human beings have perished in their endeavor to reach the shore in row boats during very rough weather; so, to avoid peril, both to passengers and vessels, many times no stop is made at Joppa, and persons having taken passage for that port are taken to Haifa or Beyrout, and sent back in another steamer to Joppa, or up to Jerusalem on horseback.

There is great competition amongst the Arab boatmen in their endeavor to secure the greater number of passengers to land, especially when a small number are booked for Joppa; these men will do anything to take advantage of each other; they will even tell passengers that the boat of the man whom they are arranging with is not safe, and that he is not able to manage it, and urge them not to trust him.

The day we arrived at the mooring the sea was very rough, and growing more so constantly. We were all deeply interested as to the propriety of attempting to go to the landing in the small row-boats, which were brought over to our steamer for us, managed by eight or ten strong men, whose skillful management of the oars was convincing that they were well adapted to the work, and could be trusted even when the sea was much troubled.

As there was no other convenience to take passengers to the shore, and to continue our journey to Haifa or Beyrout would cost fifty or sixty dollars more, we concluded to venture to make the landing in the small boat.

Although thousands of people disembark at the port of Joppa every year, no special provisions are made as to their safety. In nearly all the ports in foreign lands steam launches are provided for the safe conveyance of passengers to and from the steamers; but Joppa is the most unprotected and dangerous of all ports we visited during our entire circuit around the world.

LANDING AT JOPPA.

Within three or four miles of the shore evident signs of shoal water are prominent, which continues more and more until the anchorage is reached. Ledges of low-peaked rocks extend far out into the sea, which may be properly called the "gates of death," because of their peculiar situation.

Many vessels have been broken to pieces against them, and thousands of human beings have perished there. It is estimated that if the number of ships and human beings who have perished in those shoals could be laid over them, they would cover a space of many miles.

Only a few days prior to our arrival there were eighteen persons, who had ventured to go ashore in one of those small boats, perished in the sea, their boat capsizing during a heavy gale. Notwithstanding the very rough weather which had greatly agitated the water and was getting more intense every hour, on the day of our arrival, yet we nerved up to the strongest point and ventured to reach land in a small row-boat, placing all possible trust in the never-failing arm of the Lord.

The boatmen worked faithfully and earnestly to take their human cargo safely to the landing, and when they had gotten beyond the danger-line, there was a demonstration of gratitude akin to enthusiasm, both among the passengers and boatmen, which was not easily controlled. On entering the historic town the beauties and charms of its external appearance, which are so very attractive from the sea-view are entirely lost; and the stranger finds himself in a most repulsively filthy place, with a wild looking people, of all complexions, among whom ignorance is dominant, excepting those who have settled there from countries of progressive civilization, and you can find but few natives who have been taught to appreciate a higher state of manhood. There are no supposed antique sights to be seen in the town, except the traditional house of "Simon the Tanner." This house, which is evidently several centuries old, is used both for a mosque and lighthouse. How significant, if this is the site where St. Peter slept and was so illuminated by a mysterious and ponderous revelation from God, that his prejudice against preaching to the Gentiles was immediately dispelled; and the same house should be used as a signal-lighthouse, to guide seamen safely along a most dangerous coast. Within its walls the adoring multitude assembles daily to worship according to the custom of the Moslems.

Yet may we not feel assured that God, who showed the Apostle Peter the right way on the house-top of "Simon," will change those followers of Mohammed so that they will see and follow the "old path?" It is a singular fact, that a single revelation from God thoroughly convinced Peter that all people were alike according to His mercies and grace, and that they should not be considered unworthy of social and religious society because they belonged to another race.

Yet all the pointed revelations the Holy Bible contains cannot persuade many of those professing to be Christians, that the color of a man does not form a part of his manhood nor render him inferior to the whitest of the whites; still they declare by their conduct that those of the despised race are common and unclean, although God has cleansed them.

Notwithstanding there is but one traditional place in Joppa of Bible distinction, there is much to be seen that will greatly interest visitors, especially those who have not been made acquainted with oriental life. The streets, like those in all the cities of Palestine and Syria, are crooked, narrow, and by no means inviting, neither in appearance nor condition. Many of these passes are so narrow that a person can stand in the centre and stretch his arms so as to touch the houses on either side. These streets, with two or three exceptions, are so narrow that no vehicle can pass through them.

There are a few carriages in Joppa, which are used almost exclusively for conveying tourists up to Jerusalem and north as far as Haifa and Shechem. Men, camels, and donkeys are the burden-bearers. They can be seen from early morning until late in the evening, ladened with merchandise. Many of the men carry enough on their backs to break down two of our common laborers. Sometimes the poor, half-starved camels are so greatly overloaded they fall, and refuse to move until delivered from it.

There are several things connected with the history of Joppa, which make it one of the most memorable places in the world. It has a part of the territory allotted to the tribe of Dan. Its surrounding country is rich and highly productive. And hither came thousands of brave, earnest, and devout defenders of the cross of Christ, in the days of the prolonged conflict between the crusaders and bloodthirsty infidels (see Josh. xix. 46; 1st Kings v. 2; 2d Chron. ii. 16).

One of the most inviting places to visit about Joppa is the "*Orange Groves,*" which are close to the town; they are several miles in circumference; the fruit is delicious and healthy. Strangers are recommended to eat them when thirsty, instead of drinking the water, which is very unhealthy. Many times the trees yield so abundantly, great caution must be taken to keep them from breaking. Other fruit, such as lemons, pomegranates, watermelons, and figs are very productive. The orchards are generally enclosed by high cactus hedges, which protect the grove from public intrusion far more securely than our wooden or stone fences in this country. It is estimated that not less than three thousand orchards are located within the vicinity of Joppa. Oranges are so plentiful, in their season, they can be bought on the streets for three cents a dozen.

It should be stated concerning the American Colony at Joppa they are doing well, and have done much to change the habits of many of the natives, who, at the time they landed, were not far above the average heathen: they have built a commodious little village to themselves in the most healthy section of the town, and have organized a church and school, which has done an incalculable amount of good.

They have found it, however, to be an up-hill journey from the time they entered upon the work until the present; they find the only road to success is to teach and impress the children; this they are doing with much promise of good results.

Joppa is still the landing port of tourists and pilgrims who are going up to Jerusalem; the latter swarm there by thousands each year to visit the Holy places through Palestine on the occasion of the great Eastern festivals, and devoutly worship at their shrines; the devotees are of all conditions, rich and poor, old and young. Old men and women bending under the burden of three-quarters of a century are seen wending their way from place to place leaning heavily upon their staffs, while young men and maidens speed their way with nimble steps and light hearts, because they have been permitted to worship on the "Holy Hill of Zion." These singular people, both in dress and customs, impress one who is not acquainted with oriental habits, especially as to the attraction of their costume; some of them are attired in rich and costly dress, while others are almost bare, yet all go there for the same purpose, that is to worship and follow the walks of our Lord, to drop a tear where He shed drops of blood; to weep where He wept, and to kiss the shrine which, according to tradition, marks the site where in deep and overpowering agony, "He gave up the ghost."

The pilgrims make a visit through Palestine, in compliance with a rule taught and impressed upon them in their church; and not simply to see the country and walk upon the soil made hallowed by the feet of the Lord Jesus.

The Greek Church rule enjoins the duty upon all its followers, even at a great sacrifice, to make a pilgrimage to Jerusalem at least once in their life; therefore parents are so anxious to conform to this rule; thousands take their children with them, so as to be sure the law has been fulfilled, and will spend all they have to make the trip which is regarded as a most sacred undertaking.

During my visit to Palestine and Syria, the pilgrims were coming into Jerusalem to make ready for the great festivals, and hundreds had gathered there as early as the last of January, which gave them time to visit all the sacred places round and about the "Holy City," including all those as far as Bethlehem and the Pools of Solomon, before the time of the eastern feast. Many of the Pilgrims come from Egypt, from all parts of Syria, Armenia, Asia Minor, from Roumelia, Stamboul, and from all parts of the East. The length of time the journey requires and the great sacrifice of means necessary to the trip, are but little concern to them in comparison to the unbounded happiness they enjoy the remainder of their lives from the benefits the pilgrimage gives them.

Many of them feel, when they have passed through the gates into the great city, that they have entered the very ante-chamber of the heavenly Jerusalem. In order that they may be able to sustain themselves the poorer classes usually take with them a number of very choice articles which are anxiously sought by the merchants and vendors; these are readily sold at a reasonable price to defray the expenses necessary to the completion of their pilgrimage.

The great masses come by sea to Joppa, and travel up to Jerusalem as best they can; those who can afford it ride up to the great city on donkeys or camels, or in vehicles or by railway; but thousands walk for the sake of economy, especially when they arrive early, having plenty of time before them to make the tour to the various traditional sites between the two great historic cities, at all of which they devoutly worship.

The vessels used to transport them are generally Greek brigs and schooners; the people are usually crowded in them almost to suffocation, so that their situation would be a striking reminder of the way the slave-traders used to pack away the poor Africans during the existence of American slavery; but with those pilgrims it is a matter of choice, they travel so for the sake of cheapness. A number of families usually charter a boat and put as many in it as possible, each taking their own provision, which is generally very poor and of the most common kind. At times the voyage is very rough, causing much suffering amongst them, and even death; but in the face of peril they go, willing to endure the customary hardships rather than abandon their visit to Jerusalem that they may kiss the shrines so peculiar to the memory of the civilized world.

When they first land at Joppa it is their custom to assemble on the shore and sing a hymn of thanksgiving to God for conducting them safely over the deep sea; when this is done they arrange for their journey to Jerusalem; as soon as they get there they make their way to the open space in front of the church of the Holy Sepulchre, where they display and sell their goods. The traders know about the time they will be in the city, and are found waiting for them, so that they may be the first to procure their goods.

The busy people buying and selling in the usual boisterous manner, characteristic of oriental life, make the place more like a busy market than the entrance to the church, which, tradition says, stands upon the sacred hill of calvary and over the place where our Lord lay.

The Jewish money-changer lurks about ready to make what he can, and the vendors solicit all who pass them to examine the goods they have for sale.

The antique sights being few in Joppa, it is not the custom for travelers to remain there more than three or four hours before they start up to the "Holy City." In a few moments after passing the Orange Orchards, the plain of Sharon is entered; it is both extensive and picturesque, extending many miles; the soil is rich and fruitful, and would be much more so if the husbandmen knew how to improve it properly.

There is only a comparatively small portion of the plain cultivated; the greater part is used for pasturage, in which thousands of cattle feed every day. In the proper season a great profusion of flowers appear throughout the whole region, shooting up amidst the green grass. These flowers begin to bloom about the middle of January, and continue until the whole plain appears like a vast garden of variegated flowers. The lilies, because of their loveliness, produce the greatest attraction, and are so very numerous they often interfere with cultivation, and cause the crops to be very poor.

Those whose object is to obtain a more elaborate knowledge of *Bible History* should not fail to read the scriptural references concerning it while passing through. No doubt that when he looks at the beautiful rose and lily he will call to mind the words, "I am the Rose of Sharon, the Lily of the Valley;" also he will meditate upon the words, "The wilderness and the solitary place shall be glad, and the desert shall rejoice and blossom as a rose. It shall blossom abundantly and rejoice even with joy and singing; the glory of Lebanon shall be given unto it, the excellency of Carmel and Sharon."

The greatest profusion of flowers appear during April and May; at this season the whole plain looks like a vast district of beautiful gardens, from which is emitted such delightful odor that the visitor is loath to leave it; we feel safe within the limits of truth in saying there is no place in the world where nature is adorned with more beauty than is seen in the plain of Sharon.

The original highway prominently traveled in Solomon's time passes directly through the plain, and it is particularly interesting to be reminded, although natural changes have been made as to its condition, yet it is the same ancient route that has been traveled for thousands of years, and was traveled during the transportation of the material from Lebanon to Jerusalem for the Temple, and was thronged with thousands of busy Phœnicians and Hebrews, who were employed to carry on the work.

Of late a new road has been completed, much of which is made over the old beaten pass, while other portions run close to it. It is also highly interesting to the Christian traveler, going on his way to Jerusalem, to know that he is traveling over the same ground over which passed many of the ancient worthies, for it is this way prophets and apostles used to travel when proceeding on their mission.

Doubtless the Prophet Jonah passed over this same "Old Highway" when enroute to Joppa, to embark on the Tarsus-bound vessel; Peter came over it when he was called from Lydda to restore Tabitha to life; it is also the same route traveled by King Hiram of Tyre, Hiram Abiff, and King Solomon.

These and thousands more passed along this way, and as they crossed the flowery plain of Sharon, beholding its loveliness and drinking copious draughts of its balmy odor, it is probable the Apostles were reminded of the words of our Lord as their feet pressed the soil of this plain, "Consider the lilies of the field how they grow." There are several places of historic distinction well worthy of a visit between Joppa and Jerusalem, and those who go up on horseback have an opportunity to stop at each one of them; it is only needful, however, to pass in sight of the most of them, as many clouds of doubt cluster about the majority. There are several places whose history is so clear not a shadow of doubt hangs about them. Lydda, known in ancient times as "Ludd," is positively identified. It is southeast of Joppa, about eleven miles and a half, and is situated close to the eastern edge of the plain of Sharon. During the time of Greek supremacy in Palestine its name was changed to Diapolis, "City of Jupiter." But the original name was again adopted, which has been retained through all the painful ordeals of warfare and disaster through which it has passed.

The most important event which transpired here, of which the Bible makes mention, is the visit of the Apostle Peter; he came to Lydda to visit the saints, and found a certain man by the name of Æneas who had kept his bed eight years, being seized with the palsy. When Peter came to his couch he looked upon him and said to the poor sick man, "Æneas, Jesus Christ maketh thee whole, arise and make thy bed," and he immediately arose.

The most important attraction in Lydda is the Greek Church, dedicated to St. George, who according to tradition, was born and buried there. The church, which is handsomely embellished inside strictly according to Greek taste, is visited annually by hundreds of pilgrims, who pass up through that way enroute to Jerusalem.

In connection with the tomb of St. George, which is inside the church, under the high altar, there are many other old relics sacredly kept, all of which are carefully guarded by the officials. Lydda was a prosperous city at the time of the occupancy of the Israelites, and was inhabited by the Benjamites after the captivity. In the time of Cassius, after the death of Julius Cæsar, the whole inhabitants were sold into slavery; this caused great depression and suffering, as is natural in such cases.

The earliest calendar relates that St. George was born at Lydda; that he suffered martyrdom in Nicomedeia, under Diocletian, near the close of the third century, and that his body was conveyed to his native town, where a church was erected to his honor. (Murray's Hand-book.) It is said the building was very much injured by the Crusaders when they entered Lydda, and the revengeful Moslems demolished it, but because of the high veneration they entertained for St. George, they did not interfere with his tomb. The church was rebuilt, but in less than a century the whole town, with the church, was destroyed by Saladin; but the ambitious people determined to rebuild it, and succeeded. (Ezra ii. 33.) It is one hundred and fifty feet long.

From Lydda to Ramleh is two miles and a half. At this place the main road to Jerusalem is joined. The English interpretation of Ramleh is sandy, and it will be at once conceded that the village is not mis-named. Several writers have attempted to associate this place with Arimathæa, the home of Joseph, who took charge of the body of our Lord after his crucifixion, and laid it in the tomb in which no one had been placed.

But the evidences to the contrary make the truth of its having such a connection very doubtful. There is a Franciscan convent not far from the town which tradition locates on the site where the house in which Nicodemus lived stood. But there is no historical foundation to sustain it. The thing of greatest interest, and for which Ramleh is noted, is the great tower, now much dilapidated, situated a short distance from the main road; it is one hundred and twenty feet high, and is ascended by one hundred and twenty much-worn stone steps; it is called by the Arabs, "The Tower of the Forty," in honor of the forty companions of the prophet, and is said to be the minaret of a ruined mosque. A most delightful view may be had which will doubly pay one for the fatigue of the ascent. All the plain of Sharon, from the great mountains of Judea and Samaria, even to the Mediterranean, and as far as the base of Mt. Carmel and the deserts of Philistia, is spread out like a vast panorama. Ashdod, Askelon, Gath, Gaza and Cæsarea are plainly seen.

I remember so well the day I ascended the tower; I was the last man up, but in reality the first man down. While standing on the time-worn tower we saw, in connection with the places already named, Mt. Hermon's snowy top, and the Lebanon range on the north; the Valley of the Jordan and the mountains of Moab on the east. The view is transporting, and the objects are distinctly seen through good field-glasses. There are but few visitors who will dare venture to the top, because of its dangerous condition; the whole structure is cracked from top to bottom; one portion of it has fallen, and it will be only a short time before the whole tower must be considered among the things of the past.

The junction of the ancient highways, from Joppa to Jerusalem, and from Egypt to Damascus, which crosses near the old Tower of the Forty, caused Ramleh to be a town of considerable importance; there is an old tradition which says Joseph took this route when, in obedience to the command given him by the angel, he fled from the wrath of Herod, with "the young child and his mother," into Egypt. This is not generally credited, as it is more than likely he took the road that Joseph, the son of Jacob, traveled on his return to Hebron with the remains of his father. This seems more likely, as it is a much shorter route, and a person fleeing from danger would be apt to take the shortest and most direct road to the place of refuge.

The valley of Ajalon is crossed a few miles from Ramleh; the road leads through the most important part, which has, from the time of Joshua, been memorable because of the wonderful victory he achieved there. (Josh. x. 12.)

In crossing the valley, going to Jerusalem, the two Beth-horons are on the left, and the lofty hills down which Joshua's army pursued the retreating enemy are plainly seen. Gibeon is to the east, behind a high ridge of stones; it has a historical connection with Beth-horon in the victory so gloriously won by the Israelites; for over the former the sun, in answer to Joshua's prayer, stood still, and the moon also over the Valley of Ajalon.

ISRAEL'S FIRST DEFEAT AT AI.

After the capture and destruction of Jericho, it became necessary for Israel to go up against Ai and subdue it; for until this royal city of the Canaanites was taken, Joshua and his people must remain hemmed up in the extreme eastern confines of Palestine, and in danger of being destroyed by the combined forces of the several independent governments prominently known in the land.

Just as the ladder of Tyre was the key to Palestine, so Ai was to the passage of the Israelites to the northern country; there were only two convenient highways by which they could travel with their possessions to Shechem, where, according to the command of Moses, they were compelled to go and renew their covenant in recognition of the blessing God had given them. One of these highways runs southwest from Jericho by the way of Bethany and Jerusalem, now known as the bloody pass; the other leads to the northwest up to Bethel; this was the more direct and pleasant way for those going north, halting at Jerusalem. But to take either road they would have come within a short distance of Ai. The spies whom Joshua sent to investigate the situation and condition of this fortified stronghold of the Canaanites, returned full of confidence that it would be easy to conquer, and that it was only necessary to send up two or three thousand men to take it; but they failed in their first attempt, for the men of Ai rose up against Israel in their strength and put the three thousand chosen men to flight, thirty-six of whom were slain.

This defeat astonished Israel and caused Joshua to weep bitterly;

he solemnly took the case to God and was informed that it was a rebuke for a breach by one of his men, who had secretly hid some of the spoils of Jericho. When Joshua was thus informed he caused an investigation to be made, that the man guilty of the crime might be detected, and it was found to be Achan; he confessed his sin and was stoned to death.

The confidence of the people having been restored, Joshua went up again to smite Ai; in this undertaking he worked cunningly and successfully; he caused a large body of men to lay in ambush, and sent another number over in front of the city; then withdrew, and halted in the valley toward Jericho. The men of Ai, feeling confident that the hosts of Israel had weakened, left the city in pursuit of them. At that auspicious moment those in ambush sprang from their hiding, entered the city, burned it, and then went with all possible haste after the men who were pursuing Joshua. At the same time that portion of the fleeing army turned on their pursuers and hemmed them completely in. Caught as the men of Ai were between the two forces, they were seized with wild confusion, and were soon captured and cut to pieces. The whole of the inhabitants—twelve thousand in number—perished, and their city burned to the ground; the king also was taken captive, put to death with the sword, and his dead body hanged on a tree until evening, then taken down and buried at the gate under a heap of stones.

The main camping ground of the Israelites was at Gilgal, as usual, after the destruction of Ai; but they had obtained an unmolested sway of the highway to the north (Josh., vii-viii chaps.). There was a short period of rest given the Hebrews after they had captured Ai. They returned to their camp at Gilgal, and offered their usual tribute of thanks, and were jubilant over their triumphant conquest.

During their respite, Joshua and the Israelites went up to Shechem as directed by Moses, where they were to be further impressed as to the merits of the law of God. Joshua copied it on an altar of stones, which was erected on Mount Ebal, and caused the whole people who stood in the valley to repeat the blessings and cursings it contained.

Having returned to Gilgal to their camp after a long and fatiguing travel from Shechem, they were visited by a company of strangers, who practiced a cunning scheme upon them which was difficult to conceive. The people of Gibeon, one of the most important towns between Beth-horon and Jerusalem, and said to be the chief city of the several towns laying between Jerusalem and Bethel, like all other chief cities, had many foes who would, upon the least provocation, declare war against it. The inhabitants were interesting, industrious, and cunning. Any one who has read their history will at once concede that they were a crafty and sagacious people. These Gibeonites outwitted Joshua, as completely and successfully as he did the men of Ai, and at the same time used no violence in doing so.

The most of our readers will call to mind how the people of Gibeon, Beeroth, Kirjath-Jearim, and Chephirah planned a scheme which formed a binding alliance between Joshua and them. Gibeon was only three days' travel from Gilgal, going at a very slow rate; for, as we shall see, the whole journey was made afterwards in one day's rapid march. The movements of Joshua were known to this people, the fall of Jericho and Ai was fresh in their minds, and fearing they would meet the same fate, they went down to the camp at Gilgal, taking with them old mouldy bread and torn wine skins, and old clothes, and worn-out shoes, representing to the Israelites that they had come from a far country and desired to become servants of the God who protected Joshua and his people.

The thing seemed good in the eyes of Joshua and all Israel, so they formed a league of friendship and mutual protection. It was but a short time before the scheme was developed, but Joshua could not severely punish them, having allied himself in lasting friendship with them; but, as a stern rebuke for their deception, they were reduced to the humble rank of hewers of wood and drawers of water, which occupation they followed under Israel for many years (Josh. ix. 1–27).

The dwellers in the land of Canaan, who were composed of many tribes, had developed into several independent states, each having a chief or capital city, in which lived their chief, who was generally acknowledged as king; the territory over which the chief ruler presided, was but a small district; many of them did not cover as many miles as some of the large cities in our country. For the most part these states were hostile to each other, and had bitter and bloody contests, striving for supremacy, just as the people of Italy did before the states consolidated.

Some of these governments were monarchies, and others republican in form. The five cities or towns represented by the Gibeonites, who made a visit to Joshua at Gilgal, were not far from each other; the remotest is not more than ten miles north of Jerusalem, and were nearly surrounded by important tribes, whose war-like character had won for them wide spread fame. Those people who lived in the chief cities south-east and south of Gibeon were the most important.

When the news of the fall of Jericho and the capture of Ai spread abroad, great dread fell upon the people previously inhabiting the land. They found it was necessary to form combinations of forces, who had hitherto been independent of and hostile to each other, if they would retain the rulership of the country. To accomplish this end, the five kings of the Amorites living south of Gibeon combined to capture it.

These kings ruled over the following districts: Jerusalem, Hebron, Jarmuth, Lachish, and Eglon. These kings having combined their forces to overthrow Gibeon, caused great alarm amongst the Gibeonites, for they felt themselves incompetent to withstand them. They, having formed a league with Joshua, sent in haste to him to come up to their rescue. The commander of the forces of Israel felt himself bound to answer the summons, and started at once for the scene of trouble.

The kings forming the confederacy were greatly exercised over the alliance of the Gibeonites with Joshua, and attempted to sternly rebuke them. To accomplish their purpose the five kings, having armed themselves, drew their forces up before Gibeon. The latter, finding they were not able to cope with this formidable confederacy, became greatly alarmed; they at once dispatched a messenger to Gilgal, who informed Joshua, and said to him, "Slack not thy hand from thy servants; come up to us quickly and save us, for all the kings of the Amorites that dwell in the mountain are gathered together against us."

Joshua responded immediately to the summons, and went up in great haste to their help. The confederate kings had no expectation of seeing the army of Israel on the scene so soon, and when they beheld them in the early morning fearful alarm seized them, for they trembled even at the name of the "Lord's Host," before whom the nations of the earth fell like grass that is cut down. The whole confederacy soon became disorganized, and were ready to flee before Joshua had struck a blow. When the attack was made the Amorites made no vigorous defence, but fled in great confusion from Gibeon, and endeavored to escape down the steep rocky pass leading from Beth-horon into the valley of Ajalon, but were pursued by the Lord's host and slain in great numbers. The dismayed confederacy was hotly chased along the way leading to Beth-horon, and in this wild flight they became insanely confused and suffered great loss, as the following record will show: "And it came to pass as they fled before Israel and were in the way going toward Beth-horon, that the Lord cast down great stones from heaven upon them unto Azekah, and they died." There were more who died of the hailstones than were slain with the sword by Israel."

The Amorites in fleeing from the advancing Israelites were making their way to the valley in front of them, and in doing so they must descend about four hundred feet of a most difficult and steep mountain pass; the refugees being panic-stricken, they rushed unguardedly down the mountain without considering the danger into which they were rushing. The gathering clouds which had spread over them were charged with showers of God's indignation against them, which was about to be discharged with intense fury.

This was evidently a miraculous demonstration of the displeasure of the Almighty against the confederates, for the Israelites were not injured by them. It is reasonable to suppose that the fugitive army must have been far in advance of them, as they were dwellers of the mountains and could much more readily speed their way down the rough pass than the Hebrews, who were strangers and knew nothing of the condition of the pass (Josh. x.), and could not descend with the speed of the fugitives. As the day advanced, and the enemy was still retreating, Joshua, the man of God, became anxious to finish the combat and achieve the victory before night had settled upon them. He and his people were in a strange part of the land, and having been sent for to come up at once with all possible speed, he had not the opportunity to follow their usual custom of sending spies to ascertain the situation of the country, as had been done before they crossed the Jordan, or went against Ai.

It would, therefore, have been impossible for the Israelites to have pursued their enemy after nightfall, and even to go into camp would have been a dangerous risk, as the fleeing enemy could have had great advantage, which would have put them to much perplexity. The occasion was so momentous and anxious Joshua was deeply moved with interest for the safety of Israel and the triumph of the Lord, on this account; he uttered that wonderfully strange and sublime prayer, which seemed to have the bearing of a command; he wished the rapidly retiring sun to halt and the moon to stay its coming upward until the army of the Lord had completed its victory.

The man of God came forth in the name and strength of his Lord, as if commander of the solar system as well as the army of Israel, and with uplifted hands, one doubtless pointing to the moon and the other to the sun, he said, "Sun stand thou still upon Gibeon and thou moon in the valley of Ajalon."

In compliance with Joshua's prayer the Lord checked the passage of the sun and moon, "and the sun stayed in the midst of heaven, and hastened not to go down, about a whole day." This illustrious answer to the commander's prayer must have filled all Israel with holy enthusiasm and gave them a fresh impetus for the combat.

The army continued a vigorous pursuit after the fleeing confederate kings, who were making a rapid retreat. They were overtaken and captured, in connection with two important towns, on the border of the plain. The cave, Makkedah, where the capture of the five kings took place, was on the eastern margin of the plain of Philistia, to the south of the opening of the plain of Ajalon. The five kings were taken from their hiding-place, and the chief officers of Joshua's command put their feet on their necks, as was the usual custom in that country, as a signal of triumph.

After putting them to death they were hanged upon trees, as was also the King of Ai, until evening; they were then taken down and placed in the cave from which they were captured, for the law demanded they should spare nothing.

Joshua having won the victory took advantage of the occasion and continued his conquests from Gibeon to the desert on the south, capturing the cities of Makkedah and Lebonah.

Joshua afterwards had another tremendous foe to face, for whom he had to make special prayerful preparations, but the Lord was with him and fought for Israel.

THE NORTHERN CONFEDERACY.

The battle of Beth-horon did not cause the inhabitants of Canaan to immediately close all hostile opposition to the Israelites, and acknowledge them the rightful occupants of the land, but other States formed combinations with a firm purpose of exterminating the whole army of Joshua at a single blow. There was great alarm among the people up North caused by the sweeping victory Joshua had won over the combined forces of the South. Therefore, Jabin, King of Hazor, one of the most important cities in northern Canaan, sent messengers to the several kings throughout the country to form a confederacy against further encroachments of the great leader of the hosts of Israel. He sent for them to prepare themselves to join him to confront Joshua and crush his army at once. Jabin seems to have been a man of great influence, and the most heroic of all the kings of the North in his day. When this great man issued the call, the rulers united with him from the Trans-Lebanon district on the north and those on the south. The king in the Arabah, south of the Sea Tiberias, and in the low'and and on the heights about Dor, near the sea on the west. and from Shimron, and from Achshaph, and those from the hills of the north. The Canaanites living on the east of Hazor, and those on the west, the Amorites, the Hittites, the Perizzites, the Jebusites, from the regions in and about Jerusalem, the Hivites under Hermon, in the land of Mizpeh, all came up in response to the call of Jabin against the victorious army of Joshua. They made the strongest and most guarded preparations for the attack, having horses, animals greatly dreaded by the Israelites in war, and heavy chariots with knives or short swords fixed to their wheels. The captains were equal to the duties of their position, and the military forces were well trained. This great confederacy when united seemed to be a countless number, and in every way stronger and better prepared for warfare than the host Joshua put to flight in the South. This vast army of well-drilled and carefully-armed men of war had no other expectation than they would mow down the Hebrews like grass. The army of Joshua had neither horses nor war chariots. Jabin, having collected his allies and their forces, marched them to "the waters of Merom to fight against Israel." This lake is known as Huleh; it is about four miles and a half long, and three and a half wide, and eleven feet deep in some portions. Lake Merom is about twelve or thirteen miles north of the sea of Tiberias. It is called waters of Merom in the Bible, and by Josephus Samo-chonitis. Swamps and hedges nearly surrounded it, in which the water-fowls find safe retreat. No doubt that the level country and the abundant supply of water induced King Jabin to camp the vast confederate army there. It necessarily required level ground to manage the horses and war chariots in an engagement, for they were of no use in a mountainous region. The Israelites had no heavy arms, for they had to walk from one battle-field to another, whether far or near; and it may be they feared to confront the tremendous confederacy. But God, who had hitherto fought for them, said to Joshua, "Be not afraid because of them; for to-morrow about this time will I deliver them up all slain before Israel." The account given of this victory won by Joshua is short, but it may be inferred the panic that seized the consternated confederacy was more exciting than that encountered by the hosts of Amorites in the valley of Ajalon. Joshua and his brave men, having been assured by the Lord of conquest, used their previous method of attack. They came down suddenly upon the confederates and completely put them to flight, leaving their horses and chariots on the field, and according to the word of the Lord, Joshua cut the ham-strings of their horses and burnt their chariots. For the Lord said "Thou shalt hough their horses and burn their chariots." Notwithstanding there was no visible appearance of a physical phenomenon, as was witnessed at Gibeon and the Valley of Ajalon, this great victory was as miraculous as the one first won when Joshua went up against the southern confederacy. The all-powerful hand of God won the victory. We must concede the fact that nothing short of the interposition of the Almighty's arm could have won the battle against such a countless host of well-armed forces. There seem to have been no other strong combinations formed against the children of Israel during the life of Joshua.

EL-JIB OR GIBEON.

With Gibeon are connected many other important events, of which mention is made in the Bible. This city, which was at one time one of the most distinguished in all the country, stood on a hill about three hundred feet above the valley, very pleasantly situated, and commanded a delightful view from afar. The ancient buildings, of which the present village is composed, are sparsely situated over the summit on which stood the original city when robed in its fullest glory.

There is a large building yet standing in the midst of the others appearing like a giant among dwarfs; this is supposed to have been the citadel. Gibeon, according to the Old Testament, was one of the great royal cities of Palestine, and was the capital of those towns whose people formed an alliance with Joshua. When the land was divided among the tribes Gibeon fell to the lot of Benjamin, and was made a strong Levitical city.

The Tabernacle was brought here after the destruction of Nob, and the great altar of burnt sacrifice was built, and continued until permanently removed to the temple. The reservoir on the eastern side of the hill is supposed to be the fountain at which Abner and Joab met with the armies of Judah and Israel, and witnessed that most revolting combat between the twelve men on each side, all of whom fought until they died. And on the other hill it is thought the battle occurred in which Abner was defeated and Asahel put to death. (Josh. x. 2; ix. 17; 2 Sam ii.)

At the "stone which is in Gibeon," Amasa, who was King David's nephew, was drawn into a net by the treacherous pretension of Joab, his cousin, whose heart was full of murderous intent. Joab said to his cousin, "Art thou in health, my brother?" and, taking hold of his beard with his "right hand," as though he intended "to kiss him," he had a dart of death concealed with which he smote him (Amasa) under the fifth rib, from which he died. There is a large stone on the side of the pass leading over to Jerusalem, which is supposed to be the scene of this most dastardly tragedy.

But the day of retribution came, and Joab was rewarded for both of his murderous deeds; when despair overshadowed him he ran into the Tabernacle of the Lord for refuge, and even took "hold of the horns of the altar," but was pursued by Benaiah, the son of Jehoiada, who fell upon him by order of Solomon "and slew him."

Here ended the life of one of the most treacherous men that lived. It was at Gibeon that King Solomon offered up a thousand burnt offerings, and had the vision given him from God, urging him to make a choice of that which he desired most in life; in compliance to which he chose wisdom rather than honors, riches or longevity.

These various Bible associations which cluster about Gibeon have made it memorable to all who know its history, so that travelers to to Jerusalem are almost as anxious to see the site of this ancient royal city as any other place in Palestine. (See 2 Sam. xx. 9–12; Kings ii. 28–34; 1 Kings iii. 4–15).

NEBY-SAMUEIL, OR THE ANCIENT "MIZPEH."

This place of ancient renown, where stood one of the most historic cities in Palestine, is now a small village, and is called by the natives Neby-Samueil. It is about four hundred feet above Gibeon, and nearly three thousand above the level of the sea. Mizpeh was in the lot of Benjamin, and is only about six miles from Jerusalem, the seat of the national government. The lofty peak on which it stands is regarded as the highest in southern Palestine, and gives a most delightful view of the whole land from Dan to Beer-sheba, which is obtained if one will take the pains to ascend to the top of the mosque or minaret.

On the north Carmel and Gerizim are distinctly seen; on the west Joppa, the plain of Sharon, Lydda and the Mediterranean Sea loom up; and the mountains of Moab, east of the Jordan, are plainly seen, and the outstretched landscape of Gilead is in full view to the east and southeast. Following the sea-coast along the southern shore a mound is seen which marks the site of Ashdod, where Philip was conducted by the Spirit; and farther southward is Ekron, where the ark was lodged for a time.

The city must have been a place of great importance from very early times. After the occupany of the land by the Hebrews they used to gather at Mizpeh on great national assemblies, when representatives from all the tribes would meet to approve of some new rules for the benefit of the whole people prior to the establishment of the monarchy of Palestine. (Josh. xviii. 26).

Mizpeh was the place where all the male population gathered, even from Dan to Beer-Sheba, with the chief officers, and were filled with indignation against the people of Gibeah because of the great sin they had committed against the Levite, who went there to lodge over night; and they vowed never to return to their homes until they had avenged the Benjamites for their outrageous conduct.

The Israelites after finding their idolatrous worship had turned the blessings of God from them, met Samuel at Mizpeh and solemnly promised to forsake the gods of Baalim and Ashtaroth, and henceforth follow the God of their fathers. It was also at Mizpeh that the representatives of Israel met and chose their first king, notwithstanding the protest of Samuel; and when it was decided that Saul of Benjamin should be the monarch, a shout of enthusiasm made the mountain echo, saying, "God save the King."

When the chosen people were carried away into captivity, the Chaldean governor lived at Mizpeh and was murdered there by hostile Jews; and after the return of this people from Babylon, and Nehemiah began to rebuild the walls of Jerusalem, the men of Mizpeh joined the men of Gibeon in rebuilding one portion of them.

There are many other events of interest to the Bible student which took place at this old historic town and its environments; it was at Mizpeh that Samuel took a stone and called the name of it Ebenezer, saying, "Hitherto the Lord hath helped us."

The present village is modern and of no interest to travelers, and would not be visited were it not for its ancient history. (Judges xx; 1 Samuel vii. 6-12, and x. 17-24; 2 Kings xxv. 25.)

On approaching Jerusalem by the way of the main road from Joppa the houses of the outskirts or near the community known as the New Jerusalem began to appear. A vast improvement has been made during the last fifteen years; hundreds of nice little dwellings have been built west of the city, and inhabited by Jews, who have gone there to spend their days. In the winter of seventy-seven, when I made my first visit to Jerusalem, nearly the whole place upon which now stand seven or eight hundred houses was vacant; at that time there were but few houses west and northwest of Zion: then the tendency was to build on the north of the Joppa gate, but on my last visit I found the extension was on the west and northwest.

This New Jerusalem covers as much space, or nearly so, as the old city; on account of the zigzag survey of the highway and the hills Jerusalem could not be seen until a near approach was reached, even in those days when the hill round about on which stand hundreds of houses was vacant; but at this time when so many buildings have been erected, the city is entirely hid from view until one approaches within a short distance of the Joppa Gate.

The long and crooked street through which we pass is seemingly full of tumult, it being the only business thoroughfare outside the walls, which is by no means extensive; men and women are constantly going to and fro, carrying great boxes on their heads, while the poor overloaded camels and donkeys seem to bend in agony under their burden; there is no society for the protection of animals against cruelties in Palestine, therefore the poor beasts are treated without mercy.

PART V.

ANCIENT AND MODERN JERUSALEM.

Approaching Jerusalem—The Ancient and Modern Cities—Situation of Jerusalem—General Elevation of the City—Mountains Around the City—City Walls—Walls of To-day—Towers Along the Walls—Gates of the City—Present Jerusalem, the Modern City—Division of the City—Greek and Latin Churches—Population of Jerusalem—Its Sanitary Condition—How the Nights are Spent—Shining Light—The Jews' Wailing-place—Worship under the Church of England—Witnessing the Mournful Service—What Jerome Says of This Place—The Harem Area—Mosque of Omer—The Castle of Antonia—Mt. Moriah—Inscriptions on the Walls—Entering the Mosque of Omar—The Sacred Rock—Mohammed and Gabriel—Cave below the Mosque—Caleph Omar—Mosque of El-Aksa—Temple Courts and Foundations—Description of Temple—When Built—Its Furnishings—Old Foundations—Ancient Quarries—Ancient Jerusalem—Jebus Captured—Jerusalem the Resting-place of the Ark of God—Jerusalem During the Reign of Solomon—Decline of Jerusalem—Inhabitants Carried into Captivity—Prophecy of Isaiah Fulfilled—How Alexander the Great Met the People—Alexander and Antiochus—The Great Slaughter—Armenians to the Rescue—The Great War for Liberty—King Herod's Reign—Zion, the Centre Light—Zion, on Approaching Jerusalem—How Situated—Mt. Moriah, Ornan's Threshing-floor—David's Sin—Sacrifice Offered—Approaching Jerusalem—Inhabitants of Mt. Moriah—Mt. Akra, Mt. Bezetha—Mt. Calvary—Extension of Walls of Jerusalem—Existence of Tombs within the Present City Walls—Great Questions Discussed—The Tomb of Christ—Church of Holy Sepulchre.

APPROACHING JERUSALEM.

IT will be hard for me to tell how I was impressed at my first sight of Jerusalem. Persons entering Jerusalem for the first time cannot be other than deeply moved with solemnity when one remembers he is about to enter the most sacred and historic city in the world, around which cluster all the achievements triumphantly won by our Lord, which purchased for man the right to enter through the gates into the heavenly Jerusalem. When my eyes first beheld the holy city I was most solemnly impressed; the sufferings of my Lord came vividly to my mind, and I exclaimed: "O Jerusalem! Jerusalem! thou who hath stoned the prophets and killed them that my Lord hath sent you,

VIEW OF JERUSALEM.

how many times would He have gathered thy children together as a hen gathers her brood under her wings, but ye would not."

Indeed there was no day during my stay in the holy city that I was not moved with awe while visiting the many places of sacred memory. I am told every visitor is more or less impressed on first entering Jerusalem with the sacred character of the place. Peculiar impressions naturally seize one while visiting the ruins of ancient Rome, or Pompeii, or other places distinguished for passed greatness.

It matters not how strange or deep the impression may be in viewing these ruins of Rome or Pompeii, it is not like the impressions received when you take your first view of the holy city; it is entirely different, both in character and magnitude, from that which is felt in any part of Palestine. The time may come when the thousands who, from time to time, visit the great city on the banks of the Tiber to view her ruins, her churches, her catacombs and her spacious founts will cease; but Jerusalem the venerable—the holy city where prophets, priests and mighty kings lived, and which stands at the head of the historic world, will ever be visited by the multitudes of ardent admirers of the Lord Jesus Christ, because the proclamation of His love started from there, and in and around about it are clustered the precious emblems of Divine truth and salvation.

When the gate of Joppa is opened and the feet of the eager visitor stands on Mount Zion, his mind is immediately crowded with many events of its glorious past age. He rejoices that he is standing on the holy hill of Zion, the mount on which patriarchs and prophets have been known to walk, where the Lord Jesus once stood, and apostles preached repentance toward God and faith in Christ.

He will call to mind that somewhere near by was the throne of David, of Solomon, and others of the kings of Judah. He looks toward the great mosque of Omar, on Moriah, and thinks of the spacious temple which crowned its sacred brow, and the altars on which sacrifices were burnt, morning and evening, for hundreds of years, and its hallowed shrines, where thronged the adoring Israelites from all parts of the land, gladly embracing the opportunity to celebrate the annual feasts, perhaps using the words of the Psalmist, "Our feet shall stand within thy gates, oh, Jerusalem."

A SURVEY OF JERUSALEM.

After the stranger has finished for a time his meditation of the antique history in connection with the dawn of the Christian era, he may turn and consider the present condition of the people thronging the narrow streets of the Holy City. There is a general expression of disappointment by all who visit Jerusalem from Europe or America, both in the condition of the people and its internal regulations. The authorities have no law in force regulating the sanitary condition of the city; therefore it is exceedingly disagreeable to visit some portions, because of the accumulation of filth, from which a continuous odor is emitted, and four-fifths of the inhabitants are sadly ignorant, dejected and poor, many of whom have not sufficient clothing to render them presentable on the streets. The most of the people are very sinful and seem to glory in it. We can plainly see while looking over the city what moved our Lord to tears when he viewed it from the slope of the Mount of Olives, for even now any one who has been awakened by the spirit of Divine grace will find himself sorrow-stricken while passing from street to street, taking a general view of the condition of a people living immediately under the shadow of the Cross.

And were it not that we are assured in God's word that Jerusalem will be restored, and that hopeful evidences of its fulfilment are already appearing, the Christian visitor would be constrained to continue the lamentable strains of Jeremiah and say, "Oh, that my head were waters and mine eyes a fountain of tears, that I might weep day and night for the slain of the daughter of my people." (Jer. ix. 1.)

The information I have received from those who have visited Palestine is that none have escaped the emotions that cannot be controlled on entering the Holy City, and especially when they take a general survey of the inhabitants. It seems to me impossible for any to feel otherwise who visit there from a land of higher civilization.

SITUATION OF JERUSALEM.

It is the custom of the guides to take visitors around the walls on the outside of the city; this is the beginning of the tours in and about the city of sacred history; it is important to make a circuit of it so that it may be definitely seen. The whole of Jerusalem is built on hills, which can only be seen to advantage from lowland on the outside, especially from the Valley of Jehoshaphat and the Valley of Hinnom.

It is not a very long journey, but very tedious; from one and a half to two hours are required to complete the circuit; this could be done in one-half the time were the paths in good condition; the visitor has his choice of walking or riding; the latter is generally preferred, although some portions of the way one must alight and walk over the dangerously rough places, for should the beast stumble and fall, the rider would sustain great injury, if he did not lose his life.

But there is no more speed made by riding than walking; it is believed by those who have tried it one can make quicker time walking than riding, but it is much more fatiguing to do so. Jerusalem is situated on four hills, Zion, Moriah, Acre and Bezetha, formally separated by a deep valley which divided the city into four parts. The general elevation of the city is estimated to be about twenty-six hundred feet above the level of the Mediterranean Sea, and about twenty-eight hundred feet above the level of the Dead Sea. It is worthy of remark that persons going to Jerusalem from every direction go up hill, therefore all say, "I am going up to Jerusalem." How significant is the fact to the idea of ours about the New Jerusalem, the land of "Precious Promise"; all who travel hither express themselves as going up.

Although the Holy City is prominently situated on high elevations, it does not seem to be so when compared to the mountains round about it, but can be regarded so only when compared with the deep ravines that nearly surround it.

There are mountains around the city much higher than those on which it stands, therefore distant views cannot be had of it such as we get of Tyre, Sidon, Nazareth, Safed, Beyrout, and several other cities and towns in Palestine and Syria. The best distant view of Jerusalem is obtained from Neby Samueil on the west, Mt. Scopus on the north, and the Mount of Olives on the east; neither of these places are far from the city.

Many travelers seem to be impressed with the thought that the city is so elevated it can be seen from any quarter when approaching it, and are greatly disappointed when they find themselves within a few hundred yards of it before it is seen, except by those who come from the north. The peculiar situation of the city prevents it from being seen at a distance, except from those mountainous points already referred to.

The hills around Jerusalem are much higher than those on which it stands, so that it must be approached on all sides from deep ravines which lead up to the hills that are not far from the *Holy City*.

THE CITY WALLS.

The present city is after the manner of the *old* one, closed in by high walls and gates. These walls are by no means square, and are broken in several places; time's crushing hand is making telling impressions upon them.

They are not to be compared neither in height nor thickness to the walls around the *Ancient City* in the days of David, Solomon, Herod and others; in those days the chief object in building walls was to secure the protection of the inhabitants against hostile foes; the means of defence were meagre, therefore great caution was taken in building those fortress walls.

These walls which now inclose the city were built during the early part of the sixteenth century by order of Sultan Suleiman, who at that time ruled Jerusalem. As far as the various investigations have been made it is found that the present walls stand on some of the ground upon which the old walls of the middle ages stood, especially on the east and south sides, and contain much of the material of which they were composed, and even those of remoter times.

The measurement shows they are only fifteen feet thick at the bottom and much thinner at the top; they are from twenty-five to seventy feet high, according to the elevations or depressions of the ground on which they are built; these walls were not built to protect the people in the city, as those which were built in ancient times; since the use of modern improvements of warfare have been adopted, therefore they would be of little or no use for safety within them.

The present wall would be of no more service as a protection against the encroachments of an invading army, strong and well equipped for battle, than a steam launch could guard a city bordering on the sea coast against the approach of a man-of-war steamship, yet these walls are not wholly useless as protectors, for while they close the city in from the world without and clothe it with a garb of antiquity, they also guard it from the thieving Bedouins, whose haunts are the mountains, caves, and solitary places of Palestine, and who are generally looking about watching an opportunity to plunder, and would gladly enter the city, commit depredations after night, were it not that the wall prevents them.

All the gates are usually locked after sundown, except the Joppa gate, which is often open until nine or ten o'clock, but always strongly guarded by a detail of soldiers from the barracks. The walls are estimated to have a measurement of a-half a mile on each side, and the whole circuit of the city about two miles.

There are towers along the wall at irregular intervals which serve as supports as well as watch towers; it has been the custom of visitors to ascend to the top of the wall, near the entrance door into the ancient quarry where one of the most superb views of the city is had.

There is no danger of falling; the walls are about six feet thick on top and will allow two or three persons to walk abreast without the fear of falling; the ancient walls were three, each covering different periods; these shut in and protect certain portions of the city; the first enclosed Mt. Zion, the second Mt. Acre and the third Mt. Bezetha; those who have attempted to identify the exact locality and direction of these walls, have not been as yet satisfactorily successful in their efforts, nor have they agreed in their conclusions, but advanced several opinions as to their probable directions, especially with regard to the second wall. Much care has been taken and labor expended to find the precise location and direction of it, for if that could be discovered, the long and perplexing dispute as to the site of Mt. Calvary would be forever settled; until that is known there will be continued controversies as to the true site of our Lord's crucifixion.

Of late gratifying progress has been made which has stimulated a hope of future success.

GATES OF THE CITY.

There are eight gates in the walls of the present city: of these the Joppa gate, through which all who go up to Jerusalem from the west or south pass, is without doubt the most important; at least four-fifths of those who enter into the city pass through this gate. The new gate, which has only been placed in the walls lately, is on the northwest of the former; it has no historical importance attached to it, and was opened simply as a convenience for those living in the west and northwest.

The Damascus gate or gate of the Columns opens opposite the old road to Shechem, Samaria, Nazareth, Tiberias and Damascus; it is sometimes called the ornamental gate, because it is more richly embellished than any of the others. St. Stephen's gate, which the native Christians call "The Gate of my Lady Mary," is located on the east side of the city, and is the most convenient entrance and exit for those who are passing to and from the *Kedron Valley*. The gate is very plain, having but a single peculiar feature of distinction, that is, a sculptured lion over it. The gate of the Moore is small and used but little. It is situated on the south side of the city near the Tyropean Valley, and is the nearest exit to the village of Siloam and several other places in that locality. The Zion gate is on the ridge of Mt. Zion, and is known by the natives as the gate of the Prophet David.

There are two other gates, the gate of Herod and the Golden gate; these two are closed continually; the latter is watched zealously by the Moslems who confidently believe that if that gate should be opened their power in Palestine would be broken forever. This gate also marks the site of the ancient gate through which our Lord made his triumphant entry into Jerusalem headed and followed by a tumultuous multitude shouting His praise.

If the Golden Gate were opened it would lead from the Valley of Jehoshaphat to the area of the Mosque of Omar. It has a double arch on the valley side and inside a very well designed vaulted chamber.

THE PRESENT JERUSALEM.

The gates of the ancient city were many more than those of the present; they are enumerated in the books of Nehemiah and Second Kings. When we consider the minute description of these gates as given by Josephus and other ancient writers who remembered the purpose for which they served we cannot but conclude they were not only massive, but also very beautiful.

Notwithstanding the traveler who visits Jerusalem for the first time is seized with a feeling of disappointment when he passes through the entrance gate, from the fact nothing upon which he looks fills the measure of his expectation; but when he considers he is in the most famous city in the world, the one which is connected with the most sacred and illustrious events known in history, he then commences to realize that the ground upon which he stands is holy. Jerusalem has passed through so many bitter ordeals it cannot be expected that many of the ancient relics remain above the surface.

Jerusalem having been sacked at least seventeen times, the greater part of it lies deeply buried beneath the present city. Much of the old material, however, has been discovered by the various excavations which have been in progress from time to time; it is stated that when the foundation for the English mission church, for the proper teaching of the gospel among the Jews, was being dug on Mt. Zion, the workmen had to dig down through fifty or more feet of ruins before they came to a place solid enough to lay the foundation. (See Nehemiah, iii.; 2 Kings, xiv.)

There is a street, beginning at the Latin convent and passing through the arch, "Ecce Homo," which leads to the gate of St. Stephen, this is known as "Via Dolorosa," and is traditionally held as the route through which our Lord passed while bearing His cross to

Golgotha's summit; this has been memorable to pilgrims who still continue the custom that has existed for many years.

They do not fail to go down this pass, mournfully expressing their sympathy for Jesus who bore the cross for them. Notwithstanding there is not a shadow of foundation for locating the way of mourning to be this narrow pass beyond questionable tradition, yet it is so confidently believed by the great mass of pilgrims, they would not dare leave the city without passing through it and shedding tears in sacred commemoration of our Lord's agony. It is the prevailing opinion that if the tears of the pilgrims of many generations which have fallen upon the ground here remained, every spot of it from end to end would have been wet; how fittingly the words of our Lord apply to them, with which He addressed the mourning multitude who followed Him while bending under His *cross*. Judging from sad demonstrations they manifest, they are just as earnest in their sympathy as were those who followed our Lord.

David and Zion streets run nearly at right angles, dividing the city into four parts; on the northwest is the Christian quarter, the Moslems live in the northeast, on the southeast the Jews are clustered in their ancient looking dwellings to themselves, and from the general condition of their quarters, we feel safe to say, no one, not even the native Arabs, covet their situation.

On the southwest side the Armenians have their quarters, they seem to be an industrious and prosperous people; these four sects represent the religious communities, though divided in four general divisions, yet they embrace several different denominations; it is important that these sects should live in sections to themselves in order that peace be preserved among them.

There is an unabating hostile sentiment, fostered by them on account of their religious persecutions; it is an evil which will, no doubt, bring about results which will be sadly lamented; there are many demonstrations that indicate fearful results in time to come, unless proper steps are taken to remedy the existing evils. Some of the religious denominations which live in the same section are bitterly opposed to each other; this feeling has existed for some time among the Greek and Latin Christians, who have attempted on several occasions to take each other's lives. This outrageously hostile feeling began when the officials of the Greek and Latin churches, both in the Church of the Holy Sepulchre in Jerusalem, and that of the Holy Nativity in Bethlehem, were at swords' points against each other. It happens that their outbreaks of hostilities are many times the results of small matters, such as the decorations about the altars, or the right to enter one of the doors claimed by another, and such other correspondingly light matters.

It may seem to many, to be incredible but it is nevertheless true. guards of soldiers are kept constantly within the walls of these sacred and most distinguished buildings in the world, to prohibit an uprising and bloodshed among those who ought to be peacemakers, the "salt of the earth," "the light of the world;" yet it is sadly true they are kept under close vigilance daily, lest they should renew their hostilities.

We know this to be true, for our own eyes have seen them; it had been but a short time before I arrived in Jerusalem that a very disastrous outbreak occurred in Bethlehem, during which several of the participants were severely injured; the bitter feeling which was kindled in the breasts of these influential religious bodies, many years ago, is just as strongly encouraged now, as when it was first blown to a flame, and is likely to continue for ages to come. The population of Jerusalem is estimated to be about sixty thousand, and it is constantly increasing. Of this number, forty-three thousand are Jews, about eight thousand Moslems, nine thousand Protestants, four thousand Orthodox Greeks, three thousand and nine hundred Latin Catholics, two hundred Greek Catholics, eight hundred Armenians, one hundred Syrians, one hundred and fifty Copts, five hundred Abyssinians, and a few others; this large population living in such a small space are compelled to occupy but little house room for large families, therefore they are necessarily pressed and put to many disadvantages, which the inhabitants of our modern cities know nothing about; their homes are poorly ventilated, their cisterns and reservoirs often become stagnant. The destitution of sewerage and the total neglect of sanitary regulations, render the *Holy City* at times very unhealthy.

On this account, strangers are ordered to be specially cautious in drinking the water unless it is first boiled and filtered; otherwise it is liable to produce some troublesome disease. The violation of this advice has been woefully experienced by many. It is strange proper steps are not taken by the Turkish authorities to place the city in a more healthful condition, both for the benefit of inhabitants and those from other lands, who are yearly visiting it.

It is authoritatively stated that the refuse of the city is largely dumped into the pool of Bethesda, which is nearly adjoining the soldiers' barracks; it can be easily seen that such a state of things is antagonistic to health. It is the opinion of medical men, if Jerusalem was put under a rigid sanitary discipline it would be one of the most healthy and purest places in the world. The many pleasures indulged and patronized by the masses in countries known to be highly civilized and progressive, many of which break down in health, and hurry thousands to untimely graves, are not known in Jerusalem; just as soon as the sun dips its golden pinions into the Mediterranean Sea, the places of business are closed, with few exceptions, and all the gates but the one on the west are closed. This has been allowed to remain open longer to permit those who have been detained on business to come in; but few if any care to be out after dark; the streets are as dark as midnight, for there can scarcely be seen a ray of light anywhere, and a death-like silence reigns in all the passes and lanes almost over the whole city.

There are no church meetings at night, except at a small mission, about a half a mile beyond the Joppa gate, where meetings are held for a few persons about one hour on Sunday nights.

Jerusalem is free from all such amusements as concerts, theatres, balls, and the variety of attractions common in other lands; therefore the people have nowhere to go to spend their time, and break down their health, therefore almost all the people seem to go down with the sun and arise with it.

There are a few people seen lurking about the Cafés and drinking saloons, until nine or ten o'clock, but they are generally quiet and orderly; the poverty of the masses will not permit them to indulge very freely in spending their money for liquors; the most drinking is done by persons who visit there from countries of more advanced civilization.

SHINING LIGHT.

If a person should necessarily be out at a late hour it is important he should have a lantern, otherwise he is liable to be arrested. It happened during my stay in Jerusalem, the American Consul was compelled to be out one night very late, visiting a number of Jews who were under his supervision, and when he came back to the hotel some one had to escort him with a light. It is commonly believed that no one but thieves are out in the darkness, or some evil motive is the prevailing incentive, that would stimulate a person to prowl through the city without a light; therefore all persons who are thus found are promptly arrested, and put in the guard-house until morning, then an investigation is made in their case.

This custom has come down through the distant ages unchanged;

this same rule applies to all the cities in Palestine and Syria except Beyrout, in which there are street lamps lighted with gas.

Our Lord seems to have referred to this time-honored regulation in his memorable "Sermon on the Mount," when He admonished the anxious ones to "let their light shine before men." The illustration is so very striking no one can fail to see how fittingly our Lord applied it to the indispensable spiritual light, which alone is convincing to men, they are changed from nature to grace. (See Matt. v.)

THE WAILING PLACE (JERUSALEM.)

The Jews' Wailing Place is one of the great attractions in Jerusalem. It is sought as eagerly as any of the ancient historical places of distinction in Palestine. No visitor to the Holy City feels satisfied with his observation, nor is he willing to leave without witnessing the strikingly peculiar devotions of the Jews, which is one of the most impressive exhibitions of deep lamentations, on account of Divine displeasure, to be seen anywhere in our world. The Jews gather in large numbers along the walls of the celebrated Haram, to weep over their present condition and pray for the favor of God to rest upon and restore the city and country to them, that they may rule over it as their fathers did in their day of prosperity. The narrow lanes and passes leading to the Wailing Place are very difficult to pass through, being rugged, crooked and filthy.

The moment the Jewish quarter is entered a sickening odor, that fills the air, is prominent; but the stranger will not regret the unpleasantness of the trip when the occasion of his visit is witnessed. The Jews of both sexes assemble along the stupendous walls of the time-stricken building each Friday afternoon, and weep aloud from three o'clock until five.

These poor, dejected people, of all ages and conditions, from all quarters of the world, are seen here every week, participating in the most peculiar service, which, although strange and amusing to many, is one of the most important character in the estimation of the Jews, from the beginning to the end, and they are from all outward appearances as earnest and sincere as if their last moments on earth had come.

These poor, unfortunate people, whose misleading faith has launched them into a deep gulf of adversity, gather at their place of weekly lamentations from Russia, Germany, Poland, Roumania, Spain, India, Egypt, Africa, and other countries, wherever they are dispersed, to mingle their pensive petitions with those who dwell in Jerusalem, for the return of the blessings of the Almighty upon the people of their

JEWS' WAILING-PLACE.

race in Palestine. Some of them are seen bending under the weight of four-score years, some in the meridian of life, others in the morning of youth, all of whom have their faces turned towards the wall, presenting a deeply touching scene; their agonizing gestures and penetrating cries are almost bewildering. This method of expressing their grief because their sanctuary has become dishonored and desolate, in connection with their own destitute and humiliating condition, has been continued for many centuries, and doubtless will be perpetuated until they make a full and complete surrender of their cherished religion, and embrace the Lord Jesus Christ, which, to my mind, is only a comparatively short time.

For already hundreds of them have espoused the Christian faith and devoutly worship Christ on the hill of Zion, under the auspices of the Church of England. This practiced weeping was no doubt introduced during the Babylonian captivity, when the devout Jews remembering the devastated condition of Jerusalem, their temple and altars, mourned and hung their harps upon the willows on the river bank.

But the precedent became more prominent, about the year 362 of our era, when the Jews were not permitted to enter the Holy City but once a year, then special permission was given them to pass through the gates to weep over the ruins of the Temple. In after years, when those ostracised people were granted permission to return and dwell in their ancient city, they went every week to their present place of wailing to demonstrate their griefs, and continued to do so on each Friday. The burden of their lamentations is based upon Psalm lxxix., which they read or repeat during their service.

It has been the opinion of some visitors who have witnessed these strange gatherings, that the Jews conduct them specially to entertain strangers and enlist their sympathy, and, aside from that, the whole proceeding is a meaningless custom; but this is far from being correct: these meetings are of the most sincere character and the Jews expect as fully to obtain their desire, as the most fervent Christian, who earnestly prays for something of special interest to the world.

I had a favorable opportunity to witness this mournful service which so solemnly impressed me; it will not soon be forgotten; we saw old men and old women bending under the hand of time, young men and maidens just entering their majority, little boys and girls who are to be the future guides of their race, all bending in solemn devotion, the magnitude of which could not be fully expressed even by the flow of tears prominently falling from their cheeks.*

* Psalm cxxxvii. 1: 2.

The summit of Calvary on which the Lord Jesus died for their redemption is only a few minutes' walk from the walls where Jewish wailing is heard, yet these weeping ones have no faith in the story of the cross and they despise the Saviour of men to this day, even as did their fathers who slew Him. I felt like saying to them while beholding their devotions, Turn and look to Calvary and accept the Christ whom your forefathers crucified and all these blessings you seek will be given you for His name's sake. The Jews have worn some of the rough stones composing the Haram wall quite smooth with their heads which have pressed them for so many centuries.

The stones of which the wall is built are white marble, composed of very large blocks, some being fifteen feet long and three feet thick; as the wall became higher, in building, smaller stones were used for it, yet all of them may be regarded as unusually large; Jerome speaks of this place as the site of the Jews' Wailing Place, in the time when Jerusalem was in the custody of Rome.

He says such was the deep anxiety of the dispersed and sorrowing Jews, to be allowed to go to the walls and weep, they would pay the Roman soldiers for permission to do so. It is prayerfully hoped, as the rapidly increasing Mission Church on Mt Zion grows in numbers, its influence, in connection with others near the city, will be effectually illuminating, and instead of a promiscuous gathering of aimless people seen each Friday at the Haram, they will be found in the house of the Lord, bowing before their Redeemer.

THE HARAM AREA.

The Mosque of Omar occupies a portion of the venerable site on which was erected the great Temple and its connecting buildings; this large tract, shut in by walls, is one of the most revered and sacred places in Jerusalem; the sacred enclosure covers about thirty-five acres of space, and is known as "El Haram-ash-Sherif," or "The noble Sanctuary;" it is closed in by high massive walls in which are set eleven gates, three of these are on the north, and eight on the west side; there are three other gateways, which are supposed to occupy the sites of ancient gates; those on the south are called double and triple gates respectively, and that on the east, is the renowned Golden Gate.

These ancient gateways are carefully walled, so that no one can pass through them; the Haram is in the possession of the Moslems, who keep a close watch over it day and night. For a long time Christians were not permitted, under any circumstances, to pass the portals of its sacred enclosure, and if one would dare venture beyond the prescribed bounds the chances of his returning were as slender as a spider's web, for the alert Mohammedans would slay him without mercy.

But it is pleasing to state the barriers have been removed, and all visitors to Jerusalem are allowed to enter by paying a high fee, but even now it is not safe to attempt a visit there without having a guard. The functionary is called Kamass; he is sent, on application, by the consul of the country to which the applicant belongs.

Besides paying an admission fee of two dollars and fifty cents, each person is expected to give fifty cents extra as Bakshish to the Moslem Sheikhs, who superintend the various buildings within the enclosure. Although there are eleven gates opened into the area of the Haram, visitors generally pass in the entrance gate at the end of the street of the cotton merchants; it may be of interest to state that in all the cities of Palestine the streets are named according to the character of the business conducted in them, such as the street of the "tanners," or of the shoemakers, or of the sheep market, cotton merchants and the like.

There are streets having four or five different names, and are divided into business sections On the morning of our visit to this most memorable place there was a party of twelve of us, besides six or seven guides and as many consular guards.

Our chief guide was a converted Jew, who was one of the official ministers of the mission church, located on the slope of Mt. Zion, under the auspices of the established Church of England; he was an efficient guide, having had an opportunity to thoroughly explore Jerusalem and the country round about as far as possible.

He has acquired a voluminous amount of historical information concerning some of the most eventful places in and about Jerusalem. A moment after we passed the entrance gate he caused us to halt; he then pointed to a curious looking stone, which was in use when our Lord frequented the temple, and is supposed to have composed a part of the pavement leading to it.

MOSQUE OF OMAR.

Then said the guide, "This stone is in all probability one that composed the portion of the walk when our Lord repeated His visits to the Temple, and no doubt his feet often rested upon it when passing in and out of this enclosure." The words of our guide filled us with hopeful amazement, and when I placed my foot upon it, and remembered it was probably resting on the very spot upon which the feet of our Lord stood, a feeling of joy came over me which is impossible to describe.

Although nearly every foot of ground within the enclosure and almost every noticeable stone has been under continuous controversy, yet there is no doubt as to the existence of this rocky surface during the time of our Lord, and as it is close to one of the entrance gates it is highly probable the Lord Jesus often passed in and out over it.

Therefore there is no tangible reason to the contrary that the holy feet of Jesus many times rested upon it; there are many important traditional sites within the Haram inclosure, concerning many of which we cannot speak owing to small space, and can only give a passing notice of some of the most important places.

The castle of Antonia, built by Herod, on the site of a Macedonian fort, as an outpost and defence of the Temple Court, was in what was known as the "second circuit, or within the second wall inclosing the lower city;" it was here that St. Paul addressed the people so touchingly after having been delivered from an angry mob, who sought his life. (See Acts xxi: 34–40.)

Within the Haram enclosure is one of the most historic places in the world; it is the memorable Mt. Moriah, the site on which Ornan had his threshing floor; here, it is currently believed, Abraham brought his beloved Isaac to offer him up to the Lord; here King David came in haste, being divinely directed to intercede for his plagued-stricken people; and upon its lofty brow stood the beautiful Temple, which King Solomon solemnly dedicated to the services of the Lord, to which multitudes of enthusiastic worshipers came to pour forth their devotions to the Most High. Moriah is now covered with the Mosque of Omar, which is looked upon as the most beautiful and interesting building in Jerusalem; this building stands in the middle of the platform, which has been skillfully elevated. It is octagonal in construction, having a measurement of sixty-seven feet on each side, rising forty-six feet from the ground, and supporting a circular wall, which is twenty-five feet higher; upon this the beautiful dome is erected, which rises forty feet higher, making the building from the surface to the highest point of the dome one hundred and ten feet.

There are inscriptions of beautiful designs in pure Mosaic in several places on the walls, which must have been very handsome in earlier times; they are fast falling, and in a short time there will not be one of these precious gems left to tell of the former glory of the inner walls of the Mosque.

It would be difficult for any one possessed with reason to stand in front of the wonderful and magnificent building and view its many colored marbles as they glisten in the sunlight, as did the stones of the great Temple which once adorned this summit, without being touched with the peculiar emotions that filled the hearts of the multitude on their approach to the Temple, when the tribes came up to pay their vow to the Lord God of Israel. About this cragged summit clustered the religious, poetical and political life of the people favored by the Lord. The aggravating controversies, which have caused much uneasiness and perplexity among many leading explorers of Palestine, do not linger around the brow of Moriah, as its identity is conceded by most of the leading writers. Although there are many opinions current as to the true sites of various places, concerning which the Bible gives account, in and about Jerusalem, but few will attempt to dispute that the Mosque of Omar stands upon the summit of Mt. Moriah. The Jewish, Christian and Moslem traditions accord in the statement that the Mosque of Omar occupies one of the most sacred places in the Holy City. Those who are favored with an opportunity of entering its adored precincts are commanded to take off their shoes at the entrance door, or put a pair of slippers over them, for the Moslems will not allow any one, under any circumstances, to enter without first covering their shoes with soft-sole slippers, and this must be observed by all who gain admission, whether potentate or peasant. On first entering, the interior is very gloomy, and so dark at times that one must wait a few moments until the pupil of the eye expands sufficiently to take in enough of the dim light penetrating the crevices to overcome the darkness of the chamber.

THE SACRED ROCK.

Then the beauties of the large room begin to appear more and more until the beholder is almost amazed in wonder and filled with admiration; the gorgeous coloring of the beautifully painted woodwork, the fine marble, the costly mosaics, the great dome over head handsomely decorated with choice inscriptions finely gilded. All this splendor gleams out through the darkness, presenting a panorama of rich and rare taste; there are many other important objects worthy of admiration to be seen in the building, but all of them combined fail before the Sacred Rock in the centre of the building just under the dome, carefully protected by a wooden railing, and constantly watched by the officials of the Mosque.

The rock is exposed to every one's view who enters the chamber; its surface is smooth and bare, and is estimated to measure about sixty feet in length and forty-five feet in width; Captain Wilson says, "It stands about four feet, nine inches and a-half above the marble pavement at its highest point, and one foot at its lowest."

The surface of the rock bears prominent marks of bad treatment and rough chiselling; there are many stories of Moslem invention told visitors by the guides, simply for the story's sake, but the Mohammedans would have them believed, no matter how enormous they may seem.

The Moslems cannot, it seems, see anything but certainty in every legend transmitted to them from their ancestors; they seem to believe in them as confidently as they do in their Koran, and will brand every one as a stupid infidel who differs with them in religious persuasion.

MOHAMMED AND GABRIEL.

There are many wild and groundless legends the fathers of Moslemism have connected with the several places in and about the Mosque of Omar, that interfere very much at times with the sacred impressions made on the minds of pious visitors; for example, at one corner of the rock may be seen an indentation resembling a foot print. Moslems try to impress strangers that it is the impression of Mohammed's foot; close to it is a poorly cut hand print; this is said to be the mark of the hand of the Angel Gabriel; the current Moslem tradition is, that when Mohammed started from this world to heaven, he was standing on this rock, and such was the holy impression he made upon the rock, it lifted itself to go up with him, but Gabriel, being present, placed his hand upon the rock to hold it down, which, when lifted, left its print there; and likewise Mohammed's foot left its impression where he stood.

These marks they say have remained there until the present, and this is one of the wild statements Moslems have to relate to strangers.

THE CAVE BELOW THE MOSQUE.

Beneath the rock there is a cave, which is entered by descending a flight of eleven steps; the Mohammedans say this was the place frequented by Abraham, David, Solomon and Jesus, when they wished to pray privately, and the four niches there are respectively shown where each one used to pray.

There is also a small marble slab in the centre of the floor covering a deep cavity, in which there is an incessant rumbling sound that can be heard distinctly by applying the ear to the slab; the cause of this noise is not satisfactorily known, although several stories have been told concerning it. The opinion of Devogue Pieratte and Warren is, that the opening is connected with cisterns and sewers through which the blood and refuse ran from the Altars of Sacrifice, and passed into the valley below; this seems to be the most plausible definition of the existence of the murmuring sound in the deep cavity under the rock, which could easily be produced by the water passing through from one basin to another as it runs in by a subterranean channel from one of the pools about the city.

By tapping the sides of the cave a hollow sound is produced; on this account the Moslems insist that it is conclusive evidence the cave is suspended; but the deep hollow sound that is heard is said to be caused from defects in the plastering.

The Mohammedans think the more causalities they can show the better the visitor is pleased; there are other sacred spots about the Mosque to which are attached many legends; this Mosque is the most distinguished of all others under the jurisdiction of Mohammedans in any part of the world.

CALIPH OMAR.

The great Mosque at Damascus, St. Sophia's at Constantinople, nor the ones of proud boast in Delhi, India, can compete with the Mosque of Omar, neither in grandeur nor historic attachments; it stands on the memorable and time-honored site upon which stood the Temple which was built during the reign of King Solomon, and rebuilt by Zerubbabel and Herod; this sacred summit has been reverenced by representatives of almost all nations who have visited Jerusalem. Those who entered within her portals in triumph and those who passed through in a state of humility, have alike been impressed while beholding Moriah the Mount of God's Temple.

It is said when Caliph Omar captured the city he asked to be conducted to the place where the Jewish Temple stood; he was taken to the place, which at that time was a huge mound of rubbish, that had been lying there from the time the sacred building was destroyed by the army of Titus; Omar caused the ruins, or much of them, to be cleared, and then built the Mosque upon the same site which bears his name.

But as there is so much of the so-called history of Palestine drawn from legends or false traditions, it is not safe to accept everything we read as genuine; only those works which have been given to the world after proper investigation has been made are worthy of acceptance.

THE MOSQUE OF EL-AKSA.

The building of special attraction and importance in the Haram enclosure is the Mosque El-Aksa, or the "Distant Mosque;" it is given this name because of its position with reference to Mecca; there are many opinions as to the origin of this building, and the matter may never be entirely settled, but the most prominent opinion is, it was built by the Emperor Justinian in the middle of the sixth century, in honor of the Virgin Mary.

Our party stopped a few minutes in front of the grand portico, which is divided into seven apartments, covering the whole length of the building; the great nave extends through the centre, and is a beautiful sight to behold; it is separated by massive columns on either side and neatly painted arches. Each of these pillars bears the name of one of the prophets, or a caliph, to whom it is especially dedicated.

The nave has three alleys on each side, one of which is walled up and set off from the body of the other portion; this is known as the women's apartment; it obstructs a view of the entire sweep of the interior without passing from one side to the other. As it is, a fine view can be had of the greater part of it.

When the crusaders captured Jerusalem this Mosque was used as a Christian church. Baldwin II. occupied a part of it for a new military order, who from their connection with the Temple site took the name of Knights Templar; they built a wall in front of the great El-Aksa, which they used as a granary.

TEMPLE COURTS AND FOUNDATION.

The great Temple of Solomon, according to Josephus, stood upon a rocky eminence in the eastern section of the city, on which at first there was scarcely to be found a level space sufficient to bear an altar, the sides being steep and precipitous. King Solomon first caused a wall to be built around the summit, and one also on the east, filled in on the inside with earth, on which he built a covered colonnade, and left the Temple exposed on three sides. But in process of time the whole of the enclosure was built up and filled in to the level of the hill, which in this way was enlarged; a three-fold wall was built up from the bottom, and thus the upper enclosure and the lower part of the Temple were constructed; it was a wonderful undertaking, even to prepare the foundations of the Temple; there was a vast amount of filling up to do before the workmen could begin the foundation proper, therefore it is worthy of remark that the foundations for the Temple were built upon another foundation laid expressly for it, the whole depth of which has never been discovered, because they filled in the valleys, wishing to level the abrupt places in the city.

In proceeding with the work it was necessary to secure it against future calamities that might arise from depressions or weakness of the understructure, therefore they used massive stone, some of them being forty cubits long and bound together with lead and iron into a compact mass, so that the whole construction appeared almost as a huge block formed by nature.

TEMPLE COURT.

The whole structure when completed was enclosed into a square, measuring six hundred feet on each side, or twenty-four hundred feet in circumference; the interior of the enclosure was surrounded by covered colonnades along the walls; the portions which were uncovered were paved with beautiful variegated stones.

It became in after days a great place of resort for the people in Jerusalem; also for strangers, and finally it was noted as a public trading-place, especially on the approach of and during the annual festivals. It was commonly known as the Court of the Gentiles.

Near the middle of the Court was an ornamental balustrade, composed of large stones, six or eight feet high; this formed a boundary of a smaller enclosure, through which foreigners and the unclean were not permitted to pass; within this was another wall forty cubits high from its foundation, which surrounded the inner Court, and was surrounded on the outside by fourteen stone steps, which led up to an open space about twenty-five feet wide, from five other steps which led up to the interior. There were several gates through which this Court could be entered, the principal of which was on the east; there were no gates on the west, strange to say, but originally there were three on the north, and three on the south; the latter three were added to these three others for women, one on the east, north and south, respectively. There was still another enclosure, which was regarded the most sacred of all; this was within the second Court, into which none but the priests were allowed to enter; here within this sacred enclosure stood the great Temple.

THE TEMPLE.

The Temple was built during the reign of King Solomon, but preparations were made for it long before he was installed king of the Hebrew nation. The whole plan had been given to David in detail by God Himself, and the warlike king made great preparations for the building; but he was not permitted to build the sacred sanctuary because he was a man of blood, and was engaged in directing wars from the beginning to the close of his administration.

The duty of building rested on Solomon because there was universal peace when he took hold of the sceptre, the hostile enemies having been subdued by the victorious arm of David. This stupendous structure was the first house built and dedicated to God. Previous to this the people had for their sanctuary the ancient Tabernacle, which was a movable tent.

The Temple superseded it, and was made a permanent dwelling-place of the Most High, having some of its interior arrangments after the pattern of the Tabernacle, but had a greater capacity; the apartments were double in size to those of the movable tent, but with this additional enlargement it was very much smaller than many of our church auditoriums of the present day.

If we consider this structure by our standard of measurement, this fact will be readily ascertained. The whole length of the building was only ninety feet, with a breadth of thirty feet; it is therefore seen that in point of size it would be classed with our smaller church buildings of this age. The great chamber was divided into two parts, known as the *Holy* and the *Holy of Holies*, or the *Most* Holy Place. It had a spacious porch in front, bordered by two pillars which had no little distinction; these were Jochin and Boaz. There were also two chambers at the sides which were exclusively for the use of the officiating priests.

The small size of the Temple will not be considered as inadequate to accommodate the great throng of worshipers who went up to Jerusalem for that express purpose, when we consider the fact that it was not intended to hold a congregation for worship as our church edifices.

But one of the apartments (the Most Holy) was exclusively for the High Priest to enter to attend to his official duties, and he was only to enter once a year, officially. Its furnishings consisted of the old chest that contained the two tables of stone on which the Lord God wrote the law, which had been given to Moses while he stood upon the quaking summit of Sinai. It also "contained the two colossal winged Cherubim," which were placed over them with wings so expanded as to touch the wall on each side of them.

In the Holy Place were the tables on which was placed the Shew Bread, the Altar of Burnt Offerings, and some of the furniture used on great ceremonial occasions. The Temple, though small, was the richest building in the world; its flooring and sides were lined with pure gold, which made it so brilliant that persons standing afar off were charmed with its beauty, and the fame of its splendor reached far beyond the confines of the dominion of Constance to the Southern Queen.

OLD FOUNDATIONS.

There are only a few scattered remnants of the foundations of the temples of holy worship, that crowned the brow of Moriah; several of those massive stone blocks that compose a part of the foundation of the pavement are of the Mosque of Omar, and many others are deeply buried in the earth, from sixty to a hundred feet, which have not as yet been excavated, that formed a part of the lower structures of the ancient temple.

Explorers are clearing away the ruins as fast as they have opportunities, and it is anticipated that they will in some future period have the privilege of carrying on their investigations without legal restraint. It is the general opinion of those who have been engaged in the various investigations of the material they have excavated from the deep beds of debris, that much of it belongs to the age of Solomon.

ANCIENT QUARRIES.

Some of the blocks measure twenty-nine feet long and are broad in proportion; the quarries from which these huge blocks were cut, are partly under the city and are known as Solomon's quarries; the entrance to them is through a small doorway, hewn through the rock beneath the north wall of the city on the outside, about one hundred yards east of the Damascus gate.

It connects with a long, steep incline passage, that leads to a number of broader aisles, opening into many great caverns, which are connected by wide hallways in all directions; there are several of these caverns, which have not yet been explored and may not be for a number of years. As far as the investigations of the quarries have proceeded, satisfactory developments have led the investigators to the conclusion, they must have been the ancient quarries from which much of the material was gotton for the first temple. It is without doubt a marvelous place, and bears prominent marks of those instruments used for hewing stone in antique times. There are many niches to be seen in these rocky chambers, out of which large blocks were cut, which correspond exactly with the stones now seen in the walls of the Haram and other places about its enclosure; it is thought if they were taken over to the quarries, some of them would fit in the niches as compactly as if they had only been removed from there a comparatively short while.

These ancient quarries have become so noted they are generally visited by tourists to Jerusalem, and the greedy Turks who are always seeking to take advantage of sight-seers, keep the entrance door locked and compel every one who is admitted to pay a fee of at least fifty cents; great caution must be observed by all who enter the quarries, on account of the accidents to which they are liable; many have occurred, and some proved fatal.

In every case a guide is indispensable, and he must be a man thoroughly familiar with the complicated avenues which run in every direction, or he will be incompetent for the task; the whole place is as dark as midnight (when thick clouds cover the heavens) and very rough to walk through; sometimes a step to the right or left, when passing into some of the caverns, would precipitate one into a deep dell from which he could not extricate himself.

It was a source of great dread to me, the day we visited those deep underground chambers, fearing some calamity might be awaiting us there. But, having a careful and experienced guide, we were properly cared for and gratifyingly informed; we provided ourselves with candles and matches (without which the visit would be useless), and started to view some of the under-ground wonders of Jerusalem; there may be seen many places where pillars and blocks have been nearly cut out and abandoned before completed; it is generally believed, that the master inspector found a flaw in them and ordered the workmen to leave them. Another opinion is that there was no more material found such as that they were preparing or as was needed, hence they left their work in a half-finished condition; there are columns still lying about the quarries, seemingly without a flaw, except a little time-worn; others are broken.

It came to my mind, there must have been a great noise down in those dark caverns, while the hundreds of men were busily at work preparing the stones for the great temple, the dwelling-place of the Almighty; hammer, chisel and the heavy sledge must have made the whole place a scene of life and bustle.

But the tumult, however loud during those busy days, could not be compared with the mournful noise which took place here, when our Lord expired on the cross, and every rock throughout this ancient quarry sent forth an expression of sympathy, when they were everywhere broken.

JERUSALEM.

The best authors who have written on the history of ancient Jerusalem are inclined to the opinion, its name is the compound of two words, which taken separately composed the names of the two towns, which were afterwards blended into one; these were Jebus and Salem, the former was situated on Mt. Zion, and was the stronghold of the Jebusites, who were a people noted for their ability in warfare and belonged to the Hametic race.

The latter was situated in the lower land, between Zion and Moriah, also inhabited by the Jebusites. Here Melchisedek, a priest of the "Most High God lived," in the days "when Abraham returned from the slaughter;" others are of the opinion the territory of the Holy City was formerly called Jebus, and afterwards called Jerusalem or "Salem of Jebus." This name is said to have been given the city after the Israelites had settled in the eastern portion of it.

JERUSALEM AND JEBUS CAPTURED.

This portion of the land was allotted to Benjamin; yet that tribe did not fully possess it for five hundred years after it was given them. The Jebusites held it with unyielding grasp; and it was not until King David's time that they yielded to Israel. The mighty monarch of the new nation was determined to take possession of the hill Jebus, or Mt. Zion, as it has been known, since the conquest, and sent an army of two hundred thousand against them.

The Jebusites, placing unbounded confidence in themselves, felt absolutely secure against any attack the Israelites might make; they offered no resistance, but simply laughed at them, and to show how little and insignificant the Army of David was in their estimation, the Jebusites sent their halt and blind to defend them, and then made light of Israel because of their ineffectual attempt to storm what they supposed to be their impregnable stronghold.

But the persistent Joab felt confident of success and continued the struggle with renewed determination, rallying and encouraging his undaunted army constantly, until at length the ramparts of the Jebusites were scaled and Jebus was in David's possession, who immediately fortified it and built his palace there; henceforth the name of the place was changed to the City of David, and was made the chief city of the Hebrew nation until the revolt of the ten tribes.

There seems to have been a sudden flood of glory poured upon Jerusalem after it was made the permanent resting-place of the Ark of God, so that it became the pride of the nation and federal seat of divine worship; the king who had his seat of government at Hebron caused it to be transferred to his own city and lived there himself for thirty-three years in almost perpetual uninterrupted prosperity, notwithstanding the wars he was engaged in.

During the reign of Solomon, David's son and successor, Jerusalem reached its zenith in splendor and glory; his father, not being permitted to build the Temple, left an immense treasure of gold, silver and other valubles to assist in the erection of the house of the Lord ; there was no barrier in the way of Solomon that would interfere with him in proceeding with the work, as the people who had so greatly troubled Israel and were constantly warring against this new nation, had all been subdued; so that Solomon entered upon the duties of his office in the time of peace, having the most powerful nations in alliance with him, and his wife was a member of the royalty of Egypt.

The King of Tyre, who had subjects skilled in the work of fine arts, was in close friendship with him and rendered great assistance to the Hebrew nation, by building vessels for naval and commercial purposes. But above all God blessed him with wisdom superior to all others in his day and qualified him for the duties of his responsible office; for wisdom and peace properly observed will bring success to any one.

Many bitter ages have passed into eternity since the glory of Solomon first adorned Jerusalem ; the plowshare of devastation has robbed it of its primitive physical splendor, yet there are still to be seen a few scattered remnants of antiquity, which indicate her past glory to those anxious travelers of to-day who are so often found amongst these ancient ruins, seeking some new revelation of the Jerusalem in the time of David, Solomon and others

Although the glory of Jerusalem has long since departed and nothing remains of the splendor with which she was first adorned but a few faint emblems worn by time and defaced by the heavy sieges of warfare she has encountered, yet thousands of the most intellectual and progressive people of our world visit the Holy City to behold the faded glories of Israel's most illustrious king as it dimly shines from the granite pillars and blocks of stone in the dark halls and in the subterranean chambers, where not a single ray of sunlight has ever entered, and among the tombs or anywhere that an indication points to antiquity ; can it be astonishing then, that if men of to-day travel so far to see but the shadow of the splendor of Jerusalem, that the Queen of the South should come from her distant home, to see the glory of

Solomon and the splendors of the Temple, when it it was fresh and dazzling?

Then the whole city was aglow with its unclouded grandeur, the glory of the illuminated Moriah, and all the other buildings within and without the Temple enclosure; Mt. Zion was crowned with the stately palace of the king, whose style and beauty could not be excelled; then the great bridge that united Zion and Moriah added greatly to the glory and grandeur of the city.

These and many other additional embellishments made Jerusalem the most beautiful and inviting city in the world. But after the death of Solomon the glory of the Holy City began to decline rapidly; and although it had been the chief seat of law and religious devotion of the Hebrew nation for seventy-five years, it was compelled to yield to the dominant sway of secession, and divide her political and religious strength with the northern kingdom.

Ten of the twelve tribes had revolted against Rehoboam and elected and installed Jeroboam to the Monarchy of Israel, who stimulated the worship of idols throughout the kingdom; there seems to have been no permanent rest for Jerusalem after her decline began from the attacks of hostile foes; it fell into the hands of Nebuchadnezzar three times, whose relentless hand seemed not to tire in administering heavy strokes of intense hatred upon its people, whom he deeply humiliated. It was also captured by the Chaldeans, who took King Zedekiah into custody, slew his two sons in his presence, then led him into captivity to Babylon, and there put out both his eyes and left him blind and defenceless; not long afterwards the Holy City, the place so proudly beloved, was sacked and emptied of its immense treasures; its walls were razed to the ground and the inhabitants carried away into captivity, in which state they continued seventy years.

It was written, "God brought upon them the King of the Chaldeans, who slew their young with the sword in the house of their sanctuary, and had no compassion on their young men nor maidens, old men, or him that stood for ages. He gave them unto his hand, and all the vessels of the house of God, great and small, and the treasures of the kingdom, and his princes, all these he brought to Babylon. And they burned the house of God, and broke down the walls of Jerusalem, and burned the palaces thereof and destroyed all the goodly vessels thereof, and those who escaped the sword carried he away to Babylon, where they were servants to him and his sons until the reign of the King of Persia."

The Most High bore long and patiently with the rebellious Israelites, whose ingratitude became more prominent as they increased in prosperity, until they had thrown off almost all their obligations to Him, and even worshiped gods after the order of the heathen round about them; therefore, when they would no longer be admonished by prosperity nor adversity to honor and serve God, He allowed one scourge after another in hasty succession to afflict and distress them; but this chastisement seemed not to be competent to cause them to return to the God of their fathers and fully renounce the gods of the heathen. In several instances they had kings to reign over them who were filled with pride and selfishness, and had no fondness for the observance of the true worship, and continually led the people into deeper transgressions. For three hundred years these wicked kings ruled the people, except a few, such as Asa, Jehoshaphat, Uzziah, Hezekiah and Josiah, under whom the city had a state of prosperity. and the worship at the Temple was duly celebrated.

It is evident that the Hebrews laid the foundation of their own destruction. In the first place, the nation gave itself a deadly blow when the revolt of the ten tribes took place. "A house divided against itself cannot stand." While the two kingdoms were contending against each other, the enemy made it opportune to come up with triumphant success against them.

Then there was not only a decline of material prosperity with the people, but their liberty was checked, and they found themselves under a sceptre of a foreign sovereignty; thus the brilliant history of the people of Israel, that had attracted all nations, suddenly changed and became a story of horror and shame. It seems that for a time every nation's arm was outstretched against them: the Egyptians, the Assyrians, the Chaldeans, the Persians, the Romans, the Ethiopians, the Syrians, the Philistines, the Arabians and Turks.

The religious sects known as Mohammedans, who are composed of several different people, all in their turn at various periods have set themselves in hostility against that once highly-favored, prosperous people, all of whom have done something to assist in making the situation of the Hebrews more oppressive. As to the Holy City, it was reduced to ruins, in which state it remained for seventy years.

But at length the period of the fulfillment of the Prophet Isaiah came, Cyrus' permission to the Jews to return home, and also the privilege to rebuild their devastated city, its walls and temple, promising to restore the golden and silver vessels which Nebuchadnezzar carried away when he captured the city, but this was not done until the reign of Darius.

It will be borne in mind Jerusalem remained under the Persian Empire until the time of *Alexander the Great*, when this most distinguished warrior had conquered the Persian monarch, and brought the government under his own jurisdiction; he came up against Phœnicia, and all the countries round about that had not peaceably submitted to him; feeling the need of more men, he sent to the High Priest, who was also Governor of Jerusalem, for troops, and having been refused he became very angry, and swore he would visit Jerusalem with vengeance.

He proceeded with a large army to carry out his purpose, but a marvelous event occurred which changed his intention. It is said, Alexander had reached the heights overlooking the city, and as he looked over the city he saw a glittering procession extending from the mountain to the very gates of the city; the people were clothed in white garments, coming out to meet him, led by their High Priest, himself clothed in his purple, and wearing on his breast a golden plate, upon which was written the name of Jehovah.

They bowed to the conqueror, put their necks at his feet and prayed for mercy; the humility of the people struck Alexander with both awe and compassion, so that he at once adored the name of Jehovah, saluted the High Priest, and offered sacrifices in the Temple, and the people were saved from the destructive calamity about to be administered upon them.

ALEXANDER AND ANTIOCHUS.

But when Antiochus, King of Syria, plundered Jerusalem, he was not so merciful as Alexander, but to satisfy his bloodthirsty appetite, he caused thirty thousand men to be put to death, demolished their walls, and abolished their religion. The hand of the Lord was prominently seen defending the Hebrews and giving them wonderful success, even for a long time after they had largely turned themselves from Him, and placed their affections upon strange gods.

But when they had entirely forsaken Him, and would not be admonished to return, He left them to be driven from home and dispersed throughout the whole world.

THE GREAT SLAUGHTER.

The monarchs who ruled the Hebrews after the death of Alexander were the Ptolemies of Egypt; these kings swayed the sceptre of power over Jerusalem two hundred and fifty years; they were kindly disposed toward the people, and favored them in many ways, during which time they enjoyed a good degree of prosperity, but in the second century before Christ, Antiochus Epiphanes entered and captured Jerusalem, who, after plundering it, defiled the Temple.

About two years later he sent his general, Apollonius, to complete the barbarous work he had begun. The Israelites were a remarkably superstitious people as to the observance of the Sabbath, and would suffer the most cruel impositions rather than violate its sanctity. To engage in a combat, even with their most inveterate foes, on that day, was in their estimation an unpardonable sin; Apollonius, having a knowledge of this, took a most disgraceful advantage of their scruples, and embraced the opportunity to administer wholesale destruction to them; he turned loose his army amongst the people on the Sabbath day; all the able-bodied men were put to death, and the poor defenceless women and children were sold into slavery. Apollonius then ordered a garrison to be placed on Mt. Zion, and would not allow priest nor people, to enter the sacred domains of the Temple, so that the sacrifice of oblation ceased, and the city, in which the services of the Lord were chanted, became desolate; and the Temple, the sacred emblem of the presence of the God of Israel, was dedicated to Jupiter Olympus; and the altar, which had been devoted to those sacrifices that the Lord commanded should be offered, was polluted with idolatrous offerings. In the process of time, a priestly family appeared, known as the Asmoneans: they rose up in their might to expel these idolaters from their land, and vindicate the honor of their God by doing all they could to re-establish His services.

This attempt introduced a terrible combat, which lasted twenty-six years. Judas Maccabæus and his brethren, carried on the war with the Syrians until they had broken off the yoke which had galled the people so long, and established their independence; then a new and joyful era dawned upon them. Israel being free once more from a distressing bondage, which had been a thorn in their flesh for many years, again breathed the air of peace and liberty.

About the year thirty-four, before Christ, the last prince of the Asmonean line was slain by the Roman General of Syria, and Herod the Great was installed King of the Jews. He was born in Idumea, and was by no means kindly disposed toward his subjects, but did whatsoever he chose, without compunction; such was his rigid rulings, the poor Jews often smarted under his iron sceptre; many times their religious freedom was taken from them because of his fondness for idolatrous worship; notwithstanding all these things, Herod, it is said, was not entirely wanting in a few pleasant characteristics which

MOUNT ZION.

were commendable. He had a special regard for the prosperity of the kingdom, and did much to advance it; many large and prosperous cities were built and beautified during his reign. The most important work he did was rebuilding the Temple at Jerusalem; it was begun in the eighteenth year of his reign, and notwithstanding the principal portion of it was completed in nine years, the whole building was not completed until the end of the forty-sixth year, the beauty and grandeur of which were of the most lavish character. Now it is plain to all, who have a knowledge of Jewish history, they had many sore afflictions, mostly brought upon them by reason of their own malconduct, and one disaster after another overshadowed them after they had disregarded all the opportunities God gave them to adhere to his precepts.

But the end of their troubles had not been reached: a gushing fountain of dire calamities was lurking in their path, which they could not shun; calamities, which the mountains and valleys round about Jerusalem, could they speak, would unfold a scene that has never been described by the pen of the most graphic writers our world has produced.

And could the dead who have been sleeping so long in those ancient sepulchres about the city, rise up from their silent homes and speak, they would declare a history that our sensibilities could not endure. Mt. Zion, which at times, has been the very centre of commotion, bloodshed and slaughter, from whose summit the blood of thousands, ran in streams into the valley below, would detail some of the most shocking accounts of human sufferings known to the world. (John ii. 20; Matt. xxv. 1, 2.)

ZION AGAIN THE CENTRE LIGHT.

But it is noteworthy to state, that upon the very mount which was the scene of appalling calamities, is now the very centre of gospel influence in Jerusalem. Zion has again lifted herself from the dust, and put on her beautiful garments; upon her brow stands a Christian church, whose good work cannot be discounted by any who have availed themselves of the opportunity of attending service there, especially on the Sabbath. It is situated but a short distance from the traditional Cœnaculum, or the upper chamber in which our Lord took the passover with his disciples, and where they had assembled on the day of Pentecost, when suddenly the Holy Spirit came upon them, and gave them courage to go forth "preaching the gospel of the kingdom of heaven" and lifting up the people from sin to righteousness. If it is really the true site of the Cœnaculum, the identical spot on which stood the house the disciples were in, when the Holy Spirit came upon them. how significant that the same hill should be chosen for the renewal of the work, begun near the same spot nearly two thousand years ago!

And how strikingly applicable are the words of the prophet, who says: "Awake, awake, put on thy strength, O Zion, put on thy beautiful garments: O Jerusalem, the holy city, for henceforth there shall no more come unto thee the uncircumcised and the unclean; shake thyself from the dust, arise, sit down, O Jerusalem, loose thyself from the bands of thy neck, O captive daughter of Zion."

We earnestly trust the time is now at their door when the fulfillment of this prophecy will be realized, and Jerusalem will be fully redeemed. (Isa. liii. 2).

Then will be seen as never before, "how beautiful upon the mountains are the feet of them that bringeth good tidings, that publisheth peace, that saith unto Zion thy God reigneth." "Break forth into joy, sing together, ye waste places of Jerusalem, for the Lord hath comforted his people, he hath redeemed Jerusalem."

Zion seems to have been from the time it was taken by David until now, the most distinguished and preferable portion of the Holy City. Zion was chosen as the most fitting place for the king's palace; from it went forth the law; on Zion was the site of the shrine of the sanctuary, which had been for a long time in exile, and with tumultuous shouts it was set up. Mt Zion became, henceforth, even after the temple was built on Mt. Moriah, and the ark was transferred, the royal symbol of the kingdom of God in His church. Mt. Zion seems to have been selected as the most appropriate place for a residence of the High Priest; on it tradition says the palace of Caiaphas stood to which our Lord was taken on the morning of his betrayal. On Zion, Kings David, Solomon, and others of the royal line were laid to rest, and upon the rocky summit of Zion, the old historic Tower of David, is still standing, the most important relic of the once strongly fortified mountain.

Zion is the first of the city to be seen on approaching Jerusalem, west or east, and the last to hide from view, when leaving it. It is the first in height, importance and size. It occupies the southwestern section of the city and extends much farther south than Moriah; the west and southwest rise up almost perpendicularly from the valley of Hinnom to the astonishing height of from three to four hundred feet above it, having a bold brow on the south; while on the east, is a gradual descent into the Tyropœan Valley towards the south; on the north side the descent is very much steeper until within a short distance of the Haram, where the incline is more gradual.

On the north Zion is bounded by David street It is stated, that Mt. Zion was, before the many disasters that have so often dismantled, a level tract, extending from the citadel of David to his tomb, embracing about six hundred yards from the city wall, in length, and about two hundred and fifty in width, from the city wall to the west side of the Armenian Convent, and was the first part of Jerusalem on which buildings were built.

Upon it, as has been stated, the Jebusites, whom the Israelites found to be so hard to subdue, had their stronghold, from which the army of David had much difficulty to rout them. The kings of Judah lived on Mt. Zion, for more than five hundred years, and it is believed that fourteen of them were buried there, David being the first.

Zion was the last portion of the city to surrender to the vicious and inhuman attack of the Romans, under the generalship of Titus; it was some time after the other portions of the city had been burned to ashes and the courts of the Temple had been garrisoned by the invaders, that the remnant of the Jews, who were in the stronghold of Zion, submitted to the Romans, and perished around the palace and tombs of the kings. This is the most historic mountain in Jerusalem. (See Num. xiii. 29; Josh. xv. 63; Judges i. 21; 2 Sam. v. 5-8.)

MT. MORIAH AND DAVID'S SIN.

The next mountain in importance as to size, elevation and conspicuousness, and the one that has the first place in religious distinction, is Mt. Moriah; this is the identical hill on which Ornan the Jebusite and descendant of Canaan, the son of Ham, had his threshing floor; it is well worthy of special mention, that this man's threshing floor was the only place in Jerusalem that our Lord seemed not to frown upon, during His administration of an alarming and disastrous rebuke to King David for his flagrant disobedience, in that he numbered the people of his kingdom, notwithstanding the Lord commanded him not to do so. The Lord pungently rebuked David, by sending a devouring plague throughout the kingdom, which was killing the people at the astonishing rate of seventy thousand a day. Then was the king greatly troubled and earnestly prayed to the Lord that He would remove the plague; there suddenly appeared an Angel of the Lord, hovering over the threshing floor of Ornan with his arms uplifted as if he was about to destroy the city. David in a state of great humiliation, confessed his sin; and a prophet, under the direction of the Lord, told the king to go to the spot where the angel had been seen and build an altar there unto the Lord.

David gladly obeyed and lost no time in putting into effectual operation the advice given him by the prophet. When he had gone to the threshing floor, and made known the object of his mission to Ornan the Jebusite, and offered him a large sum for the needed preparation, the Hamite refused to accept any amount the king offered him, but willingly and gladly offered them to the king free of charge. The offer he made the king was the timber, which was his threshing instruments, and oxen for the sacrifice.

This generous offer the king refused as a gift, stating, that he would not offer to the Lord that which cost him nothing; he, therefore, bought the oxen for fifty shekels of silver, which amounted to about twenty-two dollars and fifty cents; he also paid for the whole place six hundred shekels in gold, or about four thousand, five hundred and twenty-four dollars.

Then he offered his sacrifice, which the Lord accepted, and stayed the fury of the plague; in after years the spot, which was the property of a farmer who was of the Hamitic race, was chosen for the site on which the Temple of the Lord should be built, and where multitudes of Hebrews came with their numerous sacrifices to present to the Lord of hosts.

Moriah is the place also to which, most historians are of the opinion, Abraham came with his son, the child of the promise, to offer him as a sacrifice to the Lord. This Mount is separated from Zion by the Tyropœan valley, and is bounded on the north by a small depression, supposed to be the site of the Berket Israel. The portion of the ridge that extends southward from Moriah to the connection of the Tyropœan and Kedron valleys, at the Pool of Siloam, was called Ophel.

Here lived the Nethimims; these people were Gibeonites and were set apart as sacred servants of the Lord's house; they seemed to have greatly multiplied in after years; there were a few amongst the captive Jews in Babylon, and who it is thought settled near the Caspian Sea. (2 Sam. xxiv. 24; 1 Chron. xxi. 25; 1 Kings ix. 20–21; 1 Chron. ix. 2; Neh. iii. 26 and vii. 46, 60, 73.)

MT. AKRA.

There are two other mountains of which no mention is made in the Bible, that are connected with the Holy City, and should not be passed without being mentioned here. In the time of Josephus, Jerusalem was divided into two parts, known as the upper and lower city; the former was commonly known as the City of David, and was located principally on Mt. Zion.

The latter was situated on Mt. Akra, and from the present indications was an important business centre, where the various industries were fully displayed; it was separated from Zion by the Tyropean valley, or that portion of it that ran from west to east along the course of the present David Street, it was on the north of Zion and embraced the present Christian quarter, and the space which is occupied by the Church of the Holy Sepulchre.

Josephus says Mt. Akra was at one time much higher than at present, but was leveled in the time of the Asmoneans so that the Temple might be seen above it to a better advantage than formerly. A tradition of many centuries locates Mt. Calvary, on the summit of Akra, just as Pisgah is on the top of Mt. Nebo; and the relation the present city sustains to it has caused many and uncompromising controversies as to its being identical with the scene of the crucifixion of our Lord.

Indeed, many persistently ignore the idea of its having any connection with it whatever; the matter has been under a process of investigation for a long time, and may be permanently settled soon.

MOUNTS BEZETHA AND CALVARY.

The fourth mountain within the walls is Bezetha, which also has been brought into prominent notice by Josephus, covers the space extending from Berket-Israel to the road leading to Jericho near Jeremiah's grotto. Josephus tells us it was identical with Cœnapolis, which means "Empty City," and was so named, it is supposed, because the inhabitants were not as numerous as those in other portions of the city.

In the time of our Lord the greater portion of Bezetha was outside the walls, and was not enclosed until the time of Agrippa, who built the third wall, extending over a portion of it; its breadth near the Haram is four hundred and fifty feet, and extends north more and more until it covers nearly one thousand feet. We have given a brief outline of the four hills on which the foundation of Jerusalem stands, but there is yet another, situated on the summit of one of these and within the walls of the present city, of which special mention must be made, because the glories which crown it are of the most important interest to the world. This is Mt. Calvary, the hill on which our Lord reconciled justice, and made it possible for fallen man to be at peace with God. There is no place in Jerusalem over which there has been, and still is, so much controversy, and around which so many doubts cluster as this Mount, which tradition says is Calvary. When the visitor is taken first to one, then to another summit, both of which are located as the true sites of the crucifixion, he is at loss to know which of the two is the real Calvary.

It is generally understood that special attention was paid to beautifying the walls, and great pains taken to have them as square as possible. And if the wall on Mt. Bezetha had been extended and not that on Akra, Jerusalem would have presented a shape by no means admired by the people; it would have terminated in a semi-circle on the north.

I am strongly inclined to the opinion, the whole wall from the northwest to the northeastern terminus was extended; this would form a direct line, and add greatly to the beauty of both walls and city; taking these facts into consideration, there can be no doubt that the traditional site of Golgotha, as located at present, was at a time past, outside the walls.

For it is known the Jews were careful in not permitting the dead to be buried within the city limits, and there are clear evidences that such had been done within the enclosure of the present walls. In the Church of the Holy Sepulchre, underneath the western galleries, just behind the sepulchre, are to be seen two hewn tombs in the rock, known as the burial place of Joseph and Nicodemus; these tombs are ancient, and as evidently Jewish sepulchres as any of those seen in the Valley of Jehoshaphat, or Hinnom, or those of the tombs of the kings and judges; therefore to deny these of their Jewish origin would be to deny that any of those ancient tombs round about Jerusalem or elsewhere were Jewish.

It is therefore, conclusive, that tombs did and still exist within the limits of the present walls, and that it is a fact, the Jews did not allow any burying within the city.

In thinking of Calvary we are touched with a feeling which is reverential and affectionate, for it is the most sacred of all the holy places in Jerusalem, in comparison with which all others are but dim or shadowy, and pale before it as the light of the moon would before the sun at high meridian.

Therefore in attempting to write a chapter concerning this most sacred hill, we do so with a knowledge of our great want of divine guidance, that we may be so directed in every thought that it may accomplish the good intended, and even more than we could anticipate. It is known to many that the old traditional sight of Calvary is being hotly contested, and another location is looked upon as the true site.

But if the place so long reverenced as Mt. Calvary is not the genuine site, the deep interest which for many centuries has clustered about it, gives it an exalted dignity, such as no other place in the world has attained; men have for a long time endeavored to cast a shadow of grave doubts as to the genuineness of the traditional Calvary and sepulchre, and have attempted to locate this most hallowed spot at another point on the north of the city and beyond the walls; this new site has been steadily gaining opinion in its favor, and many of those are inclined to believe it to be Calvary rather than the one so long regarded as such; it is not our purpose to enter into the details of argument presented by prominent men, who have participated in the investigations from which they have drawn their conclusion.

Those who desire a full and exhaustive discussion on the subject, we refer to the Biblical researches of Dr. Robinson, in which will be found all that is necessary, "The Holy City," by Mr. Williams, and the article by Prof. Willis on Architectural History. It will be seen by a close examination of the above references, that the whole burden of these arguments bear upon the development of two very important and intricate questions, one of which is deductive, and the other may be called scientific.

The deductive question is, the conclusion drawn from an early tradition, that the site on which the Church of the Holy Sepulchre stands, was known to be identical with the event of our Lord's crucifixion and burial, and was designated as such some time prior to the conquest of Constantine, by the Emperor Hadrian, who caused to be built on the spot a heathen temple to Venus, that the place which had been so devoutly and sacredly commemorated by Christians might be polluted.

The question that must be developed by scientific investigation is, Can it be positively proven that the present site of Golgotha, was, at the time of our Lord's crucifixion, beyond the walls of the city? The Holy Scriptures inform us the bodies of beasts whose blood was brought into the sanctuary by the High Priest for sin, were burned without the camp, and that the Lord Jesus "might sanctify the people with his own blood, suffered without the gate." The place to which Jesus was taken was close to the city, and seems to have been beside or close to a public road, for they that passed by reviled Him (Heb. xiii. 11-12; Matt. xxvii. 39).

THE TOMB OF CHRIST.

Now as to the deductive or historical question, that is introduced because of a statement made by Eusebius in the third century, saying there had been a heathen temple erected to Venus over the sepulchre of our Lord, it is the opinion of men whose writings seem to be without even the tinge of bias, that those advocates favoring the present site of the tomb of Christ as identical with the original, have never met the difficulty fairly, and that it is hardly conceivable Hadrian could have had any motive in such a purpose, when his whole object in establishing his new city, Ælia (which was the name he gave Jerusalem), was not to insult the Christians, but the Jews, from whom the Christians in Palestine at that time were greatly divided.

As to the conclusion just cited, it cannot be regarded as wholly true, especially as to the opinion of Hadrian's attitude towards the Christians. It is commonly known by all who have a knowledge of the general stand pagans take against Christians, that they are emphatically opposed to them; that whenever and wherever they have an opportunity, they show themselves uncompromisingly hostile to them. Taking this undeniable fact into consideration, it cannot be considered unreasonable to infer, that although the prime motive of Hadrian was to punish and humiliate the Jews, and not the Christians, the latter was his secondary motive, after he had vented his spite on the former; in fact, his purpose seems to have been to do whatever he could to abase the people, whether Jews or Christians.

It does not seem reasonable to suppose he would show the Christians any favors whatever, being under no obligations to them; but on the contrary he would follow the common custom of the Roman emperors. It is not likely Hadrian would be more compassionate with the Jewish Christians in Jerusalem than with the straight-out Jews whom he expelled from it, and refused permission to return.

Such a man would without compunction build a heathen temple to Venus over the Tomb of Christ if he saw it would deeply wound his followers; the Jews would not have been moved at such a procedure, for they had no faith in Christ nor reverence for the place in which he was buried; the question raised by some writers as to the probability of the walls of Herod's time running so as to close the plat on which the Church of the Holy Sepulchre is built, in the opinion of others, depends for its solution upon such excavations of the vast accumulations under which they lay (and is just now impossible), but will in some future time be so effectually conducted as to clear away the mystery of the topography of ancient Jerusalem, as in the case of Rome

CHURCH OF THE HOLY SEPULCHRE.

and other places in the old world. It should be borne in mind, as has been stated, the walls of Jerusalem were extended by order of Agrippa, who enclosed that portion of Bezetha that was outside the city limits; it looks plausible that in extending the walls he would cautiously guard against having them to appear awkwardly. Therefore, in order to make them as much as possible uniform and square, he would have extended them also on Akra, the mount on which the Church of the Holy Sepulchre stands, and as the Jews did not allow their dead to be buried within the walls or limits of the city, therefore, the walls of to-day must have been extended beyond the limits of those of ancient times, and that they occupy a portion of the site of a place of burial that the Jews used in ancient times; it is, therefore, highly probable the Church of the Holy Sepulchre is identical with or very near the spot where Joseph's new tomb was, in which no one had been placed until the body of our Lord had been laid in it.

The idea of those two tombs being those of Joseph and Nicodemus is very doubtful and even ridiculed by many. As to the objection we have no criticism to offer, having no direct evidence to sustain the tradition; indeed, we are inclined to the opinions of the objectors, as there seem to be reasonable grounds upon which to build them; but the point is they are tombs, and as such could not be placed, under any legal claim, within the bounds of the city walls.

And the plat on which the Church of the Holy Sepulchre is built being inside the enclosure, and, as has been stated, these ancient tombs being under its western galleries, are strong proofs that the whole space occupied by the church was outside of the walls.

These facts, greatly strengthen the opinion that the rock-hewn tomb represented to be the "Holy Place where the Lord lay," is without a shadow of doubt of ancient date, and may be identical with the tomb it represents; in the conclusion we have reached, we feel confident it is confined within the limits of probability, and it is our earnest hope and prayer, this conclusion has at least added a faint light upon the matter and will open up avenues for thoughts more matured and sacred; it is our opinion, as the excavations proceed, which for a long time have been in progress, such positive evidence will be developed as will settle this question forever. It is proper that a historical sketch of the Church of the Holy Sepulchre should be given here; we have stated elsewhere, the site of the tomb of our Lord, had been, some time in the third century, covered by Hadrian with a heathen temple which was dedicated to Venus.

This statement is corroborated by some of the most distinguished and reliable early writers, among whom are Jerome, Socrates and Solomon; these men, whose writings have been of great historical value, sustain Eusebius in the assertion that the Holy Sepulchre had been covered with earth, and a temple to Venus had been built over it. So that, as Eusebius put it, "That illustrious monument of immortality had been lost in darkness and oblivion."

In this condition it remained a long time, but at length we are informed by all the writers of the time of Constantine, The Great, that Helena his mother, who was a very saintly woman, being divinely directed to search for the true *cross*, and holy sepulchre, came to Jerusalem, and instituted inquiries among the inhabitants concerning the location of Mt. Calvary, but none could tell her the exact place; the fact of the ignorance of the people concerning the matter gave Helena much uneasiness and perplexity; but being hopeful of satisfactory results, she continued the anxious search, and after a time it was miraculously discovered; there is but little doubt, if any, existing as to the fact, that three crosses were found, but there have been many opinions existing as to the genuineness of them, and many seem to be inclined to the opinion that some one made them, and placed them there.

There are many other unimportant objections based upon just such frivolous foundations; it may be the crosses were not buried by any one to preserve them from destruction, as is believed by many; but they more likely fell and were buried under the debris, when the city was destroyed, and if they had been buried by the early Christians, it is not reasonable to suppose that those who lived two hundred and fifty or three hundred years afterwards, could find the exact place where they were buried, for the reason there was no historical record kept as to the place where they might be found.

And if those who buried them told any one of that locality, it was enjoined upon the person to keep the matter a profound secret, lest the enemies of our Lord would destroy it. It is thought by some, that if any one had buried the cross of our Lord, those of the two thieves would not have been buried with it. But that was very natural, as each of them embraced a peculiar historical significance, that would stimulate the Christians to preserve them.

PART VI.

EVENTS IN AND ABOUT JERUSALEM—ITS MEMORABLE PLACES.

Description of Mount of Olives—Appearance from a Distance—Fuel Used in Palestine—A View of the Country from the Mountain—Disciples Taught how to Pray—Lazarus Raised—Bethany—Tomb of Lazarus—Our Lord en route for Jerusalem—Ride to Jerusalem—Christ's Entry into Jerusalem—Our Lord Deeply Moved with Compassion—The Garden of Gethsemane—Tomb of the Virgin Mary—Description of Tomb—Valley of Jehoshaphat—How Situated—Strong Faith of the People as to the Historical Places of Palestine—Absalom Claiming Himself King—David and His Friends—The Love Attai had for David—The Returning of the Ark of God—David's Flight—David in Exile—Suicide of Ahithophel—David Numbers Those with Him and Forms Three Divisions—Absalom Hanged in the Forest—Breaking the News of His Death to David—David's Return—Absalom's Pillar—Valley of Hinnom—Valley of Giants—Hill of Evil Counsel—Potter's Field—Idolatry of Israel—The Kingdom Embarrassed—Solomon's Early Blunder—His Decline in Piety—Pools and Fountains—The Great Cisterns—Pool of Siloam—Healing of the Blind Man—Pool of Bethesda—Healing of the Lame Man—Siege of Titus—Troops Stationed at the Foot of the Mount of Olives—Titus Marches to the City—Famine Raging—War Among the Inhabitants—Titus's Anxiety to Save the City—Prophecy Fulfilled Concerning the Destruction—Burial of the Dead—Tower of Antonia Captured—The Sacred Edifice in Flames—Titus Offers Terms of Peace—Final Demolition—The Triumphal Arch—David's Tomb—Attempts to Locate it Elsewhere—How Impressed on Entering—The Conaculum—Mosque of Neby Da'rid—Description of Upper Chamber—Tombs of St. James and Zacharias—Other Tombs—Absalom's Shaft—Tomb of Jehoshaphat—Tombs of Prophets and Judges—Tomb of Helena—Future of the Jews.

JERUSALEM'S MEMORABLE PLACES.

THERE are a number of places in and about the holy city that are mentioned in the Old and New Testaments, and in the writings of Josephus, that have been identified, notwithstanding many physical changes have taken place; the most prominent of these places are Mounts Zion, Moriah, Akra, Bezetha, Olivet, Scopus and a few others.

The valleys of Kedron or Jehoshaphat, Hinnom and the Tyropœon or Cheese-mongers. The fountains and pools of Siloam, the virgin's pool, the two pools of Gihon, Hezekiah's pool, and the site of the pool of Bethesda; these places we will mention in detail as we proceed, except those of which mention has been made.

MOUNT OF OLIVES.

The Mount of Olives is one of the most conspicuous and venerated places about Jerusalem, and is generally regarded as hallowed ground, because it was frequented by our Lord, at times when He sought a quiet retreat, that He might pray without being disturbed by any one; here also He often came with his disciples to teach them lessons concerning Himself, and their work as messengers of salvation, necessary to make them competent to contend against the mighty forces that should come up in battle to drive them from their post.

Upon the summit of Mt. Olivet, the hallowed feet of this "wonderful councilor" and "mighty God" stood on the morning of His triumphant departure to the house of "Many Mansions," in the presence of great numbers of anxious witnesses, who, after hearing His last words to His disciples, saw Him borne heavenward to take His station as our federal representative at the right hand of the Father.

The Mount of Olives is about a mile east of Jerusalem; it is estimated to be about four hundred and twenty feet high from the base of Jehoshaphat, and two hundred feet above Mt. Moriah; it runs parallel with Moriah, and is divided into several peaks by intervening depressions; on the top of the central peak is a building with four towers, belonging to the Russians; from the top of either of the towers a superb view is obtained of the country around, as far as the eye can see with the aid of field glasses.

They are the first objects in the neighborhood of Jerusalem seen by those going up from Jericho. It has a peculiar appearance from a far distance, and would remind one very much of a tower suspended in the air; there are several other buildings belonging to the Russians, Greeks and Latins, on the Mount, and a small Arab village near Bethany.

These buildings greatly disfigure the mountain, and rob it of much of its solemnity, and also obstructs much of its natural beauty and loftiness. Some portions of it, especially the northern, is kept under cultivation, and seems to be productive. The olive trees become fewer each year, so that the number it contains now are not to be compared with that of antique times.

Wood being scarce in Palestine, the old olive trees are cut down for fire use, as soon as they begin to die; even the roots are dug up

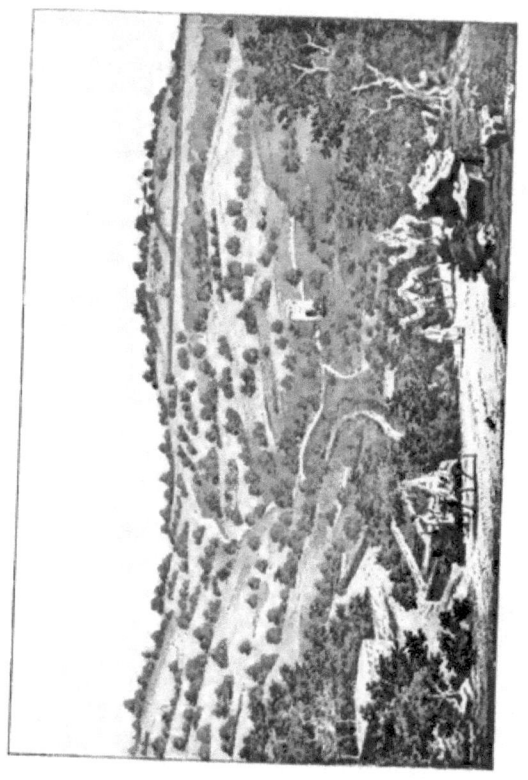

MOUNT OF OLIVES.

and burned, but the few hundred trees of the shady groves yet remaining are memorable of those of long ages past, which gave this sacred mountain its immortal name.

On the summit, a short distance from the traditional tombs of the prophets, is a building belonging to the Mohammedans, that from the early times of our era has been settled upon as the spot from which our Lord ascended to heaven; it has been so recognized since the third century, when Helena and others made extensive investigations, and concluded the rock over which the building stands, is that upon which our Lord rested while giving His disciples their final commission to preach the Gospel to every creature. In the meantime, the firmament was thronged with a multitude of adoring angels, waiting to escort "Him Home and shout him welcome."

The building now standing over the rock, is the fourth one; the first chapel was built by order of Helena, the mother of Constantine, the Great; it was replaced by another small round church, under the superintendence of Modestus; this was again replaced, in the twelfth century, by another, built by the Crusaders, but was destroyed by the hands of violent enemies, after the expiration of nearly four hundred years; there seems to have been no attempt to replace it for two hundred years.

Then the present one was erected; the building is by no means spacious in appearance; it stands in the midst of an enclosure. In the same area, is a small mosque, that is visited by all travelers who ascend Mt. Olivet to witness the remarkable echo, that may be heard from the mildest tone of the voice; the echo has a delightful sound, in some respects akin to that that may be heard in the Baptistry at Pisa.

The view of the country round about, from the top of Mt. Olivet, is very fine and impressive, especially so when the visitor contemplates the historic associations connected with the sacred mount upon which he is walking. He remembers the same ground he is traveling over, was once marked by the sacred feet of the Saviour of the world, and somewhere near here once stood a cluster of trees He frequented when burdened in spirit, heavily oppressed with the sin of the world, to commune with His Father, and drop tears of sorrow. Down the southern slope, near the tomb of His devoted mother, is the traditional spot where the disciples came to Him, and privately asked Him to teach them to pray, even as John taught his disciples; and in compliance with their petition, that prayer of prayers, which is repeated in almost every home in civilized lands, and every pious mother feels it her indispensable duty to teach the little ones of her household to say, "Our Father, who art in heaven," was formulated.

There are three pathways leading over Mt. Olivet to Bethany, one being the ancient Jericho road, and the identical one over which our Lord passed with His disciples, when He came from the City of Palm Trees and gave the blind man sight, and passed over it many times, to and from Bethany and Jerusalem. Along this road He was walking one morning, and being hungry went to a fig tree to refresh Himself with the fruit, and found "nothing but leaves," and from that moment it withered under His curse.

LAZARUS RAISED.

Jesus made His home with Lazarus and his two sisters at their little home. They loved Him and always made Him as comfortable as their means would allow. It is reasonable to suppose, the family often wished to have Him come and see them on those occasions when they needed His sympathy and soothing words; to heal them in their afflictions. It is certain the sisters did, when their brother died,—at the time, our Lord was at Bethabara beyond the Jordan with His disciples. They sent a messenger informing Him of the illness of Lazarus and requesting Him to come and heal him. It was on the account of the death of this good man, that the whole village seemed to be in a state of deep lamentation. The event opened up an opportunity for the Lord Jesus to perform one of the most stupendous miracles of His ministry, one which evidently showed forth His divinity.

The multitudes shouted His praise, and the village, that for four days had been a scene of lamentation and great weeping, instantly leaped into enthusiastic joy; for in obedience to the command of Jesus, Lazarus the beloved, who had been four days confined within the cold embrace of the grim monster, came from his silent abode full of life and vigor, a living witness of the truth, that Jesus who would soon yield to the sting of death, had power over it, and is indeed "the resurrection and the life."

Simon, the leper, lived also in Bethany, at whose table our Lord reclined, when Mary came in and anointed Him, and wiped His feet with the hair of her head (Matt. xxvi. 6–9; John vi. 1–46).

Bethany, is on the southeast of the Mount of Olives, situated in a hollow that hides it from Jerusalem; this little village may be regarded as one of the most important historical places outside of the Holy

City. Many authors give it only a passing notice, as though it had not been dignified by the frequent visits, and works of Christ.

This village is not in a very reputable standing with the masses who visit it, because of the very low and disorderly class of people who inhabit it. The Arabs call it Azariyeh, which means corruption from Lazarus, after whom they have called it; the word "Bethany" in its primitive meaning is "House of Poverty," and any one who visits there will conclude the name is specially adapted to the condition of the people generally, for they are from all outward appearances to be numbered with the poorest inhabitants of Palestine, and were it not for the sacred history that clusters within its limits, no one would care to visit the place or even view it while passing by en route to Jericho.

Bethany is a dreary, desolate and miserable place, without a single inviting natural feature; but all these physical objectionable aspects are overcome, when the wonderful fame of nearly two thousand years' standing is called to mind; it is the little village hid away behind the Mount of Olives, at a distance of a mile and three-quarters, from the great city whose fame is known to the world, that our Lord used to frequent when in the vicinity of Jerusalem.

There is a deep vault partly excavated in the rock near the centre of the village known as the tomb of Lazarus, and sacredly venerated alike by Christians and Moslems because of an old tradition, that the body of pious Lazarus was raised from it after his burial. On the day the author of this volume visited Bethany, he went down to the bottom of this historic cave, and took a general survey of its interior. It is deep and dark, having thirty-seven steps to descend before the bottom is reached; candles are furnished by the guard, who not only demands half a franc admission, but an additional sum as a present.

The last time our Lord visited here, and performed the miracle of the resurrection, was during the season of the Passover, when crowds of people had gathered from all parts, so that as usual the *Holy City* was crowded to its uttermost with admiring strangers, many of whom joined the multitude in celebrating His praise and spreading His fame abroad.

On the morning He started in triumph to Jerusalem; on the way to the city, just opposite the point where the first view of Mt. Zion is obtained, is a ravine; near it are remnants of an old village; this is supposed to be the site of ancient Bethpage, the village to which Jesus sent two of His disciples to bring the colt upon which He was to ride into Jerusalem.

It is an easy matter for the people of Bethany, as in all the villages and small towns of Palestine, to be informed when a stranger is in their midst, as there are only one or two entrances as a rule. This old rocky highway is the very same that Jesus passed over on the morning He entered Jerusalem in triumph; it was a jubilant occasion with the great multitude who had witnessed one of the most wonderful of all the miracles that had been wrought by our Lord during His ministry; there was no elaborate or costly preparations made for the event.

JESUS' RIDE TO JERUSALEM.

The Saviour requested two of His disciples to go over to the next village and bring a colt to Him on which no man had ever sat; the request was promptly complied with, and the people, whose enthusiasm over the recent resurrection of Lazarus had overflowed, were still jubilant, and anxious to spread His fame in song and with shouts of praise.

Having spread a few pieces of their scanty garments upon the colt for a saddle, they sat Jesus on him, and He started for Jerusalem. On leaving Bethany, the adoring multitudes immediately began to express their extreme joy for their Lord, by taking off their garments and strewing them upon the ground for their *Divine Master* to ride over, which was an act that strongly demonstrated the exalted veneration they had for Him.

The vast throng of admirers of Christ, sung with loud voices, praises to Him that "cometh in the name of the Lord;" a vast number of people coming out from Jerusalem to meet Him, sped across the Kedron and entered the highway, pulling off palm boughs as they passed the gardens along the way, to welcome "Him who cometh in the name of the Lord."

This multitude continued on toward Bethany, to join those whose voices were making the very air vocal with their loud shouts of Hosanna; there was a vast crowd escorting the Saviour from the home of Mary, Martha, and Lazarus, who had spent the night in their little village, and had witnessed the miraculous resurrection, and it is likely, some of them, were those who mournfully sympathized with the women who piteously bewailed the loss of their brother; these also spread palm and olive branches on the ground, in honor of the Lord Jesus, whose praises they were shouting.

CHRIST'S ENTRY INTO JERUSALEM.

As the two divisions approached each other, the enthusiasm became intense, and about half way between Bethany and Jerusalem they met, then those who went out from the city turned, forming a solid line; marched toward Jerusalem, saying, "Blessed is He that cometh in the name of the Lord, hosanna in the highest." As this long and enthusiastic procession proceeded, the little village behind them was soon hidden from their view, and the southeastern portion of the great city loomed up before them with all its glory.

This loud and triumphant shout of the multitude, was a surprise to the jealous scribes, Pharisees and elders, who had spent so many days in endeavoring to crush out the fame of Jesus, and had formed many plots to kill Him, who was "going about doing good." Just as our Lord was approaching the decline of the hill, where a view of a portion of Jerusalem was obtained, the multitude seemed to have sung with greater fervor than ever before, so much to the disconsolation of the Pharisees who were standing by, that they complained of the noise, and requested the Saviour to command them to be still; but He looked towards the ground and pointing his finger (see Luke xix. 30–40) to the rough stones along the highway, said to them: "If these should hold their peace these stones would immediately cry out." It is worthy of remark, that the stones did cry out, when there was no one by Him to speak a word in honor of his name; while hanging on the cross suffering great agony, for the sins of mankind; when the procession had moved to the depression, where the city is hid from view for a short while, their songs dispersed all the gloom that lurked about the valley, then in a few moments the steep hill is ascended, where in almost an instant the whole city is spread out to full view.

It is the general opinion, that our Lord had reached this point when his heart became so deeply moved with compassion that He wept over the fact, the time was fast advancing when desolation and death should overthrow the city. This high hill is settled upon as identical with the place where our Lord wept; because there is no other place on the road, nor on the Mount of Olives, that affords such an unobstructed and beautiful view of Jerusalem.

Just below the greatest depression of the Kedron Valley appeared, where it connects with the Valley of Hinnom, is an elevation composed of large rocks, which affords a beautiful view of the Holy City, and any one familiar with the narrative of the triumphant entry into Jerusalem of our Lord, and having an opportunity of passing along this ancient road from Bethany to Jerusalem, will be constrained to agree with the thousands of others, in their belief, that this rocky ledge is identical with the point where the Saviour was suddenly stricken with over-powering sorrow which caused a gush of tears to flow from his eyes.

While under the influence of this deep anguish, Jesus predicted the woeful fate that should come upon the people, and said: " For the days shall come upon thee, that thine enemies shall cast a trench about thee, and compass thee about and shall keep thee in on every side; and shall lay thee even with the ground, and thy children with thee, and they shall not leave thee one stone upon another, because thou knowest not the time of thy visitation."

How alarming was this prediction, and how dreadful the future of Jerusalem; a most woeful calamity was in store that should come upon the people like a devouring fire and consume them. It was only about forty years from the time of the prediction, that the sad visitation came upon the city, and the words of Christ were literally fulfilled, in the great siege, capture, and overthrow of the city, and slaughter of immense multitudes of people. The Garden of Gethsemane is situated at the base of the Mount of Olives, just at the point where the three roads up the side of the mountain diverge; a very old tradition, at least as far back as the time of Constantine the Great, locates the renowned garden here, and it has been generally believed to be identical because of its close proximity with the Brook Kedron, which accords with the narrative of the Scripture concerning it. The garden is in the custody of the Franciscan Monks; it is a square lot, enclosed with a white stone wall, about five or six feet high, and an inner fence standing three or four feet from it, on the inside. In the midst of it are seven olive trees. At one time there were eight, but the oldest one has yielded to the crumbling hand of time, notwithstanding all pains were taken to preserve it; the remaining seven are well stricken with age, and must soon succumb to the same influence their parent perished under; their trunks are much decayed, and are propped up by heaps of stone and earth; they are supposed to be the descendants of the original trees which stood here when our Lord was on earth. The traditional sites where our Lord prayed while in great agony, and where the disciples slept when they should have been watching, are pointed out; also the place where Judas Iscariot betrayed Him with a kiss.

It cannot be supposed, from the nature of things, that any one can

GARDEN OF GETHSEMANE.

place confidence in the correctness of these localities pointed out in the garden, yet they serve to refresh the mind concerning the scenes of the events. Now as to the garden, we have it recorded in the Bible, "Jesus went over the Brook Kedron with His disciples, where there was a garden into which He entered." The following is from the pen of one who regards this as the identical place of our Lord's agony and betrayal, and his opinion has been endorsed by many travelers and authors who have carefully examined the geography of the place, as to its agreement with the Scripture narrative referring to it. We copy it for the benefit of our readers because it is both pathetic and sublime: "Over there in Jerusalem His body was crucified, but here was the scene of the crucifixion of His soul; there the letter of the law was executed, but here the awful weight of the spirit was borne; there He drank the dregs of sorrow, but here the full cup was wrung out to Him; here the enemy who had departed from Him for a time returned with all the powers of hell (Matt. xxvi. 36; Mark xvi. 32) to overthrow the Son of Man; here His own familiar friends betrayed Him; here the Captain of our salvation was made perfect through suffering, and from this place, broken-hearted as He was with the cross before Him, and a heavier cross upon Him, He rose up from the garden and went forth to die."

THE TOMB OF THE VIRGIN MARY.

"Take thy shoes from off thy feet, for the ground whereon thou standeth is holy." Not far from the Garden of Gethsemane is another memorable place, that ranks in importance with most of the venerable and holy places about Jerusalem. It is known as the Tomb of the Virgin Mary. This ancient-looking tomb is situated amongst the deeply-bedded rocks at the foot of Mt. Olivet, on the western side, and according to some of the early writers, was erected by order of Helena, the energetic mother of Constantine, whose untiring labors in Palestine will ever be commended by the civilized world.

This tomb is now a place of worship, chiefly under the control of the Greeks, although the Latins and Armenians have separate apartments there, in which they hold services at stated times. The chambers of this resting-place of the sainted dead, are deep and dark, entered by descending sixty stone steps, divided almost midway by a small platform, where three tombs are placed. The two on the right are those of Joachim and Anna, the parents of the Virgin; that on the left is the resting-place of Joseph, her husband.

Proceeding down the second flight, the main chamber is entered; it is always very dark, for the sunlight never enters; therefore it is continually illuminated by lamps. On the right side, near the extreme end of the Greek chapel is the high altar, and the tomb in which the remains of the Mother of our blessed Lord were placed, is said to be under it.

The Greeks claim this place to be the oldest church in the world; it is without doubt a reverential-looking place, and if appearance is to be considered as a proof of its antiquity, we can see no reason why the claims of the Greeks may not be conceded. On entering it, one feels himself to be within the sacred walls of the last resting place of some one, whose illustrious character won for him immortal fame and honor, without being informed to whose memory the tomb is dedicated.

One noticeable thing concerning this place, that gives it prominence in history, is the fact of it not being so critically disputed as most places to which claims are laid for prominent events that occurred in ancient times.

VALLEY OF JEHOSHAPHAT.

There are in connection with the valleys already mentioned inside the Holy City, others on the outside, round about, two of which are famous in history because of the marvelous events which have transpired in them. The valley of Jehoshaphat may be consistently classed with the most renowned in all the land, in point of distinction; it is a a very deep ravine, lying between the city and the Mount of Olives, running north and south; the brook Kedron flows through it, and by which name the valley is sometimes called; it is very deep in some parts and difficult to descend, the water rises in it at times during the heavy rains in the fall, to the height of ten or twelve feet, but during the summer season is almost dry.

The Jews and Mohammedans believe this valley will be the scene of the last judgment, and Christians have also adopted the Jewish faith, with regard to the final day, and stubbornly insist the Judge of all the earth will call the nations before Him in this valley; it is thought, they base their belief on the declaration of the Prophet Joel; the Jews have a tradition that all persons not buried in the valley of Jehoshaphat will be compelled to come from every part of the world under ground, to judgment; therefore they are very anxious to be buried there and have occupied every available space for their tombs almost to Bethany; the Jews build their tombs on the east side of the valley and the Mohammedans on the west.

DESCRIPTION OF TOMBS.

These tombs are not dug as in other countries, but built up from the surface with stones, by men who follow that work daily; the dead are not kept for three or four days, therefore, thousands have their tombs built while they are alive, so that they will be sure of being buried properly. Men can be seen every day on both sides of the valley busy building tombs. (See Joel iii. 2–12.)

Some of these tombs are very ancient, and it is highly probable that the dusty remains of a hundred generations rest in them, comprising a number of the many races who in their turn controlled the country, viz.: Jebusites, Hebrews, Syrians, Macedonians, Egyptians, Romans, Persians, Franks and Turks; some of those tombs such as are known as Absalom, St. James, Jehoshaphat and Zechariah's, are supposed to be amongst the oldest in the land.

They are drilled in the rock, and from their appearance much time was expended in preparing them; about these stately monuments of the memorable dead lie the remains of almost innumerable hosts, whose names will remain unknown until the day of final accounts. This valley was the scene of great tumult when David was fleeing from the fury of Absalom, his rebellious son, who was in hot pursuit after him with murderous intent.

Jehoshaphat properly begins at the head of a valley about one mile and a quarter west of the Damascus Gate, at which point it is very shallow, but continues to deepen gradually as it goes south; the first half mile runs in the direction of the city, then suddenly turns eastward; in this course it runs for half a mile, then changes southward and becomes much wider.

The road going to Anathoth and Michmash crosses it here; the valley is said to be a hundred feet deep opposite St. Stephen's Gate, and about two hundred feet wide. It is the general opinion, the name of this valley was adopted after King Jehoshaphat had won a great victory there, one that strengthened the hearts of the Jews and made both the king and the battle-field memorable to them throughout many generations. (2 Chron. xx.)

The places of Bible mention in and about Jerusalem are now, as in earlier times, eagerly sought by the thousands of tourists and pilgrims who annually pay the Holy City a visit; the routes of daily travel from place to place are accurately arranged, so that all places visited are classed according to their distance from each other, into daily itineracies from one to eleven.

Many of the traditional places hitherto settled upon as identical with prominent events mentioned in the Bible, have been for several years rigidly investigated by men who have great ability for exploring; these investigations have in many instances been highly beneficial; several places that were not identified have been discovered through their efforts, and many that have been settled upon have proven to be mis-located.

These developments have given new avenues for thought to those who travel to Palestine in search of historical information; it is very unfortunate, however, that several places that have been believed to be identical with events narrated in the Scriptures have been disputed by some of our modern investigators, without establishing proof to the contrary, or discovering any other site that indicates their premises are properly founded.

The people of Palestine who have charge of those historical and sacred places cling with unyielding tenacity to the old traditions, believing those who lived sixteen or seventeen hundred years ago had a better opportunity to know the locality of these places than the people of to-day, and they think the places as located are genuine, notwithstanding the devastation to which the city has been subjected.

When Absalom, whose previous conduct had caused him for a time to be exiled from the embraces of his father, had been kindly restored and pardoned for his great sin, he began another cunning scheme that was so agreeable to the masses, they became willing to abandon David and took the young aspirant for their king. Absalom's ambition and treacherous disposition was of the basest character; he did not only seek to obtain the sceptre before the death of his father, but such was his ambition for it, he eagerly sought to murder him to obtain it. Many young men follow this most sinful of all examples and bring sorrow, lamentation and death hastily upon their parents, because they wish to possess their fortune.

It was too long, in the estimation of Absalom, to wait until his father died, to possess the throne, so he plotted and put into effect one of the most barbarous schemes a son could conceive against the interest of his father.

THE PATH DAVID TOOK THROUGH THE VALLEY.

Clothing himself in royal attire, Absalom appeared in the most conspicuous place and persuaded the people to rebel against the king, because their rights were being imposed upon, and if they would elevate him to power, equal justice should be the standard principle of his administration; and that his cunningly-devised plans might be attained he went to his father and obtained permission to go to Hebron, to pay a vow he had made; David, having no suspicion of treachery, granted his request; then the nature of the oath was soon developed.

Absalom, having arrived at Hebron, sent out messengers in great haste throughout the nation, that at a given sign previously made known to the people, they should unitedly proclaim him king in Hebron, the previous seat of government.

This intelligence enthused the people, and many whose sympathies were with David did not dare to express themselves in his favor; for a short time Absalom grew in popularity with the people, and his party increased rapidly. When the news of his treason had come to the ears of King David he was completely unnerved, so that his courage fell, and the man whose fame as a mighty conqueror, had made nations tremble, became so appalled that he was almost like a helpless child, and may be looked upon as a conquered conqueror.

The king in wild dismay fled from the city of David, whilst his son and usurpers were advancing on the city from the south, which was the most convenient way from Hebron. David having heard of the route the would-be king was coming with his army of revolters, ran down into the Valley of Jehoshaphat eastward, entered the path leading over the Mount of Olives and continued his flight until he found himself east of the Jordan in the land of Gilead.

Hence the Valley of Jehoshaphat has been memorable also, on account of David, who passed through it in deep sorrow, when his own son was seeking his throne and his life. The path the king took through the valley with his court, is graphically described in the Bible: "And all the country wept with a loud voice, and all the people passed over."

DAVID AND HIS SYMPATHETIC FRIENDS.

"The king also himself passed over the Brook Kedron and all the people passed over it;" the road leading over the Mount of Olives was very steep and rugged; to ascend, it is therefore clear to all, that the king had a toilsome journey from the beginning; the difficult road to travel, and a rebellious and murderous son behind him with vengeance flashing from his eyes, must have made the journey expressly solitary and bitter.

It seems to have been early in the morning when David was apprised of the rebellion and fled from the city; this we infer from the time it required him to travel the distance at rapid speed and the events which transpired during the flight, which, when taken into account, seem to justify our opinion, that the king started from his palace early; Josephus contributes more space to this event than any other; he very minutely portrays the behavior of David under his deep affliction, showing he was patient, and fervent, in his religious devotions; that in time of danger when fierce and bloodthirsty foes were persuing him, he took time to attend to his daily religious devotions.

He also speaks of his generosity, his simplicity, his forgiving disposition, but nothing of his courage, for it had left him, the weight of grief had crushed it out of him, for the time being; for a son whom he loved so tenderly, had brought him shame and burdened his heart; notwithstanding Absalom had proved himself unworthy of his father's love, yet he was dearly adored by him even when the offence was of such a nature, any other person would have been hunted down by David's strong arm and slain, but we find this "mighty man of valor" escaping from a rebel son, with all the speed he could command, having with him a multitude of grief-stricken friends who made the very hills and valleys in the vicinity of their journey echo with their doleful lamentations for miles around; there were no cheering developments along the route.

But on the other hand one event after another attended the flight of the king which served to increase his fears; when David left the City of Jerusalem a multitude of sympathizing friends left with him, including his entire household except ten women of the harem (concubines), whom he left behind to look after household effects; the mules and donkeys that were usually taken when the king started on a journey with his court, were left and all the company started on foot, believing it to be the most expedient method of traveling over the very rough pass, down to the Jordan. It was a long and mournful procession composed of the Philistine body-guard, the six hundred men from Gath, the high officers of the king's court, all the servants and many women and children (see 2 Samuel xv.).

THE STRONG LOVE OF ITTAI FOR DAVID.

There were none of those who clung to David in his state of deep distress more worthy of mention than Ittai the Gittite; although he was a stranger and also an exile, yet he was so deeply in sympathy with the king he was willing to go with him and to suffer with him, whatever calamity there might be in store; to this end he nerved himself to follow David and do all he could for him in life and in death.

The attachment of Ittai to his lord was so strong no further objection to his purpose was made; and he and those with him passed down through the valley of Jehoshaphat, beyond the Kedron, to join the mournful procession. The evidence of the king's purpose to flee in pursuit of a place of refuge was prominent, for the whole multitude instantly uttered a wail of grief that almost shook the surrounding mountains.

Then Zadok came in company with Abiathar and the Levites, bearing the Ark of God from its resting-place on Mt. Zion, intending to take it with them for the consolation of the king in his painful flight; but the treasure was so sacred and valuable, David regarded it too risky to attempt to escape, and ordered the Priests Zadok and Abiathar to return it, deeming it far better to perish himself and all those with him, than for anything to happen to the sacred Ark.

It was, according to David's command, returned to Jerusalem; the king also requested the two priests to remain with the sacred instrument and pay strict attention to the movements of Absalom, and send him word what they proposed to do, by their two sons Ahimaoz and Jonathan, who were waiting for tidings in the Valley of Johoshaphat by En-rogel. These young men were fleet as runners, and could come to the king in time to warn him of Absalom's plans.

DAVID'S FLIGHT.

The lamentations of David and those with him must have been heart-rending to those who heard them, for the thoughts of his flight and the cause that stimulated him are shocking to those living in this remote age. We are informed, David went up by the way of Mt. Olivet, and wept as he went, with covered head and bare-footed, and all those with him covered their heads, and wept with their fleeing king as they went there; when they had reached the summit of Mt. Olivet, having aching hearts and bleeding feet; the king stopped long enough to worship, and then advised with Hushai, who like a friend in the time of need, or sore affliction, having heard of David's trouble because of his heartless son, that he was compelled to flee from his palace and from Jerusalem, and seek a safe retreat elsewhere, rent his clothes, and came out to meet him, with his head covered with earth, and endeavored to persuade the king to go with him.

But the king did not want to burden his friend with his sorrows, therefore, he continued his journey, but requested Hushai to remain as one of the advisers of Absalom, feeling he could render him valuable service by doing so, as to the movements of the treacherous usurper, whose iron heart and merciless hand were greedily seeking the blood of a father whose love for his son knew no bounds; the two had not separated but a short time, before another man met David and his party.

But he was not a friend; his expressions were indicative of an enemy, in whose heart was concealed a deep-seated grudge and low cunning. It was plain, the king had not only obstacles behind him, from which he was fleeing, but gainsay and derision before him, these evils combined their influence to intimidate and discourage him.

As he proceeded down the eastern slope of Mt. Olivet, Shimei, the Benjamite, who was a relative of King Saul and unfriendly to David, met him, and went along the mountain side, and cursed him, threw stones and dust at him; the enemy embraced the opportunity when David was too much overcome with grief and fatigue to resent an insult, to drive the wedge of agony deeper into his bleeding heart, and drive him into insanity, or absolute madness, if possible.

DAVID IN EXILE.

This grave insult to the king so deeply incurred the displeasure of the high officials of David's staff, and others of the company, they for a time, lost sight of their perilous situation and were with no little effort restrained from avenging the insolent Benjamite. Abishai, who had lost control of himself, would have leaped across the ravine and smote off the head of Shimei, had David given his consent; but the king reminded them, that since his own son, whom he so dearly loved, had abandoned him and caused him to go into exile, anything could be tolerated that others could do to him.

This timely advice restrained his friends from dealing rashly with the man who attempted to assault their lord, and they continued their hasty flight until they had reached the valley of the Jordan, where they camped amongst the thickets, and refreshed themselves after a fatiguing day's journey. Here, mark the change in David's surroundings; just a day previous he was in his stately palace on Mt. Zion, in the city of Jerusalem, having at his command all that was needful to make him happy; now he is in exile among the weeds, and bushes along the banks of the Jordan, without shelter or a pillow upon which to lay his head.

Yet he seemed not to be so much disturbed about being deprived of home comforts for the time being, as he was to know the plans of Absalom, and what more was necessary to make good his escape from his son's rebellious hand. Then, suddenly, while the heavenly sentinels were advancing up their silvery paths to their meridian, they heard the sound of the two fleet-footed youths, Jonathan and Ahimaaz, coming with great speed bringing the ardently desired tidings.

On the arrival of the young usurper, which occurred a few hours after the flight of David and his company, he held a council as to the best mode of procedure, seeing his father had fled from the palace and city. The chief adviser was Ahithophel, a man of great influence, and on whom David himself relied for advice in times of great perplexity. This man had turned from the king and set his face toward the traitor son, and advised him, among other things, to pursue his father even to the banks of the Jordan and slay him, that the nation might have peace. This advice pleased Absalom, for he knew that if David could be captured and put to death, the kingdom would be safely in his hands.

When the news reached Hushai he advised Absalom differently, which seemed to be better than that given by Ahithophel, but in truth it was in David's favor. Having the full text of Absalom's immediate procedure, Hushai informed Zadok and Abiathar, and requested them to dispatch the young men to David at once, that he might cross the Jordan before his pursuers overtook him. The messengers reached the king in time to prepare him to escape. These young men, sons of the priest, were being watched with all possible vigilance, as they were suspected of being unfriendly to Absalom; and had it not been for the well in Bahurim, in which they concealed themselves, Absalom would have had them put to death as enemies of his cause and emissaries of his father, whose life he was anxiously seeking. (See 2 Samuel xvii.)

AHITHOPHEL COMMITTED SUICIDE.

Just at this time there was a break in the council. Absalom offended Ahithophel because he followed the advice of Hushai. This so troubled the aged counsellor, that he saddled the donkey on which he generally rode when going a journey, went to his home and put his house in order, then went out and deliberately hung himself. It was thought he was apprehensive of the fate of Absalom, and having joined the rebellious party, he would naturally come to shame, and perhaps lose his life in the struggle.

When it was known that Ahithophel had committed suicide, he was honored with an honorable burial in the sepulchre of his father, which was not customary in those times; it was the prevailing opinion that men who committed self-murder were not worthy of being buried with the honored dead. The death of Ahithophel was but the signal-cloud of the pending storm that would turn the tide of indignation from David, and cause his rebellious son to reap the reward of his hands.

Absalom was full of ambition, and restless anxiety to capture his father and put him to death, and all who were in sympathy with him, and to accomplish this he thought it proper to follow Hushai's instructions. Collecting a large army he appointed Amasa, his cousin, chief commander over it, instead of Joab. This young rebel was the son of Abigail. David's sister; his father was Ithra. It was thought he was not very highly esteemed by David, and this led him to join in the rebellion against him. The preparation being completed the army started in pursuit of David, whose hidings were on the east of the Jordan, with friends who were endeavoring to make him and his army comfortable (see 2 Sam. xvii. 7–24). For when it became known to the people that David had fled to them in Mahanaim for protection from the wrath of his son, three powerful officials came to his help. These were Shobi, son of Nahash, of Rabbah, supposed to have been king of Ammon; and Machir, the son of Ammiel, of Lo-debar; and Barzillai, the Gileadite, of Rogelim.

They brought beds, and basins, and earthen vessels, wheat and barley, and parched corn, and honey, and butter, sheep and cheese of all kinds, for David and for those who were with him to eat, for they said the people are hungry, weary and thirsty in the wilderness. The king, finding himself in the midst of friends, was relieved of much of his tenderness and his spirit was greatly revived. After he and his army had refreshed themselves from the sumptuous supply of choice food given them by the trans-Jordanic dwellers, David began to prepare for the crisis before him.

He numbered those who were with him and divided them into three divisions, and placed Joab in command of the first, which comprised one-third of the whole army; the second division was under command of Abishai, the son of Zeruiah, Joab's brother; and the third was in command of Ittai, the Gittite, who vowed to stand by David, and even suffer death, if the crisis demanded, before he would leave him or suffer his rebel son to triumph over him.

The king had also concluded to go into the battle with the people who had sacrificed their homes and put their lives on the altar of death to protect him; but the whole people demanded that he should remain in his hidings, for his life was of more value to the nation than ten thousand other men (see 2 Sam. xviii. 1–33).

David yielded to the earnest protest of his people, and remained at the fortress, but charged Joab, Abishai and Ittai, the chiefs in command, and all the captains in the hearing of the army going out against the rebels, to be kindly disposed toward his rebellious son, for notwithstanding all the tenderness of heart a son should indulge for a kind father, had been crushed in Absalom, by an avaricious ambition to control the nation, David still most tenderly loved him and wished his life preserved.

The great army of Israel, under the command of Amasa, in the meantime had crossed the ford and was east of the Jordan. Absalom seems not to have been advised to remain in the palace at Jerusalem, and being bent on conquest, he came with the army, to assist in anything he might do to capture and slay his father and slaughter the veteran army, whose loyalty was as firm as the hills around them.

The army of King David went up against that of Absalom, and they pitched their first battle in the forest of Ephraim, which resulted in the loss of twenty thousand of the rebel army; these men, the most of whom were unskilled in warfare, fled before the veteran army of David, and thousands of them, having lost their way to the fords, fled to the interlacing thicket, where they were pursued by the men of King David (who were far superior in skill and military strength) and slain.

During this stage of great panic in Amasa's command, Absalom himself came riding in at full speed upon his mule, and unguardedly met a squad of men of David's force; these he attempted to shun by darting through the forest in another direction and was caught in the fork of an oak (perhaps by his neck) and held so tightly he could not extricate himself, and the beast darted out, leaving him hanging. (See 2 Sam. xviii. 5–11.)

ABSALOM'S TRAGIC DEATH.

There was great anxiety as to the termination of the success of the great national conflict on both sides. But those men with Absalom were full of confidence, and had expected to capture David and his whole force that day; but when the man whom they had illegally anointed and installed king, had been caught by the limb of a tree, and had been slain by Joab, they immediately abandoned their unfortunate insurrection and were filled with wild dismay.

The man who saw Absalom hanging would have been glad to have driven his dart through him, but having heard David forbid that any one should do him harm, he was restrained, but went to Joab, the chief officer of his division, and related the story of Absalom's fate, whereupon, in an unguarded moment, Joab disregarded the admonition of his king, and took the responsibility upon himself, and slew the ill-fated son of David.

He caused his staff to form a circle around the tree where Absalom was suspended, and finished the work of death; they extricated him from the limb, and finding near them a ditch or "great pit," into that they threw the remains of the dead rebel son of Israel's victorious king, and covered it with a mound of stones.

Ahimaaz, the son of Zadok, the priest, was present and asked to be allowed to run and bring the tidings of the battle to the king; but Joab thought it would be better to break the news to David another day, when he would be better prepared to receive it. In the meantime a Cushite was dispatched to bear the news to the king of what he had seen and heard. Then Ahimaaz insisted to be allowed to run, and was permitted to go; he outran the Cushite, for he was one of the fleetest and most noted runners in the land, and was generally known afar off, by his peculiar style of running, and while yet in the distance the watchman in the lookout tower recognized him and told David, who was sitting between the two gates of the camp, awaiting the news of the battle. When Ahimaaz arrived his heart failed him, so that he could not get courage enough to break the news of Absalom's fate.

DAVID'S LAMENTATION.

But when the Cushite, the regular messenger, came to the camp, he delivered the message and told of the death of Absalom, and the destruction and confusion of his army. When David heard it he wept bitterly over the death of his rebellious son, whose hand had been so long uplifted against him.

Such was his fervent love for Absalom, he would have died in his stead; the lamentations of the bereaved king awakened deep sympathy for him among all his people; his indignation was so greatly kindled against Joab, he could no longer make him the trusty head of his army. Amasa, who was one of the most expert commanders in Israel, was appointed in Joab's place.

This action of David severed the intimate friendship between the king and the slayer of his son forever; Joab also entertained a deep-seated dislike for Amasa, which in time was clearly developed. David made preparations to return to Jerusalem, and sent the two chief priests to the city to allay any feeling amongst the people that might exist against him; this being done, the king came over the Jordan,

EVENTS IN AND ABOUT JERUSALEM. 121

followed by a large procession (2 Samuel xviii. 15–33) and marched up to Jerusalem, and was once more the victorious King David, whose fame as a conqueror was known far and wide. The bloody struggle was over, the rebellious Absalom had been slain, the remaining rebels had been subdued, peace was restored, and David himself was on the throne. But there was no lasting rest after his restoration to the throne; many things tending to perplex his soul, and reduce his pride, rushed upon him one after the other until he neared the swellings of Jordan.

A FAMINE IN THE LAND.

About the time when the many difficulties seemed to have been removed, that so greatly interrupted the prosperity of the nation, a devastating famine, which lingered three years, threw a great check upon the nation's prosperity, and the indefatigable Philistines, who had been a thorn in the path of the nation for a long time and who David thought were finally conquered, came up against them as thick as locusts, and plunged the king into a new struggle.

But these issues, sad and perplexing as they were, did not compare in magnitude to the calamitous internal conflict that was stimulated by Sheba, the Benjaminite, whose bugle blast upon the mountains of Ephraim called to his help men of war from the ten tribes, whose loyalty to his cause seemed to be unshaken, even by the hitherto powerful arm of David himself.

Now from the time Joab was dismissed by David as general-in-chief of the army, and Amasa put in his place, he was revengefully angry, and sought an opportunity to put his successor to death, but made no demonstration of his intention; David, fearing an uprising of Sheba, the son of Bichri, a Benjamite, might result seriously to the prosperity of his kingdom, sent Amasa to call the men of Judah to battle against him. And when they halted at the great stone which is in Gibeon, Joab found it opportune to murder Amasa, under the guise of friendship, then proceeded with the army, loyal to David, and defeated Sheba's forces and won another victory for the king (2 Sam. xx. 1–22).

ABSALOM'S PILLAR.

Absalom, the ambitious aspirant to the throne of his father, during his more quiet life caused to be erected a shaft or monument to his memory in the king's dale, which is in the Valley of Jehoshaphat, known in earlier Scriptures as the Valley of Shaveh. The shaft was marble according to Josephus and was built to perpetuate the memory of the young prince, because at that time he had no son to keep his name in remembrance.

ABSALOM'S TOMB.

It is stated in another chapter that Absalom had three sons, and one daughter of very great beauty, named Tamer; the general opinion is, the pillar was erected some time prior to the time his children were born. In the Valley of Jehoshaphat, on the east side of the City of Jerusalem, an old tomb is known as Absalom's Pillar; it is about twenty feet square and forty feet high from the foundation to the top of the dome.

The origin of this monument is not positively settled; some suppose it has been substituted for the one built by Absalom, others are of the opinion it is the original shaft itself; let these opinions be true or otherwise, it is without doubt one of the most prominent monuments of all those in the venerable valley. It is held expressly odious in Jewish estimation; they hate the very memory of Absalom's name, so much so, that when passing his pillar they hurl stones of indignation at it, on account of his rebellious conduct toward his father.

The whole of the shaft bears prominent indications of Jewish violence, it being full of scars from top to bottom. 2 Sam. xviii. 18; Gen. xiv. 17. The disgraceful fate of Absalom should serve as a lastingly impressive lesson of special admonition to the young, they should remember, it is far more desirable to sleep in a tomb of the blessed, than one that the living of an hundred generations will curse when they pass it, as the incensed Jews do the shaft of the rebel son of David, whose grave was a deep ditch, having a pile of stones to cover his mortal remains, in the wild forests of Ephraim, instead of being honorably buried in the rich sepulchre he prepared for himself in the king's dale.

VALLEY OF HINNOM.

The Valley of Hinnom is one of the most notable of those in Palestine and one of the most widely known in the world, because of the peculiar history connected with it. This renowned valley is situated on the west of Jerusalem, separating Mt. Zion on the north, from the Hill of Evil Counsel and the Plain of Raphaim on the south. It is first mentioned in history, in describing the boundary of the tribe of Benjamin, which is so accurately drawn that modern visitors have, with little difficulty, traced them. "The border line of Benjamin leaving En-rogel went up by the valley of the Son of Hinnom unto the southwest of the Jebusite; the same is Jerusalem, and the border went up to the top of the mountain that lieth before the Valley of Hinnom, westward, which is at the end of the Valley of the Giants, northward." The Valley of the Giants mentioned here is that also known as Raphaim, where the Philistines were defeated by King David. At the point where the Valley of Hinnom turns eastward it rapidly increases in depth, and as it passes along the southern boundary of Mt. Zion, which rises high above it, a beautiful observation can be obtained of the mountainous situation of Jerusalem.

HILL OF EVIL COUNSEL.

The Hill of Evil Counsel is on the south, which is high, steep and rugged; it contains many tombs, hewn in the rocks; the most of them are empty, the remains of their illustrious dead have been removed to other parts, and some of them, it is highly probable, have never been occupied. This will not seem strange when we call to mind that it was a common custom for people in olden times to have their tombs prepared many years before they died.

It was one of their supreme thoughts, when they came into manhood, how and where to prepare their sepulchres. This was a common custom in Egypt long before Moses led the Hebrews from their bondage. Many of those ancient tombs, that were built at a great cost, are yet standing as evidences of the fact.

It is likely, the Hebrews brought the idea with them when they entered the "Land of Promise." Absalom, who has been mentioned, had a stately monument built in the king's dale, to perpetuate his memory; Joseph of Arimathea prepared his tomb, and laid the body of the Lord Jesus in it after the crucifixion; but the intention of Joseph, when he had the sepulchre hewn, was to have it ready for his own body when death should come to him.

This Hill of Evil Counsel is the traditional summit on which Caiaphas, the High Priest, counseled with the Sanhedrim Court, to put Christ to death. Then is seen another place high up the hill, which is of great importance to visitors, if the tradition as to its identity is correctly drawn. It is called Aceldama, now known as Hok-el-Dum.

POTTER'S FIELD.

It is directly opposite to the Pool of Siloam; there are, as is natural to suppose, doubts existing among some of those who have made investigations as to the identity of this as the "Field of Blood," nevertheless it has great prominence as such because it has been for a long time greatly reverenced by Christians, and many pilgrims who died while visiting the holy places about Jerusalem, have been buried there.

The soil is believed to be expressly efficient in promoting decomposition; for this reason many ship-loads of it were taken, by special order, to the Compo-Santo, at Pisa, Italy. We were conducted to this old cemetery, while in Pisa, in which this soil was placed. It is regarded as one of the most sacred and reverential places in the city.

There are several sepulchres in the neighborhood of the Potter's Field, of Hebrew and Greek origin; many of them are very ancient. Here the betrayer of our Lord, after being seized with overpowering condemnation as a result of his vicious and deliberate crime, went out and hanged himself. This site is, therefore, looked upon as that with which the money given Judas for delivering Christ into the hands of his enemies was bought, and has continued until now to be a burying-ground for strangers.

It is noteworthy that all strangers who die in Jerusalem are buried in Aceldama. There are very many tombs here; some of them are those of hermits, who lived in Jerusalem in very early times; others are the silent homes of many crusaders who died here; others are of very recent date. Pains have been taken to have beautiful inscriptions carved on the face of several tombs.

These places, so important in sacred history, being in some way connected with the Valley of Hinnom, has caused it to be mentioned many times in connection with them, but this valley became more prominently noted after it was made the head of the idolatrous worship, for the people who had largely estranged themselves from the God of their fathers. (See Matt. xxvii. 7-8; Acts i. 19; Matt. xxvii. 3-10.)

IDOLATRY OF ISRAEL.

Many of the Israelites brought their innocent children to be sacrificed to Moloch; this was practiced there and at the high places of Tophet; which, according to Jerome, were situated at the north of the valley, near what is known at present as Bir-Eyuh. The procedure was many times revolting to humanity; the worshipers, or many of them, would freely bring their children where these terrible sacrifices were carried on, and would cause their sons and daughters to pass through the fire.

There is a Jewish tradition stating that the statue of Moloch was brass, having a body of a man and a head of a lion; its interior was hollow, and fitted up with a furnace, by which it was made red hot. The children to be sacrificed were then placed in the red hot arms of the devouring image to burn to death, and to drown their pensive lamentations and heart-rending cries men would beat drums.

This abominable institution was first established by King Solomon "Then did Solomon build a high place for Chemosh, the abomination of Moab, in the hill which is before Jerusalem, and for Moloch, the abomination of the children of Ammon" (see 1 Kings, xi. 7).

This wise king, who was specially endowed of God with extraordinary wisdom, proved himself to be at length one of the most unworthy of all the kings who had reigned on the throne at Jerusalem. The reign of this young monarch began with copious indications of being a great blessing to his people, a guide to lead them in the way of righteousness.

But when his probation was ended he left a deep black cloud, pregnant with many baneful issues, hanging over the nation, largely caused by the polygamous character he so fondly nursed. Solomon was not content with the females of Hebrew origin, but took to himself wives of several surrounding nations, and thereby brought into the capital many whose religion was idolatrous, and whose gods were not the Lord. This forbidden conduct introduced idolatry into the land, which continued increasing until it had nearly supplanted the worship ordained of the Lord.

The Mount of Offence was almost covered with idol gods, before whom the people reverentially bowed (2 Kings xxiii. 10-13; Isa. vii. 31).

THE KINGDOM EMBARRASSED.

The luxury and profligacy that became popular in connection with the fatally numerous marriages of the king, and Jerusalem being situated away from the centre of the nation, where it could not be in sympathy with the tribes of the far-away north, were instrumental in breaking the ties that bound the nation, and the increasing lust of the king for magnificence, greatly aided in the work of destruction; for it caused the country at large to become impoverished that the capital might be made rich.

Then in the extreme moment, when foes sprang up from the south and on the north, under Hadad, who dwelt among the mountains of Edom, and Rezon from the plains of Syria, Solomon found his power had departed. This young king had a most brilliant prospect before him to become the most cautious, progressive, and powerful monarch of those who preceded him, or any that should succeed him to the throne of Israel.

His mother, Bathsheba, who was formerly the wife of Uriah,

an officer in David's army, paid special attention to her beloved son, Solomon, from infancy, and trained him with all the tenderness an affectionate mother of her day could command; he was also put under the care of pious Nathan, who was one of the chief advisers of David, for mental training.

It may be seen very clearly that Solomon was specially reared in the fear of God. He being very young, not having reached his majority, when the responsible duties of the throne were accorded him, he sought direction from God, and above all other honors he prayed for wisdom. In answer to his prayer the Lord endowed him with such gifts that he astonished his subjects, and impressed them that he was the proper man to hold the sceptre of power.

The first demonstration of his superior judgment, was that most masterly decision between the dispute of the two women over the child that both claimed. The young king had a double opportunity for unlimited success; the nations round about were at peace and ready to form friendly alliance with him.

SOLOMON'S EARLY BLUNDER.

The powerful Phœnicians, who were masters of the sea, were on most intimate terms of friendship with him, and above all he had the blessing of God with him, and His hand to guide him; there was for a time nothing but success in the path of the lad king, such as had never visited Israel before. He built cities, where there had been naught but a dreary wilderness; he also built great palaces and splendid gardens, and royal stables, that furnished room for forty thousand horses, and one thousand four hundred chariots.

Solomon also caused spacious parks to be made, which were watered by aqueducts leading from the great pools, nine miles from Jerusalem. The glory and unequaled splendor with which Solomon was adorned caused him to turn his mind from the right way, and to forget the counsel of his dying father, to feel his superior importance and to incline his heart toward idolatry.

It is proper to say for Solomon that for the first few years of his kingship his administration was one that exhibited wisdom and great caution, but when his fame reached beyond the confines of the immediate surrounding nations to those remotely distant, so that potentates and rulers from far away lands began to lavish praises of high commendation upon him, Solomon grew proud and sinful. One of his earliest grave mistakes was his marriage to the daughter of Pharaoh, King of Egypt.

This woman fondly admired the idolatrous worship of Egypt, and was not slow in her endeavors to persuade Solomon to introduce it into the kingdom of Israel, and it seemed her influence had some weight with her husband, for he at length yielded to the toleration of false gods, as has been related. There was a growing inclination resting in Solomon to polygamy, and, being bent on indulging this inclination, he caused the harem to be enlarged, which was a significant indication of a great increase in the king's household; this fact was soon developed, for Solomon burdened the nation with the additional responsibility of caring for the surprising number of seven hundred wives and three hundred concubines (1 Kings iii. 15-28), whom he had chosen for himself, selected from his own nation and those of others round about. These ten hundred women were furnished with everything necessary to make them royal in appearance; they wore robes of Phœnician purple, with gold gilt, and their table furnishings were the best in the market. The great domestic expenses of Solomon, in connection with his general and incidental obligations, were more than his yearly income of six hundred and sixty-six talents in gold (which amounts to about thirty-five millions of dollars in our money). He, therefore, in order to discharge those obligations, exorbitantly taxed the people, many of whom were distressed, so that the king, who in the beginning of his reign, displayed so great wisdom, fell into a deep gulf of degradations, and when the shades of death were upon him he found himself far from the path in which he first began to walk.

POOLS AND FOUNTAINS.

One of the many embarrassments which every visitor to Jerusalem must encounter, is the liability of being made sick, and perhaps seriously so, from the use of the water; therefore, strangers are admonished by the leading physicians to guard against the free use of it, unless it has been boiled; and even then it should be taken cautiously. In many instances where this advice has been discarded the results have been deeply regretted.

I suppose no one, whose life was spared, has felt the impulse of disobedience more than the writer, who at one time seemed to be near death's door, which was the result of disobedience; it is far better to be painfully thirsty in that far-off land than to be painfully in need of a physician. Jerusalem is chiefly supplied with water from cisterns; the most of them are inadequate to hold enough water to supply the people throughout the dry season; then the public cisterns and pools furnish water, until the rainy season comes on again, when the small ones are replenished. These reservoirs are either hewn in the rock or built of stones, having arches over them, and a small opening at the top to allow the water to run into them from the tops of the houses during the winter rains.

THE GREAT CISTERNS.

Some of them are very ancient, reaching as far back as the time of the Hebrews, if not those of the Jebusites. There are also a number of cisterns under the Temple area that are very large; the ancient writers, both Jewish and Gentile, in connection with the united opinion of the Jews, Christians and Moslems, affirm there is an inexhaustible supply of water in them; those who have investigated a portion of these excavations say the greater part of the area is hollowed, containing vast caves and tunnels.

The largest of these cisterns is called the great sea; the attention of our party was specially called to it while passing through the enclosure; these cisterns are said to be the reservoirs for the water supplies in the time of Solomon, and were closely guarded by trusty men; care was also taken that the walls were kept covered so as to prevent anything being put in them that would endanger life. It is estimated that the largest of these cisterns will hold two million gallons; there is another highly important reservoir called "the wall of the leaf," having a tank, forty-two feet deep, which Professor Warren places to the northwest end of it, immediately under the Temple altar, and Prof. Candor locates the man-hole just outside the water gate.

The water supply in these reservoirs was obtained from three sources: from the pools of Solomon, the Great Cistern north of the Damascus Gate, and the rain fall on the Temple Court. There are a few pools of water in and close to the city. The renowned Pool of Siloam is located at the foot of O'Phal, near the point where the Tyrœpæon Valley opens into the Kedron on the south side of the city. This pool has been carefully walled so as to form a small reservoir about fifty feet long, eighteen feet wide and nineteen feet deep, and supplies the people of Siloam with water.

The little maidens cheerfully go to this pool with their water-pots, amusing themselves in song while bearing with a steady head a pot full of water up the hill side. The pool is considered to be highly medicinal by the people in its locality and they use it as such.

Somewhere in the vicinity of the pool once stood "the Tower of Siloam, which fell and killed eighteen men." Our Lord referred to the sad event to teach the superstitious, that calamities are not always evidences of special guilt; this pool became specially prominent after the miracle our Lord performed when He caused the eyes of the young man, who had been blind from his birth, to be healed.

This poor fellow was sitting by the wayside of the public thoroughfare, begging, which is a custom still continued; Jesus, coming along, had compassion on him and healed him; this occurred on the Sabbath-day, and our Lord had just finished administering a stunning rebuke to the Jews, which made them so deeply incensed, they had concluded to stone Him, having already gathered stones for that purpose; but Jesus eluded them, and left the temple without their knowledge. As Jesus was passing along He saw this blind young man; He went to him, spat on the ground, mixed a little clay, then anointed the man's eyes, saying to him, "Go wash in the Pool of Siloam;" he went, and washed, receiving his sight; then there was great excitement, the whole city was stirred to almost wild fury.

The Pharisees, after examining the matter, charged that Christ was not from God, nor did He do the works of the Lord, because He did these things on the Sabbath-day. How unreasonable! Well might the Lord say, they "strain at gnats and swallow a camel," for they had just attempted to do Him violence on the same day, in that they would have stoned Him, had He not escaped from their murderous hands. Now before their ire is cooled they charge that Christ is a bad man, because He caused a poor blind man to enjoy the pleasure of seeing, as they had. (John ix. 7–11.)

These would-be lights of the people, were so full of animosity against Christ, they attempted to turn the man from Him who had just had his sight restored and, who had, only a few moments prior, looked upon the world, and the face of his mother for the first time in life; but his obligations to Jesus were too sacred and binding, and the friendly act of Christ was such as none other had done or even attempted; therefore he would not take sides with the Pharisees against his Benefactor.

POOL OF SILOAM.

The pool is supplied with an imperishable subterranean current. Here the Jews came in olden times to celebrate the festival, when they would sing the twelfth chapter of Isaiah. The fountain issues from a rock thirty feet below the surface, and is reached by descending a flight of twenty steps

The traditional Pool of Bethesda, the "House of Mercy," was a place of resort for the sick of all diseases; at this pool they were constantly waiting and watching for the moving of the water, that they might be the first to enter and be healed. According to the best obtainable information, the location of the ancient pool is along the north wall of the temple area, and is at present a dry reservoir filled with *debris* from the foundations of new buildings; it is estimated to have been four hundred and sixty feet long, over one hundred and thirty feet wide and seventy-five feet deep.

To this mysterious pool an angel of the Lord came at certain seasons, and troubled the water, at which time, the peculiar healing properties would cure any kind of disease known to lodge in man; for this reason various invalids were there, the blind, the deaf, the leper, the halt, and all, whatsoever might be the malady, were found waiting for the Angel of the Lord to stir the quiet waters.

Some of the diseased would manage to get in without help; others were so greatly smitten they had to be helped in by some one who was by, when the water was moved. One poor man had been there thirty and eight years, lying on his couch waiting for some one to help him in, but had not been blessed with a helping hand from any of those who pretended to seek the good of the helpless; some one would always get in before him.

It would seem proper to infer from his continuance there, his purpose was fixed to be healed or die on the porch, where he was couching; Jesus, passing that way going up to the feast, saw the man, and, knowing his faith, had compassion on him. Christ was touched with sympathy for the man. It was likely the poor man had been there so long and been seen by so many like the impotent folks about Jerusalem at the present, no one took notice of him; there he lay poor, friendless, and nearly worn out by the constant innovations of his infirmity.

Jesus went to him and asked, "Wilt thou be made whole?" The man began relating his sad experience; his hope of being healed had been blasted so many times during the thirty-eight years of his stay there. He had made the attempt to get in, but found himself unable, having no strength, and no one offered to help; at least thirty-eight had been healed in his presence while he waited. He could only look while they leaped for joy when such an one came up restored, and wish that such would some day be his good fortune; here he was compelled to remain from year to year, hoping and trusting some one would come and help him. Jesus said to him, "Arise, take up thy bed and walk;" the man obeyed and was instantly made whole.

THE SIEGE OF TITUS.

The siege of Titus, which caused the fatal fall of Jerusalem, occurred in April A.D. 70, during the season of the "feast," when the city was crowded with adoring worshipers; who, according to custom, had gone up from distant places to worship the God of their fathers, in the courts of the temple, which was so fondly admired by every Jew in the land. When Titus stationed a portion of his troops at the foot of the Mount of Olives, east of the city, he was bent on its capture, at whatever cost or sacrifice he would be compelled to make. The events connected with this terrible conflict are regarded as the most touching, lamentable, and barbarous on record, and may be catalogued among those crimes commonly indulged by those whose ambition is only gratified when their hands are stained with the blood of their fellows. Josephus graphically discloses the shocking event that doomed to death, by a most merciless massacre, a million human beings. The Jews had for some time indicated in several ways their great dissatisfaction with their subordinate relation to the Roman throne, and had embraced several ineffective measures to free themselves The exhibition of discontentment on the part of the Jews seemed to have aroused their oppressors to be more rigid than before, and even to reduce them to a more humiliating subordination. To this end Titus, the general-in-chief of the Roman army, bent his energy; having collected a very strong and well-equipped force, composed of several legions and auxiliaries, marched to the city. When he arrived at Mount Scopus, about a mile and a half north of Jerusalem, he was joined by two more legions from the west, and the other, which was the tenth, came up from Jericho, their farthest eastern station in Palestine, and camped on the Mount of Olives, but was afterwards ordered to the foot of the mount and stationed between its western base and the Kedron, from which point they were to begin the siege; here they were reinforced, by several legions from the region of the Euphrates. The army was then making cautious preparations for a deadly conflict. There was great agitation and distress in Jerusalem, it being thronged with strangers who were not prepared for war; and in the meantime, there was bitter discord existing between the factions, who were uncompromisingly at variance with each other. Such was their blindness, they could not see the danger lurking at the gates; they were at that time doing themselves more harm than the strong forces stationed on the outside. The vast stores of provisions they had provided against the day of want were destroyed by their own hands, and was the cause of many thousands being driven to starvation a short time afterwards.

The army of Titus was besieging the city, and the outer wall, that had been extended by Agrippa, and the suburbs soon fell into his hands; but the strongholds were so fortified that the general found it required more than an ordinary struggle to capture them. He then made further preparations for his success by cutting a deep trench about the city, and compass it about with the army so as to keep the people within the walls. The plan was a great success. In a short time the stores became exhausted, and famine began to show prominent signs of a terrible crisis; for the people were dying from it in greater numbers than by the vengeance of the Roman army; and yet it is a surprising fact, that even under these circumstances, the factions were so blind to their interest, the spirit they entertained seemed to them of more importance than the union for self-protection against an invading foe; so that when there was an interval of hostilities with the Romans, these poor, foolish people, filled to overflowing with selfish ambition, and blindness, were up to their necks in war among themselves. Finally efforts were made to lay down their internal strife, and make arrangements for self-protection against the hostile enemy without, and they unitedly did good work, but it only lasted for a short while. The Romans were soon convinced that stronger and more cautious preparations were necessary for the accomplishment of the siege; and that the needed arrangements might be made, they discontinued the engagement of hostilities until they had completed them. The factions whose efforts had been united against their common foe misunderstood the situation; they supposed their enemies had given up the struggle. Feeling themselves secure from the death-dealing darts of the invaders, they returned to their work of self-destruction. Assassins prowled through the streets, and in every house the melancholy impress of death was left. In the meanwhile, Titus turned his attention to the northern wall; he threw up embankments as close to it as possible, upon which wooden towers were placed for the guards. The Mount of Olives, and other places where trees were numerous, were robbed to assist in the perparations. The Jews, seeing their true situation, resolved to unite again for their self-defense and did well for a short time. Titus showed repeated evidences of a desire to save the city from total destruction, which again caused the Jews to be misled, who took them as indications of weakness; he offered them liberal terms if they would peaceably surrender and submit themselves to the Roman power. But the stubborn Jews would not accept any of his propositions, notwithstanding the people of the city were dying like sheep on account of the raging famine; thousands of the half-starved people, not being able to obtain food in the city, ventured beyond the walls, seeking it in the valley; this procedure was fatal to many. The Romans, seeing them, would capture and slay them by either hanging, or otherwise torturing them to death in the presence of their friends who were on the walls. It is said that those tortures were so numerous that the soldiers used all the material of which the crosses were made, and were compelled to use other methods of punishment. Titus, being persuaded that he could not bring the Jews to his terms, and they had no disposition whatever to surrender, made an effort to compel them to do so, or completely reduce them by starvation. He then caused a trench to be made around the city, so as to hem the people in, and at the same time preventing outsiders from carrying them supplies; and thus increased the intensity of the famine which was then sweeping the people into eternity like a raging epidemic.

The temple siege was a literal fulfillment of the prophecy of Jesus concerning the destruction of Jerusalem, declaring it should be trenched about, and the people should be compassed by their enemies. It seems very strange they did not call to mind this doleful prediction which had only been spoken about forty years prior. They had eyes, but could not see, and hearts, but did not understand, and their enmity was so strongly expressed against our Lord, they could not allow themselves to confide in Him, although everything He had said was glaringly manifested before them. Their blindness and obstinacy led them to destruction. The plan of Titus worked well and served the purpose designed. The famine increased so alarmingly, there could scarcely be found a house in Jerusalem in which there was not some dead as a result of it; and the upper rooms of the houses throughout the city were filled with corpses. The dead bodies strewn along the streets were as thick as though they had been leveled by the army. Josephus says that the people who survived the terrible plague were unable to see to the burial of their dead relatives, and common consent was given to throw the dead over the walls into the valley. It is said that six hundred thousand were in this way removed from the city, and one hundred and thirteen thousand were buried at public expense. It is said that Titus, the lion-hearted general, wept when he beheld the work of the famine, and the deep sorrow that had visited the people, and called heaven to witness that it was not his enmity, but the madness of the Jews themselves, was the cause of such an unprecedented calamity. The crisis reached such a degree of distress, the people were final'y driven to despotism, to the extent that there was a total lack of sympathy existing even for the nearest relatives and dearest friends. The strong would hunt the weak, and if any food was found about them they would forcibly take it, even if it was in their mouths.

The magnitude of the situation can be partially estimated, when it is called to mind that a mother, bearing in her heart all the maternal tenderness possible for her child, was so frantic from the dreadful pressure of starvation, would break the ties of motherhood that entwined the babe to her by tenderness and love, and kill and cook the child, eating one portion of it one day, and the other the following.

With this, and many other insurmountable difficulties that were crushing the life out of the people, the controlling element of the Jews refused to surrender. Then Titus captured the tower of Antonia, a stronghold on which the Jews greatly relied for safety. The Jews, finding the tower in the hands of their enemies, went in wild haste to the temple, hoping to be able to defend themselves within its sacred precints. This hope soon proved fruitless; the Romans having gained control of the strong tower, there was nothing for the Jews to hope for as to their safety; yet, Titus was about to move upon them, notwithstanding he held the destiny of the people in his own hand. He again proposed terms of settlement, promising to spare them from further distress if they would agree to accept them. But the blindness of the poor suffering Jews would not permit them to agree to anything; and they determined to defend the sacred edifice inch by inch. Titus did not wish to injure the beautiful Temple, so sacredly adored by the Jews, and made memorable by religious associations for many hundred years, but without the knowledge of the general, and contrary to his wishes, a private soldier threw a firebrand into some inflammable material from a window, and set the sacred edifice ablaze, and in a short while the whole structure was burning. Such was the brilliancy of the flames, the whole country round about was illuminated. This was done some time during the night while Titus was asleep in his tent; he was suddenly awakened by the wild shrieks of horror from the Jews, who were vainly endeavoring to save the building from destruction. This demonstration of sorrow was heart-rending, so that the lion-hearted Titus could not look upon it without being touched with sympathy for the panic-stricken Jews. The general rushed from his quarters and beheld the appalling conflagration, which, with the combined efforts of the Jews and Romans could not be controlled. The crackling of falling timber, the roar of the flames, the mournful cries of Jewish indignation, the thunder of the shouts of the victors, and the priests, insane with madness, throwing gilded spikes down from the building aimlessly at the enemy, while under the influence of overwhelming grief, all added to the great sound, that made the very hills about Jerusalem shake and echo the tidings to the distant regions.

When the wild flames had finished their work of destruction, all that was beautiful of the sanctuary was in ashes, and Mt. Moriah was robbed of her precious monument, and the Jews of their renowned place of sacred worship. The precious Temple of religious devotion, towards which the hearts of thousands were turned annually, was destroyed. It would be supposed that the Jews would have accepted the situation, and surrendered immediately to the Roman sceptre without further resistance; but, strange as it may seem, they would not yield, for they were unshaken in their faith that the Messiah, whom they so prayerfully hoped for, would come even in those extreme moments of suffering and deliver them; and when there was not a fragment of assurance of sunshine left them, that prompted them to hope for victory, they still clung to the vain belief that a deliverer would come. They retired to Mt. Zion, the strong citadel, and made another attempt to vanquish the foe; here, again, Titus, still sympathizing with them in their blind and fruitless attempt for victory, offered them terms of peace, but the blind, fanatic Jews would consent to nothing. With the destruction of the Temple, Josephus informs us that six thousand unarmed people, including women and children, perished, who had been led into it by a false prophet, who made them confident their expected deliverer would come to their help. From the fact of their disappointment and false representation having reached the ears of the leaders of the Jews, it would seem that they would have abandoned all hope of deliverance at a time so pregnant with calamity and death. But they stubbornly insisted on victory, and would yield to no terms proposed; then Titus renewed the siege with the intention of making a final close of the piece-meal war he had been engaged in so long. At length prominent evidences of weakness had seized the few remaining Jews, and their defense was less than a breakfast spell to the Romans, who soon became undisputed possessors of all that was left of the once beautiful and renowned city of Jerusalem. Then the Roman soldiers were like wild beasts just from the forest, who renewed their barbarous work in every way that seemed pleasurable to them. Men, women and children were slaughtered without mercy, and, according to Josephus, about ninety-seven thousand were captured and made slaves; and the number of those who lost their lives during the siege is estimated to be eleven hundred thousand. Then Titus, to make a finish of the work of destruction, ordered the demolition of the whole city, except three towers and the western wall. The Romans, having accomplished the complete destruction of Jerusalem, and returned to Rome, were received with wild enthusiasm ; and Titus, the victorious general, was honored with a triumphal arch, dedicated to the memory of the great victory he had won. He was seated in a triumphal car, drawn by eight white horses, and driven through the arch, having a number of the captive slaves chained to his chariot, walking with bowed heads. This time-worn structure is still standing in the city of Rome, known as the "Triumphal Arch of Titus." While in the old historic city, I visited this arch and passed under it. Judging from its present appearance, it must have been a very gorgeous and costly structure. It is situated between the Capitol buildings and the old, dilapidated Coliseum. Titus did not only return to Rome with a large number of captive Jews, but a vast treasure of rich and precious spoils, comprising a number of the temple furnishings, such as the golden table, the golden candlesticks, and many other costly jewels used in the sanctuary.

The golden table, and the golden candlesticks, having seven arms, and the silver trumpets, were distinctly sculptured in the walls of the Triumphial Arch at Rome, and are clearly seen up to the present time ; also, many other trophies are represented upon it.

DAVID'S TOMB.

There are many antique tombs near Jerusalem. We have already referred to those in the Valley of Jehoshaphat and in and about the Potter's Field, and other places ; we shall now briefly refer to a few others of the vast number that nearly surround the city. Jerusalem is really environed with tombs ; they are to be seen on every hill and in the valley around it, so that it is computed that there are more tombs about the city than there are houses in it for the living. On Mount Zion is the resting place of King David and his successor, Solomon, and several others ; also, some of the members of their families. The tomb, generally believed to be David's, is outside the walls on the southern slope of Mount Zion. It has been the united opinion of Jews, Christians and Moslems, for nearly seven hundred years, that this is none other than the burial place of King David, and a number of his successors. The Jews manifest their special regard for the tomb ; when they approach it, they present a sad and reverential expression of countenance, indicative of their superior love and esteem for their ancient dead. Josephus says, the tomb was opened by Hrycanus, from which he took three thousand talents ; and that Herod the Great also attempted to plunder the tomb, but found, to his discomfiture, it had been previously opened and spoiled of its treasure. It is a solemnly strange-looking place, and all who visit its curiously arranged interior, naturally feel an unusual impression of graveness, that restrains them from indulgence in mirth. There have been attempts made by some investigators to locate the tomb of David, and those buried with him, at another place than the "City of David," now known as Mount Zion, but they have failed. This site has not only a long-standing tradition, and the united opinion of the Jews, Christians and Moslems in its favor, but the Bible also locates the area, at least, in which it is. It is expressly stated in First Kings concerning some of the successors of David to the throne of Judah, "They slept with their fathers, and were buried in the city of David." Now, what plausible reason can any one give why the locality known to the ancients, to the Apostles and others, should be changed to some other place in the latter times? Surely no mischievous resurrectionist has gone there in the death-stillness of the midnight and removed those dusty remains to one of the adjacent hills, in order that they might baffle all attempts to identify it. Men should learn the fact, that greatness does not come to us by tearing down one man's work to build up another, but greatness is brought to us by an earnest endeavor to establish the truth. It is hoped an opportunity will be given, in the near future, to make all the needed investigations, which will be the means of ending the many unpleasant disputes concerning the locality of many places now in doubt. But the Holy Scriptures must have precedence, and in them we are told in unmistakable words that kings David, Solomon, and their successors, were laid to rest on Mount Zion; and there can be but little doubt as to the place above named being identical with the tombs of the kings of Judah. The current opinion in Jerusalem among the Jews and Mohammedans is, that this building, with a few others, escaped interference when Titus pillaged and sacked the city; and they, say the earliest travelers there, found it identical with the "Last Supper." We would be understood that no attempt is made by the author to condemn the tradition as to the site,—it may be that upon which the house stood where our Lord took the passover with His disciples; but we are strongly inclined to doubt that the present building is the same that stood there in the time of that immortal event.

We entered and passed through this building, and were deeply impressed with its history; thinking that, if beneath the cenotaph in these rocky excavations the remains of Kings David, Solomon, and others were laid to rest, and if their dust has remained undisturbed until this day, how royal is the place upon which my feet stand. and my eyes are beholding! Although the illustrious dead, whom tradition informs us sleep in this stupendous Sepulchre, were but mortal, filled with all the defects of humanity, yet one feels like stepping lightly while passing through the building dedicated to the memory of some of the most illustrious kings of Judah, who, like the humble of the Potter's field, and the poor outcasts around the city, upon the hills and in the valleys, whose graves and names are not known, are awaiting the voice of the archangel's trump to call them forth. Then we passed into the adjoining room, where it is said the "passover" was celebrated by our Lord and His disciples, and is also said to be connected with the event of the "Day of Pentecost," when the Holy Spirit came powerfully upon the messengers of Jesus. The Cœnaculum is connected with the tomb, both sites being enclosed by the same building; the latter is on account of the use made of it. The "Mosque of Neby Da'ud" also stands on the southern slope of Mt. Zion, and has a very presentable minaret. There is an ancient-looking room on the left of the high steps, known traditionally, as the identical chamber in which our Lord ate the passover with His disciples, on the night He exposed the secret intention of Judas Iscariot. This place has provoked much discussion; and we think not without proper reasons, for it would seem doubtful that this old building should be left undemolished on the brow of Zion through the many bitter struggles this historic hill has passed. It does not seem probable, that after the great slaughters and demolitions, caused by the many foreign powers in whose hands it fell from time to time, that this building would be left as a souvenir of antiquity. The traditions identifying this place with the scene of the "Last Supper" originated in the fourth century; it was then brought into prominent mention by Cyril, Bishop of Jerusalem. Under the upper chamber is a crypt or lower room; this is divided into two apartments, one of these is said to be the room in which our Lord washed His diciples' feet. This custom is still continued by the Monks of the Latin Church, who wash the feet of pilgrims, Mondays and Thursdays, in commemoration of the example of Jesus. The chamber is forty-five feet long, and twenty-nine feet wide, having two aisles divided by columns. Over the western pillar of this department is seen the cenotaph; over the one below this is said to be the tomb of David.

OTHER TOMBS.

The tombs compassing the city round about are only known as such; for the most part, those of the most illustrious dead, with few exceptions, are unidentified. Several that have been settled upon by a few investigators are strongly doubted by others. Those that have been generally settled upon as correctly identified are the tombs of St. James and Zacharias. That known as Jehoshaphat, now nearly covered with rubbish, the result of many years' accumulation, is not properly identified. This tomb is a little to the northeast of Absalom's Shaft, and from what has been agreed upon by repeated investigations, the first chamber must have been used in former times as a Christian church, a custom very common in crusade times. Those devotees of the Christian religion made it a regular practice to convert tombs, castles and heathen temples into churches. Many of them bear strong indications of their religious services. About the middle of this century an odd old manuscript roll was found in the so-called tomb of Jehoshaphat, containing the Pentateuch. It was discovered by one of the members of the Armenian Church. This caused much excitement among many of the Jews, for they concluded that the tomb was that of one of the rabbis instead of Jehoshaphat—and have from that day to this sternly protested against any one entering its interior—which may be true, for the Bible says Jehoshaphat was buried on Mt. Zion. The tombs of St. James and Zacharias are a little to the south of the two last mentioned. As to the identity of these tombs there seems to be but little doubt, even with those who have been critically doubtful as to the true site of many places in Palestine, that others have settled upon without a scruple. The tomb of St. James is opposite the Mosque of Omar, or the Temple plateau, at an angle, where, it is said, the apostle was thrown headlong into the Kedron valley below, and was killed. The best place to see the great depth of his fall is in the area opposite the tomb. Here, it is thought, the wickedly insane mob hurled the man of God into the jaws of death. The tomb of Zacharias is not really settled as to which of the two it belongs. The Jews claim it is that of Zachariah, son of Jehoiada, who was stoned in the reign of Joash, and the Christians maintain it is the tomb of Zacharias, the son of Barachias, who was slain between the sanctuary and the altar. The opinions of these two religious sects being so materially divided, leave the identity of these tombs in a state of uncertainty, but it is the general opinion among Christians that they are correctly located. Over on the west side of the Mount of Olives are the traditional tombs of the prophets, and are different in style from any others seen about the hills and valleys in the vicinity of Jerusalem. It is the opinion of some, who have made examinations there, they are natural caves, artificially extended and so arranged for tombs, but not wholly finished. To descend, one must pass through a low ledge into a round chamber, in which are remnants of Greek and Hebrew inscriptions. These impress many that the tombs are of Jewish origin. But, since they have stopped burying there, these chambers have been used by Christians, most likely by the crusaders, as they commonly made use of ancient tombs to hold religious meetings in, and for other sacred purposes. One of the strongest indications of their having been used by Christians is the emblem of the cross over some of the niches on the walls; and as the cross is a sign of faith in Christ, it is evident they were cut into the walls subsequent to the period the Jews had them in charge, by those whose faith was fixed in Jesus Christ. It is, however, doubted by many who have carefully examined these tombs, that they are those of the prophets. There is another ancient burial place north of Jerusalem, about a mile, and close to the old rugged and difficult road leading to Mizpeh; in this ancient rock-hewn cemetery are many sepulchres, all of which bear prominent marks of antiquity. They are called "Tombs of the Judges" by Christians, but the Jews say they are those of the members of the Sanhedrim.

There is much confidence placed in the knowledge the Jews have of the correct location of the places in which they are interested in and about Jerusalem, inasmuch as their knowledge of them is likely to be more extensive and reliable in cases where tradition is the only source of information. These tombs are situated in a very rocky district, and it is necessary to exercise great caution in traveling over the road; for if the horse or donkey should fall, the rider would doubtless sustain fatal injuries. Those who intend entering the tombs must take candles and matches, as it is very dark in them, and many are from two to three stories deep, in each of which there are niches hewn out for burial purposes. There are dangerous excavations or under-chambers into which persons would fall, unless they could see their way from one apartment to another. There are in all, over seventy of these receptacles for the dead, in this lonely, rocky district. The entrance to these tombs faces the west, with an open vestibule about thirteen feet by nine, and a door opening into the main chamber is cut through the back of this passage. The interior is arranged as follows, which is a true description drawn from careful investigations: The main chamber is twenty feet long, nineteen feet wide, and eight feet high. In the middle of the southern wall of this room is a door by which entrance is gained into another room eight feet square; in the eastern wall of the main chamber is another door, opening into a small room, dark and lonely. Then, to the northeast of the largest chamber, is a stairway leading down into two vaults. It is only necessary to enter one of the many tombs in this locality, as we were informed that the interior arrangements were the same in each. But the most marvelous of these tombs, in the vicinity of Jerusalem, are what are commonly known as the "Tombs of the Kings." The Arabs call them Kabur es-Salatan, "The Tombs of the Sultans." Late investigators have changed the opinion of many with regard to them, and it is now believed, that they are the resting place of Helena, queen of Adiabene. There is a broad flight of well-worn steps leading down to two very large cisterns, which are hewn out in the rock; then a door opens into a large court, also rock-hewn, at the mouth of which is a rock-hewn passage leading to the tombs. At the door of the tombs was a mammoth stone, which is rolled aside. The opening is very small, and an adult must kneel and crawl through. The interior is spacious, containing many chambers, one above the other, and from two to three stories deep.

THE FUTURE OF THE JEWS.

The overwhelming power of Rome did not only conquer the Jews, sack their city, carry away the Temple furnishings, and lead thousands into captivity, but dispersed the people, broke up the nation, and banished even the remnant from their land, and issued edicts expressly forbidding them to return to their own country, especially to Jerusalem. Therefore the Jews, a people for a time happy and prosperous, as if nursed with the milk of divine love, and protected by an all-powerful hand, became scattered among nations and tribes throughout the world; wandering like sheep having no shepherd. Their own hands threw to the ground the sceptre of power (it may be said), and their feet trampled it into the dust. But the hand that so triumphantly led them from bondage and sorrows, is now turned against this wonderfully strange people. It was their own hand that destroyed them, and it is their hand that keeps their land subordinate to foreign powers. But they have a hopeful future; the time is coming when they will fully accept Christ, whom their fathers nailed to the cross, and reverently come before Him in devout worship, return to their own land, and pay Him their tribute on the very summit where the pathetic prayer was offered by the Lord Jesus, in their behalf, while the arrows of death were piercing His soul, "Father, forgive them, they know not what they do." They will return home from Syria and Turkey, from Poland and Russia, from Germany and Holland, from China and Japan, from Australia and America, and from all the countries of Europe, from Africa and the ends of the earth. Then will the poor weeping Jews, who stand along the wall of the Haram every Friday afternoon, mourning the loss of the pride of their love, turn their wailings into shouts of praise to the God of their fathers, whose Son, they had so greatly rejected, made it possible for them to return and sing His praise and taste His love on the "Holy Hill of Zion." The Jews seem to be preserved by an extraordinary providence, such as allows them to mingle with the whole world and maintain their distinct racial representation almost completely; so that they are looked upon, in whatever land they may be dispersed, as separate and distinct from all others. There are cases of intermarriages among them, but are very few when compared with other races; they are scarcely noticeable. This special care the Jews take in preserving their descendants unmixed, is unlike the tendency of all other races of men. Observations show beyond all doubt, the tendency is, to unite in marriage with the people in whatever land man's lot is cast; that is when people migrate from their own country to another. They generally take to themselves a wife or husband from among the people with whom they have settled. This will be found to be true of all people, of all complexions, races and types. I do not believe there is a country in our world, where different races are permanently settled, that this rule does not obtain. Even in Africa, where Caucasians settle permanently, they make no hesitancy in choosing one of the native females for a life companion. But the Jews, wherever found, are clinging to each other in marriage relations, so that they may preserve themselves unmixed with other race-types. The law, forbidding their ancestors to intermarry, is still in full force. It seems as though the Jews are being preserved as a distinct people for their restoration, and the inheritance of their own land as a nation. If we have noticed the predictions concerning the future of this people, we cannot be otherwise than inclined to the opinion, that a restoration of the Jews will take place; and this seems to be the general belief throughout Christendom. Christians are looking forward to the time, which to them will be a glorious event, both to the Jews and Gentiles. The time is now nearing the horizon, when the blindness of the people shall pass away forever, and the true light shall shine upon them. It is written, "Blindness is happened to Israel in part until the fulness of the Gentiles be brought in; then all Israel shall be saved."

THE TOWER OF DAVID.

It is also inferable from the Holy Scriptures, that the conversion of the Jews is a matter in which the whole Christian world will be interested, and by which all people shall be blessed. There are visible manifestations even now of the fulfillment of this blessed event; for many Jews have turned from their Judaism and embraced Christ in this and other lands; and as has been stated there is now a flourishing church on Mt. Zion, in Jerusalem, that is doing much towards the conversion of the Jews to Christianity. Therefore, when the time fully comes for the return of this dispersed people, their relations will be harmonious; those who return from other lands, will have acknowledged Christ before starting home, and those whom they greet on their arrival, will not be strangers to Him; so that there will be a union of heads and hearts, and Jesus "will be all in all." What a glorious time, what a blessed period when the people, once dispersed and unsettled, shall again " sing the Lord's song" in their own land! Then will the returning hosts set up a standard on Mt. Zion, with the motto stamped thereon, "This God is our God forever and ever; and will be our guide even until death."

PART VII.

ANCIENT HEBRON.

The Highway of Hebron and its Loneliness—General Description of the Country—Condition of the Land of Hebron—Tombs at Beth-Zur—The Highway to Hebron—Sad Reflections—Beth-Zur—Pleasant Reflections—Antiquity of Hebron—Inhabitants of Hebron—Different Names given to Hebron—Roads Leading to Hebron—Vineyards of Hebron—Watchtowers and Watchmen—Historic Pools—The Event Concerning Rechab and Baanah—Places of Interest to Tourists—Inhabitants of Hebron—Description of Streets—The Situation of Hebron—Feeling of the Inhabitants to Visitors—Meaning of the Word Hebron—The Author's Experience Concerning His Visit—Description of Ramah—Oak of Mamre—Ancient Hebron—Accommodations for Christians—Facts Connected with Hebron—Patriarchial Associations—Hebron as a Burial Place—Historical Associations of Hebron—Joseph's Mournful Return—Historical Association—Jacob's Burial—The Mosque Machpelah—The Love of the Mohammedans for the Tomb—Treatment of Visitors who visit them—Description of the Mosque by the Prince of Wales—The Entrance to the Mosque—Description of the Shrine of Abraham and Sarah—Shrines of Jacob and Leah—Shrine of Joseph—Description of the Shrine of Joseph—Historical Association of Hebron—Value of the Investigation made by the Prince of Wales—Desirable Situation and General Condition of the Land of Canaan—Ancient Inhabitants of Hebron—A great Refuge City—The Custom of Blood Revenge—Cities of Refuge in which there were Judges—Names of Cities—Hebron the first Capital during David's Reign—Installation of David as King—Hebron as Headquarters of a Latin Bishopric—Possessed by the Moslems—Jews' connection with Hebron—Treatment of the Author by Inhabitants—The Dominant Inhabitants of Hebron.

THE HIGHWAY TO HEBRON AND ITS LONELINESS.

THE road from Solomon's pools to Hebron is in splendid condition, and is regarded as the best and most carefully kept road in Palestine.

Those who have been traveling over those very rough and fatiguing passes in different parts of the country, almost imagine themselves in a country where the blessings of higher civilization and progress are enjoyed; for no one but those who have had the experience, can imagine how rough and difficult the roads are throughout the land, with a very few exceptions. There is but little of interest to be seen on the way to Hebron, except a few ancient ruins. These would no doubt be of much importance if they could be positively identified; but all that was known of them is buried in the silent past. The whole face of the country for miles around is wild, barren, and very rocky; so that one must travel for about three weary hours without seeing anything of importance to attract attention, unless, perchance, something should occur worthy of note among the shepherds and merchants who are daily on the road, with flocks and caravans. It so happens, at times, that amusing incidents occur among them, which relieve travelers of the quiet and loneliness of their journey.

The vast tract of country on either side of the highway, which, from its present appearance, would impress one that it has always been barren and worthless, produced abundantly in those early times, when the children of Israel occupied the country. But now, those fields in which sounded the busy hoe, the plow, and other implements of husbandry, nothing is seen but desolation, except here and there a small patch of vegetation is under cultivation. A few weather-beaten, shaggy oaks are standing, to indicate the possibilities of the country if proper care were taken of it. When the children of Israel received their apportionments this tract composed a part of the allotment of Judah; it was under good cultivation and highly productive, but in latter times nearly the whole region was untilled, and is naught but a dreary wilderness. As Hebron is approached more signs of life become prominent, a few dwellings stand along the way, and much of the land is under cultivation, with vineyards and fig orchards and other salable products; the ever-alert husbandman may be seen from early morn until nightfall toiling hopefully. There are several rock-cut tombs exposed to view along the roadside, especially at Beth-Zur. It is without doubt a sad reflection to a Christian, traveling along this frequented road, so prominent in the long gone-by days, because of its important events, to be compelled to pass them without having the least inkling of the places around which they centre. It is to be hoped the near future will bring to light many places and things that are at present obscure, or in great doubt. But it is a gratification to know, as we pass along the highway towards the city and home of the "Father of the Faithful," several places are seen that have been generally settled upon as identical with the names they bear. These are Beth-Zur-Maarath, Halhul and Ramah. It is noteworthy that Beth-Zur was at one time an important place, and one of the towns of Judah in the time of the allotments to the tribes; its inhabitants came up to Jerusalem to assist Nehemiah to rebuild the walls, and it became one of the frontier towns in the time of the Maccabees. (Neh. iii. 16; Josh. xv. 58.)

PLEASANT REFLECTONS.

But notwithstanding the journey from Jerusalem to Hebron is through a wild and monotonous district, where savage-looking Arabs, with their sheep, goats, camels and donkeys are almost constantly traveling, yet it is cheering to know we are en route to one of the sacred cities of Palestine, and one of the most ancient and historical cities known to the world. It is also a source of great pleasure to know we are traveling the same route over which many patriarchs, priests and Levites used to pass to and from Hebron on official business, and thousands of the most pious Israelites pressed the soil on their way to the Temple to celebrate the annual passover. This is the route Abraham traveled when on his sacred mission, in obedience to the command of the Lord to sacrifice Isaac, his beloved son, on Mt. Moriah; and when King David, the victorious warrior, sent his brave army against the Jebusites, who occupied the stronghold on Mt. Jebus, they came this same way. It is also the same route little Joseph took when in compliance with his father's request, he went to see how his brethren fared at Dothan; and when the multitudes of rejoicing Israelites had won the victory over the Jebusites they passed up this way, shouting praises to the king, whose conquering arm had won the day. It is also believed that Joseph, when he, in obedience to the command of the angel, took the infant Jesus and His mother into Egypt to escape the vengeance of King Herod, came down this route. So that not Hebron only, but almost every foot of the ground from Bethlehem to Hebron, is sacredly memorable to the Bible student and to Christendom.

HEBRON—ITS ANTIQUITY.

Hebron is the oldest city in Palestine, and is considered to be one of the oldest in the world, and is held in great esteem by the Moslems, its principal inhabitants, because of its antiquity and voluminous history. It has a large population, many of whom are in a flourishing condition. Damascus and Shechem are the only cities west of the Euphrates that are claiming an equal share in its reverence because of old age. The first name of Hebron was Kir-Jath-Arba, after Arba, the father of Anak, the giant. The Bible speaks of it as one of the earliest cities known in the world. Moses, the law-giver, spoke of it, when describing the route the spies took, when sent to survey the country, and said, "Hebron was built seven years before Zoan, in Egypt." Zoan or Tanis was the old capital city of Egypt, and situated on the eastern side of the Tanitic arm of the Nile. When Abraham settled in Hebron it was called Mamre; this name is supposed to have been given it from that of Mamre, the Amorite, who was a close, strong friend of Abraham. It was a walled city at that time, for we are informed that when Abraham went up to the city, to buy the field of Machpelah, it was in the presence of the children of Heth, "even of all that went in at the gate of the city." The reference to a "gate" is indicative of a "wall." When Josephus wrote concerning the city it was twenty-three hundred years old. It may be seen from these facts, in connection with the Bible references given below, that the claims of antiquity attaching to Hebron are not without strong evidence in its favor. Those who travel from Egypt to Jerusalem, through the desert, commonly pass through Hebron if they travel by either of the three principal routes. Should they prefer the short desert road, they generally cross over to Hebron from Gaza; if they come by the old Sinai thoroughfare, they naturally come to the old city from Beersheba, on the southwest, or from the rocky city of Petra, on the southeast. (Gen. xxiii. 10; Joshua, xv. 13–14: xx. 1–11; Num. xiii. 22; Gen. xxx. 11–19; xl. 27.)

HEBRON AND ITS SITUATION.

This ancient city is built upon a mountain slope running up from the Valley of Eshcol. There are a few buildings in the valley, but the most of them are situated upon the hillside towards the summit. Those approaching Hebron from Jerusalem, do not get an observation of it until they ascend to the top of the high hill over which the main road passes, at a point not more than two hundred yards from the site of the old entrance gate. There are an almost endless number of vineyards in the valley, which is now, as in olden times, celebrated for its fine quality, and great quantity of grapes. In each of these vineyards the old-fashioned wine-press is seen, at which several men and lads are busy, in the season, making wine. The number employed at wine-making is usually regulated according to the size of the press. There is also a watch-tower connected with them, in which watchmen are placed to look after the safety of the vineyards; this is a custom that was instituted in the prime days of the Israelites, and is as necessary now as in their times. The city is not protected by walls as in former days, although it has one or two needless gates and all persons entering the city from the north pass through the gate, which is a mere sham. There are two pools in the valley of very ancient date, encompassed by walls composed of massive stones. These pools still furnish the water supply of the city. It is currently believed, that one of these is that at which the event narrated concerning Rechab and Baanah, sons of Rimmon (an officer in the army of Ish-bosheth) took place. These young men, in attempting to exalt themselves in the estimation of David (who had been only a short while installed king), did a work that brought a most severe penalty upon them. Ish-bosheth, the son of Saul, was an indefatigable rival for the sceptre of the kingdom, after the death of his father, and having a large following sent up an army against David, but was ingloriously defeated; then Rechab and Baanah slew Ish-bosheth, and brought his head to Hebron, supposing the young king would highly commend them, and appoint them to some very honorable and exalted position. But when the matter was made known to David, he said to them, "As the Lord liveth, who hath redeemed my soul out of all adversity, when one told me saying Saul is dead, thinking to have brought good tidings, I took hold of him and slew him in Ziklag, which was the reward I gave him for his tidings. How much more when wicked men have slain a righteous person, in his own house, upon his bed, shall I not require his blood at your hand, and take you away from the earth?" Then David caused his young men to slay them and cut off their hands and feet and hang them up beside the pool in Hebron. Thus ended the existence of two young men who were guilty of double dealing. They were captains in the army of Ish-bosheth, pretending to be at war against David and the tribe of Judah, whose loyalty to him held the original kingdom intact, and at the same time sought a favorable opportunity to assassinate the man for whom they expressed willingness to sacrifice their lives. The coming of these captains to the palace at that hour created no suspicion, for the reason it was in accordance with a long standing custom, which is still observed in the East. Their business there was supposed to have been, to get wheat for the soldiers, to distribute among them, that it might be sent to the mill at the usual hour next morning; having a knowledge of the time Ish-bosheth would be taking his accustomed nap, they made it opportune to murder him. They took his head to David, the rightful king, and the man whom the murdered usurper had been endeavoring to destroy. But he could not commend their bloody deed; it was too dastardly for a man of honor to recognize; and that a lesson might be taught others, who might be inclined to follow their footsteps, he made an example of them (2 Sam. ii. 8-11, and iv. 2, 5, 6). There is a general agreement among the best authors of the land, that one of these two ancient pools in Hebron is identical with the scene of the execution of Baanah and Rechab, the sons of Rimmon, the Beerothite, of the tribe of Benjamin.

One of the most important places to which sight-seers are taken, aside from the Mosque which marks the site of the resting-place of Abraham and his family, is the pool where the punishment of these two men's crimes was meted out to them.

FACTS OF INTEREST TO TOURISTS.

The population of Hebron is estimated to be about fifteen thousand five hundred; of whom one thousand are Jews, and fourteen thousand five hundred are Molems, of the iron-clad type, who seem to care for no one but themselves. There are few strangers who care to remain there longer than to visit the ancient sites, as the accommodations both indoors and out are extremely poor. The streets are very dark generally, and especially so in cloudy weather. Many of them are arched almost from one end to the other; therefore, it is necessary, many times, to illuminate them from the early morning through the entire day. Several streets are above the others, which makes it necessary to tunnel those below, hence the darkness. The city is nearly a mile long, and extends across the valley on the south side, and occupies a considerable portion of the western slope also. All the houses are substantially built of stone, which abounds in that region, as in the most of Palestine. It is indispensable for all Christian travelers to Hebron to employ a native guide before venturing to enter the city; and he who ignores this admonition does it at his own peril, for he is exposed to insults and even violence. The Mohammedans take delight, we are informed, in imposing upon Christians, and will do so when they can trump up the most frivolous pretext. They proudly boast of the fact that no European has ever been permitted to build a house in their ancient city. It is the current belief that such a step would not be allowed; and if they could not keep a Christian out by threats, they would kill him. The reputation of the inhabitants does not by any means accord with the name of their city, which is highly significant. Hebron means "Friend." It may apply to the friendship they entertain for each other, but their feeling towards strangers, especially Europeans, is most bitter, as a rule. Having been informed of the hostile attitude of the people toward strangers, I felt very dubious about making the visit, fearing they might do me an injury. But to be so close to one of the oldest and most historic towns in the world, and not see it, although the opportunity was favorable, was more than I could consent to. I therefore became willing to attempt the journey with the disadvantages and risks confronting me. To see the old city in which Abraham, "the father of the faithful," dwelt, which many years after was the home of Jacob and his family, was an incentive so overpowering, the peril was almost lost sight of entirely, until we had come near the northern gate of the city. The morning we started from Jerusalem for Hebron, was very unfavorable; it was cold, rainy, and otherwise disagreeable. But the guide had hired a close carriage for us, to which were hitched three good traveling horses, which the driver urged almost every foot of the way, that the trip might be made in five hours and a half. The most of the way going is up-hill. Hebron is five hundred feet above Jerusalem; its altitude is estimated to be the highest of any city in Palestine. Our party had a memorable experience that day, and I am sure neither of us will soon forget it. As we drew within a few miles of the city it became very much colder, and on several occasions we got into snow-drifts, which our team refused to pull through with the load. This compelled us to get out of the vehicle and push both carriage and horses, until we had gotten through the snow, or on good pulling ground; this we had to do repeatedly.

The highest point on the way to Hebron is Ramah, which is considered the most elevated place in Palestine, and south of the Upper Galilee. It is thirty-three hundred and forty-six feet above the level of the Mediterranean sea, and is commonly known as Abraham's Hill. On the east of the road, a short distance, is the traditional site of the Oak of Mamre, and the solitary tree that stands there bearing the marks of the devouring influence of time is called Abraham's Oak. It is supposed to be on, or near the spot, where the tree stood, under which Abraham sat many times to refresh himself in the cool of the day. Continuing on the public highway a few moments, the stranger's eyes behold ancient Hebron spread out before them in almost full view, which is entered, after descending the hill, from which the town is first seen. Those going from the north enter Hebron on its extreme northern side; but if the company have tents, they remain outside on the tenting-ground in the valley near by. But if no tents are taken, travelers usually stop at a small Jewish inn, where moderately-good accommodations are obtained.

ACCOMMODATIONS FOR CHRISTIANS.

Those going to Hebron should make up their minds to calmly yield to the discomforts common to all strangers, as there is but little preparation made for public comfort. I am confident there is no large town in Palestine, that has such meagre accommodations for strangers as ancient Hebron. The truth is, the natives don't want Europeans there, and they make nothing inviting to induce them to come. It is far the best to have a tent; they are much more comfortable, even in cold weather, than the best house furnished by the natives. The little inn kept by the Jews, has the poorest sleeping comforts, and it would be far more preferable to sit up all night, than to go to bed with the expectation of getting rest. But one who takes delight in the volumes of antique history that cluster about the town, will quietly submit to the situation because of the great and lasting benefits that will redound to him from the sacrifice of the few hours' comfort he has made. It is a most gratifying pleasure to any one who delights in the searching of Bible history, to be in the midst of a town associated with events prominent in the lives of holy men, from the early period of our world. As the visitor looks over the town, and round about the hills and valleys within the range of his observation, many events connected with the patriarchs, prophets and other men conspicuously mentioned in the Scriptures, are freshly presented to his mind with renewed and deep impressions. Then when the narratives concerning them are read at or near the place they occurred, the impressions become indelible, and the traveler feels at times as though he were transported to some distant world. The connections of Hebron with the Holy Scriptures are very numerous. If we should turn our attention down the line of nearly four thousand years, that have been launched into the deep of eternity, we will call up many stupendous occurrences, that were brought into prominence on these hills, famously renowned in sacred and secular history, which will pass like a beautiful panorama before our vision. In the first place we would see many things connected with the lives of Abraham, Sarah, Jacob, Leah and Joseph, whose lives seem to be written upon the everlasting rocks round about the ancient town, whose fame is known throughout the civilized world. Abraham, the oldest patriarch and "father of the faithful," spent nearly the whole of his life in the southern parts of Palestine, the most of which was associated with Hebron and its vicinity. It was at times called Mamre, and at other times known as Kirjath-Arba.

It was to this portion of the country he came, when he first journeyed in Canaan, and on his return from Egypt, whither he had fled from the distressing famine that was in the land. During the time he was with his nephew, he spent a short while at Bethel, but returned after the unpleasantness, that became so grievous, that a separation of his herdsmen and those of Lot was made necessary, for the promotion of peace and the maintenance of friendship. Lot then pitched his tent towards Sodom, and "Abraham moved his, and came and dwelt by the Oaks of Mamre, which are in Hebron, and built there an altar unto the Lord." It was his custom, when he moved to a place to settle for a time, to build an altar, and dedicate it to God. This act of the patriarch made the place memorable, from generation to generation, even to the present day. Several of those who made investigations of the districts in which Abraham built altars have attempted to locate them, and, although the exact sites cannot be positively identified, it is a great satisfaction to the thousands who visit Hebron, Bethel and Shechem to know they are at least near the spot, if not on it, where the venerable patriarch erected his altars, to consecrate the place to the Most High. Abraham, after he had separated from his nephew, Lot, lived long enough in Hebron to form the acquaintance and win the esteem of the officia's, and people who lived there, to form a confederation with them, and pursue Chedorlaomer and the kings who were with him, when they were taking Lot and his possessions in captivity. Aner, Eshcol and Mamre, joined in friendly alliance with Abraham, and went forth to rescue the captives with the patriarch, who had a small army of three hundred and eighteen trained men of his own, and pursued the captors of Lot as far as Dan, and on to Hobah, which is on the left hand of Damascus. There he recaptured Lot, and all his goods, and all his people, and returned in triumph to Hebron and sent his nephew to his home in Sodom. Here, by the Oaks of Mamre, the venerable patriarch sat in his tent door in the heat of the day, when the angels paid him a visit, while on their way to destroy Sodom, and, on hearing of the fearful pending calamity, pleaded for the preservation of the righteous, whom he supposed were there, and the whole city, for their sake. One, standing on this site of ancient renown, may imagine he can see Abraham, at the dawn of the following morning, standing on the summit of the high hill (called after his name), stretching his vision down into the valley of Siddim, steadfastly gazing at the smoke of the obliterated cities of the plain ascending heavenward, "like the smoke of a furnace." Then he knew full well the number of righteous persons, for whom he so earnestly and faithfully pleaded, were not found, and the cup of the people's transgressions having been filled to overflowing they were consumed. It is reasonable to suppose his mind fell upon his nephew, and wondered how he and those with him fared. Abraham made Mamre his permanent home. If he left there it was but for a short while, for he was sure to return to the place where the Lord came to him in human form, and told him not only of the pending wrath hanging over the cities of the plain of Siddim, but assured him that he should be blessed with a son in the advanced age of himself and wife, whose descendants should be as innumerable as the stars of the Heaven, or the sand grains upon the the sea-shore. It was at Hebron Abraham was living, when Sarah, his beloved wife, died; here he greatly lamented her loss to him; here he bought for the first time, a plat of ground, expressly for a burial-place, where he laid to rest Sarah, his wife. Himself, Isaac and Rebecca, his wife. Jacob and his first wife, Leah—all these ancient ashes are still quietly resting within the cave Machpelah, guarded day and night by the vigilant sons of Ishmael, with sleepless eyes and attentive ears,—even the approach to the sacred precincts of their illustrious dead. (Gen. xiv. 13-18; xviii. 1-16-32; xix. 27-28.)

There was an anxious wish existing among children of olden times to be buried with their fathers, and often they would die far from home; but, according to their request, surviving friends would have them buried where they desired to rest. Thus it was with Jacob, who died in Goshen, in Egypt, but was brought to Hebron to be buried with his father. Isaac spent most of his life away from the old homestead, but returned before his days were ended, and died, having a desire to be buried with his father in Machpelah. Jacob, who in early life, fled from the wrath of Esau, his brother, returned to Hebron (after many storms of affliction passed over him), and made it his permanent home. He was living there when his sons were attending the flocks in the pastures in Shechem, and Dothan; from Hebron, Joseph, his beloved son, was sent to look after their welfare, who, when drawing near the camp where they were, was filled with joy to know they were well. But the moment his brothers saw him, vengeance was plotted, and they cruelly treated him, bringing floods of sorrow to the heart of their aged father, who with anxious desire, looked for Joseph to return home with the tidings as to the welfare of his brethren; but the lad did not return to him, nor could he hear anything from him until the plot of deception, formulated by his elder sons, was made strong enough to look plausible in his eyes. Joseph did not come to Hebron until that mournful day, when he led the heart-stricken procession from Egypt, with the mortal remains of Jacob his father, whose dying request was, that his body should be buried with his father.

JOSEPH'S MOURNFUL RETURN.

Although the occasion was sad and would naturally absorb all other reflections, yet we doubt not, when Joseph drew near Hebron, and he looked upon the home of his childhood, and upon the hills on which he used to stand in the long gone-by days, refreshing himself in the cool of the day, under the boughs of the great oaks; and as he thought of the other incidents connected with his life while at home, such as the field, in which the sheaves of wheat stood, that he saw in his dream, and his dream of the sun, moon and eleven stars, that made obeisance to him, and then of the memorable day he journeyed from home to look after the welfare of his brethren; all these incidents like a flood rushed into his mind as he was approaching the margin of the scenes of his youth. It is presumable that during these reflections, he looked down the line of the past and saw himself a boy, seventeen years old, standing before his father telling his wonderful dreams that laid the foundation for the flame of unquenchable hatred his brethren kindled in their hearts against him. He saw himself at Shechem, and Dothan, and the execution of the malicious scheme, concocted by his brethren to put him where his dreams could never be verified; he saw all the affairs concocted with the event that caused his father to weep bitterly many long years, and which caused his return that day, to the home of his infancy. These streams of reflection must have filled his heart, which was already freighted with grief on account of the death of his fond father, to overflowing and caused the suppressed tears to flow copiously, and force him to give vent to the most pitiable lamentations ever heard by the inhabitants at Hebron. The long funeral procession that came from Goshen in Egypt, with the embalmed body of Jacob, to Hebron, was in compliance with the patriarch's dying request. When the sons of Jacob gathered around his bed, just a while before he died, to receive his last benediction, he asked them to lay him to rest with his fathers. "And he charged them, and said unto them, I am to be gathered unto my people; bury me with my fathers, in the cave that is in the field of Ephron, the Hittite, in the cave that is in the field of Machpelah, which is before Mamre, in the land of Canaan, which Abraham bought with the field of Ephron, the Hittite, for the possession of a burying-place. There they buried Abraham and Sarah, his wife, there they buried Isaac and Rebekah, his wife, and there I buried Leah." Therefore, in accordance with this most fervent and pathetic request of the father of the great Hebrew nation, Joseph and the other members of the family, in connection with a great train of sympathizing friends, proceeded mournfully from Goshen to Hebron, that the last dying favor Jacob asked, might be promptly and faithfully fulfilled. It was the unfailing custom of the Hebrews to carry out the wish of their dead, especially one who was the head of a family or one who had been in authority. It will be called to mind also, that in the event of the exit of the Israelites from Egypt, they gathered up the bones of Joseph, who had been long dead, and brought them to the "Land of Promise," and buried them near the well of Jacob in the vale of Shechem, because Joseph charged them concerning his bones when he was about to die, and the request was remembered and fulfilled.

THE MOSQUE MACHPELAH.

The ancient mosque, formerly known as the Cave of Machpelah, at Hebron, is called Abraham's Mosque. It is strictly guarded by the Mohammedans, in whose absolute charge it is, as well as the whole city. The great mosque is built over the entire space occupied by the cave, and closes it in from the gaze of the outside world. The Arabs are seen about this sacred resting-place of the immortal Abraham, and others of his family, by the hundreds from day to day, fully prepared for any emergency. Such is the love and veneration for his tomb, they are willing to lay down their existence, that it may be protected against the encroachments of those whom they regard as unbelievers. With the conscientiousness with which these sons of Ishmael protect the mosque, we do not believe it to be in the least degree beyond the bounds of propriety, nor the slightest digression from the truth to say, they are as vigilant, in guarding the tomb of their great ancestor, as were the Roman guards who were placed at the sepulchre of our Redeemer. Visitors are not permitted to advance farther than twenty-five or thirty feet along the wall leading up to the entrance gate to the mosque; and, notwithstanding Hebron is one of the four sacred cities of the Jews in Palestine, they are not permitted to enter within the walls of the enclosure, nor approach nearer to it than visitors from other lands, who are not of the Moslem sect. These poor, oppressed Jews content themselves with coming to their lawful limit, at a point in the exterior wall where a portion of the natural rock is seen. Here the devout Jews assemble to pray, and impress the ancient rock with a fervent kiss. There is no division of opinion as to the identity of the cave of Machpelah, the resting-place of Abraham. Jews, Christians, and Mohammedans are united in their unswerving faith as to the undoubted genuineness of the site. Until the year one thousand eight hundred and eighty-one, but little had been known with reference to the internal bearing and arrangements of the Haram. At that time the Prince of Wales secured permission to enter, and took with him a few friends. They also made good their only favorable opportunity, and took a careful and full measurement of its entire interior. They give the following account as the result of their investigation. It is only possible for us to give a part of their statement. "The outer walls enclose a quadrangle measuring one hundred and ninety-seven feet long, by one hundred and eleven feet wide, externally. There are twenty-eight buttresses, each twenty-five feet high, standing on a base wall. The masonry of the walls resembles the olden masonry of the Jerusalem Haram, and thus proves their Jewish origin. The average height of the courses is three feet seven inches long, and three feet eight and a half inches high; the thickness of the walls is the same as that at Jerusalem, namely, eight feet and a half, and the average height at the ancient wall is forty feet. On the top of this is a modern wall with battlements. plastered and white-washed. On the north, south, and east, the enclosure is surrounded by another of more modern masonry, forming passages with two flights of steps. The four corners of the Haram point nearly to the four quarters of the compass, so that the longer sides are southwest and northeast, and the shorter sides northwest and southeast respectively. The gates leading to the steps are situated at the west and south ends of the southwest side, and both lead up by passages to a doorway in the northeast side, which is the only opening into the interior of the Haram.

"The church occupies the southeast portion of the enclosure, three of its walls being formed by the ancient outer ramparts. It is divided into a nave and two aisles of almost equal width, and its length is again divided into three bays, measuring twenty-five, thirty and fifteen feet respectively. The total length of the church is seventy feet, the breadth ninety-three feet. There is a clear story with three windows on each side above the nave, and a low-pitched gable at the northwest end, having a large window, slightly arched above, which is a round window now outside the roof of the nave, which has a ridge lower than the top of the gable. The interior of the roof is slightly pointed with flat-ribbed grain. The aisle-rafts are nearly flat, and the whole are covered with lead. The naive is supported by four large piers with clustered columns, the capitals being adorned with thick leaves and mediæval volute. The church is now a Moslem Mosque, and in the centre of the southeast wall a mihrab, or prayer recess, has been carved out. It is flanked by slender pillars having rich gothic capitals, and by two wax torches. Above it is a window of stained glass, resembling those on the dome of the rock at Jerusalem, and dating from about fifteen hundred and twenty-eight. The mimbar, or pulpit, stands on the right of the mihrab and resembles that in the Mosque Aksa. It was constructed in the year ten hundred and ninety-one, and was given to the Mosque by Saladin, in eleven hundred and eighty-seven, after the capture of Askelon. The merhala, or reading-platform, is similar to that of other Mosques. In the east corner of the northeast aisle is a Greek inscription built into the wall, apparently of the time of

Justinian, containing an invocation to Abraham for a blessing on those who erected it.

"The entrances to the cave below are closed with stone flags, and are never opened. The caves could only be reached by breaking up the flooring of the Mosque, which would be regarded by the Moslems as an unpardonable act of sacrilege. The cave, however, is said to be double, as the word 'Machpelah,' signifies, and in the middle ages it was called 'Spelunca duplex,' in consequence. Two entrances are supposed to lead into the southwest cave, and one into the northeast. In these caves are said to be the graves of six Patriarchs—Abraham and Sarah, Isaac and Rebekah, Jacob and Leah.

"Over the supposed positions of these tombs are placed cenotaphs. The shrines of Abraham and Sarah, stand within two octagonal chapels in the porch, which is double; the vaulted, grained roof, resting on heavy piers, and, according to an inscription, was restored in seventeen hundred and fifty-five. The shrines are covered with green and white silk, embroidered with green Arabic texts in gold thread. The entrances are closed and opened by barred gates of iron, plated silver, of the date twelve hundred and fifty-nine. The walls are cased with marble, having Arabic inscriptions near the top. Silver lamps and ostrich shells are hung before the cenotaphs, which are each eight feet long, four feet broad, and eight feet high. Copies of the Koran on low wooden seats surround the cenotaphs. The shrines are lighted by stained glass windows. To the northwest of the porch, is an open court-yard, in which is a sun dial, and on the other side of the court are the buildings enclosing the shrines of Jacob and Leah. Behind them are two small chambers now used as lumber rooms.

"A long chamber is situated at the southwest end of the buildings, and a door leads from it through the ancient rampart wall to another chamber fifty feet long, by twenty feet broad, which apparently leads to the shrine of Joseph, which is reached through a vaulted gallery, in the corner of which is Adam's foot-print. This relic, brought from Mecca six hundred years ago, is a slab of stone with a sunken portion resembling the impression of a human foot. It is enclosed in a recess at the back of the shrine of Abraham. A small lead dome stands above the gallery close to this place. The shrine of Joseph consists of two chambers, one over the other, in each of which there is a cenotaph, as in the 'Tomb of David,' at Jerusalem. The whole is surmounted by an octagonal lantern, with a dome covered with lead. Each cenotaph is covered with green silk. The lower chamber is entered by a passage just within the west gate of the Haram. The shrine of Joseph is of Arabian workmanship, and is evidently much more modern than the other shrines in the Haram. The mosque has two minarets. The dates of the various portions of the Haram are probably as follows: The outer walls, or ramparts, are Herodian; the mosque or church is crusading, and was built between the years eleven hundred and sixty, and eleven hundred and eighty; the shrine of Joseph, the outer passages, door-ways and steps are Arabic, and date from the fourteenth century; the stained-glass windows belong to the sixteenth century; whilst certain restorations in the court-yard, and additional adornments of the shrines are of the eighteenth and nineteenth centuries. The pavement is comparatively modern ("Murray's hand-book of Palestine and Syria"). We are indebted to the Prince of Wales for the above description of the mosque surrounding the cave of Machpelah. Had it not been that he was permitted to visit and investigate its interior by a special dispensation, the outside world would have been ignorant until the present, and perhaps forever, of the arrangements of this most stupendous building, that closes the eye of man from the sight of a renowned rock, in the cavern of which, the mortal remains of the father of patriachs were rested, to await the awakening voice of the arch-angel's trump. This ancient tomb makes Hebron more sacredly remembered, because the grave of Abraham is there, than it was when the sire was actively engaged in the natural pursuits of life, in and about it. It is likely there will never be another visitor (who is not a Moslem), permitted to enter within the gates of the Haram enclosure again; especially while it is under the control of the Mohammedans. Therefore, all Christendom should appreciate the information we have concerning it, through the princely son of England.

There are many events of great interest to our world, which cluster in and about Hebron, that are detailed in various scripture narratives, and in the writings of ancient historians, that would compose a large volume. Concerning these things we shall be able to give only a passing account. The first evidence of the abundant products, the richness and desirable situation, and general condition of the "Land of Caanan," that stimulated the children of Israel to possess it, was the fruits brought to the camp by the spies, who had been sent out to obtain information as to its general condition. The men who continued their survey from the border land east of the Jordan, even into the valley of Eshcol, took back with them bunches of grapes, and reported, saying, "The land is good, and we are fully able to go up and possess it." Caleb and Joshua, who were the senior representatives of the tribe of

Judah, seem to have been so well pleased with Hebron that they requested to be allowed to make it their home, notwithstanding the Anakim giants lived there.

A GREAT REFUGE CITY.

After the children of Israel entered upon their several allotments throughout the land, Hebron was constituted one of the cities of refuge, and within its gates, many poor, fleeing Hebrews, found security from the wrath of the avenger. The law, demanding "an eye for an eye and a tooth for a tooth," was practically enforced in the early days of the Israelitish occupancy of Palestine, and that a person might have a chance for his life in cases of accidental injuries, six cities of refuge were established in different localities, and corresponding distances, known as Levitical cities. The custom of blood revenge was prominent among the Hebrews, and many times they would commit grave blunders, and frequently charge the wrong man with the crime for which they sought revenge. These visitations of revenge became so generally indulged in by the Israelites, even while they were yet in the wilderness, that they were common occurrences, and the practice would have grown more popular and tyrannical had not the Lord checked or modified the custom by ordering Moses to appoint cities of refuge, in which there should be judges to investigate the case (Deut. iv. 43; xix. 1-10; Josh. xiii. 26; xx. 8; Deut. xix. 7-9; Josh. xx. 2-3-8; 1 Kings xxii. 29) of each person who fled to them from the wrath of his pursuer, whether he should be a Hebrew or a stranger. And if the crime be one for which the refugee should atone, the avenger had the liberty to slay him; but if after due examination, it should be found the killing was not an act stimulated by deliberation and intent, he was set free. At first there were six of these cites, three on the east side of the Jordan, as follows: Galon, in the territory of the tribe of Manasseh, on the northwestern border of the kingdom of Bashan; another was Ramoth Gilead, or Ramoth Mizpet, in the confines of the tribe of Gad; and the third was Bezer, situated within the territory of Reuben. The three on the west of the Jordan were Kedesh of Naphtali, in northern Palestine, Shechem in the territory of Ephraim. Hebron became the city of next importance for all the people living in southern Palestine, not only because of its physical attractions, but it was the great haven of security for many whose lives were unjustly sought by the avenger of blood. Travelers who go over to Hebron by the different ancient highways may think of the flight of many, who, in the early days of the children of Israel, sped their way over the same road in pursuit of a safe retreat, while the sun was pouring out its melting heat upon them, yet they persevered to the end.

HEBRON—THE FIRST CAPITAL OF DAVID.

Hebron was the capital of the loyal portion of Israel during the first seven and a half years of David's reign, and it was from there his army was sent forth, under the command of Joab, to war with Ish-bosheth, the son of King Saul. And to Hebron, the remains of Abner were taken, after being cruelly slain, and honorably buried by David, who piteously mourned his death. It was also the scene of great jubilation on the memorable day, when David was installed king over the whole nation. The chief men of all the tribes, east and west of the Jordan, came in teaming multitudes to Hebron, with many precious fruits of the land, such as "bread and meat, meal, cakes of figs, and bunches of raisins, and wine, oil, oxen and sheep abundantly." They came on "donkeys, camels, mules and oxen." The rejoicing multitude made the hills and valleys echo with their shouts of high praises to their new king.

When the Jews returned from their captivity at Babylon, and rebuilt Jerusalem, they also renewed the waste places of Hebron. But it was not permanently held by them. The Edomites, who were deadly enemies to the Jews, captured the ancient city and controlled it until Judas Maccabæus rescued it from them. It fell into the hands of the crusaders, and was made the headquarters of a Latin bishopric, in the year eleven hundred and sixty-seven, and remained, partially under their control, for nearly two hundred years, but the formidable Moslems finally gained possession of it, and have the absolute control of it until the present. But alas, Hebron, the ancient city, in and around which cluster so many important events connected with the history of the world, the city whose fame is immortalized because of the distinction given it by Abraham, the father of the faithful, has greatly fallen from the glory with which it was crowned, in the years those ancient hills echoed songs of praise to the Lord of Hosts, chanted by the patriarchs, Abraham, Isaac and Jacob. The many events, recorded of old, concerning Hebron are still fresh in the memory of Christendom, and will lose none of their influence to the end of the world, so that, from one generation to another, the historian, the tourist, the Jew and Mohammedan will fondly turn their attention to Hebron, and seek to know something of the early greatness of the once happy home of the early fathers, from which evolved much of the primitive history of the religious world. The descendants of those whose prominence and piety so greatly distinguished the city, have lost their control of it, and are now subordinate to the sons of Hagar, who, with relentless ostracism, refuse them permission to look upon the site in which are deposited the dusty remains of their illustrious ancestor. These self-destroyed people, who, in the morning of their glory, boasted in the fact that Abraham was their father, may be seen every day standing by the wall enclosing the rocky chamber, of which his sepulchre is composed, and drop a tear, impress a kiss, and then mournfully return to their homes, having no real prospect of ever being permitted to gaze upon the sacred tomb, or even enter the gates of the Haram leading to it. They prayerfully wait for the time, when those who oppose and cause many sorrows to depress them, will be compelled to surrender the Machpelah cave to them without a struggle, and yet they have not learned to trust in Him whose arm alone can help them. I feel it to be my duty to mention a word or two as to the treatment I received from the people of Hebron, while in their ancient city. It will be remembered, I stated elsewhere, how hostile the Arabs are said to be to European visitors and Christians generally, who go there sight-seeing, and how dubious I felt about making the trip, when we started from Jerusalem under very unfavorable circumstances. But, to my great surprise and gratification, the people who have been known to impose upon and even injure those who have visited there, treated me with the utmost kindness. Their expressions to me seemed to be full of the most cordial welcome and good will. I am of the opinion these poor Ishmaelites have been often driven to take harsh measures, with many strangers who have come among them, because many advantages are taken of them in various ways.

It is many times the case, that those who visit Palestine have first made a tour through India or Egypt, where the natives allow all kinds of impositions; and these same people, who have been masters of the situation in those countries mentioned, many times attempt the same kind of bossism in Hebron; but the people will not allow it. This often brings about trouble, and the inoffensive and offensive are served alike. These people are ever ready to stand in their own defence, and when there is the least indication of imposition, they are ready to resent it severely. It is also true, no doubt, that many of them, because they hate strangers of Christian bearing, who come among them, will seek a chance to misuse them, and upon the least provocation will assault them. When they see a white man coming into their town, he is at once looked upon as an enemy; therefore, they want nothing to do with him, and feel relieved of a burden when he leaves their borders.

I can say of them gladly, their treatment of me, as far as I observed, was as good as any one could hope for, from a superstitious people whose "hand is against every man." Indeed I fared as well in Hebron as in any place in Palestine, so far as being kindly treated is concerned. I was somewhat of a novelty to them, not because of my complexion, for they are nearly all colored, as is common to their race; but because I was dressed in what is known as European style of dress, and looked so different from them, whose scanty habits are such as are commonly worn by the Orientals. When they saw me, they looked as if struck with profound astonishment, and seemed to express the wonder, if I had once been a Mohammedan and turned from their faith to embrace the Christian religion. But as I could not speak Arabic and they could not speak English, we were shut off from immediate intercourse, and the only thing we did was to bow and smile at each other. I was the only one in our company they seemed to express a desire to have any communication with. Nevertheless, I was glad when the time allotted for our stay was spent, and our faces were again turned toward Jerusalem. There is no necessity to remain in Hebron more than two or three hours, as all that is to be seen of interest to travelers may be visited in that time. It is to be regretted, that of the fifteen thousand inhabitants of the town, not one of these has embraced Christianity, and we are persuaded it is next to an impossibility, for a Christian to live there while it is under Moslem rule. The one thousand Jews who are there, we understand, are not accorded the freedom the Arabs have, and are but a small consideration in the estimation of the dominant race.

VIEW OF BETHLEHEM.

PART VIII.

FROM JERUSALEM TO BETHLEHEM.

Places of Interest Along the Road—Valley of Giants—Well of the Wise Men—Tomb of Rachel—Well of David—Church of the "Holy Nativity"—Ancient Inns—Description of the Holy Nativity—Altar of the Magi—Joseph and Mary Journeying from Nazareth—The Advent of Jesus—Solomon's Porch—Solomon's Gardens and Orchards—Mar Saba—Site of the Convent—Places of Interest from Bethlehem to Jericho—The Well Bir Essuk—Character of the Beduoins—Wilderness of Judea—Wilderness of Engedi—Dead Sea—Mountains of Sodom—Cities of Sodom and Gomorrah—The Vale of Siddim—Location of Zoar—Earthquakes as a Work of Destruction—The Amorites—The Hot Springs—Judah and Israel Combined Against Moab—The Valley of the Jordan—Plain of Jericho—City of Palm Trees—The Jordan River—The Faithfulness of the People of Palestine for their Church Services—Nebo and Pisgah—The View of Moses—Joshua Camped at Gilgal—The Three Jerichoes—Spring of Elisha—The Second Jericho—The Brook Cherith—The Highway to Jericho—Mount of Temptation.

BETHLEHEM, House of Bread, now called by the natives Beit Lahm, is about five miles and a half from Jerusalem, a little to the southwest, and eighteen miles from ancient Hebron. The road is in splendid condition and speed can be kept up, after the Valley of Hinnom is crossed, as far as Rachel's Tomb, which is a pleasure greatly admired by travelers in that country, because it so seldom happens that good roads are made. Starting from the Joppa gate for Bethlehem, or Hebron, or any of the country on the south and southwest of Jerusalem, the descent into the valley is so very abrupt, that it is necessary to ride very slowly and cautiously, for if the animal should fall the result might be fatal to the rider. This highway is not only made lively by the multitudes who are continually going and coming, but the visitor is kept busy looking at the many places that make up much of the history of Palestine; prominent among them are as follows: The Plain of Rephaim, also known as the Valley of the Giants, which is mentioned in connection with the Philistines, who spread themselves here when they sought David and were defeated. It is a broad plain, and was in olden times very rich and productive, and extends several miles. The Germans have a colony settled in one portion of it, not far from the main road leading to the south, and are doing well. It will be largely occupied by Europeans no doubt in the near future, as those who have settled in the "plain" are meeting with great prosperity. The next place of interest is the "Well of the Wise Men," situated on the roadside. Here, tradition says, "Those men, who were guided by a star from their eastern home to Jerusalem, stopped after being sent by Herod to search for Jesus. The star having disappeared during their conference with the king, they came down and stood by this ancient well, and looking down saw their guiding star reflecting in the water, and they starting anew on their journey, came to the place where the Saviour was born. The renowned well is on the right of the road, near the convent of Mar-Elias of the Greek Church.

RACHEL'S TOMB.

The next place of special historical importance is the "Tomb of Rachel." The present building standing over the tomb is not ancient; it may be that a portion of its foundation is, but the structure is comparatively modern. The genuineness of the tomb, as being identical with the burial-place of Rachel, is generally conceded by the most stubborn critics, who have examined into the legality of the claims of those who identified it. It is a small building with a dome or oval top, very much the shape of an old-fashioned bake oven. The tomb is reverenced by Jews, Christians, and Moslems alike, all of whom look upon it as a place of sacred memory. The following we copy for the enlightenment of those who may be in search of more information as to the tomb: "The original building was opened with four arcades supporting the dome. The arcades, however, have been filled up except at the east, where a second chamber has been added. The square building measures twenty-three feet each side, the arches having a span of ten feet. The height of the walls is twenty feet, and the dome is ten feet higher. The east chamber is twenty-three feet long by thirteen feet wide. A covered court with a window, and Mihrab (praying niche) on the south, and a double window on the east, and measuring twenty-three feet square, is situated at the east end; it is used as a praying place by the Moslems. The inner chambers are locked and the key kept by the Jews; here they pray every Friday. A modern cenotaph stands immediately under the dome." (Murray's Hand-Book.) The Jews have charge of this tomb, and they appreciate it most dearly, as there are but few historical places in Palestine they are permitted to control. Here they meet each Friday to pray.

The walls of the building are much defaced, caused by the pilgrims and other devotees, who cling to the tradition that the spirit of Rachel visits her tomb, and is active in granting the prayers of the faithful who implore her agency. There are many who have but one opportunity in this life to visit this ancient resting-place of Jacob's second wife, and believing she is busily engaged in answering petitions, they, therefore, scribble their prayers on the wall indulging the hope she may see them. This is a custom of long standing in Palestine and all the sacred places where it is allowed have almost numberless prayers written upon their walls. Just a few steps south of the tomb, the road forks, and the main road to Hebron is direct, and that to Bethlehem is on the left. From this point to the little town so very unworthy of historic mention, before the birth of our Lord, is only about one mile to the southeast.

WELL OF DAVID.

The road is not in good condition, and the horses must go slow. Just as the outskirts of the town are entered, the well of David can be seen by any one who will take the pains to go to it. It is located on the left of the road in a small open space, which is entered through a narrow and difficult pass. This well is regarded, both by tradition and the best evidence obtained by investigators, to be identical with the well "at the gate," the water of which David so eagerly longed for while he was in the cave of Adullam, and three of his valiant men having heard his ardent wish put their life in peril that his desire might be gratified. The well is rock-hewn and deep; the water is cold and very pleasant to drink, but care should be taken by strangers not to drink more than two or three swallows, as the free use of it is apt to make one sick; my own experience of freely drinking from it has admonished me to give the warning against its free use. I would advise travelers who may visit the well to be strictly cautious, and drink but little, no matter how thirsty they may be. If I did not give this advice, I should feel that a grave duty had been neglected. Those who live immediately adjoining the well are ever alert, and when a traveler comes up, they will run with a glass or some other vessel for him to have a drink. Of course they expect to be compensated for their kindness, and are seldom disappointed. It is highly probable that thousands of dollars have been given from time to time by the many visitors, for the water from the well "at the gate." If before entering the town the traveler will halt and take a survey of the landscape, and the country round about, he will call to mind much of the history of the far distant past. He may think of Naomi wending her way home in poverty and distress, bereaved of her affectionate husband and two loving sons, in company with Ruth, her widowed daughter-in-law, who would not forsake her in her distress. And should he look upon the fields, on either side the way, in which the husbandman is gathering the beautiful products of his labor, he will doubtless remember the womanly Ruth, who in meekness and great thankfulness followed the reapers of Boaz gleaning in one of these fields. And such was her loneliness and winning demeanor, she captured the heart of Boaz, whose love and tenderness for her were inexpressible, and in a short time afterwards became his wife, also the grandmother of David, the ancestor of Christ. He may also see a shepherd coming along having a flock of sheep behind him; he will make some kind of noise as if speaking to them; they follow close after him without turning to the right or left. This scene is a forcible reminder of the saying of our Lord, "My sheep know my voice, and they follow me." Now if one should take time to go to one of the fields in which several shepherds are attending their flocks, it might puzzle him to know how one shepherd divides his sheep from another's. But the difficulty is soon solved. It may be that one of the shepherds wishes to go to another place or home, and he will make the sound or tone of voice usually known to them, and immediately all his sheep gather together and follow him. The sheep are so well trained to follow and come when they are called, it is scarcely necessary to count them to see if any remained behind. It is highly probable that David was minding his father's flocks in one of these fields, when Samuel went to Bethlehem to anoint him the future king of Israel, and somewhere in these regions round about, while the young shepherd was looking toward heaven in deep meditation, he sang his nocturnal song, which has been prayerfully repeated by millions of the blood-washed army: "The heavens declare the glory of God, and the firmament showeth forth his handiwork." 2 Saml. xxiii. 15–17; 1 Chron. ii. 15–19. The stranger having meditated upon these events, is prepared to enter the heart of the town where other scenes will further refresh his mind concerning its historical importance. Before entering the shepherd fields just east of Bethlehem, other important events may be profitably contemplated. He will call to mind that somewhere here within the limits of my immediate surroundings, David, the grandson of Ruth, was born and reared, on some of those glens. On the outside he fought with a bear and a lion and slew them. From this town he went in the strength of God and met Goliath, the Gathite, and won a triumphant victory for Israel. Should the stranger take a few moments' walk to the southeastern terminus of the town, he will see just beyond him the fields in which the shepherds were watching their flocks on the early morning, the angels of the Lord descended and informed them of the birth of the Redeemer. Having finished his meditations and observations of the many places and events referred to, the stranger may with great benefit turn to the scenes connected with the advent of our Lord. But before we proceed to examine those places, especially referring to the history of our Lord in His infancy, it is proper that a historical sketch of this little town should be noted. The ancient name of Bethlehem was Ephratah, Ephrath, which means fruitful (1 Saml. xxvi.; 1 Kings ii.; Matt. i–v.; Ruth ii.); it is first mentioned in connection with Rachel's death, and spoken of again in the narrative of Ruth and Boaz, in which it is called Bethlehem Judah, to distinguish it from Bethlehem in the territory of the tribe of Zebulon. It was called the "City of David" in honor of him after Samuel anointed him to be the second king of Israel. It was not considered an important place until after the birth of our Lord; but since that auspicious event, it grew rapidly, both in size and popularity, and became more prominent after the church of the Holy Nativity was built, and thousands of adoring pilgrims visited there every year. Bethlehem is a Christian town containing about seven thousand inhabitants, of whom about thirty-five hundred are members of the Latin Church, twenty-five hundred belong to the Greek Church, about eight hundred are Armenians, and the remainder are Protestants. As strange as it may seem, there is not a Mohammedan in the town; although Jerusalem, which is only six miles away, is one of the Moslem strongholds. It is noteworthy to state that there seem to have been no special attractions in Bethlehem for our Lord after He left there in His infancy. It may be to many when considering the natural influence the place of birth has over mankind, a wonder why He manifested no disposition to visit the home of His childhood once, at least, especially when He so often came up to Jerusalem and Bethany, and other places not far away. Gen. ii.; Gen. viii. 7.

It is not recorded that our Lord ever visited Bethlehem, and it is presumable, He did not see it again after His parents took Him to Nazareth. It may be there was nothing to do more than had been done during His short sojourn. The message the angels brought, the narrative of the shepherds, the visit of the wise men from the east, and the mysterious flight of Joseph with Jesus and His mother, were evidences strong enough to arouse the whole town to embrace their Saviour and King. It should be remembered, Christ did not come to earth on a visit, but on business; and He never visited a place except upon such matters of business as strictly accorded with His divine mission. Ever feeling deeply impressed with the burden of His responsibility, He could spend no time except in those places where it was absolutely needful He should go. His duration was short on earth, and must be spent to the very best advantage to the world. On this account, Jesus worked hard all the while, and found no opportunity to pay the friends of Bethlehem a visit, simply to see the place of His birth. If our position is properly taken, we have clearly shown the mission of Christ. It demanded His untiring labor from the time He began to be active until He returned home. But the influence He left in Bethlehem has been working as leaven in the three measures of meal.

Bethlehem stands on a high hill, and is estimated to be at least three hundred feet higher than Mount Zion. It is properly called "the House of Bread," for the hills and valleys are clothed with olive groves, vineyards, fig orchards, and other fruits, all of which yield abundantly and fill the markets. The wheat, barley, and other products thrive richly. The people are generally employed, and are not seen following travelers through the town by the dozens crying "backsheesh," every step they take, as in most of the places in Palestine. It is noteworthy, that in every place where the Christian religion prevails, beggars are fewer, and strangers sustain but little if any annoyance. The Christian training of the Bethlehemites has given them a physical and moral bearing, very different from their Moslem neighbors, in other towns and cities round about them. The complexion of the females is fair; their dress, although Oriental in style, is neat and clean; and their head-dress differs from those in any other part of the country. They are generally busy at something of benefit to themselves and the community. When not employed with domestic duties, they manufacture fancy articles, and make relics out of pearls, olive-wood, cherry-stones and sea-stones; these they find ready sale for at the relic stores, and to tourists. As soon as it is known that strangers are approaching town, the young men who deal in souvenirs hasten to meet them, present their business cards, and endeavor to secure their promise to give them a call, and buy from them whatever goods they wish. It is of no use to tell them you don't want anything, for unless you are really without money, it will be next to an impossibility to leave Bethlehem without purchasing a number of articles. They have an eye to business, and know how to display their goods to make them inviting and salable. But few, if any, leave the town without making a purchase. But the great attraction in Bethlehem is the church of the "Holy Nativity." It is regarded as one of the most sacred sites in Palestine. It is said by Jerome, who lived in the town a short while after the

CHURCH OF THE NATIVITY (INTERIOR), BETHLEHEM.

erection of the church, "It was really built upon the site of the khan or inn at Bethlehem." It is also known that these khans, situated on great caravan highways, were always stationed (as is the case at the present day) at certain distances as nearly as possible, and retained their respective positions from one century to another; therefore, the ancient inn at Bethlehem, in the time of Jerome, was known to have been located on the grounds upon which the church of the "Holy Nativity" was built; and on this same spot occurred the mysterious birth of the Saviour of the world, on the night Joseph and the Virgin lodged there.

Justin Martyr, who wrote concerning it in the second century, said: "The stable of this inn was a rock-cut-cave." These ancient rock-cut stables are by no means uncommon in Palestine; several of them have of late been found on Mount Carmel and in different parts of Galilee, and will remain there to testify to travelers their ancient usefulness for many ages to come. It is common even to this day to have stables situated under the first floor of inns, both in Palestine and Syria. Those who go up to Jerusalem from Joppa by the old highway, usually halt at Babel-Wad for luncheon, in a small inn by the wayside. Here the traveler will find a genuine old-time stable, just under the main floor. There is a much stronger illustration of the Bethlehem stables at Sidon; when the upper portion of the house is full, the people frequently spend the night in the stable below with the horses, and many prefer lodging there for the sake of cheapness. It may be seen from these references, it was not an uncommon occurrence for people to sleep in stables in Palestine and the circumjacent countries. This was the cause why Joseph and his espoused lodged in the stable. "There was no room in the inn."

CHURCH OF THE NATIVITY.

The church that has been substituted for the tavern, stands in front of a large open space which is used for a "market place," and for a camping-ground for the market-men and merchants coming in from the country. Every day dozens of poorly-dressed, and half-savage-looking "Bedouins," congregate there with tents and luggage and remain sometimes through the day. The entrance to the church is from the space in which these wild-looking men are lurking. On approaching the door, travelers are followed by a number of men and boys, who vie with each other for the right of holding the horses, hoping thereby to earn a little backsheesh. They are so persistent in their endeavors for the privilege, the dragoman is often compelled to abruptly dismiss them to restore peace. The entrance door to the church is about four feet high; it opens into a vestibule that is very gloomy; this is the entrance to the spacious and beautifully-decorated building. The church proper stands inside a monastery which belongs to the Latins, Greeks and Armenians alike; each having their separate apartments, because the brethren do not by any means " dwell together in unity," but entertain the most hostile feelings towards each other. The church is free to all Christians to visit, and, if desired, devotional services may be held without interference in the open chambers, but no one, not officially constituted, would be allowed to officiate at the altars. There are evidences at times of encroachments, both in the interior and outside the church. Much of its embellishments have faded and crumbled off, so that in several places the walls are very much defaced. It was built in the year three hundred and twenty-seven, and is supposed to be the oldest Christian church in the world. There are different opinions as to who caused it to be built. Some think Constantine the Great, founded it; others say it was erected by the order of his Christian mother, the Empress Helena, who in the day of her energy and zeal for the progress of Christianity in Palestine, built many churches, chapels and convents throughout the country; and from the weight of evidence, it seems highly probable, she built this memorial basilica at Bethlehem over the rock-hewn manger of "Him who was born King of the Jews."

The measurement of the church is estimated to be one hundred and twenty feet long, one hundred and ten feet wide. It has five rows of marble columns, some of which are said to have been used in the Temple at Jerusalem, and were transported here for the use of this memorial building. The chapel of the "Holy Nativity" (one of the basement chambers) is a rocky cave, about twenty feet below the main floor of the church, which is approached by two flights of stairs. It is low and dark, so that lamps are kept burning day and night; in addition to the lighted lamps, each visitor is furnished with a candle to assist him through those dark places, where there are no lamps. The chapel is thirty-eight feet long, and eleven feet wide. In the pavement, may be seen a marble slab having a silver star in the centre; this is the traditional spot where our Lord was born, having the following inscription placed around it: "Hic de virgine Maria Jesus Christus natus est"—Here Jesus Christ was born of the Virgin Mary. This grotto is generally conceded, by those who have made exhaustive investigations, to be identical with the site of the manger in which the Lord Jesus was born. On this account, thousands of devoted Christians of all lands reverently bow at this holy shrine, and pour forth floods of praise and thanksgiving to the Lord Most High, for the gift of Jesus, His Son, who consented to be born of a woman, in a lowly stable, and in a rock-hewn manger, for dying men. Never can the writer forget the feeling of profound gratitude that pervaded his heart, the day he knelt by the stone that marks the site of the place where Christ first entered our world in flesh. There is a tradition, circulated extensively among the people, stating that the manger was found and taken to Rome, and placed in the church of St. Maria Maggiore. This is one of the many stories that have but little weight among the people at large. There is also an altar dedicated to the memory of the wise men, called the altar of the Magi. It designates the place where those eastern seers stood, when they presented their gifts to their infant king. There is another apartment called "The Chapel of Joseph," and is supposed to be the place to which he retired when the Saviour was born; and where "the Angel of the Lord appeared, and commanded him to take the young Child and His mother and flee into Egypt." The Altar of Innocence is dedicated to the memory, it is said, of twenty thousand male children who were murdered by the decree of King Herod, when he vainly sought the life of Jesus. There are several impressive paintings suspended over and about the altar, representing the inhuman massacre. There is not the least doubt in my mind, that some of the chapels and altars are fictitious, and gotten up upon mere conjecture, as many so-called sacred places in Palestine are, by many who have been too ambitious in locating the places where events took place of which the Bible gives account, or by some persons who had no conscientious scruples as to veracity. It is a common occurrence in Palestine, both with the Greeks and Latins, to fix upon places as genuine sacred places, without real foundation. There are many places purporting to be authentic, which cannot be satisfactorily established. But it seems to be the general opinion, that the place designated as the site of our Lord's birth is at least not far from the place, if not identical with it. It was accepted as such, as early as the time of Justin Martyr, and it must be conceded that at such an early date accurate accounts could be given. But one thing about which there cannot be a shadow of doubt, and naturally gives great comfort to the visitor is, he is confident that while walking from one recess to another through this ancient grotto, it is the identical inn in which the Son of God was born, and somewhere within its rocky confines is the sacred spot where the blessed virgin brought Him into the world.

There is another marvelous place in this cave, or rock-hewn inn, and that is the Chapel of Jerome. It is a rough chamber hewn in the solid rock, and is known beyond doubt, to be the room occupied by that most eminent and self-sacrificing follower of the Saviour for thirty years, who met the end of his life full of good deeds and works. Here he prayed, examined and studied; here he fasted, mourned and wrote, that he might be instrumental in making the world better and rekindle the sacred flame in Palestine, that it might burn from age to age, until every heart should be opened to receive the Saviour's love, and every knee should bow at His Holy Shrine. Here he gathered around him his devoted followers in the small communities which afterwards formed the beginning of Conventual life in Palestine, to instruct in the doctrines of the Word of God. Here he wrote letters and commentaries and sent them forth to the world. These chapels or grottoes have been sources of much contention and bitterness among the rival religious sects, who have specific apartments under their custody, and had it not been for the interposition of the civil authorities, there would have been on several occasions very disastrous results. These people have had dangerous outbreaks, it is said, simply on account of a few inches of wall, or a fractional portion of one of the altars, which in some of the rooms is so divided as to devote a portion of it to the express use of each denomination: they are generally divided by a heavy curtain which may be moved at will, so as to encroach upon the other officials, and when this is supposed to be, or is really done, the act has always been the harbinger of a row. Much trouble has occurred on several occasions about opening and shutting the doors. It is currently circulated that such inconsiderable matters have been so sternly rebuked by the parties who were dissatisfied, or felt to have been imposed upon, that they have nearly precipitated a war upon the people. It is an appalling outrage that it has become necessary, in order to protect life, and preserve nominal peace, that a guard of Turkish soldiers is stationed inside the church of the "Holy Nativity," to prohibit the Christian priests of the Latin and Greek religious sects, from doing violence to each other. Several times shameful outbreaks have occurred and much blood spilt, and lives have been lost within the precincts of the venerable church that marks the site where "The Prince of Peace" was born, by those who claim to be His followers, and the higher lights whose life is consecrated to the work of illuminating this dark world, that men may find their way to God. It is certain that if the Lord Jesus should sit in their midst as with His disciples and the multitudes on the mount, He would not say to them, "Ye are the light of the world." A deep-seated unfriendly feeling exists between the Greek and Latin priests, which seems to be impossible to exterminate. Just about one mile east of the church of the "Holy Nativity" is the shepherd's field, enclosed by a stone fence having several Olive trees in it. The grotto of the shepherds is also there; it belongs to the Greeks and is sometimes called the chapel of the shepherds. It is evidently of comparative modern date, and sometimes services have been conducted in it. On entering the chapel the transition is so sudden and marked, it is necessary to rest the eyes for a while so as to allow the pupil to expand sufficiently to become adapted to the change, because of the darkness that pervades the interior of the building.

This chapel marks the site where tradition locates the shepherds watching their flocks, when they saw the company of angels, who informed them of the advent of Jesus into our world. There is but little if any confidence attached to the genuineness of the statement with reference to the exact site of the shepherds' location on that memorable morning, or that those men used to rest themselves there, as some would have us believe. It is the general opinion of those who have made investigations of the place, that it was built in the time of the crusaders, who were distinguished for having occupied every historical place they found, and built either a chapel or convent to perpetuate its memory. But it is firmly believed that this dark chapel is in the neighborhood of the site at least, where the heavenly messengers came and for the first time proclaimed "peace on earth and good will to man." The olive trees are generally sought by travelers from Christian lands, from which they take a sprig or two of leaves. Every one who has heard the story of the glorious advent of Our Lord and Saviour, knows something of that stupendous event, and notwithstanding it will be an incomprehensible mystery down to the remotest ages, it is nevertheless the chiefest of the sources of consolation to mankind; and when one avails himself of the opportunity to visit the land in which the Saviour was born, and many of the places chiefly connected with His glorious mission, it is an unspeakable gratification to him.

THE JOURNEY FROM NAZARETH.

When Joseph laid aside his carpenter's tools, and closed the door of his workshop in Nazareth, and left home with the virgin, his betrothed, in obedience to the Emperor's mandate, to be enrolled for taxation in their own district of Bethlehem Judea, they had not the slightest idea that this wonder of wonders would occur before they returned to their home in the far-away hills of Galilee.

It was God's plan that, in accordance with the prophecy, our Lord should be born in Bethlehem, and so ordered it in His mysterious arrangements that Joseph should start with the virgin mother, so that they might arrive in the town designated for the miraculous birth of the Messiah, just at the time of the expiration of the period when she should be delivered. Joseph fulfilled two decrees in going up to the city of David to be registered. Cæsar Augustus, who was the first of the Roman emperors, demanded that a uniform taxation should be levied upon all the subjects of his vast dominion, and that none might escape, he decreed that each person should be enrolled in his own district, and Joseph, being of the house and lineage of David, went up to Bethlehem according to law to be registered, and thus, as a loyal citizen, fulfilled the decree of Cæsar Augustus, his earthly monarch, and inasmuch as Mary, his betrothed, was of the house of David, he took her with him, and while there the days were accomplished that she should be delivered. This wonderful event fulfilled the decree of the Lord, who by the mouth of the prophet declared that Christ should be born in Bethlehem Judæa.

The multitude of people who went over to the city of David in compliance with the decree of Cæsar Augustus, were, it seems, in advance of Joseph and Mary; and having arrived at the humble inn first, secured every available room and bed in it. Therefore, they were compelled to submit to a resting-place in the stable, or have none at all. Just a little longer and it would have been too late for the fulfillment of the event at Bethlehem. But God, whose purpose cannot be overruled, knew the day and hour to start Joseph to the place designated for the entrance of Christ into our world.

THE ADVENT OF JESUS.

When Joseph arrived at the inn, with Mary, his espoused, no one sympathized with her so as to arrange for her comfort. But if there had been a prophet of the Most High, in whom the people confided at the little inn, and if he had told them (Luke ii. 1–5; Matt: i. 25) Mary was the vessel God had chosen to bring the Redeemer into the world, and that her coming on to little Bethlehem would not only dignify it with her own presence, but it would be supremely exalted because she would be delivered of the Holy One, of whom Moses and the prophets wrote, and it was important that suitable arrangements at once be made for her comfort. I venture the assertion, that every one who had procured a room would have been ready to vacate for the accommodation and comfort of the Virgin Mother. But the birth-place of Jesus was one of the most humble that could be found; yet He was willing to become meek and lowly, that men might be exalted to the right hand of the Father. It may be seen that God causes men to carry out His plans when they have no intention or disposition to do so. It had been prophesied seven hundred years prior, that Christ should be born in Bethlehem; and, inasmuch as Joseph was a poor carpenter working at his trade over in Galilee, it is not probable he would have laid aside his work to go over the rugged highway up there unless urged by indispensable business; therefore, Cæsar Augustus became the efficient instrument in causing Joseph to go to Bethlehem, in company with Mary, just in time to establish the fulfilment of the words of the prophet. It so happens in many cases that men even attempt to thwart the purpose of God's work and His wishes. It is a tremendous truth, although carelessly observed, that "God moves in a mysterious way." To illustrate the thought, we call attention to the conduct of Joseph's brethren, who resorted to extremely criminal measures that God's purpose, as indicated by their brother's dreams, might not obtain; but they were the mediums through whom the ultimate purposes of God might be effected. It is also further demonstrated in the dream of Pharaoh. It was important that Joseph should suffer, that in the time when his talents were expressly needed, he would come from his prison-home, to take his exalted station as governor of Egypt. That he might attain to the position, it was needful that the king should dream such a mysterious dream that none but Joseph could unfold, and that the lineage through which Christ should come might be preserved, God caused Ahasuerus to spend a sleepless night, and to wile away the night-watches by listening to the reading of the book of record, in which was found the disclosing by Mordecai of a vicious plot concocted by two men to take the king's life. For this he had not been rewarded; and the king there and then put Mordecai in a position that saved his own life, and all the people who had been doomed to death by Haman. The case of Belshazzar further illustrates the evolution of God's plans, which were mysteriously hidden from human observation. When no man amongst the most learned of his kingdom could be found to make known his dream, Daniel was brought before the king; he made known his dream, and the interpretation of it. This act of Daniel promoted him to a high official position, and revealed the supremacy of the God of heaven and earth; also, ultimately delivered the Jews from their captivity. So it may be seen, that God used Cæsar as an instrument, in fulfilling His decree and establishing His truth; for in serving his own mission he also served the end of his Maker. If there had been general information given as to the exact time of the coming of the Messiah, how He should come, and where He should first appear, the plan of the Almighty, as to the place of His birth, would doubtless have been carried out differently. Joseph and Mary would have gone up to Bethlehem without being urged by the decree of Cæsar; and the multitude, instead of going up to be registered, would have gone to the city of David to be ready to shout an enthusiastic welcome to the King of kings, who had come to redeem them. They would have been as eager to worship Him, as were the wise men who came from their eastern home to bow at His feet, and present their gifts as a token of their admiration for Him.

But such a demonstration would not have been consistent with the prophecy concerning Him; also, it would have been an open door for His enemies to find Him. But whatever the results may have been, the wisdom and prudence of Mary, who was guided by the Holy Spirit, kept the whole matter from public attention. She left the disclosing of the wonderful advent of Jesus Christ to the heavenly songsters, who thronged the firmament of the Bethlehem pasture, and to the wise men of the East, who came over in search of Him. They broke the news and held the first jubilee over the matchless event. From these shining messengers the jubilating song started to enthuse the world; and from the morning of their memorable visit to the shepherds of Bethlehem (who were blessed above all other men on earth, in that they heard with their own ears a chorus chanted by angels, and saw them with their eyes while they rested in the firmament upon expanded wings, and sang as if Heaven in its fulness had come down to earth), it has cheered mankind. When the men had regained their composure, how edifying must have been the occasion, and how loth they must have been to have them leave!

SOLOMON'S POOLS.

Three miles from Bethlehem, a little to the northwest, are situated the renowned pools of King Solomon. These reservoirs are believed to have been constructed when the man, whose name they bear, was king over Israel, and remain until this time to assist in perpetuating the memory, and genius, of those workmen who lived nearly three thousand years ago. There are three of these pools, arranged in a line along an elevation, one a little higher than the other, and supplied from four springs. One of them has a vault built over it; this is the principal one of the four, and from it the pools receive their main supply. It is the general conclusion of those who have made investigations, these pools were built especially to have a larger and more healthy supply of water furnished in Jerusalem. There are yet to be seen remnants of the original aqueduct, exposed above ground within the neighborhood of the pools. The conduit was composed of stones; each piece is about three feet long, and about two feet thick, having a hole chiseled through the middle, and so shaped at its end as to allow it to fit in the piece to which it is attached. It is an ingenious display of mechanical skill, and was in all probability done by the workmen from Tyre, or conducted by them, at least, as they did the most of Solomon's artistic work. It would be in our times a very costly contract; but in those ancient times, when labor was done at a very meagre cost, and often just for what the workmen ate, large contracts could be accomplished for a small sum of money. It is true even of our present age, that men in the far eastern parts of the old countries, especially in Asia and Asia Minor, work for from seven to seventeen cents a day; and hundreds of them, I have been credibly informed, work just for something to eat. On such cheap bases the pyramids of Egypt, and the mammoth palaces and monuments of India were constructed. Taking this view of the manner men were compensated for their labor, there can be no wonder, that such giant structures were built for the use of kings in antique times; and it may be understood how Solomon could so elaborately surround himself with every convenience, competent to make him happy. The pools which Solomon caused to be built nine miles away from Jerusalem, with the acqueduct connection, would, in the present age, tax the financial ability of the Turkish government, to have it done with the same kind of material and implements, at the cost of mechanical labor in America. These pools are so constructed, that the bottom of each is higher than the top of the one next to it. The reason for this was to collect as great a quantity of water as possible. They are in such a splendid state of preservation, that it seems difficult to be persuaded they were constructed in the time of King Solomon. But as to the fact of their being erected in his day and by his order, there seems no reasonable cause of doubt; but it is the opinion of many, they were repaired, by order of Pontius Pilate. The first or upper pool is three hundred and eighty feet long, two hundred and twenty-nine feet wide, at the western terminus, and twenty-five feet deep at the eastern end. The middle pool is one hundred and sixty feet from the upper one, and is four hundred and twenty-three feet long, thirty-nine feet deep at the eastern end, two hundred and twenty-nine feet wide at its west end, and two hundred and sixty feet on the east end. The lower pool is two hundred and forty-eight feet from the middle one; this is the most spacious of all and commands the greatest attention. It is five hundred and eighty-two feet long, and is fifty feet deep at its eastern terminus, one hundred and forty-eight feet wide at the west end, two hundred and seven feet at the eastern end. This lower pool supplied the aqueduct that conducted water by the east side of the hills, past Bethlehem, and onward to Jerusalem.

That these reservoirs and aqueducts have an antique origin is seldom questioned, by the most critical investigations, notwithstanding there is no direct reference to them either in the Holy Scriptures or in the writings of Josephus. It is the opinion of some of those who have investigated these pools and the country immediately circumjacent to them, they are identical with the place referred to in the declaration of Solomon, "I made me great works, I planted me vineyards; I made me gardens and orchards, and I planted trees in them of all kinds of fruit; I made me pools of water to water therewith the wood that bringeth forth trees."

SOLOMON'S GARDENS AND ORCHARDS.

The valley just below the pools fully accords with Solomon's expressions, and is even to the present very beautiful and inviting to look upon and pass through. Not far from the pools of Solomon is situated in a narrow valley, a little village called Artas, surrounded with fine gardens and trees, and several ruins of ancient bearing here, and there strewn about. It is supposed this little village is the Ethom of Solomon's time; if so, he used to take daily drives from Jerusalem to these gardens and orchards in the early morning, to refresh himself, and enjoy the fragrance of his rich and handsomely arranged pleasure grounds. It is thought to be the place referred to in Ecclesiastes. The village was built by Rehoboam when he built fortifications about Bethlehem.

One of the most marvelous places in Palestine, and one that should not be passed unnoticed by any traveler from abroad, is the convent Mar Saba. It is situated in the wild and dreary wilderness of Judea, among a forest of rocks, in the very centre of extraordinary solitude. The route from Bethlehem is one of the roughest in eastern Palestine, and very fatiguing to both man and beast, and one of the most lonely roads in all the land. After passing the shepherd's field, just east of Bethlehem, there is nothing seen to interest a traveler especially, the entire length of the route; but one is kept busy picking his way over the very difficult and dangerous pass, lest a misfortune might occur

CONVENT OF S. SABA.

(Ecclesiastes ii. 4, 5; 2 Chron. xi. 6; and were it not that the horses are so well trained to these rough roads, many accidents would occur of a very serious and even fatal character.

SITE OF THE CONVENT.

The convent is about fourteen miles from Jerusalem, and to reach it, one must travel over high hills, and through deep valleys, leading through narrow passes, beside which high massive stones project, so that in many places it is necessary to lift your feet almost even with the back of the horse, to save them from being injured by some of the more prominent cragged rocks along the paths. It frequently occurs that the pass is close to the edge of a tremendous precipice, at points, along which the slightest misstep of the horse would precipitate its rider into a gulf three hundred feet below, where he would be broken to pieces among the sharp pointed rocks by his dreadful fall. There are several white hills seen in the distance, which have a very strong resemblance of the sand hills of North Carolina; and were it not for the peculiar situation the traveler is placed in, he might for a while imagine himself in America. The convent is in the midst of an utterly barren and desolate, wild wilderness, where naught but solitude is supreme. Those who wish to visit the convent of Mar Saba, must first procure a letter of commendation from the Patriarch at Jerusalem; without such a paper no one need apply for admission. There have been foul measures taken with the inmates of some of these institutions, which may be the prompting cause why they so cautiously guard the entrance door; otherwise persons with murderous intent might enter and deal treacherously with them.

Mar Saba was visited a good many years ago by a number of savage men, and over forty of the monks were slain. From that day to this, the convent has been cautiously guarded against the admission of any other than worthy persons. The entrance door, which is iron, is always securely fastened, and those applying for admission must knock upon it very loudly with a stick or stone. On being heard, the keeper will come and open a small wicket, into which the visitor or his guide places the letter of commendation, which, if found to be genuine, is so recognized, and the door is opened to admit him. If the visit is for the purpose of lodging during the night, the guest is escorted to the room especially kept for strangers, situated at the bottom of the institution. Ladies are not allowed under any circumstances whatever to enter it. Should a female be in the company, they have a small tower adjoining the convent where they are permitted to spend the night; but this does not occur once a year; for when females are traveling, caution is always taken to provide tents and beds for the trip, with all other needed accommodations, and they generally pitch the tent in the valley near the convent, where the whole party stay together. On entering the outer door of the institution, a long deep flight of steps must be descended, and these are intercepted by another iron door very heavy; then another long flight of steep steps lead to the third door. When this is passed, the stranger enters within the precincts of a marvelously contrived habitation, and one of the most solitary places of retreat known in the world. The visitor, who hitherto has been stout-hearted and even dauntless, will feel somewhat intimidated although he may try to maintain his former courage. I know nothing with which this isolated place can be more adequately compared, than the Doubting Castle, so minutely described in Pilgrim's Progress. The room at the eastern end of the convent, into which strangers are first taken and in which they are to spend the night, is a small, gloomy, and a very uninviting place. The hard bed is put on the stone floor, and is very uncomfortable, and one must be almost dead for sleep to secure any rest whatever; even then he will arise in the early morning feeling as though he had been lying on a bed of stones during the night. The convent is composed of a number of deep dells, with walls of natural rock, connected with artificial walls upon them. There are several holes or caves in the walls where the monks stay; and a person unaccustomed to a place of the kind would be astonished to see men walking about upon the ridges of the massive walls, then suddenly disappear. Each of the holes seen above are sleeping apartments, where a lawful number of the sixty or seventy people composing the inhabitants sleep; therefore, the monk who had been seen by the awe-stricken visitor, darted into one of them. The convent is so expressly complicated, none but those familiar with it could find their way through, without some one to guide him. There is no attempt undertaken by the inmates to take advantage of their guests in any way; they do not as much as ask for backsheesh, which is the custom commonly indulged by people in Palestine; nor do they make any charges for stopping there a night, but naturally expect something as a present. The history of this convent is most peculiar, and much of what is circulated as history is but a combination of fables. This monastery is the property of the Greeks, and under the supervision of the Patriarch whose headquarters is in Jerusalem; and notwithstanding its appearance is somewhat modern, it was founded as far back as the fifth century. St. Saba (as he is called), the monk, whose name the convent bears, has the reputation of having been a man of great piety. He was born in the year four hundred and thirty-nine of our era. It is recorded concerning him, that the people had the fullest confidence in him because of the piety he manifested, and thousands became his devout followers. He was born in Cappadocia, and at an early age devoted himself to convent life, in view of which he went to Palestine, and after having gone from one place to another, without settling himself in retirement, came to this place about the year four hundred and eighty-three, and began forming a religious community, and sometime afterwards founded the Mar Saba convent.

The Patriarch at Jerusalem, seeing the faithfulness and earnest, untiring efforts of "St. Saba" to stimulate a general religious sentiment amongst the people, exalted him to the position of Archimandrite of all the Anchorites of Palestine. It is said, Abbot Saba took a leading part in the vexing controversy raised about the Monophysite heresy, and at one time collected a company of his followers and marched up to Jerusalem, forced the enemies to leave the city, notwithstanding they had a squad of the imperial troops to aid them. This courageous step of Abbot Saba, gave him additional fame, and he was looked upon as a hero of the superior type; and, as it might be supposed, the people spread his fame far and near as one of the greatest men of his age. It seems, from certain legends, many looked upon him as almost superhuman, and really adored him. As it was usual, with the most of the ascetics of strong piety and zeal, at that time, to have the word "Saint" added to their names, it was, by general consent, agreed to call this man, so distinguished for piety, St. Saba; afterward his name became associated with a number of fables descriptive of miraculous achievements, which the monks, who conduct visitors through the convent, take pleasure in relating. St. Saba died at the age of ninety-four, after having spent a very useful and most eventful life, struggling against hosts of foes, and winning many precious victories of great importance to his followers. The convent of Mar Saba has been anxiously sought by many strong foes, and has had a hard struggle to maintain its existence. It was several times attacked and much damage done to both the institution and its inmates. It was plundered by the Persians under Khaasau in the year six hundred and fourteen, and forty-four of the monks were brutally murdered; and several times afterwards it was entered and robbed of what valuables it contained; and when the great war was in Palestine between the Crescent and the Cross, Mar Saba passed through many bitter changes. And to the present, it is said, the Bedouin Arabs are often seen lurking around the massive walls seeking an opportunity to enter and rob the inmates of their meagre possessions. It is commonly believed by those robbers, whose lurkings are amongst the rocks and caves of the wilderness of Judea, that rich treasures are hid in some private vault in the convent, and they are anxious to come in possession of them. It may be that at some unguarded moment they will gain an entrance and do much damage both to life and property. But the monks are aware of the malicious purpose of these roving demons, and are at all times on the alert, closely guarding their interests.

There are generally from fifty to seventy monks living in the convent, who are not the most tidy people to be found, yet they are polite and inoffensive. It is said some of these men have been placed in the monastery because of some violation of their church rules; they are sent there to pass a certain term of months or years, as the case may be, and those who are guilty of graver offences are sent there to spend their lives. It is said, there are some apartments of the convent, expressly for the insane who are sent there from other monasteries. The institution is sustained by charities, and the monks who are there are not much inclined to industry.

There are only a few things of interest in this lonely place to be seen; but any little thing that would not be noticed on the outside, is attractive to visitors who are shut up within the impregnable walls of the deep solitude for which Mar Saba is noted. The first place to which strangers are taken is the tomb of St. Saba, the illustrious founder of the convent, which is in the centre of the court near the steps leading down from the entrance gate. The remains of the Abbot are not there, having been removed to Venice, Italy; but his vacant tomb is venerated by his followers as a most precious relic. Behind a screen in the St. Nicholas Chapel is a vault, in which have been placed the skeleton heads of the monks who were murdered by the Persians in the seventh century; and the site is by no means coveted, especially in such a desolate place. Then there is another small chapel, called the Church of the Convent; it has a small bell in the tower, which is rung every night at twelve o'clock, at which time all the monks in the building are compelled to assemble for religious services. It seems rather strange to one who has not been accustomed to such a procedure, to hear the bell in the dead stillness of the night, and the inmates leaving their various rocky-chambers to attend religious worship. The bell in this convent is the only one, east of Bethlehem, in Palestine. The monks are handy with the knife. They employ a portion of their time cutting various kinds of souvenirs of olive wood, cherry-stones, and other materials, all of which are readily sold to strangers who go amongst them, and to the shops in Jerusalem and Bethlehem; these men might do a good business at this work were they more industrious, but they seemingly, do a little occasionally to pass the time and earn a few pennies. It is certain my visit there will not be forgotten while my memory is good. The evening I entered this most solitary convent, a feeling of uneasiness seized me, that grew more intense each moment, until I found myself trembling, as if a severe ague had control of me; and when conducted to the vault in which the skulls of the murdered monks were exposed to view, I had an impression that they might be the skulls of visitors who came there to remain over night; and whilst steadfastly looking, absorbed in curious imaginations that were akin to insanity, I inquired within myself, "Are these the heads of the monks who were slain here by the Persians a long number of years ago, or are they the heads of strangers who came into this 'Doubting Castle' to tarry for the night?" and I said, "I wonder if my poor head will be there soon?" These unpleasant thoughts, troubled me so intensely that sleep left my eyes, and although I lay down on my bed, I was on watch all night. It seemed to me there was nothing in my possession too dear to give, just for one more opportunity of looking up to the heavens at the stars. So about midnight, I ventured to open the heavy iron door that shut me in from the world, or even the notice of those in the convent. When I managed to open the door, I just put one foot outside to get myself in position to have a good look at the stars, and as I looked up I saw one of the monks, who had been attracted by the noise I made opening the door, looking down on me; well, indeed I went back and stayed back, awaiting whatever fate that would come to me. But when the day was about to dawn, and my guide indicated his purpose arranged for starting, I was one of the happiest men in Palestine. We left the old convent never to return again, and that purpose is still prominent in my mind. The guides, who are compelled to go there many times during the season, while traveling through that country, say they dread Mar Saba more than any other place in Palestine. It may be of interest to state, that my visit to this old convent was during my sojourn in Palestine in the winter of eighteen hundred and seventy-eight; and during my recent visit around the world, I met my old guide in Jerusalem. He called my attention to the night we spent at Mar Saba, and asked if I remembered the circumstance? I assured him I did, and the scene was so fresh in my mind I had no disposition whatever to return. This convent is the only convenient place on this route between Bethlehem and Jericho, and those whose time is very limited are usually brought down this way, on what is known as a three days' journey. It embraces a visit at Bethlehem, Rachel's Tomb, Solomon's Pools, Ethom, Mar Saba the Dead Sea, Gilgal, Jericho, and the Jordan.

The return journey to Jerusalem is up the "Bloody Pass," or the old highway from Jericho. This route is several miles nearer and can be traveled in about eight hours. Proceeding to the Dead Sea from Mar Saba, the road is more solitary and desolate, than that from Bethlehem to it. The scenery is wild and savage, and the fearful, deep chasms along which travelers are compelled to ride, produces a feeling of dissatisfaction that is dreadfully annoying until they are passed. It is indeed a wild wilderness, which has no charms to invite the delay of any one, not even the wandering Bedouins who are accustomed to living in the mountains. It is the desert country, called in the Bible Jeshimon, or the solitude; the highest point is called Watch Tower, and the surrounding district is called El Hadeidun, which is in harmony with the Hebrew "Hidoodim" which was the name given to the wilderness to which the scape-goat was led, that symbolically bore away the sins of God's people from His gracious presence.

There is a well close to the old pass leading up to Jerusalem, called Bir-essuk, the existence of which is regarded as an evidence of the identity of this wild wilderness as that to which the scapegoat was led. The messenger, who was authorized to lead the scape-goat into this wilderness started from the "Holy City" on the Sabbath day, and that he might avoid breaking the law, he took a tent with him; this he would pitch at the limit of a Sabbath day's journey, at which point he would rest for a while to eat and drink; after this he could lawfully pursue his journey for another limited distance. Between Jerusalem and the point where the scape-goat was set free were ten stations, and the last one where the tent was pitched was called the "Well of Suk."

A BEDOUIN CAMP.

There is nothing more of historical interest, to be seen until the Dead Sea is sighted in the distance. It is not an uncommon thing to pass a Bedouin camp along the way; these roving people usually go in companies of about twenty-five or thirty families, with their flocks and all they possess, and move from one pasture to another, where they find good water convenient or within a mile or two. They are a vicious people, made up of thieves and men who would commit murder and all kinds of crime to accomplish their thievish purposes.

On account of these characters, it is indispensable to the safety of travelers to have a guard of soldiers to escort them the whole journey during the three days' travel. The tents in which the Bedouins live are made of camel's hair; they are generally small, not more than six or seven feet long and from four to four and a half feet high. They are very black, and to each is tied a dog in the front to keep watch, and they invariably give notice when they see strangers approaching. Then there is a sharp lookout by these people to see who is coming, and a stranger would have a poor chance for his life, if there were no soldiers nigh to protect him against these desperadoes. But the sight of a guard or the wave of his hand will at once suppress any move they attempt; for all of them are cautious of their conduct, in the presence of the officers, who have authority to dispatch them on the least attempt they make to do violence to strangers.

THE WILDERNESS OF JUDEA.

This wilderness, in which they are generally found, is mentioned repeatedly in the Scriptures. There are different names given to separate portions of it. The southern portion is called the wilderness of Maon, so named because a town of that name was at one time situated in this district, near which Nabal lived, and there David took refuge from Saul. A little to the north of it is the wilderness of Ziph, named after a city or town four miles to the southeast of Hebron; to both of these places David fled from King Saul, who was hunting his life from day to day. It was near the latter place he remained hid for a long time. And farther on northwards, is the famous wilderness of En-gedi. This is the most elevated of the whole wilderness of Judea. The entire region abounds with caverns and cragged rocks, and furnishes one of the most retired lurking places for thieves in the entire district. The height of En-gedi is fifteen hundred feet above the level of Dead Sea. In this place David spent many lonely hours, wandering from place to place in his endeavor to escape the vengeance of Saul, and it is probable, he made his home for a time, in some of the caves that are still to be seen. The region, as has been mentioned, is frequented by outlaws, who make it a part of their business to rob whomsoever they can, whether native or stranger, when the least opportunity can be obtained. It was in this wilderness, the author was confronted by several of these wild barbarians, and had it not been for the prompt interference of the guard, the results would no doubt have been serious; but, thank the Father of Spirits, the guard was just around the bend of the road and reached the scene in time to avoid a calamity. I do not know of a more wild and desolate place in Palestine, except the thieves' valley, than the lonely and cheerless wilderness of En-gedi. As far as one can see, naught but a succession of mammoth rocks, deep chasms, alarming even to look into, and barren mountain ridges for miles around, and occasionally a Bedouin can be seen walking cautiously along the margin of the precipice, look wistfully down on the passer-by, and would compel him to stop, if it were not for the guard, whom they so greatly fear. These outlaws, always have a long gun swung to them, so that they are prepared to make an attack upon a traveler at any moment, for they know well how to handle the instrument. From the present barren state of the country, one would not think it is the En-gedi that at one time flourished with vineyards, concerning which the Holy Scriptures give account. And were it not that so much incontrovertible evidence of the identity of the place still remains, to declare it to be the genuine site, it would be sternly doubted. The wise man, in speaking of the former flourishing condition of the place, said, "My beloved is unto me as a cluster of henna-flowers in the vineyards of En-gedi." Now, how can this be explained to human satisfaction in such a wild, dreary wilderness, and where, in all the length and breadth of it could a vineyard have been found? The word En-gedi means "Fountain of the Kid." As the traveler proceeds down towards the Dead Sea, he will see nearly opposite the mouth of the River Arnon, a fine and copious spring or fountain, called by the natives Ain Jedy, which means En-gedi. The water streams forth from the rocks about four hundred feet above the level of the sea; this is the most beautiful and cheering place along the journey, and is identified as the ancient En-gedi. This district was at one time very fruitful, but has become fruitless from being neglected (1 Sam. xxiii. 29; xxiv. 1-2) for many centuries, so that nearly all the soil in the greater part of it has been washed away by the heavy rains, common in Palestine during the winter season. Indeed, it seems strange, that much of the country, throughout eastern and southern Palestine, in the time of the Israelites the most productive, is now wild, desolate and covered with beds of deep-seated rocks, from one end to the other, and must remain so forever, for there is no possibility of ever causing it to produce again.

THE DEAD SEA.

The most mysterious body of water in Palestine, if not in the world, is the Dead Sea. It is situated in the lowest portion of the ravine that extends from the northern to the extreme southern portion of Palestine. This body of water is regarded as one of the great wonders of

DEAD SEA.

the world, and has been a subject of discussion for many ages, by the most learned scientific men, our world has produced. Although they have discovered and brought many things of interest to light, yet there is a deep mystery clinging to it, which has baffled the most talented scientists of the world to demonstrate. Many have consented to accept the Scripture narratives concerning it, as to its origin, whilst others have endeavored to trace its origin to some other cause, but without satisfying themselves, after years of research and much loss of time. All these great investigations of men who undertake to set aside the word of God, as taught us in the Holy Scriptures, by endeavoring to establish other theories, suitable to their own fancies, have been a succession of failures, so glaring that many have become disgusted with their own folly and abandoned the contest. It must be admitted, however, we have been much enlightened as to many of the characteristics of the Dead Sea, that for a long time were not properly understood before the various investigations took place. There were many opinions as to its nature, and these became so very complicated, that there seemed to be less information furnished the world as to its true character, than existed prior to the time men began making tours to it. But when investigations were being held, it was seen that many wild legends were in circulation, concerning this wonderful body of water, which were too glaringly weak to find a resting-place in the hearts of an enlightened and progressive people. There is a general belief that the Dead Sea occupies the area where the cities of the plain once stood, and here righteous Lot, after parting from Abraham, settled down amongst a very wicked and Godless people, who vexed his soul because of their persistent evil doings.

The Dead Sea lies about twenty-five miles southeast of Jerusalem. The ravine or basin, in which it is confined, connects with the depression which extends from the foot of Mount Hermon, on the north, to the Gulf of Akabah on the south. This ravine, running from the north to the southeast, is for more than one hundred miles of its course, below the level of the Mediterranean Sea, and falls lower still, so that when it reaches the Dead Sea basin, it is thirteen hundred and twelve feet below the western sea. The waters of the river Jordan are continuously pouring into the Salt Sea on its north, and those of the Wady el Jeib on the south. Yet there seems to be no overflow of water caused by these immense tributaries, nor has any place been found where the waters find an outlet. There have been many theories and conjectures as to the outlets of the Dead Sea, but none of them have been so clearly and definitely demonstrated as to establish a certainty, except that of the immense evaporations. This is regarded by many to be the only means of carrying off the great quantity of water coming into it from the Jordan.

The Wady el-Jeib and other smaller tributaries flow into it. It has been thought there is a subterranean communication, between the Salt Sea and the Red Sea, into which it empties a great volume of water; but this theory has not been sustained. This body of most bitter water, frequently called in the Holy Scriptures, the Sea of Lot, is, so far as development has revealed, solitary and alone in a deep bed, shut in on the east and west by high limestone borders, which at points, dip into the sea, not leaving margin enough to walk on. It is forty miles long from the northern to the southern extremity, and the widest portion is about nine miles; but it becomes narrower until its widest northern point is only five miles, and its area about two hundred and fifty miles. It has the enormous depth of one thousand and eighty feet in some places, and from this many variations are found, ranging from one thousand and eighty, to only eleven feet deep. These differences of depth are caused by the elevations and depressions of the caldron in which the sea is confined.

Those who visit the Dead Sea from Jerusalem descend thirty-one hundred and fifty feet below the Holy City before the sea is reached. It is the most depressed body of water on the globe; and when the traveler finds himself standing upon the margin, he would do well to call to mind he is nearly thirteen hundred and fifty feet below the great sea on the west, and more than three thousand feet below Mt. Zion; above all he should bear in mind, his feet are pressing the soil of the very lowest spot of ground known on the face of the earth. To have such a distinguished privilege, is worth more than the cost and fatigue of the journey. It is excessively warm there, the sun seemingly shining in its most oppressive strength. Those who visit the Dead Sea in the months of March and April, are specially cautioned against exposing themselves to the sun, lest they receive a sun-stroke. It is so very warm there, many times in the spring, that persons visiting Jerusalem from Europe are not allowed to travel in the middle of the day, but must, for the sake of their own safety, go out sight-seeing in the early morning and late in the evening, to avoid being out in the intense heat.

When nearing the borders of the sea, it appears as if it was a beach of pure white sand, or a bed of snow had whitened its whole expanse. But it will soon be seen, as a nearer approach is gained, that the whole surface of the ground is covered with salt. In many places on the north side, salt can be gathered into little balls during the warm season; and on the east side the salt abounds in a much greater quantity, which is seen to a greater advantage if no rain has fallen for a few days

There is nothing green, nor any kind of produce to be seen on the border of this salt sea, nor has there been, since it supplanted the cities of Sodom and Gomorrah. Lying, as it does, in this deep dell, nearly immediately encompassed by cragged rocks, and having, during the long hot season, the intense rays of the sun pouring constantly down upon it, nothing could be looked for about it, but barrenness; and those who desire to take in the products of nature must remain about the regions of Jericho and the Jordan. It has been ascertained, the immense evaporations which cause the ground to be whitened all around the sea with salt, are produced by the intense heat, common to the deep caldron in which it is confined.

The atmosphere is necessarily heavy from its connection with the constant evaporations, which cause it to have a heavy and dark appearance; and the marshes of the Ghor, send out an unhealthy vapor, that connect with the already heavily charged atmosphere, and renders the country round about very unhealthy; so much so, that the people are generally feeble and short-lived. On the south of the Dead Sea are situated the remarkable salt hills, which have been so largely discussed, and with which many fables have been associated. They are called by the natives Jebel Usdum, or the "Mountains of Sodom." There are deep impressions, and many interesting reflections to engage the attention of any one while passing round the shores. The natural curiosities about the shores, and in the basin leading up to the sullen-looking waters, of this ancient renowned region are few, but those to be seen are different from any in other parts of Palestine; especially the Dead Sea stones, that are so highly praised by the relic-dealers in Jerusalem and Bethlehem. But there is so much history connected with the country, within the limits of one's observation, there is but little time spent in hunting souvenirs. The waters of this wonderful, mysterious basin, are so very salt, that it contains twenty-six pounds of saline to every one hundred pounds of water. This naturally makes it fatal to animal life—nothing lives within its solitary deep. But it is not true, that birds flying over it fall dead in the water, as has been erroneously stated by persons who we feel never visited this sea, or if they did, had no respect for the truth. Birds do fly over it every day and hour, by the hundreds; we have seen them in great numbers, going from the western to the eastern shore, and they fly over just as safely as they would over any other body of water. It has been also stated, that men cannot breathe its heavy atmosphere, even for a very short while, without being in eminent danger of fatal results. This is another ill-contrived fabrication, which cannot bear the light of truth. Pilgrims go there, sometimes by the hundreds, especially immediately after the Easter Festival; and hundreds of tourists, also, during the traveling season, visit there, and breathe in the air as freely as if in a more agreeable climate, without incurring any injury. There is danger, however, in strangers remaining too long; for, notwithstanding the atmospheric odor is not disagreeably unpleasant, strangers are cautioned not to camp out over night on the shores of the Dead Sea, as the locality is generally unhealthy during the heavy evaporations, which are much more prominent after sunset. Strangers who are exposed to it, are liable to be stricken with a fever that might terminate fatally. Much of the physical condition of this mysterious body of water has been brought to light, and many wild stories concerning it put at rest, by the energetic labors of the American exploring expedition. The scientists composing it made investigations from one end to the other, and gave the results to the world, which have been of great benefit. What was more misleading than the story of the "Pillar of Salt" into which Lot's wife was changed? It had been currently circulated that persons who had visited the shore of the Dead Sea, had seen her, broken off a piece of her finger or toe, to take home as a relic; that the mutilated finger or toe would grow again in a short time and become fully restored. This flagrant misrepresentation was credited by many, and is still believed, by some, to be true. It is true there are a number of salt mounds or pillars about the sea; but no one can tell which, if any one of them, is that of Lot's wife. It should be borne in mind, the Lord did not turn her into a statue, but a pillar. If a statue, she would have had bodily form, with accurately defined limbs, such as a statue naturally must have. But she was turned into a pillar. Therefore, it can at once be seen, that no one can tell which, of the many mounds or pillars of salt is that to which Lot's wife was turned. It was supposed for a long while, there was a deep abyss in the centre of the Dead Sea, into which flowed the accumulated waters of the Jordan, and other streams would carry it off as fast as it ran in. But it has been finally agreed by the most talented explorers, that there is no outlet; the whole domain of the amazing sea has been thoroughly explored, and nothing indicating an outlet has been found. But careful observations have satisfied those who have made repeated investigations, that the evaporations produced by the intense heat of the sun, are equal to the amount of water flowing into it. Great are the works of the Lord, and marvelous are His ways.

It would be of great benefit to the world, if all persons who visit the Dead Sea, other places in Palestine, and elsewhere for historical purposes, would make correct notes of the things they intend giving to the world. I am sure it would be the means of harmonizing the true state of things, in many places that have been greatly exaggerated, by those who have not been careful to minutely record what they saw and heard. It many times occurs, that persons who go to the Holy Land, visit a few of the most convenient and memorable historic places, but on account of fear or disinclination, fail to visit the more remote and difficult places, because of the many dangers to which they are constantly exposed; yet they desire to impress others that they have seen them, and having obtained an incorrect account of them from what they have read, form an opinion very foreign to the real condition of things, and put it in circulation as truth. Many persons who visit Jerusalem, and a few places round about it, content themselves with taking a view of the Dead Sea from the Minaret of Helena, on the Mount of Olives; from which point of observation the water appears as black as ink, and just as still as death. It also occurs, sometimes, when travelers are not careful as to the fitness of the guide; untrained and know-nothing men, will impose themselves upon tourists, who will tell them anything to pass off the time and entertain those in their care. This is often the cause of many of the misrepresentations given by persons who are ignorant of their mistakes. Those who visit the Dead Sea, after viewing it from the summit of Olivet, find a marked difference as to its real condition. If the day is cloudy and a strong wind is blowing, it will be very much agitated, and the waves can be heard roaring almost equal to those on the Mediterranean; and the water that seemed to be as black as ink, when viewed eighteen miles away, is seen to be a beautiful sheet of deep blue. Out from the border and near the point, where the Jordan is pouring into it, the water is transparently clear. The Dead Sea has a specific gravity, so great, that a heavy man can stand erect in some parts of it, and not sink above his knees, or he may lie down as upon a sofa in perfect safety. Many travelers go in, so they may experience the peculiarly strange sensation it produces. But I am frank to inform all who may wish to know, I did not try it. The peculiar sensation of my surroundings was sufficiently impressive, without going in those Sodomic waters to intensify them. It is said after the bathing is finished, the salt causes every portion of the body to tingle, and often produces an eruption known as the "Dead Rash." Those who venture to take a bath, are advised to ride as fast as possible and bathe in fresh water thoroughly, so as to remove the saline effects of the previous bath; which if allowed to dry in the flesh, will produce a cuticle disease from which it is hard to recover. It is strange that people will allow their better judgment to be overruled to the extent, that they venture, in the face of the peril of being sick, into the Dead Sea simply to gratify a greedy ambition.

The malignant character of the sea is attributed to the extraordinary amount of mineral salts it contains The analysis of chemists, show that it contains twenty-six per cent. of saline matter, an amount fatal to animal life. It can be readily understood why nothing can live in it, for it is freighted with death. The different chemical results are accounted for, according to the portion of the sea the specimens were taken from, the season they were collected, as well as the distance they were, when procured, from the point the Jordan flows into it. If they were collected in the early spring or during the warm, dry season, their analysis will largely differ from those collected in the winter. Water taken from a point near where it receives the Jordan flow, is much fresher than that taken a greater distance from it. The water in winter taken from any part of the sea, will contain less salt, and be less bitter than that taken in autumn. One analysis shows chloride of sodium, eight; potassium, one ; calcium, three. The above facts ,were obtained ,after careful analytical investigations were made by leading scientists; and taking it for granted their conclusions are correct, the buoyancy of the water is easily understood. We have also the results of the masterly expedition of Lieutenant Lynch, who surveyed the whole of the Dead Sea thoroughly, and ascertained its geographical situation and much of its mineral contents, as well as its depth, its width, its temperature and the velocity of its tributaries. He collected all obtainable specimens, and noted the currents, the changes of weather and a variety of other useful information which has been of great benefit to those who have been searching and collecting its history. The following will be read with much interest, it being a portion of the statement of Lieutenant Lynch : " Everything said in the Bible about the Dead Sea and the Jordan, we believe to be fully verified by our observations. The inference from the Bible that the entire chasm was a plain, sunk and overwhelmed by the wrath of God, seems to be sustained by the extraordinary character of our surroundings. The bottom of the sea consists of two submerged plains, one elevated and the other depressed, the former averaging thirteen feet, and the latter about thirteen hundred feet below the surface. Through the northern, and longest and deepest one, in a line corresponding with the bed of the Jordan, is a ravine at the south end of the sea. Between the Jabbok and this sea, we unexpectedly found a sudden break-down in the bed of the Jordan. If there be a similar break-down in the water-courses to the south of the sea, accompanied with like volcanic characters, there can scarce be a doubt that the whole Ghor, has sunk from some extraordinary convulsion, preceded probably by an eruption of fire and a general conflagration of bitumen which abounded in the plain." The danger which seemed to be imminent, during Lieutenant Lynch's exploring expedition of the Dead Sea was alarming. At times it seemed to him as if the Almighty had frowned upon their attempt to explore the dreary regions of the mysterious sea, under whose foaming bosom, are entombed the once proud and sin-cursed cities of Sodom and Gomorrah; and in whose depths nothing can breathe life, and around which naught but solitude reigns, as an ever-present memento of the creation of Divine wrath. But, although the expedition of Lieutenant Lynch was, according to prediction, to be a failure, and the tradition of the Arabs, that no one can venture upon the sea and live, was at times gaining strength in the opinion of some, who were nearly overcome with the threatening attitude of the sea, yet the little ship made the harbor safely with all its human cargo. One standing on the northern shore of the Dead Sea, taking a careful survey of its situation, would conclude, that the silence prevailing throughout its circumference, the desolation prominent everywhere to be seen, the deep mystery still enveloping much of its history, and the repulsive character of the water, all associate their strength and stamp upon the character of the sea the veritable image of death. It is, therefore, properly named "Dead Sea."

It was an opinion of long standing, that the Jordan flowed directly through the deep chasm, that extends from the southern end of the Dead Sea to the head of the eastern arm of the Red Sea, and in this way the water of the Jordan might be discharged. But recent investigations have proven that such a channel did not exist, and it is also shown to be impossible that such a subterranean connection could be between the Dead and Red Seas, through which the water of the former could be conveyed to the latter, from the ostensible fact, the depression of the Dead Sea basin and the whole Jordan valley is so much lower than the Red Sea, that if such a passage were open, the waters of the Red Sea would flow into the Jordan, in such volumes it would flood it as far north as the base of Mt. Hermon, and fill its eastern portion several hundred feet deep. There is a conflicting opinion as to the condition of the Dead Sea at present and that of earlier times with reference to its increase in territory. The general belief is, this sea holds its own, and has not increased nor decreased to any perceptible degree, since the Divine Being caused it to exist. The evaporations are so intense, that they absorb nearly as much water as the Jordan and other streams pour into it. But Dr. Robertson and others are of the opinion, the Dead Sea is larger now than in former times. The northern portion of it is known to be much deeper than that on the south, the former being many hundred feet deep in every part, while the latter measures but a few feet in depth, and in summer becomes a broad lagoon, so very shallow it may be forded in several places. It is supposed by many Biblical scholars, this shallow portion is of late formation, and think it was at some time, long since passed, a fertile plain. It may have been at the time of Lot, a part of the well-watered and beautiful plain, which won his affections and caused him to pitch his tent towards Sodom. This was without doubt, the land of the cities of the plain, upon, at least a portion of which, some of them proudly stood. No one can stand on the dismal shore of this historic sea, without having many sad reflections concerning the event which brought it into existence, and the dreadful calamity on the proud and Godless people, who at one time reveled in the most daring and vicious crimes against the Lord. One may imagine he sees Lot running for his life, his wife suddenly turned into a pillar of salt, and people falling under the wrath of God. We see the first mention of the locality of the Dead Sea in Genesis, referring to an incident that took place nearly four thousand years ago, when there was an increasing dissatisfaction, and ill-feeling existing between the herdsmen of Abraham and Lot, growing out of misunderstandings, it is thought, concerning the rights of each other as to certain pastures. The hard feeling grew more aggravating and became a very serious matter, tending towards a little strife, that would have eventually interfered with the ties of friendship, which bound Abraham and Lot together. The senior patriarch was apprehensive of the inevitable calamity should they continue together; therefore, he advised that a friendly separation take place, to avoid a permanent fraternal dissolution. Then Lot looked down from the high mountain summit just above Bethel, and beheld the plain of the Jordan, and the cities which were very beautiful to look upon. He was at once attracted by its fertility, and drawn by the prospect of having in that part of the country all that was needful to make him prosperous and happy. He, therefore, gathered together all that belonged to him and moved down toward Sodom.

SODOM AND GOMORRAH.

Almost every one who has been favored with the opportunity of taking a view of the plain of the Jordan from the heights above Bethel, entertains the belief that the cities of Sodom and Gomorrah, were situated to the north of the Dead Sea, instead of the south side, as some have located them; otherwise when Lot looked down from the summit, where he stood, he could not have seen the cities of the plain, unless a great change has taken place in the natural situation of the country. The Bible tells us Lot saw the condition of the land from where he stood; for he " Beheld all the plain of Jordan, that it was well watered everywhere," before the Lord destroyed Sodom and Gomorrah, " even as a garden of the Lord, like the land of Egypt, as thou goest unto Zoar." "Lot therefore chose him all the plain of Jordan, and dwelt in the cities of the plain, and pitched his tent toward Sodom." The portion of the plain seen by Lot from Bethel, is north of the sea, as the south side is not visible from that point. It is the prevailing opinion that Lot came to the northern portion of the plain first, and went southward from time to time, until he at length reached Sodom, as the whole of the southern plain was well adapted to afford abundance for his flocks.

He having entered Sodom, it is reasonable he would seek the acquaintance and friendship of the inhabitants. He next indicated his intention of remaining there, by marrying one of the maidens of the sin-smitten town, and reared a family, and in some respects he became socially identified with the people, who were not lovers of the God of Abraham, and remained with them until compelled to "escape for his life," from the pending wrath of God, which was suspended to allow him to shun it. The plain in which the doomed cities stood was called "The Vale of Siddim," and we are informed in the Scriptures, it was full of slime-pits, of which several relics are still to be seen. Those who have been at Jericho in the rainy season, and have gone to the Dead Sea on a horse, have witnessed something of the condition of this slimy district, which will give an idea of its former status, when the pits were numerously dispersed throughout the whole region, and he may also faintly catch a glimpse at a panoramic view of the ancient cities, which once flourished in the neighborhood of the place over which he rides. The whole scene of the ill-fated cities came before my mind, while standing on the shore of the Sea of Lot (Dead Sea), so vividly, I seemed for a while to be living amongst the scenes of nearly four thousand ages past. The hasty flight of Lot to Zoar, the gathering fire-clouds in which were the magazines of God's wrath, the falling storms of the arrows of death clothed in flames, the consternation of thousands who felt the terrible effects of the calamity, and their fruitless attempts to seek places of refuge, all came before my mind so clearly and pungently, that my imagination almost persuaded me I was in the midst of the scene.

The Bible narratives relative to the eventful occurrence, inform us of the overthrow of the cities of Sodom and Gomorrah, and the preservation of Zoar, which God permitted to remain for the security of Lot, who was fleeing to it for refuge. This little city to which Lot escaped was near Sodom, on the south of the plain where the ill-fated cities were located.

LOCATION OF ZOAR.

There seems to be but little, if any, doubt as to the location of Zoar by those who have carefully investigated the country round about the Dead Sea, and that it was situated on the south of the plain, becomes more evident, when we take into consideration what is said concerning the view of Moses from the summit of Mount Pisgah. Whilst standing upon that lofty eminence, the man of God surveyed the land of promise, the wide prospect opening to actual vision, and as suggested by this to the imagination is represented as being bounded on the south by Zoar, which must be a natural boundary if the above view of the situation of Zoar be correct.

This little city, which, perhaps, was the most humble of all the flourishing cities in that region, suddenly became the chief city of the whole district, for it was left alone. Here Lot stood early in the morning, and having looked towards the plain, he saw the smoke of the condemned and consumed cities ascending, for all their former glory had melted, under the awful displeasure of the Almighty. It is highly probable, Zoar grew to be a very important place after the destruction of its neighbors, and flourished as such for a long time after the death of Lot.

It is said to have been a place of much importance in the time of Josephus, and was known down to the time of the Crusades. According to the Scripture, Sodom and Gomorrah were demolished by fire and brimstone, which were rained down upon them from Heaven, as a result of their unbearable sins. It came upon the inhabitants suddenly, at a time when they were indulging in their usual wickedness, and from their conduct towards Lot; the same evening a messenger came down from Heaven; it may be said they were even more daring than ever before, for they seemed to have spent the greater part of the night indulging in crimes and shame, which is not customary with the people in that part of the country. The early part of the evening is usually spent in whatever pleasures are sought, and before midnight everything is perfectly quiet.

But these people, while standing on the verge of an awful calamity, were more intensely lost in wickedness (from their attitude toward Lot and his divine guest) than they had showed themselves to be at any other time. Being too blind to take warning, they were found without a place of refuge or a God to help them when the cup of their doings was falling upon them. Every attempt to escape was in vain, because of the extent of the calamity. It visited all the cities of the plain instantly, so that every one was in the same condition; and it became suddenly overwhelming, so that no opportunity was given the people to follow in the direction Lot fled, which was known to some of them, at least.

The command given by the angel to Lot was expressly urgent: "Escape for thy life, look not behind thee, neither stay thou in all the plain; escape to the mountain lest thou be consumed." Abraham, who lived in his tent on the plain of Mamre, having been informed of the purpose of God with reference to the wickedness of those cities, arose early in the morning, ascended to the peak of a high hill, near his tent, and looked towards Sodom. He saw the smoke of the whole country of the plain going "up as the smoke of a furnace;" there was naught but solitude to express the woe that had been brought upon the people by their own doings, so that those who had flourished in the morning, prior to the fatal visitation of destruction, were all dead the following morning, except righteous Lot and his two daughters, who had found a safe retreat. Thus ended the career of the famous cities of the plain, whose dreadful doom has turned the attention of the civilized world to the renowned Salt Sea, that largely covers the space where once lived, the proudest and most sinful people of their generation known in the world.

In closing this chapter, it may be of interest to present one or two leading thoughts, upon the agents used to accomplish God's purpose in the miraculous overthrow of the cities of the plain and their entire inhabitants save three. This fearful and complete destruction, visited upon the ill-fated district, is presented in such plain words, no one can fail to comprehend them if they will pay the least attention to their teachings.

The cities with their inhabitants, the entire surrounding country, together with all the fruitful fields and beautiful pastures, which charmed Lot and so attracted him he dwelt there, and all the glory of the region round about were overwhelmed and completely destroyed beneath the devouring flame of the wrath of God. It is written in unmistakable words that, "God overthrew the cities, and all the plain, and all the inhabitants of the cities, and that which grew upon the ground." It is noteworthy, that nothing is said, in the narrative, which discloses the most wonderful catastrophe, of water as an agent in the work of destruction, in the form of a flood overwhelming the plain as some would dare assume; but the agent at work was fire and brimstone, elements that were sure and speedy in the accomplishment of their work, not only in the destruction of man and beast, but to the ground; so that all that was beautiful, rich and fruitful, in a few moments became barren and dead. The people and the land on which they dwelt were blotted out of existence forever. Scientific men have indulged much speculation concerning the Dead Sea, and the cause which brought it into prominence, but left their investigations under a deep cloud of supposition and doubt. But when we consult the Sacred Word, the only true and safe guide, we must conclude that, upon the borders of this lonely sea, Lot made choice of a home for himself and all his possessions; that it is the veritable vale of Siddim which was full of slime pits, and into which the kings of Sodom and Gomorrah fell. These kings and Lot were captured by the forces of Chedorlaomer, but were recaptured by Abraham and his confederates. Here were situated the cities of the plain whose cup of wickedness had filled to overflow. Somewhere within the limits of observation, Lot was speeding his flight, and as he ran, he found, after a short while, his wife was not with him; her heart longed for the pleasures of Sodom, and she was turned to a pillar of salt. These, and many other thoughts, crowd the mind of the visitor while passing through this district, whose sin-smitten neighborhood is still forsaken by man and beast, since the day when the fiery indignation of Jehovah destroyed Sodom and Gomorrah.

EARTHQUAKES' WORK OF DESTRUCTION.

The district has been repeatedly visited with earthquakes; and there are hot springs near the shore, which continue to send out steaming hot water, much like that coming from the extinct volcano Solfatara, near Pozzuoli, Italy. The appearance of these springs, indicates the existence, of a fiery chamber somewhere within the region close enough to communicate with them. Sulphur has been plentiful about the sea-shore, and sometimes a small lump is found by the Bedouins; also bitumen, or, as it is called, asphaltum is often found in large quantities. It is said after the earthquakes it is seen in abundance in the southern regions of the sea; the Arabs gather it, after it becomes hard from exposure to the heat of the sun, and find ready sale for it in Bethlehem and Jerusalem to the relic dealers. There is but little of this substance found of late. It may be, that it has become about exhausted. But the evidences of the past eruptions are yet prominent along the way between the northen shore of the sea and the Jordan. This region is a silent witness of the overthrow of the cities of the plain as narrated in the Bible.

After the Israelites settled in Canaan, the borderland of the Dead Sea was a familiar battle-ground, just as the plain of Esdraelon became later on. It also formed the boundaries of the territory of some of the tribes, as is indicated in our introduction. The districts round about the sea, especially those on the east and west, furnish much important history, showing their connection with some of the most interesting events mentioned in the early history of the Hebrews. Lot had two sons, Moab and Ammon, whose descendants were called Moabites and Ammonites, respectively. These tribes inhabited the valleys on the east side of the Dead Sea, and the descendants of Esau, known as Edomites, lived on the south side. They were a powerful people, very numerous, and occupied a large tract of country which extended from the southern border of the Dead Sea to the eastern, or Elamitic Gulf of the Red Sea, embracing a district about one hundred miles long and fifteen or more wide. When they grew to be numerous and powerful, they established a kingdom, and were ruled by kings, instead of governors and princes, as they formerly had been. These people were bitterly hostile to Israel from the time they entered their borders until the time of their subjugation by the Romans, and were ready to lend their aid to any foreign power who came up against Jerusalem. When the Israelites were journeying to Canaan their route was through their confines, and as soon as they arrived at the western borders of Edom, they were confronted and refused a peaceful passage through their country to Moab. Then the children of Israel forced their way through, and the result of their triumphs purchased the enmity of the Edomites against them, to the remotest generation.

THE AMORITES.

About the time these sons of Esau were strongly opposing the children of Israel, a powerful foe came up against the descendants of Lot, who were living on the southern border of the Dead Sea, drove them back eastward and southward, establishing themselves in the borderland along the sea, and the hilly country of the lower Jordan.

These new occupants, who supplanted the Ammonites and Moabites, were the Amorites (Gen. x. 16; xix. 37), a powerful tribe who descended from Emer, the fourth son of Canaan, the son of Ham. It is noteworthy the descendants of Ham were numerously settled in those regions on the east and south sides of the Dead Sea, as well as throughout the most fertile portions of Canaan. The Amorites first appeared in small communities on the west of the sea, in the mountains in the neighborhood of Hebron, but rapidly increased, so that they spread their borders and took possession of the most fertile territory of the Moabites and Ammonites. But they were subdued by the Israelites in the time of Moses, while Sihon was their king; their provinces on the east of the Jordan were allotted to Reuben, and those on the west were possessed by Judah. It is of great historical interest to travelers to make a tour around the shores of the Dead Sea, especially the most eventful portions; it will enable them to more clearly outline the districts inhabited by the various tribes who in their turn possessed them. The route for those visiting the Dead Sea from Jericho, with the intention of making a tour of its shores, is to start from the northern bank and proceed south. After traveling a few miles a point is reached where there is a break in the high mountains, at the base of which, a small stream flows into the sea; and a short distance up the valley, among the cragged rocks, are hot springs, which are supposed to be the En-eglaim of Bible mention. Here, according to Josephus, Herod the Great came a short time before his death, seeking in vain its healing virtues, that the loathsome disease which had seized him and was tormenting his life, might be exterminated.

Proceeding on southward, the ancient river Arnon, which is so greatly renowned in history, is reached. It was the chief river east of the Dead Sea and the Jordan, at one period; and before the Amorites drove out the Moabites and Ammonites, it formed the boundary between those tribes; later on it marked the division between the Amorites and Moabites, and lastly between the latter and the tribe of Reuben, who supplanted the Amorites. Still proceeding a few miles south, the country of Moab is entered, and twelve miles farther south is located the site of ancient Zoar, the little city to which Lot fled. It may be seen from the above description, the distance from Sodom to Zoar was many miles, and Lot must have, of necessity, sped his journey to reach the refuge, before the storm of God's indignation came upon the cities he left behind. If the mountains and rivers were the same to-day as when Lot was making his flight to Zoar, one might map in his mind the route he took on that memorable night. From the northern shore of the Dead Sea, which we have made our starting point, and following the southern shore several miles, we have roughly calculated the distance from that point to Zoar to be thirty-two miles. But is is not to be inferred, Lot had that distance to travel ; in the first place, it is not known which of the cities he was living in at the time he was commanded to leave ; nor how close that city was to the place of his escape. It is certain some of them were farther south than others, and Lot may have lived in one of the most southern cities ; if so, his journey was many miles shorter. The route he took is not known. Before the physical changes took place, caused by earthquakes and natural developments, there were doubtless other ways leading to Zoar, than that commonly traveled at present. It is currently stated, that along the southern end of the western shore of the sea, the hills which hitherto margin the shore, recede far in the distance, and gives the sea a much wider space. Here the water is shallow, and the immediate space connecting with the shore is marshy, and very hard even in the best places to travel. In the summer months and early part of the fall, when the usual winter flow from the Jordan and the Arnon is very much reduced, and the greatly increased heat causes greater evaporations, the sea bordering along these muddy flats becomes dry, and a large portion of the shallow margin extending into it, takes the place of the outer shore. Now it seems clear from this fact, that the only outlet to the Dead Sea is the immense evaporations and the spreading out of the sea over several miles of territory on the southwestern side, where the mountains greatly retire. If there was an outlet, through which a volume of water flowed from the bed of the sea, in connection with the wonderful evaporations constantly going on, the decrease would be so vastly more than the increase, the lowest portion of the "Vale of Siddim" would be visible during the latter part of the hot season. For on some portions of the shore of the sea, especially the northern, southern and eastern shores, salt is abundant ; sometimes lumps are found a foot or more thick. This shows the immense evaporations which absorb the water and fill the districts around for miles with beds of salt. If there were other avenues for the water to escape, it is plainly seen there would be a diminution, so great, that at least one-half of the water would be drained out. For when the decrease is greater than the increase, the chief reservoir must become exhausted ; and if the evaporations are sufficient to keep the present increase in bounds a subterranean passage would exhaust it.

When the children of Israel changed their government into a monarchy, many important events transpired, on or near the shores of the Dead Sea, under the reign of different kings; and those tribes living nearest the historic lake, were the most prominently active in their opposition to the new nation. King David, the man of war, had several touching experiences with them, and subdued all the nations round about, who were hostile to him. The tribes east and west of the Dead Sea, also submitted to his authority, after several bitter conflicts had proven their inability to contend against him. These new accessions to the sceptre of David brought to him large tax incomes and greatly strengthened the government revenue. David's reputation as a man of war, had been so widely circulated, the kings of the earth and the mighty men feared him; but after the death of Solomon, when rebellion and rivalry divided the nation, those tributary states began to show themselves unwilling to remain under the sceptre of the Hebrew kings, and began to throw off the yoke of subordination by degrees, until an opportune moment came for them to strike for their independence; at length they became so bold, they were not content with their own freedom, but remembering their past subordinate relation to Israel, endeavored to serve them in like manner.

That their purpose might be accomplished, the three restless nations, whose former territory about the Dead Sea had been allotted to the tribes of Reuben, Gad, Manasseh and Judah, formed a confederation, to subdue Israel. These restless nations were the Ammonites, the Moabites and the Edomites. It was during the reign of Jehoshaphat, that these governments formed a confederacy, to overthrow the kingdom of Judah, in the most secret manner. The Ammonites marched over to Moab, and were joined there by the Moabites; then the two armies went over and joined the Edomites near Mount Seir, and the three potent and over-confident armies, marched in a solid phalanx, up the western shore of the Dead Sea, until they had arrived at the Fountain of the Kid.

During this whole journey, it seems, their march was not observed or known to the people of Judah until they came to Engedi. Then the approach of the armies, suddenly burst upon the sight of the people and filled them with wild dismay. The news of their advance towards Jerusalem was soon dispatched to King Jehoshaphat, which greatly alarmed him. The following was the announcement: "There cometh a great multitude against thee from beyond the sea, on this side of Syria; and behold they be in Hazazon-tamar, which is Engedi." This happened just at the time when hosts of people had gathered from all parts of his kingdom at the Temple, and the king, as did Solomon when the dedication took place, led the services.

It must have been an impressive sight, to see all Judah standing before the Lord with their wives and children, while the king poured forth his supplications to the Most High, a part of which was as follows: "And now behold the children of Ammon, and Moab, and Mount Seir, whom Thou wouldst not let Israel invade when they came out of the land of Egypt, but they turned from them and destroyed them not; behold, I say, now they reward us; they come and cast us out of our possessions, which Thou hast given us to inhabit. O, our God, wilt Thou not judge them, for we have no might against this great company that cometh against us, neither know we what to do; but our eyes are upon Thee."

Just at this stage of the king's prayer, one of the Levites was endowed with the spirit of prophecy. And in those moments of extreme alarm, the Lord gave a message of blessed consolation to the king and his sorrow-stricken people. He advised them to go out to meet the confederate forces the next day; He also told where they would be found, and assured the king, the victory would be given Israel without having to strike a blow. He said, "Behold they come up by the cliff of Ziz;" which is a rugged pass near Engedi. This pleasing prophecy greatly encouraged King Jehoshaphat and the people. They, having the fullest confidence in the prediction of the young Levite, went out the following day to meet the invaders, and were victorious. The Lord who had never failed to come to the help of Israel when they prayed to Him, heard their supplication, and came to their help in a miraculous manner. The confederate army, having learned the army of Israel was approaching, became alarmed and blindly confused, so that they mistook their own forces for Israel and began to slay one another with great slaughter, and fled in wild confusion, and, as had been predicted, the Israelites did not strike a blow; their enemies' own hands destroyed them. The king and those with him, having seen the fulfillment of the prophecy in the destruction of the enemy, went over to the camp, gathered the spoil and returned in triumph to Jerusalem, and offered up their renewed thanks to God for having delivered them from the powerful hand of relentless foes.

JUDAH AND ISRAEL COMBINE AGAINST MOAB.

While Jehoshaphat yet reigned over Judah, and Jehoram, son of Ahab, was king over Israel, the king of Moab, who had been burdened with tax by Ahab, concluded to throw off the yoke that was so sorely pressing him. Jehoram, feeling himself incompetent for the pending crisis, appealed to Jehoshaphat to assist him in the suppression of the rebellion, which he readily complied with, and emphasized his willingness as follows: "I will go up: I am as thou art, my people as thy people, my horses as thy horses." And in answer to Jehoram's question, Jehoshaphat advised they should go up against Moab by the way of the wilderness of Edom, which was a little to the south of the Dead Sea, bordering on Moab and is known as Mt. Seir. It must have been a fatiguing march to the army; for the route they took was circuitous and hard to travel, requiring at least seven days' steady marching to accomplish the journey. Many of the men became thirsty and discouraged because there was no water, neither for themselves nor their beasts; for they were traveling through a desert country. The water supplies they had provided were exhausted, and they must continue on, through the wild wilderness, before water could be secured. It is the case, now that persons passing over this route and several others in Palestine, must take a supply of water with them or they will greatly suffer; and if the want of a little water, even in the time of peace, is so discomforting, what must have been the distressing situation of this vast army of men and beasts, who were worn down with thirst, passing through the wilderness on a mission of war! They found themselves in a perilous situation; for unless they obtained water, they must surely perish. But the Lord, who is at all times equal to every emergency, informed the discomfited people through the prophet Elisha, they should have a plentiful supply of water the next day, although it would not rain; and in the morning, as had been predicted by the prophet, all the ditches were filled with water. The Moabites, looking toward the plain on the borders of the Dead Sea early in the morning, just as the sun was reflecting its light over the valley, saw the water in the trenches the Israelites had prepared the previous day, and supposed it to be blood, for it had a blood-red appearance to them, because of the peculiar reflection of the sun. They seeing this, said to each other, they have smitten one another, and at the same time they may have remembered their own mistake at Engedi, how they slew one another instead of Israel, and supposed they made a similar fatal attack upon themselves.

Feeling assured Israel had been its own destroyer, the Moabites came down from their heights to capture the residue and gather the spoil, but were seized with wild dismay when they saw the hosts of Israel in battle array. The panic-stricken Moabites fled in great haste and confusion. This was another signal victory the Lord gave Israel on the old battle-ground near the Dead Sea, where on other occasions He showed His love for that people, notwithstanding they so often rebelled against Him. Just at the time the Moabites were indulging in exalted expectation, of reaping bountiful spoils from the camp of Israel, near the Salt Sea, where they had stationed themselves, they were driven into confusion and into the jaws of death. They were not only driven from the field, but pursued into their own stronghold; for they were shut up in their capital city, Kir-haraseth, one of the most carefully fortified of all their cities. It may be seen, therefore, the Dead Sea is not only famous because it occupies at least a large portion of territory, on which the cities of the plain stood, but also for the many memorable battles fought along its border, and the manifestation of God's power in fighting for Israel. (2 Kings iii.)

THE VALLEY OF THE JORDAN.

The Jordan Valley, so named because of the great historic river that flows through it, is one of the most interesting ravines in Palestine. It has been several times explored by some of the most expert scientists of our globe, and has provoked many very earnest discussions as to the prime physical causes of its formation, and is regarded as one of the most remarkable depressions in the world. It is situated between the Sea of Galilee on the north and the Dead Sea on the south; its width is from five to ten miles, the widest portion being at Jericho, where it is known as the Plain of Jericho; here it assumes the appearance of a tremendous expanse, inclosed on the east and west by mammoth mountainous ridges, known as the mountains of temptation, and those of the spies. These heights are barren, rugged, and steep. On the south the Dead Sea appears like a continuation of the plain; but in the distance it has every appearance of a beautiful little lake. Its northern bank is nearly level with the water and therefore has a similar resemblance to the plain at first sight on approaching it.

The present aspect of the Plain of Jericho is not to be compared with that described in the Holy Scriptures and by Josephus. He pronounced it the most beautiful tract of country in the entire district of Judea, a blessed region full of fatness; and in referring to the fountain of Elisha, he said it watered the country seventy stadia long by twenty broad, covered with luxuriant gardens and palm groves It was so thickly studded with these orchards, it was called the "City of Palm Trees." But this product of the land, which was so greatly esteemed by the ancient inhabitants of that once proud city, has passed from its borders, and the thorny bramble and other small trees have taken their places. All the rich products which so bountifully flourished, have seemingly fallen with the city never to rise again.

The Jordan valley is remarkable as to its physical situation, when compared to other deep ravines in that country and in the world. Its surface is estimated to be six hundred feet below the level of the Mediterranean, at the Sea of Galilee, and continues increasing in depth southward, so that at the Dead Sea, its depression has the enormous depth of thirteen hundred and twelve feet below the western sea.

This tremendous valley, the most remarkable for depth in the world, on its extreme southern terminus, has puzzled the most expert geologists on the globe, in their endeavors to investigate the physical causes that produced it; and various theories have been drawn as a result of their opinions, the most acceptable of which is that given by the Palestine exploration survey, found in the fourteenth chapter of Condor's "Tent Work." They have concluded that "a violent and sudden collapse of the whole of the Jordan valley, south of the Sea of Galilee, probably occurred at a late geological period, and that was followed by a further catastrophe of considerably later date, caused by volcanic action." It is also thought by others, from certain developments, that the Dead Sea, at some distant period, extended much further north than at present. This opinion is drawn from the fact that four distinct beaches have been discovered. The first is about thirty feet above the present high-water mark, and the others are situated one, two and four hundred feet from each other. Others have drawn the theory that the Dead Sea had assumed its present proportions before the age of man. Therefore, it is impossible for the cities of the plain to have occupied the space or any part now covered by it. The above theories clearly show the inability of scientific men to produce absolute harmony, by their investigations, independent of Divine revelation, although they earnestly endeavor to do so, and that God's word is the only true and safe guide for mankind. The Bible teaches, that at least a portion of the cities of Sodom and Gomorrah, stood on the site now occupied by the Dead Sea. Now we know that in the time of Lot this was the most fertile of all the land in southern Palestine; and so inviting that cities had been built upon the plain, and thousands of inhabitants lived in them, and were in a highly prosperous condition. Taking into account the character of the sea, that it is destructive to vegetation and human life, it is not likely, the people in those times would have made choice of the most deadly tract of country in the whole land, to establish their cities, when they could have made choice of other sites more healthy. Again, we are taught in the Holy Scriptures, these regions were flourishing with fruits, pastures and vegetation. We are just here very forcibly reminded of the stupendous question of the Scriptures, "Can a man by searching find out God?" and the declaration, "As high as the heavens are above the earth, so are my ways above thy ways, and my thoughts above thy thoughts." From the fact that men of the most progressive science differ in opinion, as to the origin and character of things, and if these extraordinarily profound matters, with which they have interested themselves, are hidden from them, it is clearly evident that they are not to be relied upon in their conclusions, of things of a graver and more intricate nature. But historians have been greatly aided in their investigations, so as to understand much that has been tangled, by having acquired a thorough knowledge of the native tongue; so that many words of the Hebrew language, when compared with corresponding words in English, furnish a key to the original meaning. Take, for example, the Arabic word for shelves, or beaches, as above referred to; it is Lidd. This is found to be a derivation of the term Vale of Siddim. It is plain, therefore, if the Vale of Siddim was located at the southern end of the plain of Jericho, there can exist no reasonable doubt as to the site of the cities of the plain, which must have been situated on the north. The great depressions of the plain, being protected on each side by lofty mountains, render the climate the hottest of any in Palestine, which eminently qualified it for the growth of palm trees and other highly esteemed fruits, such as are produced only in very warm countries.

It is stated, that during the time of the crusaders' control of Palestine, sugar cane was cultivated in the plain of Jericho, and it was during that period the aqueducts and pointed arches were constructed. Remnants of them are still partially standing at the entrance of the "bloody pass" coming up from the city of palm trees. At this period, under the activity of the crusaders who made an effort to restore the former fertility of that region, and make it again the garden of Palestine, much time and labor were spent to reinstate it, but they were not successful. It is at present under the jurisdiction of Arabs, who seem to know but little about cultivation, and care less; therefore, much of the best land, that, with a little care, would produce good crops is not noticed. There is no doubt that the plain of Jericho would be more fruitful than any portion of the country between Jerusalem and the Jordan, if those controlling it would bestir themselves a little more industriously. It is in my mind, only a question of comparatively short time, before this valley will bloom again as a rose. These miserable offensive Arabs will be crowded out, by an industrious people from Europe, who are already settling in various portions of the country in small communities, and producing fine crops in those districts that for a long while were left idle. I suppose those rich fields would have been settled upon long since, had it not been for the dangerous barriers, which must in time be removed.

THE RIVER JORDAN.

The Jordan is the most distinguished river in Palestine, and one of the most noted in the world. Its name is said to be a compound of Jar or Yar, and Dan, because its rise is in the vicinity of Dan. It is the chief river in Canaan, and runs from north to south, dividing the country into two parts; the larger portion is on the west and is the most important. There are two streams claimed to be the sources of the Jordan, one is at Barket-es-Ram, known in the writings of Josephus, as Phiala, from its bowl-like shape. For a long while this was supposed to be its chief and highest source. The water running from it is slimy and offensive. It has been found since, the main source is a spring of considerable size, which issues a stream from the western base of a Tell (Hill) at Dan. This is regarded as one of the largest fountains in the world, and without doubt the largest in either Syria or Palestine. It will be called to mind that Dan is the most northern point occupied by the Israelites. At Banaias or Cæsarea Philippi, not far from the site on which once stood a shrine erected to the god Pan, is a great cave called Rasen-neb, regarded as the "fountain head." From this fountain runs one of the sources of the Jordan. It is situated on the side of a perpendicular cliff estimated to be one hundred feet high. These three fountains have been the prime feeders of the great historic river ever since its name has been known to man, or has had a beginning in the world. The river Jordan is without a parallel on the globe. It is shut in from the great western sea by high mountains, and pours its contents into the great Salt Sea, at the lowest point of surface known in the world, it being thirteen hundred feet below the level of the sea on its west side. It gathers the water from the melting snows along the highland as it proceeds south, and thus became a stream of considerable size. The length of the Jordan from its source to its mouth, if it continued in a direct line, would be about one hundred and four miles; but because of its tortuous course, it travels two hundred miles before it reaches its terminus at the Dead Sea. It runs rapidly down a continuous plain, interrupted at different stages by twenty-seven cataracts. It is not traveled by vessels, and there is not a flourishing city along its banks, as is commonly the case in other lands. But instead of lively towns and cities along the border land, the oleander, the tamarisk bushes and the willow, are plentifully seen fringing

VIEW OF THE JORDAN.

the banks forming a deep border; the weeds and bush-wood grow uninterruptedly and have become so very thick, a person has much difficulty to work his way through them. These closely grown thickets afford convenient homes for beasts of prey. The wild boar and the leopard frequent them. Therefore, it is highly important that great caution is observed by all who pass through this trackless mass.

The half-savage Bedouin, whose chief ambition is to plunder and steal whenever an opportunity is presented, often finds it unsafe to enter this wild forest alone, although he would find a safe retreat from those who may be in pursuit of him. Jericho is about ten miles west of the Jordan, and is the only place of importance along the valley until the Sea of Galilee is reached, on the shore of which the little village of Tiberias stands. From the above outline it may be seen that the banks of the Jordan possess no charms of interest; and were it not that the traveler is on the margin of the river where some of the most remarkable events known to the world took place, no one would care to waste time and means in traversing its borders. But the historical associations connected with the Jordan are so full of interest, one who travels its shores for the sake of informing himself as to location where these wonders took place, does not take any account of the labor and trouble of the journey. The traveler becomes more deeply impressed with the many events prominently narrated in the Bible, that occurred at the Jordan, by visiting the scenes where they took place. He may think of Lot, who, being allured by the richness of the plain along which it flows, because it was well watered and full of verdure, sought its benefits. And to these fords, came the great army of Hebrews, after their wanderings of forty years in the wilderness, and crossed over on dry ground, until all the people were passed to the other side, to possess the goodly land which the Lord had chosen for them to dwell in. Their crossing was miraculous and a most striking evidence of the presence of the Lord. This wonderful event occurred at a season when the fords, where it was usually shallow and easy to cross, were swelled so greatly that no one could pass them. For it was during the April harvest, when the overflow of the inner banks, had caused the water to flood the whole space between the outer and inner banks. This overflow visits the Jordan annually, and is caused by the melting of the snow on Mounts Hermon, Lebanon and the neighboring highlands. The sudden breaking up of the ice and snow rushes into the river and causes it to swell rapidly, so that its inner banks cannot contain the volume of water passing between them. "For Jordan overfloweth all her banks all the time of harvest, that the water which came down from above stood, and rose a great way off, at Adam, the city that is beside Zaretan: and those that went down toward the sea of the Arabah, even the Salt sea, were wholly cut off; and the people went over right against Jericho." Here also Elijah and Elisha crossed; on that memorable day the Jordan was divided, by a single stroke of the prophet with his mantle, in the name of the Lord. It is noteworthy that the Jordan was commonly fordable during the dry seasons, when the water was low at the fords. Jacob, David, Abner, Absalom, and thousands of others crossed the Jordan after Israel entered the land of Canaan. It was a common thing for the Jews, living in the northern and southern districts, whose prejudice would not give consent for them to pass through Samaria, to cross the Jordan when visiting each other both on business and social relations. At present the inhabitants on either side of the Jordan, cross it at the fords as often as their business demands, during the dry or summer season. They know the time when the "swellings of Jordan" forbid the passing of any one. Then even those who are most expert in crossing at such a stage of the water, that hundreds would not dare venture, would not attempt to pass over at the shallowest ford, fearing they would be swept away with the torrent. It may be inferred, therefore, it is not an uncommon thing for men to cross the Jordan, as it is an ordinary custom. But it is not in any natural way possible to cross during the season of the overflow. And nothing but a miracle wrought by the Almighty could enable a person to do so. Had the Israelites crossed at the time the river is usually fordable, there would have been no reason for surprise, for it would have been crossed just as the people ordinarily did at that season. (Joel iii. 15, 16.) But crossing as they did at the time of the great overflow, and the miraculous circumstances connected with the event of their passage, make it a most stupendous wonder. The ark was carried by the priests who were in advance of the people, and a monument of stones was built in the midst of the Jordan, in the place where priests who bore the ark stood, and the forty thousand prepared for war, "passed over before the Lord unto battle to the plain of Jericho."

Again, when Gideon went out against the Midianites, he lay in wait for them at the fords; and there the men of Gilead slew the men of Ephraim; and here David crossed and found refuge in Mahanaim. But none crossed at the time of the overflow. There are several tributaries to the Jordan; the largest one, between its source and the Sea of Galilee, is Lake Merom, or Hulek, from whence it flows with increased rapidity and volume into the Lake Gennesaret, through which it passes, exhibiting most clearly the course of its passage. My attention was drawn to the beautiful line formed through the lake from north to south, while standing on the shore at Capernaum, and it attracted me so, I for a while was completely absorbed in admiration, for it seemed so strange, that the Jordan could flow through a body of water as large as the Sea of Tiberias as if confined within the limits of its banks, without being at least partly hidden from view. There is a continuous depression in the course of the Jordan from its northern extremity to its mouth. During the whole distance of its passage, it falls twenty-three hundred feet; seventeen hundred feet of this fall is embraced in the first twenty-seven miles, that is, from its source to the Sea of Tiberias; this gives it an average fall of about sixty-three feet to the mile in its upper course, and eight feet in the lower. Therefore, the first fall of twenty-seven miles is very abrupt, but the greater distance is gradual; it also becomes deeper and wider during the winter rains. At this season it is not uncommon for the river to be from eighty to one hundred and sixty feet wide, and from five to twelve feet deep. Then the water becomes very muddy on account of the collection of clay it gathers from the banks. Those who visit the Jordan from Jerusalem, usually take luncheon at the ford opposite Jericho, which is the traditional site of the crossing of the Israelites; and some say, our Lord was baptized at or near the same place; and that Elijah crossed here with Elisha, when he was taken to heaven. It is an inexpressible pleasure, to the Bible student, to have the privilege of visiting the shore of the Jordan and its historic fords, with the Bible and guide-book, scanning the narratives of events having transpired at the place where he stands, or near by.

In connection with others, he might fix his mind on Elijah and Elisha, who crossed here at the lower ford opposite Gilgal, and the return of the young prophet alone to the same crossing, for his father had been taken up in a chariot, and the only thing belonging to him, in the keeping of Elisha, was the familiar mantle. With this precious relic the young man came in triumph to the Jordan, which had assumed the same attitude it presented when he first approached it in company with Elijah; but remembering how the water parted when his father smote it, and having unshaken faith in the same God, Elisha stood on the east bank, while the young men, who came to witness the miracle, sat on the west, looking on, and Elisha struck Jordan with the same instrument, and said, "Where is the Lord God of Elijah!" and again Jordan parted to allow the young prophet a passage over it. The young men who so eagerly watched the movement of Elisha, having seen the miraculous display of the power of God working in him, proclaimed: "The spirit of Elijah doth rest on Elisha." From that auspicious moment, the young man who had left his plow and parents, to follow the man of God became his successor, and went forth in the strength of God, working wonders, and delivering such messages to men, whether kings or peasants, as were given him from God. One, in a highly spiritual state, may imagine, at times, while standing on the bank of the Jordan, he can see the wonderful event taking place.

At the brink of this river came Naaman the Syrian, burdened with a loathsome disease. Being directed hither by Elisha that he might be healed, and be persuaded thereby, that there is no other supreme being but the God of Israel, the advice given him by the prophet was simple and at first disregarded. "Go wash in Jordan seven times," was the recommendation of Elisha to the captain. But he despised this counsel, and would have returned home, filled with indignation, had not one of his attendants urged him to try the remedy. Being finally persuaded, he dipped himself seven times in this historic river, and was every whit whole; for his "flesh was like unto a little child's" But while these events referred to, are stupendously wonderful, they are but stepping-stones to those of which the New Testament gives account. 2 Kings ii. 1-15.

JOHN THE BAPTIST'S VISIT AND WORK THERE.

Here at this Jordan and near (according to tradition) where I took luncheon at the ford, the voice of John the Baptist "was heard preaching in the wilderness," in tones so awakening that all Judea and Jerusalem came down to hear him, and he baptized them, confessing their sins. It was along the western bank of this Jordan, that our Lord came walking, to be introduced to the multitude that had assembled to hear John, and to enter more fully upon the work of His divine mission. It was while Jesus stood on the bank of the Jordan, that the heavens opened and the Holy Spirit descended, looking like a dove, and lit upon Him. Here our Lord made the river memorable forever, by having the rite of sacred baptism performed upon Him by John.

It is proper to state, there exists a division of opinion as to the site where these latter events took place; one tradition favors the lower ford opposite Jericho, near the crossing of the Israelites; another has settled upon the next ford on the north, as the place. But the old crossing opposite Gilgal, is the place generally believed to be the original site, and here hundreds of pilgrims come every year and take a bath, after the close of the Easter Festival. We were informed that they rush to the Jordan in great crowds—sometimes a thousand or more—and without ceremony, or even halting; without doubting or intimidation; without taking off any of their clothing, they plunge into the muddy, yet sacred stream; then they vigorously and prayerfully bathe; then lie down, with a hope that the new baptism will cleanse them from whatever stains of sin they may possess and will bring to them many blessings.

It is certain, if their faith in the Lord Jesus, whose example they attempt to follow, is as strong as it is in the Jordan, they will not come short of the blessings they so ardently seek. The clothing in which they bathe is supposed to be made holy by the cleansing influence of the water, therefore they are carefully preserved, to be used only to bury them in as their winding-sheet; and they also indulge in the anticipation of entering in through the gates into the city of the heavenly Jerusalem, in the sacred garments with which they bathed in the Jordan.

The Oriental pilgrims who visit the sacred sites in Palestine from far-distant lands seldom have more than one opportunity to do so in life, and they esteem it next to the hope they entertain of heaven. It is the same case with the Moslems; it is enjoined upon all the followers of Mohammed, to visit Mecca at least once in life, even at a tremendous sacrifice; and many spend the last mite they possess to comply with this rule. And so the Greeks have a similar rule for the adherents to their faith. This is the reason the many thousands go up to Jerusalem, from remote parts of the world, feeling it to be their duty if possible to make the pilgrimage, confidently believing it will be of spiritual benefit to them. It so happens at times some of these people are unable to return to their homes, both those who go to Jerusalem and to Mecca. It seems that the people in the far East and Palestine take great delight in carrying out their obligations to the church, however great a sacrifice they must make to perform them. This example should be noted. But if we properly look into the conduct of these devotees, we will see the necessity of a general circulation of the Holy Bible and a proper instruction of its teachings. It may be seen from their custom that the old Jewish idea is still indulged by many of the Gentiles, especially the ancient custom of going up to Jerusalem to worship. While they do not hold to the opinion, it is the only place to engage themselves in sacred devotion, they do believe a visit there, and to the holy shrines and sacred places, adds greatly to their standing in heaven; and like the Samaritans of old, who supposed Mount Gerizim was the most acceptable place to worship, so the Mohammedans believe Mecca is the most sacred spot on the whole earth, and they must by all means go there once in life to bow at the shrines and kiss the tomb in which this illustrious founder's remains were deposited. By so doing they think it will bring to them blessings, such as nothing else can. These gravely sad errors obtain because the Holy Bible is not generally circulated among these people, as well as a great lack of receiving proper instruction from those in whom they confide as teachers. These are plain cases of " blind leading the blind." But the Holy Bible, the Book of books, opens the understanding of all who will consent to abide by its teachings. It is suited to all men, of all ages and conditions. We learn that the wise, the ignorant and poor, the humble and despised, all may draw bountiful supplies from its inexhaustible fullness without fear, for all are welcome. It is not, as many may think, a mere pastoral book, or one that is adapted to certain classes who live in cities and towns, who may read it merely for historical information, but it is given to all men; to the end they may have an abiding knowledge of the will of God and be conducted in the path of holiness; its various forms of conveying the truth adapts itself to all phases of human condition, and these diversified forms of truth, at once commend their teachings to man as the word of the great and all-wise God, and impress him that it is not needful he should go to Jerusalem, nor to Mecca, to worship, but in every place where men call upon the Lord, He will hear them and come to their help. Again, the Holy Bible has helped men as nothing else could, in developing much ancient history which would not have been understood without it. For this most precious of all books, like the inscriptions carved on tombstones, tells the story of the past.

NEBO AND PISGAH.

We might pass from one part of Palestine to another, viewing its rivers, seas, brooks and the various places of historical value, and would know but little, if anything, of the wonderful events that took place there, had not the Bible revealed them to us. Take for example the lonely peak of Pisgah, on which Moses, the illustrious leader of the Israelites, ascended when he viewed the land of promise; its geographical location, could not have been satisfactorily settled, had it not been so minutely defined in the Bible. In it we are informed that, " Moses went up from the plain of Moab into the mountain of Nebo, to the top of Pisgah, that is over against Jericho." This definition is so distinct and evident, that visitors even in these times have but little difficulty in identifying Mounts Nebo and Pisgah, from the other mountains of

Moab; and in whatever direction one may go in central or southern Palestine, and many parts in the north, the mammoth mountains of Moab can be seen prominent.

THE VIEW OF MOSES.

Very soon after the plain of Sharon is passed, on the way up to Jerusalem from Joppa, and the western point of the highland of Judea is passed, this range, of which Nebo forms a part, appears to view along the eastern horizon about thirty miles away, but does not seem more than half the distance. It is also seen from Mizpeh and the sacred Mount of Olives; then a little to the north of Jerusalem on Mt. Scopus, the range is distinctly seen; then, southeast, as far as Bethlehem, and south, as far as Hebron, views are had of these mountains. On the north they can be seen from Bethel, Shechem, Ebal and Gerizim. One who has viewed them from the Jordan particularly, will be able without difficulty, to point out the historic mountains from all others in the range, even from the far northern points of view. Although Pisgah belonged to the Abarim range, there seems to be, when viewed from the Jordan or the Plain of Jericho, a depression breaking the range a little, near Nebo; this gives it distinction, and as there is no visible elevation behind the summit of Pisgah, which is a peak on the top of Nebo, it has the highest and most conspicuous altitude in its neighborhood. Standing as it does, the foreground of the mountain range, it affords a more prominent view of Palestine than any other round about it. Therefore, Moses, the servant of God and faithful leader of the Hebrews, was directed to ascend to the summit of Pisgah, that he might obtain the best observation of the land of Canaan, the future permanent home of the children of the promise. Although Moses had reached the advanced age of one hundred and twenty years, he was not embarrassed by feeble sight, nor was his natural physical force abated. This is evident from the fact, he was able in his old age to climb to the heights of the lofty Pisgah, then stand and view the land, until he had gotten a general observation of the whole country: "And the Lord showed him all the land of Gilead unto Dan and all Naphtali, and the land of Ephraim and Mannassah, and all the land of Judah, unto the uttermost sea (Mediterranean); and the south, and the plain of the valley of Jericho, the city of palm trees, unto Zoar." This loftly summit was the most prospective peak of the whole range. It is so situated, both as to elevation and location, that an unobstructed view can be had over the mountainous country of Palestine, and over the sea on the west.

On the top of this mount Moses stood, about the time he was nearing the end of the long, weary journey through the wilderness, and his career on earth, and looked with extreme delight, upon the beautiful country the Lord had chosen for a heritage of the people, with whom he had so long suffered many heavy trials, during their forty years' wandering from the land of Egypt, the land concerning which, under Divine direction, he had written so strangely, and where Abraham, the father of the faithful, had sojourned five hundred years prior. While viewing the many hills and mountain tops, doubtless his ravished eyes glimpsed Mount Moriah, and he thought of the morning, when Abraham took his son Isaac to sacrifice him to the Lord, and how in the moment, the faithful father stood with uplifted hand to slay him, the voice of the Lord stayed his hand. As Moses looked westward and downward, the bold Jordan had flooded its banks, in proud defiance of the multitude below, who were soon to stand upon them, eager to enter into the country on the margin of its western shore.

Just across this narrow stream, which, from the height of his view, must have appeared almost beneath him, near the base of Nebo, was the beautiful plain of Jericho, and little Gilgal, where his people should build their first altar in Canaan. Then looking a little to his left, he saw the dreary waters of the Dead Sea, the border-land of which still bore prominent signs of the wrath of God. Then casting his eyes northward, Mounts Tabor, snowy Hermon, Ebal, and Gerizim were in full view before him; and on the west could be seen Carmel, Lebanon, and the hills of Galilee, and all the country as far as Dan, the most northern limit of the land. It may be imagined, how unusually happy, the old care-worn and age-stricken man of God felt, as he stood upon this lofty peak, far away from the communion of the people, whose constant inclinations to rebellion and mistrust, many times chafed his soul and caused him to weep bitterly, especially when he heard them murmur against God and charge Him with dealing unkindly towards them. But for a short time, while holding special communion with the Lord, who had taken charge of him, his soul enjoyed undisturbed rest, and there was nothing to disturb the thoughts passing through his mind. Therefore he was permitted to drink to his fullest satisfaction, the blessing so desirable to man, while standing on the narrow margin of death. He also enjoyed the blessing of having a most delightful view of the land, soon to be inhabited by the people whom he had endeavored to encourage and counsel all through the journey of the wilderness; the land that should produce abundantly, the "land of milk and honey." And although he would not be permitted to conduct them beyond the narrow confines of the Jordan, or spend another hour with them on earth, he was willing to surrender his responsible charge to Joshua, whilst he waited patiently for the summons that should end his long and trying probation. We may suppose, without transcending the limits of propriety, that the transporting views Moses had of the goodly land, gave him as much pleasure, as if he had been permitted to have entered and enjoyed its fruits. How greatly he drank in its delectable impressions is not known, as he died upon the mount without communicating it to the people. But it is no stretch of imagination, to suppose, his satisfaction was so complete he was willing to die, and let his spirit wing its flight to the upper Canaan, to join the ranks of the glorified hosts, who bask in the splendors of the golden city beyond this chilly vale of tears.

The heart of Moses, while looking upon these scenes, must have had much satisfaction in the contemplation of the fact that the journey of the people would soon be ended, and everything they could consistently hope for, would be obtained in the land whither they should soon enter. And could Moses have commanded enough power while there to communicate with his weary people, in the camp at the foot of Nebo, his graphic description of the country, would have caused new inspiration to arouse the anxious multitude, with a full determination to enter upon their long-sought possessions.

Upon the lofty summit of Pisgah, Moses, whose patience had been taxed for forty dreary years, finished his observations of the country before him, that lay just beyond the Jordan, finished the number of his days in the world, and immediately opened his eyes on the most glorious land, promised to all who will take up their cross and follow Jesus. How transporting was the sight! The very first look upon the heavenly land, was far more glorious than all the country he had been surveying from the top of Pisgah. We venture the assertion he became lost in amazement. But what a marvellous funeral the great prophet must have had, although the usual ceremony was not performed; the long procession was not seen, following him to the tomb, while the weeping ones were filling the air with bewildering lamentations. No human orators were there, delivering long eulogies, setting forth in strong terms the sacrifices Moses made for the good of the people; but God, who had led this, the greatest of men for one hundred and twenty years, took charge of the funeral on the mountain top, far from mortal sight, and saw to it that this hero, whose presence upon Pisgah immortalized its name, should be honored with a burial such as man never had. It may be imagined that hosts of angels came and rested their feet upon Pisgah's rocky summit, while the remains of the man of God were laid to rest, where no mortal could know or identify his grave.

JOSHUA CAMPED AT GILGAL.

Joshua, the successor of Moses, led the people into the promised land. Gilgal, the place so distinguished in sacred history as the first camping-place of the Israelites, after entering Canaan, is southeast of Jericho. Nothing marks the site of that anciently renowned place, so sacredly memorable to the Jews, but a small, shapeless ruin. But they highly reverence the locality because the Ark of God remained there, until it was removed to Shiloh. It is about four miles southwest of the Jordan, and five miles from Jericho. There were several places in Palestine bearing the name of Gilgal: one on Mt. Carmel, another near Kefr, Suba, and another near Singel. But this one near the Jordan, southwest of Jericho, is the historic place which the Hebrews looked upon for many ages with profound, if not adoring, reverence. The twelve stones taken from the bed of the Jordan were carried to the hill Gilgal, where they were piled ; and all the Israelites were circumcised, and there made it a place of rest. The headquarters of the camp, for a long time were there. After they had rolled away the reproach of Egypt from them, they celebrated their first passover there, in the land of Canaan.

It was from Gilgal Joshua went up to Jericho, and saw over against the wall one whom he supposed to be a man, who informed him, he had come "as captain of the Lord's host." In the immediate neighborhood, a school of the prophets flourished in the time of Elijah. It was from Gilgal the army of Israel, marched when they won the great victory over Jericho without striking a blow, until after the walls tumbled down. This proud city was situated in the Jordan valley, about ten miles from the river, and was shut in by a high mountainous fortress, which is known as the mountains of the spies, because the men were directed by Rahab to hide in them three days. The only way for Joshua to march against Jericho, was from the south or southeast portion of the plain. This route was not obstructed by mountains, and the Israelites had a pleasant plain to march through, up to the city. There are three Jerichos known in history; these are, the ancient city, which was in a flourishing state when the children of Israel entered Canaan ; the Jericho of Herod's time, which is known to have been a city of great importance in the time of " Our Lord," and the modern village now standing, which is a little dilapidated place known to the Arabs as Eriha; its inhabitants have the reputation of being a very dishonest people, and by no means trustworthy. They do but little work, as the tillable land of the plain clearly shows. One of the attractions about Jericho is the famous fountain, or spring of Elisha, which is in the immediate vicinity of the site of the ancient city, and is the life of the present community. Its water is perennial and copious; so that it not only furnishes supplies for the people and cattle, but for irrigation also. It is cool, bracing and pleasant to the taste. A small reservoir receives its flow, from which it is carried off by several little channels, cut through a portion of the plain, for the purpose of watering the gardens in the dry season. This is the spring, which, in the time of Elisha, contained bitter water, and the men came to him complaining of it; when the prophet heard this, he had compassion on them, and healed the spring so that it was made sweet immediately, and has continued so to the present. As to the fact of its sweetness, I can candidly testify; for while there I drank abundantly of it, and found it not only sweet, but delicious. This seems to be the candid conclusion of all who have drunk of it. Were it not for this spring, the inhabitants would be compelled to travel to the Jordan, which is at the nearest point about ten miles, for water. There are seasons they could get it from the brook Cherith; but the greater portion of the year it is dry or so low water could not be gotten. There is nothing to be seen at the site of ancient Jericho, to indicate its passed history in any way, for it is "an heap," where not even its ruins are visible. But it is the opinion of many, that if at this late date, money enough could be appropriated to excavate some of the old mounds, many valuable and interesting relics would be found. We rode entirely around the site of the ancient walls, talking of Joshua and thinking of the great victory he won, and of the triumphant shouts of the multitudes, when they saw the massive walls falling level with the ground, when the seventh round had been completed. But now all is desolate and dead. On the high mound above the spring, a good view can be had over the plain, and of the mountains of Moab from which the children of Israel fondly gazed, upon the country they should soon enter and enjoy. Just under our feet were the woeful remains of the once popular and prosperous city to which Joshua sent men from beyond Jordan to spy. Just behind us on the west, are the bold mountains, to which the men fled to evade the wrath of their pursuers.

The most conspicuous memorials of the ancient city, with its mighty gates, massive walls, monumental towers and Edenic gardens, are a few withering mounds, under which lie buried all the dusty remains of that great city. Lying, as it does, under these mounds, in a deep depression nearly thirteen hundred feet below the level of the Mediterranean Sea, and more than thirty-one hundred feet below Mt. Zion, and being nearly closed in by high mountains, a temperature rises so intensely hot, it would almost seem as if the fire of divine indignation was still being poured upon it, that others may be aware of His wrath. It may be that upon this very spot over which we rode, Joshua stood forth in the presence of all Israel, and pointed his victorious hand towards the masses of ruins that comprised the renowned city of Jericho, which had fallen beneath the displeasure of the Almighty; and in the name of the God who made him conqueror, pronounced a curse upon the man who should at any time thereafter attempt to rebuild it: "Cursed be the man before the Lord that riseth up and buildeth this city Jericho; he shall lay the foundation thereof in his first-born, and in his youngest son shall he set up the gates of it."

It is worthy of remark, that notwithstanding this awful malediction, in about five hundred years after it was pronounced, a man came forward to test its validity, or defy its authority, and made an effort to rebuild the city upon which the wrath of God was still abiding. This man was Hiel, the Bethelite; he rebuilt the old sin-cursed city, but to his bitter sorrow witnessed the literal fulfillment of the woe pronounced by Joshua, upon the man who would dare to do it; for his children suffered the fate of his folly. The second Jericho, is that which existed in the time of our Lord, and was located at the entrance of the hill country of Judea; it was known as the city of palm-trees, and was founded by order of Herod the Great.

Several traces of old ruins are prominent, that indicate the existence at some time of a flourishing and inviting city. But like the great city Heleopolis, that has but a single shaft remaining, to tell the story of its past existence, so at the second Jericho, a small tower about thirty feet high, is the most conspicuous object of the remains of the city of palm-trees. In connection with the tower are a few scattered remnants of the old aqueduct, as we proceed towards Eriha, the present Jericho. It is noteworthy that there is not a city to be found on the plain. Our Lord visited Jericho and spent some time with Zaccheus the publican, who was a tax-gatherer; and somewhere in the region over which travelers usually ride, may have been the spot along the wayside, where poor blind Bartimeus, son of Timeus, sat asking alms, because he was suffering from two serious afflictions, blindness and poverty. The Saviour had mercy upon him and restored his sight. The modern Jericho dates from the time of the Crusaders. Just outside of its low mud walls are the hotels, at which visitors put up, and find them very comfortably arranged. The most of the houses composing the village are composed of mud, but those who seem not to care to live in them, have small black tents, which are not strong. The most of them are worn with age and constant use. Joshua vi. 26; 1 Kings xvi. 24.

The last night I spent in Jericho, one of the most fearful land-storms swept over the plain, I ever witnessed. It shook the hotel as if it were but a reed, and almost persuaded me at first, it was built upon the sand; for it was shaking so alarmingly, it seemed as if down it must come; and great would have been "the fall of it." It was with difficulty, the guests could compose themselves; not one of us retired until after midnight, fearing the building would be blown to the ground. How strikingly clear the words of Jesus were comprehended, as to the difference of the house founded upon the sand, from that one built upon a rock, in the time of great storms! If that hotel had been built upon a solid rock foundation, it would not have been moved; and although it was not wholly on the sand, the soil is so very light, one would feel as if it was. It did not fall, but we saw in the morning that it had sustained considerable damage. Some, if not all, the little black tents in Eriba were torn to shreds. It is a living truth, sandy foundations will not stand heavy storms, neither spiritual nor physical. Luke xviii. 43; xix. 1-10; Matt. xx. 29-34.

THE BROOK CHERITH.

The Brook Cherith, called by the natives Woody Kelt, though very small and generally dry, during a part of the hot season, when the rain is suspended, yet it is highly interesting because of the peculiar history associated with it, in connection with the sojourn of Elijah there. The event of chief interest, that seems to have caused more discussion than anything else that occurred there, is the supply of food Elijah, the prophet, obtained from day to day for a year, while hiding from Ahab, king of Israel. The ravine, through which the brook flows, crosses the Jericho road about three miles north of Elisha's spring, near the entrance into the bloody pass. This ravine, especially that portion in the region of the convent of Elijah, is one of the most sublime in Palestine. It is from four to five hundred feet deep, and very narrow at the bottom, only wide enough to permit the little stream to pass. The highway to Jericho, passes for some distance along the border of the deepest southern part, and from top to bottom, high sharp rocks line the gorge, so that it is solemnly grand to look into. On the nothern bank is situated, in absolute seclusion, in this deep depression, the convent of Elijah, which is under the management of the Greek church. It is supposed to be located at or near the place, the prophet was hiding, during the exhaustive search king Ahab instituted to apprehend him. The path leading from Jericho to the convent, is very rugged and difficult in many places to travel; yet the monks who live there, seem to go over it without fatigue; but persons who are accustomed to good roads find it a most tedious journey, even riding a horse. It will be remembered, here, we are informed in the Holy Scriptures, that while Elijah was hiding by the historic brook, the ravens furnished him bread and meat daily, and the brook, until it became dry, furnished him with water. The food which the man of God received has of late caused many lengthy and profitable discussions. These arguments are not in opposition to the fact that Elijah was fed by the ravens; but who were these ravens, men or birds? This has laid the foundation for discussion. Many are inclined to the opinion, that the ravens spoken of in the Bible in connection with the prophet Elijah, were men and not birds, as is held by others. 1 Kings xviii. 3-7.

On this subject, much has been said, and many important facts have been advanced. It has been strangely doubted that the Lord would make choice of a bird so very unclean as the raven, to feed his servant, especially in a country where so many clean birds exist. To the north of the modern Jericho, three or four miles, is a high hill having a projecting peak. The Arabs call it Osh-el-Ghoreb, or "The Raven's Nest." This hill is in the locality of the brook Cherith, and not far from the traditional site where Elijah hid. It is said the whole district around the hill Oreb was inhabited then, as at present, by nomadic tribes, who are supposed to be Orebim, or, according to the English, the Ravens, or citizens of Arabah, the town, that rabbinical authority says, was near Bethshan. Jerome, who spent his life in Palestine hunting up facts for general information, and whose writings are regarded as authority, says the inhabitants of this town furnished Elijah with food. This statement, coming from the pious Jerome, as early as the fourth century, who wrote his convictions after careful investigation of facts had convinced him, must of necessity be entitled to our esteem. And it is found that the Arabic version of the word Orebim, in this passage, means people known by the name of Raven, either as a tribe or a family name, or after the town in which they live, and not that of birds. It is also worthy of remark, that the Jewish commentator, Jarchi, who wrote with great care and caution, his convictions, interprets the words in the same light, and adds his opinion, that " it was impossible that the Lord's prophet should receive food from creatures declared by the law unclean."

The arguments insisting that the ravens who fed Elijah morning and evening for one year, were human agents, and not unclean birds of prey, have grown in popular favor, and many are of the opinion that the only likely interpretation of the passage is, that the Orebim (Ravens), who brought food to Elijah, were a class of people so called from the town in which they lived. Murray thinks this is a plain and simple explanation, of a fact connected with Elijah's sojourn in the neighborhood, of the people whom God impressed to care for his servant, " which, from want of knowledge of the locality and its surroundings" (Josh. xv. 6; xviii. 18.), has been misunderstood, and wrongly interpreted by those who had the responsible and stupendous task of translating the Bible into English. Therefore, "they have perverted this text into a miraculous and supernatural incident; and that whenever an incident in the scriptural narrative can be explained in a plain and straightforward manne, rit is a mistake to import any elements of supernatural miracle into it; consequently, it is a matter of satisfaction that here we have an explanation so plain and rational, of what hitherto proved a stumbling-block to not a few minds." There are strange arguments produced by Dr. Paxton and others, favoring the English translation; that is, Elijah was fed by that class of birds known as ravens. But there seems to be more than a simple collection of ideas, in the arguments which favor human agency, in administering daily food to God's servant, and whatever may have been the characteristics of the men known as ravens, God could have easily caused them to take care of His prophet, as He did the widow of Zarephath, or the Shunammite woman who provided for Elisha. And may it not be possible after all, that Elijah received his daily food, during the twelve months he was hiding from Ahab at the Brook Cherith, from men living near-by? I am frank to say this interpretation seems to have a shade of plausibility, that is worthy of toleration, so that I find myself inclining to the opinion, those ravens may have been men.

The Brook Cherith will be ever memorable to me. When I returned from Jericho en route for Jerusalem, during my first visit to Palestine, our party had a puzzling time in crossing it. The previous night a heavy rain fell, (but not half so stormy as that of my last visit there), which caused the water to run from the surrounding mountains so rapidly, that by eight o'clock in the morning, the brook had swollen so tremendously, it was with much difficulty our horses crossed it.

We were compelled to ford it, as there are very few bridges to be found anywhere in Palestine. When my horse started over, I was so anxious to cross that, in my random, I pulled him too far to the left; the guide said, had I gone three feet farther that way, we would have gotten into a deep place over our heads, and that he feared to tell me while crossing, lest he would have excited me. Now, strange as it may seem, the last visit I made to the Jordan, we crossed the same brook at the same place, and just a few days later in the same month, and it was nearly dry. A short distance seemingly from Jericho, about three miles, the quarantine or the noted Mount of Temptation, upon which our Lord was led in the spirit to be tempted of the devil, can be reached easily and seen plainly from any portion of the plain, east or south. The side of the mount nearest to Jericho, has many hermitages drilled in it. These were the habitations of hermits, who came there to fast and pray, in imitation of the example of our Lord. Persons who desire, are allowed to visit them; but the fatigue of the trip would be too great for a visit of such little value.

PART IX.

FROM JERUSALEM TO SHECHEM.

Preparation for the Journey—The Customs and Situation of the People in the Interior—Places of Interest on the Damascus Highway—Mount Scopus—The Last Sight of the Holy City—Scenes along the Road—The Village of Sha'fat—Ancient Nob, Its Memorable Events—Gibeah, the Birth-place of Saul—Rizpah's Devotion—The Levite and Benjamite—Ramah of Benjamin—Situation of Beeroth—Ramah and Its Population—The Character of the Mohammedans—Bethel and Its Condition—The Altar of Abraham and Jacob—Bethel a Judicial Station—Jeroboam's Idolatrous Worship—Dan and Bethel as Two Places for Worship—Reign of Josiah—The Reign of Ahab—The Reign of Solomon—Rehoboam's Reign Over Israel—The Reign of Pious Asa—Victory of the Cushite King—Number of Kings After Asa—Bethel, the Home of the Prophet—Present Situation of Bethel—Ancient Shiloh—History of Shiloh—Important Events at Shiloh—The Present Appearance of Shiloh—The Road From Shiloh to Labonah—Ancient Tombs—The Plain of Mukhna—Mt. Hermon Seen From Mukhna—Well of Jacob—History of the Samaritans—Conversation Between Our Saviour and the Woman of Sychar—Temple on Mt. Gerizim—Jacob's Well and Its Surroundings—The Tomb of Joseph—Shechem and Sychar—Moses' Relation to Mt. Gerizim and Ebal—Historical Association of Mt. Gerizim and Ebal—View from Mt. Gerizim and Ebal—Backsheesh.

THERE are elaborate preparations made generally by those who have charge of persons intending to travel northward, especially the extended tour to Damascus, which is the most tedious and dangerous of all the itineraries throughout the country, and the most dreaded of any I had taken during my tour of the world. It may be of interest to many to read a brief sketch of my own experience prior to leaving Jerusalem for the far north. Many discouragements had been set before me by attempts being made to increase the price first agreed upon for the tour; but when it was understood I intended to withdraw from the parties with whom the arrangements were first made, and go with one of the rival parties, they agreed to carry out the stipulations that had been made. On the evening before the morning we were to start, the dragoman who had me in charge, came to my room, at the Grand Hotel, in Jerusalem, to inform me he was going to make the necessary preparations for our journey, and would like me to be ready by nine o'clock in the morning. I told him I would be ready at the time stated, but I was seized with a trembling at the thought; for I had been told so many discouraging things concerning the roughness, distance, inconvenience, and danger of the route, my courage was fast failing. It is not common for persons to undertake the journey unless several are in a party. But there was no one of all the travelers in Jerusalem at that time going north, but myself. I began thinking of the loneliness of the tour, as no one would be with me but my dragoman and muleteer. Having a knowledge of the hostile Bedouins, who lurk in convenient places along the road for the sake of plunder and murder, it became a task for me to gather myself together enough to prepare for starting. Then the inopportune season was embarrassing, it being just the time when heavy rains were usual in the south, and deep snows in the north often rendered the roads impassable. All these obstacles greatly added to my discomfort and caused me to feel as if I were undertaking a risk that no sane person would. The guide who was appointed to go with me from Joppa up to Jerusalem, fearing he would be sent through the interior, and dreading the trip, used his best endeavors to persuade me to abandon the journey, by saying there were not suitable accommodations. I would be obliged to sleep in native huts, which were very dirty, in connection with several other inconveniences that were expressly disagreeable to me. Well, I was almost persuaded to give up the idea, and partially concluded I should not reach Nazareth, Tiberias and Damascus, nor any of the historical places in the north. But after soberly reflecting over the matter, I concluded to go even if I should be compelled to sleep in open air. But I was assured by Mr. Clark, the chief tourist agent at Jerusalem, there was no real inconvenience in my way, except the weather might hinder me from getting through; but all possible efforts would be made to accommodate me

Another dragoman was chosen to go with me, who was very encouraging as to the comforts of the interior, saying "they would be as good as any one could expect in a country like Palestine." This I found to be true, for the beds, both in the convents and inns, were just as comfortable as those in hotels of Jericho or Jerusalem. We had all needed comforts except fire. There are no conveniences for warming in the country; the people have neither fuel nor stoves, except in some of the larger cities, such as Joppa, Jerusalem, and a few of the cities in the North; even in them there are poor fires. The fuel mostly used in the interior is charcoal, which they burn in small heaters, such as plumbers use for heating their tools. These are the only stoves used in the coldest weather, and the natives do what little cooking they have by them It is hard for me to understand how the poor manage to live without fire, or even other home comforts. Their dwellings are miserable little huts, without bedding or furniture; not even a chair or stool is to be seen, and not enough clothing to comfortably cover themselves. Many women and children have so hardened themselves to the cold weather that they go about barefooted in the snow, just as happily as if it were warm. There are .thousands of old men and women who have not had a shoe on in their lives, yet, with all their poverty and ignorance, they seem to be as cheerful and happy as those whose circumstances place them beyond the disadvantage of poverty. I was up bright and early for the journey, for my ambition to visit the towns and villages, made memorable by the presence and labors of our Lord and His disciples, overruled my fears of the hardships that were so appallingly described. I became anxious to start without delay. The guide was not promptly on time, being an hour and a half later than he proposed.

It is generally a scene of excitement when tourists start for the north from Jerusalem. It is a lonely and perilous journey, and if a person should chance to start without being in company with other travelers as I did, the excitement becomes more intense. Such was the scene on the morning we bade adieu to Jerusalem. The American consul attended to the getting of my passport, which must be issued by the Turkish authorities, so as to permit one to pass through the country, and secure protection in times of trouble. Everything being ready necessary for the journey, a company of friends escorted me to my horse, among whom were the hotel manager, the chief tourist agent, and several others who wished me good luck and bade me a friendly good-bye. We started up David Street, and passed out the Joppa gate, and in a few moments were beyond the walls, leaving the Holy City, never to enter within the sacred walls again. Having before me nineteen days of rough travel, I thought at times it would dampen the pleasure with which my heart was filled at the starting; this small obstacle was soon banished by the anticipation of visiting some of the most important places of which the Bible speaks. Passing along the Damascus road, the tombs of the Judges are passed on the east; this is the usual route taken by those leaving Jerusalem for the north, and is regarded the best way to go. Those starting from Jericho, who do not wish to return to Jerusalem, may go direct to Bethel and on to Shechem; but with the exception of traveling the old road that was used by Joshua and his army, there is but little of Bible interest to be seen until Bethel is reached. Those who start northward from the Holy City have the advantage of passing several important places before arriving at Bethel; the journey lies in the heart of the country in which many great events occurred in ancient times, especially after leaving the tombs of the Judges, the first three or four hours.

VIEW FROM MT. SCOPUS.

Several of these antique places are close to each other, so that not long after one is passed, another is in sight. And soon Mount Scopus is reached; this is the famous peak from which Titus took his first view of Jerusalem, and where he was joined by several other legions. It is the unerring custom for all tourists going north to go to the top of Mount Scopus to take a farewell view of the Holy City and its surroundings.

It was from the summit of this memorable mount that my eyes beheld the immortal city for the last time. The occasion is just as fresh in my mind as if the day had just passed; the impression was so pungent we cannot forget it. I beheld the whole of the Holy City; the Church of the Holy Sepulchre, Mosque of Omar, the Jews' Synagogue, the Citadel of David, and several other buildings, could be distinguished. A little to the east, the Mount of Olives and its several buildings were seemingly just a short distance from me; westward, Mizpeh, the mountains of Judah, and other places having prominence in history, were in full view; then stretching my vision far eastward and southward, the mountains of Gilead and Moab, the valley of the Jordan and the wilderness of Judah were visible. As I looked, my heart was filled with solemn emotions. Thinking my eyes were beholding Jerusalem for the last time, I found myself involuntarily saying, "Farewell, Jerusalem! farewell, Jerusalem!" At the same time I could only by a strong effort restrain the tears from flowing copiously.

Passing down the northern side of Mt. Scopus, the city was soon hid from view, and we entered upon the most sterile and stony road I had ever witnessed. In the winter months the road is much more encumbered and unpleasant to travel than at any other season; it becomes indescribably muddy, which, in connection with the large stones promiscuously scattered along, greatly impede the travel, which is but slow at best. Many camels and donkeys are met and passed, and the road being very narrow at places, the travelers are compelled many times to allow their horses to go at camel speed until a place can be reached in the road wide enough to pass them. Sometimes long trains of them are overtaken ladened with merchandise, and the vicious Arabs seem unwilling to make room enough to permit a horse to pass them. It is not uncommon for the dragoman to hold contention with them before they will give travelers the right of way by turning a little to one side. In those parts of the road where it is sufficiently broad to allow others to pass, the camels are generally in the middle, and often must be driven to one side by the dragoman because of the indisposition of their drivers to give place Like the streets in the cities, the roads are too narrow to allow a vehicle to pass through them, except a very few ; indeed, many of the highways are but little wider than a common path, and the horses can scarcely go faster than a walk. There is a good carriage road from Joppa to Jerusalem, and from Jerusalem to Hebron, and one or two other short roads ; the rest are simply paths. There is a railway in operation from Joppa to Jerusalem; also one was being laid between Beyrout and Damascus, and another from Haifa to Tiberias. These roads will greatly help merchants and native travelers, but it would be very unwise for tourists to travel in cars, as many places of importance would be passed unnoticed, several of which are distinguished in Sacred History.

The condition of most of the public roads greatly impedes travel ; on this account many complaints are made against the Turkish government for criminally neglecting them ; but the unyielding Turks do not pay any attention to these complaints, but just continue in any way that suits them best. The horses do well to make an average of four miles per hour, and that could not be done were it not that at times a tolerably good portion of the road is reached, when the horses can gallop for a mile or two. It often happens that the poor, heavy-laden camel falls by the way under his load, which causes the entire caravan to stop for several hours, unless it is apparent the beast will not recover; in such cases the load is usually divided among some of the stronger ones that have already been burdened with as much as they should carry. Camels cannot travel over those rough roads at a faster rate than two miles per hour, and many cannot do that. The northern country, from Jerusalem to Damascus, by the way of Mount Hermon, is very much broken up ; and at times the road leads through a deep ravine caused by the water ; often heaps of stones are found in them, yet they are much better to pass through than what is known as the main highway.

The husbandmen till every conceivable spot of ground they can find, and in many places plow the highway, so that it would be impossible for a stranger to find his way through some parts of the north, if he had to depend upon the road as a safe guide. It is common to ride through wheat and barley fields, those parts bordering on the highway, especially if the road is very rough. The rough roads are encountered soon after leaving Jerusalem if the traveler is going north or northwest, and in some instances they continue so for miles. One would be worn down with fatigue, were it not that so many places of Bible mention are seen at short intervals, that completely absorb the attention of those who are seeking a more definite knowledge of the Bible-land. Soon after leaving Mt. Scopus, a small village is passed called Sha'fat. It is situated in the midst of a cluster of Olive trees, and old ruins of a church or tower, and a few cisterns supposed to be of very ancient date. This little place is thought to be the ancient Nob, to which David came, hungry and weary, in company with a few friends, and ate the shew-bread.

ANCIENT NOB.

It has been discovered that Sha'fat is from the plural form of the Arabic word Sha'f, which means hill-top, this (it is said) exactly corresponds with the Hebrew word Nob. When David went to Nob and ate the shew-bread, he was fleeing from the vengeance of King Saul, who was anxiously seeking him. David obtained from the officiating priest, Ahimelech, the consecrated bread and the sword of Goliath. The priest did not know of the existing strife between King Saul and David, or he doubtless would not have consented, without remonstrating against his conduct in taking the bread and sword, for he knew it was putting his own life in danger, to allow such a privilege to one whom the king regarded as his potent enemy. But notwithstanding the ignorance of Ahimelech of the feud between the king and the young man whom God had caused to be ordained to succeed him, Saul would not excuse him, for his wrath was kindled, and some one must suffer the penalty even if the offense was a small one. He, therefore, put the work of destruction into the hands of his servant Doeg, the Edomite, who put Ahimelech, and all the priests of Nob, to death; about eighty-five; and his work of death-dealing did not subside until all the inhabitants of the place were slain: men, women and children, none escaped. There is but little of value to be seen at Nob, for the town has long since fallen; the only attraction to travelers is the ancient history clustering there. A good view can be had of Mt. Zion and some of its buildings; this is the only portion of Jerusalem that can be seen from that point. How pleasant it must have been for the priests, who lived in this little village, to look upon the great Hill of Zion while absent from Jerusalem in their quiet homes at Nob! The Tabernacle and the Ark of the Covenant were located there in the time of King Saul. After leaving this priestly town, going northward a short distance, Gibeah, the birth-place of Saul, is reached. It is proper to state, this site like many others is disputed, but it is settled upon by the majority of those who have carefully investigated it, as the identical place where ancient Gibeah, the home of the first king of Israel, was located, and was the headquarters of King Saul, the greater portion of his reign.

RIZPAH'S DEVOTION.

It was at Gibeah the seven descendants of Saul were hung by the Amorites; and here one of the most touching exhibitions of maternal love, known in the world, was demonstrated. A loving mother had two sons among those slain; they were put to death in the first days of the beginning of the barley harvest, and Rizpah, the daughter of Aiah, took sackcloth and spread it upon a rock from the beginning of harvest until water dropped upon them from the heavens, and would not allow birds nor beasts to rest upon them by day or night. Here the poor, distressed woman watched the remains of her dead sons for six months during the hottest days of the year, with a devotion that none but a fond mother can possess. It was at Gibeah, that the shocking event occurred that revealed the woeful narrative concerning the Levite's wife, who was brought to an untimely death by the outrageous conduct of some of the townsmen. The Levite was on his way from Bethlehem to Mt. Ephraim with his wife; he came from Jebus (Jerusalem) late in the day, and his servant endeavored to urge him to remain there for a night; (1 Samuel xxi. 1-6; Neh. xi. 32; Isaiah x. 32); but he would not do so because they were strangers, both as individuals and racial connections; therefore, fearing there might be some unkind feeling against him, he preferred going over to Gibeah, and tarrying with those who were "bone of his bone and flesh of his flesh," feeling it would be pleasanter and more safe for him with a people of his own kindred and tongue than with the children of Ham. And he said unto his servant, "Come, let us draw near to one of these places and lodge there all night in Gibeah or in Ramah." It was agreed to remain in Gibeah, so they journeyed on, and before they had arrived in the town, the sun had set behind the western sea. But it was a sad night for him, for the conduct of some of the townsmen towards his wife was so vicious and brutal it caused her death, and introduced a conflict of a most bloody and disastrous character, so that the people suffered most bitterly for their crime, for they were slain without mercy. Gibeah is now, like most places in Palestine that flourished thousands of years ago. "It has fallen." There are a few small huts, the abodes of the half-civilized Arabs, but the old town with its glory is buried in the ages past, leaving nothing but desolation and dreary solitude for those of to-day to behold.

RAMAH OF BENJAMIN.

The next place of interest along the old highway northward is Ramah of Benjamin, which is only a few moments' ride from Nob. It is not to be identified as the home of Elkannah, Hannah and Samuel; their home was another Ramah in Mt. Ephraim. But Ramah of Benjamin is situated on a hill close to the old Damascus road about six miles north of Jerusalem. It is a place sacredly memorable in Jewish history, for it was the place where they assembled, after Nebuzaradan had wrecked and destroyed Jerusalem, to bid adieu to each other and their country, which was so dear to them, and go into captivity in a strange land and become the subjects of a strange people. It must have been a day of great lamentation, when the multitudes took the parting hand, pressed the cheek with endearing friendship, then parted, many of them to meet no more.

The feelings of the Jews caused by that great affliction cannot be understood better by any people than those in America, who, in the dark days of a terrible bondage, had to part from near and dear relatives, having been sold to distant lands, one from the other, in strange parts, and among strange people, to tyrant owners. 2 Sam. x. 26; xiv. 2; xvi. 10; Judges xix. Those who left their loved ones with bleeding hearts and dejected heads could tell what were the feelings of the Jews when they bade farewell to each other at Ramah. It is presumable, from the usual custom, that those who pass the old solitary site, sadly remember the event and sustain emotions of sorrow. It was at Ramah, that Rachel is represented by the prophet as being in great sorrow and weeping for her children, refusing to be comforted. But when the captives left this place, such must have been the wailing and mourning that the hills and valleys around about echoed the sound even to Bethel and amongst the hills of Ephraim.

The next town of any historical interest beyond Ramah is Beeroth, situated on a high summit, so that persons approaching from the east can see it several miles away. It is a large village having well-built houses and many comforts not usual to villages in that part of the country. There is an old church on the western border of the village that is still in a good state of preservation (Josh. xviii. 25; Jer. xi. 1; xxxi. 15), although time has made a perceptible impression upon it. This church was built in the twelfth century, and is one of the many belonging to the Holy Sepulchre. There are about one thousand people living in Beeroth, of whom a small number are orthodox Christians. In olden times it was one of the cities belonging to the Gibeonites, but was allotted to Benjamin when the children of Israel took possession of the land, and is said to be the birth-place of one of the mighty men of King David, known as Naharai, the Beerothite. Some of the early inhabitants of the town were among those who returned from the captivity with Ezra.

There is a tradition connected with this place from an early Christian period, stating it was at Beeroth that the parents of our Lord missed Him on their return to Nazareth from Jerusalem, and returned to seek Him, continuing their search until they reached the Holy City and found Him in the Temple, discussing deep subjects with the most talented men of that age, notwithstanding He was but twelve years old. The village is near the border line of the tribe of Ephraim, and but a short distance from Ramah, the home of Samuel, which is also called Ramathaim, and some who have taken pains to investigate certain parts of the interior have located Arimathæa here, the town in which the disciple lived who obtained the body of Jesus and buried it. There are two places to which claims are laid as the original Arimathæa, and it is highly improbable the matter will be settled as to the real site, unless some undeniable evidence should be developed sufficiently clear to settle the perplexed question for all time to come in favor of one of the two places.

The other place, supposed to be Arimathæa, is west of Jerusalem, just nine miles from Joppa. Beeroth occupies a commanding situation, and good views can be had down the mountains of Ephraim and Benjamin, and as far west as the Mediterranean Sea. Ramah is a large town, compared with others in Palestine, and its population adhere to the Latin and Greek Churches, except a small number who are Protestants. It is noteworthy that the Christian people throughout the land manifest a far more friendly spirit toward strangers than the other natives, who are of the Moslem faith. (Josh. ix. 17; 2 Sam. xxiii. 37; Ezra ii. 25; Luke ii. 44–45.) They have clean huts, although humble, and are clean and tidy generally. Their attitude towards foreigners is genteel, polite and friendly, while those belonging to the Mohammedans are entirely the reverse. They have a look expressive of ill-will; sometimes this is emphasized in their conduct.

It is a part of their religion to be unkind to those who are not of their faith, and on the least provocation to use the harshest means to punish them. This is well known by their conduct toward the Christians in Damascus and other parts of Palestine and Syria. These were people who were to the manner born, and it may be inferred what would be the treatment they would administer to those of foreign birth when an opportunity would permit them. This is one of the chief reasons guards are stationed through the whole country, and were it not for those officials, Christians would have a hard time to live anywhere in Palestine. We just arrived in Beeroth in time to witness a very strange sight, which so greatly attracted me I could not enjoy my meal, or even pay proper attention to the wild-looking scenes about the hills and mountains around the country. There was a large gathering of young men and maidens on the hill, about two hundred yards away, who seemed to be engaged in a strange exercise, such as I had not seen in any part of the country. I asked my dragoman what it meant, and was informed it was a marriage celebration; and from what could be seen of the performance from where we were, I concluded they were having a big dance. But it was at length found to be a solemn gathering, for it was a funeral. One of the young people of the village had died, and the friends met at the grave to bewail the loss of one of their companions. But one not acquainted with the custom would not have the slightest idea the people had gathered to pay a tribute of respect to the dead. They had formed a large circle around the grave, with their hands joined, passing round with quick pace, hallooing and jumping, very much like our young people in some of their plays. Those who were not in the circle were busy in throwing old tins, cans, or some old pieces of garments and other things, as high in the air as they could throw them. Then they would break out anew with wild shouts, and mournful lamentations, as touching and deafening as it is possible to describe. It is a custom rarely witnessed in any part of the country, and, when once seen, we do not think any one would care to see the same kind of performance again. We are not prepared to state how long the people kept up their doleful lamentations. Our sojourn there was an hour or more, and we found them deeply engaged in the service when we entered the village, and they were just as active when we left as when we first heard them. It seems that they offer prayers for the dead, and refer to him in song. The pieces of clothing they throw up may be those that belonged to the deceased friend.

BETHEL AND ITS ENVIRONMENTS.

The next place of particular interest is Bethel, but a short distance from Beeroth, on the east. Any one passing the little uninviting town, not knowing it to be the site of ancient Bethel, would not be likely to see any attractions worthy of delay. The present village is situated on a high hill, and is composed of huts which are by no means tidy. I am sure persons of advanced civilization would much prefer taking a night's lodging out of doors than in one of the native huts.

But Bethel is one of the most frequently visited places in Palestine, especially by those going north, and but few places in the land have more attractions. There is but little of the remains of the material, of which the ancient city was composed, visible. Some of these are used in the present buildings composing the village. There is also a remnant of the walls of the church, supposed to be not older than the twelfth century, and built during the time the crusaders had control of the country. There is an old time-worn tower, which is supposed to have belonged to a monastery that was converted into a fortress; the ruins occupy an area of about one hundred and sixty feet in length and one hundred feet wide, with chambers along the walls. The old reservoir indicates the importance of the ancient city, which in the days of its greatest progress was the pride of Israel. This old lake received its supply of water from two springs which are so close together that they are known as the "double spring." It is estimated to be three hundred and fourteen feet long and two hundred and seventeen feet wide. A portion of the old walls that enclosed it are still standing, but are well worn with age and exposure. Those who will take the trouble and risk to ascend to the top of the old tower above mentioned, or what is less trouble, and far better, one may go to the top of one of the highest hills near by, and from a few of the highest houses, a view of the Mosque of Omar at Jerusalem, twelve miles away, can be had, with good field glasses. It is therefore evident that those living in Bethel in the days of Jeroboam and his successors, could see the Temple of Solomon. One soon becomes interested in the history, both antique and modern, connected with the places around him. Bethel is one of the household words of Palestine. Here Abraham pitched his tent to settle for a time before he had a permanent habitation; and it was between Bethel and Ai he built an altar, and called on the name of the Lord, more than nine hundred years before the national sanctuary that crowned Moriah had the first foundation stone laid. When he returned from Egypt, whither he had fled from the famine that oppressed the land, he was mindful of the place that had been consecrated to the Lord, and went there to pay his devotion to the Great Being who had sustained him. It was at Bethel that Jacob saw in his dream the ladder reaching from heaven to earth, and the angels of God ascending and descending; the sight was so glorious that Jacob called it Bethel or "the house of God, and the gate of heaven."

On his return to his native land from Haran, about twenty years later, he came to Bethel and built an altar, and erected a memorial stone because the Lord met him there and talked with him. It was here that Abraham and Lot separated, and the Lord renewed his covenant with the father of the faithful, which was first made known to him in Shechem; that the land wherein he was then sojourning should be given him and his seed, for an everlasting habitation. While the Patriarch was standing on the mountain summit east of Bethel, he had a commanding view of all the country round about; and the Lord said unto him, "Lift up now thine eyes and look from the place where thou art, northward, southward, eastward and westward, for all the land which thou seest, to thee will I give it, and to thy seed forever."

And when the Israelites had established themselves in the land, Bethel was allotted to Benjamin, and Ephraim joined him, for his border skirted the place where the altar had been built by Abraham. When Bethel was taken by the tribe of Ephraim, the Benjamites seem to have surrendered their claim to it, and it became a part of the territory of the former. When Joshua was making his victorious expedition through Canaan, he conquered the king of Bethel which was called Lud, before the wonderful vision appeared to Jacob when he was fleeing from the hand of Esau. It seems remarkably strange that attempts should be made to change the memorable name of this highly reverential place, but that each generation would sacredly cling to it, and re-dedicate the spot made memorable by the vision of angels and the presence of the Lord, remembering most fondly, that Abraham, whom they so greatly admired, held the place in great reverence (Gen. xxvii. 11–19; xxxv. 14–15), and Jacob erected a pillar and anointed it with oil, as a memorial for all generations, that they might regard the place as he did to be the house of God and the gate of heaven. But men who have no respect for their fellow and but little for the Lord, will do almost anything they feel disposed, especially if it will be offensive to their neighbors. The enemies of the Hebrews, by whom they were subdued, changed the names of the most important towns and cities, Jerusalem itself not escaping.

But there are other things of great interest attaching to the

the history of Bethel that should be noticed here. It was a judical town, where Samuel came at stated times to hear such cases that came under his official notice as judge. It is noteworthy that Samuel was a circuit judge; Gilgal, Mizpeh, and Bethel seemingly to have been the chief stations of his court sessions. It seems his usual route was from Mizpeh to Bethel, then down the rugged highway through which Joshua and his army passed when he marched against Ai When the revolt of the ten tribes took place, Bethel was in Ephraim's possession, they being with those who rebelled, and was one of the greatest cities belonging to the Kingdom of Israel. It appears that Benjamin was dispossessed of this important city when the other tribes made war against them, on account of the sad affair that occurred at Gibeah.

When Jereboam became king of the ten tribes, caused by the great dissatisfaction with the conduct of Rehoboam, which had been kindling from the time of King Solomon's installation, if not from David's time, the religious reverence that had been given Bethel for many ages by the pious fathers, because of the services conducted there by Abraham, Jacob and others, is supposed to have been the cause that stimulated this king of the rebel tribes, to choose it as one of the chief seats of his idolatrous worship, as well as for the convenience of the people who lived east of Samaria. This ambitious man, whom the people had called to rule over them, was not interested in directing the minds of the people to the worship of the God of their fathers; but having been reared amongst the Egyptians, he had greatly imbibed their flickering religion, and was little more, in point of piety, than one of the stubborn heathens who knew nothing of the wonderful works of the God of heaven. Fearing the people of his kingdom might be induced to follow the worship of their fathers as taught by Moses, Samuel and others, he caused all the Levites to be expelled from the various cities that had been allotted to them, and in their stead he established a priesthood founded upon his own selfish contrivance, and appointed such men as priests whose means allowed them to make liberal contributions to his stores, that the people might not indulge an anxious desire for the services of the Temple at Jerusalem, and finally return there on the great feast days, and seeing such a practice would soon bring his idolatrous religion to naught, he abolished all the established festival days, except the Feast of Tabernacles, which continued regularly on the same day. Jeroboam was not moved by a truly religious motive, to allow the feast to be observed on the usual day, but he wished the people to gather on that memorable day and pay homage to him and renew their faith in him. It is noteworthy that the celebration of the feast only, was continued (1 Samuel vii. 16; Gen. xiii. 14-15; Josh. xviii. 13-22; xxviii. 16-22), but the regular day for holding this anniversary was changed to another, chosen by the king himself. It is plainly seen from the general conduct of Jeroboam, that he utterly disregarded the true worship, or any other, only so far as it served to extol himself and keep the people, whose mode of public service was not such as met his idea, in accomplishing his design. In order to succeed he knew the people of his kingdom must be kept within its borders in celebrating various festivals commonly conducted every year; and those customary feasts, if continued, would naturally draw the minds of the people from him to the regular place for holding them. This he could see from the tendency of some of the more enthusiastic; who, rather than abandon the privilege of the various religious entertainments, willingly left the northern kingdom, although they were in great sympathy with it and were members of the same tribes composing it. Therefore Jeroboam, seeing what he regarded to be detrimental to him and a signal failure of his government, on account of those people's fondness for the worship of the Temple, which would naturally win the people to it, unless something could be substituted in the northern kingdom to entertain the people, cunningly devised a plan which fully accomplished the end in view.

It may be stated that the people belonging to the kingdom of Judah were not sacredly devout in their religious celebrations; for they had wandered from God little by little, by partaking of the worship of the idolatrous nations round about, so that their devotion had largely become shadowy, and anything in imitation of them would have its weight with his people. So he appointed two places as religious headquarters; one was Bethel, a place held in great esteem by the people of both kingdoms; the other was Dan, on the extreme north, for the special convenience of the people living remote from the former. At each of these places the king set up a molten calf, and introduced a worship to supersede the original one held at Jerusalem, and exhorted the people to embrace it, telling them it was too far to have them go up to Jerusalem, as had been the custom previously. It was not a hard thing to persuade the people to follow his scheme, and thus they were permanently drawn from the Temple, which was twelve miles west of Bethel. The prompting idea of the calf-worship may have been from a traditional account he had of the method Aaron took to quiet the people at the foot of Sinai, when Moses went up to commune with God, and receive the law for their government. Or, what seems more probable he desired to introduce this service, because he knew how fondly the people of Egypt were drawn to it. Bethel, that had been a sacredly adored place by many of the pious Hebrews, suddenly became a scene of wild confusion; and the people, whose ancestors built an altar and bowed before the living God, were seen developing into gross idolatry, within a few hours' walk from the Holy Hill, Moriah, on which stood the most glorious monument of Divine honor in the world. This very city, that had been made so memorable by the altar of Abraham and Jacob, had been turned into heathen worshipers' headquarters. It is supposed by many, that Jeroboam was sincere in his religious views, and that they had been cultivated while in Egypt, because of his long associations with the people of that country, who were wholly idolatrous. Having become enamored with it affectionately, his faith was weaned from the worship of his fathers. His marriage to an Egyptian princess greatly influenced him to adopt the false worship. If these opinions are well founded, it may be inferred, that notwithstanding the people were not in the least disposed to accept the teachings of the nation under whom their forefathers so greatly suffered, especially that pertaining to their religion; yet, because of their inclination to adopt the popular heathen worship, they followed the very teachings they had been so many times admonished to carefully avoid. It is well known the calf and other animals were worshiped by the Egyptians, as fondly as the most devout of Israel served the living God. This worship was not confined to Egypt, for it had been adopted by all the tribes and nations of the eastern world, and was prominent among the various tribes when Israel entered the promised land. But it seems Jeroboam's chief interest in the introduction of this worship was especially to aggrandize himself; he did not make it obligatory upon all his subjects when it was first established; he allowed the people to accept it of their own choice (1 Kings xi. 14–39; xii. 26–33), without a code of laws exacting their faithful adherence to the new religion; but while this was true, he clustered it with so many allurements that were winning, he felt confident results would follow, that would steal the affections of the people to the extent they would confidently and firmly embrace the new national religion he had so cunningly planned It is not to be wondered that a people would so readily change their idea, when we remember the eagerness they had manifested for a long time to have full liberty to worship other gods.

The fact should be remembered, that notwithstanding Jeroboam and the great majority of his subjects had adopted a false worship, which they conducted so exultingly at Bethel, just within sight of the pinnacle of the Sacred Temple, they entertained a fondness for the worship of their fathers, and attempted to hold on to the weak cords of the faith they had been admonished to observe. That this is true, none will dare doubt, if they consider the address of Elijah to them, when, in connection with other things, he asked how long they would "halt between two opinions." This scene occurred many years after the time of Jeroboam, which is an evidence that the primitive teachings never left them. It is also known that Jeroboam himself had abiding confidence in the God of his fathers; and when the time of trouble came, he did not do as the false prophets of Baal on Mt. Carmel, but fell back on the religion of his early instruction. He built an altar to his idol gods, and a prophet was sent to cry against it, and God confirmed the mission of His servant by a most striking incident. The altar was rent in pieces by unseen hands and its ashes were poured out. The king, in his insane madness, stretched out his rebellious arm against the prophet, and it became withered that instant, and continued so until the compassionate prophet appealed to the Lord to restore it.

This miraculous rebuke which Jeroboam received, for his rude conduct toward the messenger God had sent to him to condemn his altar and false worship, caused him to boldly acknowledge that the Lord of heaven is the only true God. It is noteworthy, also, that when the child of this sinful and idolatrous king was stricken with sickness, he did not send for one of the false prophets that could have been so easily gotten, for he had no confidence in them, nor in the images he set up in the days of his pride, but he sought comfort from God, whose worship he had so wickedly ignored. He sent his wife in disguised dress to seek consolation from a true prophet. This act of Jeroboam is a strong evidence of the faith he had in his idol gods and false prophets. This is one of the many cases shown that men of high standing and empty pride, who have dared to insult the Lord of Hosts, and even rule Him out of their consciences while basking in the pleasures of sin, have been compelled to return to the Lord in the time of deep affliction and humiliation and seek His protection. No people have indulged the habit more than the kings of Israel and Judah and the people under them. But the house of Jeroboam was doomed, the malediction pronounced, and it was sure and inevitable. The sins of the father were embraced by his children, therefore, the chastisement of the Lord visited them, and the prediction of the prophet was signally fulfilled upon the whole house of the first king of the northern kingdom, for his family perished. His son, who succeeded him to the throne, had anything but an honorable reign. Josiah, King of Judah, utterly destroyed every memorial of the idolatrous worship the unworthy Jeroboam had established, and spared nothing in the city except the sepulchre of the man of God from Judah, who was divinely commissioned to "cry against the altar," because Bethel was made the chief headquarters of false worship. Its name was changed to Beth-a'ven, the house of idols.

What a wonderful change! Jacob said it was none other than "the house of God and the gate of heaven," but in after years "bone of his bone and flesh of his flesh," said, it shall not be the house of God, but that of idols. How differently did the Lord deal with the kings of Judah, for, although they many times turned from the Lord, yet the worship at the Temple, the place where His honor dwelt, was generally respected. So, instead of changing the dynasties as did Israel, there was a continuous succession of the royal line of David without any interruption. But the kingdom of Israel was begun in a tumult and continued so until it was finished. But there were ambitious persons in both kingdoms, always eagerly seeking the sceptre. This disposition is so manifest in men, we should entertain no surprise that it prevailed among the Israelites. (1 Kings xiii. 1-2; 2 Kings xxiii. 15-20.) Jeroboam had reigned twenty-two years, when death summoned him to lay down his sceptre. It may be said his whole term of office was strangely eventful. He was succeeded by his son, Nadab, who only ruled the kingdom two years; then the sceptre departed from the house of Jeroboam forever. Nadab was succeeded by Baasha, his captain, who was a man full of courage and very prominent as a warrior. He was succeeded by his son, Elah, who was not in much esteem among his people and had a short reign of two years, when General Zimré, of the staff of Elah, supplanted him. Just as he had gathered the reins of government firmly in his hand, he was assassinated, while indulging in a drunken spree, and was succeeded by Omri, who was chosen by the army. He ruled the kingdom of Israel twelve years, and was succeeded by Ahab, who was one of the most notorious idolatrous kings that had occupied the throne. It was during his term Elijah, the prophet, was sent to the palace to declare the pending famine. This wicked man was in power twenty-two years, and his work of evil would fill several large volumes; but death ended his shameful career, and the sceptre was put in the hand of Ahaziah, who, after two years' reign, was compelled to surrender. After him, eleven others are named down to the time of the captivity. The last one was Hosea. The nineteen kings mentioned were of no particular family, that is, of any special line, but belonged to several districts; therefore,

16

they were known as dynasties. The most of these men ascended to power through stratagem and much bloodshed. There was a different state of things in the kingdom of Judah after the death of King Saul. David, who succeeded him, was exalted to the throne by divine appointment, and held the sceptre for forty years amid very serious changes and conflicts. He was succeeded by his son, Solomon, who had a peaceful reign the first few years, during which he displayed wonderful wisdom and shrewdness, so that all he attempted to do for the welfare of the kingdom prospered. But pride and self-indu'gence so greatly controlled him, that, in the very time of life his piety and wisdom should have been most prominent, he became as weak as a little child, having, it seems, no control of himself whatever. Although he was permitted to reign forty years, he did not grace his position in the latter years of his administration. He was succeeded by Rehoboam, his son by Naamah, who was an Ammonitess woman. He was a man of more years than either of his predecessors when he was installed king, and should have been competent, both because of his age and experience, to have shunned the calamity which nearly destroyed his kingdom. His unwise policy gave great dissatisfaction to the people generally, and ten of the tribes left him. He was full of self-will and would not be guided by the counsel of the old men who knew what was best to produce harmony in the kingdom, but went directly opposite to the wise and safe instructions given him. He reigned at Jerusalem seventeen years, during the whole of which his people were involved in bloody strife. Rehoboam ruled the people but one year before the rebellion, after which his kingdom was known as Judah, and that established by the ten tribes, with Jeroboam its acknowledged king, was called Israel. Rehoboam was succeeded by his son, Abijah, who soon obtained great fame as a man of war, but gained very little distinction as a wise and judicious ruler, having occupied the throne but three years, and seemed not to profit by the evil example of his father, but followed his unwise teaching.

Asa, the son of Abijah, was the next king. He was a very shrewd man and gave strong evidences of piety from the beginning of his reign, being devoted to the true worship, and restored it wherever he found it had been supplanted by idolatry, and expelled those whose superstitions had made them slaves to false gods, and cleansed Jerusalem from every vestige of idol worship. Such was his firm purpose to restore the true worship throughout his kingdom, he took the position of queen from his own mother, because she caused an idol to be built to Ashtaroth, which was one of the prominent idols of the Phœnicians. He reigned forty-one years, with a degree of commendable prosperity. In the eleventh year of his reign, he won a great victory over the Cushite king, who came out against him with a vast army His heart was strengthened and encouraged by the Lord, who guarded him and gave him success because he followed His counsel. Yet it is strange that this man, who, under the direction of the Lord, seems to have known nothing but success, was found yielding to human frailties in his latter years, and thereby was not free from reproach. It is stated that when Baasha, king of Israel, opposed the work of reform Asa was conducting under divine direction, he sought not aid from heaven to assist him in the great work, but went over to Syria for help, which was a great mistake, and one with which the Lord was not pleased. But the kingdom of Judah had not been presided over by a more prosperous king since the revolt, than he. And the people enjoyed a state of happiness such as they had not enjoyed for a long time. So it may be said of Asa, taking all his surroundings into consideration, he was of great service to the people, and left the kingdom in a state of piety that it had not known for many years. There are seventeen other kings mentioned after Asa, some of whom were weak and idolatrous, so that there was no real prosperity for any considerable period for the kingdom of Judah (2 Chron. xvi. 12; 1 Kings xxii. 43; 2 Chron. xx. 32). The whole number of kings of the southern kingdom according to the chronological account, from Saul down to the captivity, were twenty-three. Bethel fell again to the Benjamites for a short while, but it never rose to its former importance after the return of the people from bondage. It was strongly fortified in the time of the Maccabees.

BETHEL, THE HOME OF PROPHETS.

After Ahab ascended the throne of Isreal the worship of Baal became so general, that the calf-worship established by Jeroboam at Bethel went down, and Bethel became the home of the sons of the prophets, and the sturdy form of Elijah was no doubt seen among them several times. It is certain he was there, in company with Elisha, just before he was translated. This old, familiar city, in which so many amazing events occurred, suddenly dropped from the record of the Scriptures, and is not brought into prominence again except by early writers. Bethel was captured by Vespasian whilst on his way to Jerusalem. At that time it was maintaining some of its former prestige; but it was fast ebbing, so that in the fourth century its glory had finally departed, and it had become very weak and unimportant. But during the Crusade rule in Palestine, Bethel is said to have revived a little.

It is visited in these times simply on account of the ancient history for which it is celebrated, as there is nothing to be seen but desolation and ruin. The prediction concerning Bethel has been strictly fulfilled, for it has come to naught.

Those visiting this ancient site purely for historical purposes can have some very profitable observations, which will be of lasting benefit to them. If travelers will take pains to ascend the high hill, and look southward from its summit, they will have an extensive view of the country round about for many miles. It may be readily understood why Lot pitched his tent towards Sodom rather than those pastures in the neighborhood of Bethel; for the country environing the latter is one of the most stony of all the pastures in Palestine. For this reason the dissatisfaction took place between the herdsmen of Abraham and Lot; as the flocks of each were large, and the pastures not being sufficiently extensive for both sets of cattle, it would naturally cause the men to endeavor to get the best places, even if a little advantage had to be taken to do so; hence the ill feelings. It is plain to be seen (Ezra ii. 28; Neh. xi. 31), that Abraham was a lover of peace and would rather be imposed upon than to do his fellow an injustice. He being the oldest naturally had the right to choose another place for his cattle when it became necessary for them to separate; but lest Lot should feel his uncle had taken advantage of him, the senior patriarch gave the junior the right of choice. Lot looked toward the southeast and saw the plain in the Jordan valley, that it was every way adapted for the use of his flocks, and afforded abundant pasture for all his possessions; that several towns and cities flourished in that region where he could find ready sale for his cattle, and that no other part of the country, as far as he could see, was so inviting; therefore, he parted with his uncle and went toward Sodom. But Abraham contented himself with the pasture land about Bethel, until he fixed his mind on the land near Hebron, known as the plain of Mamre, where he was found when the Lord made known to him the early fate of the whole country whither Lot had settled. It would be worthy of the time, and fatigue necessary to the trip, to make a short visit to the Rock Rimmon, which can be reached in a short time from Bethel,—down a steep hill. This rock was where the six hundred Benjamites hid themselves when fleeing from the vengeance of the other tribes, who were in hot pursuit after them.

JIFNA AND ITS SURROUNDINGS.

The next point from Bethel is Jifna; there is no special history attaching to the town, except, Titus camped there with his army when on his way to take Jerusalem. It is usual for those going north to remain here all night, as good accommodations can be obtained at the Latin convent, or at the house of a Syrian lady, who is a school-teacher and missionary. The most fatiguing road I experienced in any portion of the world, was when we were making our way from Jifna to the main road to Shiloh and Shechem. Were it not for the sake of getting a good place to lodge for the night, it would be far better not to go over there.

The road or narrow gorge leads up a high mountain, through a continuous bed of solid rock, very crooked and cragged; sometimes the turns are so very narrow the horse can scarcely get through; and there are other places that seem to be impossible for the poor beast to pass through safely, but they are trained to the work, and, if they are allowed to take their time, they never fail to reach the summit safely. The journey up this rugged, steep mountain gorge is about two or two and a half miles, and requires about two and a half hours to ascend to the top. It is advised that horses be rode up, as it is better for both the man and his animal. But to me it looked cruel to attempt to ride, and I am sure an officer in a country in which a law exists against cruelty to animals, would indict the first person he saw riding up such a terrible road on the back of a horse. I attempted to get off the one I rode, but the guide advised me not to do so. But I am confident it would not have been more fatiguing to have walked, for I was so completely unnerved when the summit was reached, I could have pleasantly rested the remainder of the day, but there was no time for halting until we arrived at Shiloh, for we were compelled to go as far as Shechem that day, and to do so an early start was necessary. The landscape from the summit is very cheering after traveling up such a terrible road; and the indications of an improved condition of the soil, and evidences of more cultivation are seen as far as the mountains of Galilee. Fig, orange and olive orchards, proved beyond doubt we had entered a fertile and more thrifty district. But very soon another dreary waste was entered. As the hill is descended a deep, narrow gorge, caused by a winter torrent, is passed through. It has been deepened by the flow of water descending from the mountains during the heavy rains, and at times the travel is almost, if not entirely, cut off, for it swells from five to thirteen feet. We passed a very lonely and wild glen, called by the natives Wady-el-Haramyeh, or "the robbers' valley." Progress through it is made necessarily slow on account of the great rocks that are so thickly scattered in every part of it. It is a place for robbers who lay in wait for any one from whom they are likely to gain spoils. Natives and strangers dread them alike. Near the northern end several caves are pointed out in which robbers usually hide. I rode up to them and viewed them. It would be useless to attempt to escape should they pursue one, especially a stranger, for the horses cannot walk through safely unless they go very slow, almost at a rate of about two miles per hour, and the robbers walking could make much faster speed than a horse. I could see no way of escape in case they should come to attack us. So I had arranged to surrender if the crisis came. It would have been the only safe way out of the difficulty, for I was informed it would be certain death to attempt a combat with them. The valley is something over a mile long. Near its northern end is a fine fountain, called "the robbers' fountain," and a few steps to the north of it are the caves in which these fiends have their hidings. Soon as the valley is passed the country begins to assume a more cheerful aspect, and the whole region round about presents a beautiful appearance, and the traveler passes from a rocky, sterile wilderness into a cultivated and fruitful tract of country, which changes the dull, solitary monotony he had been depressed with for a few hours.

ANCIENT SHILOH.

In order to make a visit to ancient Shiloh it is necessary to leave the main road and travel to the northeast a mile or two. The pass is very narrow, and leads through a very deep valley, then up a high hill and through cultivated fields. The site of the old historic town is about half way between Bethel and Shechem. There are no visible attractions at Shiloh; nearly every portion of the land of this once busy and sacred place is under cultivation, except the rocky summit on which it is supposed the Sacred Tabernacle stood. When the Israelites removed it from Gilgal, with its precious furniture, they set it up at Shiloh, where it remained three hundred years. The exact spot on which the holy tent stood is thought to be on the circular hill, at the northern terminus of the small plain, over which a number of ruins are scattered from one end to the other. Behind it is a very deep valley; the descent into it is very abrupt and above the ruins is a terrace with rocky sides, and other terraces below it. The whole length is five hundred and twelve feet, by twenty-seven feet wide; upon this terrace it is supposed the ancient Tabernacle rested. Shiloh is chiefly noted for its connection with the sanctuary. But there are other important events connected with it which are of vital interest to the world The remaining tribes who had not gone to possess the portion assigned them, met at Shiloh and arranged their meeting tent, after which they, at the solicitation of Joshua, dispersed to take charge of their allotments. It must have been a pathetic scene, when they fondly embraced each other, then separated, many of them never to meet again. At Shiloh the tribes annually assembled to celebrate the great feast, and renew their friendship. On these occasions, the village maidens, living nearby, would want to enliven the festival by interspersing the various amusements with dancing. The vineyards were just a short distance from the main road, in which the Benjamites hid themselves at one time when they came up to the feast, and came out suddenly from their hidings, when the daughters of Shiloh were going up to the dance; and each man took one for a wife, and fled to their district. While Samuel was yet an infant he was brought to Shiloh by his mother and dedicated to the Lord; and there he had his vision. It was at Shiloh, Eli died when in very advanced age; and although it is not known to any one, yet it is the general opinion, the old sire was buried in one of the many rock-hewn tombs around the mountain slope. It is a blessed thing his resting-place has not been identified, or the relic-seekers would have taken every particle of rock composing it, and many of them would have reverenced the stony fragments as they do their Lord. It is really astonishing how adoringly men appreciate a small stone or stick coming from one of the sacred places in Palestine. The Prophet Abijah also lived in Shiloh, to whom came the wife of Jeroboam to seek consolation as to the future of her child who was ill. When the ark of God was captured by the Philistines it did not only cause the death of Eli, but of Shiloh also, for her glory departed. It is not definitely known when the Tabernacle was removed from Shiloh. But it is understood, the people who joyfully went over to Shiloh to the annual celebration, lost their ambition for visiting there after the Ark of God had been taken; and it may be presumed with some assurance, that very early after the death of Eli, the Tabernacle was transferred (Hos. v. 8; Judges xx. 45-47; xxi. 19; Josh. xviii, xxii.; 1 Sam. iii. 18-21; iv. 12-18; 1 Kings xiv. 2-16); for Shiloh seems to have gone into a state of almost profound silence. It is also noteworthy that while Samuel himself was busy in his official office, offering sacrifices upon many altars on the high places throughout his circuit, he did not officiate at the altar at which he was solemnly dedicated to God. Very soon after Saul of Benjamin was installed king of Israel, the Tabernacle is known to have been in Nob; this is the cause of such a collection of priests there, for at this place the most of their official labors were performed. The situation of Shiloh was most graphically detailed by the elders, who advised the small number of Benjamites, who survived the war, that nearly exterminated the entire tribe, which was precipitated upon them by the Gibeonites, because they had broken the covenant made between the latter and Joshua, to go up to Shiloh and take to themselves wives; and although it was only ten or twelve miles away, they deemed it advisable to minutely describe the locality, that there might not be any mistake, and thereby prevent themselves from taking wives from any other town or village in the neighborhood, or any other part of the country except Shiloh. They said to each other, "Behold there is a feast of the Lord from year to year in Shiloh, which is on the north of Bethel, on the east side of the highway that goeth up from Bethel to Shechem, and on the south of Lebonah."

The directions given here are so distinctly clear the Benjamites could not mistake their way. The destruction of Shiloh was made known to the prophets, who lifted up their voices and proclaimed the calamity that should lay the glory of that festive city in the dust. When the prophet Jeremiah solemnly warned Jerusalem, he referred to Shiloh. "But go ye now into my place, which was in Shiloh, where I set my name at first, and see what I did to it for the wickedness of my people, Israel." Those interested in the fate of Shiloh are recommended to carefully read the seventy-eighth Psalm, and see what was the character of the wickedness indulged in by the people, that provoked the Lord to anger with them and their high places and caused His indignation to frown upon them It seems plainly evident that God forsook the Tabernacle services at Shiloh, because the people who pretended to celebrate His praise had virtually turned from the God of their fathers, and substituted the image-worship with enthusiastic devotion. It seems the tribe of Ephraim, above all others, would have unyieldingly clung to the Tabernacle and its services. As they were its close guards while coming from Egypt to Canaan, for they had their position nearest it, it seems this alone would have so won their love and veneration for the precious sanctuary that nothing upon the earth could have broken it, and that they would have been eager to defend its sanctity, when it was set up at Shiloh, as their fathers were, who guarded it through the dreary wilderness so many long and weary years. But we find Ephraim had no stability nor any pious attainments worthy of the blessings that distinguished them from the other tribes. It is not unlikely that, while under the influence of pride and selfishness, Ephraim many times boasted of being distinct from their brethren, because they came down through an unbroken line, from Joseph, the ruler of Egypt, as did the nation in the time of our Lord (Josh. xviii. 1; xix. 51; 1 Sam. i. 2, 3, 4; xxi.; xxii; Judges xxi. 15), of being the children of Abraham, which filled them so full of vainglory and foolish conceit, they thought themselves better than any other men, humanly speaking. The Lord would not suffer the meeting-tent to remain at Shiloh, but caused it to be moved entirely from their borders. It is written, "The Lord refused the Tabernacle of Joseph, and chose not the tribe of Ephraim, but the tribe of Judah, the mount of Zion, which He loved."

It is certainly a great treat for any one who is in search of more light on the history of Shiloh, especially its general situation, to take time enough to visit it, notwithstanding the road leading to it is by no means inviting. My guide did not care to go over there with me, because it was two or three miles out of our way; but I insisted he should go, and it was to me a great satisfaction. The scenery round about the place deeply interested me first of all, for I had not conceived the least idea of its situation. It is next to an impossibility to do so; though we may read of a place until we get its history so definitely as to repeat it verbatim, and then minutely consider its locality and situation, as well as any one can without seeing the place, we will find on approaching that our conceptions were far from being correct as to its general situation. I found this to be my case everywhere I went.

THE PRESENT APPEARANCE OF SHILOH.

The whole area composing the site of Shiloh is like a dreary wilderness, except here and there where the husbandman was plowing the ground and sowing seed. I looked over on the knoll where the sacred Tabernacle, in which was placed the Ark of God, stood, and viewed the whole situation the best I could under the circumstances. It seemed to me at first to be a strangely-situated place to set up the sacred Tabernacle. But it is not the Shiloh now that it was when Eli lived, and the whole face of the country for miles around was almost like a beautiful garden, and the firmament was echoing from hill-top to valley, the songs of thousands of happy voices, that sang their heart-felt praises to the Lord of Hosts; and the whole place was filled with the presence of the Lord, who met His people there and blessed them. One will soon change his opinion as to the propriety of locating the sacred tent and ark here on a second sober reflection. It is also natural to suppose that there must have been a large community about Shiloh and its environments in the time of its prime glory. This is evident from the fact, the Benjamites came over and took wives to themselves of the maidens living there.

The site of the Tabernacle being remote from the main road, and on a hill a little below the surrounding mountains, seems to have reminded the worshipers who came to it of the sacredness of the Holy Shrine; that as Israel was shut in from other nations, both socially and religiously, so was the meeting-tent shut in from the rest of the world, and the whole region within its mountain-walls was dedicated to the Lord. And even though many ages have been launched into the deep abyss of eternity since the Tabernacle was taken from Shiloh, and the physical features of the country greatly changed, the songs of high praises having long since been hushed, except those chanted by the birds who still linger about the site of the ancient meeting-tent, though all nature seems cheerless around this once sanctified spot, yet to me the whole scope within the surrounding mountains seemed to have an air of sacredness that indicated the presence of the Holy One, still lingering about the place once occupied by the sacred shrine. I felt like saying, "Put off thy shoes, for the ground on which thou standest is holy;" for the valleys, the hill-tops, and the mountains round about that formed the spacious enclosure, seemed to be clothed with a majesty not common to others not entitled to sacred distinction.

LEBONAH AND ITS ANCIENT TOMBS.

On leaving Shiloh for Lebonah, the pass is a long, deep descent, through terraced fields of wheat, barley, and other products, and cross-ditches in every direction; finally the main highway is reached, at a point where tradition says our Lord rested for a night or more, and just above the plain, along the hillside, is ancient Lebonah. There are many tombs cut in the rocks about this region; in some of them it is thought the remains of several Israelites were interred about the time Shiloh was aglow with prosperity. The traveler having entered the ancient highway to Shechem and the far north, he may be assured that he is passing over the very same ground the patriarchs and prophets of old frequented, the very route our Lord passed through with His disciples, and the same way Saul of Tarsus went when on his way to Damascus to persecute the church.

The knowledge of the fact we are traveling the same highway frequented by the Lord Jesus, both in His youth and while going to and from Judea and Galilee, on His mission of mercy and love, expels the fatigue of the rough and stony way. After passing a short distance beyond Lebonah the plain of Mukhna is entered. Here a beautiful sight looms up to view, and many objects of interest absorb the traveler's attention. The plain is about seven miles long and two miles wide. On its east side the line of hills is low, dark and rocky; the hills on the west side are much higher, and very rugged and barren. On the very highest point projecting into the plain, can be seen from the distance a white tomb, situated on one of the peaks of Mt. Gerizim. Many of them are seen, both in Egypt and Palestine; they are always erected upon the highest summits to be found in the country, and can be seen several miles away. Pains are taken, by those having them in charge, to keep them beautifully whitened, especially during the season when the most travel through the country is usual. They are known as tombs of men whose self-denial and religious devotion caused popular opinion to regard them as saints or holy men. When these distinguished characters die, their remains are laid to rest in one of these whitened sepulchres, which are generally prepared by the persons whilst in health. It is strange that there is never more than one of these tombs found on the same hill, no matter how much space it occupies, and they are usually several miles apart. It is the opinion, some rule or understanding existed, that the remains of but one person could be burried on the same summit. The people are astonishing imitators, and some are always found to follow the examples of the ancient fathers, and it is highly probable, the desire of this peculiar class of men, known as holy or saintly people, to be buried on the highest summit of the most lofty mountains, has existed from the time that information of the burial of Moses upon Mt. Pisgah was made known to the world.

The point in the plain of Mukhna from which this tomb is seen is about six miles away, and far in the distance Mt. Hermon's snowy heights are so distinctly visible, one, not acquainted with the geography of the country, would suppose it was not more than ten or twelve miles away; but you would have to travel at least forty miles, the nearest possible way, before the base of the mount could be reached, and several more before the region of the snow is entered. The air is so very rare, that distant objects seem very near. When the weather is bright Mt. Ebal cannot be seen at the point Gerizim is first noticed, because it sets in farther northward. The plain now known as Mukhna was formerly called Moreh, signifying a camp. It is the place where the Israelites halted when they came up to Shechem to renew their covenant with the Lord, after their conquest at Ai. Hence, the name of the plain was given it because of that event. A few miles from Shechem, the road forks, both leading to it. The one skirting the foot of Gerizim is the main highway, and is used mostly in dry weather, or by those who wish to go the shortest way. But the road through the midst of the plain is the more important to sight-seers, and also easier to travel. There is a village near-by, opposite the fork, on the slope of a hill called in Arabic, Awertah, having two ancient tombs on its most prominent point called el-Azeir and el-Azeirat. There is a tradition, which identifies the tombs as those of Eleazar and Phinehas, the son and grandson of Aaron, respectively. This tradition is so generally credited, that the most critical explorers of that country have confidence in it. Therefore, the village Awertah is the ancient Gibeah of Phinehas. These tombs are regarded by all capable of investigating their origin, to be Jewish of very ancient date, and they believe them to be the resting-places of the persons above mentioned.

JACOB'S WELL.

Not far from the tombs, the plain is crossed at the north side; at which point the valley of Shechem is entered; and just here the old historic well of Jacob is located. It, like all other places of sacred memory in Palestine, is under the care of some religious denomination, who guard it with the most cautious vigilance. The well is in the custody of the Greek Church. It is in the midst of an area enclosed by a thick stone wall, very low and in some places very weak; as an entrance can be obtained without passing through the entrance gate. When we arrived there it was getting late in the afternoon, and for some reason the keeper was absent, and as I was especially anxious to see it that day, for it would have taken too much time to return from Shechem the next morning; having to go a long journey northward, we concluded to climb the low wall and enter the enclosure regardless of consequences. We found it an easy matter to accomplish and were soon standing over the famous well of the illustrous patriarch, who was the great ancestor of the children of Israel. I came from the scene feeling fully satisfied that my visit was highly profitable. About the identity of the well, there is not a shadow of doubt, for all sects regard it as the ancient well, planted thousands of years ago, by the man whose name it bears; Jews, Christians, Samaritans and Mohammedans alike confidently believe this to be the original well. The land immediately circumferencing it is the land Jacob bought from the sons of Hamor, the father of Shechem. Here the patriarch built an altar which he called El-Elohe-Israel.

This well is regarded as a very sacred place by all Christians, and there can be no reasonable doubt that our Lord sat here at noon, on the day He came to the district of Samaria with His disciples en route to Galilee; and being thirsty, He stopped at the well to refresh Himself. The fields round about, upon which we had the pleasure to gaze, are those corn-fields to which He referred when He said to His disciples, "Lift up your eyes and look on the fields, for they are white already to the harvest." One can scarcely realize he is standing on the ground and by the well made memorable and hallowed by the presence of the Son of God, whose voice uttered such pungent truths, while sitting upon a stone-seat, that the whole village of Sychar was aroused to a sense of duty. Jesus was going over from Judea to Galilee on a missionary tour, and the nearest and most direct route was through the district of Samaria (Deut. xi. 30; John iv. 35; Joshua viii. 30–35; xxiv. 33–38; Gen. xii. 6; xxxiii. 20). Our Lord exhibited an entirely different spirit from the Jews; who, rather than pass through Samaria, would take the trans-Jordanic road by the way of Perea, that they might shun the Samaritan people, between whom and the Jews there were no fraternal relations. It is an easy matter to understand the intense bitterness they entertained against each other, if we consider the event which caused the breach. But Jesus, having a tender feeling for the Samaritans and desiring them to be partakers of His mercies, preferred going the more direct way over to Galilee. When our Lord started from Judea to the northern district, in company with His disciples, "He must needs go through Samaria." The Jews maintained a relentless hatred against them, which was reciprocated by the Samaritans. This feeling seems to exist at present just as strongly as in the time of our Lord. We deem it best at this point to examine the history of this people and some of the peculiarities common to their character, before we give an outline statement of the events that occurred in and about Shechem. The Samaritans are a mixed people, and were very numerous in the time of our Lord; but at present there are few remaining who can claim to have regularly descended from the original stock. There are a few living in Shechem, who cling with precious fondness to their primitive religion; and to speak in the mildest terms, they hate the Jews with an unyielding hatred, too intense to be expressed. Not long after the abolishment of the northern kingdom, and the transportation of the people beyond the Euphrates, a new state of things took place in Shechem. It was at this time and under these circumstances this new race appeared. The origin of the Samaritans is disclosed in the first and second Kings. In these we are told the Assyrians removed the Israelitish inhabitants as captives of war to their own land, and colonized a number of the people of their own government in Canaan, to take charge of the places made vacant by the capture. The people colonized from Assyria, being comparatively few, were not capable of protecting themselves nor the country; so that the wild beasts, that had been kept under control by the former inhabitants, increased so greatly they distressed them as if a devouring epidemic had visted their homes. They were a very superstitious people, and attributed the great influx of wild beasts to their lack of knowing the religion that was usually known to the Israelites. That they might be instructed in its merits, one of the priests who was taken into captivity was sent to them. He made Bethel his headquarters, and taught the people the form of the worship of the Lord. This new form of service was adopted by them, but they did not abandon their heathen religion; they held to both the God of the Israelites and their own dumb idols. Now, as to how this people so greatly multiplied is a matter upon which many opinions have been founded.

HISTORY OF THE SAMARITANS.

Some think the Samaritans are wholly of heathen origin; others believe they are a mixture of the Israelites and Assyrian colony. It is not to be supposed all the Israelites were carried away into captivity; it is not known in the annals of warfare that the victors have captured all the vanquished and transported them, especially where they were very numerous, as were the Israelites. It is also known that in all cases of conquest, social and matrimonial relations existed between the conqueror and conquered, when they mingled together in the time of peace. It is known that such relations existed among the very highest officials of the two kingdoms of the children of Israel, notwithstanding the Lord had forbidden such relations. It can be readily inferred that a people like the Assyrians, who were under no restrictions in this regard, would unhesitatingly have social and conjugal relations, with the people they found in the country, in which they were colonized. Josephus, to whom we must concede great liberality in his voluminous writings, was not free from partiality; and we must conclude his feeling towards the Samaritans was not of the most friendly character. And, therefore, he naturally would, in the absence of positive proof, hesitate stubbornly to claim any consanguineous relation to them. When we consider the various circumstances connected with the condition of these people, socially and otherwise, we do not think it a step beyond the limits of an ordinary prerogative to say that the great

Jewish historian was in error when he disclaimed that any social or matrimonial relation existed between the two races. Indeed, it is clearly evident the burden of proof is against him. We know from the record of the Holy Scriptures the people sent up to Samaria, to occupy the country in place of the Israelitish captives, were of several race types. "The King of Assyria brought men from Babylon, and from Cuthah, and from Avva, and from Hamath, and from Sepharwaim, and placed them in the cities of Samaria, instead of the children of Israel, and they possessed Samaria and dwelt in the cities thereof." These various race-types settled in the country among the remnant of the Hebrews, who had not been carried to Babylon, and it is not reasonable to suppose those who were left in the land ostracised themselves from the fraternal association of the people, by whom they had been subordinated, any more than it could be reasonably supposed that the Africans, who were in a state of slavish subordination in this land, could have kept themselves free from such relations with those who ruled them. It should be remembered there was no law against matrimonial relations between the Israelites and other peoples, upon racial lines, but it was a religious necessity. The proneness of the Hebrews to embrace the religion of heathens made it impossible to have free and full intercourse with them and maintain the true worship of God.

This barrier, if it was considered at all by the remaining Iraelites (which is very doubtful), was removed when the people partially embraced their religion, after the priest had been returned to them from among the captives, to teach the new-comers the principles of the Israelitish worship. It is also known that there are even to-day, among those claiming to be Jews, a comparatively small number who have come down unmixed from the primitive Israelitish progenitors. It must be agreed, therefore, that although we must accord to Josephus a large degree of liberality and fairness, his opposition to the Samaritan sect caused him to greatly blunder when he tells the world there were no social or matrimonial relations between the Israelites and the people colonized among them from Babylon.

Having stated the above facts, which to me seem perfectly clear, I must frankly confess my opinion is that the Samaritans are a mixed people composed of several races (2 Kings xvii. 24), Jewish included. Josephus, referring to the vacillating character of the Samaritans, says; "When the Jews are in adversity, they deny they are of kin to them, and then they confess the truth; but when they perceive some good fortune hath befallen them, they immediately pretend to have communion with them, saying, 'they belong to them, and derive their genealogy from the posterity of Joseph, Ephraim and Manassah.'" It is certain they claimed this relationship in the time of our Lord, which He did not dispute; and when we consider the pains He took to settle vexed questions, we incline strongly to the opinion, that if the Samaritans had been ignorant of their origin, or had knowingly or wilfully claimed a relationship they knew to be false, He would have corrected them and set the matter aright.

The woman of Sychar, while conversing with Jesus at the well, said to Him: "Art Thou greater than our father Jacob, who gave us this well?" claiming, in these words, Jacob as their great ancestor, and themselves as having descended through his line. She also said to the Saviour: "Our fathers worshiped in this mountain," evidently referring to Joshua and others, who worshiped there in early days. Now, inasmuch as our Lord did not dispute this claim of blood-relation to the patriarch, nor of the fathers to the woman, or any others during the two days He remained in Sychar, it seems consistent to infer that He indorsed her statement in regard to the matter.

There is another matter of importance necessary to be considered before leaving this point: the expression of the Samaritans to Zerubbabel and his assistants when re-building the Temple; they, wishing to be allowed to assist the workmen, presented their plea as follows: "For we seek your God as you do, and we do sacrifice unto Him since the days of Esar-haddon, King of Assyria, who brought us hither." It will be seen, if a little time is taken to investigate this peculiar application, that it has no bearing on the fact of their relation to the Jews. It refers especially to the words "which brought us hither." It is certainly known the petitioners were not those who had been transferred to Samaria by the King of Assyria, but descendants of them, therefore, the words, "which brought us up hither," refer to their fathers who settled (2 Kings xvii. 24) in the land seventy years prior. This was a usual expression among the Jews when referring to their fathers' deliverance from Egypt; the words, "brought us up out of Egypt," were many times addressed to the generations who lived hundreds of years after those who entered Canaan were dead. These petitioners meant by their statement, that they were in the land by virtue of the colonization of their forefathers, and not that they themselves were "brought hither." On the self-same principle, the African race in America say, We were brought here from Africa; it is evidently known that reference is made to the early fathers and not to the present generation; for millions of them have never seen that far-off land and do not care to see it.

We have presented these items of history to clear away any clouds of doubt that might hinder a clear observation of the fact as to the relation between the Jews and Samaritans. Those of this mixed race living in Shechem at present are the only representatives of the ancient stock. They closely resemble the Jews in their features and general bearing. They are as ever greatly opposed to their long-standing enemy, and have no more dealings with them now than in those days when the woman met our Lord at the well. It is generally believed by those who have expressed themselves on the subject, that the Samaritans are the descendants of the Jews who were left at the time of the captivity; that intermarriages took place between them and the new-comers, the result of which being, the introduction of a mixed people. When the Jews were permitted to return from Babylon, the Samaritans' chronicles state, a portion of the congregation followed Sanballat, the remaining portion adhering to Zerubbabel. It seems that among the many things that caused ill-feelings between the two races was concerning the proper place of worship; the Jews thought Mount Moriah was the place, and the Samaritans contended for Mount Gerizim. But there are indications, that the Samaritans became willing to unite with the Jews, in rebuilding the waste places of Jerusalem and the Temple, that there might be a common interest existing between them, and we have not found it recorded or implied that any arrangements were being made for the erection of a temple in this district until after their offer to help the Jews had been refused. But being denied, they became exasperated and used every means possible, fair and otherwise, to oppose them. The Samaritans introduced every measure they could conceive, to interfere with their Jewish neighbors. They calumniated them in the most bitter terms, and brought indictments against them to the king of Persia, and even searched the records to find something written that would stimulate them to divide the religious sentiment permanently.

Finding the command of Moses, that on entering the land, the people should proceed to Mt. Gerizim, and one-half should stand on its slope and respond, amen, to the blessing pronounced by the Levites, it was deemed by the Samaritans that this mount was a proper place to build a Temple. Therefore, they set themselves to the work to accomplish it; they also instituted an order of ceremonies according to the letter of the law. About the time of these movements, which so rapidly followed one another, a great tumult began in Judah concerning some of the officials in high position over in Jerusalem who were charged with unfair dealing (Ezra iv. 1-4; Neh. iv.; Deut. xxvii.

11-13). Many of the Jews, feeling their rights had been greatly imposed upon, left and went over to Samaria, and assisted in building the temple on Mt. Gerizim. It is said, one of the causes of this movement of the Samaritans was the expulsion of the son of a high priest from Jerusalem, because he had married the daughter of Sanballat, a Samaritan governor. It is supposed this man was afterward made high priest of the temple on Mt. Gerizim. It then became a familiar custom for dissatisfied Jews to go over to Samaria and join the people in their worship claiming to be disgusted with the manner the services were conducted in Jerusalem. The Samaritans, like the Jews, firmly believed in the coming of the Messiah, and entertained a hope He would descend from them, and not from the remnant of the restored captives of Judah who had come from Babylon. The sacred books of the Jews, that had been partially countenanced by the Samaritans, were at once stubbornly rejected, except the Pentateuch. There seemed to be an endless chain of incidents that bred strife and unyielding enmity between these races; so that they seemed not only to hate each other, but the very ground they walked upon. Therefore, the Jews living in the northern and southern districts, would go miles out of their way rather than go through Samaria; and the enmity existed equally as strong between those Jews who left and went over to the Samaritans, and their kindred whom they had forsaken, as if they were full-fledged Samaritans. Now, after all, it is strikingly wonderful what a tremendous flame of hatred a small matter can kindle. It no doubt has puzzled many to understand why these people were not allowed to test their sincerity, when they made such a strong appeal to assist in rebuilding the Temple. But a close examination will reveal the fact, that the Samaritans were only partially converted from heathenism. The priests sent to them did not succeed in influencing them to wholly abandon their native religion; and it would have been most unfortunate to the true worship, to have admitted them fully into the fellowship of the Jews. It would have been a most blessed thing if there could have been a harmonious relation among the people, so that there would have been but one people, one God recognized, and one religion known. But the proneness of the Jews to follow strange gods is well and widely known; and if the Samaritans had been permitted to associate with them in repairing the city and Temple, their influence over them would have been disastrous to the true worship. It were far better to have the two races at variance forever than to insult the Lord whose hand of tenderness had led them from captivity and restored them to their own land, than to have contaminated themselves with a people whose religion was not approved of by Him.

THE WOMAN OF SYCHAR.

When the Lord Jesus came through Samaria He found the most bitter feeling existing between the Jews and Samaritans, and when He sat upon one of the stone seats at the well, while His disciples went to get food over in the town, a woman from Sychar, a small village a few hundred yards away, came to draw water and saw a Jew sitting there. She paid no attention to him whatever, nor would she under any circumstances have passed the usual friendly courtesies if the Saviour had not approached her in such tones as to cause her to enter into a conversation with Him. And before she consented to comply with His wish, or allow herself to be detained, she wished first of all to know how it was that He, being a Jew, would ask a Samaritan for a drink, for the feeling between those people was so strong that a Jew would have died before he would have asked a favor so small even as a cup of cold water; and, as has been stated, they would not pass through the country unless their business was such that they could not avoid it. It is worthy of remark that the woman of Sychar was not surprised to see a Jew sitting at the well, for no doubt she had seen others there from time to time, whose business called them through that way, and, as the plain of Mukhna is hot and shadeless, they would naturally come to the well to draw a cool drink of water to refresh themselves; but such was not often the case. It is also noteworthy the Jews invariably took with them their vessel to draw water, for they would not drink from one used by the Samaritans; hence, the woman said to our Lord, "Sir, thou hast nothing to draw with, and the well is deep." She had no idea He would drink from her vessel, or, if He would, it would have been a blight on her to have permitted it. Therefore, she could see no way to comply with the stranger's request. The way was then open to begin a sermon to the woman, by the old historic well, that she would remember to her latest days, and that would reach all the people in the town, although they did not hear Him deliver it. He had time to make known His mission to the people, and the method used to open the way was a sermon preached to a lone woman, with as much power and earnestness as if the whole area encircling the well had been crowded with attentive hearers. Surely an important lesson is taught all those who profess to teach the Gospel; that the good done does not depend upon the number of people within the sound of their voices, but the earnestness they command to discharge their duty, though there may be but one present. It is now, as in antique times, the custom of all travelers, whether natives or strangers, to carry vessels with them to draw water, for they are just as necessary as it is to take provisions for the journey. The wells are far apart, and often travelers must go ten or twelve miles before they come to one. There are but few brooks or running streams in Palestine, and only two or three of them clear enough to drink. But in the event one is come upon which may be used for drinking purposes, and it is necessary to have a vessel to dip with, it would be a very strange request, if not insulting, to ask any whom we might meet at one of the wells to allow us to drink out of their water-pots; indeed, it would seem to them as inconsistent as it did to the woman of Sychar, whom Christ addressed.

The women and young maidens are still the water-bearers. They often go in small companies, especially when they have a distance of two or three miles to go, and can be seen almost from early morning until late in the evening, waiting for their turn to draw water. They seem to have a regular system in procuring it. The first comers are the first served, no matter how small the company may be. And should there be one who would dare intrude upon the one who had come first (as the shepherds of Midian did to the daughters of Reuel, whom they would not allow to draw water for their flocks until their own were served, when Moses interposed for them), there would be such an uproarious tumult that a stranger would be impressed that some one had met with a lamentable misfortune. But such a thing seldom if ever occurs, unless by special consent one may allow some others to take their place. When the woman, by her slowness to comply with the request of the stranger with whom she was talking, strongly indicated her unwillingness to do so, He said to her, "If thou hadst known the gift of God, and who it is that sayeth to thee, Give me to drink, thou wouldst have asked of Him, and He would have given thee living water." She was immediately aroused, and became curiously anxious, to know something of the water that would keep her from thirst and save her the trouble and labor of drawing from the well, for it is evident she did not comprehend the meaning of our Lord, although His words were plainly presented. She was so absorbed in His remarks, she had forgotten her errand to the well, and that she was having a friendly conversation with a Jew, which was a thing not to be tolerated among the Samaritans. She had become extremely desirous for "living water." Our Lord, seeing He had sufficiently won her attention, further informed her as to the conditions upon which she could obtain it. That there must be a change in her internal and external life, both with regard to herself and to the Jews whom she and her people inveterately hated, and that she must comply with the law of Moses to whom she claimed relationship whose law she professed to observe. Jesus was leading her into a state of mind that would enable her to look upon her own life, and allow her to see how deeply her lewdness had covered her, and the immediate need of being delivered from such a life. To accomplish this, Jesus made an impression upon her conscience so effectual, she was compelled to open another door for the truth to uncover her sins and bring her conduct of the past and present before her, to an astonishing if not alarming degree; for the conversation that followed touched the very quick of her soul. That He might reveal His divinity to her and make her feel that the person with whom she was conversing was more than the ordinary Jew, she had been accustomed to see passing through the country, or sitting at the well, He impressed her that it was necessary to have her husband present, before the "life-giving water" could be given to her. Therefore He said, "Go call thy husband," that both might enjoy the blessing. She, with an innocent expression that was doubtless endeavoring to hide the guilt then disturbing her conscience said, "I have no husband." He endorsed her answer, and at once entered into the secrets of her life with such exactness she was overwhelmed with amazement. Jesus uncovered her life more and more, as if reading a correctly written diary, telling her all she had done. The woman must have been profoundly astonished, while the secrets of her inner life were being unfolded by the Master so accurately; she could only stand and wonder who the wise stranger could be. And when He had gone farther and deeper into her social life, she concluded the stranger must be a prophet; and as it was commonly believed Elijah must come before the appearance of the Messiah, she may have thought it was he, for there were no prophets among the Jews at that time, nor had there been for centuries, except John the Baptist, who was not generally regarded as such. So she said to Jesus, "Sir, I perceive that thou art a prophet;" or, I feel you have told me the whole truth,—"who art thou?" It should be called to mind that Jesus selected an opportune time to unfold to this woman her conduct, when no one was near; not even the disciples heard the conversation.

This is a most important lesson, and would be of unspeakable benefit to us all if followed. Feeling satisfied she was in the presence of a man of God, as the prophets were called, she wished Him to settle the long-agitated and most vexing question that had been a source of contention ever since the return of the captives from Babylon; one that had formed a mountain wall of division between the Jews and Samaritans which seemed impossible to penetrate, for they had no dealings together. The woman did not change the conversation simply to avoid a further disclosure of her life, for Christ had told her, according to her own words, "all things that she had done." But as she was in conversation with one who was familiar with the facts, she wished that question of questions to be settled in her mind. Therefore, in order to draw from the stranger's mind something that would explain the question over which there had been so much dispute, she said to the Saviour, "Our fathers worshiped in these mountains" (referring to Ebal and Gerizim, which were in front of her, a short distance to the north and west), and ye say that Jerusalem is the place where men ought to worship." It is very clear that Jesus had so won the confidence of the woman, she was ready to implicitly confide in whatever He might tell her concerning the matter; and inasmuch as He had told her such pungent truths as to her own life, she could not believe He would do otherwise in this gravely perplexing question as to the proper place of worship. Her spiritual appetite had been so thoroughly aroused, she seemed to be ready to go wherever the proper place was, so that she might secure the approbation of the Lord; indeed, she was deeply and keenly convicted. Her people were of the opinion, because of a tradition of long standing, that there was no other place under the sun more sacred and holy than Mount Gerizim, and that from its soil the Lord made Adam, and on its brow was situated the Garden of Eden in which he was placed; and from its lofty summit the tree of life lifted up its boughs, in connection with all the other precious fruit trees of the garden; that here, Noah landed his precious cargo after the flood, and here he built an altar and sacrificed to the Lord; that Abraham came with his son Isaac to this same mount, to offer him up in obedience to the command as a sacrifice to God upon the altar of fire; that Jacob, when on his way to Mesopotamia, seeking a refuge from the wrath of Esau, rested his head upon a stone here, on the night he saw in his dream the wonderful ladder reaching from heaven to earth, and the angels ascending and descending. Here, and not at Gilgal, the twelve stones were set up which the children of Israel took from the bed of the river Jordan. But notwithstanding these flattering traditions attaching to the mountains before her, the woman wished to hear the decision of this wonderful personage, whose words of truth had won her soul. The Saviour knew the feelings of the woman—that she was ripe for instruction, and He took time to explain the matter to her, even though the disciples were opposed to it. They were of the opinion it would be of more profit for Him to eat something, than to spend time talking with the woman, whose race they had been taught to despise and to have no dealings with, except purely business transactions. But Jesus knew the importance of the moment, and used it to a most beneficial advantage. He at that opportune moment unfolded the truth to the woman so clearly that men of every generation since her day have gladly embraced it. She heard the explanation, that it was not material as to the place where men should worship the Father, but the manner was the matter of chief interest, that is, He must be "worshiped in the spirit and in truth."

It can be seen how easily Christ discharged this vexed question without deciding with either party, and at the same time brought a great truth to the surface that settled the matter for all time to come. The woman is inclined to think the Messiah had come, of whom Moses and the prophets wrote, and was talking with her; or some one gifted as man had never before been known to be in the knowledge of explaining the deep things of God. "I know that the Messiah cometh (which is called Christ); when He is come, He will declare unto us all things," said the woman. Then Jesus said, "I that speak unto thee am He." On hearing this, she left her water-pot at the well and ran to the city and said to the men, "Come, see a man which told me all things that ever I did; can this be the Christ?"

Jacob's well is seventy-five feet deep, and seven feet six inches in diameter, partly inclosed within a stone building so as to prevent the public from seeing it, as are all the places in the land where it is possible to do so. About the middle of the fourth century there was a church built over it, said to have been cruciform, with the well in the centre. There are a few old pillars and other ruins near the well, which, it is supposed, were used in the old church building. It was a pleasure to me to have an opportunity to stand upon this renowned spot and take a survey of the country round about, especially the bald mountains at which the woman of Sychar pointed while conversing with Jesus, and to meditate concerning the things that occurred there thousands of years gone by.

In the plain near the well, Abraham built an altar while sojourning as a stranger in a strange land; and here, many years later, Jacob came and settled for a time; having bought a plot of ground, he dug a well for the use of his household and flocks. Notwithstanding he bought the land and paid for it, attempts were made to dispossess him of it, but he managed finally to regain his legitimate claim. After he moved down to Hebron, he sent his sons over there with the flocks to pasture them on his own fields. Jacob referred to the event when, nearing the end of life, he said, "I took it out of the hand of the Amorites with my sword and bow." Joseph, whom God had raised up to save his father and all his household from the distresses of the seven years' famine, came through this field in which the well is located when in search of his brethren. It may be, that while I walked about there, my feet marked the soil where Abraham, Jacob, Joseph and our blessed Lord walked when in that region. Here by the well sat our Lord in the hottest portion of the day, and drew an illustrious comparison (Gen. xii. 6: xxxiii. 19: xxxvii 15: Josh. xviii. 22) between the effects of the water which He asked of the woman and that blessed stream which continually flows from the throne of God, from which He preached one of the most memorable sermons of His life to a poor woman, and it has come thundering down the ages with all the freshness and power it had when first proclaimed, so that millions of thirsty souls have heard the good tidings and prayed, "Lord, give me evermore of this water."

THE TOMB OF JOSEPH.

Just a few hundred yards north of the well is the tomb of Joseph, whose bones were, according to his dying request, brought out of Egypt by the Israelites and buried in that portion of the ground bought by his father. It is venerated by all the native religious communities. It is specially remarkable that Joseph's remains should be brought over from that far-away country, and rested in the very field through which he passed the last time he was in the neighborhood, when but a lad seventeen years old. Sychar, the town in which the woman lived who was so graciously entertained by our Lord, is a little to the northeast of Joseph's tomb, and is a small village six hundred yards north of the well. It is noteworthy, that the extortionate Arabs have not selected a site in the neighborhood of the location of the woman's home, as seems to be the rule. It must be remembered that Sychar and Shechem are distinct places; sometimes they are taken for the same place, and thereby the student gets greatly confused and misrepresents the one or the other when referring to certain events of antique times. This shows the importance of making the closest examination of history before one attempts to instruct others; for a single error may lead thousands, historically astray, even without the knowledge of the author. Shechem, which was in later times called Neapolis, or New City, by Vespasian, who while emperor caused it to

NABLOUS (SYCHAR OR SHECHEM).

be rebuilt, is at present called by the Arabs Nablous. But Sychar, now called Iskar, situated a few hundred yards north of Jacob's well, just at the base of Mt. Ebal, accords with the ancient town of the same name referred to in the New Testament. When our Lord came to the well, it is written, "He came to a city in Samaria called Sychar; near to the parcel of ground that Jacob gave his son Joseph; and Jacob's well was there." The description of this town is so very minutely defined, it would seem that no mistake could be made in locating the little city the Saviour entered on the day He sat at Jacob's well. Several authors have said, He came to Shechem first, and it was called Sychar in the New Testament. But it seems to me altogether improbable. For we are to remember that on coming to the well our Lord was fatigued; and had He passed around the foot of Gerizim to Shechem and then come back to the well, He would have walked six miles farther than He should have; for the city is at least three miles from the well. Now when we take the Bible for our guide and read, "He must needs go through Samaria," there can be no other conclusion than that He came the old highway by the way of Lebonah up through the plain of Mukhna, direct to the well. St. John says, "He came to a city called Sychar—and Jacob's well was there." The village called Sychar accurately accords with the definition. The town in question is only about six or seven hundred yards from Joseph's tomb, which is in the parcel of ground Jacob gave him, and about the same distance from the well. But Shechem is at least three miles away. It is, therefore, clear that our Lord came to Sychar en route to Jacob's well, and not Shechem. We make this point in the face of opposition, for the reason our Lord could have come no other way to go through Samaria; and the same highway is open now that was traveled in His day, and we do not see how any one could otherwise conclude who has visited that portion of Palestine.

ANCIENT SHECHEM.

Shechem is an ancient city, about thirty-five miles north of Jerusalem, and three miles from Jacob's well, having the Jordan on the east and the Mediterranean on the west. Situated between Mounts Ebal and Gerizim is the valley of Shechem, surrounded by beautiful olive groves, and is said to be watered by eighty springs, which is a blessing that no other city in Palestine enjoys, not even Jerusalem, and cannot be surpassed by any other city in historic events, except Jerusalem, Hebron and Bethel. The name Nablous, given it by the natives, is a contraction from Neapolis, by which it was known for many years. But anciently it was called Shechem, or Cheshem. The Canaanites were in possession of this country when Abraham first came to it, and it is therefore regarded as the oldest city in Palestine of which there is any knowledge. The inhabitants boast of it as being the oldest city in the world, having, as it does, a history reaching four thousand years into the past. When Jacob came and settled in the vicinity, it is said that the city of Shechem and the country round about, was in possession of the Havites, having Hamer, the father of Shechem, for governor. There is a long train of historical events running through many centuries connecting Shechem with the old and new dispensations. It is mentioned prominently with the early events of the New Testament, and alike conspicuous during and after the time of our Lord and His apostles. It was in all probability about the time of the great persecution of the church at Jerusalem, during which the Jews killed Stephen, and the apostles were all scattered abroad throughout Judea and Samaria, that Philip, Peter and John preached the gospel of Christ in Shechem. It was also one of the Christian strongholds in the time of the supremacy of the Crusaders in Palestine. Like many other cities in Palestine, Shechem has passed through many bitter ordeals from foes without and within. It is one of the principal cities visited in the Holy Land, and ranks in this respect with all the cities and towns except Joppa, Jerusalem, Jericho, Bethel, Bethlehem and Hebron. When these places are visited, the traveler turns his face towards Shechem and its environments. Jacob's well and Joseph's tomb are as eagerly sought by the sight-seer as the plain of Mamre, and the great Mosque, Machpelah, where the mortal remains of Abraham and a portion of his family are buried. The indignation of Simeon and Levi was kindled against the city, on account of a grave insult committed by the male inhabitants; they therefore rose up in their might and slaughtered them, and captured the city. This was the beginning of a woeful future for the old historic city, that brought to the people untold misery. When Jacob left Haran with his family and possessions he demanded all the strange gods in their possession, and when they were given him he hid them by an oak near Shechem. It was the place of the great convention of the ten tribes or their representatives, when they revolted from the dominion of Rohoboam and organized a new kingdom, with Jeroboam as king. The first mention of Shechem in the Bible is concerning the sojourn of Abraham there as mentioned above. It was strongly urged by many who were in the northern kingdom that the king should establish his headquarters there permanently, but this failed, Tirzah and Samaria being more preferable as the seat of power. In the days of the Judges Shechem became a Levitical city, and it was here that the men of the town assembled for the purpose of crowning Ahimelech, the Shechemite, son of Gideon; and it was from the summit of Mount Gerizim, Jotham, his brother, who alone escaped, when Ahimelech caused seventy of his brethren to be massacred, addressed the men of Shechem in flaming words concerning the tree and the bramble. The conspiracy (which was a common occurrence in those times) caused the overthrow of the city. The people expressed their preference for an iron-clad heathen of the Shechemites to rule over them, and shut the gates against Ahimelech, whereupon he captured the city, beat it down and sowed salt from one end to the other. It was rebuilt by Jeroboam soon after he was chosen king of Israel, and made his capital for a short time, when it was moved to Tirzah. It so deeply afflicted Shechem that it never fully recovered, for just as soon as the seat of power was removed, the city suddenly sank into a state of almost profound silence, and from that time forward but little mention is made of it during the two hundred and fifty years of the independence of the northern kingdom.

There seems to have been, after the permanent establishment of idol-worship in Israel, a continuous downward tendency of the ancient city. It was invaded and plundered by the formidable Saracens in the middle of the twelfth century, and again in the latter part of it. At the beginning of the thirteenth century, an earthquake occurred, which did a great deal of damage to the country round about, and Shechem was not spared; it is said to have sustained great damage. The Saracens were compelled to abandon the city about the middle of the thirteenth century, and have never been able to regain it, although attempts were made. The Moslems were found to be a powerful foe, entirely too strong for their enemies. There are several mosques in Shechem. As might be supposed, the most celebrated of them is called the Great Mosque. This seems to be a favorite name with the Mohammedans, as "Metropolitan" is among certain Christian denominations in America. This "Great Mosque" was at one time a Christian church. There are many buildings used by the Mohammedans as mosques, that were originally erected by Christians for church purposes. When the crusaders were in power they had churches in every city and town in Palestine, all of which, with rare exceptions, were converted into Moslem places of worship after the great victory Saladin achieved, on the fifth day of July, eleven hundred and eighty-seven, who nearly annihilated the crusaders in the memorable conflict.

Shechem was visited again with an earthquake, in the first half of the nineteenth century, and nearly overwhelmed; and soon after that destructive visitation Ibrahim Pasha plundered it and distressed the people greatly. But of late there has nothing of a serious nature occurred to mar the peace of the inhabitants, and there is comparative peace between the several religious sects who live there. The whole population is estimated to be twenty thousand, of whom one hundred and sixty are Samaritans, and nineteen thousand and forty are Mohammedans of the most radical character. They are full of selfish pride, and classed with the most bigoted people in the land. It is of great interest to travelers through northern Palestine to go up to the summits of Mt. Gerizim and Mt. Ebal, although the ascent is long and tedious, but, like Tabor, Carmel and other mountains, it well pays one for the toils and hardships of the journey, when the top is reached, to view the extensive ruins dispersed over a large tract of country. The principal ruins of Mt. Gerizim, are seen on the top of a very rocky hill; some being the remains of buildings erected by the Samaritans when they were in a high state of enthusiasm, over the religious subject that had been so hotly discussed and caused much excitement a question that remained unsettled until Christ met the woman at the well. There are other ruins that date back to the time of the crusaders.

Moses, the man of God and great leader of the Israelites from bondage, had been made familiar with these two mountains, that stand out like mighty sentinels guarding the sacred spot in the valley below, where, for the first time, an altar blazed with a sacrifice acceptable to the Lord, in the land of Canaan; and where God made a covenant, to give the beautiful and fruitful land upon which he looked, for an everlasting inheritance to him and his descendants. He knew of the plot of ground Abraham bought from the sons of Hamar, and in his prophetic visions saw other important events that had transpired there, and, therefore, gave a special charge to the people, that on coming into the land of their inheritance, they should proceed to the place which was dedicated to God by their forefathers, and made hallowed by the presence of the Lord, and solemnly renew their covenant before the Most High. In obedience to this command, Joshua, as soon as the way was clear enough to make a safe trip (after the capture of Ai), went over to Gerizim and assembled the hosts in the valley of Shechem that they might prepare for the solemn service that should soon follow. This scene is fully recorded in the book of Joshua and should be carefully read by all Bible students. The people assembled on the side of the mountains and in the valley, while the Levites assembled on the mountains; from the summit of Ebal smoke was seen ascending from the altar that Joshua had built of "unhewn stones," according to the directions of Moses, and he wrote a copy of the Law upon the stones in the presence of all the people. The stipulations of the Law were read in their hearing of all Moses commanded. It is clear from the command of Moses, which was faithfully observed by Joshua, that the Israelites were divided by tribes while the law was being read. Simeon, Levi, Judah, Issachar, Joseph and Benjamin, were to stand on Mt. Gerizim; Reuben, Gad, Asher, Zebulun, Dan and Naphtali, on Mt. Ebal; and the Levites repeated with a loud voice the word of the law, and all the people at the end of each command said, "Amen." It is a singular fact that by reason of the formation of the mountains into an amphitheatre, a natural sounding-board is constituted by which persons can hear each other distinctly talking in an ordinary tone of voice from either side, or conversations can be had with persons in the valley by those on the summit of either mountain just as plainly as though they were standing at an ordinary talking distance.

THE VIEW FROM GERIZIM AND EBAL.

These two historic mountains, standing so prominently along the plain of Mukhna and the valley of Shechem, furnish many topics for the Bible student's perusal. Both are nearly three thousand feet high; Ebal is said to be about three hundred feet higher than Gerizim. The view from either is sublime; the plain and valley seem like a beautiful green carpet under you. The hills of Moab and Gilead are in full view on the east of the Jordan, while Sharon, Joppa and the Great Sea, are plainly seen on the west; Hermon and the mountains of Galilee loom up on the north and northwest and all the highland round about. The sides of Ebal are more difficult to climb than Gerizim, having a very narrow path winding up to the summit, which has on its highest point an enclosure ninety-two feet square, with walls said to be twenty feet thick. It is the general opinion that these ruins are the remains of a fortress located here by the crusaders, as it was a familiar custom with them to strongly fortify their highlands.

The Samaritans are very much reduced numerically, so that there is but a small community left. They live in Shechem, and have a small building which they call "The Samaritan Temple," on the slope of Mt. Gerizim. In it they keep the Roll of the Law, which no one is allowed to examine except by special permission from the High Priest, which must be done in his august presence. It is not often permitted; therefore, a person may feel himself highly favored who is given liberty to see them. These ancient documents have given rise to much discussion, especially the oldest, which they claim was written in the time of Moses, and the production of the grandson of Aaron. But while it is very stubbornly doubted that these old, time-worn manuscripts were written in the time of Moses, or by the grandson of Aaron, it is certain they are very old, and were written long before the Christian Era. The oldest one is much worn with age, and so defaced (Josh. viii. 33: Deut. xxvii. 13) that those who have charge of it can only read a little here and there in it.

The Temple is surprisingly small and low, having a plain, old-fashioned interior that would remind one of a small country church, with a white-washed finish rather than a temple. But the people are anxious to have it look as ancient as possible, and anything that will give it that appearance is appreciated by them, and they seem to be just as proud of it as though it were a spacious house. It is located in a very quiet and lonely part of the city on the northwest, and one must prepare for a very unpleasant trip to reach it, for it is a half hour's walk from the convent, including the short time required to view the bazaar, which is uninviting. The Temple cannot be reached conveniently riding, on account of the crooked and roundabout way leading to it, therefore it can be made in less than half the time walking. The passes or narrow streets are winding, rough, dark, and shamefully filthy. When we arrived there it seemed a pleasure to the priest to open the door to admit us. In a few moments the High Priest appeared, who, after the usual salutations, began to exhibit the precious relics it contains. The recess where they are kept is called Mizbah; it is about five feet square and generally covered with a veil. It is so situated, that the worshipers, in looking at it, are always facing their sanctuary on Mt. Gerizim. There is a striking resemblance between the Jews and Samaritans in worship, which is a clear evidence that they largely embraced the Jewish mode in the early ages. The High Priest chants the service like the Rabbi, and generally takes the place of that functionary in administering the higher order of service. It requires but a short time to see all there is on exhibition; and were it not for the ancient manuscripts it would not pay any one to go there.

The Samaritans seem to be a people well-disposed towards strangers, and are glad when they pay their little Temple a visit. But the majority are said to be a do-less people, depending more upon charity than labor for their maintenance. They have, for many ages, withdrawn themselves from the social communion of other races in the vicinity, so that, in their present reduced state, they must necessarily marry their blood-relations, which, to my mind, is the major cause of their sickly expressions and the fast rate in which they have thinned out. It will not be a century before there will not be a full-blooded Samaritan in the community, and their existence will be a thing of the past. They still hold their passover on Mt. Gerizim, and the ascent to the ancient site is generally made by tourists.

The following is in part a description of a method of conducting the feast, copied from Murray's Hand Book: "We proceed along the due east toward a conspicuous hill on a rocky knoll, and in fifteen minutes reach the base of the latter. Here we observe a few perches of tolerably level ground, where the Samaritans encamp at the feast of the passover." On its eastern side is a small rectangular area, surrounded by stones like the foundation of an old building. In its centre is a trough about a foot deep, and four feet long, filled with ashes and calcined bones, the remains of the passover lambs, which are burned with fire according to the command of the law. Beside the enclosure is a circular pit three feet in diameter and eight or ten feet deep, in which the lambs are roasted. The Samaritan passover is rigidly observed in accordance with the exact directions laid down by Moses (Exodus xii. 3–28). In this respect it differs considerably from the modern Jewish rite, and is in consequence far more interesting. The tents of the community are pitched around the inside of the enclosure formed by rough walls, which is called Khurbet Luz, from a Samaritan tradition which makes Gerizim the scene of Jacob's dream. The Tabernacle stands at the southeast corner of the camp close to the rough trough. On the afternoon preceding the eating of the passover, the scene is animating and picturesque; the younger men complete all the necessary preparations, and some of the older ones recite portions of the law, but the most of them are inclined to take things easy. They remain in and about the tents enjoying solid comfort. As the approach to sunset comes on, they collect in the tabernacle and the women and children take their positions in the doors of their tents. The men are generally clothed in long white garments, surplice-like. The ceremony now begins with prayer and a spreading out of hands. Six or seven lambs are kept in readiness in a space behind the tabernacle door; a careful watch is kept on the downward progress of the sun, and as he dips into the west and hides from mortal view (Gen. xxviii. 19; Exodus xii. 10), the High Priest comes forward out of the tabernacle accompanied by the white robed men, who form a group around the place of sacrifice. When the sun is down the priest repeats in a loud voice, and very rapidly, the Samaritan version of the latter half of the sixth verse of the twelfth chapter of Exodus. In an instant the lambs are seized, and passed from one to another of the sacrificial ministers until they reach the white-robed men, whose business it is to slay them. As they lay quivering in death, two or three of the surpliced young men catch the blood in basins and proceed around the camp, sprinkling the upper sides of the posts of the tent doors, and the faces of the women and children, with blood. The lambs are then examined, and if pronounced faulty, they are rejected and consumed in a separate fire. If passed as without blemish, their fleeces are stripped off and the entrails are extracted; each lamb is then pierced lengthwise by a wooden spit with a cross-bar near the extremity, and carefully placed in the circular pit, which has been heated like an oven. When all are finally deposited, the mouth of the pit is closed with sticks and mud, and there they remain until fully roasted. Unleavened bread and bitter herbs having been already prepared, as soon as roasting is complete, which is not as a general thing until midnight, the whole male community gather around the oven, the covering is torn off, and the roasted lambs are dragged out on their long spits, black and charred. Then the eating begins, which is done literally according to law, with loins girded, shoes on, staff in hand, and in haste. In less than ten minutes, almost every vestige of the meat is consumed; the women and children being supplied in the tents. The remnants are carefully gathered and thrown into the fire, and "nothing remaineth until morning." It is said that large numbers of natives gather on Mount Gerizim to witness the passover; and even the Mohammedans who live in and about Shechem are no less curious than those who happen to be passing through on a tour northward. When the time of the passover approaches, occurring annually, those who are in Jerusalem, going over to Galilee or Syria, are advised to arrange to start in time to witness this strange feast. It is also an occasion of great annoyance to strangers on account of the incessant begging so commonly indulged throughout the country. The native children and adults of both sexes pathetically implore every stranger for "Backsheesh," and to say no to them is simply to say ask me again, for they will follow one, and every step he takes a dozen voices will call out "backsheesh." I became so very accustomed to them, it did not annoy me but little to have them follow me. It will not do to give one of them anything, unless you have concluded to give a dozen or more something, for they will not allow one a moment's rest until they all fare alike. It seems to be the first word the Arab children learn to speak, for surely it is the first word in Arabic the stranger learns, and that he learns too well.

PART X.

SAMARIA—ANCIENT AND MODERN.

The Road from Shechem to Samaria, or Sebastiyeh—The Pool of Samaria—Kings of Israel—Change of Dynasties—Jehu's Reign—Temple of Baal—The Syrian Invasion—Jehu Anointed—Death of Joram—Death of Jezebel—Reign of Jeroboam—Reign of Shallum—Pul, King of Assyria—Attack Upon Israel—Shalmaneser Invades Samaria—Description of Ancient Sites—The Situation and Environment of Dothan—Plain of Esdraelon—Mount Gilboa—Cities of Philistia—The Site of Ancient Jezreel—Naboth's Vineyard—Ancient Nain—Historical Associations—Visit to Shunem.

THE ROAD FROM SHECHEM TO SAMARIA.

LEAVING Shechem, the present Nablous, for Sebastiyeh, the site of ancient Samaria, the direction for about one mile is southward along the Joppa highway, which is very pleasant to travel, and the traveler has time to prepare for the journey before the rough road is encountered. The road is well paved and kept in good condition the whole way from Nablous to Joppa, but only a short distance of it is enjoyed by those going over to Samaria. Just as soon as Shechem is left the road winds down into the valley, through a succession of orchards of fig, apricot, apple, pomegranate and olive trees. On the hills are several villages, one after another, so that the country is aglow with life and prosperity. After the distance of a mile is traveled the tourist leaves the pleasant carriage-road and sets his face westward. The road to Sebastiyeh is not a difficult one to travel; indeed, it is very good when compared to the ancient highway, but the change is so very great between it and the one leading to Joppa, one feels it keenly; and were it not for the many attractions along the way, the change would be deeply lamented. But the natural scenery along the route is so charming one has no time to think of the roughness of the path he is traveling; especially are the scenes delightful as viewed from the top of a high mountain. Here the whole west opens to view like a vast map, and the Mediterranean appears as though it were only five or six hours' ride westward, but I was informed it would require two days' constant travel on a horse to reach the nearest point. It is believed that some of the many villages dotting the high mountains have been there ever since the time the Canaanites had possession of the country, and others were inhabited by the Israelites, afterwards by the Samaritans; yet many of the houses seem to be as firm as they were the day of their completion. The country round-about is one of the most beautiful in the whole land. I frequently found myself standing still in the road looking over the beautiful landscape, the lovely hills, valleys and plains filled with wheat, barley, rye and other products. On reaching the valley from the high mountain, on which such a fine prospect is obtained, a spring of good water is seen, and close to it are ruins of an ancient building. The spring is supposed to be the Pool of Samaria, in which the blood-stained wheels of Ahab's chariot were washed when he received his deadly wound in battle. After crossing this memorable pool a short, but very steep, hill is ascended, on which was located Samaria, the ancient capital of Israel, and one of the most historic places in the northern kingdom. Here is a site of a once powerful and proud city, in which many events took place that the Bible speaks of, which caused the Lord to withhold His hand of protection from them; and "the holy men of old" wrote many lamentable prophecies concerning it.

Not long after the ten tribes had established their new kingdom, Samaria became the seat of power. The Lord sent to this place many warnings of her fate which would surely come, if she did not repent. Prophets came with plain and painfully sad messages, to urge the people to observe the commands of the Lord. She was visited by famine and great loss of life, to warn her of the inevitable judgment that would bring her to naught. The city was situated upon a high eminence, a little lower than the surrounding mountains; its elevation, surroundings and other conveniences made it more desirable than Shechem. It would not be a hard thing for any one who had the choice of one of the two places, Samaria or Shechem, to see the former is far more desirable. When Omri procured this tract of land, he saw that it was suited in every way (at that time) for his capital; so, the place chosen for the erection of the city, is an elevation in the centre of a basin nearly five miles in diameter, and almost surrounded by lofty mountains whose summits form a natural fortress. Such a situation would at once attract the attention of a political chieftain far more than a city located as is Shechem in a valley between two lofty mountains, where an invading foe could pounce down upon them, no matter how strongly their walls were built. But, although there seems to have been great precautions taken in the selection of a site for the capital, there were some things connected with its situation that made it unsafe when confronted by a powerful enemy. One of the objectionable features of its situation was, its isolation from any of the stronghold cities in the kingdom ; and such a condition in olden times would naturally make it the object of attraction to those powers who were unfriendly to Israel. Therefore, it was liable to be completely hemmed in by foreign foes, which was one of the principal battle-plans in ancient times. It is well known the inhabitants of Samaria were several times invaded and greatly embarrassed by the presence of powerful enemies who came up against their capital, and shut them within the gates causing great, suffering among both men and beasts ; especially was this the case, when the city was besieged by Benhadad, King of Syria. The hill on which the city was built seems to derive its name from Shemer, from whom King Omri purchased it. This is an instance that shows how a small matter can immortalize a person's name, and will serve as a stimulant for those who are seeking distinction, to "sow beside all waters." If Omri, King of Israel, had not bought the ground from Shemer, it is likely his name would never have been mentioned in sacred history or any other. It is not the man at all times who performs the giant work, who wins an imperishable name; it often occurs that men do things, who only have in view something of a temporary character, without having the slightest idea of extraordinary results which will follow. The author's name has been kept alive for a hundred generations; such persons are known to almost every one in the civilized world (1 Kings xvi. 24).

CHANGE OF DYNASTIES.

The kings of Israel may be regarded as a succession of dynasties ; the first began with Jeroboam and ended with his son Nadab. The former died from natural causes after a reign of about twenty-two years, having won great distinction in infamy and shame. The latter had but a short reign of two years, and was assassinated. He followed the path of his father in wickedness, and the Lord cut off the house of Jeroboam forever. With the death of Nadab came the end of the first dynasty; and from that moment an endless succession of disgraceful hostilities began in Israel, which at length blotted the kingdom from existence. Men of various grades of position began to fix their eye upon the sceptre, and resorted to every possible intrigue to become the rulers of the kingdom ; therefore, the chief office did not remain in one household but a short time before it was transferred to another. Jehu's family governed the kingdom for about four generations, which was longer than any other dynasty of Israel.

When the capital was removed from Shechem to Tirzah, which became the seat of power for fifty years, Omri then removed it to Samaria, where it continued for nearly two hundred years; but when Ahab, the son of the latter, was installed king, a strong effort was made to have the capital transferred from Samaria to Jezreel, a town beautifully situated on a small ridge in the plain of Esdraelon, about twenty miles north of the capital. The feeling of the people to have the capital established there may have been stimulated on the grounds of its being the home of Jezebel, and the place where the worship of Ashtaroth was permanently established. But it was not changed from Samaria, although Jezreel was in some respects looked upon as such. At Samaria a temple was erected to Baal, in which several hundred priests officiated, and at its shrines thousands poured forth adoring strains of devotion. This was a fearful period; the people had become steeped in idolatry and swallowed up in iniquity; therefore, God sent several prophets to them, who, in unmistakable terms, made known the fact that their sins would be visited with severe chastisements from the Lord.

The great founder of the capital at Samaria was buried there. It may have been by Omri's request, or, that his friends wished to lay their dead kings to rest at the capital just as the people of Judah did theirs. Ahab, seventh king of the northern kingdom, married Jezebel, the daughter of Ethbaal, king of Phœnicia; she exerted a wonderful influence over her husband (1 Kings xiv. 17-18: xviii. 46), who seems to have been completely controlled by her. Jezebel insisted that the worship of Baal should be adopted in Israel. Ahab had, in compliance with this wish, proceeded to build a temple to Baal on the hill of Samaria. The eminence on which the temple stood was one of the most beautiful and commanding hills about the city enclosure. A few of the colossal pillars are yet standing just above the ground, and others are completely hidden from view.

Notwithstanding the gross wickedness indulged in by his predecessors, Ahab was the most depraved and daring. He did more evil in the sight of the Lord than all the kings of Israel. The Temple was destroyed by Jehu, an account of which will be seen on another page. The Syrians, who were potent enemies of Israel, did everything they could to vex them; they continuously assaulted the people, although one of the most striking evidences of the Lord's care for that people had been seen in the case of Elisha, who captured a whole army of Syrians and led them to Samaria. The distress brought to Samaria by the Syrians is more than can be adequately described by the most gifted tongue or the most graphic pen (1 Kings xxi. 17–20; 2 Kings vi. 8–23).

When the alarming crisis came, caused by this determined foe, who had besieged the city, and hemmed the people in for a long time there was a deep gloom haunting every household, from the king to the most humble inhabitant. Benhadad's army was stationed completely around the city, so as to prohibit any one from escaping, supposing they could by that method starve the people, or compel them to open the massive gates, which were too strong for the besiegers to break down, and had it not been for a miraculous interposition of the Lord, all the dwellers of Samaria would have perished. Their food supplies began to diminish more and more as the days passed, until they were about exhausted, so that a very sore and distressing famine was raging, and the people were dying like sheep, when a contagious disease comes among them. Mothers, whose love for their children was as pure as the morning air, consented to put some of their infants to death and cook them for table use, that the others might live a few days longer. Such was the rage of the death-dealing calamity that the king became insane with anger, trouble and fear. He put on sackcloth and walked upon the walls, swearing vengeance against Elisha the prophet, who was living there at the time, and sent a messenger to sever his head from his body, following close behind the man himself to see that the deadly work was performed. The prophet had delivered an encouraging prophecy, which the king thought would not come to pass, because the condition of the people was growing worse day after day. When the man sent on the errand of death arrived at the humble dwelling of Elisha, the king was just behind him, leaning on the arm of one of his captains. The man of God was not alarmed when the messenger came to him, but calmly waited until the king came. Then Elisha delivered a wonderful prophecy as to the abundance of food at the disposal of the king the next day. But the faithlessness of the captain caused him to flatly deny the words of the man of God. For this cause a prophecy was pronounced against him, which was fulfilled to the letter. Elisha declared to them that a blessed change was at hand, when each one in the city would have abundance, saying: "To-morrow, about this time, shall a measure of fine flour be sold for a shekel, and two measures of barley for a shekel in the gate of Samaria." The captain on whose arm the king leaned said, "Behold, if the Lord should make windows in heaven might this thing be." Elisha answered him, saying, "Behold, thou shalt see it with thine eyes, but thou shalt not eat thereof." Just as was predicted, the thing happened. The Syrians were panic-stricken by a miraculous event. The king of Syria, having heard a great noise, as if a strong army was coming against him, and supposing the king of Israel had formed an alliance with other kings, or had hired them to assist him, caused his whole army to beat a hasty retreat from their camp, leaving everything behind them. It was an anxious time with the king of Samaria and his starving people, who had heard what the prophet had said. Some of them were no doubt like the captain, did not credit what was predicted, while others at least believed it to the extent that they were hopeful it might be so. It is certain king Joram had faith in the statement of Elisha, for he had spared his life, awaiting the results of the following day. It so happened there were four lepers sitting at the entrance gate in a starving condition, who concluded to go to the Syrian camp to beg something to eat; "for," said they, "if we remain in this state we will die," and they could suffer no more than death if they went to the enemy's camp. So they went, and, to their surprise, found the camp vacated, but all the abundant supplies left there. This was reported to the king, and everything Elisha had said came to pass just as was predicted. The captain who doubted Elisha was placed in charge of the gate, and the rush of the nearly starved people trampled him to death. Truly he saw it with his eyes, but did not taste it. Seeing how triumphantly the Lord had delivered them from their relentless foes and from the very jaws of death, it would seem that the king and all his subjects throughout the kingdom would have immediately abandoned every shadow of idolatry and turned themselves in fervent devotion to the God of their fathers, but they ate, drank, and filled themselves with the spoils and returned to their idols.

The intrigues of Jehu add to the history of Samaria a page of infamy of the basest character. This young man was commander-in-chief of the army of Israel, and about this time a fierce conflict was going on between Syria and Israel, as had been during the whole of Elisha's prophetic life (2 Kings vi.; vii.). In the earlier days of the Syrians, they were not regarded as an important people, and were not dreaded by the northern kingdom; but by reason of the consolidation of the various independent states they suddenly grew rapidly and became a powerful nation, and because of their bravery had gained a wide-spread reputation as shrewd warriors. Israel, seeing how warlike they had become, feared them; and had there not been a true prophet among them, their condition would have been hopeless, for they were the most timid people in the world when left to themselves. It is known to be a fact, that every victory Israel won from the time they left Egypt until taken into captivity, was given them immediately from God; and when they marshalled themselves against their foes, if God did not interpose for them in some wonderful way, they invariably lost the battle. Therefore, when Israel knew their northern neighbors had gained power so rapidly, they became alarmed when compelled to confront them in war. The Syrians, feeling they were competent to subordinate Israel, began to impose upon them by taking portions of their territory, little by little. The intention of the Syrian monarch to reduce Israel to a subordinate kingdom became so evident, that it was found expedient for the latter, if they would preserve their safety, to contend for their rights, and even unite their forces against this common enemy, as they did in the time of Ahab and Jehoshaphat. These two kingdoms, which were so strongly opposed to each other on account of the revolt, found it to their advantage to become friendly, so that their united powers might be exerted against the Syrians. Had it not been for the continued interference of this new kingdom in the far north, the people of Israel and Judah would have remained unfriendly. The Syrians were encroaching upon the dominion of Israel; they had possessed Ramoth-Gilead, on the east side of the Jordan, in the time of Ahab, by the walls of which he received his death-wound; and it remained in their hands until after his death. When the furor created on account of the murder of Benhadad, king of Syria, by Hazael, an officer in his court, caused the Syrian army to abandon Ramoth-Gilead for a time, and it was occupied by Jehu, the general-in-chief of Israel, who was known to be a very brave man and an expert in horsemanship. At this time Joram, Ahab's son and successor, was king of Israel, and was at Jezreel, very ill from the effects of a wound he had received at the same place his father had been mortally wounded; and Ahaziah, king of Judah and nephew of Joram, had come over from Jerusalem to pay him a visit.

These two monarchs were in conversation in the summer palace at Jezreel, and the army was in charge of Jehu at Ramoth-Gilead. Just at this time, Elisha sent a young man over the Jordan to anoint Jehu to be king of Israel. When the messenger arrived and informed him of his mission, he received it with great composure, not wishing to disclose the matter until his plans were fully matured; but his companions were apprised of the secret, and hailed him with shouts of praise as their future king. Then, without delay, the young prince entered his chariot, escorted by some of his close friends, and made all possible speed for Jezreel, where Joram, the wounded king, and Ahaziah, his nephew and king of Judah, were. When Jehu was seen from afar, his coming had a suspicious bearing, although he was not recognized from the distance, he was at first seen about six miles off. There was a watch-tower in Jezreel, in which a man was stationed to keep a close lookout and give notice when he saw anything worthy of attention approaching. These towers were thought to be indispensable, in those days, in all the strongholds or important places in Palestine and Syria, and many are still in use. The watchman was steadfastly looking in every direction of the approach to Jezreel; and as he turned his eyes down the road that is between little Hermon and Mt. Gilboa in the plain of Esdraelon, he saw a rapidly-advancing chariot accompanied by an escort, coming with great speed, and gave notice to Joram of the approach of some one whom he did not recognize. Then the king ordered that a messenger should meet the company and ascertain who was coming, and whether they were on a visit of peace or war. He made haste to execute the command, but did not return; for, when he drew near to Jehu, and asked if his coming to Jezreel was for peace, he answered, "What hast thou to do with peace? Turn thee behind me." The watchman noticed this strange procedure, and informed the king that "the messenger cometh to them, but cometh not out again." Another was dispatched with the same message, and was treated as the first one. Then the king became alarmed, for he was apprehensive that a foe was advancing with treachery in his heart. By this time Jehu had reached a point in the road where the watchman partially recognized him by the way he drove; for the general was well known as a fast driver. He then informed the king, it must be "Jehu, the son of Nimshi, for he drives furiously." On his approach to Jezreel, Joram arose from his bed, mounted his chariot, having Ahaziah by his side, and went with haste to meet him. When he approached within speaking distance, he cried out, "Is it peace Jehu?" He answered, "What peace?" adding that the conduct of Jezebel, the mother of Joram, was disreputable and unbearable; for she was leading a life of lewdness and indulging in witchcraft. The king became alarmed, seeing Jehu was about to bring trouble, turned immediately and fled, saying, "There is treachery, O Ahaziah." But without further warning, Jehu drew his bow with all his strength, and sent a dart of death into the wounded body of Joram, which resulted in his speedy demise. It happened just as he was passing through Naboth's vineyard, and his body was thrown in the same plot of ground his father so unjustly took possession of, to satisfy a covetous ambition. Ahaziah fled, but was pursued and slain. In the meantime, Jehu went with haste to Jezreel; Jezebel, being old and feeble, endeavored to hide her age and feebleness by artificial means, but was not spared; for Jehu caused her to be thrown from the window out of which she was looking, and the hungry dogs devoured her flesh, just as the prophet had predicted. When Jehu understood how completely the dogs had done their work, he said, "This is the word of the Lord which He spake by His servant Elijah, the prophet, saying, 'In the portion of Jezreel shall the dogs eat the flesh of Jezebel.'"

The new monarch proceeded to destroy the household of Ahab. His next command was, that the seventy sons of Ahab should be put to death; all of whom had hoped to hold the sceptre of power at some time in the future. Thus it is seen, the very beginning of Jehu's reign was a scene of murder and tyranny, which continued until he had destroyed all those connected with Ahab's family; even the house of Ahaziah did not escape his wrath. The house of Ahab was not permitted to control the kingdom, because it would follow the evil example of their father, who was one of the most wicked men of his day. Not one member of the house of Ahab, of the large number it was composed, escaped the sword of Jehu. He proceeded immediately with all possible haste to Samaria, after putting the sons of Ahab to death who lived in Jezreel, and conceived a scheme which succeeded in accomplishing the destruction of the remaining members of that household; and when he had done this fully and completely, he turned his attention toward the utter demolition of the images of Baal, and immediately put an end to that famous worship that had been so enthusiastically conducted at the renowned capital of Israel and other parts of the kingdom. Jehu's method was a cunning one, which gave him an opportunity to make a clean sweep of all against whom he had plotted. At the same time he pretended to the officials he had great zeal for the worship of Baal, and commanded that those who were of that faith, both priests and people, should meet at the temple of that deity at a certain time, for special worship; to which call, all the interested people responded with great pleasure, expecting to enjoy a season of extraordinary pleasure, so that the temple was crowded with Baalites. Jehu, having pre-arranged all his deep-laid plans, so as to carry into effect his murderous purpose, ordered that every one should be slain, which was almost instantly done. Not one of the followers of Baal remained alive. Then the images of the gods were brought out and broken; the temple was demolished, and its place was devoted to purposes highly questionable. There would seem, from a casual observation of Jehu's distaste for the Baal worship, to be a disposition in him to bring about a creditable religious change in his kingdom; but his idea of true reformation was not half complete; for, when he destroyed one form of idolatry, he established another. The old custom of worship ordained by Jeroboam, which had sunk into insignificance, was revived, and again took its original station as the religion of the kingdom, so that the people were no freer from idol worship than they were before the ambitious and deadly Jehu destroyed the Baal form.

There was a foul and deadly purpose hidden in the heart of Jehu when he caused all the Baal-worshipers throughout his kingdom to be put to death under the pretense of reorganizing the true worship of Jehovah. His intensely proud heart seems to have been filled to an overflow with an insatiable lust for his own aggrandizement, so that everything like lasting preference, devotion and zeal, relative to the true religion, could not obtain, although he is regarded as an exception to those who succeeded him. Every one of his successors cultivated a ravenous passion for the idol-worship established by Jeroboam, and Samaria was not at any time entirely free from the humiliating practice of idolatry. The laws of the Lord were not looked upon as a standard-guide of human conduct; they trampled upon them as unworthy of toleration, and expelled them from their thoughts. Jehu had the most favorable opportunity, had he been truly sincere, to have rooted out every phase of idolatry, and with ease established the true worship, for he had from the beginning of his control of the kingdom everything under his sway. The whole dominion felt his masterly hand and stood in great fear of him. Therefore, his was the pivot-reign, for no monarch succeeding him had such a commanding control of the people. The destruction of the Baal worship, which was done at such a tremendous sacrifice of life, was in fact but disguised mockery, for Jehu had no intention of reorganizing the people according to the will of Heaven. The house, of which he was the acknowledged head, was the largest of all the dynasties in Israel, and had the kingly control for the period of one hundred and three years, with the following members of his house upon the throne, viz.: Jehoahaz, Jehoash, Jeroboam, the second, and Zechariah. None of these are known to have exerted any manliness worthy of note, except Jeroboam, who won several important victories, and did much towards advancing the prosperity of his kingdom during the forty-one years of his reign, and yet added much to the guilt of Israel. The kingdom, having an ambitious man as king, whose heart was full of selfishness and death-dealing, was still in a state of woeful corruption. His thirst for blood did not abate when his destructive hand had wiped from existence the wickedly-licentious occupant of the throne and his household, but his influence was strongly exerted in Jerusalem through Athaliah, whose mother he had slain. This woman united with Jehu in carrying out his deep-laid plans to destroy the royal house of Judah. She even caused all her own children to be put to death that she might be permitted to remain queen. Only the infant, Joash, who had been hidden by his aunt and reared in absolute secrecy, was left alive, for if Jehu, the blood-thirsty monarch, or Athaliah, his infamous mother, had known where he had been hidden, they would have secured him for slaughter by some low-cunning means. There was not much interest attached to the administration of the house of Jehu in Samaria after his death, who seems to have left but little bloody work for his successors to perform. Bethel was again chosen as the chief place for calf-worship, and idolatrous priests, under the reign of Jeroboam. the second, who was the third king from Jehu, officiated. He seems to have had a good degree of prosperity during the time of his reign. But it is clearly evident that Bethel became once more the seat of great corruption, for the prophets who watched Samaria with incessant vigilance suddenly turned themselves towards Bethel and fixed their attention on the place where the people bowed with enthusiastic devotions to the calf. These men of God, who had been appointed to warn the people against the bitter results of idol-worship, were almost constantly busy in the discharge of their duties, and were just as determined to do the work of their calling when their messsage was woeful as when it was pleasant. There was no period during the time of the prophets that one could not be found who was ready for duty. (2 Kings viii. 28–29; ix.; x.; Amos vii. 10–13.)

Jeroboam extended the border of Israel, and subdued Damascus, the capital of the Syrians; a people whose continuous efforts to capture Israel kept them in constant dread of the vengeance of their relentless ire. The last king belonging to the house of Jehu was Zechariah, who only was permitted to reign six months, when he was ruthlessly slain by Shallum, son of Jabesh, an ambitious aspirant, who after committing the fiendish deed usurped the crown. His aim was accomplished, but like many whose ambition overrules their judgment, Shallum had not gotten the sceptre in his hand before he was in turn slain by Menahem, in Samaria; for it was just at the end of one month's reign, when he was dispatched to eternity. About this time a new and powerful nation rose into prominence on the east beyond the Euphrates, who increased so rapidly in strength that Judah and Israel watched her with a suspicious eye; for there were evident indications that a woeful crisis would seize the two kingdoms of the Hebrews, if this nation continued to grow. These new people were the Assyrians, who afterwards proved to be the mightiest foe the Israelites had known. An alarming signal of their power was developed by Pul, king of Assyria, who resented the conduct of Menahem, who caused the inhabitants of Tiphsah to be slaughtered Pul became indignant, and suddenly rose up with his forces and descended upon Israel with vengeance, carrying a large number into captivity, but spared Samaria and the immediate districts around it. Yet, while Pul was disposed to be gracious enough to save the capital of Israel from destruction, he brought the tyrant Menahem under heavy obligations to the Assyrian government, by compelling him to pay a tax amounting to a thousand talents. It is said this attack was made upon Israel, by the king of Assyria, through the mountainous country east of the Jordan, and north of the plain of Esdraelon. The attack was so very sudden upon the people, they were not in condition to defend themselves. The event was a manifestation of the weakness of Israel, and the maiden test of Assyrian strength. This was a warning to Israel, and should have admonished them sufficiently to awaken them to a sense of their duty to the God of their fathers, who had so frequently fought for them, and never allowed them to lose a battle while they were under His command The Assyrians continued to increase so rapidly that other nations were beginning to notice them and fear their power. When Hoshea, the last king of Israel, was ruling, he attempted to sever his subordinate relation to the Assyrian empire, by forming an alliance with the king of Egypt; and no doubt would have effected his plans, had not Shalmaneser been apprised of the plot in time to prevent further negotiations between the two monarchs. So, an Ethiopian, who was second king of the twenty-fifth dynasty, was the ruler over Egypt at the time the proposition for an alliance was offered by Hoshea, king of Israel. It would have been a wonderful addition to the strength of Israel, had an opportunity been given the king of Egypt to help Hoshea But as soon as the news reached Shalmaneser, he at once came up against Samaria with a large army, and besieged it for three years; at length the people became so greatly reduced they could hold out no longer, but surrendered to the powerful foe, who was determined to capture the city (it seems), even if they starved every inhabitant to death. The king was captured also, put in bonds, and carried with the people away into captivity. This struggle terminated the existence of the northern kingdom, which had been prominent for two hundred and fifty years, under the most variable circumstances of any kingdom known in the world, considering the length of time it existed.

The people, whose hearts were brought low because of their bondage, were dispersed throughout the Assyrian empire, and many endured great afflictions under their new rulers; but the Lord allowed them to remain there until the expiration of seventy years. There were no more attractions in the city of Samaria for a long time; her doom had come; her rich treasures had been carried away, and her glory was in the dust. This was about the year seven hundred and twenty, before the Christian era, when this final calamity visited the kingdom of Israel, which completely demolished it. It is thought by several eminent scholars, that the new-comers, who were transported to take charge of the country, occupied the city of Samaria as their headquarters for a while, then went down to Shechem and made it their permanent and chief city. It is plain to be seen, that the Israelites, who revolted and established a new kingdom, began it with a malicious spirit, and proved themselves unworthy of the protection of the Lord almost from the beginning to the end of their national independence. They went from God to the idol calf; then to Baal; then to Astarte, and a number of other images. After the captivity, which caused the downfall of the kingdom, but little is known of Samaria for several centuries.

The next important development in its history was in the time of Herod the Great. It having been given him by Emperor Augustus, the king rebuilt Samaria and adorned it, changed its name, which is known to the Greeks as Sebaste, but is called by the natives Sebastiyeh. It is said that Herod left an open area of nine hundred feet in the centre of the city, surrounded by some of the most costly buildings; upon this area he built a most magnificent temple to the emperor. It is supposed to have stood on the summit of a hill, which is an eminent site, and must have been highly attractive to those approaching the city from the east or west. It is also believed, from a number of developments, that Ahab built his temple to Baal upon this same site. There are many remnants of the long colonnade which winds around the hill, several of them remaining where they were placed by the workmen. They extend as far as the village in the western section. Sixty columns are yet standing; several have been broken, and others are full of scars, many of which have been caused by relic-seekers; but time's hand has crumbled them more than the hand of man. It is the general opinion that the colonnade was erected to beautify the great street of the city, just as those in other cities in the East, especially Damascus, Palmyra and Constantinople. It is thought that the large building which stood on the corner of the hill facing the north was intended for the celebration of the great festivals or on other occasions when jubilees were held. From what has been stated concerning the new city built by Herod the Great, it may be concluded that he did not spare pains or expense in making it a stupendous palace. But Samaria, the beautiful, has fallen to rise no more, for it has become a wreck.

The little village that crowns a small portion of the site of the ancient city, called Sebastiyeh, is composed of about sixty houses and four hundred inhabitants. It is built upon an old terrace, about the middle of the eastern side of the hill, and is almost entirely composed of the old material of the former cities. Many of the carefully carved blocks of stone, which formed a portion of the beauty of the capital of Israel, and the Sebaste of Herod's time, are carelessly laid in the walls of the present huts of which the whole village is composed.

The first attraction on entering Samaria is the church of St. John, standing upon an elevation on the east of the village. Its entrance-door opens from a court which is a little lower than the grade around it. The low door passed through to enter the building is said to belong to the time of the Crusaders; and it is currently believed that it stands over the grave of John the Baptist.

The church had almost become a ruin for a long time, but efforts were being made to remodel and change it into a Mohammedan mosque. It is one hundred and eighty feet long and seventy feet wide, having a small dome over the cellar, under which is the traditional tomb of John the Baptist, which is reached by descending thirty-one stone steps into a very dark and lonely chamber. This is partitioned from the tomb by a thick wall. The graves of Elisha and Obadiah are traditionally located here also. Josephus says: "John was beheaded at Fort Machaerus, east of the Dead Sea," but many of the foremost writers and scholars are of the opinion that Herod Antipas did not select such an out-of-the-way place as that was to hold a jubilant feast. There is a tradition, reaching back to the time of Jerome, which says: "John was beheaded at Samaria." It is thought to be the more likely place, as it corresponds with the vicinity where he performed his latter work, which was only a few miles east of Samaria, at the head of Wady Far'ah, which is between Ænon and Salim. It is also supposed John was in one of the prisons in Samaria, either the one connected with the palace or the one common to prisoners in general. It is certain the place of John's confinement was not far from the place where the feast was held. Jerome, who was a man of great piety and candor, says, "John met his death at Samaria," which seems to be the more likely place from the connecting circumstances. The traditional tomb of John is much older than the building over it, and may be the place where the great prophet and forerunner of our Lord was laid to rest. This being the Samaria of the New Testament times, and no doubt the city to which Philip on his evangelistic mission came and preached the gospel, and here preached Peter and John also. When the Crusaders were in power, Samaria was their headquarters and the seat of a bishopric, at which time it had regained a portion of its former importance. It was about noon when we arrived there from Shechem, and on approaching the village we turned to the northwest to make a tour of the site of the ancient cities, and see the remaining ruins that are visible. I had for some time been very dubious of visiting Samaria, having heard of so many unpleasant things as to the conduct of the natives toward strangers. The inhabitants have the reputation of being the most vicious of all the people in Palestine, and they have on several occasions driven strangers from the place with stones and deadly instruments. I nerved myself for the journey, with the purpose of making the very best I could of the worst that might come. According to custom, when we drew near the village every one that could came from their humble dwellings to see who was approaching. We made the usual circuit of the whole place, and it is but just that I should say for the inhabitants of Samaria, I did not find in all my travels through the land a more friendly and quiet people. Not one of them gave me an ill-look or a cross word. There is a small native school kept in an apartment in which several important relics are stored, some being images that were worshiped in ancient times. Just as I entered the room the teacher ordered the children to rise and make obeisance to me, and they did it with as much delight seemingly as though I were one of the high officials. I thought they would immediately take their seats, but when it became apparent they would stand until I left the room, I told the teacher, through my guide, to seat them. We remained some time in Samaria, visiting the many scenes of remarkable ruins. We rode around the elevated terrace on the west side to the leper's gate, and took a passing view of the ruins of the ancient colonnade, which we followed to the end, where heaps of stones are promiscuously piled up. Many more columns are yet standing in the line they were placed in Herod's time.

The colonnade begins on the west, where there is a large mass of ruins, which are supposed to have been a triumphal arch. It runs about one thousand feet eastward in a direct line, then turns a little southward, following the hill until the terminus is reached, which is a little to the southeast of Sebastiyeh. There about sixty of the old columns standing on the west side, which indicate by their irregular positions, the depth of the ruins about them. Some of them are several feet above the ground, others are not more than a foot or two above. Not one of them is as high above the ground as when first put in position, but several are high enough to indicate their former heights, and the depth of the ruins about them; and there are reasons to believe, from the heights of some of the mounds between many of the columns, that several of them are completely covered up by higher piles of ruins. There was a double range of these columns, at a distance of about fifty feet, supposing to have extended about three thousand feet. The shafts are sixteen feet high and two feet in diameter. These colonnades are supposed to have been the centre of attraction in the main street of Samaria; but their glory is departed, and, like a man who has descended from riches and plenty to poverty and want, they stand to tell all who visit them what they were in other days; stationed as they are in a place of solitude, surrounded by great masses of ruins, it cannot be conjectured by any one who has not witnessed the sight, what a strikingly sad spectacle they present. Here stood clustered in dazzling splendor, the glory of Samaria and Sebaste in the days of their prosperity, when their proud heads were lifted to the sky, and their envied fame was spread to the ends of the earth, but now all lies deeply entombed in the dust; for the mighty cities have fallen. Who can look upon these heaps of desolation, under which the crumbling remains of the two great cities are buried, without dropping a tear of deep sorrow because of human weakness? Who can ride around the hillside and in the valley of this wrath-smitten place, and look in the valley and on the hill upon these broken columns, standing among the wild vines, olive trees and green corn, looking like an old dead trunk of a once flourishing and fruitful tree, or see them surrounded with heaps of stones, which at some age of the distant past occupied their place in one of the lavishly embellished buildings that adorned the hill with splendor, without feeling most pungently the sacred words, "Thy sins will find thee out;" or, who can look at the heaps of stones, which have been carefully carved by skilled workmen, to be placed in some of the most spacious buildings crowning the hill, now serving as the bases of terraces in the corn and barley fields; or, upon the many beautifully-hewn and costly stones strewn along the valley, as if tossed by a mighty tornado or a tremendous upheaval, and not see the revelation of the handwriting on the wall, "God hath numbered thy days." The prediction of the prophet Micah, as to the fate of Samaria, has a standing testimony of its fulfillment in the piles of ruins from one end of its original boundary to the other. "Therefore, will I make Samaria as an heap of the field and as the planting of a vineyard; and I will throw down the stones thereof into the valley, and I will discover the foundations thereof." I did not see in any other portion of Palestine such a tremendous profusion of ruins as are prominent in Samaria; and any one passing through the old ruins, having a knowledge of the predictions concerning it, could not otherwise conclude than that every word has been literally fulfilled. (Micah i. 6.)

There are several interesting places to visit while passing around about the ruins, among them the most interesting is the site of the "Leper's Gate," to which the poor, starving men came on the night the Syrians abandoned their camp, leaving everything and fleeing in wild dismay, supposing a reinforcement was on the way to capture them. The site of the "camp" is supposed to be the beautiful little plain on the northwest side; certainly, it is the only convenient place about the city for a camp, and we have no doubt that it is identical with "The Lepers' Gate," and the scene of the great press of half-starved people, who came out to get food when the captain was killed. The traditional tomb of John the Baptist is also worthy of visiting. It is down in a dark crypt, and the person who intends entering must brace himself strong with courage or he will not be able to go into it. I am not ashamed to confess my timidity when about to make the trip. Not to descend looked cowardly, and to do so seemed to be a venture of imminent peril, and to allow that opportunity to pass would be giving up the only chance I should ever have to see the place, where it is said a portion of the mortal remains of one of the most pious and distinguished men of the world was buried. I, therefore, concluded to go down into it whatever might occur. The lights were arranged and we started down the journey of thirty-one steps to the little, dark chamber at the bottom, where a ray of sunlight cannot enter, and perhaps has not since the sainted dead was first rested there. The keeper of the sepulchre went in advance, followed by one of his companions; I followed them and my dragoman came behind me. My nerves had gotten to an exciting point, and many unpleasant ideas came unbidden to my mind. At one time I was about to give up the trip and intimated my purpose to the dragoman; he insisted I should continue, so, mustering all the courage possible, I started again, and finally we reached the chamber. I was conducted to the partition which divides the tomb from the main room and shown an opening in the wall. Through this visitors look upon the traditional tomb of John. I was soon satisfied with what I had seen and ready to return towards the earth's surface, and came up feeling rather pleased with my visit. There could be a fine museum of Ancient Statues in Samaria if the people knew how to arrange it and could appreciate its value, for hundreds, if not thousands, of such relics could be found under the mounds; if the people would command enough industry to dig for them they might find other valuables which would place every inhabitant above the sills of poverty. But they are under the Turkish Government, which seems to be disinterested in making investigations. One unfortunate thing about Samaria is there are no Christians residing in it. I feel safe in saying if the present villagers were blessed with native Christian neighbors a greater state of progress would soon be seen, for it is noticeable in all the cities and towns in Palestine where Christians form a part of the inhabitants there are evident indications of progress, and where they are not found signs of improvement are wanting. It is a fact, as plainly demonstrated as two and two are four, that Christianity is lifting the world, and is the light of it in every sense pertaining to human elevation. The road from Samaria northward is, for a few miles, "beautiful for situation," and when the high hill is reached travelers usually halt to take their last look at the scenes just left and the fine country round about. Close to the halting place is a small village called Neby Lamin, or the "Levite Prophet" Near by is a tomb supposed to be that of Sanballat, who was a very prominent governor of the district of Samaria.

Proceeding a short distance, the plain of Esdraelon is seen a few miles away; and a stranger finds himself nearing one of the most historical districts in the world; for it is filled with memorable associations from one end to the other. To just give an outline of all the events of this plain, several volumes much larger than this would be required. About midway the beautiful valley leading to the plain, just east of a flat-top hill that stands out from the surrounding mountains, is an opening to the northeast. This is Dothan. It was on this rich plain that the sons of Jacob were feeding their flocks, when Joseph was sent to see if they were doing well. On the hill-sides are yet remaining several ancient pits, one of which Joseph, no doubt, was put in before he was sold to the merchants who were going down to Egypt. It is well no one has been able to identify the pit of Joseph's incarceration, or a mosque would have been placed over it, and every one visiting there would be required to pay for entering. One of the most important events connected with the life of Elisha transpired at Dothan, and should have special mention here (2 Kings vi. 8–23). When the king of Syria was haunting the king of Israel, many cunning and deep-laid plans were arranged by him and his council to capture the kingdom. To accomplish this design he would get information as to the route the king of Israel's army would take, or where they were likely to camp, and lay in ambush so as to come out against it suddenly and capture it; but Elisha warned the king of these cunning intrigues, and the Syrians were unsuccessful in their plans that had been so carefully formulated in great secrecy. The king of Syria was puzzled to understand how his plans were exposed to the king of Israel, unless some of those of his own council were traitors. He therefore called a council that he might find who was the man so shamefully untrue. It was made known to him that his suspicions were misplaced; that none of his council were false, but that there was a prophet in Israel who told these things and knew his most secret plans. Hearing this the king of Syria became almost insanely excited, and sent out spies to apprehend the prophet. Poor fellow, he did not seem to know that if the prophet could tell all his secret plans, he could also know when spies were seeking him and could, if necessary, elude them. But Elisha had nothing to fear, and therefore made no effort to flee. The spies soon returned with the information that the prophet was in Dothan, which is about ten miles north of Samaria, a little to the northeast of the main road to Jenin and Nazareth. The king, hearing where the prophet was, sent a large army by night to capture him and bring him to Damascus. The army obeyed the order; and on their arrival at Dothan concluded to wait there quietly all night and make the capture in the morning. That they might prohibit his escape, the soldiers surrounded the mountain so as to hem in the village completely. But, without their knowledge, another army appeared on the scene.

The Lord, whose messenger Elisha was, sent an army of angels from heaven to guard his interests; much larger than the King of Syria had sent to capture him. When the morning came, and the servant of God was ready for the engagement, he simply prayed that his enemies might be smitten with blindness, and it was instantly done. He then led them into the city of Samaria as blind captives. Surely, "one can chase a thousand."

I took great care, on our arrival at Dothan, to survey its situation; and especially the location of the mountains where the Syrians encamped, awaiting the morning dawn, that they might execute their mission. The village is nearly surrounded by a double range of mountains, the inner circle being very near it, but the outer one a mile (we think) away. It is, therefore, reasonable to suppose that the Syrians formed their circle around the heights of the inner or smaller range, for it would have required a very large army to have encircled the outer and more extensive mountains. The small circle does not connect on the northwest, the narrow space between them forming a beautiful little plain, extending to the village. At present there are but two or three houses, a mill, and a shed or two in Dothan. It may be we passed the site of Elisha's house. (2 Kings vi. 8–23; Gen. xxxvii. 15–28).

The next point of importance north of Dothan is Jenin, the ancient Engannim. It was one of the Levitical cities, belonging to the tribe of Issachar, and stands on the border terminating Manasseh. In the time of our Lord, Jenin, also, was the extreme northern border of the province of Samaria. It is pleasantly located along the highway, and is very important because of its abundant supply of water; its present name, Jenin, signifies "much water." It is one of the most convenient towns for travelers of any in the interior of Palestine especially between Samaria and Nazareth and points along the sea. Those not going to Jezreel, Shunem, and the north, can find a road from the vicinity of Jenin in any direction usually traveled. The main road passing through it is the same ancient highway along which Ahab traveled in the days of his pride when passing to and from Samaria and Jezreel, and the identical road that the iron-hearted Jehu passed over when he went to Samaria on his mission of death, about the time he cunningly devised the scheme which resulted in the massacre of all the worshipers of Baal. It is believed he was on this road, near Engannim, when he received Jonadab, the son of Rechab, into his chariot.

The beautiful plain of Esdraelon is entered just at the northern end of the town; here, a fine prospect of the country for miles around is spread out to view. In the far north, Hermon is seen; a little to the northwest, Gilboa and Little Hermon appear in sight, and on the southwest, Carmel is seen stretching herself to the sea. It almost seems to one who has been traveling through the interior a few days as if he was coming from behind a dark cloud, such is the pleasant change of nature. The beautiful lilies are seen in every direction, and life seemingly begins anew.

This large tract of land is known in the Scriptures as the plain of Jezreel, which is the Hebrew form of the Greek "Esdraelon." This plain was the frontier of Zebulun, and the special portion of Issachar;

it passes through the country east and west from the valley of the Jordan to the Mediterranean Sea. That portion north of Mt. Carmel is known as the Plain of Acre; the central portion is called the Valley of Megiddo, an immense triangle, having its highest point towards the west, at the eastern end of Mt. Carmel. It is estimated to be about fourteen miles long on the north side, seventeen on the east, and twenty on the southwest The plain is cut by the interference of Little Hermon and Mt. Gilboa, so that it became three separate valleys of equal proportions; the centre one is the noted valley of Jezreel, stretching gently into the valley of the Jordan.

The plain of Esdraelon is not only famous for its superior beauty, but as a battle-field; some very memorable battles were fought in different parts of it, and Israel has sent up many shouts of joy along its bordering mountains, because of the victories the Lord won for them. Among the most prominent battles fought in this plain were, the one between the Israelites and Syrians (Josh. xvii. 16; Deut. xxxiii. 18), in which Deborah, Barak and Sisera, were the most prominent factors; another with Israel and Syria, in the reign of Ahab; also, one between Saul and the Philistines, in which the king received his death-wound; and one between Gideon and the Midianites. There was also a fierce battle encountered here between Josiah and Pharaoh-nechho, in which the former was slain; here, the Romans fought sore battles when contending for the supremacy; and the Crusaders, when contending for the right of Christianity, found Esdraelon a convenient battle-field. In this plain over against Mt. Tabor, the French engaged in a deadly conflict with the Turks; fifteen hundred of the former battled against twenty thousand of the latter for thirty-five hours and were rescued by Napoleon. There are many places to be seen in and about the plain, the names of which are familiar to Christendom on account of frequent mention being made of them in the Bible. Several are in nearly a direct line to Nazareth, and can be visited by making short detours. We shall mention them as we proceed, for there are so many historical localities in the midst of this plain and along its border, we deem it best to refer to them, if only slightly, as we come to them. Engannim is the usual halting place over night for northern-bound travelers (Judges vi. 33; iv. 14; 2 Kings xxiii. 29; 1 Samuel xxix. 1), it being the most favorable place from which to reach Nazareth in one day's travel, and allow a visit to the several important places along the way. The whole journey through the plain is enjoyable, especially to those who are attracted by the fragrance of a vast variety of flowers; for the whole expanse is aglow with some of the most beautiful lilies, roses and many other kinds of wild flowers that nature can produce, so that the scene is really dazzling. Several ancient villages and places of historic importance are in view on either side of the highway as we proceed toward Jezreel; some of them are so surrounded with flowers they appear like a paradise. There are but few elevations in the plain proper; therefore, the whole landscape from the base of the mountains, on either side, is comparatively level; and instead of draining off the great flow of water that is poured into it from the mountains during the heavy rains, it soaks the ground and makes traveling very difficult for man and beast. Some portions of the plain are like a marsh for three or four miles, which at times becomes impassable. It has been several times the case, that animals have stuck fast in the mud and were obliged to remain there a day or two. It has also been the case that tourists have had to get down in the midst of the worst of the marsh and make their way out as best they could, leaving their horses stuck fast, and were compelled to unload them before they could be released. This difficulty exists because of the great lack of water-courses. The water which accumulates from day to day during the season of the heavy rains, must remain in the low land until it settles in the earth, except in those parts near a regular stream or winter torrent. The river Kishon and its few small tributaries are of great benefit in taking the water from the plain about Jenin and along their coasts. Through these small channels, the drainage from the foot of Mounts Gilboa and Tabor flows to the western sea; there is a small winter stream that flows through the valley of Jezreel to the Jordan. It will be called to mind, that these two streams run in direct opposite courses; the former flowing to the west, the latter, to the east; were it not for these little streams, many parts of the plain would be so greatly soaked no one could travel through it in winter, especially from Jenin to Jezreel, for the mud and water would form a complete blockade. Soon after leaving Jenin going northward, Taanach, Gath-rimmon. Kedesh and Lejjun, the ancient Megiddo, are passed at a short distance, but can be distinctly seen. Mt. Gilboa lies a little to the east of the main road, but as Jezreel is approached, it skirts its border. This famous mountain of the Scriptures lies northeast and southeast, and is estimated to be eight miles long from Jellron to Zer'ain, and six miles wide from Beitkad to Mujedd'a. It contains several peaks which are intercepted by small villages, its highest summit being nearly seventeen hundred feet above the level of the Mediterranean Sea. Some parts of Gilboa are very rocky and desolate, while in other portions spots are seen at intervals which show evidences of fruitfulness, and the husbandmen are busily at work from day to day, tilling the soil, planting and reaping. The most barren land is on the north side, and there is nothing seen on the south but clusters of shrub-bushes and dwarf trees. There is nothing of special interest to a traveler upon Gilboa except a more definite knowledge of its general condition. The journey is very fatiguing and monotonous even to the natives themselves. There was a bitter feeling existing among nearly all the tribes and nations against the Israelites about them; these, in connection with their domestic troubles, kept them almost constantly at war with foes within and without; for when they were free from internal struggles, they were engaged in battle with some foreign power whom, at times, they found to be more than a match for them. It may be said of Israel, it was a target for all other tribes and nations; but of the numerous foes who gave much trouble and perplexity to them, none were more vexing than those imposed upon them by the aggressive tribes of the desert on the east and south of Palestine, known as the Amalekites and Midianites, who for centuries sorely troubled this famous people, whom the Lord had brought into the land. These sons of the desert first opposed them while on their way to the "Land of Promise." They followed them after they had settled themselves in their homes, and continued their assaults upon them in every way they could. They came against Israel with a tremendous force in the time of Gideon, but the Lord greatly discomfited them, and gave the victory to the small army of brave men, who had the courage to confront them. The Amalekites lived in Arabia Petræa, between the Red and Dead Seas; they are supposed to have been a migrating people, being very powerful and warlike. It is the opinion of many, they were more numerous in that territory south of Palestine, between Mt. Seir and the border of Egypt; but they did not seem to have many cities; as a rule they lived in caves and tents. Soon after the children of Israel crossed the Red Sea, they were opposed by them in the desert of Rephidim, and they slew all the Hebrews whom they found straggling behind the army. This conduct greatly incensed the Israelites and they concluded to exterminate them; but this determination was not executed, for they made another attack upon Israel, or some of them, when they were on the border of Canaan.

The inhabitants of the desert had a hatred against the Hebrews, which nothing but vengeance could satisfy, and every generation came into activity with the same feeling of unfriendliness, and were engaged warring against the Israelites after they had established a kingdom.

The Midianites were descendants of Midian; they were a wandering people, living largely in Arabia, and are said to have been very numerous, having rich possessions, consisting mostly of flocks, herds and camels. It seems as though they lived mainly on the east of the Elonitic branch of the Red Sea, about the location of Midian. These people became very numerous, and spread themselves over a large tract of the desert, and when their own land seemed too narrow for them they came east of Mount Seir to the border of the Moabites, and on the other side to the region of Mount Sinai. They were the descendants of Ishmael, but the two tribes seem to have been so intimate or mixed they are sometimes called by the same name, or by both, as the case may be; that is, at times they would call them by the one name, and at other times by the other (Exodus xvii. 8–16; Num. xiv. 45). Their capital was called Midian as late as the time of Jerome and Eusebius; much of its ruins were to be seen. It was situated on the river Ornon, south of Areopolis. They were, as all their kindred tribes, idol-worshipers, and many times Israel became anxious to adopt their gods or mode of worship. Therefore, when the Midianites were not in open contest with the Hebrews, they would be inducing them to pay their devotions to idols. At other times they would sorely oppress them, and cause their hearts to bleed because of the outrages perpetrated upon them. Many times it occurred that when the Israelites were about to gather the produce, for which they had toiled hard, the Midianites would suddenly come down upon them and drive them from the field and gather the harvest themselves. It is written, "The Amalekites and Midianites, children of the desert, would come down like locusts in countless swarms, with their cattle and tents and camels, to devour and carry off the fruits of the ground." They would come with their arms, ready to do violence, or even murder, if they could not drive off the Hebrew farmers by mere threats. Hence the poor husbandmen, who had been toiling all the season, were many times compelled to flee for their life, leaving all their possessions (Isa. ix. 6; Acts vii. 29; Exodus iii. 1; xviii. 1; Num. xxii. 25–31; Judges vi 8; Gen. xxv. 2–4), and seek places of refuge in dens, caves, and in the solitary mountains, where they must remain until their thieving foes had satisfied themselves with plunder and retired. At one time, when these outlaws came on their mission of plunder and death, God commissioned Gideon to deliver the people, whose hearts had often bled because of these malicious foes. He entered into the conflict against a great multitude, but God commanded his little army, and gave him the victory. It may not be out of place to state here that the Ishmaelites of the present age are followers of their ancestors in all the malicious work they indulged and fondly practiced; therefore they may be justly classed with them in the commission of the meanest and most murderous crimes of which mankind is guilty. They are constantly on the alert, seeking plunder, and are not only dreaded by strangers, but by natives as well. At the time in question Gideon was a Judge in Israel; he was a very prudent and just man, living in the fear of the Lord, and resided on the east of the Jordan in Ophrah, and, no doubt, witnessed many of the disadvantages which the people over whom he presided were compelled to endure. Moreover, as he was a judge, it is likely the people often complained to him of the conduct of the Midianites, for many living in his district suffered on account of them, and when he heard the news he was greatly pained. It is highly probable Gideon cried to God daily in behalf of the people, and asked Him to interpose for them. Many times the people "sowed in tears," thinking of what was likely to occur about the time of harvest.

The Lord called Gideon to go forth and drive from the land those barbarous people who were a thorn in the flesh of Israel, that they might have rest from continued hostilities. And that he might be assured of success, God showed him signs from heaven which stimulated him for the battle, for he was so nerved by them that he was as certain of the victory before the engagement was begun as if it had been already practically won. The tribes of the desert formed a combination and invaded the land, intending to make a sweeping raid everywhere throughout those parts inhabited by the Hebrews. They crossed to the west of the Jordan and entered the plain of Esdraelon, and proceeded beyond Carmel and Charon to the confines of Philistia, having multitudes of camels and cattle and a great number of tents, preparing to settle in the country so as to be ready at any moment to do violence to the Israelites whose kindred they had inhumanly destroyed on the east of the Jordan. (Judges vi. 7.) The presence of these wanderers filled the people with great fear; indeed, their fears were well founded, for their crops had been destroyed, their pastures filled with strange cattle, and they had to escape for their life. Gideon, himself, had suffered much by the intrusion of these plunderers, and his brothers, who had gone over to Mount Tabor, had been overtaken and slain by the princes of Midian. He, therefore, attempted to collect a large army to drive the intruders out of the land, but this he found to be a hard thing, the men being timid because of the past offenses. Gideon was of the tribe of Manasseh, whose allotment in

Canaan was on the southern border of the plain of Esdraelon. He succeeded in collecting his forces, which at first were thirty-two thousand men, but fear seized twenty-two thousand of these, who, in accordance with the command of Gideon, left the army and went to their homes. Nine thousand and seven hundred more, because of faintheartedness, refused to "lap water like a dog," and were therefore excused. The daring Midianites and Amalekites were camped in the valley of Jezreel, a little to the east of the city, between Little Hermon and Mount Gilboa, known as "the hill of Moreh." Gideon, the man of valor, came down from the hills of Manasseh with his men, pitched his camp beside the well of Harod, which is believed to be the fountain of Jezreel, now known as Gideon's fountain, having only a small number of men upon whom to rely, who, rather than be subjected to the outrages of the invaders, would sacrifice their existence. The commander went in the dead stillness of the night over to the camp of the enemy, and just arrived there in time to listen to one of the Midianitish soldiers relating his dream to one of his fellows, which clearly indicated a defeat and assured Gideon of a glorious victory. His next movement was very unlike the usual custom of procedure when an army is about to attack an enemy; he was totally without the ordinary weapons of defense, but he marched silently forward, unseen and unheard. The invaders were quietly sleeping, many of whom lay down expecting to make a sweeping dash upon Israel the next day. But Gideon with but three hundred men, these each armed only with a pitcher, a lamp and a trumpet. This strangely equipped company came cautiously up to the camp of the combined foes and spread their line out the whole length of their camp, which would appear like a vast army to any one suddenly aroused from sleep. Then instantly, as if a mighty thunder had disturbed the midnight silence, or a shocking earthquake had shaken the ground, the thunder of the smashing of three hundred pitchers was heard, three hundred lamps flashed with fire, three hundred trumpets were sounding, and three hundred voices cried out, "The sword of the Lord and Gideon."

The sleeping multitudes of the Amalekites and Midianites were immediately aroused from their quiet, filled with alarm and being wild with confusion did not take the time to notice who were friends and who belonged to Israel; but began striking right and left, killing each other at a rapid rate, mistaking their own men for those of Gideon. At length they fled from the camp, madly running towards the ford of the Jordan near Succoth, hoping to be able to cross there and escape the vengeance of the Israelites. A few made good their escape, but the large majority were captured and slain. Israel was once more free from a most bitter and annoying foe. But there was not a complete subjugation of these people, for, down the line as far as the time of King Saul, they were seeking Israel. The causes which provoked the bitter feeling of those powerful tribes against Israel, is an illustration of the enmity that was fostered from one generation to another, as has been stated. These people sought to revenge Israel for an action of Moses against their forefathers. When the great leader and law-giver of the Hebrews was journeying to Canaan with his vast army, he camped for a time within the confines of Moab, at the time Balak was king; he, fearing his country would become impoverished by the multitudes who had appeared in his territory, or that they would overpower him and take possession of the land, was anxious to get rid of them. He therefore appointed a large delegation to wait upon Balaam, and solicit him to come and curse Israel. That the petition might be as strong and influential as possible, the king requested that a delegation of the Midianites should accompany his men and jointly present their wishes. When this matter was made known to Moses, he severely punished both Moab and Midian, causing their king and male population to be slain, their cities and strongholds to be destroyed, and all their possessions, together with their wives and children, were carried to the camp of Israel (Num. xxxi.). The residue united their efforts, and within two hundred years became a numerous and powerful people. And having had the conduct of the Israelites, with reference to the massacre of their ancestors, transmitted to each generation, with the ill-advice that they should retaliate in the same way even to the last generation, the Midianites sought the life and property of Israel whenever the slightest opportunity was presented; and this was the chief cause of their attack upon them in that memorable engagement in which Gideon was the most conspicuous factor. Before going to Jezreel or Shunem, it is customary with travelers to make a detour to the fountain of Gideon, which is called by the natives Ain Jalud. It is about one mile and a half or two miles east of Jezreel, under the northwestern end of Mount Gilboa, and sometimes called the "Well of Harod." It is a large stream gushing from the crevice of a mass of rocks, which seem as though they had been deranged by an earthquake. Just at the foot of the mountain, a few feet from the point where the water spouts out is a natural reservoir, quite narrow at the end next the mountain, but suddenly widens, so that it is about fifteen feet wide with a diameter (according to estimate) of fifty feet. As the word Harod means trembling, it is highly probable the name was applied to it because the men of Gideon, who did not lap water, were so greatly overawed with fear they shook while standing there; therefore, the name is highly appropriate.

The brave and heroic leader and commander of the stalwart three hundred fearless men who composed his army, came here, lapped water, as a signal of their willingness to go out against the Midianitish hosts, and under the guidance of the Lord and Gideon. put them to flight. The fountain sends forth a stream of crystal-like water, very delightful to drink. The Lord assured His servant that He would deliver Israel out of the hand of their enemy and save every one of the three hundred dauntless men whose confidence was strongly fixed in Him, although their enemies were as numerous as grasshoppers, and their camels without number, as the sands of the sea. There never was a general who entered upon the field of battle against a foe with stronger confidence of a triumphant victory than Gideon. Men of to-day would have branded him with insanity, as they did John Brown, who marched to Harper's Ferry with a few men and struck an effective blow for the freedom of four and a half millions of poor colored slaves.

The little army of Gideon was not provided with the current deadly weapons of warfare, but with such keen-edged instruments as were not known to the foes against whom he marched. The sword of the Lord and Gideon was the armor of the three hundred, which cut down the enemy like grass, and caused a shout of triumph to go up from the small army that made the regions round about echo. It is also noteworthy, that when the hosts of Philistines had gathered in battle array against Israel, they camped just across the plain near Shunem, and King Saul pitched his camp near the fountain of Jezreel, where Gideon and his brave three hundred had their headquarters. The Philistines were anxious to subordinate the Israelites, and resorted to all manner of schemes to accomplish their wish. They made a strong effort in this direction in the youthful days of David, and felt confident of gratifying results through the conquering arm of Goliath of Gath, whom they pitted against any man Israel might produce; and had it not been for the heroic courage of little David, the contest would have been deeply perplexing to Saul. The lad sent a stone well directed from his sling, which brought Goliath low. This great victory weakened the Philistines and gave fresh courage to Israel. But these people prepared to renew their strength, and came with more energy than ever before. It may be said of the Philistines, that no people in Canaan, except the Phœnicians, were so well equipped for warfare; they were indomitable in spirit, and marshalled one of the most warlike armies known in the land, with stores of wealth to sustain them; so that when they came over to Mt. Gilboa to attack Saul's army, they seemed as numerous as the locusts of Egypt. In this conflict Saul fell. Before entering into the particulars of the battle in which King Saul received his death-wound, it may be of interest to give a brief sketch of this war-like people, who so often made it opportune to oppose Israel.

The Philistines, from whose general name the promised land is called Palestine, were very numerous on the borderland along the southern coast between Joppa and the northwestern border of Egypt. They had established themselves there at a very early date, and had formed a government with a king over them when Abraham came in the land and had built several small cities. There are divided opinions as to from which of the three great ancestors they descended; some think they were of the race of Shem; others believe they were of Japhetic origin; and a third opinion is that they were racially identified with Ham; or may have been a mixture of one of the two other races. However, it is the settled opinion that they came from Egypt first and settled on the Island of Crete; from there they migrated to Southern Palestine and planted themselves on what is known as the Plain of Philistia, between the sea and the western boundary of Judea.

About the time Saul began his reign, this people had multiplied very greatly. It may be that they were not all of one race, for as the word Philistine means "stranger," it would apply to all persons coming there of foreign birth; and it is generally known that in all large communities, in those times as now, other races settled among those who were known as the primitive inhabitants. Such a custom prevailed from very early times, and it was the case in Israel, notwithstanding a law existed among them forbidding their mingling with other peoples. It is also known that it was an ordinary thing for different political states and tribes to combine in a common cause to protect themselves against other powers; and such an alliance naturally introduced social relations. This is one of the reasons, and perhaps the major cause, that brought many of the high officials of Israel into social intercourse with other nations and tribes. Therefore we feel competent, with these facts in view, to venture the assertion that much of the numerical growth of the Philistines was caused by the migration of other people. As the growing population of the world made it necessary for those who were confined in a straightened district or province to seek localities more suited to their wants, men began to migrate in small colonies to other parts which were not burdened with inhabitants. Therefore this was no doubt the stimulating cause that impelled the Philistines, formerly known as Cretens or Caphtorims, to leave their island home and come over to Canaan. Being pleased with both the availableness and richness of the country, they established themselves in the southern portion along the sea, adjoining the territory settled by the Hamites. The Philistines, having become a strong political people when the Israelites entered Canaan, it was not an easy matter to dispossess them of their territory. Joshua did attack them, but it seems they suffered but little inconvenience from it, if any. Their portion of the country was very rich and fertile, and when a sore famine raged in other portions of Canaan, the Philistines had abundant supplies. When the seven years' famine was greatly distressing the land, and the beautiful rich plain of Esdraelon was parched and unyielding so that want and suffering prevailed, Elisha the prophet sought refuge in Philistia, as did the Shunammite woman who had cared for him so faithfully. The Philistines had five principal cities that were thickly inhabited, namely: Gaza, Ekron, Askelon, Ashdod, and Gath, the home of Goliath, the great champion upon whom they so strongly relied; who, when they demanded that Israel should send out a man to contend against him, when seeing little David, the youngest son of Jesse, coming down the hillside to strive against him, became madly insane. These people troubled Israel and even alarmed them for about one hundred and twenty years, because of their aggressiveness, and their armed forces were always a signal of discomfort to them. King Saul himself was seized with dismay when he saw the armed multitudes of their dreaded enemy encamped at Shunem. The Philistines watched Israel with a jealous eye; and when they knew of an extra large gathering of them, spies would come up from Philistia to see and hear what it meant. But there was a sudden increase of strength and courage in Israel when they assembled at Mizpeh, about twenty years after the Ark of God had been recovered from the Philistines. The people had returned to the Lord to the extent that a religious reformation obtained among them, through the blessed influence of their pious leader and adviser, Samuel the prophet, who was also the last regular judge divinely appointed over them.

The Israelites, having seen their unfortunate situation, became anxious for the return of the favor of the Lord in their midst as in other days, when He led them triumphantly in every struggle against their enemies. They therefore put away their strange gods and earnestly cried unto the God of their fathers to mercifully return unto them and lead them, pledging themselves to observe His commands.

They then, in accordance with the call of Samuel, assembled at Mizpah to renew their vows, and solemnly engage themselves in religious devotion to the God of heaven and earth. When the Philistines saw the people thronging the highways in multitudes to attend the convocation their suspicions were greatly aroused, thinking they had mischievous aims in view, so they came up from their lowland cities, armed with deadly weapons, against the assemblage, thinking the knowledge of their presence would intimidate Israel and confuse their purpose. But Israel, having newly and solemnly dedicated themselves to God, immediately received a revival of their former courage, and once more the people went out in the strength of the Lord, the God of their fathers, who fought for them and gave them a glorious victory. The Philistines fled from the presence of Israel in great alarm, but were pursued, and numbers of them were overtaken and slain. Then Samuel set up the memorial-stone and called it Ebenezer, saying, "Hitherto the Lord hath helped us." Such was the success of the Israelites in their engagement, the Philistines restored to them the cities they had captured, even from Ekron to Gath, and the coasts thereof. Then there was peace, for the great victory of Israel so subdued the Philistines they did not attempt an open attack again until the reign of King Saul. During his long and perplexing rule those people of the lowland began to renew their encroachments upon the children of Israel, with almost continued success. It appears they renewed their usurpations about the time Saul was inaugurated, and continued them with increasing vexations until the day that monarch died on Mount Gilboa. The first war these lowlanders had with Saul they brought up a tremendous army, having thirty thousand chariots of war, six hundred thousand horsemen, "and people as the sand of the seashore in multitude." This vast number came up and camped at Michmash, a little to the south-east of Bethel. The Israelites along the route they marched were greatly alarmed, so that many left their homes and took refuge in caves and dens; others fled to the east of the Jordan; but Saul came out with his men of war and slew them right and left. So vigorous was the conflict that the Philistines fled from the field, and the victorious Israelites pursued them as far as Ajalon, cutting them down as they ran. This is the fight that took place after Jonathan, the eldest son of Saul, performed that brilliant exploit when he entered the garrison of the Philistines without the knowledge of any one except his armor-bearer, who went with him, and threw the whole camp into a state of confusion. This act of heroism has made the name of Jonathan memorable to the present generation. But there seems to have been a restless purpose existing in the Philistines never to abandon their endeavors until they had become the acknowledged masters of the Israelites. Therefore, if they lost a battle, it only served as a stimulant for them to renew their attack.

From the day Samuel died a train of alarming adversities began to be strewn in the path of King Saul, which haunted him through life. This young, promising king, who thrilled the hearts of his subjects into a high state of enthusiasm when he appeared before them at Mizpah, and fixed himself affectionately in their esteem, soon began to show evidences of weakness, which indicated that he was being controlled by a spirit not of God. In the meantime the Philistines, who had made several unsuccessful assaults upon Israel, prepared themselves for another, more vigorous than any of their previous attacks, intending to subdue them or crush their kingdom. To this end they marched up for a deadly encounter, and, notwithstanding their plans were cunningly devised and arranged in profound secrecy (1 Sam. xiii. 3; xiv. 1-52), their movement was bold and daring, and yet so unexpected to the Hebrews, that King Saul and all his army were troubled. The Philistines came up from their lowland homes and proceeded northward, making a long march through the plain of Sharon as far as Mount Carmel, then crossed to the plain of Jezreel and camped on the southern slope of Little Hermon, near ancient Shunem. King Saul also came with his forces and camped by the "fountain of Jezreel," on the northern slope of Mount Gilboa. These camps were so near each other that Saul could look across the narrow neck of the plain from his camping-ground and distinctly see the army of the Philistines, who were so very numerous; his head bowed, and sorrow, fear and weakness seized his frame. Then he began examining himself. Samuel, the man of God, who had cautiously advised him, was dead; the priests of Nob had been put to death, to appease his wrath, by his own command; and, more than all, he had allowed his proud to turn him from God, so that he could not commune with Him nor receive an answer to his most fervent inquiries. Saul was left to himself in the darkest moments of his life; he had no Samuel, no priests, and no God from whom to obtain a word of counsel, which he so greatly needed. He sought it in dreams and asked it of the Urim and inquired of the prophets, but could find no consolation; then the bitter anguish of his heart was pressing him sore, even to despair. After deep reflection Saul could see only one thing to do that might relieve his fears or disclose to him the results of the pending conflict. The little village of Endor was not far distant, in which lived a woman known to be a witch. Saul desired to consult her, for he was willing to court the favor of any one who could by any means give him a word as to the turn of the battle. He wanted to hear from Samuel concerning the matter, although he did not treat the old man with due respect while he was living, and received a stern rebuke by him for his untowardness, very early after he was anointed to be the King of Israel. Saul must have felt his situation most keenly, for we venture the assertion that no man was brought into a deeper state of humility than the falling king. He had two great impediments to encounter in attempting to effectually carry out his design. He wanted to go over to Endor to consult the witch, and to do so he must run the risk of being apprehended by the Philistines, for they were in camp in the direction of Endor, and to get there he must pass beyond their lines. The next obstacle was his mission to consult with and ask a favor from a woman who was one of the class of people whom he had manifested uncompromising opposition to, for he had ordered all the witches in the land to be put to death. Therefore, to be compelled in an extreme moment to go to a person for favors whom he had commanded should be killed, must have been a most painful thorn in his side. But, as humiliating as it was, he could see no better course of procedure; hence, of the two great dilemmas, he chose what seemed to him the less. King Saul then disguised himself and started in the thickest of the darkness to find the woman of Endor, to implore her to bring up Samuel, that he might consult with him.

It can be clearly seen that Saul was a believer in witchism, although he ordered them all to be put to death. He found the woman, and when she apprehended him, she feared his visit was for a deadly purpose, or that he would attempt to set a snare for her; but he swore to her that she should not die. Having heard his oath, she consented to do the work he so anxiously desired her to perform. She said to Saul, "Whom shall I bring to thee?" "Bring me up Samuel," was the answer of the consternated king. She gave a cry and said, "Thou hast deceived me! I saw gods ascending out of the earth." And in answer to Saul's question as to the appearance of the objects seen, she said, "An old man cometh up, and he is covered with a mantle." The king hearing this, feared the spirit of Samuel and bowed himself to the ground, and heard a voice saying to him, "Why hast thou disquieted me?" he answered, "I was sore distressed, for the Philistines make war against me, and Jehovah is departed from me, and answereth me no more." Then said the voice to him, "Why ask of me, seeing Jehovah is departed from thee and become thine enemy? He hath done to thee as He said, and has given thy kingdom to David, and He will deliver thee to the Philistines, and to-morrow thou shalt be with me, thou and thy three sons."

Then Saul was nearly helpless; in an instant he became as helpless as a baby, and gave up in hopeless despair, for his doom had been declared, and he was of no more service to himself nor his army. Saul had the fullest confidence in what he heard; therefore, it is not hard to understand why his strength left him. The proud and selfish king felt himself no longer the successful leader of Israel, for his hope had vanished like a dream, and his courage melted into weakness. The next day the fierce battle was begun; but Saul and his army being overpowered with fear, fled. The people having no commander or leader, and no one to advise the discomfited men in their alarming peril, all their courage left them, and the wildest confusion prevailed. Those who, in their disorderly flight, could not keep up with their comrades, were captured and slain wherever found, so that the whole line of retreat was marked by dead men.

The king, being conscious of defeat, and alarmed by the doleful tidings he received at Endor the previous night, fled with his three sons to Mt. Gilboa, hoping to find a safe retreat within some of its hiding-places; but nothing could save them. They were hotly pursued up the rugged slope by the courageous Philistines, and before they could elude them, Jonathan, Abinadab and Malchishua, sons of Saul, were slain in the front of the fight, and Saul himself was sorely wounded by an arrow hurled into his doomed body from one of the Philistines. The ill-fated king knew his army was powerless and that the potent enemy was master of the situation. He at the same time remembered he had been a proud and victorious king, the pride of Israel and the great leader of a hitherto victorious army; and the very people who were then slaying his sons, cutting down his army, and had sent a dart of death into his own body, had been made to tremble and flee from the vengeance of his sword in the recent past; then, to be captured by them, and be compelled to bow at their feet, was a matter he could not endure. He then piteously entreated his companion-in-arms to kill him; but he sternly refused to comply with Saul's petition. Then the doomed king drew his own sword, fell upon it and died.

It is sadly painful to be compelled to record the fact that the first king of Israel committed suicide. His head was severed from his body, and sent with his armor to Philistia as a signal of their triumph, and his body was hung upon the wall of Beth-shan, on the west of the

Jordan, about twenty-five miles south of the Sea of Galilee. When the tidings of Saul's death came to the knowledge of David, it overwhelmed him. Indeed it is an event deserving more than a passing notice. David's most relentless enemy was King Saul, who hunted him with his heart flooded with vengeance and would have murdered him if he had not eluded him from time to time; yet David loved Saul because he was the Lord's anointed and would not injure a hair of his head. It was also known to David that he was to succeed him as king of Israel, but he was not anxious that that monarch should die, that he might control the nation. The extent Saul's death affected David should increase our esteem for him, so as to hold up this unprecedented example to every young aspirant to the position of others, that he should do nothing to indicate an anxious wish to step in the place of another before his time comes. But we find so many in our times seemingly so anxious for the place occupied by another, they restlessly wait and long for it while the rightful incumbent is active. But David's conduct was the reverse; for he wept bitterly and became author of one of the most touching funeral dirges ever conceived by man. The words which fell from his lips, when informed of Saul's fate, are strikingly sublime and touching. David was aware the Philistines would raise a tumultuous shout of joy when the news came to them of the death of the king of Israel, and the triumph of their own army. "Tell it not in Gath, proclaim it not in Askelon, lest the daughters of the Philistines rejoice; lest the daughters of the uncircumcised triumph," were the touching words of the son of Jesse. But the exultant victory of the Philistines was not permanent. The lost cause of Saul was a rebuke from the Almighty because of his waywardness; but when David ascended the throne, the Philistines found him competent to withstand them; and it was not long after this young man was acknowledged king of Israel, that they came up against him. They marched to the southwest of Jerusalem, and halted in the plain of Raphaim; but King David was more than a match for them; he repulsed them and finally subdued them, so that their government became tributary to David. Then there was an end to hostilities for a time by these people who had been a sore plague to the children of Israel. The whole narrative of the memorable battle between the Philistines and the Hebrews, can be drawn before the mind like a panorama, from the hill on which ancient Jezreel stood. It is along the edge of the plain, and one may station himself for a while, facing the north, and look over the plain toward Shunem where the camp of the Philistines was located in the neck of the valley, and while reading the history of the battle, can almost imagine himself in the midst of the real scene. Then turning towards Gilboa, he can see the place where Saul was in camp with his timid army, at the foot of the mountain. It appears from the present situation of the place, Saul made a blind attempt to gain the heights of Gilboa; for the Philistines had a favorable opportunity to capture and slay him as they were coming from Faku'a, marching along the crest of the mountain. And as we look upon this memorable battle-field, high upon Gilboa, we pause and ask the unanswerable question, Where among these mighty rocks did Saul, Israel's first king, draw his own sword with a quivering hand, and then with all the force of his death-stricken frame, covered with his own blood, rise up, fall upon it and die, a self-murderer?

Ancient Jezreel, called by the natives Zer'ain, has been so clearly identified that there have no objections appeared as to its certainty. It is said there are but few places in Palestine whose original site is so generally agreed to as Jezreel, the home of Ahab and Jezebel. It has been minutely defined by many of the foremost and most critical explorers of Palestine. The principal mention of the ancient city is largely connected with the life and character of the cunning Jezebel, and her barbarous husband, Ahab, and the daring Jehu, the son of Nimshi. The present village is by no means a pleasant place to visit; the little half-mud huts are anything but tidy, and the whole place is disorderly, if not filthy. I would have refused to pass through its narrow and crooked lanes, had it not been for the ancient history attaching to it. It seems that the whole village is filled with beggars; and just as soon as a stranger enters it, they come out of their little huts, like locusts coming out of the ground. Sometimes twenty or thirty children will be heard shouting at the top of their voices, "Backsheesh, backsheesh;" and keep the strain up until the stranger leaves the place, and the sound is lost in the distance behind him. It was a great relief and pleasing satisfaction to me when I had left the place; for I was not only relieved of the troublesome beggars, but had the privilege of inhaling the pure air once more. There is a tall house in the centre of the village, which is approached by passing through the site of Naboth's vineyard; it is not an ancient building, though it bears the marks of age. It is the general opinion that this house stands on the spot of the famous watch-tower of Jezreel, in which the watchman stood when he saw Jehu approaching in great haste. From the top of this building a splendid view may be obtained of the valley as far as Beth-shan, on the southeastern border of Galilee. There is a very steep pass leading down from the village into the adjacent valley toward the east. Along the side of the hill, are several ancient wine-presses cut in the rock; this is believed to be the plat of ground known as Naboth's vineyard, and the wine-presses were used in his day, and probably hewn out by his own hands. A little north of the village is a fine well at which the maidens of Jezreel may be seen in small companies awaiting their turn to draw water. Another remark concerning ancient Jezreel may be in place. It can be discerned without much research, that a prominent vein of Hamitic influence ran through both Judah and Israel from Solomon's time down to the captivity. The latter married a daughter of one of the kings of Egypt who greatly influenced him to consent to the toleration of idolatrous worship, which was the beginning of the decline and ultimate fall of the chosen people; for this state of things continued at intervals to grow in popular favor, until the daring Jeroboam became the acknowledged head of the revolting tribes and established his kingdom upon the rotten foundation of idolatry, with Bethel and Dan as headquarters. It is a fact that cannot be reasonably denied, that these giant departures from God are invariably traced to the immediate or remote influence of tribes or nations not of the household of Israel. One of the chief ideas for referring to this state of things among the children of Israel is, to indicate the fact that the Hamitic descendants had a strong grip upon the two kingdoms. This matter will be presented in another page, we hope, so clearly, that no room will be left for reasonable dispute. It is marvelously strange that the people of antique times had no prejudice as to color or race, but recognized man as man, even as far back as the beginning of civilization, and have not changed their faith in this regard to the present; the only distinction being that of a religious or class line, which is the same among all of whatever complexion, in the old world. And then to see such a spirit of racial distinction in a country that proudly boasts of its civilization and Christian brotherhood, as is fostered in America, shows clearly there is a great lack of the spirit of justice existing here, and that those who profess to be religious, are as largely idolatrous as were the Israelites whom they pity. They worshiped gods made of their own hands; but the dominant race of this land worship their complexion. Which is the greater sin?

It may be of interest to note, there were two Jorams or Jerams or Jehorams, as the name has been pronounced at different times; both of whom were blood relatives and connected with the two kingdoms by virtue of their birth-right. The one in question was the son of Ahab, king of Israel; the other, a son of Jehoshaphat, king of Judah. This latter Joram married Athaliah, daughter of Ahab and Jezebel; therefore, their son Ahaziah was a nephew of Joram, king of Israel, and were contemporaneous monarchs over the southern and northern kingdoms. When Ahaziah learned of the illness of his uncle Joram, he went over to Jezreel to see him, which happened to be about the time the young man sent by Elisha was anointing Jehu to be the tenth king of Israel. He was an admirer of the administration of the house of Ahab, and followed it as did his father Joram in the house of Judah. But he was permitted to rule the kingdoms but one year, before he came to an untimely death by order of Jehu. It may, therefore, be reasonably inferred that both the kingdoms of Judah and Israel were largely controlled by Phœnician influence. Jezebel, the daughter of the king of Sidon, held for many years the ruling sway over the northern kingdom, for it seems as if Ahab, her husband, became so completely wound up in the net of her cunning schemes, he did all she desired. It was through her persuasions, the groves were arranged at Jezreel and the altars were built to Astarte, at which four hundred priests officiated, and her daughter Athaliah, who was the wife of Joram, king of Judah, followed as near as possible the footsteps of her mother, who was living at the same time in Jezreel, and was untiring in her efforts to add to the strength she possessed over the kingdom of Judah, to bring it into political and religious harmony with that of Israel. If we consider the laws that led to the assassination of Naboth we cannot fail to see that Ahab was a selfish, covetous and dishonorable man; and that Jezebel was a cunning, shrewd and a daringly adventurous woman. She was ever ready to plan and formulate deep schemes for the successful accomplishment of any issue that gave her much concern. Ahab, in his desire for gains, was not content with the enjoyment of his beautiful palace and the general comforts with which he was surrounded; his parks and gardens were of the most spacious and fascinating character, all of which were attached to his family palace, to embellish and make it a lovely paradise. But his envious and greedy disposition caused him to long for a plot of ground belonging to Naboth, the Jezreelite, in which were a wine-press and vineyard. Ahab requested the owner to let him have the plot, saying he wanted it for a garden of herbs. But Naboth would not consent to the proposition of Ahab, because the land in question was bequeathed to him by his father and kept as a sacred memorial of him. The king, seeing he could not persuade his neighbor to part with his cherished possession, went to his palace with bowed head and (pretendingly) a heavy heart Such was the sad expression of his countenance, the curiosity of Jezebel was greatly aroused, who seemed to have a balm for all her husband's wounds and a remedy for every fear.

To express the depth of his trouble Ahab went to bed, turned his face to the wall and refused to eat bread, because of the grief he suffered from the disappointment caused by Naboth's refusal. When Jezebel entered the room and found her husband in such deep distress she became alarmed, and when she learned the cause of his discomfort she urged him to eat bread and be merry, for she would see that his desire should be obtained. She then ordered a feast to be made ready, to which Naboth should be invited, and at which time men were to stand ready to stone him to death. The order was carefully observed. The charge against him was that he had sinned against God and the king. After the tragedy, which resulted in the death of Naboth, Jezebel went to Ahab, who was pretending to be grieved because he had not gained consent to take the property he so greatly coveted, and said to him, "Rise and go, take possession of the vineyard." In compliance with the ill-advice of the cunning woman, King Ahab went and seized it. And while there, feeling jubilant over the accomplishment of his aim, Elijah, the prophet, met him with a message from God. When Ahab saw Elijah he said to him. " Hast thou found me, O mine enemy?" "I have found thee," said the man of God. He then pronounced the fate of Ahab, of Jezebel, and the entire royal house, telling him not one of them should be left, and that upon the same ground where the dogs licked the blood of Naboth, should dogs lick his blood. When Ahab heard this doleful message he came to himself, but it was too late; his doom was fixed, for the mouth of the Lord had declared it, and the whole calamity came to pass. The next place of importance is Shunem, about three miles north of Jezreel. There is nothing antique to be seen in the village, and therefore no halt is made there, except it is for luncheon. It is likely there would have been no mention made of it had not Elisha, the prophet, been so kindly cared for by the Shunammite woman. It is also a satisfaction to travelers to look over the plain westward and take an observation of the route the poor, distressed woman took when she went with great haste to Elisha on Mount Carmel, to consult him about the death of her only child. There are a cluster of villages and other places of historic interest situated at short distances in the vicinity of Shunem. To the northeast about three miles, upon the margin of Little Hermon. Nain is situated. It is a very small village, bearing no signs of importance whatever, and would be passed unnoticed, as many other places are, were it not for the miracle which our Lord performed the day He made a visit there.

This present little village occupies the site of the ancient town in the time of our Lord, near the gate of which He performed one of His greatest miracles. He met the funeral of a young man who was the only child of a widow; he was her only support. Christ caused the bearers of the dead to halt, and in a few moments the man who was being carried to the tomb, was restored alive to his mother. It is noteworthy that the number of persons our Lord restored to life accords exactly with the number of days He suffered himself to be under the dominion of death. He raised three persons to life, and He came forth from the gates of death on the third day. There is a small mosque at the edge of the village, standing on the spot designated by tradition as the scene of our Lord's miracle, and is known as the "Shrine of Christ." Very early in our era a Christian chapel stood upon the same site, and it is supposed, the title of the mosque is the name by which the original chapel was known. (1 Kings xx. 1–23.) An opinion has been advanced that Nain was not a walled town, as there have been found no traces of its ancient foundations by those who have made investigations, as is usual in many cases. But there are two things that would incline us to believe the opinion is not well founded.

It should be considered, in the first place, that if it was unprotected by walls, it would have been exposed to the danger of being taken at any moment by foes, who were prowling like wild beasts through the land, hunting prey, and the people living in the various towns and cities in Palestine did not fail to protect themselves in the surest possible way, especially with walls and gates. Therefore it is not likely that the inhabitants of Nain would content themselves to live in an unprotected town, under a thousand liabilities to hostile attacks, when they had ample means and opportunity to secure themselves as other places were, against the entrance of those who sought their discomfort. Secondly, it is plainly stated in the Bible concerning the visit of our Lord there, "When He drew near the gate of the city." This is a clear evidence, the city had one gate at least, and without a wall it would have been but mockery. It is also known that the people in those days did not build ordinary fences, and the gate must have been placed there to pass in and out of, because the little city was surrounded by a wall. The town is small and uninviting, as are nearly all the villages in the interior. But it gives the Christian traveler supreme consolation, to make a visit there and other places of sacred memory, because the same road was marked by the feet of our Lord while going about doing good. On entering the road to Nain new thoughts enter one's mind, and a change naturally takes possession of a traveler's feelings, he having for several days been busy with the scenes of the idolatrous tendencies of Israel, and the many chastisements God gave them, and the wars they had with foes without and within, a'l have a tendency to make one feel gloomy and wish for a change. Then having so suddenly entered upon another scene so very touching and cheering as the mission of Christ to little Nain, it seems to one as though he had been transported from a dark, dreary, monotonous land to one full of beauty and pleasure. It certainly is a change from a sad and unenviable state of mind to one that is full of good cheer. And although the foot-prints of our Lord cannot be traced, we know He came over this plain and visited a little city called Nain, on the eastern side, and did a work of love that hushed the noise of lamentation, checked the flow of a widowed mother's tears, and made a multitude of poor weeping ones jubilant over the restoration to life of a young man, whom they were about to lay in the tomb. Indeed, he was known to travel many times over the plain of Esdraelon, a little to the west of Nain, so the place was familiar to Jesus and His disciples There seems to be no doubt as to the identity of the place as being the site of ancient Nain. Our Lord had been in Capernaum, attending His mission and healing many who came to Him from afar. But He suddenly left them and came to Nain, a distance of about twenty miles, and just reached the gate in time on the next day to perform a most stupendous work. We venture the opinion that our Lord came up to this little border city of Esdraelon, especially to perform the miracle of life-giving. What a tremendous excitement must have prevailed when the dead man was restored to life and to his weeping mother! Those walking in the procession did not pay special attention to the man approaching the gate, but when He had made them astonished, every one wanted to see Him. It is likely some of those attending the funeral were from Nazareth, and knew Jesus as the son of Joseph and Mary, but not as "the Mighty God," for the two cities were only about four miles apart, and the inhabitants were often going to and from them. (Luke vii. 11–18). It is certain they had heard of Jesus; the fame of His miracles had spread over the land. Not far from Nain was another small village prominently mentioned in the Bible in connection with King Saul's nocturnal visit. This is Endor, where the famous witch lived, whom he sought in the time of his grief.

When the allotments were apportioned, Endor fell to Manasseh, and was a flourishing place as late as the time of Eusebius. But nothing remains there now to attract any one, except the caves in the hillside; the curiously shaped one near the village is supposed to be the one in which the witch lived. The country round about presents a beautiful appearance as far as one can see. The soil of the plain of Esdraelon is one of the richest and most productive in Palestine. The shepherds and wandering Arabs take advantage of the beautiful pastures, and hundreds visit them daily with their flocks. If the husbandmen were adapted to the modern customs of farming, the products of the plain would be at least ninety per cent. more abundant. But they do not seem to care for the general cultivation of this most fruitful tract of country (1 Sam. xxviii. 7-25), and content themselves with tilling it in small patches. The half-wild Arabs, who migrate from place to place, make this plain one of their most favorite resorts. They take their herds, tents and families, with all their possessions, and camp there for weeks, and often for months, seeking the pastures for their herds by day, and at the same time watch for an opportunity to plunder by night. It is not infrequently the case that they commit these depredations in the open day whenever the slightest opportunity is presented. They have been known to hotly pursue travelers on several occasions, before the government of Turkey placed guards through the country, to give strangers the much-needed protection now given them.

Sometimes, persons going from Shunem to Carmel and from Jezreel to Tiberias have been compelled to escape for their lives. The matter became so alarming that the Sultan of Turkey has caused a military force to patrol the country, so that travelers may be permitted to pass through safely, and that farmers may be encouraged to pursue their work without entertaining fears of being deprived of enjoying the fruits of their labor at the time of harvest; for the native husbandmen have not escaped (in many cases) the murderous intrusions of the Bedouin highwaymen, who would kill them for the purpose of plunder just as readily as if they were foreigners. It is reasonable to suppose that those husbandmen sowed in tears, not knowing whether they would be permitted to reap what they so earnestly labored for. But we think the days of these outlaws are passed, and a more healthy state of things exists.

The greater portion of the plain was in the bounds of the territory allotted to the tribe of Issachar, who seem to have been a people not very much noted for bravery, but were quiet and passive, disposed rather to suffer intrusion than stand out boldly for their rights. This feature of their character is demonstrated by their humble submission to the Canaanites of the adjacent towns and cities, especially the Phœnicians along the sea-coast between the Ladder of Tyre and Sidon. It is said that the tribe of Issachar, or a goodly number of them, were not only the burden-bearers of the Canaanites, but were in a semi-slavish state, and were content in having a menial relation to them, their occupation being such as mule-drivers, wood-choppers, and the general handy-fellow. Their situation accorded exactly with the prophecy of Jacob concerning them, when about to die: "Issachar is a strong ass crouching down between two burdens; and he saw that rest was good; and the land, that it was pleasant; and bowed his shoulders to bear, and became a servant to tribute." It is proper to remark at this point that it would be well for those who believe and teach the doctrine, that the curse pronounced upon Canaan, was to continue down the line to all the descendants of Ham, and that his progeny have no higher calling than that of menials, to consider this fact, that the very people who they say are to be kept down and deprived of an opportunity to demonstrate their manhood as others, were the masters of those who they say are divinely set apart to rule, and their will was submitted to with humble obedience.

Those Canaanites, whose ancestor was Ham, and who were more the typical Hamite by far than ninety per cent. of the colored population of America, were of the direct class these false teachers would have the world believe, were born under the curse of the Almighty, and that Shem and Japheth are appointed to execute it throughout all generations. The above is but one of the many proofs of the downright absurdity of the damaging doctrine so earnestly taught by those whose blindness have hidden "the truth as it is in Jesus" from them. "God is no respecter of persons." The very foundation of the northern kingdom was built upon elastic premises, and, therefore. was unstable from the day Jeroboam was proclaimed king to the lamentable day when Hoshea, the last king, being overpowered by Shalmaneser, king of Assyria, carried him and his subjects into captivity. There was a constant tendency among the people to emerge into the darkest shades of idolatry, so that when Ahab, the seventh king, ruled Israel, the people had so generally given themselves up to idol worship, there could be found of the vast number comprising the population, but seven thousand who had not bowed their knee to Baal.

This is the number the Lord informed Elijah had been preserved from the seductions of the established idolatry of the kingdom of Israel. There seem to have been two modes of making proselytes to Baal adopted by Ahab and Jezebel: one was seduction and the other intimidation. When favors were to be granted, personal and otherwise, the recipients would be those who had become Baalites; and as there were many positions of honor at the disposal of the king, and men were in those days, as at present, eager to become the honored incumbent of an office of high trust in the government, they would go over to Baal simply for the sake of an official position, or indulging the hope of obtaining one. Those who would not be induced by these and other seductive allurements were doomed to death. Such was the wholesale slaughtering of those who were strongly inclined to the worship of the God of their fathers, that Elijah was of the opinion, when the Lord called him from his rocky retreat at Mt. Horeb, he was the only one left who had escaped Jezebel's murderous hand.

Jezreel and Samaria were dotted with idolatrous priests, four hundred of whom were chosen to officiate in the former city, and four hundred and fifty in the latter; their altars were constantly blazing with sacrificial fires, and the lower atmosphere was darkened with smoke. The name of the great idol was sacredly adored, and devoutly praised by multitudes who had forsaken the Lord. Notwithstanding the tendencies of man are evil, and the Hebrews were surrounded by idolatrous tribes and nations whose examples were of the most degrading nature, there is no excuse for their wilful departure from the God of their fathers, knowing, as they did, the wonderful things He had done, both in delivering them from the bondage of Egypt and sustaining them during the many years of their national independence. The Lord intended these people should have a religious government, or one in which the light of the true God should flame so brilliantly that the heathen about them might be persuaded to adopt their worship and become admirers and servants of the God of heaven; but we find Israel just as eager to depart from God and wholly abjure His worship, as were the idol-worshipers who never knew Him as such.

There seems to have been no trouble for Jeroboam to establish his calf-worship among the people; they took hold of it with a greediness that was hard to satisfy. Israel may be compared to a young person, or a youth cautiously trained, and who is surrounded by others who have been given a wider privilege, so that they do as suits them best. The youth who has been carefully disciplined, seeing the wide scope of liberty seemingly enjoyed by those in his neighborhood, becomes dissatisfied with the rule of his own parents and seeks to break them down and follow the example of those whose restraints are very meagre. He begins to extend his privileges little by little, until he finds himself indulging in whatsoever he wishes, and only finds out the danger of his course when it is too late to redeem himself. This is about the status of Israel. They felt that the laws of God were too exacting; that they were kept in a position which cut them off from those enjoyments others indulged in, and hence they longed to abjure the law of the Lord and become their own keepers. This tendency was fostered in Samuel's time, and was often rebuked by him, for he did not fail to tell the people of the calamity that would follow such conduct. But their evil passions seem to have mastered their judgment, so that they would not be admonished.

It was one hundred and twenty-one years from the time Saul of Benjamin was anointed king at Ramah by Samuel, to the time of the revolt of the ten tribes, when Jeroboam was installed king. Under this monarch the long-sought opportunity to indulge in open idolatry, without lawful restraints was accorded to all who desired it, and from that day the Israelites went into deeper sins, until their desire for the worship of the true God became a thing of the past. So that when Ahab was made king, fifty-six years from the time Jeroboam took the sceptre, the people had gone so far from the God of their fathers (with few exceptions), they were ready to do anything that might be suggested by their ruler. Ahab has the reputation of being the most wicked and daring king of the six preceding him; and finding the subjects of his kingdom completely in his hands, he ventured to go farther into idolatry than even Jeroboam, who practically established it. Most authors seem to be in sympathy with Ahab, and even apologize for his conduct by charging Jezebel, the Phœnician princess, with influencing his course of procedure. This seems to be a strange apology, one having no more force than that made by Adam, as a reason for violating the command of the Lord, when, to satisfy his disobedient inclination, he took the fruit from the hand of his wife and ate it.

Men who send out their thoughts to the world for its enlightenment, ought to clothe every idea with candor perfectly free from bias. It is a fact known to the world that Ahab was king, and as such held the sceptre of power in his own hand, or had the authority to do so. He was not a feeble-minded man, as some authors would have us believe he was, from the manner in which they record his life; but a sturdy, brave and daring man, full of ambition, pride, covetousness and vanity, caring for none but himself and household any farther than to serve some personal end in view. He was also the husband of Jezebel, and was to some extent, by human and divine law, a king or double ruler over her; first as husband, and second as monarch of the kingdom in which she was living. Therefore Ahab's malicious conduct was the outgrowth of his own diabolical inclinations, intensified by an insatiable disposition to be regarded the greatest man on earth. Jezebel was equally anxious for his success in the direction he aimed; she, therefore, put almost an endless number of plans in motion to accomplish it, and having been reared amid heathen influences and by parents who were fervent adherents of Baal, it cannot be expected she would incline to any religion except that taught her from babyhood, especially when her husband was willing to abandon the God of his fathers and those ordained by Jeroboam to adopt the religion of the Phœnicians.

The fact seems clear to my mind that Ahab was the worst of the two, according to the opportunities each had in life to know the true God. It does, therefore, seem unjust that the malicious conduct of Ahab should be charged to Jezebel, his Hamite wife, but on the other hand her husband, who was the acknowledged sovereign of Israel, was guilty of allowing his wife too much ruling authority, which was many times the cause of much trouble. The northern kingdom was ripe with idolatry, when Ahab ascended the throne, for the calf-worship had gained strong hold on the people in the fifty-six years of its establishment, and the future outlook had become alarming, so much so, that God raised special messengers to warn the king and subjects, from time to time, of the pending calamities with which they would be plagued on account of their rebellion against Him.

There had been several prophets in Israel from the time Jeroboam expelled the priests and Levites to the occasion of Ahab's accession to the throne, but none of them were endowed with the characteristics of Elijah. It became necessary for God to raise up a host of these special agents, from time to time, to admonish Israel and declare His judgments. Many of them were bold, stern and faithful men, going through the land, prefixing their message with the words, "Thus saith the Lord." Many times it was one of death, but they declared it with the same boldness they did those that delighted the receiver. Their authority was generally recognized, and what they declared was confidently expected, whether to an individual or to the nation.

These prophets were not looked upon as leaders of the people politically, or rulers, nor did they so regard themselves; they were not consecrated priests in the ordinary sense of the word, therefore they did not attempt to officiate at the altars as such, but they were persons chosen from the people of whatever tribe the Lord selected them, without respect to priestly descendants. Yet there were times when a prophet seemed to rank above both priest and king, for both of these functionaries were often confronted by them with a message from God to which they would listen and respect. Not a few times these mysterious messengers would be sent to the chief officials of the country, both religious and political, to denounce their conduct, without being interfered with; sometimes they would speak most bitterly against king, priests and people, and yet their authority would not be questioned, although the parties concerned would at times become enraged. There can be no doubt that these messengers of the Lord were sustained by Him, to the extent that their enemies became powerless when listening to the word of the Lord sent to them. That the prophets were specially constituted by God, cannot be consistently doubted. It is a known fact that what they said was fulfilled exactly according to the time they predicted, and much of their prophecy has been fulfilled in our time, and is yet being accomplished in every age.

Let us consider the call of Jeremiah, for example. "The word of the Lord came to me saying, 'Before I formed thee in the womb I knew thee; and before thou camest forth I sanctified thee and ordained thee to be a prophet unto the nation.'" Then said I, "Oh! Lord, behold I cannot speak, for I am a child; but the Lord said unto me, Say not that I am a child, for thou shalt go unto all that I shall send thee; and whatsoever I command thee thou shalt speak." It was likewise with Hosea, Ezekiel and Amos among the herdsmen. The mysterious voice of the Lord told them to go, and they promptly obeyed. The first class, as we have designated them, were the most notable. They were as a rule bold, fearless and pointed in their addresses, regardless of smiles or frowns. Our imagination can draw the appearance of one of these wonderful men before us. We see him with rugged countenance, flowing hair, stern voice, clothed with the skin of beasts, or in garb worn by the peasantry, and with keen eyes flashing—as it were—the message of their mission. Sometimes they appear suddenly in the presence of a rabble multitude, at the door of the temple, or in the presence of a king, or meet some one while on a journey to do some act highly offensive to the Lord, and, with a thunder-like voice, pronounce a doleful message from God to them, and and then disappear as mysteriously as they came. And if, in our day, one of those inspired messengers should appear in a church congregation some Sunday morning, just as the people were about to engage in their formal worship, and should suddenly pronounce words of condemnation against those who came with but a form of Godliness, and were he to single them out one by one, telling them, You draw nigh to God with your lips, but your hearts are far from Him; and suppose he should tell them of their unchristian discriminations, of the contempt with which they look upon the poor, of the bitterness they entertain against those whom God in His wisdom has permitted to be born with a darker complexion; and should he sternly rebuke the rich for oppressing and grinding the life out of the poor, by refusing to reward them properly for services rendered, and tell in detail, in words that could be distinctly understood, of all the inhuman deeds committed against those who could not defend themselves, what would be the result of such a message?

It seems to me that if an earthquake of extraordinary force should occur, it would not produce a greater consternation. And what would the minister think of his course of procedure, who attempts to declare the word of God to the people and so arrange his subject as to evade the duty of pointing out their wrongs? I imagine there would be such a stir, with both pastor and people, they would go down in the dust of humility and cry against themselves. It is also known the prophets were often abused and even murdered. In one period of Elijah's time the persecution of these servants of God became so great many were slain, others were faint-hearted, being overcome with fear, for they were all doomed to death. It would seem there were two classes of prophets; one, those who were moved by the Spirit to go forth bearing messages without having passed through the preparatory schools; some were without the meager education the ordinary people were taught; indeed, it might be said, many were without any knowledge of letters, but God took them up and demonstrated the possibility of an unlearned man's powers to accurately comprehend and declare future events through the agency of the Holy Spirit. The work of this class was somewhat peculiar. They wrote and posted no messages along the highways to be read by those passing through the land, but delivered them to the person or persons concerned face to face, except in a few instances when one was sent to perform a work in their stead, as was the case when Jehu was anointed to be the tenth king of Israel.

Sometimes the work of these prophets was confined to a single case, as that of the young Levite in Jehoshaphat's time, when a confederate army was marching against Jerusalem. The other class were those who were especially trained for the work in the several schools which seem to have originated in the time of Samuel. There were schools located at Gibeah, Naioth, Bethel, Gilgal, Jericho and Mt. Carmel; in these, young men were carefully trained in the religion of the Hebrews, to conduct the services and to teach the people the will of God. These doctrines were in opposition to the religion established upon the rotten foundation of idol worship; therefore, they were antagonized by the kings and other authorities who followed the teachings of those whose god was not the Lord. This class, in addition to their teaching as to the proper and only true worship, would write messages and post them along the public highways for the good of all who read them. But we need not have a prophet sent to warn us against the toleration and practice of such conduct. One has been here, the greatest of all prophets, even the author of them, whose voice can be heard in thunder-tones by all who will give attention. He has had our duty, which must be observed by all generations, plainly recorded: "As ye would that men should do unto you, do ye also unto them."

The prophets were reformers of the people; they exerted their uttermost powers to keep them in the ways of the Lord, but many living in their day lost sight of the words of warning until it was too late; their fate came finding them away from God. It is, therefore, easily discerned who were the divinely appointed men and who were false. The words of the self-constituted prophets died with them, and were buried in the same grave. But the predictions of the true prophets (many of them) are with us to-day. Their prophecies are given us in detail in the Scriptures so distinctly that evidences of their fulfillment are developed in numerous instances to those living in this age, which are powerful demonstrations of the divine authenticity of the men who uttered the predictions. Every one who reads the Holy Scriptures cannot fail (if he takes time to examine them carefully) to see the prophecies continue through both the Old and New Testaments, embracing the vast extent from the fall of man to the end of time, and that at first they were delivered at long intervals, but at length they became more frequent, and were uniformly carried on in the line of one people, the seed of Abraham, who were separated from the rest of mankind to be the unyielding witnesses of the true God and the custodians of His precious oracles; and that with some intermission the spirit of prophecy continued with men down to the close of the life of Malachi.

That Jesus and His apostles exercised the same power in the most conspicuous manner, and that they left various predictions on record of a most sublime and glorious character, are yet to be developed, but are just as sure to be accomplished as if already fulfilled, for the mouth of the Lord hath spoken them. From the beginning of the kingdom of Israel to the end, it was found necessary to have these prophetic reformers constantly engaged in urging the people to abandon idolatry and return to the God of their fathers; and there was no time in the history of this people when they needed the teachings of the prophets more than when Ahab was ruling. As has been intimated, this notoriously wicked king ventured beyond the limits of the idol-worship established by Jeroboam and adopted by his successors, and did just what his evil heart inclined to. His reign over Israel was one of the most remarkable for idol worship in the annals of their history. He was not only an admirer of the idolatrous examples of Jeroboam, but leaped beyond them, and planted his kingdom in the very heart of that practiced by the heathen or that so fondly adored by Ethbaal, king of Phœnicia and father of Jezebel.

When Jeroboam established the calf worship it was more intended as a state religion than to settle down in idolatry. That is, he wished to confine his subjects within the bounds of the northern kingdom, and thereby lead their minds from the worship at Jerusalem. It was a cunning deception, leading the people to believe that they were paying due homage to the Lord, by presenting their devotions to the images. It was indeed idolatry in disguise, and the entering wedge which sundered the people from the God of their fathers. But Ahab was not content with that form of worship; he seems to have entertained an opinion, he should be looked upon as deity, and lost no time in introducing every scheme his wicked heart could conceive to bring about the result. It was a matter of impossibility to firmly establish the worship of Baal (the religion his wife sacredly adored and lent her strongest influence to establish it in Israel), and hold to the form adopted by Jeroboam, and greatly admired by the people. He, therefore, caused the calf worship to be abolished, and planted the Baal worship in its stead. Then the new idol was generally endorsed by the state and adored as god. The kingdom had had several severe blows from its own hand, but this was the most serious of all. It was a willful departure from God, and a wholesale turning over to Baal.

During their fifty-six years of calf worship, under the guise of paying devotions to the God of their fathers through them, God bore it with great patience and chided them in various ways, sending prophets to them, who in ungarnished terms denounced their fostered inclinations to evil, and told them of the ultimate end of their conduct; but they went from bad to worse, until they compelled the Lord to withdraw His hand of protection from them and give the kingdom over to the keeping of Baal. Having ignored the teachings of Moses, Samuel and others who had been raised up for their betterment, they lapsed into the deepest slums of iniquity. At the same time it is but natural to suppose, Jezebel, whose ambition to supplant the existing state religion by that she ardently loved, did all she could to welcome and establish the Baal form of worship throughout the kingdom, putting a law in practical force that any who refused to adopt it, were doomed to terrible persecutions; the real torture of which could only be known by those who were the victims. Ahab was not inclined to build a temple to Baal at Bethel, the headquarters of the calf worship; he, therefore, caused one to be erected in the city of Samaria of a stupendous character, both in proportion and embellishment, as the headquarters of the services of Baal. Fragments of this temple remain to the present; and a grove was also prepared and dedicated to the new divinities at Jezreel where four hundred priests were employed.

These gorgeous preparations and elaborate ceremonies so completely enchanted the people, they fondly adored them and were ready to slay any one who avowed their intention to worship the true God. The altars that had been erected to the Lord were torn down, and others were set up to Baal in their stead. The prophets of the Lord were slain, and those of Baal were appointed in their stead. The crisis had come when the large majority of the people in the northern kingdom determined to bring the whole people to Baal, if not by common consent, they should submit by force. The music, dances, and songs of praise that were fondly lavished upon the idols, were at times tumultuous, so that it seems as if the whole people had become wild over their new state religion, and Baal was the cry from all quarters by old, young, wise and ignorant; all sang songs of adoration to Baal in exulting strains. Just then when the enthusiasm of the people was the most marked, their hopes highest, their joys brightest, their shouts loudest, and their prospect of future prosperity most encouraging, a strange man, whom they had not seen or even heard of, suddenly appears. He had no one with him, and from his general bearing one would suppose him to be a man whose calling was not by any means enviable. His manner was uncouth, his step firm with an air of independence and carelessness, his expression was stern and bold; his voice was heavy, impressive and daring; his garments were composed of sheep-skin, and his girdle was leather; he walked with the dignity of a king, although his appearance was like a green countryman, who knew nothing of the courtesy common to city life; yet he moved on in this unusual way to the residence of the king, and suddenly appears before the palace, in the august presence of the mighty king of Israel with a special message from God. Who was the stranger, and from whence came he? It was the prophet Elijah, a native of Gilead, but of unknown parentage and early history. All we can learn of his early life is, he was born east of the Jordan, somewhere among the mountains of Gilead; his bearing gave evidence that he was trained in the highlands and looked much like the wandering Bedouins of the present time, who are often met in Palestine and Syria. Elijah had been commissioned of the Lord to cross the Jordan and go over to Jezreel with a special message to Ahab. It was not lengthy, but woeful as to the future of Israel.

This careless-looking man did not shrink from the responsible duty, nor did he go down to Joppa and embark for some other country, rather than go to the people, who were swallowed up in idolatry, but fearlessly went directly to him to whom he was sent, without alarm, or offering any apology for his coming, nor did he present himself to the haughty Ahab in an humble way. He was bearing a message to a king from the King of kings, under whose protection he had the liberty to go with manly boldness and with an uncompromising expression depicted upon his countenance, and with undaunted earnestness flashing from his eyes. When such a man, who was unbidden, unknown and uncouth, approached the king of Israel, it must have been an exciting scene, especially so when he began his short speech with a sacred oath, and then pronounced the calamity that was at the door. If an unexpected thunderbolt had struck the palace, it would not have excited more alarm than the words of the stranger who stood before the king. The prophet did not dress his message with an alluring introduction charged with flattery, but began at once to disclose his mission in the strongest and most positive terms at his command. "As the Lord the God of Israel liveth, before whom I stand, there shall not be dew nor rain these three years, but according to my word." This was an astonishing message, one that foretold a pending calamity, freighted with great distress and death; yet it was but the beginning of a continuous flow of Divine indignation, that would not stop until the kingdom should be leveled with the dust, and its inhabitants led into captivity.

When the message had been delivered, the prophet did not wait to hear the king's reply, for none was needed; but as suddenly as was his coming he departed, leaving the king to ponder the words of his strange visitor. Ahab, in his blindness, allowed himself to become enraged and swore vengeance against Elijah. It may have been he did not wish to show weakness in the presence of Jezebel, who was ever ready to cheer him and prompt him to deeds of violence on the least seeming provocation. He resolved to have the man of God put to death, and commissioned his officers to hunt him down and slay him. But where was he to be found? No one knew. (1 Kings xvii. 1).

It seems not to have occurred to them that the God of heaven, who sent Elijah would surely protect him against the wrath of wicked Ahab. So they made a diligent search for him, but could not apprehend him or hear of him through any one. Where is he? was the anxious inquiry escaping thousands of lips.

ELIJAH'S RETREAT.

It is highly probable all the officers of state, high and low, were hunting God's messenger with excited eagerness, hoping to have the honor of bearing the news to Ahab that the daringly arrogant fellow, whose presence had disturbed him so much, had been hunted down and slain. But the Lord had provided a place of security for His servant, and arranged for his sustenance there for a year. It is remarkable that Elijah did not go east of the Jordan to elude the officers in search of him, but was hiding within a few miles from the place where he delivered the words of his message to Ahab. He, being directed by the Spirit of the Lord, fled to the narrow confines of the brook Cherith, and made his home in one of the solitary caves in a deep and wild ravine (traditionally) located on its northeastern bank, a few miles north of Jericho. There were no fears lurking in the breast of Elijah as to his safety, for he knew the Lord would sustain him amid the rugged clefts of the Cherith, just as He did while living at the house of his childhood, among the mountains of Gilead. There were four or five hundred more prophets in Israel against whom Ahab vented his wrath, Jezebel, his wife, being the chief directress of the massacre. Obadiah, who was chief of the household, took a hundred of the prophets secretly from the slaughtering huntsmen and hid them in caves by fifties, and fed them with bread and water, without the knowledge of their wicked persecutors. Some of the number, it is feared, became timid and changed their conduct so as to please Ahab, or refused to pronounce as before against the idol worshipers. The brook, which was Elijah's only water supply, became dry. This was not an uncommon event, as some have supposed, but an annual occurrence. This brook is a winter torrent, which carries off the water during the rainy season from the heights along its course, and receives other small streams caused by the rains. But when these feeders fail to supply it the water ebbs, day after day, until the brook becomes dry. But it is reasonable to suppose its water gave out earlier the season Elijah was hiding there because of the lack of the usual rains. The time had come when the people throughout the kingdom hopefully looked for the return of rain, to replenish their cisterns, which were about exhausted, but no rain fell. Then Ahab and Jezebel, who doubtless in their madness were eager for the life-blood of Elijah, began to awaken and remember the words uttered by the strange visitor, who so abruptly approached the presence of his august majesty, and told him there would be a cessation of rain and dew for three years. Soon a scene of desolation was prominent over the whole kingdom. The fruitful fields and vineyards, the perennial springs and streams became dry. The fig, olive and all other trees began to droop under the pressure of the drought. The cattle and flocks were dying in astounding numbers, while the people were famishing. Elijah's water-supply was also cut off, for the brook went dry. But the Lord had made other provisions, as He always does for those who follow Him. He ordered him to Zarephath, the Sarepta of the New Testament, a city near the coast north of Tyre, and gave him a home in the house of a poor widow. It is noteworthy that each of the places selected for the prophet were such as would not be suspected by those who were hunting him. It did not enter their minds he would be among the rugged clefts of Cherith, where the needed friendly aid to sustain him could not be had, nor did they suppose he would escape to any of the cities of Phœnicia, because he was religiously unfriendly to the people and could expect no protection from them. But the Lord chose these places for him and raised up friends to His servant in a marvelous and miraculous way. The first work of mercy the prophet did on entering Zarephath, was a miracle which recruited the woman's meal and oil until the return of rain.

The famine had waxed sore, even in Phœnicia, and when Elijah drew near the house the Lord had selected for his home while there, the poor, heart-broken widow came out of her door to perform the last domestic work of her life. Her meal, except a handful, was entirely gone, and the cruse of oil was also about gone, except enough to prepare a small cake of bread, all of which she was preparing to bake for herself and son to eat—then die. But the prophet being weary with his long journey, hungry and thirsty, asked her, in connection with the water she was about to get him, to bring also a cake. The poor woman related her sad situation, telling Elijah of the small amount of meal and oil she had, but the man of God assured her, if she did as he requested, her meal and oil should not give out until the Lord should send rain. Ordinarily this would have been an exorbitant request, but, under the circumstances, she was simply blessing herself abundantly by blessing God's servant a little. This act of the widow met the approval of the Almighty; she did not refrain from giving a part

of the small remnant of meal she had to a stranger, and did not fail
to receive her reward. The least we may suppose as to her faith henceforth, is she became soundly drawn from the faith of Baal-worship and
served the God of Elijah. This did not take place, however, until her
only son, who died, was restored alive to her by Elijah, for she said,
when he was returned to her, "Now, I know that thou art a man of
God, and that the word of the Lord is in thy mouth in truth." After
a time it so happened, the famine was raging so greatly in Israel, the
king, his household, his full-blooded horses and cattle were threatened
with death.

Seeing the imminent peril the royal household was placed in, Ahab
became alarmed and concluded he would go himself in search of water
and grass for the perishing animals, hoping he might find some green
spot somewhere within the domain of his kingdom; and a running
stream, though it might be very shallow, that would serve to keep the
beasts alive. That a thorough canvass of the kingdom might be carefully
made, the king requested Obadiah, who had charge of the affairs of
his household, to assist in making the search. It is just that we say,
Obadiah was in great sympathy with the prophets and the remaining few who adhered to the religion of their fathers, and he reverenced
and feared the Lord (1 Kings xvii. 10-24). It is likely he was many
times found in the same attitude of the earnestly devout worshipers
who bowed their knee to Baal. For it is not perceivable how he could
be in the confidence of Ahab without indicating his belief in and
devotion to the worship of their god. It is our opinion, therefore, that
while Obadiah often bowed his knees before Baal, he did not bow to
him in his heart; but like Naaman, when he entered with his master
the house of Rimmon, he only bowed his knee, but his heart took no
pleasure in it. These two men of high distinction divided the whole
kingdom between them, to go in diligent search for water and grass
among the ravines and low lands far and near; Ahab going in one
direction, and Obadiah in another.

ELIJAH'S RETURN TO AHAB.

This occurred about the time that the Lord ordered Elijah to appear
again before Ahab, which was about the end of the third year of the
famine. The prophet had left his temporary home in Sarepta, and was
again in Israel, wending his way towards Jezreel to meet Ahab, in the
same stern and fearless manner he approached the king on his first
visit. Obadiah was out earnestly hunting for grass and water, having
no idea of meeting the man of God, for whom a relentless search was

being made, and against whom vengeance had been sworn; but Elijah went on fearlessly, for the Lord had sent him. He said to Obadiah (who knew him), "Go tell thy lord, Behold Elijah is here," and assured him he would appear before the king that day. The prophet, true to his word, met Ahab, not to declare the continuance of the famine, but to assure him that the end of it had come, and there would be an abundance of rain. It is probable that when the king saw Elijah all the indignation of his soul was kindled against him for a moment, but was suppressed just as soon as the messenger of the Lord opened his mouth to him. "Is it thou, thou troubler of Israel?"

Elijah was not alarmed at the presence of the man who had sworn vengeance against him, but addressed him with the same sternness he did when he met him three years prior. In reply to the king he said, "I have not troubled Israel, but thou and thy father's house, in that ye have forsaken the commandments of the Lord, and thou hast followed Baalim." Is it not marvelous that Ahab at once seems to have lost all the bitterness he so long entertained for Elijah, and became as though he was but a subject standing in the presence of a king? Indeed Elijah did, for a time, ascend in point of power above the king of Israel and commanded him to do a work which was faithfully fulfilled. So it may be said of the prophet, he for a short period while filling his mission as a divine messenger, acted as king of Israel in that he commanded the king to assemble all the people before him (Elijah) on Mount Carmel, and the four hundred and fifty prophets of Baal, and the four hundred prophets of Astaroth. In compliance with the request of the messenger of the Most High, Ahab had messengers dispatched calling the people to meet Elijah on Mount Carmel; and when they had come, the man of God asked in thunder tones the momentous question, which has been repeated with equal earnestness by many thousands who have been chosen messengers under the Lord Jesus Christ, "How long halt ye between two opinions? If Jehovah be God, follow Him; but if Baal, then follow him."

The people followed Baal because they wished to please Ahab, and be favored with the positions of state at his disposal; at the same time they wanted to hold to the God of heaven, that they might respect the opinions of their fathers. But their inclination for the worship of Baal was fast absorbing them so completely, they were claiming for him the same authority the true follower and prophet of the Almighty God claimed for Him. Now Elijah wished to have the matter fully and fairly tested, that it might be settled for all time. Therefore the stern, dauntless prophet stood the lone representative of the God of heaven, against eight hundred and fifty of those representing Baal, who had a host who were in open sympathy with them. It may be that Obadiah and a few of the seven thousand who continued true to the God of their fathers were present, but did not dare make known their preference. Hence Elijah practically stood alone; yet he was brave, confident, and full of good cheer. The prophet proposed that a settlement of the question, as to who had the right to be acknowledged the true God, be made; and that there might be no disadvantage taken, he gave the Baalites the first opportunity to test the authority and reality of their god.

The matter of demonstrative answers to prayer had never been tested by the officials of this heathen deity, and yet they had full confidence in him, and believed he would make known himself in showers of fire that day, to the jubilant gratification of all the people assembled on the mount and to all Israel throughout. The mode of testation was the consumption of a sacrificial bullock laid upon a new altar, expressly erected for the tremendous event. They, after carefully arranging their sacrifice, began to send out a wild and tumultuous cry, "Come, Baal, O, Baal, hear us!" But he did not hear them, nor come in that extreme moment of anxious hope. To give them a good chance to vindicate their cause, Elijah told them tauntingly and ironically to "Cry aloud, for he is a god; either he is amusing himself or is gone aside, or is on a journey, or peradventure he sleepeth and must be awakened." Then the scene that followed must have been amusing to the prophet, for they became really wild with clamorous shouts, and dancing about the altar, even cutting themselves with their lances. But Baal did not come. Jezebel, who was equally concerned as to the result of the test, no doubt heard the cries of her confident prophets, and sat at the highest window in the palace of Jezreel, or in the tower, anxious to witness the flow of fire stream from heaven in answer to the faithful call of the priests of Baal; and Ahab, who had become greatly humbled in the presence of Elijah, was stationed at a convenient distance from the scene in hopeful expectation of a triumphant victory for Baal.

After these priests had made a thorough test of the capacity of their god and signally failed up to the time of the offering of the evening sacrifice, Elijah, the lone representative of the God of heaven, called the people around him, that they might witness there was no unfairness in his dealing with this monstrous test. He then rebuilt the altar of the Lord that had been thrown down, and took up twelve stones, each one representing a tribe of Israel, and built an altar in the name of his God. He cut the bullock in pieces and put it upon the altar, and then drew water from the perennial spring (which is still located) and poured, or caused to be, twelve barrels on the altar, so that the bullock, wood and altar were overflowing, and the trench around it was filled. Now all is in readiness for the test of Elijah's God. The prophet was not only confident, but full of assurance. He drew near the altar and prayed, saying: "O, Lord God of Abraham, of Isaac and of Jacob, let it be known this day that Thou art God in Israel, and that I am Thy servant, and that I have done all these things at Thy word. Hear me, O Lord, hear me that this people may know that Thou, Lord, art God, and that Thou hast turned their hearts back again."

ANSWER TO ELIJAH'S PRAYER.

At the moment Elijah had finished his pathetic prayer, fire from the Lord God fell from heaven, consuming the sacrifice, the wood, and to the astonishment of all, the very stones of which the altar was composed were melted by the fire, and the water in the trench was consumed by the flames. When the multitude of witnesses saw it, they suddenly fell upon their faces and cried out, "The Lord, He is God; the Lord, He is God." Elijah immediately became the acknowledged master of the situation; therefore the people, and even Ahab, stood ready to observe whatsoever he commanded. All the false prophets of Baal, without an exception, were captured. They were then led down to the foot of the mountain and slain by the brook Kishon. Then Elijah came to Ahab, who seems to have been as meek as any of his subjects, and said: "Get thee up; eat and drink, for there is the sound of abundance of rain." The king reverentially obeyed, for Elijah was the commander-in-chief for the time being, and every order was carefully observed. But there was yet another thing to be done according to prophecy—the rain which had been stopped for three years must come in abundance.

The man of God ascended to the top of Carmel in great humiliation, and sent his servant up to another peak to look toward the sea for signs of the gathering clouds, for he was expecting rain, but he soon returned without having seen any visible indications of the pending storm. But the prophet sent him again, even until he had gone seven times. Then he reported he saw a cloud about the size of a man's hand, as if rising out of the sea. Elijah sent word to Ahab to have his chariot in readiness, to make all possible haste to his palace, lest the rain should prevent him. Such a message would doubtless have been as an idle tale to Ahab under ordinary circumstances; but it came from Elijah, and he believed it to be true, notwithstanding there were no indications of a storm as far as he could see. Elijah ran before the chariot of Ahab, like an Egyptian courier, to the gate of Jezreel. In the meantime the heavens became black with clouds, and the rain descended in torrents. Ahab, having witnessed the wonderful demonstration of the power of God through Elijah, did not come forward like an honorable man and destroy every image of Baal he had set up, and order the people to return to the religion of their fathers, but went home sheepishly to Jezebel and told her all that had come to pass. The woman was viciously angry, and sent a messenger to Elijah with this woeful message: "So let the gods do to me and more also if I make not thy life as the life of one of them by to-morrow about this time."

When Elijah heard this, he became alarmed and fled to Beersheba, in Judah, and left his servant there. The conduct of Elijah has been harshly criticised by some people because he allowed a woman to so alarm him; but it should be remembered that all that the prophet did of a superior character, was by the direction and under the influence of the Holy Spirit, and without its dictation he was simply an ordinary man. It would have been a hard thing to have found a man who, under the circumstances, would not have done the same. When the man of God had finished the work assigned him on Mt. Carmel, and escorted Ahab to the gate of Jezreel, all that was intended for him to do at that time was accomplished. It should be remembered, also, that Elijah was of the class of prophets that were given certain messages to carry immediately, and not as those whose prophecies were many centuries developing. He did not write his predictions as did those whose names are used as the title of a number of books in the Old Testament, but was a reformer of men, and a messenger from the Lord, going from man to man, rebuking and commending as the case might be. If God had ordered Elijah to carry a message to Jezebel, he would have returned with the messenger that she sent to him, and delivered it. It was the Lord's will he should do as he did, and caused Jezebel to notify him of her intention, that he might have ample time in which to escape. It was not the will of the Lord to reveal to Elijah the calamities that should visit Ahab, Jezebel, the city of Samaria, and the whole kingdom, which would be of such a destructive character that the king should be swept from his throne and the nation brought down to the dust; but it seems He intended to show the prophet, who, but a few hours prior, was the hero of Mt. Carmel, that he was but a frail man, and could do nothing without divine help.

ELIJAH'S FLIGHT.

It may have been that Elijah's triumph over the eight hundred and fifty priests of Baal, and over Ahab himself, would have caused him to become a little pompous; therefore, the Lord allowed this sudden withdrawal of spiritual force to keep His servant humble and ever mindful that he was but an humble instrument through whom the Almighty worked His sovereign will. When Elijah was moved by the Spirit to leave Beersheba and flee into the wilderness, he seems to have comprehended the magnitude of the situation, and left the lad, his servant (who, a far-fetched tradition says, was the widow's son whom he restored to life, and the Jonah who was sent to Nineveh), and went alone to the solitary wilderness, and sat down under the shady branches of a juniper tree, and wished he might be permitted to die. Here we find the bold, indomitable, indefatigable Elijah, weary, thirsty, hungry, and preferring death rather than the ordeal through which he was passing. But the eye of the Lord was watching him to guide and comfort him along the lonely road. While he slept, an angel brought him bread and water, which strengthened him forty days and nights. "The eye of the Lord is over the righteous, and His ear is open to their cry." Elijah journeyed from thence to Mt Horeb, and took refuge in one of the huge caves, once more far from those who sought his life, and in a place far more dreary than his rocky chamber by the brook Cherith. He was a ready man, and moved by divine command the moment he was called upon.

It did not matter to him what the character of the message was, to whom it was to be delivered, nor how far he must go to bear it; he was ready and willing for the task. There were many prophets sent among the people, but none more impressive and distinguished than this stern Tishbite, whose second coming was confidently expected prior to the advent of the Messiah, to recognize the chafed Hebrews who were groaning under the reward of their hands. When Malachi was finishing his prophecies, he referred to Elijah as the great central figure in turning the hearts of those who had become estranged towards each other; and it is reasonable to believe his name was carried down through that long period of over four hundred years of profound silence, which causes a deep and dark chasm to be placed between the closing of the Old Dispensation and the beginning of the New. This idea is clear from the statement of the woman of Sychar to our Lord at Jacob's Well. "We know Elias must first come and restore all things." And those who were about the cross when Jesus cried out,

"Eloi, Eloi, lama sabachthani," supposed He was calling for Elijah, and waited to see if he would come and deliver Him. It is worthy of remark that the Lord never removes one of His messengers from labor without having some one to take his place, if another is needed; for it occurs at times that the entire work belonging to certain developments is allotted to one person, so that in hundreds of instances we have but one man for some peculiar work, whose singular characteristics and fitness prepared him to discharge the duties enjoined. There was in fact but one Moses, one Samuel, one Elijah; and so we might trace this line of singularly fitted men down to our time, and find them in the persons of John Wesley, Richard Allen, Daniel A. Payne, John Brown, Abraham Lincoln, Charles Sumner, and others. When the time of their demise came, the living wondered who would take their places and carry on the work they were so faithfully pursuing; but as time passed it was found that the work in this particular was so well developed that another to follow in their identical sphere was not needed. The Lord appointed Elijah to perform a peculiar work that required a man with just such singular fitness as he possessed; one who had the courage to strike heavy and effectual blows at the very heart of idol-worship, and cause the powers that upheld it to tremble. But before the time came for Elijah to be called from the field, God made choice of another who was to enter upon the work in his room, but conduct it under different circumstances and in another way.

ELIJAH COMMANDED TO RETURN.

When the Lord came to Elijah, while he no doubt was in deep meditation in his rocky home in Mt. Horeb, and informed him, to his great astonishment, there were yet seven thousand in Israel who had not bowed to Baal, He commanded him to "return on the way to the wilderness of Damascus: and when thou comest, thou shalt anoint Hazael to be king over Syria; and Jehu, the son of Nimshi, shalt thou anoint to be king over Israel; and Elisha, the son of Shaphat of Abel-meholah, shalt thou anoint to be prophet in thy room." This young man, who seems to have known nothing but country life, having been reared as a husbandman, was chosen of God to the high official office of Elijah. The prophet went from his solitary hiding with the full intention of fulfilling the commands he had received, but only had an opportunity of performing one of them in person. He anointed the man named as his successor the first of all, instead of going down to Damascus to anoint Hazael to reign in the stead of Ben-hadad, or Jehu to take Ahab's place.

We know human beings are so constituted they are seldom willing that another should succeed them in honorable and exalted positions, whether in church or state, notwithstanding the burden of more than three-score and ten years, united with failing health which disqualifies them to discharge the duties their position enjoins. But there was no feeling existing in Elijah, for he manifested no disposition to stand in the way of another whom God had chosen. It was important Elisha should be anointed and receive a primary knowledge of the work before he (Elijah) was called home; others could fill his place in setting apart Hazael and Jehu, but no one could anoint his successor. Therefore, he performed the more important duty first. We feel confident that every fair-minded man will indorse Elijah's conduct in this all-important matter, and his affectionate disposition towards Elisha the remainder of the time allotted him before the chariot separated them. Elijah took the young man as his son from the day he anointed him, and acted like a loving father to the end of his pilgrimage on earth. Indeed they seemed more like close companions than predecessor and successor, for they affectionately lived together, going from place to place with all the fondness that they could possess. Nor was Elisha willing to leave Elijah when the day of separation came, although he could not fully enter upon his work until his father had left the world. This young man's conduct towards his senior was a manly example that would be of great benefit to many in our day if they would follow it.

It should be borne in mind, Elijah did not leave the world for several years after his return from Mt. Horeb, and pronounced doleful predictions against Ahab and his house. After the separation, Elisha devoted much time to the sons of the prophets, giving them counsel in the work they were to pursue as teachers in the vineyard of the Lord. On one occasion his presence saved many of them from a sad and deadly calamity; when the poisonous plant had been unintentionally put in the pot of pottage. He was active in admonishing the kings, and giving such warnings from time to time as the Spirit of the Lord dictated. One of his great acts was the advice to Naaman the leper, as has been stated. There is an incident connected with the life of Elisha most touching and instructive. It was his custom to make frequent visits to Shunem; and in time, the attention of a wealthy woman, whose household consisted of herself and husband only, was drawn to him. She is called in the Bible, "a great woman;" and she proved herself worthy of this distinguished recognition, as her history shows. It occurred one day, when the prophet entered the town, she gave him a cordial invitation to stop at her house any time he passed that way; she also proposed to her husband to build a special room apart from the main building "for the man of God." When it was finished she furnished it with whatever was necessary for his comfort.

Elisha was grateful for her generous considerations and felt himself under obligations to her, and felt it his duty to do any kindness for the family he could, whenever an opportunity was presented. He asked what returns he should make to repay her for her favor; asking if he should speak of her commendably to the king or the captain of the hosts. But the woman did not do this deed of charity that she might be extolled or brought into high favor with the powers that be, but for "the man of God's" sake. "I dwell among mine own people," said she, or she would have Elisha understand she took more pleasure with her husband and home, than to be in company with the king or the high officials of the kingdom. Elisha was informed by Gehazi she had no children, and told her she would be a mother (2 Kings iv. 13). The statement seemed to her so very unlikely, she said to Elisha, "Nay, my lord, thou man of God, do not lie to thine hand-maid." But the prediction of the prophet was fulfilled, and this woman in advanced age embraced a son, who seemed to have been the idol of her heart. At length the child became suddenly ill, at a time when Elisha was not there, but at his own home at Mt. Carmel. This little child finally died in its mother's arms. It was a most bitter affliction to her; yet she had strong faith in Elisha, and without any demonstration of grief, she laid her dead child on the bed of the prophet, and fled with haste across the plain, enduring the pressure of the burning sun, to the home of Elisha on the mountain.

When he saw her coming he was impressed that something of a very urgent character impelled her to come to him so far through the intense heat, and being anxious to know what the cause of her visit was, he sent Gehazi to meet her and inquire if all was well. But she was not willing to make known her sorrows to the young man, so she kept the object of her mission within her own sad heart until she came into the house of the "man of God." On arriving at the house she fell in an exhausted state at his feet. When she sufficiently recovered to break the news, she told what had happened to her son. Elisha immediately sent his servant ahead with his staff to lay it on the child, for the woman would not leave him, so he arose and went with her. On entering the room where the dead child lay he prayed to God from the depth of his soul for his restoration, and soon it revived and was restored to the mother. When the famine was raging in the land this woman, by advice of Elisha, left her home, and went into Philistia and remained seven years. On her return home she found that her property had been seized by an enemy.

When court opened she went up to lay her complaint before the king. On her arrival at the palace Gehazi was there relating the whole circumstance; and seeing her enter, exclaimed: "My Lord! O! king, this is the woman and her son whom Elisha restored!" After hearing her story the king ordered her property returned with all the benefits it brought during her absence. There seems to have been a divine purpose, not known to Elisha at the time he turned his attention towards Samaria as a residence, instead of Bethel, for he arrived there just about the time the two kings, Jehoram or Joram of Israel and Jehoshaphat of Judah, had formed an alliance to go up against Mesha, king of Moab, and his allies, as mentioned in another chapter (2 Kings viii. 2), and he gave Joram the needed advice for Jehoshaphat's sake. It occurred also that a poor widow, who had been the wife of one of the prophet's sons, was in deep distress: her husband, who had been very poor, died in debt, leaving nothing to settle the amount due his creditors. And as the law permitted the person seeking satisfaction to seize all the dead man left, even his wife and children, to recover his money, the creditor, taking advantage of this law, was about to take the two sons of this widow to make them work for him until the debt was settled. This rule still obtains (we are informed) in Damascus, Bagdad and other places in the East. She complained to Elisha of her situation, and the prophet asked what she had in the house; she told him, nothing but a pot of oil. Elisha ordered her to borrow all the pots she could find among the neighbors far and near that were not in use; this she did, fully expecting good results, although she did not at first know what the prophet would do with them. But she felt it her duty to carry out to her uttermost ability the advice given. Elisha told her, when she had finished bringing the vessels, she should shut the door upon herself and sons so as to be secluded from any one, and pour out in all the vessels, and set aside those that were filled. This the woman and her sons carefully did. When all were filled, she went to Elisha and told him. He said, "Go sell thy oil and pay thy debt, and live, thou and thy children of the rest." It is useless to add more than this—a poor widow's heart was made to rejoice, her sons were saved from bondage, and the name of God was glorified.

It rarely occurs that men whose dispositions so widely differ live together such a long time as Elijah and Elisha did in harmony. But we find these two servants of God just as lamb-like as if they possessed the same peculiar characteristics, but as men there was a vast contrast between them. In the first place, Elijah was odd in his dress, so much so he was known by it; it is likely that many who met him, who had never seen him before, knew he was Elijah by his clothes. He was in that respect like many who live in our time, that seem to take pleasure in being odd from their fellows. In connection with the oddness of Elijah's dress, he was equally so in his general bearing, yet he was kind, manly and sympathetic. But Elisha was full of life, having gentle manners and mild speech; and yet between the two a fervent friendship was kindled that continued as long as they remained together. (2 Kings iii.; iv.) When Elisha was called from his plow to be a prophet he immediately consented to the will of the Lord without a murmur, notwithstanding but little could be expected as to his prosperity at that time, for the whole land in which his services were wanted, had gone astray after idols. And when the mantle of Elijah fell upon him he entered the work under different circumstances and a heavier responsibility than he had yet experienced.

It was not until the translation of his father that he was to become a full-fledged prophet; hitherto he was a disciple sitting at the feet of Elijah. But the trouble came to him when his father was taken away. It was far more easy for him to divide the Jordan with the sheep-skin mantle, than to stop the flow of idolatry that was prevalent in the land. It was much easier for him to make the bitter waters of the spring of Jericho sweet, than change the bitter water flowing from a wicked heart to a sweet and pure spring from which might flow the water of life. It was much less troublesome to cause the oil to flow into vessels that enabled the widow to save her sons from bondage, than to persuade men to receive the oil of eternal life. One of the greatest examples of rebuke on record, is the calamity that visited the children who made open sport of Elisha while en route to Bethel. It is one that should be deeply impressed upon the minds of the young, that they may feel it necessary to their existence to respect the aged, although they may appear at times somewhat untidy, especially an ambassador of the Lord. It should be carefully taught them that they put themselves in the way of calamity, when they make the people of God the objects of ridicule. The children in question reproachfully cried after Elisha and said, "Go up, thou bald head!" He invoked a visit of divine displeasure upon the children, and immediately two female bears came suddenly upon them while they were enjoying the playful amusement, and slew forty-two of them. Elisha was not insulted as a man, but as God's messenger and successor of Elijah, who the people of Bethel knew well, was to be respected, even at the cost of many lives. It is likely the whole people round about Bethel and throughout eastern Palestine had heard of the mysterious translation of Elijah, and many were glad to learn he had gone, for they feared him. When these children saw the young man coming, whom they had seen passing along the highway with the old prophet, they doubtless proposed to have a little fun to themselves. But the Lord intended that the man he appointed to take the place of Elijah should be reverenced.

THE LESSON IT TAUGHT.

Therefore the lesson was a lasting memorial for those who did not share in the fate of those who attempted to make sport of the young messenger of the Lord. This pungent rebuke established the fact that Elisha was a man of God, and sent by him in the room of Elijah. This is not the only insult hurled at him during his official life; but he did not rebuke them in the same way. Yet he did not fail to rebuke them in a manner sufficiently clear to warn others of the results of wicked insults offered him by those who should have sought his counsel.

It is said that Elisha was about to make his home in Bethel, but the conduct of the inhabitants was so vicious he suddenly changed his mind, and went to Samaria. These fearless and determined men went forth inspired of the Lord to bear His message; and they went dauntlessly proclaiming themselves prophets of the Most High, and demanded that their message should be heard and obeyed. But it should be borne in mind that all who claimed to be sent to prophesy were not chosen of God. There were false prophets in those days; that is, men set themselves up as prophets whom God had not ordained, pretending to be divinely inspired (2 Kings ii. 24). And it is noteworthy that a class of men have been found in every age of the church to our day, who claim to be teachers sent of God, that have never been appointed by Him. Indeed we find false prophets were prominent as far back as the time of Moses; they were so active in their work of deception, that it was commanded they should be put to death.

The Hebrews were often alarmed by the declarations of men claiming to be sent of God, who assumed the position of their own accord. Jeremiah says, "The prophets speak lies in My name; I sent them not, neither have I commanded them, neither spoke I unto them; they prophesy unto you a false vision, divination and things of naught and deceit of their heart." Ezekiel was disturbed by them, also, and said,

"The word of the Lord came unto me saying, Son of man, prophesy against these prophets of Israel, and say unto them that prophesy out of their own hearts: Hear ye the word of the Lord. Thus saith the Lord, Woe unto the foolish prophets that follow their own spirit and have seen nothing. O Israel, thy prophets are like the foxes in the desert." It would seem, from the above references, that false prophets acted so much like those whose commission was from God, that it was not easy for the people to distinguish them; and it is not to be wondered at, when we remember the same characters exist to-day in the person of many who attempt to teach God's word simply as a business. It was but a short time after our Lord went to the house of "many mansions," before false teachers came forward and attempted to teach the principles of Christianity, who had not known the love of Christ experimentally.

PART XI.

NAZARETH.

Nazareth the Home of Our Lord—The Visit of Jesus to Galilee—Phœnician Possessions in Galilee—Hamitic Possessions in Galilee—Christ's Removal from Bethlehem—Childhood of Our Lord in Nazareth—Baptism of Jesus—First Miracle—Establishment of the Christian Church—Church of Annunciation—Feeding the Five Thousand—Christ's Social Life—Why Jesus was Rejected—Mount of Precipitation—The Ministry of Our Lord—Village of Gath-hepper.

NAZARETH, THE HOME OF OUR LORD.

NAZARETH, the home of Joseph and Mary, is indeed, a village among the hills; and though it is much lower than its immediate surroundings, it would be regarded as a mountainous city in many parts of our world. Those approaching Nazareth from Endor or Nain can see it five or six miles away. It is situated on the slopes of a basin formed by fourteen high hills; the approach to it from all points is rough, steep and fatiguing; but the view of the village is cut off on the north and northwest on account of the mountains; so that it is not seen until the top of the mountain overlooking it is reached.

It is generally conceded that Nazareth is one of the most prosperous inland towns in Palestine. It is not mentioned in the Old Testament, as nothing transpired there during the old dispensation connecting it with the Holy Scriptures; and it is strikingly strange that Josephus did not mention it. There is no place in Palestine, except Bethlehem and Jerusalem, that is more admired by Christians of all lands and denominations than Nazareth, the home of our Lord's childhood, and where He remained until He began His soul-saving work. It was in this place He suffered much and was bitterly opposed by His own townsmen, who sought to kill Him, just as eagerly as those who afterwards nailed Him to the cross. Nazareth is a very lively place; every one seems to be doing something; it has a large population for its size, which is estimated to be twelve thousand, of whom nine thousand are Christians and three thousand are Moslems.

Strange as it may seem, there is not one Jew living in the village. It is a very secluded place, which is regarded as an essential fitness for

NAZARETH.

the scenes of the history it contains. Although Nazareth is not connected with the sacred history of the old dispensation, it composes a part of the early history of the Christian era, and is mentioned in connection with the visit of the angel who brought the news to the Virgin concerning the birth of Jesus. It is mentioned as the home of Joseph, who was a carpenter, and was espoused to an inestimable maiden named Mary The Lord made choice of her to become the mother of Jesus Christ, whom He promised to the world as a Saviour.

Nazareth, being separated from the scenes of the busy world, and less popular in public estimation than the other villages and towns in the district of Galilee, was chosen as the retired home of the Son of God until He entered upon the work of His holy mission. The inhabitants of this world-renowned village, in the time of Joseph and Mary, were considered by the people of the neighboring communities unworthy of friendly recognition, and, therefore, held the least communion with them possible. These people, living high up amongst the hills of Galilee, grew up rough, and, in many respects, unmanly; so much were they given to gross sins that they were unable to appreciate their own prophet who had been reared among them, whom they knew to be perfect and exemplary from His youth, and had seen Him daily in the town, many of whom, no doubt, had talked with Him. It may be understood how they were regarded by the more advanced people of Galilee and other portions of Palestine. if we consider how greatly Nathaniel, who lived in Cana, about three miles from them, was astonished when he exclaimed, "Can any good come out of Nazareth?" But out of that town, which was so very low in the estimation of all the people round about, came the most holy and distinguished being that our world ever knew.

We know that Jesus was not born in Nazareth, but it was there the first quickening inspiration of mortal life entered His infantile body, and He lived there with His espoused father and virgin mother after His wondrous birth in Bethlehem of Judea, and performed the most of the mighty works He wrought in the district of which Nazareth formed a part. It was His custom to make annual visits up to Jerusalem to celebrate the passover, but He would soon return home in company with His parents. The first bold attack made to take the life of Jesus after the great massacre of the young children in Herod's time, and by his command, was by the people of Nazareth, when He preached that short, pointed and mighty sermon in the synagogue. Such was their anger and murderous excitement, they sought to kill Him, and did succeed in thrusting Him from the house and the city. They even led Him to the brow of the hill now known as the Mount of Precipitation, with the full intention of hurling Him headlong that they might dash Him into the arms of death and thus put a sudden stop to His career. But Jesus, in some way unknown to them, escaped from their midst and prevented the success of their purpose. It must be admitted that the people who were acquainted with Jesus in the town in which He was reared, knew Him to be a most exemplary, pious person from His youth up, or the officials of the synagogue would not have consented to allow Him to officiate on that memorable Sabbath, when they became so greatly enraged that attempts were made to kill Him. Indeed, it was commonly known by those with whom Jesus came in daily contact, that His piety was decidedly more marked than that of any of the devoutly religious in the town; and it is reasonable to suppose that they often spoke of Him as an example for others to follow. As a citizen, He strictly conformed to the law, so that none ever complained of Him as an offender until He began to perform works of great power.

It is likely that Jesus attended the services at the synagogue every Sunday, with Joseph and His mother during His childhood; and it is certain they made it a yearly custom to travel with Him up to Jerusalem to celebrate the great feast. When Jesus stood to read the Scriptures, no one objected; no one said a word against His morals, notwithstanding they knew just who He was and how He had spent much of His life as a townsman with them. It is evident from their conduct that they would have branded Him as one of the foulest of men, could they have found any stains attaching to His character. The keeper of the Sacred Records, who must have known Jesus, had given Him the volume containing that portion of the prediction of Isaiah referring to Himself as the divine healer of men. It so happened that that was the passage that came in the regular order, according to their custom of reading the Scriptures; it was not especially selected for Him; any other person who might have been requested to conduct the reading at that service in the synagogue would have been given the same lesson. Jesus came just in time to read a passage which gave Him a favorable opportunity to introduce Himself as the personage the passage referred to, and invite their adherence to His teachings.

After the reading was concluded, He closed the book, returned it to the minister, then sat down to address the eager listeners. There was something so very inviting in the tone of the Saviour's voice that every one present was drawn firmly towards Him, and all listened with the closest attention to His remarks. According to custom in those days, those conducting the services stood to read, and sat to deliver the address. Our Lord did this in keeping with the form. When beginning to explain the passage He had read, the first utterances surprised them beyond recovery. He said to them, "This day is the Scriptures fulfilled in your ears." When He began to unfold the meaning of the passage they had heard so clearly, those present knew He was referring to Himself. Then they became greatly incensed, and were ready to murder Him, without even the form of a trial. This action proved them to be more lawless than those who crucified Him, for they consented to have a trial, although their purpose was fixed before the authorities took the case under consideration. It was the Sabbath-day, which was supposed to be most sacredly observed by the Jews, and yet they were so indignant that their respect for the sacred day was overruled, so that by unanimous consent they attempted to lynch Him in a most brutal manner. They considered it a crime for a man to work his ox on the Sabbath, but they could commit murder without remorse.

How stinging must have been the words of Jesus to those viciously desperate people when He told them the thoughts they were pondering in their hearts. "Ye will surely say to me, Physician, heal thyself; whatsoever we have heard done in Capernaum, do also here in thy country." It may be seen they had heard of His work of healing down in the capital city of Galilee, and were of the opinion some miracle would be performed by Him at the home of His childhood, but Jesus gave them to understand the inutility of a miraculous work among them by referring to the prophet Elijah, that while there were many widows in Israel who perished by the great famine, he was appointed by the Lord to go over to Sarepta and perform a miracle at the home of a poor widow, which increased her meal and oil until the rain fell. She was a heathen, and had not been taught to fear the Lord, as had been the widows in Israel. Also, He called attention to the many lepers in Israel, and but one person was cured by Elisha and he was a Syrian. The inference is that He had lived in their midst from childhood, and His life, as seen by them, was enough to convince them, to believe without having to perform miracles.

When our Lord returned in the power of the Spirit to Galilee, He did not go immediately to Nazareth to introduce His divine mission, but went to other parts of the province, preaching and teaching in the synagogues, and was glorified in all. From the beginning of His ministry His fame spread so among the people that they sought Him.

Therefore when the time came for Him to return home, the people had received information of His wonderful power, and this should have made them the more anxious to prepare in every way possible that would give evidence of their faith in Him. But selfishness and unbelief overcame them; so much did they manifest their opposition to Christ they were ready to dash out His precious life among the rocks. This action severed the domestic relation with Him and the people of Nazareth, and only on one more occasion did He pay them a spiritual visit. Then He could do nothing for them because of their infidelity, except heal a few sick folks by laying His hands upon them. It may have been an insincere motive that prompted the people to have Christ conduct the service. They, no doubt, were more anxious to see some wonderful miracle performed than to hear the word of God expounded. It should be remembered, the people did not have Jesus conduct the service on the Sabbath He entered the synagogue because they considered Him a master in Israel, for it was not an unusual thing for persons who were not rabbis to address assemblages in synagogues. It was a custom of long standing for men known to be strictly pious to be invited by the officiating ministers to read the Scriptures and explain them to the people. Therefore Jesus was not given an extra honor by being permitted to do so; any other truly pious person would have been invited to do the same. The people were not inclined to bestow any act of high honor upon Christ that they would not willingly confer upon others whom they considered worthy. Those authors who would have us believe that Jesus was accepted as a rabbi because he was permitted to read and expound the Scriptures, are at least guilty of false representation, or of a blunder caused by premature conclusions.

St. Paul was invited under the same rule at Antioch, in Pisidia, as was our Lord at Nazareth and other places The people knew Paul was a very pious man, and from his knowledge of the Scriptures was able to explain them; they, therefore, asked him to conduct a part of the service. The home people heard of the great satisfaction Christ had given many in other synagogues, and the wonders He did among the people, and having, as has been stated, a knowledge of His piety, they became anxious to hear Him. The whole life of our Redeemer was simple, which is a characteristic not generally common with rabbis, and upon no occasion did He allow the people to be misled as to who He was. It is true, in the general acceptation of the word, Christ was a rabbi, but not in the peculiar sense it implies, and it is, therefore, unfair to intimate that our Lord accepted the appointment to address the people at Nazareth under the guise of a Jewish rabbi in the sense in which such officials were known. For while we must freely admit our Lord was a rabbi in the most exalted degree, He was not so recognized at home by the people among whom He lived. It is plain that Christ made no pretentions of the kind, for as soon as He began explaining the Scriptures He endeavored to establish the fact of His mission as Messiah, and not as an ordinary rabbi. He knew what a tumultuous uproar His remarks would produce, but He had the duty to discharge just at this time and place.

CANA OF GALILEE.

It is noteworthy that Jesus did everything at the time it should be done, fearless of what might follow, so that nothing that should have been done to-day was postponed until to-morrow. Therefore, each day had a finished record of all that belonged to it so far as the work of Christ was concerned. The beginning of our Lord's miracles, at Cana and Capernaum, were great agents in causing His fame to be generally circulated. The first miracle was wholly unexpected, as He had not fully entered into the work of demonstrating His divinity through miraculous developments. It may be said the wedding at Cana was the most illustrious one known to the country. Two of the most distinguished people in the world were there. Mary, the mother of Jesus, the most important woman of the globe, was invited, and went over from Nazareth to attend it. It may be that one of the contracting parties was a relative or a very dear friend of the family. Our Lord was also present, having been absent from His mother preparing for the work before Him (Mark vi. 5) He joined her at the marriage at Cana. The presence of Jesus and Mary made this occasion the most memorable of any wedding on record. It was likely this is the only one our Lord attended while on earth, and it is certain there never was a greater surprise at a feast than that caused by the miracle He wrought, which changed water into wine. It was conducted in private; even the governor of the feast was ignorant of what had taken place, and supposed the best wine had been retained to serve last. The bridegroom was just as ignorant of the miracle as the governor; but those who were serving the wine knew why it was brought to the company last.

This miracle, which was witnessed by the servants and the few disciples Jesus had chosen, made a deep impression upon them, so that their increasing faith in the God-man became greatly strengthened. It should be borne in mind, this increase of wine at the feast was not to gratify the appetite of wine-drinkers, but to open the eyes of those who saw the miracle, and others who would hear of it, to the fact that Jesus of Nazareth was He of whom Moses in the law and the prophets did write. It was wine made of pure water. It will not be surprising to learn there are three places in Galilee claimed to be the ancient Cana (St. John ii. 1–11.), where the miracle of the changing of water to wine was wrought. It is an ordinary thing in Palestine, when the least opportunity is presented for the over-anxious people, who wish to have the honor of living in the place where something miraculous or wonderful occurred by our Lord or His disciples, to dispute the right of one place, that the one they favor may be acknowledged the proper site of the event.

At Reinch, a Christian village, but a short distance from Nazareth, on the Tiberias road, is a spring called Ain-Kana, and this place has been located by a few persons as the scene of our Lord's miracle. There is another place, now in ruins, eight miles north of Nazareth, called Khurbet-Kana, and the third place, called Kefr Cana, is situated three or four miles from Nazareth, on the direct road to Tiberias, and is generally settled upon as the true site of the miraculous change of "water to wine." It stands on an incline bordering a narrow valley, and is regarded as a very progressive village, nearly surrounded by fruit trees, such as figs, pomegranates and wild olives. About one hundred or more yards from the west end of the village is a copious fountain, which supplies the inhabitants with an abundance of water. This is supposed to be the identical fountain from which the water was taken for the making of the wine. This opinion is well founded, for there is no other place about the village to get water, nor anywhere in the neighborhood.

There is a small church near the east end of the village, which, according to tradition, stands on the site of the house in which the marriage-feast was held. It is divided by a partition into two distinct churches, owned by the Greeks and Latins respectively. In the apartment belonging to the latter are several old relics, such as old pictures. Several of these old pictures are hanging around the walls. Near the altar are two ancient water-pots, very large. These are said to be the vessels into which the water was poured when our Lord made the wine. It may be understood from this badly-gotten up tradition, how unlikely many things are that the authorities would have strangers believe. The officials were very kind to us, not only in showing the old relics, but doing other things to make us comfortable. On the west of Cana a short distance, there is a village called by the natives El-Mesh-hed. It is supposed to be the ancient Gath-hepher, sometimes called Gettahhepher, and is said to be the birth-place of the prophet Jonah. An old tradition, sanctioned by Jews, Christians and Moslems, locates the prophet's tomb on a hill, which is conspicuously seen from the road near the village. The action on the part of our Lord's townsmen made it necessary that He should teach and preach in other cities in Galilee instead of His own home.

Our Lord did visit towns and cities in southern Palestine, the district of Samaria, and visited some of the people east of the Jordan; but the greater portion of His time was spent in Galilee, and Galilee received His first visit after the resurrection; for He left Jerusalem before all of His disciples saw Him and went to the district where so much of His time and labors had been spent. It may seem strange to many, that during the whole of the ministry of Jesus, He did not make a visit to the little town where he was born. Bethlehem is only six miles from Jerusalem, and Jesus went to the latter several times from the time of His childhood to that of His crucifixion, and passed to the east of His birth-place, coming from Jericho to Bethany, but never saw the rock-cut manger after Joseph fled with Him and the Virgin into Egypt; but one thing is sure, our Lord left a most hopeful influence there, for the inhabitants of the town are strong believers in Him; so staunch are they in the faith that He is the Messiah, Mohammedanism has no footing there.

It is evident our Lord loved Galilee most dearly, notwithstanding the insults that were hurled at Him from many of those who lived there and saw His mighty works. Therefore, for some reason unknown to man He returned there very soon after His resurrection. The angel who rolled the stone from the sepulchre told the women to inform the disciples, their Lord had gone over into Galilee and they should see Him there. Having heard this, the eleven went over there and assembled upon the mountain that had been designated by their Master, and saw Him. It is worthy of remark that Galilee, which means "round," was selected as one of the districts for a city of refuge. There were six of these cities, three on the east side of the Jordan and three on the west; the one in the north was Kedesh in Mt. Naphtalim. The four northern tribes inhabited the district of Galilee, which embraced the tract of country between the upper Jordan valley (including Lake Meram) and Lake Tiberias on the east, and the Mediterranean Sea on the west, and between the mountains of Samaria on the south and Mt. Lebanon on the north.

The four tribes living in this territory were, Issachar on the south, occupying the most of the beautiful plain of Esdraelon; Asher on the west, along the plains of Acre and Phœnicia and the hills adjoining; Zebulun and Napthali possessed the great tract of hill country, the territory of each opening on the Sea of Galilee. This part of the district contained the places in which Christ did the most of His works of power. Therefore, it is readily observed how definitely the prophetic declaration representing the presence and labors of Jesus, in the territory mainly controlled by those two tribes, were described when He foretold the joy that would enthuse the people on account of His visit there. "The land of Zebulun, and the land of Naphtalim toward the sea, beyond Jordan, Galilee of the Gentiles: the people which sat in darkness saw great light; and to them which sat in the regions and shadow of death light is sprung up." (Matt. xxviii. 7, 16, 17; Matt. iv. 15, 16.)

GALILEE.

The province of Galilee was important in developing the general history of the Israelites, and was one of the most desirable divisions allotted to them. Much of the land was highly productive and afforded excellent pastures for the numerous cattle owned by the people within its boundary. The references made to this district in the Scriptures strongly indicate its importance. Speaking of Issachar it says, "His rest is good;" "The land is pleasant;" "Rejoice, O Issachar, in thy tent." Zebulun, nestling amid the hills of lower Galilee, "offers sacrifices of abundant flocks nourished by their pastures." "Asher yields royal dainties;" "His bread is fat." Naphtali is described as "satisfied with favors and with the blessings of the Lord."

The portion of Asher bordered on the Mediterranean Sea, the plain and coast belonged to the Phœnicians, and the portion of territory under their jurisdiction occupied by Asher was by their permission. Those people, in whose district thousands of Israelites lived on amicable terms, were of Hamitic descent, owned twenty cities in Galilee which the Israelites inhabited and paid tribute for their privilege to Hiram, king of Tyre. This will be seen more fully in another chapter. There existed, as far back as the Old Testament times, a cold feeling between that portion of the Hebrews who lived in Jerusalem, Shechem, Samaria and their environments, and those living up' north, especially in Nazareth. It is likely the revolt was the premature cause of much of the bad feeling in connection with the change of customs and other minor things that assisted in keeping the ill-feeling alive. Isaiah, in speaking of the district, calls it "Galilee of the Gentiles," and represents the people as sitting in darkness and in the region and shadow of death. Such were the extensive social relations between the

Israelites and Gentiles, that the pure Hebrew had become much broken in the time of our Lord (Gen. xlix. 20-21 ; Deut. xxxiii. 23-25).

CHILDHOOD OF OUR LORD IN NAZARETH.

How marvelous are the ways of God, and how tenderly is His care made known to the children of men! When the King of kings came into our world, He appeared first in a small town, that was regarded as worthy of but little notice, notwithstanding it is within six miles of the capital city. Christ came humble and poor, preferring rather a place among the beasts than the inn, and a stony manger for His bed rather than the best chamber that could be found in the little town. When Christ was removed from Bethlehem permanently, it was by order of the Lord to Joseph to make a hasty flight into Egypt by night that He might safely hide the young child from the massacre of King Herod. And when by the will of the Father He left the land of Egypt, Joseph must take up his abode again at his home in Nazareth, and keep the child Jesus in seclusion for a time from the outside world. Therefore Jesus was not known as God-man to the people in whose midst He lived, for neither Joseph nor Mary declared to their townsmen the wondrous events that attended His birth, nor how they had preserved Him from the decree of King Herod by fleeing to Egypt, having been ordered by an angel to do so. If they had told such a wonderful story to the people, they would have had no confidence in their words, and at the same time there would have been an ill-feeling existing of a most disastrous character.

It is noteworthy that the home selected for our Lord was in a town whose inhabitants were regarded by other communities as the worst of all people in the land. Yet it was the will of God that His Son should grow to manhood in this place and preserve Himself spotless. He could have lived elsewhere with the same influence upon the world. He could have been reared in Bethlehem, where He was born, or in Jerusalem, where He was crucified; but it was not so ordered in Heaven. Our Lord was the humblest being known to the world; for though He was the Son of the Highest Being, He became so humble that it was not offensive to accompany Joseph to his carpenter shop and assist him in such things as He was requested to do.

When but a very small child, He was no doubt often found going in company with Mary, His affectionate mother, to the fountain to draw water, and many times His parents took Him over to Jerusalem to witness the yearly feast. From Nazareth our Lord went to the Jordan to be baptized of John, and after a temptation of the greatest

test. returned with a few followers to Cana of Galilee, and performed His first miracle; from there He went to Capernaum. His life then began to be sought by those whom He came to save; but with all the opposition produced by adversaries, our Lord was willing to bear all the impositions of men that He might open their eyes to the light of immortality. Since the events connected with the life of Jesus in Nazareth have been made known, all Christendom has turned its attention towards the little isolated town where He spent the most of His life.

When the Crusaders were in possession of Palestine, they built a Christian church there, which was afterwards destroyed by the Turks when they came into power. The Christians made several efforts afterwards to establish themselves there again, but could not succeed until the eighteenth century; but when they were permitted to reorganize themselves, they took a firm stand (it seems) for the cause of Christ, and their work has been crowned with great success. It is, therefore, a pleasant fact to note, that three-fourths of the inhabitants of Nazareth are Christians, and no barriers are fixed to interfere with their religious devotions. The various denominations do not meet under the same roof as in Jerusalem, Bethlehem and Cana; therefore, they are at peace. It seems impossible for peace to obtain where these different denominations meet under the same roof, notwithstanding they have separate apartments; many serious troubles have occurred, especially with the Greek and Latin monks. The latter have the greater religious influence; their church and convent are the chief places of interest, both to tourists and pilgrims. They are surrounded by high walls. The Church of the Annunciation is the most important of all the visiting places in the town. It is really astonishing to know how eagerly the people attend the services, and with what sincere devotion they bow in holy reverence to Him who was once one of the humble citizens of the town, and was compelled to abandon it for doing good. It may have been clearly seen that the prophet saw the results of good works when he advised us to cast our bread upon the waters, for it should be found after many days. Our Lord did this on the Sabbath, He conducted the service in the synagogue, and now it is found throughout the town. In the time of the ministry of Jesus, but few could be seen in Nazareth who consented to follow Him; but at present, nine thousand profess His name and publicly acknowledge Him as their God. In His time, the people of Nazareth were mean, murderous, and a byword for all other communities; to-day, they are peaceable and exemplary. Then, it was generally thought that nothing good could come out of Nazareth; now, it is looked upon as one of the most Christian communities in Palestine; then, the people sat in great darkness; now, the light of blessed hope shines upon them; then, they did not want Christ for their Saviour; now, they cling to Him.

The province of Galilee abounded with rich pastures, olive groves, and other pleasant attractions, which drew many people from other parts to it. Josephus, who was a chief military officer shortly after the time of our Lord, is authority for the statement that Galilee had a teeming population, and was dotted over with towns and villages. He was of the opinion that an army of one hundred thousand men might have been raised from its male population, who were able to do service in war. The labors of our Lord in Galilee must have been immense, for He visited all the towns and cities in the province, teaching and preaching the gospel of the kingdom of Heaven. How tremendous must have been the multitude that followed Him! At one time He fed five thousand men, besides women and children, and we feel satisfied in venturing the opinion the latter classes outnumbered the former. It is not unreasonable to suppose there was at some period of His ministry a greater number following Him than the above-named. It may be readily inferred that our Lord spent a busy life from the time He entered upon the work of His mission until it was fully accomplished.

Jesus made three distinct itineraries through Galilee, on which occasions He was kept constantly busy from the early morning to late in the night, preaching, teaching and healing all kinds of diseases and casting out devils. At one time His near relatives felt concerned as to His sanity, and went in search for Him, with the intention of urging Him to retire from His work and return home, but such was the importance of His engagements, the persuasive entreaties of His fond mother could not influence Him to abandon it. This was not that He feared to return to Nazareth, where He had been so shamefully opposed, for when the time came for Him to go to those wicked people again He went boldly. But the people were just as blind to their welfare as when they attempted to kill Him.

NAZARETH—OUR LORD'S INCREASING FAME.

Jesus loved the people of Nazareth. He would not forsake them, even if they did threaten His life, but returned there to teach them lessons of peace, that they might flee from the wrath to come, and finding them unyieldingly obstinate, He left them. How sadly stubborn they were! Jesus had gained great fame when He made His last visit to Nazareth, for it had spread over into Syria, Phœnicia, and all the country round about Galilee, and it is highly probable several people living at His home had been amongst those who followed Him in other portions of the province, and witnessed some of the mighty works He did. Yet their sins had so deeply overshadowed them, they closed their eyes and stopped their ears, so that they could neither see nor hear. Finding nothing could be done, Jesus left them. It must have been a sad time with our Lord when He thought of the final state of those who refused life, and though no tears were seen coursing down His cheeks, there were deep emotions disturbing His soul. The people of Nazareth, or a portion of them, seem to have been religiously inclined, for they had a synagogue, in which services were regularly conducted by the proper officials. This would suggest at least the existence of a species of the formal piety current amongst the Jews in those days; therefore the people were not entirely without moral precepts and teachers. But it is apparent the example was sadly wanting.

It is also known, the whole people could not be justly pronounced as singularly depraved, although the city was universally scorned; for we know Joseph, Mary and their children were exceptions, and several others, no doubt, whom they associated with, were truly pious. But the great majority were both wicked and vicious. The grounds upon which they founded their objection to Jesus, was from the fact that He was a fellow-townsman. This seems to be the view of our Lord as to the situation, and we know His views were always correct. It is also remarkable, He did not condemn them harshly at the time the people rejected Him, but simply said, "No prophet is acceptable in his own country." It is likely He was consistently familiar with the young people of the neighborhood of His home, for when they were listening to His discourse, they marvelled at the knowledge He possessed, for they knew Him as Joseph's son, and knew all the family. It is certain, not one who knew Him could say a word against His character in any way, or they would have done it while their rage was kindled against Him.

HIS SOCIAL LIFE.

The older people (many of them) were associates of Joseph and Mary, and in keeping with the custom of friends, they often called to pay them a visit, taking their younger children with them, as is usual to the present time; and it is not unlikely some of their children were about the same age of Jesus. Therefore, many formed His acquaintance in early childhood, and grew up to manhood, somewhat familiar with Him. It was customary also for those living at a distance from Jerusalem to go up in companies to the annual feasts, as the pilgrims do now on the return of the Easter celebration each year. It is known the parents of Jesus took Him with them from time to time in company with their friends and children. Hence the people, young and old, had many opportunities of seeing Jesus and knowing something of His piety. If He had been reared in obscurity and had come before the public suddenly, they would have more readily received Him, even as they did John the Baptist. But Jesus was objected to because He was a fellow-townsman and was known It really should have been the chief reason for accepting Him as Christ, knowing as they did He was correct in all His ways from childhood and that none of the young folks in the town had such a clean and sinless record as Jesus. But He came to His own, and they rejected Him.

It was not a question of a popular city or town with our Lord in selecting a home on earth, but putting Himself in touch with the poorest and most depraved of mankind. When the life of Jesus is well studied and understood, it will be seen that His great condescension to come into our world and make His home in a city so wretchedly sinful as Nazareth, was an evidence stronger than can be described, that "He came into the world to save sinners;" and that He might accomplish the purpose in view, He consented to become poor, dishonored and humbled. The lesson we learn from our Lord's humiliation is this (St. John i. 45), He became meek, so that none would feel embarrassed in approaching Him. The king and peasant alike might come without feeling unwelcome. He knew the masses of the people composing our world were poor, and had no social relations with the rich; therefore, to come to the latter adorned in costly garments would be to estrange Himself from the very people who would be more likely to accept the kingdom of God first.

Riches are a tremendous barrier against the full exercise of sympathy for the condition of the poor. For a person who fully understands the situation of his fellow must have some practical idea of it. Our Lord became experimentally conversant with the great masses of those in a state of absolute poverty by becoming poor Himself. It is known His parents were in humble circumstances. Joseph was a poor man, working daily at the carpenter-bench, to sustain himself and family; and in those days it was not an easy thing for a poor mechanic to move his family and effects into a strange city and establish himself in business. Therefore, it was important he should remain where he was generally known. It is also noteworthy that our Lord's home was near the place where the majority of men lived whom He chose to become His disciples, and where the most of His mighty works were done. Therefore, He was perfectly willing to endure the many hardships and privations of life, both as to society and luxuries, that the gospel might be preached to the poor. And should we notice the class of people who express the greatest fondness for the cause so richly purchased by the Saviour, and whose devotions for His cause are the most earnest, we will see at once the wisdom He displayed in providing for the poor, that the "word of life" might be preached to them.

The life of Jesus is without doubt a tremendous example to those who prefer to follow Him. It admonishes them to become meek, that their influence may reach the poor; that their preaching should be to win souls to Christ, whether their hearers be rich or poor; and they are not to use the gospel as a medium through which their talents may be displayed or education admired, as we fear many do, but to preach the word in its simplicity, having in view the same purpose our Lord had. He was not satisfied in having the poor know the gospel was preached only, but that it was preached to them in the same manner and for the very purpose it was preached to the rich. Nor are those who stand in Christ's stead to content themselves with having a rich and fashionable congregation to preach to from time to time, but they should seek the poor and lowly, and even the meanest men, that they may bring them to the foot of the cross.

If the world is to be saved, those who stand as watchmen on the walls of Zion must take the same general method Jesus took to save it. They are not to feel themselves too important to go down to men who are held in derision, in popular estimation, as were the people of Nazareth, among whom Jesus lived the most of His life. It is absolutely strange that many men who claim to be masters in Israel, sent of God to preach His word to men, are so very select in their pretended efforts to save. Thousands of poor, unfortunate men and women would be brought to Christ if the preacher would show them by his friendliness he is anxious as to their future and eternal welfare. It was a very pleasant afternoon the day we left Nain and Endor behind, and came into the town made sacredly memorable as the home of our Lord from infancy to manhood.

On account of the elevated situation of Nazareth, it can be seen afar off. It is very attractive when first viewed. The valley of Esdraelon, with its great profusion of variegated flowers, begins to lose its charms, and the approaching traveler draws his attention to the beautiful town before him. Notwithstanding I had carefully read the history of this little city among the hills, I am frank to confess that my idea of it was but meagre, as was the case with regard to all other cities and towns in that land. Just after leaving the plain, the ascent of a high and rugged hill begins, which is difficult and fatiguing to travel. It is just west of the Mount of Precipitation, the traditional hill to which the enraged citizens led Jesus to hurl Him to death among the rocks below. A full view is obtained of it as the town is approached from Nain. After the rough hill is ascended, the traveler enters a good road; here we could travel much more comfortably. In a few moments after reaching the eastern edge of the town, we halted at a little hotel, at which I spent two nights pleasantly. The Greek church and convent are seen first, on arrival at Nazareth, from the south and southeast. The Latins have the most important historic sites under their control. It is really wonderful to learn of the shameful amount of deception practiced upon strangers in various portions of Palestine by the two rival churches, the Greeks and Latins.

In Nazareth, both churches claim to occupy the site of the home of the Virgin Mary where she was visited by the Angel Gabriel, who informed her that the Lord had chosen her as the medium through whom the advent of Christ should be made into our world. But the site held by the Greeks is wholly repudiated by those who have made investigations; and the general opinion inclines to the site of the Latin Church. The officials are very generous, and take great pains in conducting visitors to the various sacred sites they have in charge. It is also worthy of mention that they do not allow any of their officials to take pay from those who go through the church and convent, which is an honorable exception to the general rule, for in many places they are so greedy, a visitor is perplexed with their importunities for contributions.

There are many things of interest to see in the Church of the Annunciation. The high altar, which is approached from the broad marble steps, is dedicated to the Angel Gabriel, and is supposed to be near the spot where he stood when he announced to the Virgin that she should be the mother of our Lord. "Thou shalt bear a son, and His name shall be called Jesus." The altar is handsomely decorated, and presents a very impressive scene; but the interior of the church is plain, having a few fairly good pictures suspended along the walls. Below the altar is an apartment called the Chapel of the Angels, adjoining which is another small chamber known as the Chapel of the Annunciation. In this room is seen a marble altar containing the following inscription: "Hic verbum caro factum est."—Here the Word was made flesh.

There are several other sites within and about the church to which visitors are conducted, such as the Visitation of Mary, the Worship of Joseph, the Fountain of the Virgin, the Mount of Precipitation, the old synagogue in which our Lord delivered His first sermon, etc. As these places are, with two or three exceptions, wholly traditional, they are not to be relied upon as identical with the events they represent; yet, they are highly interesting to visit, because of the history clustering about them. The very high mountain northwest of the town called Mount Nazareth affords one of the grandest views to be had in Palestine. One standing upon this lofty summit can look over to Nain, Endor, and upon the highest peak of Mount Tabor, all of which seem to be only a few hundred yards away. Turning westward, the Mediterranean seems to be only a mile off. The whole view is superb!

PART XII.

MOUNT CARMEL.

Description of Mount Carmel—The Athlit—Simon Bar-Cochebas, or "Son of the Stars"—Situation of the Carmelite Convent—Location of Acre—Pasha of Acre—The Ladder of Tyre—Sidon the Mother of Tyre—Situation of Tyre—Shalmaneser's Invasion of Tyre—Nebuchadnezzar's Invasion of Tyre.

MOUNT CARMEL is one of the most famous of all the mountains in Palestine except Zion and Olivet. It is regarded as sacred by the various Christian denominations in the land, and reverenced by them next to the Holy Mount in the City of David. It is not a single mountain, as many suppose, but an extensive range of about thirty miles in length, having many ravines and peaks of different degrees of altitudes and depths. Carmel separates the Sharon plain from that of Esdraelon, forming it into a triangular shape. It is very dismal to travel, and were it not for its historical associations no tourist would consent to make a trip over it. The whole range is wild and uninviting, having a hugh limestone surface here and there; from one end to the other, great ledges of these rocks pave the pass leading up the mountain from the base to its summit. But a much wilder scene is presented while passing over its steep hills and winding paths, studded with monstrous rocks from beginning to end. It is not a wonder the Prophet Amos referred to it as a place of retreat for refugees. It has many secure hiding-places, which are sought many times by the Bedouins, who endeavor to elude their pursuers. It is said there were many large trees covering several of the hills and vales of Carmel in the near past, but nearly all of them have been cut down by the charcoal-burners for the markets. This fuel is mostly used in the interior of Palestine, and is in great demand in the cold season. The herdsmen, who are very numerous in the locality of Carmel, have destroyed much of the timber-land to procure pasture for their cattle. They have set fire to large tracts of it, so that they may get fodder from the tender branches which grow the following spring. This procedure has caused many of the vicious wild animals, that have made their homes in the dens and caves so frequently seen, to abandon them and hunt homes in other parts of the country; yet there are a few remaining among the wild haunts, such as the leopard, hyena, porcupine, weasel, wild boar, wolf, and a few of the minor classes. The jackals are the most numerous, not only in the wilds of Carmel, but in almost all parts of the northern and western portions of Palestine and Syria. It is said many venomous snakes lurk in several of the more dreary places, but it was my good fortune not to see any of them. It is very evident from the number of ruins scattered over certain portions of Carmel, that a large population lived up there in earlier times, who had comfortable homes. The present inhabitants are Arabs and live in their usual characteristic huts, mostly composed of sun dried clay. It is supposed the greater portion of the ruins on the southeastern side of the mountain are the remains of a Jewish village in which a synagogue was built. It is, therefore, evident there were several thousands of them inhabiting the southeastern district, and that they settled there after their return from captivity, because the Jews did not have such buildings previously. Great precautions seem to have been taken in building the town, both in arranging for comfort and protecting themselves against the encroachments of invaders. The Crusaders partially renewed the place and made a long jetty to land their fellow-pilgrims who came over from Europe.

It may be of interest to state, that in connection with the many ruins remaining on Mt. Carmel, are those which, from their architecture, are supposed to be of Phœnician origin. One of these is an antique chamber hewn out of the solid rock, and is likely to have been used as a guard-house by that most progressive and war-like people, during their occupancy of that portion of the coast. The old, weather-beaten rock, that has been pelted by the storms of four thousand years, still bears visible impressions of the instruments used by the workmen. And there are many other old ruins scattered over the mount, which are evidences that the ancients caused the dreary wilderness to be a busy scene, when they were the custodians of this most noted mountain. But now solitude reigns supreme almost from one end to the other, except the few Arabs who inhabit it; whom to look upon, many times causes a stranger to feel more lonely than if he had seen nothing but the occasional wild animals which still find a home in the dens and caves.

THE ATHLIT.

The site of the ancient town and fortress lies beyond the ruins of a gateway, about which may be seen great masses of crumbling pillars and blocks of stone of various shapes scattered over a large space.

This is where the Athlit was located, historically known as the Castellum Peregrinorum, or "The Pilgrims' Castle." It was the landing-place for the new recruits in the time of the Crusades, for more than two hundred years. It is the general opinion of those who have made examinations of the numerous ruins, that the fortress and castle were built by the Knights Templars early in the thirteenth century. It has been discovered that there are prominent traces of masonry that belong to the age of the Phœnicians and Canaanites among these vast ruins promiscuously strewn over the mountains. It is highly probable that the Phœnicians had one of their strongest fortifications here, when they were guarding the coast along their territory. The natural situation of the place forms a monstrous citadel in itself, and when combined with art it must have been the most stupendous of all the fortresses of the coast, and those whose good fortune it was to be residents of the mount, felt themselves perfectly secure.

The greatest historical interest of the Athlit lies in the fact of its being the last Jewish, and also the last Christian possession in the Holy Land. In the year one hundred and thirty of our era, Simon, the son of Bar-Cochebas, commanded the last Jewish insurrection against the Romans in the time of Hadrian. It is said the whole plan was cunningly formulated by Simon, who was a skillful man, but amazingly superstitious. He called himself Bar-Cochebas, or "Son of the Star;" claiming that the prophecy of Baalim was centred in him, saying, "There shall come a star out of Jacob." The Jews had the greatest confidence in Simon, as the man whom God had raised up to deliver them, and believed the above prediction would be fulfilled in him. Therefore they were ready to follow whatever commands he might give them. Feeling assured their commander was the gift of God, the Jews entered into the conflict with great energy, and through the whole struggle, which lasted three years and a half, they possessed indomitable courage, winning one victory after another until fifty towns and cities that had been dispossessed by the Romans, were captured. But after a little more than three years had elapsed, Julius Serverus, Hadrian's commander-in-chief, came upon the scene, and cut down the hitherto victorious Jews like grass; many thousands were slain, others were captured and executed, and the residue were subjected to the most rigid discipline. This was the final Jewish struggle for independence in Palestine, and the one which caused them to be dispersed over the face of the whole earth.

FORTRESS OF SIMON "BAR-COCHEBAS," OR "SON OF THE STARS."

During this conflict Athlit was the main stronghold, where "the son of the star" garrisoned his forces. It is still celebrated in Jewish literature as a memorial of the last foothold of land in Palestine they possessed, while making their final contest for national independence. The new-comers to this land of Bible renown, having a knowledge of Athlit, made it the stronghold of the Crusaders; and although a thousand years had passed since Simon and his brave army were in camp there, it was found to be in such a good condition, but comparatively little work was required to make it the strong fortress it was in former times. But it is very evident the Crusaders greatly increased its dimensions and fortifications. It was attacked by Sultan El-Melek Moaddham, and sometime afterwards the famous Bibars vainly strove for seven years to capture it. But when Acre, just three or four miles away, had fallen into the hands of the Moslems, who had control of every inch of Palestine except Athlit, the Crusaders were compelled to abandon their fortress. Before they finally left it, those who escaped the sword of their foe came together the night prior to their departure and held a memorial banquet.

It is very evident this part of Mount Carmel was chosen as a fortress, because of the memorable victory won by Elijah the prophet near the place of Athlit. But aside from the sacred history attaching to this mountain, the events that transpired upon its summit in later times makes it one of the most interesting places in Palestine, for it is a historical reservoir. Mount Carmel first came into imperishable distinction as a battle-field when the prophet Elijah went up against the hosts of Baal, to decide who was the true God. This of all the events for which Carmel is noted is the most important. As has been stated, Carmel has been from ancient times to the present a refuge for all classes of men. It is as much sought at times by those fleeing from justice as were the ancient cities to which refugees escaped from their pursuers.

It is regarded as a fruitless procedure to attempt to hunt down one who has time enough to reach the hiding-places of Carmel before the officer of the law overtakes him, for some of the caves and dens are so secluded that it is impossible for those who are well acquainted with them to capture a man without running a sad risk of his life. It is said one might be in the same cave where his pursuer is, and within arm's length of him, before he could see him. This is also true of several other mountains in Palestine and Syria, such as the mountains of the spies of Jericho, the Frank mountain, east of Bethlehem, the Lebanon and Anti-Lebanon ranges in Syria, and a few others. But none of these seem to be so abundantly supplied with retreats as Mount Carmel. Those who have traveled over it had an opportunity to see many of its secluded retreats.

The pass leading to the summit on its western border begins at Haifa, and requires about one hour and a half to ascend it. Some portions of the pass are mediumly good, but from the half-way station to the top it is most difficult. It is with much labor and fatigue the animals are enabled to carry a person up. Many will not venture to remain on their horses when the most dangerous places are to be traveled, and it often occurs that people walk the whole way from the base to the summit. There are open places along the extreme narrow portions of the pass as it approaches the edge of the sea, along which are gorges several hundred feet deep. It is alarming to pass them, either riding or walking, for if the least blunder should happen to be made, the unfortunate person would fall headlong down among the pointed rocks and be broken to pieces in an instant.

There are still to be seen several caves in the mountain-side which were occupied in earlier times by the Anchorites. The most celebrated of them is near the foot of Carmel, between Tel-es-Samak and Kaifa, known as El-Khudr, or "the evergreen." This is the name the natives gave the prophet Elijah. But English-speaking people call it the school of the prophets.

On arriving at the gateway, at the top of the mount, the visitor passes into a beautiful yard where green grass and various flowers abound. The buildings round about compose the Carmelite Convent. It is estimated to be forty-five feet long, twenty-seven wide and fifteen high, the whole of which has been excavated out of the solid rock, having a modern building on each side of it. In the central chamber is a broad stone seat, about two feet high, hewn out of the rock; and in the east wall is a recess carved from the huge limestone bed composing it. This cave is sacredly reverenced by Jews, Christians, Moslems and Druses as the identical site of one of the schools of the prophets. The convent is located near the sea-border, and is one of the most desirable situations of the entire range. The custodians are very polite to strangers who visit the convent.

THE BROOK KISHON.

The Brook Kishon is one of the great historic streams of Palestine. It came into prominence on the day the false prophets were so shamefully defeated by Elijah, on Carmel, who in their vain attempt to escape the sword of justice, were slain near this brook by their enraged pursuers.

The Kishon takes its rise in the plain of Esdraelon, near the foot of Mount Tabor. It flows through the memorable plain, gathering more strength from its tributaries along the way, which swell it in the winter season to a deep and rapid current. For a considerable distance it runs along the base of Carmel, and pours its contents into the sea, a short distance from Acre. During the latter portion of the summer the brook is generally dry about its source, but in that portion that runs along the foot of Carmel the water remains the year round, because it is continually receiving supplies from the perennial springs flowing down into it. When the rainy season is in its height the brook's fords become so greatly swollen it is impossible to pass over them. It was just such a season when the army of Sisera was drowned when fleeing from the army of Israel. Here the Arabs were most sadly defeated while fleeing from the memorable battle of Tabor. This brook, Kishon, will ever be memorable to the author of this volume, for it was by a slender chance his life was preserved.

The dragoman having me in charge feared we would not be able to cross, as the water was running rapidly, and was getting deeper seemingly every moment, as it had been raining hard several days. As we approached nearer, evidences were prominent that it would be difficult to cross the ford. We went to the lower ford, which was a good deal nearer Haifa, but not near as crossable as the one a mile or two above in the time of heavy rains. On our arrival at the usual crossing the water was running in torrents, but we concluded to make an effort to cross. My horse being very thirsty stopped, after entering a few feet, to drink; and there being a great accumulation of mud at the bottom he sank into it several inches, so that when he attempted to recover himself it was with much difficulty; and twice while attempting to free his feet the poor horse came near falling. Just at that time it seemed impossible for me to free my feet from the stirrups; but, by the mercy of God, he finally recovered, and we reached the other shore safely. Had he fallen we would have both perished. But O! what joy when we reached the land! I cannot ever forget the experience We reached Haifa in the early afternoon very much fatigued; but it was only a short while after dinner when we were again in the saddle ascending the rugged path to the summit of Mount Carmel.

LOCATION OF ACRE.

Haifa is supposed to be the site of Misheal or Mishbal of the Scriptures. Acre is known by different names. It is sometimes called Akko (Accho), also St. Jean d' Acre It is a small city, situated along the sea-border about ten miles north of Haifa. It is a place of great historical importance, notwithstanding it is not prominently mentioned in the Scriptures, yet we find it mentioned in the Old Testament as Accho. In the New Testament it is called Ptolemais. Akka is the name by which it is known in Arabic. The French call it "St. Jean d' Acre," and the English have named it "Acre." This little city contains about seven thousand inhabitants, all of whom are Moslems, except about one thousand who have espoused the Christian faith. The situation of Acre with reference to approaches to it by sea and land were so peculiarly difficult it was for a long time called the key of Palestine. Those entering the Holy Land from the north had to come this way, over the very narrow and rugged pass known as the Ladder of Tyre, then through the plain of Acre.

When the children of Israel entered upon their tribal possessions, Acre was allotted to Asher. This tribe seems to have lived on terms of peace with the Canaanites who inhabited the place, as they were never expelled from it. The following towns, according to the Scriptures, were held by the Canaanites after the allotment was made and Asher went up to dwell in the country as apportioned. "Asher drove not out the inhabitants of Accho, nor the inhabitants of Zidon, nor of Ahlab, nor of Achzib, nor of Helbah, nor of Aphik, nor of Rehab; but the Asherites dwelt among the Canaanites, the inhabitants of the land, for they drove not them out." The Jews regarded the city as abhorrently unclean, and excluded it from the boundary of the Holy Land, confining it to the walls of the town. The same opinion has come down through the ages of Jewish traditions to the present, so that the Jews of to-day in Palestine adhere as strongly to the idea as those of the earlier times. They abhor the name of Accho, and will not consent to die there under any circumstances if they can avoid it. They have a small cemetery on the east of the town just outside the wall, which they claim is within the limits of the Holy Land. Here the Jews are willing to be laid to rest until awakened by the trump of the resurrection.

Acre, being the key of Palestine, caused many hostile nations to turn their attention towards her. These came up against the little fortress city from time to time, until seventeen heavy sieges were encountered, during which it was captured several times. The city and district were for some time divided into seventeen parts, each being under a separate jurisdiction. "It had many sovereigns, but no government." The kings of Jerusalem and Cyprus, of the house of Lusignan; the princes of Antioch; the counts of Tripoli and Sidon; the great masters of the Hospital, the Temple, and the Teutonic Orders; the republics of Venice, Genoa and Pisa; the popes, the legate, the kings of France and England, each assumed an independent command, so that seventeen tribunals exercised the power of life and death (Gibbon). This complicated state of things introduced many sad events, so that mob-violence was often indulged in and blood freely shed. The Turks finally gained possession of Acre and placed it under the control of a pasha.

In the latter part of the eighteenth century, a very cruel and heartless official ruled the district, whose administration was so inhumanly outrageous that he became generally known as the Jezzar, or the "Butcher." There are many things stated as to the atrocities committed by this man, of which the following is a sample: He caused his fifteen wives to be killed to appease his wicked passion, and tortured his banker to death. This young man was a Jew belonging to Damascus. He was very handsome and generally admired. Jezzar was very jealous of him. He passed a high compliment on him for his beauty one day, and while he pretended to be playing with the young man, put one of his eyes out, so that he might be robbed forever of some of his beauty. The young banker afterwards so adjusted his turban as to hide the disfigured eye. Jezzar, seeing this, drew his sword and smote off the man's nose. He then, at short intervals, committed other brutal assaults on him, until at length he caused him to be beheaded. It is said, that aside from his cruel disposition, Jezzar Pasha was a most prosperous and energetic ruler, and largely extended the pashalik of Acre while he was ruling. There is a mosque in the town bearing his name that was built by his direction. The New Testament mentions this town by its new name, Ptolemais. St. Paul came here and remained a day when on his way to Jerusalem. This seems to be the only mention made of it in the New Testament.

THE LADDER OF TYRE.

After the fatal battle of Mt. Hattin, when the Crusaders were vanquished, Acre fell into the hands of Saladin, and in four years later the Crusaders recaptured the city after a heavy siege of two years, which cost the lives of sixty thousand men. But there was a constant uneasiness prevailing among the people on account of repeated attempts on the part of the enemy to capture it. Just about one hundred years after this great struggle, the Crusaders were again compelled to abandon Acre after a strong resistance of one month. This was the last desperate struggle the Crusaders engaged in, for they had become hopelessly overpowered and their doom was sealed in the "Holy Land." About twelve miles north of Acre the narrow pass is crossed on the slope of the hill skirting the sea; this is called "The Ladder of Tyre." It well deserves the name, for it is very steep and dreadfully rugged. After ascending to the summit, the northern descent is so very steep and dangerous, but few will attempt to ride down it; even the natives dread it, and dismount when they begin the descent. Some portions of it have openings to the sea; and the pass is so close to the edge of the gulf it is really shocking to pass them; should you fall here nothing could save your life. Just as the pass is crossed the border of Phœnicia is reached. The road leading over the Ladder is one of the most ancient highways in Palestine, and, as has been stated, was the only over-land entrance to Tyre.

Through this narrow head-land hundreds of thousands of mighty men of war have passed in olden times to battle and to death. When Rameses II., sat himself against Asia Minor to subdue it, he caused his large army to pass this way; and according to information the Bible gives us, the Assyrians were sent over this critical pass on at least five missions of war and death. At one time they came over under the leadership of Pul; once under Tilgath-Pileser. Shalmaneser led his forces over it, Sargon's troops came over it with a greedy expectation of victory; and here came also Sennacherib with his tremendous host. The Syrians came down like a flood over this pass more than twenty-five hundred years ago; and hither came the proud Rameses more than three thousand years ago to lift his conquering sceptre over the land. This monarch was the Sesostris of Herodotus, and the Pharaoh of Moses. Many other victorious armies have marched over this narrow Ladder since those ancient warriors have fallen asleep.

This pass is called by the natives Ras en-Nakurah, and is known to the Romans as Tyriorum. Soon after leaving the northern base of the pass, a countless number of ruins are exposed to view, extending over several miles. Some of them are piled in mounds and others are scattered in every direction. This is an evidence that the whole district was an unbroken succession of cities and towns, in which lived many hundred thousands of Phœnicians. But how sadly those mighty cities have fallen! They were once a scene of busy life; now the whole region is a vast wilderness. There is not a sign of life to be seen in the most of it except a traveler here and there passing through. These ruins are strong evidences of Phœnician genius, whose knowledge in sculpture was the most skillful of any people in the countries round about them.

Ancient Tyre is supposed to have been one of the first cities of our world, running back into prehistoric times. It was built and inhabited by Phœnicians, who settled in the country early after the dispersion of men over the earth. They were descendants of Canaan, the youngest son of Ham. These people became so very numerous, the whole country was named after them prior to the time the children of Israel took possession of the greater portion of it. Tyre is the word from which Syria takes its name, which means "the Land of the Tyrians." With reference to its antiquity there can be no doubt, for it is spoken of as such in the Holy Scriptures. Isaiah, in speaking of it, says, "It is of ancient days." It is an established opinion among authors that Tyre was founded nearly three thousand years before our era; and, according to William of Tyre, its founder was Tyras. Herodotus says the city was in a state of prosperity as far back as two thousand and fifty years, B.C.

SIDON THE MOTHER OF TYRE.

It is evident that Sidon was a much older city and was known as the mother of Tyre—indeed, she was the parent of all the cities, towns and villages along the coast. This statement will not be questioned if we confide in the words of Isaiah, who calls Tyre the daughter of Sidon. But it seems that the former suddenly grew and became the most important city the Phœnicians possessed, for it became the most noted of all others known in the land. Ezekiel's reference to Tyre is most graphic and expressive of the wonderful powers of the people whose influence had spread over sea and land as that of no other people had. These two great cities of the Phœnicians were well known to Jacob before he left Hebron for Egypt, and when about to die he named them as the boundary of the portion of Zebulun. The Phœnicians were a powerful people and were dreaded by the nations around them, notwithstanding their country was allotted to Asher, that tribe never took possession of it, but remained in a subordinate relation to this warlike people whom they found inhabiting their portion.

PHŒNICIANS AND ISRAELITES.

The Phœnicians, however, seemed to have lived on the most friendly terms with Israel, and rendered them great service. And, although numerous wars and quarrels continued so many years between Israel and other nations, we have no knowledge of any contentions having existed between them and the Phœnicians; notwithstanding in some portions of the country they lived together; and in cities adjoining each other, they were on most intimate and friendly terms. We know there was, in the time of David and Solomon, a strong friendship existing between the two nations, that bound them almost as one people. It is known that King Hiram of Tyre rendered great assistance to King Solomon in the construction of the Temple, and we have reasons to believe these friendly relations continued without any serious interruption, for when Ahab reigned over the northern kingdom he married Jezebel, a Phœnician woman and daughter of the king of Phœnicia. It seems strange that these people should be so wholly lost in idolatry, especially when they had for neighbors a people who professed to be children of the living God. But instead of being turned from their idols through the influence of the chosen people, they caused Israel to turn wistfully towards their gods, and even devoutly worshiped them.

Tyre is situated about twenty-five miles south of Sidon, on the eastern shore of the Mediterranean Sea. Its inhabitants in early times endured some of the most hostile attacks that were ever made against a people in the history of wars. She withstood them for a long time, and proved herself mistress of the situation; for these brave people either put their foes to flight, or so persistently withstood them that they considered it a fruitless procedure to contend against them. The Phœnicians had both harbors securely garrisoned by a powerful and alert fleet of well-equipped men, who were ever ready to defend their government against the encroachments of an invading foe. The Phœnicians were masters of the sea, and possessed unequaled skill in their day, in arming and commanding vessels. This superior knowledge not only prepared them to maintain their prestige as seamen, but placed them in a condition to successfully contend against forces much larger than their own. Many times the enemy came against them, whose numbers were by far the greater, who, after a long and bloody conflict, resulting in the loss of many lives, were compelled to return to their home covered with shame and defeat.

Josephus says: "Shalmaneser went up against Tyre with sixty vessels, having eight hundred men manning the oars. The Tyrians met them with only twelve vessels and discomfited them. They captured five hundred of the Assyrians, and put the remaining fleet to flight." But the land force of Shalmaneser was not so readily subdued; they could fight better on the land; moreover, they were very numerous. This vast army camped before Tyre five years, and did much damage to the outskirts of the city and the water-works; but at length they became hopeless of accomplishing their aim and gave up the contest, leaving the Phœnicians masters of the situation. Nebuchadnezzar stood out against Tyre with a strong army, who besieged it for nineteen years, using every means at their command to overthrow it, but were finally compelled to abandon their effort as a fruitless task. Until Alexander the Great came up with his conquering army, the Phœnicians maintained their jurisdiction over Tyre.

But when this conqueror of conquerors came upon the scene, with his invincible host, one of the most bloody and deadly conflicts began that had visited the Phœnician citadel. The people fought bravely and desperately, but were compelled to surrender their cherished city to the superior strength of Alexander's forces. The island city withstood the invaders seven months; but they also were finally subdued and captured after the enemy had united it to the mainland by forming a mole of massive stones and timbers from the ruins of the old city. This little isthmus was so well constructed, that it gave Alexander an opportunity to seize the island city with but little trouble, although the Tyrians fought with great determination to maintain their position; but they were too weak for their powerful foe, and were compelled to submit to him. The most decided encounter of the Greeks against the Tyrian-Phœnicians was an illustrious fulfillment of the graphic prediction of the Prophet Ezekiel. He so clearly disclosed the scene that it could not have been more definitely narrated if he had been looking upon the event when it took place. This shows how clearly and adequately the Lord inspired human beings to foretell events hundreds of years before they came to pass.

ANCIENT TYRE.

Tyre is now called by the natives Ras-el-Ain. It is located about three miles from the island city on the south. The present town occupies a portion of the site on which the latter city stood, in and about which many ruins of the former city are to be seen. Investigations have strongly indicated that old Tyre occupied all the space from the southern end of its ruins to the island. There are remnants of the ancient reservoirs, still in a medium state of preservation, into which several perennial springs flow. These reservoirs formed a portion of the water supply of the renowned city, in ancient times, through an aqueduct. It has been discovered that the vast tract adjoining the reservoir was made into a succession of beautiful gardens. It is supposed they contained some of the most lovely flowers known in the East. There were also fine shade-trees, beautifully arranged, so as to make the gardens not only inviting to look upon, but pleasant to visit. The reservoirs are believed to be those which King Solomon gave to Hiram, King of Tyre, as a compliment in recognition of the efficient aid rendered by the latter in building the Temple. The following is the current tradition concerning them, which is credited by the people of Tyre generally.

Hiram, the great King of Tyre, having made a tour of the twenty cities in Galilee, which Solomon had presented him in return for the services he gave him in building the Temple, perceived at once that the possession of them might bring him more annoyance than benefit, and thinking that Solomon had only presented them to him to get them off his hands, expostulated indignantly with Solomon on the nature of the proffered gift. Nay, more, in accordance with a genuine and universal mode of proceeding in the East, he intimated his unwillingness to accept the gift or acknowledge it in the light of a friendly recompense, and forwarded to Solomon one hundred and twenty talents in gold, a little more than a just equivalent of the value of the villages. Thus far the Tyrian tradition is simply in accordance with the Biblical record; but the sequel, which is perhaps the most interesting part, is not to be found in the Bible. "Solomon, having received the money, well understood that Hiram expected something further in the way of recompense from him." He therefore sent an embassy to Hiram to inquire what he most desired, and the King of Tyre replied: "A proper supply of water for his great city."

Solomon accordingly dispatched to Tyre the masons who had built the Temple, and constructed the magnificent reservoirs and aqueducts of Ras el-Ain. Hiram, in return for this, presented Solomon with the beautiful garden which he caused to be laid out around the reservoirs; and it is to this very garden and to these springs the Hebrew King alludes when he says: "A garden inclosed is my sister, my spouse; a spring shut up, a fountain sealed. A fountain of gardens, a well of living waters and streams from Lebanon. Awake, O north wind, and come thou south; blow upon my garden, that the spices thereof may blow out." (Murray). It is said that the above tradition is of very ancient date, and from the general connection it has to the situation, credence is given it by many close observers. The situation of old Tyre corresponds minutely with the well-defined description given it in the Song of Solomon. The well of living water is fed by streams from Lebanon. And the most healthy and bracing winds come from the north and south. Were it not for the overwhelming sands that have covered much of the remaining beauty of the reservoirs and gardens, no doubt many traces of them would be prominent which are now hidden. There are sand-beds spread over the garden many feet deep, caused by the winds which blow fiercely in the winter season.

Tyre was conveniently located for a commercial city, and was doing business in all ports of the commercial world. The inhabitants were the most expert navigators of their day, and delighted in doing business over the sea. It is called the "merchant city" in the Bible, and is also called "the crowning city, whose merchants are princes," and whose traffickers are the honorable men of the earth. These merchants and traffickers traded in every land, so that their bazaars contained the most important and richest goods from all the trading countries known to them. Merchants from afar came to this city, having for sale the choicest products of their country invitingly displayed in the markets of Tyre. It can be assuredly said, that the most precious fruits of the genius and industries of the people of every tribe and nation, along all the shores of the Mediterranean Sea, were on exhibition in the business places and markets of ancient Tyre. They came from Damascus, Jerusalem, Egypt, India, Arabia, and from the islands of the sea, seeking the trade of this most thrifty city of the world.

GENIUS OF THE TYRIANS.

Tyre was also widely known as a place in which some of the most skillful workmen in fine arts known in the world lived. In the time of David and Solomon, Hiram, King of Tyre, was applied to for skillful artists to assist in fully carrying out the original design in building the Temple. He sent cedar timbers to Joppa, and skilled workmen to Jerusalem, whose ability to execute the work far exceeded the most expert among the Hebrews. Solomon himself acknowledged the superior skill of the Phœnicians when he sent to Hiram asking the favor. "There is not among us any that can skill to hew timber like unto the Sidonians." Solomon also procured from the king of Tyre, Hiram, a widow's son, whose services were indispensable in fully accomplishing the work of the Temple. He was an expert worker in brass. The most celebrated of all Phœnician goods manufactured was the Tyrian purple; it had the distinction of being the richest of all other goods in the world. It was great gratification to a person to be able to dress in this renowned purple that was eagerly sought by the kings of the earth and mighty men, who thought their wardrobe incomplete without a garment made of this material. It is said that this famous dye was extracted from the glands of a peculiar species of shell-fish found in the Mediterranean, called " murex trunculus," small quantities of which are still found, but not to be compared in quantity to that obtained in the prime days of the ancient city.

The spirit of development was so replete in the Phœnicians, they did not content themselves with the territory they possessed on the east in Canaan, but established several colonies; among them were Leptis, Utica, Carthage, Gades and others, in all of which the progress and enterprise of Phœnician industries were clearly developed. After the fall of Tyre, before the victorious arm of Alexander the Great, it was again partially restored, but never attained to its former distinction. There were several rivals who clamored to be its acknowledged ruler. It is said the greatest contentions were stimulated by the rival successors to the great conqueror, who, because of greedy ambition, caused Tyre to suffer greatly. It passed from one ruler to another, according to the amount of power he exerted in warring against it. It fell into the hands of the Mohammedans in the early part of the seventh century, A. D., who, it is strange to say, agreed to spare the lives of the inhabitants and their property, provided they promised to build no more Christian churches, and that they should ring no bells, nor ride on horses, nor offer insults to the Mohammedan religion.

Tyre was retaken by the Christians in the early part of the twelfth century, who controlled it one hundred and sixty-seven years; but was recaptured by the Moslems and became hopelessly lost to the crusading Christians. These insanely cruel people completely demolished this once-famous city, which, for several centuries, had been pining more and more, from time to time, like the fading moon, until finally her last ray was extinguished. The present town is small, but it has grown rapidly within a few years. At present there are prominent indications of a revival in business to a medium degree, but it is not thought in business circles that much can be done to enhance the interest of Tyre while under Turkish rule. In the time of our Lord's ministry, His teachings so greatly aroused the people of Sidon and Tyre, that they went over into Galilee in great numbers to see Him and taste of His love. And we have reasons to believe that many of them were so influenced by His word that they followed Him, and on their return to Tyre they separated themselves into a Christian society. If this was not done while our Lord was yet on earth, it existed in the early age of the apostles. It is certain that St. Paul found a church (on his arrival in Tyre, when en route to Jerusalem), in a progressive state, and publicly declaring their faith in Christ.

It may have been on account of the eagerness manifested by the people of Sidon and Tyre to hear the instructions of our Lord, and the readiness with which they received it, that He favorably referred to them while denouncing Capernaum, Bethsaida and Chorazin. Paul remained here seven days with the disciples, and when the time came for him to leave them, the farewell meeting was most touching. They accompanied the apostle outside of the city with their families, then all of them knelt down on the shore and fervently invoked the blessings of God upon Paul; and when they took leave of each other, he entered the vessel, and the friends returned to their homes. This is a clear evidence that a small congregation, at least, of faithful Christians, who gave public expression to their faith in Christ, lived in Tyre. When the Crusaders took possession, the whole city came under Christian influence, and remained so until the force-rule of Mohammedanism compelled many to espouse that religion.

THE FALLEN CITY.

The ruins of the spacious cathedral built by the Christians are still to be seen. These remains of the cathedral would be extensive were it not for several small buildings which have been built in the centre of the nave They greatly obstruct the sight, and prevent an extensive observation of the space occupied by it. There are a few capitals and broken column-bases of white marble strewn about; and with them can be seen several slabs of white marble supposed to have belonged to the front. The building was erected some time in the twelfth century, and occupied the site of that built early in the fourth century by Paulinus. One passing among the ruins as they lay about in various portions of the present town, can only with an effort persuade himself that his eyes are beholding the mouldering remains that formed one of the most distinguished cities the world ever knew—a city with towering walls, and massive gates, through which the merchants passed from all lands, seeking the richly woven materials and skillfully carved metals wrought by the genius of the Phœnicians.

Tyre was, in her prime days, the centre of attraction from which the superior skill of the children of Ham flowed to all the world.

And notwithstanding the proud city and its teeming millions of busy people have returned to dust, much of their genius lives to benefit the world. It is strange such a limited number of those who pretend to be seeking to find something worthy of mention performed by the Hamites along the line of their existence fail to remember the Phœnicians were racially identified with them, who, aside from their idolatrous tendencies, deserve the praise and appreciation of the civilized world. They were not only skillful workmen, but inventors of such great distinction, that they have furnished the world with some of the most important developments that move the progressive people of our globe. Their works stand to the present as monuments of their power and genius. Tyre is many times referred to in the Bible; in fact it became the burden of prophecy, for six of them were divinely commissioned to speak against her and declare its utter destruction. Isaiah, Jeremiah, Ezekiel, Amos, Zechariah and Joel, all prophesied against Tyre with such accuracy, power and firmness, there can be no doubts entertained as to their being supernaturally inspired to foresee her downfall.

But how hath the mighty fallen! Tyre, the great and beautiful city, that in the days of her glory was mistress of the sea, has been brought low; she has become a heap of ruins, and her glory and pride have come to dust. Her spacious towers and massive walls, her splendid arches and deep vaults, are crumbling beneath the hand of time. That which escaped the instruments of war, the earthquakes finished; and many of her rich treasures, that for centuries were buried under massive ruins, have been washed into the sea by the innovations of the billows. The towers of the old city, it is said, could be seen from afar as the trading vessels approached; and the high walls formed a fortress that defied the arm of the most powerful foe for a long time. Her vigilant fleet was ever alert, guarding with care the approaches to her portals. But they have all disappeared forever. Her beauty and pride, her spinning-wheels and tools for the work of fine arts, her merchants and merchandise have all been brought low, even into the dust.

BURIED TREASURES.

The final demolition of the city, which occurred near the end of the thirteenth century, left nothing but mounds of stone and debris, much of which was transferred to Acre and Sidon for building purposes. The present town is built over ruins of the city of the Crusaders, which lies buried several feet beneath it; and deeper still are the dusty remains of the Mohammedan and early Christian city of Tyre. But the great and beautiful ancient city, that was mistress of the sea and pride of Phœnicia, over which King Hiram swayed the sceptre, and was, after a most bloody and deadly conflict, captured by Alexander the Great, lies deeply entombed under the cities that have been built over her grave. It is currently believed, from evidences several times developed, that there are many valuable treasures yet remaining among the deeply-buried ruins, as various denominations of ancient coins have been found in those parts that have been washed out by the waves of the sea. But the inhabitants seem to have no disposition to seek it; they lurk around the place where the waves are likely to undermine, to pick up what they can find, but exhibit no ambition to seek further. Many valuable metals have been found after the high tide abated at various times, that would be highly appreciated by all tourists could they procure them.

While in Tyre I stopped at the Latin Convent, and one of the officials presented me with several pieces of old coin; some of them were current in the time of King Solomon and King Hiram. It was a very acceptable gift to me, and one that will ever be gratefully remembered. In almost every direction in and about the town deep caves exist, caused by the sinking in of decayed ruins. Many look as though they would afford safe retreats for bandits and other outlaws, whose presence in the country is so greatly dreaded. Just about six miles south-east of Tyre is situated on the hillside, near the Safed road, the tomb of one of the most celebrated and illustrious men known to the Phœnicians. It is the monument beneath which lie the dusty remains of King Hiram of Tyre, the memory of whom will go down to the latest generation. This venerable relic stands alone, out from the scenes of busy life, but is looked upon as one of the most remarkable sepulchres in the world, because of the distinction the character achieved whose remains are resting there. It is an immense sarcophagus of limestone, hewn out of a single block, and standing on a base formed of three courses of large, white stones, nine feet and eight inches high. The sarcophagus itself measures twelve feet and two inches in length, and seven feet and nine inches in width; it tapers slightly towards the top. The lid is made with large ridges in the direction of its length, and is three feet seven inches high in the centre, and two feet ten inches at the sides. Immediately at the north side of the monument two flights of rough steps lead to an artificial cavern, ten feet long, eight feet wide, and five feet high. There is a general agreement as to the identity of this tomb as that of King Hiram, the ally of King Solomon, whose skilled men in fine arts greatly assisted the latter.

Close to the tomb of Hiram is another, which, in some respects, resembles that of the illustrious king of Tyre, and is generally regarded as the resting-place of Hiram of Tyre, the widow's son. There seems to be several well-founded reasons for regarding this tomb as identical with that of Hiram Abiff. Not far from these tombs are several others, differing widely from the above, in which it is thought some of the most distinguished Tyrians have been buried.

In one of those tombs is a remarkable group of fifteen stone figures that were carefully carved, representing male and female; all but three or four are standing erect, with their hands placed one upon the other in front of their breasts. It is said this is the usual attitude of the Phœnicians when they paid their devotions to Baal and Astarte. The statue in the midst of the group is supposed to represent Baal. Towards this deity three men and a woman are approaching. The statues are much disfigured, no doubt by the hands of invaders, which is a common custom in the East. In this way all the statues of ancient date in Egypt have been mutilated. It is likely that all the great images the Phœnicians set up have been destroyed in this way. If these ancient tombs could have been preserved in Phœnicia as in many other places, the historians would have had a greater advantage in obtaining a correct idea of the characters they illustrate, for instead of probability there would be certainty designating each of them.

Ten miles and a half north of Tyre the site of ancient Zarephath or Sarepta is entered. This is the town to which the Lord directed Elijah to journey, and make his home with a poor widow, when the brook dried near which he was hiding from the wrath of Ahab While here he raised the widow's son, who had suddenly died. There is nothing to be seen in the place now, except great masses of ruins covering a large space. The town was abandoned by the inhabitants in the thirteenth century, because of the insecurity of the plain in which it was located, and they built up a village on the side of the mountain, not far away, and named it Surafend. Some have supposed this old site to be identical with Misrephoth-maim. There is but little known of the inhabitants of Palestine and Syria, prior to the settlement of the Hamites, who came in the land in large companies, and made vast improvements in all parts in which they located, so that in process of time, it became one of the most progressive countries in the world.

PRIMITIVE CANAANITES.

The Canaanites were divided into eleven tribes, according to the information the Bible furnishes us. This great Canaanitish nation must be acknowledged, by all fair-minded people, as one of the most progressive people the world contained. It may be of interest to mention the tribes respectively, and the parts of the country they inhabited when Joshua entered Canaan with the children of Israel.

The Phœnicians settled along the shores of the Mediterranean from Gebal, on the north, to Acre on the south. It is also evident they occupied the tract between Acre and Haifa, for they had a garrison on the west border of Mount Carmel. The Hittites were descendants of Heth, who was the oldest son of Canaan. This tribe was divided into two divisions: those on the south occupied the territory around Hebron; the northern division lived back from the sea in the northern districts of Syria, and along the Orontes valley; their capital city was Kadesh. The Jebusites selected the country in and about Jerusalem; Ornan, who had the threshing-floor, in the time of David, on Mount Moriah, was of this tribe. He was an important helper to the king in the time of his great trouble. The Amorites were a powerful people; they were also divided into distinct portions; those on the south settled west of the Dead Sea, in the district of Engedi, a very mountainous and wild country. They afterward crossed the Jordan and established two highly prosperous kingdoms known as Heshbon and Bashan.

The northern Amorites settled in the plain of the Beka'a, between Lebanon and Anti-Lebanon, on the south of the Hittites. The Gergasites occupied the district which was known in later times as Decapolis. The Havites were a very popular tribe, and finally divided into two distinct portions; that on the north selected their portion of territory on the Anti-Lebanon district, extending as far as Hamath, which seems to have been the most northern limit of the Canaanitish territory. The Havites, on the south, settled at Shechem, and the whole country round about as far south as Gibeon. The Arkites settled in the plain on the north of Lebanon, which was well watered and fruitful. The Sinites occupied the whole of the mountain tract of Lebanon. The Arvadites lived along the seacoast on the north of Sidon, having their chief seat on the Island of Aradus. The Zemarites also inhabited a portion of the coast (it is thought) between the Phœnicians and the Arvadites. This tribe seems to have been one of the smallest of the Canaanites. The Hamathites settled in the city of Hamath, and this district divided the Hittites from the Amorites along the Orontes. It should be remembered that these various tribes were called Canaanites, because they descended from the same chief ancestor. The most of the tribes were progressive, industrious and brave, but the most important of them in point of prosperity were the Phœnicians.

The country inhabited by the Canaanites, and afterwards given to the children of Israel, has been known under several names; the most prominent was "Canaan," after the general name of the people whose influence and progressiveness were known throughout the realm of civilization. They were inventors of the most intricate arts and sciences of their age. There are several who have written historical sketches concerning this wonderfully progressive people, who have failed to appreciate them properly for the enterprising spirit they exhibited; and others seem to have been puzzled to know to which race they belonged. Attempts have been made to take the Phœnicians out of the Hamitic stock and give them to Shem or Japheth. Others say they were of doubtful origin, and therefore fail to give them to either race. It is strange that all other races can be traced to a distinct origin and placed with the class to which they properly belong.

Because these Hamites were an important people attempts have been made to rob them of their proper place in the catalogue of races. The Bible tells us plainly the Phœnicians were descendants of Canaan, the son of Ham, and any one who will take the time to read the Bible account of their origin must concede the fact. It is well understood the youngest son of Ham was named Canaan, whose posterity was very numerous, so that it became necessary for them to seek a new territory. They migrated from their home and settled along the eastern border of the Mediterranean Sea, north of Mount Carmel; then spread themselves over much of the interior, as described above. The first city founded by them was called Sidon, after the first son of Canaan. Making this city their capital, they began to spend over the most fruitful districts in the land. They settled in communities, calling each by a particular name to designate one from the other. But the country became known by the name of the ancestor of the people, "Canaan," whose name was adopted by all his descendants. The following is recorded in the Scriptures concerning them: "And Canaan begat Sidon his first born, and Heth, and the Jebusite, and the Amorite, and the Girgasite, and the Hivite, and the Arkite, and the Zemarite, and the Hamathite; and afterward were all the families of Canaan spread abroad." "And the border of the Canaanites was from Sidon, as thou goest toward Gerar, unto Gaza; as thou goest toward Sodom and Gomorrah, and Admah and Zeboim, unto Lasha. These are the sons of Ham after their families, after their tongues, in their lands, in their nations."

The Hittites appear to be the most numerous of all the tribes; they soon became a powerful and warlike people. They formed themselves into a separate government entirely independent of the other tribes, submitting themselves to one general head instead of having independent rulers over each town and village, known as the Sheikh, which seems to have been the custom of a majority of the tribes, which was the cause of many severe internal struggles. The Hittites were the descendants of Heth; their first settlement was on the west of the Sea of Tiberias, but in time they became so numerous it was necessary for them to divide, and as early as the time of Abraham a great number of them had moved to the south and settled about Hebron. This was a brave, warlike and progressive people. Many emblems of their chariots and other war implements are still seen among the broken shafts and monuments in Egypt.

It was to the Hittites Abraham applied for a burial-place to lay the remains of Sarah to rest, and purchased from them the cave Machpelah. It seems that this tribe was not lost sight of, until after the Jews returned from captivity. Uriah, one of David's royal officers whom he caused to be treacherously put to death, that his adulterous conduct with Bath-Sheba (Uriah's wife) might not be unfolded, was a Hittite It will be seen by this, the Hamitic race were not only the menials in Israel, but held royal positions. It seems the Arvadites and Zemarites, because of their position along the coast, became blended with the Sidonians so intimately, that they were known by the same name, and became a portion of the most enterprising, skillful and prosperous people of the Canaanitish families. The origin of the Phœnicians, therefore, is perfectly clear and distinctly stated in the Bible. They were first known as Sidonians for many ages (2 Sam. xi. 3-27; Gen. x 15-20; Ezra ix. 1), because they were descendants of Sidon, the oldest son of Canaan; and Canaanites because Canaan was their great ancestor. But they were called Phœnicians by the Greeks and Romans. This was the name given to the district in which they lived rather than a racial title; just as it is common to call a resident of Washington, a Washingtonian.

HISTORICAL ASSOCIATIONS.

The name Phœnicia was given to a tract of country in Palestine, embracing a narrow strip of frontier land, between the hills of northern Canaan, the mountains of Lebanon on the east, and the Mediterranean on the west. But notwithstanding the title given the district by the Greeks and Romans, the inhabitants clung to their original name and called themselves Canaanites. The accounts given us concerning these people are but meagre; for their real history was destroyed. But enough has been gleaned from the Bible and other places to assure us they were of Hamitic origin, and known to belong to the families of Canaan, who spread themselves over the land. They developed into a great people, possessing a high degree of literature, and kept accurate records of their history; and had not the most important accounts of their progress been destroyed, we should be much more enlightened as to their wonderful intellectual powers and historical value. The numerous manuscripts, compiled by their scribes, were committed to the flames by foes, who after many attempts succeeded in overthrowing Tyre, their capital, and demolished everything valuable.

There have been exhaustive investigations made by men of brilliant minds to find something reliable that would allow them to trace the origin of the Phœnicians to Shem or Japheth; but they have failed in their attempt. The Bible account of their racial descent is conclusive; and were it not for this, Ham would no doubt be robbed, in general estimation of his fatherhood, of one of the most energetic and skillful people known to the world in their day. Although we have the clear facts of the word of God concerning them, there seem to be a few authors who fail to comprehend them, and contend that the Phœnicians are descendants of Shem. Rawlinson is quoted as having said, in giving the world the benefit of his convictions as to the origin of this people: "On the whole, it may be concluded, that the Canaanites and Phœnicians were two distinct races; the former being the original occupants of the country, and the latter being immigrants of a comparatively recent date." This is a tremendous step backward to dodge a plain Bible truth, which teaches to the contrary; for every one who has examined the Holy Scriptures, concerning the origin of the people known as Phœnicians, must, in all fairness, conclude that they were composed of the Sidonians, Arvadites and Zemarites, in connection with a few from some or all of the other Canaanitish tribes. These, without a doubt, were that great people, called by the Greeks and Romans, Phœnicians, but known in the Scriptures as Canaanites and the descendants of the fourth son of Ham. There is but one conclusion for all unbiased and reliable authors, who claim to be guided by the standard of truth, and that is, the Phœnicians were, beyond all question, Canaanites, whose great ancestor was Ham.

It is lamentably true that this wonderful people, so full of progress and genius, were ignorant of the true God; notwithstanding there must have existed among them a traditional knowledge of His dealings with the people whose sins became unbearable before the flood was visited upon them; yet they were so allied to Baal, their false deity, that their eyes were closed against the true God. They were most stubborn in their idol worship, which, without doubt, brought down upon their government repeated visits of God's just indignation.

THEIR WIDESPREAD INFLUENCE.

But when we turn from this dreadful and most damaging evil, and look upon this people's progress in art and science, the fact must be conceded, that we cannot point to a civilized people on the globe where Phœnician influence is not felt. There were no people living, in the age of the Phœnicians' greatest advancement, who surpassed them in skilled workmanship and naval achievements. Their vessels were built so as to be used for battle-ships in the time of war, and trading purposes in peace. It is said they had such a well-defined code of laws for the government of their fleet, that Athens, the foremost maritime state in Greece, was not equal to her in disciplinary regulations. Hence, when the officials of Athens wished to improve their military laws, Xenophon referred to the Phœnician vessels as the best-known in the world for orderly regulations and skillful management. The Phœnicians were, also, the great leaders in the use of astronomical science in navigation; until they introduced it, the world was ignorant of its value to navigators.

The connection of the moon with the tides, and how it influences their ebb and flow, was first brought into prominent notice by the Phœnicians; and it is one of the great sciences that aid shipmasters in many ways to-day. Many precious lives have been saved by a knowledge of it. Each of the Phœnician cities along the sea-border was noted for some specialty that particularly characterized it. The manufacture of the world-famed purple dye, which the Tyrians prepared from a certain shell-fish, gave them celebrity throughout the civilized world. The people of Sidon were celebrated because of the knowledge they had in manufacturing glass. Its invention and use in Palestine were first introduced by the Sidonians. Some authors say this people were the first inventors of glass; but this is strongly doubted by others, who are inclined to give Egypt the honor of introducing the use of it, and that men skilled in the art were sent over from that country to Sidon to carry on the work.

It is known, however, that glass was first discovered by the Canaanitish seamen on the banks of the Belus River, near Acre; and there is now to be seen at Ain Musheirifeh a well having faint traces of an old foundation near it. This is supposed to be the site of ancient Misrephoth, the limit to which the Israelites caused the Canaanites to retreat, and the identical place where they established a glass factory long before the Hebrews entered the country. It is likely that the old ruins scattered about are the withering remains of the ancient glass works founded in the time of the Hamites' occupancy of Canaan. Now it cannot be regarded as a matter of very great importance, whether glass was first invented in Egypt or Canaan, so far as it pertains to the race to whom the honor of bringing it into use is concerned, for in either case the Hamitic race is entitled to the first honor. It seems the Phœnicians were inventors of several musical instruments, which they played with great skill. With one or two exceptions, there was a general idea of government existing among the tribes, which they endorsed early after settling in Canaan. They had no disposition to form a general government under a chief executive and become a strongly fortified people, but each city was a kind of independent sovereignty in itself. The stronger cities were usually looked up to for protection by the dwellers in the towns and villages in cases of necessity. This gave the ruler, who guarded the welfare of the neighboring towns, the right as chief adviser, which the people felt to be under obligations to observe. This state of affairs introduced many disastrous troubles, which would have been avoided if they had formed a general government. The Tyrians had a large slave population, which seems to have been more numerous than the free citizens. These slaves were taken from various parts of the world by traders, somewhat on the plan African slaves were obtained in the United States of America. At times the bondsmen would cause the Phœnicians much trouble, which on one occasion at least caused great torture, much bloodshed and the loss of many lives. All of this could have been instantly checked if the people had been united in a general government; but under the circumstances the Tyrians were compelled to fight their own battle when domestic trouble confronted them. When foreign invaders came up against them the whole people would unite to secure the general welfare of their country.

The best evidence obtainable as to the founding of Sidon and Tyre, the two most important Phœnician cities, shows that the former was built about fourteen hundred years before King Solomon's time, and the latter at an early subsequent period. With the beginning of Solomon's reign a historical notice of their doings is recorded. The king succeeded by Hiram was Ahibal, from whose time a written sketch has been preserved. It is thought by many that the Phœnicians reached their meridian in progressive development about the time Solomon came into power. Hiram Abiff was one of the most skillful workmen in the country at that time, and was master of the artistic workmanship in carving gold, silver, brass, iron, stone, and timbers, and was equally expert in preparing the purple, the blue, the vine levin, and the various engravings. Therefore King Hiram sent him to look after the work of the Temple. It was, it seems, an ordinary custom with the Phœnicians to carve their names in some of the foundation stones of buildings of extraordinary character. This they did on some of the stones composing the foundation of the Temple.

It has been discovered that several stones of the ancient Temple that were used in the foundation have the names of the Phœnicians carved on them. We were informed, while passing through the Temple area, old foundation stones are found as the work of investigation proceeds. These are very deep down in the earth, and all that had been found bearing inscriptions were those that had been carved by the Phœnicians. We have reason to believe the Israelites were employed, in common with the Canaanites, in preparing stone for the building; but they failed to set their mark upon it, that their work might be distinguished from their Phœnician associates. There is a remarkable coincidence in the reign of Solomon and Hiram. Under their official jurisdiction both kingdoms were prosperous, and reached the highest point of their national greatness, and when these monarchs died the gates of success, hitherto opened to the two kingdoms, were suddenly closed, and they began to decline. It is stated Hiram was succeeded by Baleastartus, his son, whose reign was comparatively short. This decline took place in the tenth century B.C. Then domestic troubles became prominent, and the kingdom of the Israelites divided, and at the same time foreign nations were covetously looking towards Phœnicia. Indeed, the government of Tyre never became prominent after the decline began. It was continually haunted with "fightings without and fears within." The last representative of Hiram's family who held the sceptre of power was Philetus, who fell in the second year of the ninth century by the murderous hand of Ethbaal. "Ethbaal," who assumed the ruling jurisdiction of the kingdom, thereby formed a new dynasty, causing the kingdom of Tyre to pass into the hands of his own family in regular succession. It seems that during his reign Ahab was installed king, to succeed Omri, his father. The king of Tyre (Ethbaal), like the former rulers, was on intimate terms with Israel, and gave his daughter Jezebel in marriage to Ahab.

Sidon, the mother of Phœnician cities, was one of the most ancient cities in the world. It is mentioned in the early writing of human progress, and is supposed to have been built very soon after the dispersion, or about twenty-three hundred years before Christ. It is mentioned in connection with the first events, when the world began to increase in population, of the Land of Promise by the Canaanites. Josephus says the city was built by Sidon, the oldest son of Canaan, and named after him.

Long before the children of Israel entered the country from their wilderness wanderings, Sidon had a wide-spread fame, and was known as Great Sidon, so called by Joshua in distinguishing it from another city of the same name in the interior, because of the wonderful achievements the people had made in progress. The inhabitants were a thrifty, energetic, and prosperous people, doing everything they attempted in the best possible way. Their indomitable spirit of enterprise made them not only an equal, but superior to all other nations who followed the same employments. The ancient writers unite in their statement concerning the people of Sidon, that they were progressive citizens and stood in the front ranks of the cultured classes of their day. Their architects were the best in Syria, and they seem to have maintained that character during the many ages of independence. Strabo says, the Sidonians were celebrated in astronomical science, in geometry, navigation and philosophy. This must be true, otherwise the people would not have reached such a high state of prosperity and distinction.

SOME OF ITS STRUGGLES.

The situation of Sidon was far more exposed than Tyre, and was much less trouble to attack. It was captured in seven hundred and twenty B.C., by Shalmaneser, who became famous as a great warrior on account of the many victories he won while king of Assyria. It was also subdued by Artaxerxes, king of Persia, several years later. But when Alexander the Great went up against the city, the people regarded any attempt to withstand his army but a fruitless issue, and surrendered immediately. In this, the difference between Sidon and Tyre is seen in regard to their situation in case of an attack. When the great conqueror attempted to besiege the latter, he found it much more difficult. The city was well fortified and hard to approach. The Tyrians were not willing to surrender without compelling him to win, by a great struggle, every inch of ground upon which his men should set their feet. Therefore, he was withstood most manfully for seven consecutive months before his victory was complete.

Sidon was captured at least six times after the death of Alexander, at each of which the whole city was plundered and ransacked, so that it finally became deserted, and remained so a long time before signs of a revival were hopeful. Finally, the city was partially restored, and at present compares favorably with the majority of small cities and large towns along the Mediterranean coast. There is but little of antique importance within the city limits of interest to historical visitors. But some of the ancient tombs, a short distance from it, are regarded as highly important. The most renowned of them are those of Ashmanezer, Sidon's greatest monarch, and Alexander the Great, the world's most famous conqueror. The tomb of the former was discovered in January, eighteen hundred and fifty-five; the latter, thirty-seven years later. The remains of each of these great and mighty men were removed; those of Ashmanezer were taken to Paris and placed in the Louvre, and those of Alexander were placed in the Museum at Constantinople. There are many beautiful orange orchards about Sidon, which are very fruitful, and are regarded as some of the finest in all the land.

Now, when we take into consideration what the Canaanites have done for the good of the world, and that many of the inventions produced by their progressive minds have been improved and are still being used by land and sea, we cannot fail to see that the descendants of Ham have been as much (if not more) benefit to the world as any other race in it. To say these Phœnicians were not of the families of Canaan is to deny the word of God; and to affirm as some do, without a single evidence, they became extinct before the period of the great achievements made by the people called Phœnicians, by whom they were supplanted, is worse than folly. For it is well known the original Phœnicians did not lose their identity in the country until after the captivity of the Israelites.

THE LEBANON RANGE.

The range of Lebanon is one of the most noted in Syria and Palestine. It is very low, continuing many miles in length, connecting with a number of parallel ridges and peaks having deep valleys between them. There are other portions containing a number of transverse valleys, some of which are beautiful and green, affording rich pasture for thousands of cattle.

This great mountain chain of Lebanon, which, to look upon, seems as if it were struggling towards the region of perpetual snow, but has not as yet reached the line of its destination, affords enough atmospheric pressure to hold the barometer to a point where snow can be kept the year around in sheds or storage provided for that purpose. Its highest peaks are situated at the southern extremity of the chain; were they to the extreme northern limit, it is likely snow would be on them almost the year round. Those parts of the country which cluster around the base of Lebanon are furnished with a beautiful supply of water and heavy dews constantly, while those more remote parts are scantily watered. This towering mountain yielding its moisture incessantly is the life of Damascus; without it she would not be the beautiful city of gardens, which she has been always called. There is but one road leading over the mountain between Damascus and Beyrout, which is known as the "Diligence Road." This is one of the finest highways in the land. It belongs to a French company, and is kept in the best repair, so that the stages, by making an early start, drive the whole distance of seventy miles between Damascus and Beyrout in one day. There are several stations along the road where the teams are changed.

When the mountain ascent is begun, the elevation is gradual until a half mile is traveled. The road then begins to wind in a zigzag style up the lofty mountain side; sometimes it runs along a ridge which abounds with wild, romantic scenes, and soon the traveler will find himself about five thousand feet above the level of the sea, where the scene is wilder than any of those previously seen, and the only pleasant attraction is a large grove of several thousand small cedar trees. Very nearly all the climates are passed through while making a passage over the mountain of Lebanon and Anti-Lebanon, from an ice-cold to a blood heat. The rocks in many parts of the mountains are very porous, and have been worn by the action of air and water into many deep caves and hollows. These afforded safe retreats for many persecuted Christians and Jews, who fled from the wrath of their pursuers, on occasions when dreadful religious mutinies suddenly matured to exterminate them. It seems as if God caused these caves to be opened against the day of conflict, as a refuge for His people.

The tillable land of Lebanon is very fertile, and many of the farmers are in a state of commendable prosperity. But the country comprising the Anti-Lebanon district is wild, barren and desolate; some portions of the road through this scene of desolation were noted as favorite lurking haunts for robbers. At Hameh, a few miles from Damascus, a favorable change begins, from the wild and lonely scenery to verdure and fertility; more and more the way becomes cheerful and lifelike. The river Abana with its tributaries flows directly from the heights of Anti-Lebanon to the plateau at the eastern base, giving Damascus a beautiful girdle of gardens. The cedars of Lebanon became celebrated and widely known from the time of the building of the Temple; because the hewers in great multitudes, both

Israelites and Phœnicians, were sent to cut down the trees and prepare them for the use of the building. It is reasonable to suppose there was in those days a very extensive forest of large and beautiful cedars from which the workmen selected the best to send up to Jerusalem.

It is often a disappointment to travelers going from Beyrout to Damascus, over a portion of the most mountainous region of the Lebanon range, not to see the lofty cedars, of which so much has been written, both in sacred and profane history. The remaining large cedars are situated on a group of knolls, in the middle of a vast seclusion in the central ridge of the mountain range, at the head of Wady (valley) Kadisha. It is not a large forest; those who have had time and means for surveying it, estimate it to be about three-quarters of a mile in circumference, and containing about four hundred trees. On approaching them from a distance, they appear so small that one feels he is not half compensated for the pains it requires to go to them. But when the small forest is reached, after a fatiguing ride for one or two hours, the full size of the trees is seen and one's fullest expectation is at once gratified. Some tourists have pronounced it the most lovely specimen forest they have ever beheld. One thing which greatly heightens the appreciation of visitors, is the comfort it affords after a weary horseback ride through the mountains and valleys under the severe pressure of a burning sunny day; then suddenly entering into a lovely shade, it would seem as though one escaped the heat of a furnace.

One of the most interesting features of this forest was its deep solitude; but that has been largely removed by the erection of a chapel on the site where it is supposed many of the timbers, which composed the Temple, were taken from. There are about a dozen of the most ancient trees yet standing. It is not known how old they are, but some of the guides would have us believe they are coeval with those that furnished timber for the Temple in Solomon's time. It is known that cedars, under favorable circumstances, live to a great age; but we cannot suppose there is a tree standing on Lebanon, which had an existence when the busy hewers were leveling and trimming them to take their place in the first house built for the worship of God. If there could be found such an antique cedar in any portion of the mountain range, it would be worth a double fortune to the owner; for souvenir-seekers would give a large amount of money for a small piece of it, and the greatest impositions would be practiced by venders. These trees vary in size, as may be supposed; the older ones—at least two of them—measure forty feet in circumference; the others are not more than five or six feet in diameter. Many of them are scarred with the names of travelers who have visited the forest. This is not to be wondered at, when it is remembered such a custom has existed for many years, wherever it has been allowed.

Lebanon has been visited by thousands who seem to be satisfied if their feet can press the honored forest from which the timber was taken for the Temple. And when we remember the antiquity of the trees, their ancient glory, their world-wide fame, and the holy uses for which the cedars were hewn, we can readily understand why so many pilgrimages have been made to it from century to century. The cedars of Lebanon were greatly venerated by the Hebrews as emblems of power and majesty. These groves on Mount Lebanon were doubtless very vast in olden times.

PART XIII.

DAMASCUS AND ENVIRONMENTS.

Situation of Damascus—River Barada—Saul Arrested while on his Mission of Persecution—Its Buildings—Some of her Rulers—First View of the City—Present Inhabitants—Annual Pilgrimage to Mecca—Principal Places of Amusement—The Great Café—Its Walls and Houses—Mohammedans Hatred Towards Christians—The City Seized by Timour—The Street Called "Straight" and Others—The Great Mosque—House of Rimmon—Greek Inscription on the Wall.

DAMASCUS.

DAMASCUS is one of the chief cities of Syria; but Beyrout is much larger and more progressive. The latter is along the coast of the Mediterranean Sea; therefore it possesses many advantages over the old capital which are common to seaboard cities. It has been said Damascus is the oldest city in the world, but there are objections to this tradition; some incline to the opinion that Hebron is the oldest, others think Shechem is entitled to the honor; but it is certain Damascus is a very old city, having a history extending back into the dim regions of antiquity, and it was widely known in the time of Abraham's sojourn in Canaan. It is situated in a beautiful, luxuriant plain, about thirty miles in diameter, between the eastern base of Anti-Labonus and the desert, about fifty miles southeast of Beyrout, its nearest seaport, and one hundred and thirty miles (by the way of Tiberias) from Jerusalem, but much further if the trip is made by Tyre and Sidon.

Notwithstanding Damascus sits in a valley, it is estimated to be about two thousand and three hundred and forty-four feet above the level of the Mediterranean Sea. This valley is supposed to be one of the richest and most fertile tracts of land in Syria. Its fertility is due to the river Barada, the Abana of the Scriptures, which became so widely known because Naaman referred to it when recommended to dip seven times in the Jordan. This life-giving stream, though very small, waters the plain. We are told by Josephus that Damascus was founded by Uz, grandson of Shem; therefore it takes its station among the oldest cities known in history, although it was not generally popular until the time of King David, who subdued it when the Syrians of Damascus came up to assist Hadadezer to fight against Israel. David's army slew twenty thousand of them and took charge of their city. But the Syrians waited their opportunity, and recaptured it in the time of Solomon under the dynasty of the Hadads. Damascus became the capital of Syria, when it began to rise into power, and exerted itself in every possible way to become the equal, even the superior, of the kingdom of Israel. Syria became involved in several wars from the time it began to struggle for superiority until late in the ninth century before Christ, when it was captured by the Assyrians. One of the most interesting events connected with the high officials of Damascus was the miraculous cleansing of Naaman (Gen. xiv. 15; xv. 21; 2 Sam. viii. 5, 6; 2 Kings v. 1–27), the commander-in-chief, of the leprosy. Syria, like the surrounding kingdoms, passed through many bitter ordeals; for she had foes within as well as without. There was always some one who did not belong to the royal house looking up to the throne with an anxious hope of becoming the ruler, and would even take the life of their king, to satisfy their wicked ambition, as did Hazael, after he was anointed, to change the dynasty of Benhadad. Damascus fell into the hands of Tiglath-Pileser, king of Assyria, about the middle of the eighth century, B.C., and lost her independence from that moment; yet it seems her commercial prosperity was not materially impeded for a long time. There are many references to Damascus, especially with regard to the many conflicts it had with Israel and the Assyrians, which caused much bloodshed, suffering and great loss of life.

In the latter part of the fourth century before Christ, Alexander the Great captured Syria, and sometime afterwards it fell into the hands of the Ptolemies; then of Aretas, King of Arabia, and was finally captured by the Romans, and subjected to the emperor of Rome in the time of our Lord. The Romans strongly fortified Damascus, so that it became one of their main strongholds. It finally fell into the hands of the Turks, under whose sway it remains to the present, and is made the headquarters for their military barracks in the middle district. Damascus, like all the principal cities of Palestine and Syria, has had its severe ordeals, although it escaped the total demolition, which many of the others suffered; for while they have been so terribly wrecked that not one stone was left upon another, this old capital has partially maintained its original status; 'but she has changed many times from one nation to another. She passed from the ruling authority of the Hadads, and was subordinated to the kingdom of Israel during the reign of David. The Assyrians, under Tiglath-Pileser, captured it; after a time it fell into the hands of Alexander the Great. The Ptolemies in turn were over her, and several other foreign monarchs swayed the scepter of power over this antique Syrian capital. When Philip, the tetrarch of Ituræa and Trachonitis, died, those states were annexed to the Roman province of Syria (Isa. xvii.; Jer. ix. 23–27; xi.; Ezek. xxvii. 18; 2 Kings v.; vi.; viii. 7–15–28, 29; x. 32–38; xii. 17, 18; xvi. 3–7–17, 18–22–25; xiv. 5–12; 2 Chron. xxiv. 23; xxviii.; Song of Sol. vii. 4; viii; xi; Amos i. 3–5), which was on the border of the government of Aretus, the Arabian, who gave his daughter in marriage to Herod, the tetrarch whose lewd passion caused him to put away his wife and take Herodias, the wife of his brother Philip, for which he was strongly rebuked by John the Baptist. The daring act of licentious indulgence aroused the indignation of Aretus, father of Herod's lawful wife, and he marched an army against him and captured Damascus just about the time of the death of Tiberius Cæsar at Rome, which was in the year thirty-seven of our era.

When Saul of Tarsus went to Damascus on his mission of persecution, it formed a part of the Arabian kingdom which was held by Aretus under the Romans. The place where Saul, "when he drew nigh unto Damascus," saw a brilliant light which caused him to fall to the ground, is still pointed out to travelers as identical with that memorable event.

Early in the seventh century Damascus was taken and ruled by the Moslems, and twenty-seven years afterwards it was made the capital of the Mohammedan empire by Moamyah, the first Caliph of the Omeiyades. This powerful dynasty swayed a widespread influence, and several other nations fell under Moslem dominion. Europe, Africa and Asia were under its iron hand, so that Damascus could boast of being the great centre of one of the most extensive empires known in the world.

The city, while under the control of the Omeiyades, was much improved with many spacious buildings, both for residence and worshiping places; he having used some of the most costly and carefully prepared materials the city contained; such as the Roman Colonnades and porticoes; and other costly structures were partly, if not entirely, demolished to erect them. But this Moslem sway was only for a comparatively short duration.

The people, content with the victories they had won, and supposing their stay permanent, made themselves contented without fortifying against outward foes, and went from one degree of moral and physical degeneracy to another, until they became steeped in licentiousness, and the glory they had faded like a rose; and Damascus, the city of their pride, was taken from them. Damascus passed from one conqueror to another during a stormy period of four hundred years. The Tulumides and Fatimites of Egypt possessed it, and from them it was taken by the Seljuks, who were a roving Turkish people. In the year of our Lord one thousand one hundred and twenty-six, when the Crusaders were making successful attacks in Palestine and Syria under Baldwin, Conrad and Louis VII., they attempted to enter Damascus, but were not successful, and the Crescent banner of Syria still proved to be the honored emblem of the great capital, which gave great joy to its admirers.

In the second half-quarter of the twelfth century Damascus was captured by the Mongols, but was only a short time under their control when it was captured by the Bibars; about the beginning of the fifteeth century, she was again siezed by Tamerlane, who dealt with the people in a most barbarous manner. He did more to injure the inhabitants than all the previous conquerors together. The whole place was exposed to the most outrageous assaults known in the most barbarous countries of our world. The Turks captured Damascus about a century later, and were one of the last masters of the situation, whose rule was of no benefit to the Syrians; on the other hand, they seem to be draining the whole country dry by extorting from the people heavy taxes, and other heavy burdens that will not allow many of them to get beyond the limits of stringency. It is thought one of the chief reasons for pauperism and theft originated from the refusal of thousands to work on account of the heavy heel of taxation, which continually grinds them down.

Many cutting criticisms have been published against the Turkish rule in Palestine and Syria, but it does not seem to amount to anything so far as changing the condition of the people is concerned. Without doubt Damascus was a renowned city in the earlier historic times; it was known in the days of the pioneer Patriarchs, and continued through the multitude of ages to modern times. During its existence other powerful cities have risen in many parts of the eastern world that vied with her in strength and beauty for a time, then decayed and came to naught. But Damascus, notwithstanding she has passed through the furnace of many bitter ordeals, has maintained an unbroken space in history from the time it was founded to the present. She has been robbed of much of her glory and early greatness; but her claims to antiquity must be respected by all the world. It was founded before Baalbec and Palmyra, and has outlived each of them. These two great cities, in connection with Babylon, Tyre and Sidon, and many others of proud boast in the East, have come up and passed out of existence in the swift train of time and left this old Syrian capital, the lone star, to point the traveler to their ancient greatness. It was in a most flourishing condition in the time of the Jewish kings; this is evident from the caution David took to place a strong garrison there, after his army had captured it, and from the stand it took against King Solomon, who vainly attempted to hold it under his sway. This proud city must have been from very early times attractive to men as a place of habitation, as the adored Nile, the life of Egypt, has from time immemorial been the centre of attraction to the population of that country in all generations to its living waters.

Damascus abounds with water-courses for miles around; in all directions may be seen an unbroken forest of beautiful gardens containing many acres of ground, and everywhere can be heard the murmur of rivulets, breaking the silence of the night. Abana and Pharpar, those ancient rivers which were the proud boast of Naaman, constantly pour their contents into these little canals, so that from those parent streams the whole expanse of country in which the city and gardens are located is fed and kept alive. Such are their beauty and enchantment, that when the first view of the city is obtained from a distance, it appears like an earthly paradise; and the astonished beholder is ready to cry out, Great is Damascus! Although she has lost much of her splendor, riches and antique embellishments, she is now the most important city in Syria. It contains a busy population, many of whom are thrifty, prosperous and healthy.

The inhabitants of the city are estimated to be one hundred and eighty thousand, of whom one hundred and fifty-two thousand are Mohammedans and twenty thousand are Christians of various denominations, and eight thousand are Jews. These Jews and Christians are much hated by the dominant class, and are often cruelly treated. Were it not for the military troops, who are constantly stationed there, it would be impossible for them to live among them. As it is, there have been alarming outbreaks, caused by the ever-flaming fury of indignant Moslems, who swept the Christians away by the thousands. There is a deep and permanently-seated ill-feeling existing between Mohammedans and Christians, which will require many years to obliterate. There was one of the most shocking and bloody massacres occurred in this ancient city in eighteen hundred and sixty, known in history, the effects of which are keenly felt to this day in Damascus; notwithstanding, many of the churches and dwellings, which were destroyed, have been rebuilt. The story of the terrible and heartless tragedy is pathetic in the extreme, and would seem to be more like a carefully-written myth, conceived in the mind of an expert novelist, rather than a true historical account of a recent event.

There was one imposition after another heaped upon the Christian population, until a great fire of indignation suddenly burst upon them with fearful violence and destruction. It is said, by those living near the dreadful scene, that by sunset, on the ninth of July, 1860, the whole space, known as that portion of the Christians' quarters, was a broad sheet of flame. The water supplies were cut off, so that it became impossible for them to extinguish the fire in any of the burning buildings, nor could they leave their fast-consuming quarters themselves, being hemmed in and closely quartered by infuriated Moslems, who stood ready with instruments of death to murder any one who attempted to escape. Caution was taken not to begin the bloody work until the Christians, who were in other parts of the city attending to their avocations, had returned to their homes, so that all of them, if possible, might be burned to death or slain at the same time.

It is pleasant to know that the whole plan did not succeed; for many, having received help from a source the blood-thirsty Moslems did not anticipate, were rescued from their murderous scheme; and yet it is estimated that five thousand Christians were killed in cold blood, and many thousands more, who escaped, perished, shortly afterwards, from fright, famine and other agencies. Recruits were pouring into the city to join the rioters from the neighborhood to put a final end to all the Christians. During the entire night and following day the shameful massacre went on. Hundreds fled to the caves and dens in Mt. Lebanon for security, homeless, penniless, naked and wounded. Thousands of those who could not escape were treated in a most shameful manner. Many, to save their lives, were compelled to deny the Christian faith and espouse that of the Mohammedans. The scene was one which has but few parallels in the history of the world. Damascus is the capital of the eastern district of Syria, under command of a governor-general, and is the headquarters of the army of Syria. The commander-in-chief is called Seraskier, and the space occupied for himself and the command is very large. The soldiers are compelled to patrol the whole country.

There are no police officials or constables to guard the interest of the people in any part of the Turkish dominion; therefore, the soldiers are sent out in all directions to look after the general welfare of the country. Sometimes they are sent out in small companies, especially in the most dangerous portions of the Lebanon and anti-Lebanon districts. They have the fastest horses in Syria, and a person would have a hard time to escape them. As there are no color-lines drawn in the Turkish government, nor any other outside of America, as far as I have seen, no distinction is made in forming companies. There can be found among the soldiers complexions from a coal-black to the ordinary white, forming the same company without a murmur; all are fellowshipped upon the most friendly relations. They go on patrol duty together, eat at the same table and sleep in the same bed. Damascus is the great centre from which the annual pilgrimage starts for Mecca, so as to be convenient to the commander of the army, whose duty it is to go with the pilgrims or send an official in his stead. These pilgrimages are composed of Moslems, who, in compliance with their law, make a journey to the citadel of their religion at least once in life.

These people make the greatest sacrifice to accomplish it. Many are very poor, but they do without the comforts of life to lay up a fund sufficient to enable them to go to Mecca and pay their devotions at the great shrine. Those who can, take all their family, so that if the children find it impossible to go when they become of age, the law will not hold them responsible. Pilgrimages are made from China, Japan, Ceylon, India, Syria, Palestine, Egypt, and all parts of the world where Mohammedans are in large numbers, and when they all reach Mecca they sometimes number three or four hundred thousand. The principal places of amusement or public comfort are the baths and the "Great Café," which are almost continually thronged with the pleasure-seeking classes of all grades of society. The cafe is generally visited at night or after working hours, as many of the public parks of our American cities are by those whose employment occupies their time during the day. It is simple in its construction and general arrangement, consisting of several shed-like buildings, situated in the midst of a number of rapidly running streams, which are roaring constantly and producing a deafening noise, which is greatly augmented by the inharmonious sound of hundreds of voices that make a stranger feel as though he is in the antechamber of Pandemonium. The place is illuminated dimly when compared to our modern illuminations. There is no gas or electric lights in Damascus. Small oil lamps are used, which, from their sparseness, make a very poor light; these lamps are suspended on ropes from one limb of a tree to another, at a considerable distance apart, and many are hid from view on account of the hanging branches of the trees.

The greatest attraction to a stranger is the beautiful coloring it gives the white foam of the waters as they dash against the rock. The whole space, which is very large, is filled with people, even the banks of the little streams are crowded. The café is a common resort for men and children. The streams passing through it are made by digging deep trenches, into which the waters from Abana, which is now, as in the days of Naaman, the great river of Damascus. It has been the life of the city from its beginning. To these waters she is indebted for her beauty and fertility, and in this water Naaman, the leper, thought he might wash and be healed.

The city is walled in, but the wall is not very strong; while there is much material that was in the former walls composing those of to-day, the most of the composition is sun-dried mud, which makes them appear ragged and dilapidated. In several parts of the wall, small houses are built, which is a custom brought down from the earliest times. They are quaint in appearance, and so situated as to compose a portion of the wall. It can be readily understood how the house of Rahab, Elisha, and that from which St. Paul was let down over the wall in a basket was constructed, by closely examining these houses built now on the wall of Damascus. The site of that eventful escape of the apostle is still pointed out, as is also the site where he fell to the ground, having seen a light above the brightness of the sun. On the south side of the city, where the walls contain the models of masonry of almost every age, the foundations are of Roman origin mostly. In some parts the character of the work shows they are of great age, no doubt from the early days of the ancient city. Farther southward to the boundary is still standing the foundation of the ancient wall; the present is not connected with it, a deep ditch being between the two.

The Mohammedans of Damascus are intensely opposed to Christians, and were it not that they fear the authorities it would be impossible for any to live there, or even visit. In all my travels it is the only place where I noticed any attempt of an outrage upon me. I noticed on two or three occasions, while riding down the streets in a carriage, stones were thrown by some one at me; and on the day we visited the public garden, it seemed to me, for a while, they would take us by force, but we fortunately got off without injury. One fellow threw something at us; I do not think it would have done much damage if it had struck me. The native Christians must at all times be alert lest they are outraged by these midnight disciples of Mohammed, who hate them as poison. They have no more relations with them than the Jews and Samaritans had in the days of our Lord. It will be no surprise if at any time they should rise up against them. Damascus has been famously known for its wonderful steel sword-blades, which in olden times were so very elastic they could be bent until the point reached the hilt, and sharpened as keenly as a fine razor. But after Tamerlane or "Timour" (the Asiatic, as he is called by some writers) seized the city and committed many vile depredations and carried off its wealth, its stores of antiquity were pillaged and robbed, all the costly fabrics were taken, its beautiful palaces were ransacked and burned to the ground; its great libraries, filled with valuable literature, were destroyed, and its noted armors and keen-edged steel swords were carried away to Samarcand and Khorassan, which places from that time supplanted Damascus in the art of making the famous steel swords.

It seems the people could not regain their original expertness in finishing those noted blades, although they do what they can to imitate them, and many of all sizes are seen lying in piles in the bazaars, selling at low prices. There are many bazaars in Damascus which form an almost perfect labyrinth of narrow lanes and alleys, connected by dark passages, some of which are so very narrow two persons cannot walk abreast, and often on meeting each other in certain parts of them, pass with difficulty.

Many of the streets where they are located are completely arched over, so that it is necessary for lamps to be lighted in the stores all day. This is also true of the street called "Straight," which is to the present day a great feature and thoroughfare in the city; not only for its busy markets and stores, but for its important connection with Ananias, who lived on this street when Saul and his associates came down from Jerusalem with a commission to disturb the believers in Christ. The street is not entirely straight all the way from east to west, but it seems to be in a direct line for a considerable distance. It is mostly a business street, and crowds are in it all the day. The greater portion of the streets in the city are narrow and dark, and ancient in appearance. There are but few that will admit a vehicle to pass through them. Many times it is necessary to alight from the carriage and walk through certain streets and meet at another point; for many of the narrowest are the most important for sight-seers. They do not excel in cleanliness, especially in the Jewish and Christian quarters; and no one accustomed to streets having proper sanitary provisions will regret having to leave these hovels so entirely wanting of purifying water. The Mohammedans' quarters are much more inviting: caution is taken to keep them clean and pleasant. Those whose condition will allow it, have richly furnished houses paved with marble, and beautifully adorned with fountains, flowers, fruit-trees, and other things that embellish and make home inviting and cheerful.

The city is two miles or more in length from its extremity on the northeast to that of the southwest, with a comparative breadth in some portions, and densely filled with a varied population of all classes, conditions, races and complexions. These people can be best seen on Friday, which is the great market day. The Jew, with long, curly locks and turbaned head, can be seen with his sack and stool in some locality of the market, carrying on the money-exchange business. The Arab looks as if he were ready to pounce upon any one who ventured to stand before him; the waddling Turk, who seems too lazy to walk; the African, who looks amazed at one of his own color dressed in European clothes; the philosophical-looking Afghan and the dusky-looking Algierian, all pass together. One of the greatest attractions in Damascus is the great Mosque; not because of its superior character in architecture or magnificence, for it is very inferior to the great Mosque of Omar in Jerusalem, or that of St. Sophia of Constantinople, though it is called the great Mosque. Any one who first visits either of the two last named, would not be much impressed with that at Damascus, except on account of its historical association, which runs back into antiquity.

The price of admitting a party into this mosque is exorbitant, and would be checked by law were it located in a country where people pay some attention to the admonishment of conscience. Twenty francs is the amount charged for a party. The usual preparations must be made on the outside. If the visitor has no slippers of his own, he may rent them from the bookseller, who has a stand close to the entrance door kept for that purpose, as no one is allowed to enter without them. In connection with the things shown inside are the Fountain of Ablution, and the tomb in which the traditional story locates the burial-place of the head of John the Baptist. This structure is four hundred and thirty feet long, and one hundred and twenty-five feet wide. Its greatest attraction is, its being situated on the site once occupied by a heathen temple, which, it is stated, covered six hundred square yards; and a number of its broken columns are here and there seen among the bazaars near by. In the time of the splendor of this building, when the people devoutly kneeled at its shrine, it was somewhat on the order of the Temple at Jerusalem. It contained rows of columns forming a colonnade, with everything else needed to make it alluring to the thousands of her devotees who knelt at the shrine. This is supposed to be the identical site of "the house of Rimmon," to which Naaman referred, and in this temple was erected that altar, the beauty of which, so won the admiration of Ahaz he ordered one like it made for the use of the Temple at Jerusalem.

It is stated that the temple in which heathens used to worship was standing during the first century of our era, and "was destroyed by Theodosius in the middle of the fourth century; and that a Christian church was built on the site out of a part of its ruins by Arcadius, in the beginning of the fifth century, which was dedicated to John the Baptist, whose head was said to have been buried there." This church continued under the control of the Christians for three hundred years, after which it was divided between the Christians and Moslems, each of them having separate apartments; but later the Christians were routed by the Mohammedans, who took absolute control of the whole structure.

There has been allowed to remain on the outside of the south wall a most **significant** inscription in Greek, which some think the Moslems have overlooked, or their blindness hides it from their view, which contains the **following**: "**Thy** kingdom, O Christ, is an everlasting kingdom; and **Thy** dominion endureth throughout all generations." The wonder **prevailing** among Christians is, how it has escaped the notice of the Mohammedans, who for over twelve hundred years have been the sole custodians of the Mosque. The inscription is in an obscure place, and was discovered by persons who were closely examining the building historically. The Mosque has three minarets, one of which visitors generally ascend to get a good view of the city, which enables them to have an almost perfect idea of it and its environments. The street called Straight, the various orchards, streets and lanes, the bazaars, the crooked shape of the city, together with the surrounding hills, are all open like a map to the eye. These are some of the wonders of Damascus. (2 Kings v. 18 ; xvi. 10–16.)

PART XIV.

THE SEA OF TIBERIAS AND THE NOTED PLACES ROUND ABOUT.

Route from Nazareth to Tiberias—View of Mt. Tabor—Ascent of Mt. Tabor—Journey from Tabor to Tiberias—Caravan Road from Jerusalem to Damascus—Character of the Natives—The "Mount of Beatitudes" or "Horns of Hattin"—Time Spent in Galilee—The Environments of the Sea of Tiberias—Visit to Decapolis—Visit to Magdala—Visit to Cæsarea Philippi—Mt. Hermon—Sea of Tiberias and its Situation—Fish of the Sea of Galilee—Custom of the Fishermen—Town of Tiberias—Plain of Gennesaret—Springs of Lake Gennesaret—Old Testament Association—Ancient Magdala—The Latin Convent—Ruins of Chorazin—The Two Bethsaidas.

FROM NAZARETH TO TIBERIAS.—APPROACHING MT. TABOR.

THERE are two routes from Nazareth to Tiberias; one leading through Cana, the other by the way of Mt. Tabor, both of which are full of interest. It is customary for persons going no farther north than the lake, to go down via. the latter route and return by the former. Indeed, it would be of benefit to those going to Damascus to arrange with the authorities to return by the Mount Hermon route, so as to get a nearer view of it than that obtained from Capernaum, and also have the privilege of returning to Nazareth, by the Mount Tabor road. In this way a traveler has the benefit of both routes; that is, he may go down through "Cana of Galilee," and return by way of Tabor. When the Israelites received their allotments, the frontier boundaries of Zebulun and Naphtali were marked by Tabor. It is a most commanding mountain, which at first sight strikes the attention of the beholder as a place of historic importance. Tabor is very lofty and sloping at the top. This princely mount stands alone in the plain, looking as if it were frowning down upon the few minor elevations that connect it with the mountains of Galilee. This monarch of the plain is estimated to be over two thousand feet above the level of the sea, and thirteen hundred and fifty feet above the surrounding hills. It is attractive from any point of

MT. TABOR.

view, whether from a long distance or near by, and presents a different scene from each quarter. One standing on the south will notice it has a steep, rough and rugged slope, from base to summit with mammoth rocks, seeming as though they were ready to fall, clinging to it. On the north its general features are changed so greatly, that it does not seem like the same mountain. The whole slope from bottom to top is covered with green foliage and small trees.

It is usual for tourists, who are not pressed for time, to make a trip to the summit. A comparatively good road winds the slope, and thereby renders the ascent much less fatiguing than might be supposed. There are two convents on the peak, belonging to the Greek and Latin churches respectively; at which fairly good accommodations may be obtained for the night. There is a tradition of several centuries' standing that upon Mt. Tabor, the scene where the transfiguration of our Lord took place, and those who have had an opportunity of investigating its general situation, have concluded it is beautifully adapted for the occurrence of such a transportingly grand event. Its beautiful and inviting landscape round about, its shady depressions in connection with its general adaptability for such a memorable conference as was held at the time in question so prominently combine, that the top of Mount Tabor is believed by many to be the hallowed place that our Lord ascended with Peter, James and John, when Moses and Elijah came down to commune with Him. But as no one knows it to be the real site of the event, the visitor cannot go one step beyond probability, for opinion is divided between Tabor and Hermon; and, notwithstanding critical examinations have been made, no definite conclusion has been reached by candid and unbiased minds that are capable of settling the difficulty. The Greeks and Latins, who seem to be ever ready to draw definite conclusions from mere traditions, many of which are founded upon unjustifiable premises, claim Tabor as the real site of the stupendous transfiguration. It is also true that many of the best examiners believe, from the circumstances connected with the event, that Hermon is the most probable mount of its occurrence. This opinion is established upon the fact that two of the three evangelists, in referring to the matter, speak of Cæsarea Philippi immediately before the event took place. It is supposed by some that their statements warrant the belief that the event took place on Mount Hermon. But those who incline to Mount Tabor as the scene of this stupendous event, hold the argument in favor of Mount Hermon, is based upon the fact of our Lord being at Cæsarea Philippi with His disciples a few days prior to the transfiguration, which is claimed to be insufficient to justify their position. It is evident a week had elapsed between the time He questioned the disciples as to the opinion of men concerning Himself and the conference with Moses and Elijah on the mount, which would allow ample time to travel from Cæsarea Philippi to the summit of Tabor. St. Matthew and St. Mark use the same words as to the time Jesus went up into the mountain. They say, "after six days," etc. St. Luke says, "about eight days after" the Saviour was teaching the disciples at Cæsarea, He ascended the high mountain with the three in whose presence the transformation took place. There is no conflict between these two statements with reference to the time of the occurrence; two of the evangelists say, "after six days," which may be the seventh or eighth day; the other says about eight days, which may be a little less than eight full days, and surely after six had passed. It is not stated by either of these disciples where Christ went, or what He did between the time He ended His teachings relative to the great sufferings He should soon encounter and the glorious change of His person, when visited by the two great lights of the church who came down to commune with Him. It is certain, therefore, that neither Tabor nor Hermon can be definitely settled upon as the real site of this overpowering event. But there can be no doubt that it transpired on one of the two. The convents belonging to the Greeks and Latins, respectively located on Tabor, are both claimed to be on the site of the transfiguration, which is not a strange occurrence with those two religious bodies; their bitter opposition to each other seems to forbid the one from having in charge a traditional site without the other having one close by claiming the same thing. It is so with reference to the Church of the Holy Annunciation in Nazareth, and the site of the changing of water into wine in Cana; and we might mention many other places of similar occurrences. It is sadly unfortunate that such is the case, for many times a person is placed in a state of doubt as to the identity of a place when he is standing on the exact site where certain Bible events took place. In fact, both of these sects should be branded with deception; for if it could be established that Tabor is the mount upon which the hallowed transformation took place, no one could tell the exact site. There was no altar or tabernacle built as suggested by Peter, or even a stone set up to mark the site of the event; and yet men dare, in this date of our era, to tell to the world that they have discovered the identical spot of the transfiguration. I do not hesitate in saying it would require Peter, James and John, the three who witnessed the glorious occasion, to return to earth and point out the spot before it could be definitely located.

Notwithstanding this fact, thousands of poor, ignorant pilgrims are decoyed by this glaringly deceptive delusion, and climb to the top of Tabor expressly to worship on the traditional spot of the transformation of their Lord. The summit of Mount Tabor is broad, although it seems to be very narrow from a far view, and contains many ruins of buildings which in earlier times dotted it. It is highly probable that a small village was built there in the time of the Hebrews, or later. The ruins consist of walls, towers, houses, cisterns and vaults, all of which, though greatly decayed, are sufficiently preserved to indicate the use made of them when they were erected. The view from the peak of this lofty mountain is better than that from Mt. Nazareth in some respects, but not so general, for several points can be seen from the latter that are not prominent from the summit of the former. Investigations have shown the ruins scattered over Tabor are of Jewish, Byzantine, Crusading and Saracenic origin. There are indications of several cisterns having been cut in the rock, which are supposed to belong to the Jewish period, and are likely to have been cut out during the time Josephus had command. The descent from the mountain is not dangerous, as might be supposed, but very tedious; many times it is found best to alight from the horse and walk over the very rough places; persons are advised to make this descent in the cool of the morning; therefore an early start is necessary, so that Tiberias can be reached in time to make a trip across the lake to Capernaum and Bethsaida on the same day.

Now, if this majestic Tabor is the place where that memorable transfiguration of our Lord occurred, how hallowed is its lofty summit, and what a gush of divine glory covered it when the immaculate feet of the world's Redeemer rested upon its rocky surface! The beauty and majesty in which the Saviour appeared to receive His heavenly guests, cannot be described even by those who had an opportunity to behold Him for a moment. There was no change in the nature of Christ, although His form and appearance were marvellously transformed; but in substance His body remained the same as when the angelic host proclaimed in song His entrance into the world, or as when He ascended the rocky summit. The cause for which Christ went up into the mountain was unknown to the three witnesses, for our Lord did not give them the least intimation of the event. And when it took place, they were so greatly overwhelmed they could not maintain strength enough to catch but a slight glimpse of the splendor with which He was adorned, however desirous they may have been to witness the whole transaction. The sight was too effulgent for them to gaze upon fully at that stage of their spiritual adoption; they were not members of the council, but taken up there simply to witness the glorious preparations for it. Therefore, they were not permitted to hear what was said during the conversation; they simply saw the transformation of Christ, and the two members of the Holy Convocation appear upon the scene, then they fell into a state of death-like stupor, and remained so until the conclusion of the conference. What less could Peter say than he did, and what more could he have proposed to express his willingness to be shut in with Jesus from the communion of the rest of mankind? He exclaimed: "Lord, it is good for us to be here; let us make three tabernacles, one for Thee, one for Moses, and one for Elias." It may be said of Tabor or Hermon (for this scene occurred upon one of the two beyond all doubt), that the most stupendously glorious conference ever conducted upon the face of the earth known to man, was held on the occasion of the transfiguration of Christ.

Two patriarchs of the militant church had come to pay honor to the Saviour, and to talk with Him concerning His death, which was soon to take place over at Jerusalem. Moses, the distinguished leader of the Hebrews, came as the chief representative of the law that was given him on Mount Sinai, which he made known to the people in his charge. Elijah came as the chief representative of the prophets, who gave unmistakable evidence of our Lord's coming. The condition of the three witnesses during the time they had to catch a glimpse at the likeness and distinguish the two ancient worthies, must have been to them a transporting scene. But neither of them could take such advantage of the event as to listen to what was being said, or see what those distinguished representatives did; the whole transaction was as a blank to them; it was a secret council. Therefore, beings who knew nothing practically of the state beyond this life could not be permitted even to hear what was being said. It must have been a most glorious sight, and, notwithstanding we were not with the favored three who saw the beginning of the transfiguration, we join St. Peter in the statement, it was good to be there.

The journey from the foot of Tabor to Tiberias is not a pleasant one, but the thought of visiting the place where our Lord did many of His mighty works makes the travel much less fatiguing. The whole route, except in two or three places, is dreary, rough and monotonous. There are no shade-trees along the way, and those traveling that route in April or May, experience a most unpleasant and tiresome journey. When the descent into the plain is made, Tabor is seen in its majesty, lifting its summit beyond the lower clouds, and presents a form more amazing than from any other point hitherto seen, especially when an unobstructed view from its base to summit is obtained. There is but one place of material interest along the route, which is the old caravan road leading from Jerusalem to Damascus. This is crossed at a place called Khan-el-Zejjar, the merchants' caravanserai. This is the identical road Saul of Tarsus went, in company with his little band of men, on his mission to Damascus to persecute the saints. It is also thought they stopped for the night at the old inn, just at the cross roads we have named. This is a very dreary place, and deadly quiet, except one day in each week it is a scene of tumultuous confusion.

The merchants assemble here from all parts of the country for miles once a week to conduct their sales; many are found there from day-break until late in the afternoon. When they all arrive, the space used for the market is well filled with men, camels, donkeys and produce of various kinds; then a scene of wild confusion begins, which would seem to one unaccustomed to their mode of transacting business, that a mob, with the serious results of great loss of life, had occurred. But no trouble of a dangerous character happens; the natives are a very excitable people, and make the greatest fuss over small matters. We have witnessed many occasions when from the conduct of the people nothing short of a hard battle was looked for; but all soon became quiet without having struck a blow. When the afternoon advances, the merchants and dealers quietly disperse from their wonderful market and return to their distant homes, leaving the place to resume its usual solitude. I had not the opportunity of witnessing the market at Khan-el-Zejjar, but formed an opinion of it from the conduct of the people at others we had seen.

The Saturday I left Nazareth for Tiberias, was very unpleasant. It began raining in the morning and continued all day, and, although we had made careful preparations for the weather, it was so piercing that our clothing was very wet when we reached the little village on the shore of the lake. Our horses were faithful, and took us down in good time, but they showed evidences of being much worried by the storm. There are many places and things to interest the traveler round about the Sea of Galilee. Our Lord spent much time here, doing wonderful works, and establishing his Messiahship to the great satisfaction of thousands. Thronging multitudes followed Him from place to place around the sea, and made the hills echo with their importunities to be healed of deadly diseases with which they had been grievously tormented for many years. From here His fame spread to all the nations and people in far-away countries, as a wonderful physician, whose healing power had never failed to instantly exterminate any disease the people were afflicted with.

It is noteworthy that our Lord did not leave His home in Nazareth simply to build for Himself a great reputation as a healer of all complaints so as to display His divine power, for He would have gladly done for the people of His home all these things which were so greatly beneficial to those of other towns and cities, if they had not murderously rejected Him. The time having come for Him to openly work the works of the Father who sent Him, and being forced to leave the home of His childhood, our Redeemer came down the mountainous region of Galilee, entered Capernaum and temporarily established His home there. He immediately began anew His mission of mercy and love that the dwellers of Nazareth so blindly rejected.

St. John tells us our Lord went from Cana in company with His mother, brethren and disciples down to Capernaum, where He only remained a few days, as it was about the time for Him to attend the Jewish Passover at Jerusalem. On one occasion He found the Temple desecrated by those who had made it a trading place, at which the Lord became disgusted and whipped them out. These occasions were very exciting in Jerusalem; the people in all parts of the land looked with eagerness, hoping to be able to go up to the great feast. When the time drew near, large companies from every section of the country would wend their way to the great festival, which grew more attractive each year; that is, it became less sacred and more for pastime, and what we would call miscellaneous pleasures. The venders of doves, pigeons, oxen, sheep, etc., and the ever ready money-changers usually made extra preparations for the entertainment. The people began gathering several days before the feast took place; the throng was so dense during the celebration that accommodations could not be had for all in the houses or public inns; hence it became necessary to put up tents on Mounts Zion and Bezetha beyond the confines of the walls.

The Easter feast now celebrated in Jerusalem is not to be in any way compared with the ancient Jewish feast, neither in the number of attendants, nor the character of the feast. But if we could witness one of the annual celebrations at Mecca, when from two to three hundred thousand people have gathered, we could form an idea of the gathering at the great Jewish feasts in the time of our Lord. Now if we could fix our minds on a scene of this character, composed of men, women, and children of all grades of society and dispositions, crowding the Temple that had been built especially for the worship of God, degrading its sacred precincts with merchandise, and defiling its sanctum by cheating and robbing, we would not wonder that Jesus, who was full of compassion, became indignant at such inexcusable wickedness. To look at the conduct of our Lord from a natural standpoint, we might be amazed at the fact that the many who were selling and buying in the Temple, allowed one man to drive them all out with a cord without remonstrating. But there was a power in Him they keenly felt and feared; therefore they fled from His presence. This alone should have convinced them and all the people in Jerusalem of His divinity.

It was during this visit to Jerusalem the conference took place between our Lord and Nicodemus, who sought an interview with Him in the night, and was kindly listened to by the Saviour, who afterward delivered a powerful sermon to him, assuring him that the simple fact of his being persuaded that Jesus was sent of God to teach and enlighten men was not sufficient—he "must be born again." It is reasonable to suppose Nicodemus returned home fully convinced of the authority of Christ, and saw his own condition as never before. Some authors criticise this night visitor for not telling his associates of the conference he had with Jesus; but to my mind it was better, under the circumstances, that he should hold his peace.

When the time came for Jesus to depart from Judæa, He returned to Galilee through the district of Samaria, and stopped at Jacob's well, as has been stated in another chapter. After two days, He left Samaria and came into Galilee, and was gladly welcomed by the Galileans, for many of them had been up to the feast at Jerusalem and witnessed the works of power He did there; then Jesus came again to Cana, where He had changed water into wine. This was a timely visit, just as were all the others made by Him. He was anxiously desired at the time by a nobleman in Capernaum, whose son was very ill, and nothing that had been done for his restoration to health was effectual.

THE NOBLEMAN'S SON HEALED.

The news of our Lord's return spread through the land as if sent by electricity; every one passing through Cana, which is on the road leading from Nazareth to Capernaum (and people were passing to and from those cities constantly), told the news that Jesus had returned to Cana. It is highly probable He was expected; for although He had been absent about nine months, it was generally known in what part of the country He was laboring, and when He resolved to return to Galilee, we have no doubt the news reached the province, and likely the capital, in advance of Him. The nobleman, hearing that Jesus had returned to Cana, which was about twenty miles from him, made all possible speed to go for Him to come and heal his son, who seemed to be in the arms of death. When the man found Him, he made a touching appeal: "Sir, come down ere my child die," was his beseeching petition. This was a glorious opportunity for Jesus to manifest the power He had over a dreadful fever without being by the bedside of the sick, or sending anything to be taken. It was a real faith cure. "Go thy way, thy son liveth," said the Lord. The nobleman took Christ at His word, firmly believed his son would be healed, and returned home filled with hope. He was met by his servant the next day, as he was approaching the house, with the glad news of the complete restoration of his son to health, and that the fever that held him with a deathly grasp had left him about one o'clock the previous day, which corresponded exactly with the time Jesus assured him the boy should be healed. What news could have been more joyful to that father, whose interest in the health of his son compelled him to travel over the rough and dangerous mountain road to procure the services of Jesus, the Great Physician, who alone was able to exterminate the deadly disease that was surely stealing away the life of his son; and what could have demonstrated to him more pungently the divinity of Jesus, than the favor so mercifully conferred? The meeting at home must have been one of great emotion, intensified with the tenderest embraces. It is certain the nobleman did not leave the presence of Jesus doubting, nor did he entertain a moment's mistrust during his return, for he was about twenty-four hours in returning, which could have been traveled ordinarily in eight hours, and by forcing the journey, it could have been made in six, for nearly the whole distance is down hill. He seems to have been several hours longer going home than he was coming over to Cana, which is an evidence that he came in haste to find Jesus if possible before the lad died. But having had the promise that his son would live, he went home slowly.

THE VISIT TO CAPERNAUM.

There seems to have been an interval of several months between the time of the miraculous healing of the nobleman's son and the visit the Saviour made to Capernaum. He returned to Nazareth after He had spent the time allotted Him in and about Cana; in the mean time He was preparing to enter more largely upon the work of His mission of healing the sick, casting out devils, and raising the dead. Our Lord made Cana His temporary headquarters or the point from which He started on His mission of mercy through all that region. Luke says, "He taught in their synagogues and was glorified of all." (John iv. 50; Luke iv. 15). This is the time He went to Nazareth, the home of His parents, where He had been reared from infancy; and the people, having heard of His wonderful works, invited Him to conduct the reading and address the people in their synagogue on the Sabbath. The result that followed has been stated on another page.

Being compelled to leave home, Jesus came to Capernaum, where He had several friends, who would receive Him most gladly. The nobleman, whose son He healed from the deadly fever and all his house, were His friends, and would have arranged to accommodate their benefactor during His stay; but our Lord preferred a more humble residence,—one that the poorest of men would not fear to approach. Therefore He came to the house of Peter, the poor fisherman, and seems to have made it His headquarters while in that city. Jesus, having settled upon Capernaum as His future home, entered with great power upon the work of teaching men the way of salvation; confining His labors largely to the province of Galilee, through which He made three special itineracies, working many miracles, and healing all kinds of diseases. How blind the Jews were; all of them looking steadfastly for the coming king known as the Messiah; and according to their instruction, they expected He would first appear in one of their four sacred cities; therefore they were found each year there looking for him, and as Tiberias was one of these cities, it would be filled with Jews each year about the season they expected their deliverer would come. But when He came in their midst and performed such things as no one but God can, they turned themselves from Him.

How assiduously our Lord labored for the good of men! For beside doing the wonderful works daily, He walked over all the ground, making three circuits over Galilee, passing through Samaria and Judea, through a portion of the country beyond the Jordan, and we hear of Him being out in the northwest as far as the borders of Phœnicia. We do not hear of Him riding at any time until He entered in triumph into Jerusalem; at this time He rode a donkey from Bethany to the Holy City. When the fame of Jesus had spread over the land as a great teacher and healer, multitudes came to Him, so that many strangers were seen in Capernaum. Many no doubt came just to see the man about whom so much was being said; some came to be healed of their disease, or brought their friends to have their ills exterminated.

When Jesus went from the synagogue to the house of Simon Peter, He found Simon's mother-in-law very sick with a tormenting fever. He rebuked the disease, and it left her immediately, so that "she rose up from her couch at once and ministered unto them." This was on the Sabbath, and the news was soon dispatched through the city, of the miraculous healing of the mother of Peter's wife, which created a great desire in many to apply to Him to cure them. It must have been a time of great jealousy among the physicians, who so suddenly lost their prestige. It is reasonable to presume they would have gladly expelled Him from the city if it had been in their power. The people were ready to go at once to have our Lord heal them, but many were prevented by those who pretended to scrupulously observe the Sabbath, insisting they should not visit Jesus on such business until after the hour which closed the Sabbath day, teaching the poor sick ones the moral law, forbidding them doing anything of the kind on that day. Several observed their request and waited with impatience until the blast of the trumpet announced the close of the Sabbath. Then the multitude made a dash for the house of Simon Peter to see Jesus.

Our Lord had been teaching the multitude, and being greatly pressed, it became necessary he should enter a boat and move a little from the shore. It was Peter's fishing boat He entered, and Peter at that moment was off with his brothers with their nets. They had been fishing all night and caught nothing; therefore they were much discouraged. After the Saviour finished speaking to the people, He told the men to put out a little into the deep and prepare for a draught; they did so, and caught so great a number their boats began to sink. They became convinced of His divinity, and at the command they followed. He first called, according to the evangelists, Simon Peter, and Andrew, his brother; James and John, sons of Zebedee. These first disciples seem to have followed our Lord on his first itineracy through Galilee. They left their nets and came into Capernaum with Jesus, and went in company with Him to the synagogue on the Sabbath. This is the occasion when He expelled the unclean spirit from the man in the presence of all the people. The unclean spirit objected; but He bade him come out of the man, and he obeyed.

In a comparatively short time the house was crowded, and a multitude, being unable to get in, remained about the yard. Jesus without a murmur attended each case in regular order. "He laid His hands on them all and cured them." It was a busy night with Christ, but He took pleasure in healing each one of whatever disease he possessed. It must have been a wonderful sight, especially when the devils came out of some of them "crying out and saying, Thou art the Son of God." The number of persons healed was very great, and no doubt it was a late hour before He had a chance to take His rest. He could have healed every one with a single word, but did not choose to adopt that method; having many ways at command to cure, He preferred to work with His hands that night, although it required several hours to lay them on that vast multitude of infirm people.

But the Saviour was not fatigued, for when the day broke He rose up and sought a place of retirement that He might commune with the Father before the busy scenes of the day began. It is likely the multitude who had been healed spent a sleepless night with their friends holding a jubilee over the result of the event that restored them to health, and no doubt sent word to all whom they knew to be troubled with disease, to come over quickly and apply to Jesus for relief. At any rate the news quickly spread, and an early start was made for Peter's house by a host of sick people possessed of various diseases.

They must have been greatly exercised when it was made

known the Lord was not there, but had left early in the morning, saying nothing as to His destination, nor when He would return. But Jesus was at the time out in the quiet desert having uninterrupted communion with the Father. This seems to be the first recorded instance of our Lord going out to engage in private devotion at the early dawn. Simon Peter, who seems to have known where the Lord was, seeing how disappointed the people were, concluded to lead them to Jesus, and when he had come to where He was, he told Him how eagerly the people sought Him. But He said to Peter, "Let us go to the next town that I may preach there also, for therefore came I forth." It is plain that Jesus did not wait for the people to come to Him, for many living remotely from Capernaum had no way to reach Him, and wishing all to be beneficiaries of His blessings, He was anxious to visit them.

The impression made by our Lord in Capernaum before starting on this mission was so great, the people spread His name through all Galilee, so that the whole country was excited over His good works. All the people of the cities and towns received Him gladly, except those who were ambitious to be lords, such as the Scribes, Pharisees, Elders, and rulers of the people. These classes generally opposed Jesus secretly, and when there was no danger of an uprising against them by the people, they made open opposition to His claims. But His ability to heal the poor sick folks, who had been many years pressed down under incurable complaints, was so clearly demonstrated, no persuasions offered by these malicious enemies could deter the people from seeking Him from every part of the country round about. These good tidings had reached those living in Judea and beyond the Jordan, many of whom came seeking Him over in Galilee.

It is a most pleasant thought, that of all the varied cases presented to Christ not one was too hard for Him to master; whether the persons were blind, halt, dumb, deaf, covered with leprosy, possessed with devils, or dead, He controlled every case and set the captive free. It was many times so very exciting in those parts Jesus visited, the people left their daily work for a while and followed Him into other towns and cities.

One of the most touching appeals was made to our Lord by a poor man who was smitten with leprosy. It seems to have been a very severe case, for the Evangelists say, "He was full of it;" and, having heard of Jesus' wonderful cures, he came and fell at His feet saying, "Lord, if thou wilt, thou canst make me clean."

Jesus immediately had compassion on the man and healed him. What a gracious change! The disease had not only made its subject miserable, but ostracised him from the society of his friends. It is a most dreaded and destructive affliction; when it takes hold of one it never releases its victim until death discharges it. Would any one wonder that the man spread the news everywhere, telling all whom he met what Jesus of Nazareth had done for him, and what great joy there must have been at his home when his friends met and embraced him!

It was the custom of Jesus to so arrange His tours of mercy to be in a community on the Sabbath where a synagogue was located, that He might teach the people and open their understanding to the things pertaining to their peace with God. The pressing demand to hear Him was so great that the officials always invited Him to explain the Scriptures. Therefore Jesus taught and preached in all the synagogues throughout Galilee. The whole country was dotted with these places of worship. They were built for the convenience of the people after the return of the Jews from captivity. To build a synagogue was regarded as a mark of piety; hence, if it was found that a community of ordinary wealth was without such a building, it was as surprising as it would be to those of our times should they enter a large town or city in which there is no Christian church, and no one directing the people to the Lamb of God. There were also many people dispersed through Galilee who could not attend the services at Jerusalem on those great occasions to worship, while others could only, with much difficulty, manage to go once each year. The synagogues served as a kind of substitute for those who, by reason of physical and domestic inabilities, were unable to go up to the Temple with the hosts that assembled there. They were so constructed that the faces of the people who went into them to worship were turned toward Jerusalem. They were allowed to be built any place where the community was large enough to form a medium congregation. They all contained special seats for the elders, which were known, being higher than the others; usually invited guests sat on them, and they were commonly called "the chief seats." The Pharisees, who were always anxious to be conspicuous, generally sat in them, so that they might be looked upon with a high degree of veneration. Jesus referred to them when He was administering a searching rebuke to these selfish men.

The synagogues were usually built by personal gifts, as churches are in our times. The people would come together wherever their means would justify such procedure, and give according to their ability money enough to build a house of worship suited to the number of attendants. Sometimes one person who desired to immortalize his name would build a synagogue for the people. Those who came to Jesus in behalf of the Roman nobleman's servant, regarded the recommendations they gave him of the highest importance when they said, "He is worthy that thou shouldst do this for him; for he loveth our nation, and himself built us our synagogue." While the services were being conducted the strictest decorum was enforced and any manifest tendency to violate the rule was sternly rebuked.

It is estimated that there were four hundred and eighty of these buildings in Jerusalem alone. These places of worship contained two apartments, one on the west, the other on the east. The former was the repository of the chest in which the books of the law and the sections of the prophecies were kept; and, to distinguish it from the main room, it was called the temple; the other apartment, in which the congregation assembled, was known as the synagogue. The men and women had separate seats; the former occupied the main floor and the latter had seats arranged in the gallery secluded behind lattice-work. The last of the services was the reading of certain portions of Scripture, and the preaching was done by the officials or some one chosen by them. It can be understood from this how our Lord had so many opportunities to read and preach in synagogues. He was generally known and sought by the people in every city He entered; and many times the officials were just as eager to hear Him as those who followed Him; hence it was no trouble for an opening to be made to have Him preach at each place He was found on the Sabbath day.

When Jesus had completed the first itinerary through Galilee, He came back to His "own city," to attend to those who sought Him there, and to work wonders in the presence of great multitudes from all the country around. His fame had so attracted the people in all parts of the land that "everybody was talking about Jesus." This intensified the malice of His opposers to the extent they determined to spare no pains in securing His capture. The Pharisees and doctors from all the villages and cities in Galilee and Judea, and those at Jerusalem, rose up as if drawn by magic, and came down to Capernaum to criticise Jesus, and use their uttermost endeavors to turn popular opinion against

Him. They assembled at Peter's house, mingling with the anxious throng that had gathered from every direction. Just then four men brought one of their friends lying on his cot helpless, stricken with palsy; and when they found it impossible because of the multitude to get to the door, went on the house-top and let him down before Jesus that He might heal him. He turned His attention to the man and said, "Thy sins are forgiven thee." Then a general murmur was indulged among the Pharisees and doctors, claiming that "none but God could forgive sins." Jesus, perceiving their reasonings, clearly demonstrated that the Son of Man had power to forgive sins, by commanding the man to rise, saying, "Arise, take up thy couch and go unto thy house," the man quickly obeyed, to the amazement of all present; so much were they astonished, they said one to the other, "We have seen strange things to-day."

Our Lord, having silenced these critics, left the house and went along the sea-shore, followed by an enthusiastic throng, and saw Levi, a tax-collector, sitting at the customs office, and He said to him "Follow me;" he immediately rose up, left all, and followed Him. This man may have seen Jesus, but never as at that time. As a public acknowledgment of his thankfulness of the favor of being counted worthy of being a follower of Christ, Levi gave a great feast in honor of Him, to which he had invited a multitude of publicans. The Pharisees regarded that class as too mean for them to associate with, just as many of the same spirit do to-day. But Jesus was teaching the fatherhood of God, and the brotherhood of man; that, whether Jew or Gentile, they were but men. This Levi was the St. Matthew who wrote the first book of the New Testament.

It was a busy day with Jesus on the Sabbath. He restored the poor man whose hand had been paralyzed a long time. The Scribes and Pharisees, whose teachings were very unlike that of Jesus, were jealous of the great fame He had won in all parts of the land, for about that time the masses of the people of all classes had turned their attention to Him, which was one of the reasons no effort was interposed to keep Him from teaching in cities and towns. But wherever Christ went, the malicious Scribes and Pharisees were found watching Him and endeavoring to measure every word and work He did, hoping by that method to catch Him committing some deed or saying a word that would give them an opportunity to charge Him with violating the law. It was very grievous to those who would be lords to find that their influence had so suddenly left them and everybody seemed to follow Jesus. It was no use for them to openly attack Him, for the people would have interfered, and they could do nothing with Him in arguments, for they would soon become tangled so greatly that the people would see their weakness, as had been the case the last time they attacked Him.

The thing they tried to establish in popular estimation was that Jesus was a Sabbath-breaker and was generally lawless. Now as He knew their viciousness, that they were attempting to persuade the people He was not observing the law, that He would do whatever He chose on the Sabbath day,—and no doubt one of the strongest points was the permission He gave the disciples to pluck the corn on the Sabbath; in connection with this, they insisted that the work of healing on the Sabbath was a gross violation of the law. Jesus went into the synagogue as usual, followed by a number of Scribes and Pharisees, who were always after Him, and while there He saw a man having his right hand withered. Jesus found it opportune to put a stunning question to these false pretenders, who would have the world believe that they were strict conformists to the law, and that Jesus was one of the chiefest of sinners. He commanded the afflicted man to stand up, that all the audience might see his condition; the man immediately did so. Then, when all eyes were fixed upon him, and saw how deplorable his case was, and no doubt all who looked upon him greatly sympathized except the heartless Scribes and Pharisees, and having drawn the attention of the sick man, He asked the pretenders if it was "lawful to do good on the Sabbath or to do harm?" "to save life, or to destroy it?" They would not answer the questions, for they did not dare to say it was not lawful to do good on that day, and they also knew to restore a palsied arm would be a most benevolent work; therefore they thought it more to their interest to say nothing. Jesus, seeing their indisposition to be honest and manly, gave them a look of condemnation that must have touched the very quick of their souls and filled them with torturing emotions; then turned to the paralytic and said, "Stretch forth thy hand;" he immediately did so, and found it to be as strong as the other. The Scribes and Pharisees, finding themselves in another dilemma, went out to hold a council against Him to see if there was not sufficient magnitude in the procedure of our Lord in the recent case of healing to formulate a lawful indictment against Him. What gratitude the poor man naturally entertained for the blessed Christ! It is probable he went home spreading the news and praising God for the wonderful blessing he had received.

The increasing labors of the Master pressed Him so heavily about this time (for the people were coming to Him from all the countries), that He withdrew from the busy scenes for a while, that He might choose from those who followed Him the competent number needed to be His apostles. Before making the final selection, our Lord went into the mountains and engaged all night in prayer. When the morning star rose, it found Him in the same place the evening star left Him; and when the day-dawn kissed His holy cheeks, He was still in the same place where the night shades covered Him. It is reasonable to suppose that the Master was praying for direction in the selection of twelve men who were to stand before the world as its lights. It was a momentous time, an occasion that should impress those who are to select men to stand as the great leaders of the Christian Church. The result of our Lord's selection comprised the following: Simon Peter, Andrew, James, John, Philip, Bartholomew, Matthew, Thomas, James, the son of Alpheus, Simon, which was called the Zealot, Judas, the son of James, and Judas Iscariot.

After the selection of these men our Lord solemnly set them apart as His future messengers. Afterwards He preached to the people who followed him in great multitudes from Galilee, Decapolis, Jerusalem, Judea, from beyond the Jordan, and from Sidon and Tyre, who were possessed with divers diseases, and He healed them. Jesus ascended the mountain, sat and taught them. The newly-chosen apostles stood close to Him listening to the words of power the Saviour was declaring. He gave a clear exposition of the spirit of the law, which had been so grossly corrupted by the Scribes, Pharisees and rulers of the land. St. Matthew gives a lengthy statement of this wonderful sermon which should be read and pondered by all men. The traditional mountain, on the brow of which Jesus delivered this exhaustive sermon, is about seven miles west of Tiberias and a little to the north of the road to Cana. It is called the "Horns of Hatten," from the two ridges resembling horns or arms connecting with it. It is remarkable that Moses gave the letter of the law from Mt. Sinai, but Christ gave its spirit from Mount Hatten, or one of the mountains near the sea of Galilee. We do not wonder that the people were greatly astonished and said, "He taught as one having authority, and not as a scribe."

When Jesus had finished teaching the multitude, He returned

to Capernaum followed by all who heard His words; for they were not weary, notwithstanding He had held them spell-bound for a long time. It was not long after His arrival that a Roman centurion stationed there sent for Him to come and heal his servant. To make the request impressive, he sent a delegation of Elders to recommend him, should a question arise as to the propriety of entering his house. He had done several favors for the Jews; the most commendable of them was building a synagogue for them with his own money. But without cavil Jesus started at once to heal the sick servant; and as He was approaching the house the Centurion seems to have suddenly felt the weight of his unworthiness to have one so kind, loving and holy as Jesus come into his house, and he at once sent others of his intimate friends to apologize to the blessed Christ, and tell Him not to come because the man, whose house He was approaching, felt, after a careful examination of himself, unworthy to have Him come, or go to the Master in person; therefore he asked through the messengers that Jesus would speak the word where He was, and his servant "shall be healed." Our Lord commended the man's faith, telling those following "He had not found such faith in Israel." He then informed the messengers it should be as they had believed; and when they returned to the house they found the man entirely restored.

We next hear of Jesus over at Nain restoring the widow's son, as has been mentioned in another chapter. We find our Lord, after this first miracle of resurrecting the dead, taking dinner with Simon, the Pharisee, at Capernaum. This was the occasion when Mary Magdalene came in and anointed His feet with tears and wiped them with her hair. The conduct of the woman astonished the Pharisees; but Jesus put them again to silence. He made a second tour through Galilee with increasing fame, preaching again in the cities and villages to multitudes of eager hearers, and was attended during this itinerancy by the twelve disciples, Mary Magdalene of Magdala, out of whom He had casted seven devils, Joanna, wife of Chuza, Herod's steward, Susanna and many others who had ministered unto Him. The people thronged Him as usual, but He slighted none.

It is generally known to those familiar with Bible history, that our Lord spent the most of His life in Galilee; not only while a quiet citizen in Nazareth, but the greater part of His busy missionary life was spent in that province. The inhabitants of Galilee were not looked upon with much favor by those of the southern district, and were criticised by them harshly. There were many Gentiles living among them; they were therefore looked upon as a mixed people and ignored in many respects by the more secluded or distinct communities of Jews over in Judea. Yet these very people, who were so unpopular among their fellows, were more susceptible to the teachings of Jesus than those who looked upon them with contempt. Our Lord found it far more pleasant to be with them than those round about Jerusalem, because they sought and welcomed Him to their towns and cities. He always addressed the people plainly and pointedly without being liable to be mobbed by those self-important false teachers, who held themselves up as lights of the people.

Galilee was the most favorable district for our Lord to prepare His disciples for the duties they were to discharge when they should enter upon their mission after His departure; for a work so full of interest to the world could not be successfully accomplished where exposure to numerous assaults were common. Therefore He chose Galilee as the more favorable place to train the disciples for their soul-saving work. Again, Galilee was better adapted for the mission of Christ than the southern province for the reason which has been stated; the people in that far-off district were anxious to have Him with them, and received Him with enthusiasm. But in Judea, the Pharisees, Rulers, and Elders were more numerously seen in the multitudes ready at every opportunity to incense the people against Him. But it is noteworthy that most of the mighty works of Jesus were performed about the Sea of Tiberias, although Galilee at large was His chosen field of labor. This region was made the centre; from here He made visits through the country, frequently returning to Capernaum, remaining there for a time, giving the needed attention to those who came seeking His aid, then away again to another part of the district.

The Sea of Tiberias was environed by towns and cities, some being very important, especially Capernaum, Chorazin, Bethsaida, Tiberias, Magdala, Gadara, and Bethsaida Julius. These were bordering on the sea or near it. In some of these cities many Gentiles lived; and it was of equal importance that they should have the benefit of our Lord's labors; for He came "to save that which was lost." There were other advantages that made this region a convenient field for the wonderful works of Christ. Many synagogues were located in these cities by the sea, all of which He labored in; this naturally required a long time. The sea was to be a scene of several of His stupendous works and the deserts were chosen as the tramping ground of multitudes of hungry people, who followed Him, and were bountifully fed. The country about the lake was very favorable for His labors, because the great highway to Damascus went through Capernaum, and to the western sea from Tiberias. Through these roads people were constantly traveling, many of whom had an opportunity of witnessing His works, and spread the news among the people where they lived. It is not unnatural that the Scribes and Pharisees should leave Jerusalem and go down to Galilee in pursuit of Christ, for although He was not working in their immediate district, such was the holy influence exerted by Him, the dwellers in Jerusalem and Judea talked of the greatness of His labors as much as if He were at the time in their midst. The merchants from Damascus and the cities about the sea brought fresh news of the wonders being done daily, as they came to Jerusalem. It seems highly probable the people asked every new-comer where Jesus was, that they might find Him. This exasperated the Pharisees so greatly, they went down to use their influence against Him.

One of the most touching visits our Lord received was that of a small band of friends, who came from Nazareth with His mother and brothers to take him home. Reports had reached Mary at her home that Jesus was not sane; and they, fearing it might be so, came to plead with Him to return with them. On their arrival at the house, they found such a dense crowd, it was impossible for them to get to the door. The Pharisees, who had come down from Jerusalem, were found mingling with the multitude in the yard, charging Jesus with black art, or being possessed with a devil and working through the agency of Beelzebub, the prince of devils. But He soon put them to silence, as He always did; that their ignorance might be exposed to ridicule. He showed them in a few words, a house divided against itself could not stand, and if He cast out devils through the agency of their prince, their kingdom must fall.

About this time some one informed Him of the desire of His mother and brothers to see Him; Jesus took the occasion just then to show the relation which those who are the children of God sustain to Him: "Who is my mother and my brethren?"—then, looking upon his disciples, said, "Behold my mother and my brethren, for whosoever shall do the will of God, the same is my brother, my sister, and my mother." Our Lord did not allow the pleadings of a fond mother to interfere with the work of His mission. The people, who heard the teachings of Jesus, became so enraptured they would not leave Him, notwithstanding the opposition of the Pharisees, who were using the greatest exertions to have them look upon Him as a man entirely influenced by the prince of devils. Poor, stupid fellows; how keenly they must have felt their defeat when they saw their uttermost endeavors could not turn the people from following the man who, day by day, was curtailing the sway they had so long held among them!

The people thronging the house where Jesus stopped at Capernaum, He withdrew to the sea-side, and taught the multitude many things in parables. This was a change from the mode hitherto adopted. He had been refuting in word and deed the doctrines taught by the Scribes and Pharisees; and having confounded them, He begins to teach the people the practical side of His mission, that they might fully comprehend their duty. The parable of the sower must have been strikingly illustrated. Not far from the sea-shore, where He was addressing the multitude, were the fruitful fields, just where the people could look upon them and see the stony places, the thorn bushes, the wayside path, and the good ground. This lesson being brought before them with a glowing illustration before their eyes, must have been most impressive; and if it happened at a time when the sower was scattering the seed, they saw he was laboring just as hard at those spots that were unyielding as on the good soil. This would have illustrated the efforts of their Divine Teacher, who at that time was working just as earnestly to save the poor, stony hearts in His presence as those who allowed the word to sink deeply in them. Surely those who were husbandmen clearly understood this lesson.

The last of the many parables Jesus taught at this gathering was the illustration of the drag-net, which contained all kinds of fish, good and bad. Our Lord at this time was in a small fishing-boat, having many fishermen near Him who had experienced the practical side of the parable; hence, the lesson was equally as impressive to them as the other was to the seed-sowers. These teachings must have carried their whole weight to the conscience of the amazed Scribes and Pharisees, who had begun to fall before Him as Haman fell before Mordecai. The physical bearing of this little plain is beautiful when contrasted with the surrounding country, and gives a lucid illustration of the parable of our Lord concerning the sower. Such is the literal development and impressiveness of this wonderful lesson, its spiritual bearing is clear to the most ordinary mind.

This wayside is trodden by hundreds who have passed over it from time to time. These are what we would call near cuts; those who do not wish to follow the main highway, take the wayside path to save time and labor. They are sometimes made directly through the centre of a field of wheat or barley. Such a procedure would be regarded as a lawless act in our country, unless consent be given by the owner; but in Palestine they have been used to it so long people regard them as highways. Many of these wayside roads are much better for man and beast to travel, because the main highways are not kept in traveling condition; in certain seasons they are used in preference. These paths are usually plowed every year by the husbandmen, but their direction is so well known by the natives they soon beat them down. It is often the case while he is plowing one portion or sowing the seed, the other portion is being trodden by passing natives. This fact we experienced soon after leaving Shiloh. My dragoman wished to take the wayside path leading to Lebonah, it being much nearer than the main road. He therefore started for the familiar, intersecting path; on reaching it we found the husbandman plowing through it in connection with the other portion of the field. But the dragoman knew where the wayside was, and went along just as if he had not been interrupted.

Some of these waysides, or what we call byways, have been used from the time of our Lord, and are regarded now as public thoroughfares; hence, the husbandmen offer no objections to the use being made of them, notwithstanding they lay through the midst of fields in which they have sowed their seed, much of which falls by the wayside as they scatter it with their hands. This the fowls of the air are more likely to see "and pluck up," because it is glaringly exposed to their keen eyes. Birds are very numerous in Palestine and Syria, and are generally found in great numbers in newly-ploughed fields seeking food. They appear to know about the time the grain will be sown, and are ready at the first opportunity to get a good portion of it, especially when it falls by the wayside. The "stony places" are prevalent and conspicuous; in the plain a stranger cannot pass them unnoticed. It seems very strange to those who live in countries like Europe and America where large tracts of farming land are almost stoneless, to see how the husbandmen of the eastern world manage to cultivate those fields which abound with rocks; many of them have sheets of rock extending several feet above the surface, some just on a level with it, and others about an inch or two below. These are so close to each other in many places the sower unavoidably casts the seed as he scatters it over the field in these stony places, "where there is not much earth."

While looking over one of these fields in the neighborhood of the scene of the multitude, on the day our Lord addressed the people in parables, it seemed to me as though the seed sown "in the rocky places" was the more prosperous; it had sprung up and looked beautiful and green, while that sown "in good ground" was just making its appearance. I could see then, as never before, the force of the parable of the sower. The matter was plain that the seed, looking so beautiful and green here and there over the field, had but little depth of earth, and therefore soon came up and would be blasted, no doubt, as soon as the sun shone upon it with more power; but that which seemed sparse and unyielding, had taken deep root, and would bring joy to the heart of the husbandman in the time of harvest. This most valuable lesson I learned along the plain of Gennesaret, so clearly unfolding the parable of the "sower" to my mind will never be forgotten. Those of the multitude who had a practical experience of these teachings must have felt their force vividly while the blessed Master was presenting the truth so distinctly.

St. Mark says, "Our Lord went on the same evening with the disciples to the other side of the sea." This was the night the waters of the little lake became exceedingly troubled, and great fear filled the disciples, so that they went to Jesus and aroused Him from sleep to interpose for them. Here was another opportunity for Him to demonstrate His authority over nature; He commanded the waters to be still, and the sea instantly obeyed His voice. When the country of the Gergesenes was reached, they saw a most distressing sight—a poor man over among the tombs, wholly under the control of devils, so that he was killing himself by degrees without knowing what he was doing; such was his madness, nothing could hold him, strong cords with which he was bound being broken as if they were cotton strings, and every one feared even to pass along that way. When the blessed Christ was approaching him, while a considerable distance off, the devils endeavored to practice deception on Him, as if they could mislead Him to the extent to cause Him to believe the man was objecting to His presence. "What have we to do with thee,

Jesus, thou Son of the Most High God? art Thou come hither to torment us before the time?" was the language coming from the mouth of the man, but not from his heart, for it was the sentiment of the controlling devils; He knew what the man would do if he could have the liberty to exercise his own will; therefore, He said to the demons, "Come forth, thou unclean spirit, out of the man;" at this command the devils came, and on being asked their name, "Legion," was the answer, "for we are very many." He permitted them to enter a herd of swine, which became crazed and were choked in the sea.

The poor man expressed his gratitude for the unspeakable goodness of Jesus by sitting at His feet clothed in his right mind. But the people of that country besought Christ to leave there. This He did; and when He reached the other side, Jairus, a ruler of the synagogue, met Him and fell at His feet, praying that He would heal his little daughter, who was at the point of death. He consented to go with him, and while on the way a poor woman, having an issue of blood twelve years, came out and pressed her way through the throng, touched His garments and was restored immediately.

It is noteworthy that every case Jesus handled was such as proved His divinity. The man over in Gadara had everything done his friends had a knowledge of to help him; but nothing reached his case, not even to the extent of keeping him from doing personal injuries. They gave up all effort to further assist him; fearing he would be a serious pest to the neighborhood, they let him wander about among the tombs where Jesus found him. The woman, who for twelve years had suffered with an issue of blood, not only spent all her means to procure a remedy, but had baffled the skill of the most distinguished and learned physicians, without success. He healed her without looking at her; simply by the touch of faith. The daughter of Jairus had every attention that could be given, and every remedy applied to produce restoration, but nothing could be done. The last resort was Jesus. The distracted father came and fell prostrate at His feet, overwhelmed with grief, praying that He would go with him to the bedside of the child and heal her. But lo, a messenger came, informing the ruler that his daughter was dead; therefore Jesus, the Great Physician, was not needed, for all was over. But He continued with Jairus, and, on entering, found the friends in tumultuous lamentation over the demise of the child. Jesus, being full of comforting words, told them the maid was not dead, but they did not believe

Him. They even scornfully laughed at Him; but our Lord had been doubted and laughed to scorn so often that He paid no attention to the scorners, but immediately approached the bedside of the dead child and restored her to her parents. When He came down from the ruler's house two blind men appealed to Him, and in the presence of the multitude He gave them sight.

Each of these cases was such that all the skill of man failed to remedy, so that not one could say, If I had seen these afflicted ones, the same restorations would have been made. Jesus, after these things, turned His steps toward Nazareth, the home of His childhood, from which He had been so cruelly forced by a murderous crowd. But he did not abandon them because of the first rejection. He came again to urge the people to accept salvation. This visit was as fruitless with the masses as that when they attempted to kill Him. It would seem that His home-folks, having heard of the mighty works He had wrought in other communities in Galilee, would have received Him joyfully. For they did not only hear of His works, but many Nazarenes had witnessed them; and yet, in the face of ocular demonstration, they still insisted that Christ was a blasphemer and unworthy of their confidence. "We know Him," they said, "Joseph, the carpenter of the town, is His father, and Mary, a woman living in our midst, is His mother; we also know His brothers and sisters, and have known Him from youth up; we will have nothing to do with Him; let others follow if they choose." Jesus, seeing their unbelief, and the extreme hardness of their hearts, could do nothing there except lay His hands on a few sick folks. He then left the city never to visit it again officially, and traveled through the country, the people every where receiving Him with great joy. This seems to be his second tour through Galilee, and He was followed by tremendous multitudes anxious to hear Him.

It became necessary, because of the increasing greatness of the work, to send forth the disciples to preach, teach, cast out devils, and do many works of power. The instructions they had received from their Lord during a year or more they were with Him, amply fitted them for the duties assigned them as apostles. Having qualified and commissioned them, they went forth in His name doing wonders. They were sent two and two, each couple going in different directions, as the Master appointed them, which seems to be as follows: Simon Peter and Andrew went first; James and John, the two sons of Zebedee, came next; then Philip and Bartholomew went out in another direction; Thomas and Matthew, the publican, were associates; then James, the son of Alpheus, and Thaddeus were sent; the last were Simon, the Canaanite, and Judas Iscariot.

These men went forth by authority of their commission, taking nothing to provide against the discomforts of their journey, but a staff in hand. They were commanded to take neither bread, wallet nor money. They began their mission most hopefully, healing many that were sick of divers diseases and did many wonderful works. After they had been away from their Lord for a time they returned to Him, who had come again to Capernaum to report the success that attended their mission. Jesus said to them, "Come ye yourselves apart into a desert-place and rest awhile." It was a busy time with Him and the apostles, for crowds were thronging them so that they had no chance to take a meal.

They were soon in a boat with Jesus, sailing for the other shore; but the multitudes preceded them, and ran with great haste to shore where the boat was heading, and reached there before Jesus and the Apostles, for when the boat arrived at the landing, a great multitude awaited them. He was moved with compassion on account of the people, and began teaching them immediately. "When the day was far spent," the Apostles desired that the people should be dismissed, that they might go out and get some food for themselves. But, in answer to the question of our Lord, it was found that the disciples had "five loaves and two fishes." Then, by command, the multitude was seated on the grass by companies of one hundred, and fifties. Then Jesus took the bread and fishes and gave them a wonderful extension. This small amount of food would not have been, under ordinary circumstances, enough for the disciples; but, in this extraordinary case, five thousand men ate and were filled, after which they took up twelve basketsful of the pieces left from the meal.

Jesus, wishing to have a few quiet hours to commune with the Father in prayer, ordered the disciples to enter the boat and return to the other shore, while He sent the people away. No doubt everything looked favorable to them: the sky was clear, the water placid, and the breeze coming from a direction to make them hopeful of a smooth and swift passage to their destination. But their prospects were soon blighted, for the wind changed in an opposite direction and was blowing furiously. The water became greatly troubled, so that one high wave after another lashed the little craft and swept over it. The sails were useless, and the oars were incompetent to make headway. The scene became alarming; the Master had commanded them to go to the other shore; therefore they must not go back to the desert where they left Him, but bend to their oars with their greatest strength to carry out the order. Their whole journey from the shore was but four miles and a half, and although the disciples started about dusk (St. Mark vi. 30-32), they were found, just before daybreak the next morning, but a little beyond the middle of the lake, or about three miles from their destination.

He, having finished the private interview with the Father, came down from the mountain to assist the distressed disciples, for it was a momentous time with them. Just when their trouble was greatest, and despair was making a telling impression upon them, Jesus walked out to them. The appearance of a human form on the sea amid such an overpowering storm, struck them with dreadful alarm, for they supposed a spirit had come as a signal of their speedy calamity. This troubled them more than the horror of the sweeping storm. Jesus said to them, " Be of good cheer; it is I." Then all hearts were light. Peter, having received permission from his Lord, leaped into the water to walk to Him; he soon began to sink. On this account he made one of the most earnest and pathetic prayers of his life. "Lord, save; I perish," was the short but earnest petition. The blessed Saviour saved him, and both of them entered the tempest-tossed vessel, and soon all were safe on the other shore at Bethsaida. He had reached the landing but a short time, before the news of His arrival spread, and the people who had sought Him, brought their sick on beds and otherwise that they might be healed.

The people in other cities and villages came in multitudes, and finding neither Jesus nor the disciples at the place where the miracle of feeding the five thousand occurred, they came over to Capernaum; and, when they found Him, said: "Rabbi, when camest thou hither?" This opened the way for our Lord to preach another most memorable sermon. He told them it was not because they saw signs leading them to believe in His Messiahship they were stimulated to seek Him; not that the words He had spoken and the miracles wrought by Him had caused them to hunger after righteousness, but because He fed them the day before in the desert to their full satisfaction. Jesus then preached a most pungent sermon on the " bread of life." There were great objections to His remarks, so much so that a general murmuring was indulged in by the Jews; several of the disciples (not the chosen) became offended and refused to follow Him. (St. Mark vi. 44-56.)

This seems to be the time several Scribes and Pharisees had come down from Jerusalem, charging that the disciples transgressed the traditions of the Elders. Jesus in answering them showed they were not only guilty of violating traditions, but the commandments of God. He then called the multitude and taught them what defiled a man, and proved the fallacy of the doctrines taught by the Scribes and Pharisees.

After these things our Lord went from Capernaum through Galilee, and continued His visit as far as Sidon and Tyre in Phœnicia. It is the opinion of many of the most learned authors that Jesus went there to conceal Himself from Herod, who had put John the Baptist to death. But it seems highly probable He went there especially to administer to that heathen Canaanitish people the "bread of life." He knew there were people along the route and in that country waiting for the glad tidings. They followed the God-man from village and city unto the cities of the coast; but He had not been there but a short while when a woman of Canaan, a Syrophœnician, came imploring Him to help her poor demon-possessed daughter. Jesus told her "it was not meet to take the children's bread and give it to the dogs." But her answer was so remarkably touching, He commended her faith and expelled the evil spirit from her child.

Jesus left the border of Tyre and went about twenty miles further north to Sidon, then made a long circuit through Galilee to the district of Decapolis. This is the country in which He was rejected by multitudes of citizens, when He expelled the legion from the man who was out among the tombs. The conduct of the people towards Jesus had entirely changed, for they sought Him. One of their highly respected friends was deaf and had an impediment in his speech; they petitioned our Lord that He would heal the man. This He readily complied with, and he was restored. There were tremendous throngs following Him, and again He fed them with seven loaves and a few fishes. On this occasion four thousand men were fed, besides women and children; and after all were filled, seven basketsful of pieces were left. Jesus then crossed the sea with the disciples and went to Magdala, on the northwest shore, the home of Mary, out of whom He had cast seven devils. This seems to have been the first visit He made here, although He had been in the neighborhood several times. The Scribes and Pharisees met Him again, but received a stern rebuke.

Our Lord then embarked and went up to the head of the sea to Bethsaida Julias on the northeast. Here a throng of people met Him, among whom was a blind man they brought to Him to be given sight. Jesus took the man from the crowd to the outskirts of the village, anointed his eyes and the man received sight. He then proceeded northward to Cæsarea Philippi, where He informed the disciples concerning His death, and received through Peter their faith as to who He was, and impressed them with the importance of their mission, instructing them it should be more dear than their life. This was but a short time before the marvelous transfiguration. When He came down from the mountain He restored a lad to health who was severely controlled by an evil spirit that had baffled the faith of the disciples; then He went over to Capernaum, and sent seventy disciples out to prepare the way before Him towards Jerusalem, whither He was about to go (St. Mark viii. 22; ix. 1-38; St. Matt. xv. 21-28; xvi. 1-4; xvii. 14; St. Luke x. 1-16).

One of the most wonderful mountains in Syria is Hermon. Those approaching it from the east see its snow-clad summit plainly as soon as they enter the southern border of the plain of Esdraelon, and it continues visible, except at short intervals, for at least forty miles. Those who have had the courage to ascend the old tower of the forty martyrs at Ramleh could see Hermon's snowy cap, looking like a small white cloud hovering over the northern sky. It can be seen also from an elevation near the Dead Sea along the wilderness of Judea, but from both of these remote points a clear day is necessary for the view. Hermon marked the boundary of the most northern extension of the territory of the Israelites, and is known as the Sheikh mountain of Syria. There are three prominent peaks connected with this mountain; of these the one on the north is the highest; the southern cap comes next in height; the one on the west is the lowest. When the author was in its neighborhood, it was too cold to attempt to ascend this stupendous mountain; in fact, it was impossible to do so, on account of the deep snows which completely blocked the road; it was impossible for either camels or horses to pass. Therefore, that we might reach Damascus, our final destination in Syria, we were compelled to return to Nazareth and go by the way of Mount Carmel, Haifa, Acre, Tyre and Sidon, which required three days longer to make the journey; this would not have been necessary if the snow had not prevented us from continuing along the base of Hermon.

The most favorable months to ascend this mountain are June, July, August and September. Hermon is not the highest mountain in Syria, notwithstanding it would seem so from the presence of snow almost the year round, because of its being so far north. Its highest peak is estimated to be nine thousand feet above the level of the Mediterranean Sea, whereas the highest point of Lebanon is eleven thousand—nearly two thousand feet higher. Snow seldom appears on the latter after the extreme hot weather sets in. Lebanon is the most conspicuous mountain range in Palestine or Syria, as well as one of the most historic in the world. The southern cap of Hermon is supposed to mark the site of one of the high places where the worship of Baal was conducted during the reign of Ahab. One of these peaks is supposed by some authors to be identical with the scene of our Lord's transfiguration. But, as has been stated, we incline to Mount Tabor, as the site of this wondrous event. But this is a thing not known to man, and must remain a mystery forever. The opinion favoring Hermon seems to be based upon the fact that Jesus was in that region about eight days prior to the event. This we know to be true; but the presence of the Lord at Cæsarea Philippi at that time is not sufficient proof to settle upon Hermon as the scene of the transfiguration. Herod caused a temple to be built at Cæsarea, in honor of Cæsar Augustus, and changed the name from Paneas (the name given it by the Greeks in honor of the god Pan, to whom they built a shrine here) to Cæsarea. But after Philip became tetrarch of the district, he added Philippi to it, so as to distinguish it from the Cæsarea on the Mediterranean coast. This seems to have been the farthest northward our Lord traveled.

The time having come for Jesus to go up to the feast at Jerusalem, He returned to Capernaum for the last time, without money enough to pay the lawful tax, and the disciples were in the same impoverished state. This duty had been levied by the Roman government, and was greatly opposed by the Jews, who had, on many occasions, made known their opposition to it. The Scribes and Pharisees were, it seems, constantly agitating the people in opposition to the payment of the tax, yet they were unable to release them. Jesus had not decided that the duty imposed was legal, although He was asked at one time to give His opinion concerning it, when the Sadducees and Herodians came to Him with the penny on which was the image of Cæsar. But, on this occasion, Jesus agreed with Peter that the claim was not just, but that they might not be considered offenders, He agreed to pay it, and told Peter to go to the sea, and the first fish he should catch, open its mouth and he would find a piece of money, with which he should pay their tax. After this, He set out for Jerusalem, where He must meet the demand of justice, and reconcile the Creator to the creature. This had to come when the most eventful life ever spent was about to close.

There is no place north of Jerusalem of more interest to the Christian traveler than the Sea of Tiberias and its environment. Here our Lord spent much time during His public ministry. This small body of water is nearly surrounded by mountainous elevations, so that from almost every quarter a beautiful view can be gotten of the lake and country round about. Those going down to Tiberias from Nazareth via Cana, have a most delightful view from the summit just east of Mount Hatten. The beautiful expanse of water appearing from the distance, like an extensive sheet of glass, is spread out fourteen hundred feet below the summit from which the first glimpse of it is obtained; from this point, the whole of the northern and central portions are visible. One has a most touching impression while looking upon the lake the first time; many incidents connected with the life of Christ naturally flood one's mind, and if he is a Christian, a fervent expression of thankfulness will fill his heart.

The country round about the sea is the theatre of many of our Lord's miraculous works. Teeming multitudes made the shores and wilderness ring with their shouts of praise to the King of kings, and hundreds who were brought to Him here, burdened with deadly diseases, went to their homes nimble as young lambs. Here the Pharisees, Scribes, and Elders came with vengeance in their hearts, bent on influencing the people against the Son of God, and if possible, to turn a flood of indignation against Him. Just over there is Bethsaida, and beyond it the site of ancient Capernaum; at the same point between the two cities our Lord called Peter and others from their nets to learn from Him how to catch men. These poor men, unlearned and possessing but little of the goods of the world, were called to be the first ministers of the new dispensation; men whose experience of trials and hardships fitted them to endure the various physical encumbrances they would necessarily meet with in attending to the work of their mission.

The Sea of Galilee is one of the most renowned of all others in the world. This eminent distinction is given it because of the frequent presence of our Lord about its shores, and crossing from side to side when visiting the cities round about it. Those who have read of the labors of Jesus in Galilee know He was often seen on the shores of the sea surrounded by great multitudes who came from various parts to see Him, and have the opportunity of witnessing some of the mighty works for which He had become so distinguished. This lake is estimated to be thirteen miles long from the northern to its southern terminus; its widest portion is six and a half miles, and its deepest portions range from one hundred to a hundred and seventy-five feet. The water is beautiful, transparent and excellent to the taste. All the inhabitants round about its border get their water supply from it. As in the time of Peter, James, and Andrew, this little body of water furnished a living for many fishermen; so it does at present; every hour in the day when the weather permits, men can be seen along the Bethsaida shore with their nets fishing.

While stopping at the little hotel in Tiberias, I ordered a fish supper for the sake of eating some caught from the Sea of Galilee, which was a delicious luxury to me. The fishermen seem to be fearful of leaving the shore to catch the great swarms that are to be seen out in the deep.

One can imagine Peter's position when Jesus bade him "go out into the deep and prepare for the great draught," on the occasion when he had been lingering about the shore so long making a fruitless effort to catch them. Indeed it seems to have been the custom from the early times not to go far from the shore; for when our Lord was passing and called the sons of Zebedee to leave their nets and follow Him, they were so near the shore His voice could be distinctly heard in an ordinary tone. It is highly probable that this custom was observed because of the sudden storms that sweep over the sea which would damage the little vessels, and many times prove fatal to life were the fishermen caught in them; hence the caution. The same custom is adhered to now; the boatmen will not venture from the shore during a storm. It seems as though the fish take advantage of the timidity of their pursuers, and the hosts of them are generally to be seen out in the deep.

While passing from Capernaum to Tiberias we saw multitudes of fine fish out in the middle of the sea, sporting and jumping as if they were laughing to scorn the power of the men who were

THE SEA OF GALILEE.

lingering close to the shore near the site of ancient Bethsaida. It is true there were many shoals of smaller fish near the shore, but they were not the kind mostly desired by the fishermen. While looking at a man preparing his net, opposite Bethsaida, I remarked to one of our company that that man may be just about the spot Peter was when our Lord advised him to "launch out into the deep and prepare for the draught." It may be of interest to many to read a brief description of the situation of the sea. It is located in a surprisingly deep depression, nearly surrounded by mountains; some are a little remote from it, while others are so close that no margin is left to walk between them and the water, and at the southern end they do not appear at all.

It is thought, at some period in the past, mountains were prominent on the south, but became extinct by powerful volcanic actions. The mountains on the east seem to have corresponding altitude along the entire border, while those on the west are much broken by intervening depressions; and yet these do not come down so abruptly upon the margin of the sea as those on the southern side.

Here, there is a wide space forming a shore between them and the lake, on the margin of which the renowned city of Tiberias is located. On the north the mountains assume the form of a semi-circle, and are farther distant from the water than any of the neighboring hills round about; and here Gennesaret is spread out. It is called by the natives "el Ghuweir," meaning little Ghar. At the foot of the hill, on the north border of the plain, are a number of ruins. Many of those who have made examinations of this region, locate Capernaum here; but later and perhaps more scrutinizing examinations have rendered this opinion unpopular. There are many fruitful trees in the plain of Gennesaret. The whole of this district is well watered, which alone makes it much more desirable than any other tract of land in the region, and it has been looked upon, from olden times to the present, as a paradise.

This section of country has been visited with volcanic disturbances, remnants of which are yet to be seen. The stones near the shore are cemented to shells towards the southern boundary of the lake, which indicate the presence of the alarming earthquakes that repeatedly visited this region. There are also springs called Hammam, or hot baths, situated near the southern extremity of a small plain. There are four of them, one under the old ruins of a building, the other three being a little farther south. The water issuing from the springs is very salt and bitter, constantly emitting a strong sulphurous odor. These springs are highly valuable in curing rheumatism, and those afflicted with it endeavor to bathe at the boiling springs on the southern shore of Lake Gennesaret. The depth of the lake below the surrounding country is the cause of the extraordinary heat that prevails around its shores, and is said to be the reason also of the sudden high winds and storms so frequently witnessed on it.

It happens many times, that travelers experience great disappointment who go down to Tiberias, especially to have the inexpressible pleasure of crossing over to Capernaum, the Bethsaidas, Magdala, and Gadara, because they are prevented from doing so on account of prevailing storms; they come, many times, so suddenly and unexpectedly that the oldest inhabitants cannot foretell their approach. At times they continue two or three days; then again, they are over in a few moments. When the wind comes up steadily and increasing in force from the southwest, entering the Jordan valley, it sweeps violently along the whole length to its mouth on the north. But when the weather is calm, it is a most delightful gratification to have the privilege of sailing upon this little sea, to the various places about its borders, and think of the wondrous scenes that transpired here by our Lord, when the vast multitudes followed Him from hill to hill and around the shores, seeking His mercy.

Travelers often go around the seashore to Capernaum and other places on horses, when it is too stormy on the lake, but not with much comfort. This little body of water is often referred to in the Bible under different names. It is known in the ancient Scriptures as the sea of Chinnereth, and it is supposed, a town was located on or near the shore from which the sea's name was taken. In our era its name was changed to Tiberias, after the city which was founded on its southwestern border; it is also known as Lake Gennesaret, after the beautiful plain on its northwestern border, and is familiarly known as the Sea of Galilee, the name of the district in which it is embraced. The latter is a Gentile name, and the sea is commonly called by this rather than the other.

The Old Testament associations with this lake are but few; it is specially mentioned in designating the portions allotted to Zebulun and Naphtali, but the references to it in the New Testament are many. The western shores and border-land of the sea must have been the most important as well as the most business-like portion of the whole province of Galilee. The most of the large cities and towns were round about it, and the people from the various parts of the country came to transact business and for other causes. Trains of camels and donkeys, heavily ladened with rich merchandise from Egypt, Jerusalem, and Damascus, came this way, and a mixture of races inhabited Galilee at the time our Lord opened up a travel through these parts, especially for a variety of people not of the Jewish family.

Tiberias, on the southwest shore, is supposed to have contained a larger Gentile population than any other city in Galilee. It was founded by Herod Antipas, and was made the capital of the province. This city is not specially referred to in the Scriptures as such; St. John, in speaking of the Sea of Galilee, mentioned its name by way of reference. It was not founded until the twentieth year of our era, and there is no record of our Lord having ever visited it during His ministry. Tiberias soon became the chief city of the Galilean province, and was beautified with many handsome buildings, among which were the royal palace and the amphitheatre. Tamud says, "The site of Tiberias was formerly occupied by a city called Rakkah." It became the seat of the Sanhedrim, and the chief city of Jewish literature after the fall of Jerusalem. It is now looked upon by the Jews as a sacred city, and they reverence it as such. Many of their most learned rabbis lived, taught and died here, and many prominent tombs are seen, which are supposed to be their silent homes.

The present population is something over six thousand, of whom two-thirds are Jews, three hundred are Christians, and the remainder Mohammedans. The Free Church of Scotland has a mission here, seemingly in a flourishing state. There is not a radical numerical change manifest, but those who do come from under the heavy yoke of Judaism or Mohammedanism, seem to be staunch for the cause of Christ. The present town is small, partially surrounded by walls, very low and very weak. This renowned city, like all others of fame and high distinction in Palestine, has suffered greatly on account of wars and other calamities. Under Constantine's administration it was set apart as the Episcopal See; many Christians settled here and built several churches, in which the services of God were conducted enthusiastically. Justinian rebuilt the walls, which had been demolished, and for a time the city prospered religiously and otherwise. But the Persians, under the generalship of Khosrus, or Khosroes, captured the city about the year six hundered and fourteen, and in twenty-three years afterwards it was taken from them by the Arabs, Moslems, under the leadership of Omar. At the time of the Crusade conquest Tancred captured it, and renewed the bishopric. But this victory was not permanent, although it may have seemed so for a while. The indefatigable Moslems came up more powerful than ever under the victorious Saladin, and swept everything before them. Tiberias and all Palestine was forced to surrender to them. The battlefield where the great victory was won is called " The Horns of Hattin." There are a few remnants of the ancient city yet remaining in the southern portions of the present town, which largely consist of old foundations and ruins of the original walls. There is a small space of old Mosaic, still in a mediumly good state of preservation, at the foot of the hill where the gorgeous palace of Herod stood. These are about the only remnants of ancient relics to be seen.

The Jews of Tiberias, are generally recognized on sight, by their odd appearance from the other people of the town. Many of them wear high, black hats, wholly rimless, and sloping towards the top; they also have long hair, hanging in ringlets about their shoulders. They generally look pale and despondent. Some of them are conducting a small business about the bazaar and the most prominent thoroughfares; but the greater number of them have the reputation of being paupers. It is with much difficulty that those who made investigations have agreed as to the identity of some of the sites; but there seems to be no disagreement as to the site of Tiberias.

About three and a half miles from this town, on the northwestern shore, is a very uninviting little town known as Mejdel, and the only inhabited place in the plain of Gennesaret. It only contains about twenty or thirty huts and the ruins of a tower. But the site is one of the most ancient about the sea. The distinguished Magdala, the birth-place and home of Mary Magdalene, was located on this ground now occupied by a few miserable huts. Our Lord made a short visit here. The best time to make a start to visit these ancient sites is in the morning early, as they are several miles apart. It will require a day to see some of them properly. It seems that all visitors to the Sea of Galilee are enthused with the same spirit when they arrive at Tiberias; that is, to make a visit to Capernaum first of all.

The present Capernaum has been settled upon as the identical site of the flourishing ancient city that, until Tiberias rose into fame, was the capital of Galilee. It was the most flourishing of all the cities about the lake in our Lord's time, and the city He chose for a home after leaving Nazareth. The site of this ancient city is now called by the natives Tell-Hum. There are two ways by which Capernaum may be reached; one is by skirting the shore as much as possible over-land; the other, by crossing the historic lake in small boats especially built for that purpose. The latter is far the best way; it affords a good opportunity to see both the southeast and northwest shores to a greater advantage, and also the hills and valleys round about. Another advantage of crossing in the boat is, the visitor may avail himself of the opportunity of reading up the topography of each place before arriving, which will be a valuable aid to any one who seeks to obtain the general history of the place about to be visited. We have found in several instances, the guides must be questioned by those whom they have in charge; otherwise they will furnish but a meagre account of some of the most historic places.

It is proper to state that the site of ancient Capernaum has long been disputed, as all other places whose identity has not been developed beyond all possible doubt; the reason for these unsettled opinions has been explained. But there have been recent developments, caused by more minute examinations, which point to Tell-Hum as the most probable site of ancient Capernaum. One of the most important discoveries is the ruins of an old synagogue, and several ancient tombs. There are many fragments of the old synagogue scattered over the ground which have been carefully examined; and from the many illustrations they develop, it has been concluded they are the remains of the synagogue built by the Roman centurion, who sent for our Lord to come and heal his servant, and afterwards thought himself unworthy for Him to come under his roof. If the opinion with regard to it is true, it is also the place in which our Lord delivered that most impressive sermon on the "bread of life." (St. Luke vii. 5). Up the slope behind the synagogue, are many ruins of an ancient city, spreading over about three-quarters of a mile; and it is evident the greater number of them have not been discovered, for they are deeply buried under ground.

Capernaum is called by St. Matthew our Lord's "own city;" the Holy Scriptures refer to it many times, but it has come to naught; and any one walking amidst the ruins of the fallen city, cannot fail to see the literal fulfillment of the Lord's prediction as to its dreadful fate. There is at present a small Latin convent at Capernaum, near the site of the old synagogue; it was not finished at the time of my visit, but was in hopeful progress. The custodian was very polite, and seemed to be willing to do all necessary to make strangers comfortable. It is the usual luncheon place for those who arrive there about noon. One can almost imagine himself to be living in the time of our Lord, as he walks amid the scenes of those ancient localities where He performed many mighty works, although he looks in vain for the beautiful cities that once crowned the hills round about, through whose busy streets thousands passed in haste, on their way to the sea-shore, looking for "Jesus of Nazareth." Yet there is something impressive in "Capernaum," especially when one is standing on or near the place it stood (exalted in glory), that produces an impression hard to explain. But where now is the mighty city that made the hill on which it stood vocal, by reason of multitudes of voices of Jews and Gentiles? Where are those mighty buildings that changed this solitude into a paradise? All have fallen to rise no more, for the "mouth of the Lord hath declared it." About two miles north of Capernaum are the extensive ruins of Chorazin, having many visible remnants of its ancient buildings. There seems to be no doubt as to its identity. The Bethsaida, which seems to have been largely inhabited by fishermen and their families, is believed by those who have carefully examined the site to have been located near the present Tabighah, close to the edge of the plain of Gennesaret, where the German Roman Catholics, have founded a colony. It is regarded as the most desirable place along the northwest shore for a fishing village to be located. This site seems to accord with the description the Scriptures give of it, as being near the sea.

It is also gratifying to make a short visit at least, over to Gergesa, where once stood the city of the Gergesenes, in the district of Gadara, to view the "steep place" where the swine ran down and "were choked in the sea," when the legion entered them. If there have been no changes in the physical condition of this portion of the sea-shore, there is no doubt as to the identity of the site of the event. It is the only spot along the eastern shore that corresponds with the narrative. The hill is very steep and runs abruptly into the water, without having any margin to allow one to walk; but there is a narrow strip of shore, everywhere else wide enough for persons to walk between the sea and hills; sometimes the space is so narrow only one can pass at a time, but the "steep place" runs down directly into the sea. It has been said that travelers sometimes become confused in regard to the several names given this part of the country in the Bible, and some have been disposed to become somewhat skeptical, thinking the Evangelists contradict each other.

St. Matthew speaks of the Gergesenes in his narrative, and St. Mark and St. Luke call them the Gadarenes. But it should be remembered St. Matthew speaks of the people as inhabitants of a city in the province, and St. Mark and St. Luke refer to them as citizens of that country. For example, we may, in speaking of a person or people, call them Marylanders, meaning they live in that State; or, we might call them Baltimoreans, meaning they live in Baltimore; but this would not conflict with the fact of them being Marylanders. Gadara was the district. Gergesa was a city in the district; therefore the Gergesenes were Gadarenes, and the statements of the Apostles are in harmony. There are three or four other places in the region of the sea usually visited that should be at least briefly mentioned. These are the two Bethsaidas, Gadara and the Jordan.

On the northeast side of the sea stood, in our Lord's time, a beautiful little city which Philip the Tetrarch enlarged and embellished, calling it Bethsaida Julias, in honor of Julias, daughter of Augustus of Rome. This name also distinguished it from the Bethsaida on the edge of the Gennesaret plain on the northwest shore.

It has been a question with some authors as to whether there existed two Bethsaidas in Galilee; but careful investigations, in connection with what has been gleaned from the Scriptures, have disclosed the fact of their existence to the satisfaction of all who have taken pains to find out the facts in the case. It is believed both places were comparatively large for the time, and were thickly settled with a busy population; one of them was located on the northwest, adjacent to the plain of Gennesaret, where Peter, James, John, Andrew, and Philip lived, at least for a while; for we have reason to believe that the former afterward moved to Capernaum. The Bethsaida Julias was situated on the northeast of the sea, and north of Gergesa. There are several references made to these Bethsaidas in the Scriptures, which will prove interesting to the Bible student. Bethsaida Julias was nearly opposite Capernaum. The disciples went there after the miracle of the desert, just before our

Lord went with them to **Cæsarea Philippi.** Close to it the place is located where, it is supposed, the multitudes were fed when Jesus blessed the seven loaves and few fishes. St. John says, "The multitude found Him on the other side of the sea," which is an evidence that two Bethsaidas existed at that time: for the one in which the fishermen lived was on the northwest. It will be found by any who will examine the Scriptures, the feeding **of the** four thousand men and a large number, probably, of women and children, was not in the same place the five thousand were fed; the **former** was near Bethsaida Julias.

INDEX.

	PAGE
ABANA, River	385
Abraham	151–235–244
Absalom	112–120
Absalom's Pillar	121
Acre	363
Acre, Plain of	363
Ahab	310–317
Ai	51
Ajalon	51
Allotments	21
Antonia	134
Arimathea	49–233
Armed Merchants and Shepherds	15
Ashdod	50–302
Asher	23
Assyria	3
BEEROTH	232
Beersheba	22
Benjamin	23–236
Bethany	104
Bethel	235
Bethesda, Pool of	70–129–130
Beth-horon, The	54
Bethlehem	168
Bethsaida	431–439
Bethsaida, Julius	439
Beth-zur	145
Bezetha	95–99
Boundary	2
CÆSAREA Philippi	402–440
Calvary	96–98
Canaan	1
Canaanites, Primitive	375
Capernaum	409

	PAGE
Carmel, Mt.	357
Cherith, Brook	221–325
Chorazin	438
Climate	10–11–18
DAMASCUS	388
Dan, Territory of	238
David's Tomb	92–136
Dead Sea	186
Decapolis	417
Decline of Two Kingdoms	309–315
Dothan	290
EBAL, MT.	269
Ebenezer	60
Edom or Idumea	2
Eglon	54
Egypt	256
Ekron	302
Ehud	26
Elah, Brook	6
El-Aksa, Mosque of	80
Elijah	323
Elisha	333
Elisha's Fountain	219
Endor	313–314
Engannim	292
Engedi	185
Enon	286
En-rogel	122
Ephraim, Territory of	22
Esdraelon, Plain of	292–313–314
Eshcol	158
Etham	178
Euphrates	131

INDEX.

	PAGE
FALSE Teachers Rebuked	315
Farming Implements	14
Frank, Mt.	361
GAD	22
Gadara	439
Galilee, Province of	348
Galilee, Sea of	434
Gath	50–302
Gaza	302
General Character of Hebrews	20
Gergesa	439
Gerizim	257–268–269–272
Gethsemane	108
Gibeah	231
Gibeon or El-Jib	58–121
Gideon	297
Gilboa, Mt.	292
Gilead	113
Gilgal	218
Golgotha	96–98
Gomorrah	195
HAIFA	362
Harod, Well of	298
Haran	74–236
Hatten, Mt.	417
Hazor	50
Hebron	146–152–113
Hermon, Mt.	429
Hermon, Little	292
Herod	76, 200
Hinnom, Valley of	122
Holy Nativity, Church of	169
ISRAEL, Idolatry of	124
Issachar	314
JACOB'S WELL	252
Jabin	56
Jebus	85
Jehoshaphat, Valley of	113–136
Jephthah	30
Jerichos	218
Jerusalem	62

	PAGE
Jezreel	308–309
Joppa	43
Joram	310
Jordan, River	208
Jordan, Valley of	208
Joseph's Tomb	264
Judah, Kingdom of	238
Judea, Wilderness of	185
Judges	25
KEDESH Naphtali	294
Kedron, Valley of	131–139
Khan	405
King's Garden	178
Kirjath-Arba	151
Kirjath-Jearim	53
Kishon, Brook	361
LEBANON, MT.	384–430
Landmarks	16
Lebanon, Anti-	385
Lebonah	250
Levi	23
Levites	24
Lydda	49
MACHPELAH	153–155
Magdala	436
Mahanaim	118
Makkedah	56
Mamre	150
Manasseh	22
Mar-Saba	179
Mecca	394
Merom, Lake	57
Midian	296
Mizpeh	59
Moab	200
Moriah, Mt.	93–101–135
Mukhna, Plain of	251
NABOTH'S Vineyard	310–311
Nain	311–313
Names Given Palestine	1–2
Naphtali, Tribe of	23

	PAGE		PAGE
Nazareth	340	SAMARIA	273
Nebo, Mt.	215	Samuel	31
Nebo and Pisgah, View of	208	Scopus	131–228
Neby-Samuel	59	Seir, Mt.	295
Neby-Da'rid	138	Shamgar	27
Nob	230	Sharon, Plain of	47
		Shechem	153–265
OBADIAH	325	Shiloh	246
Olives, Mt. of	103–107–131	Shunammite Woman	335
Old Judges Revenged	16	Siddim, Valley of	207
Omar, Mosque of	75	Sidon	366
Ophel	128	Siloam, Pools of	129
		Simon, Son of a Star	359
PALESTINE	2	Sodom	195
Permanent Homes	17	Solomon	176
Persians	182	Sychar	259
Philistia	4	Syria	3
Phœnicia	5		
Physical Formation of the Country	3–7		
Pisgah, Mt.	214	TABERNACLE	23
Political Status	7–10	Tabor	400
Pools of Solomon	176	Tell-Hum	409
Potter's Field	123	Tiberias	419
Prophets	318	Tirzah	276
Proselytes to Baal	315	Titus	131
		Tyre	128
RACHEL'S TOMB	164	Tyropean, Valley	128
Ramah of Benjamin	232		
Ramah of Samuel	233	ZEBULUN, Territory of	23
Ramleh	49	Zion	101–135–143
Reuben	21	Zoar	200
Rimmon, House of	397		

www.ingramcontent.com/pod-product-compliance
Lightning Source LLC
Chambersburg PA
CBHW051232300426
44114CB00011B/704